SUPPLEMENT VIII
T. C. Boyle to August Wilson

American Writers
A Collection of Literary Biographies

JAY PARINI
Editor in Chief

SUPPLEMENT VIII
T. C. Boyle to August Wilson

Charles Scribner's Sons
an imprint of the Gale Group
New York • Detroit • San Francisco • London • Boston • Woodbridge, CT

Charles Scribner's Sons
1633 Broadway
New York, New York 10019

1 3 5 7 9 11 13 15 17 19 20 18 16 14 12 10 8 6 4 2

Library of Congress Cataloging-in-Publication Data

American writers; a collection of literary biographies.

Leonard Unger, editor in chief. p. cm.

The 4-vol. main set consists of 97 of the pamphlets originally published
as the University of Minnesota pamphlets on American writers; some have been
rev. and updated. The supplements cover writers not included in the original series.
Supplement 2, has editor in chief, A. Walton Litz; Retrospective suppl. 1, c1998, was edited by A. Walton Litz & Molly Weigel; Suppl. 5
has editor-in-chief, Jay Parini. Includes bibliographies and index.
Contents: v. 1. Henry Adams to T. S. Eliot - v. 2. Ralph Waldo Emerson to Carson McCullers - v. 3. Archibald MacLeish to George
Santayana - v. 4. Isaac Bashevis Singer to Richard Wright - Supplement/[s]: 1, pt. 1. Jane Addams to Sidney Lanier. 1, pt. 2. Vachel
Lindsay to Elinor Wylie. 2, pt.1. W.H. Auden to O. Henry. 2, pt. 2. Robison Jeffers to Yvor Winters. - 4, pt. 1. Maya Angelou to Linda
Hogan. 4, pt. 2. Susan Howe to Gore Vidal. 5. Russell Banks to Charles Wright.
ISBN 0-684-19785-5 (set) - ISBN 0-684-13662-7
1. American literature-History and criticism. 2. American literature-Bio-bibliography. 3. Authors, American-Biography. I. Unger, Leonard.
II. Litz, A. Walton. III Weigel, Molly. IV. University of Minnesota pamphlets on American writers.

PS129 .A55 810'.9 [B] 73-001759

ISBN 0-684-31230-1

Acknowledgment is gratefully made to those publishers and individuals who have permitted the use of the following material in copyright.

Joseph Brodsky
Excerpt from "Great Elegy for John Donne," translated by George L. Kline, from *Selected Poems* (New York: Penguin, 1973). Copyright © 1973 by George L. Kline. Excerpts from "January 1, 1965," from *A Part of Speech*. Copyright © 1980 by Joseph Brodsky. Excerpts from "Odysseus to Telemachus," "Nature Morte," "Nunc Dimittis," "The Funeral of Bobo," and "Lullaby of Cape Cod" from *Collected Poems in English*, edited by Ann Kjellberg. Copyright © 2000 by the Estate of Joseph Bridsky. Excerpts from "May 24, 1980," "Lithuanian Nocturne," "Roman Elegies," "The Hawk's Cry in Autumn," "Gorbunov and Gorchakov," and "To Urania" from *To Urania*. Copyright © 1988 by Joseph Brodsky. Excerpts from "Song of Welcome." "At a Lecture," "An Admonition," and "Star of the Nativity" from *So Forth*. Copyright © 1996 by Joseph Brodsky. All reprinted with the permission of Farrar, Straus & Giroux, LLC. W. B. Yeats, excerpt from "The Second Coming," from *The Poems of W. B. Yeats: A New Edition*, edited by Richard J. Finneran. Copyright 1924 by Macmillan Publishing Company, renewed 1952 by Bertha Georgie Yeats. Reprinted with the permission of Simon & Schuster, Inc. and A. P. Watt, Ltd. on behalf of Michael B. Yeats. W. H. Auden, excerpt from "In Memory of W. B. Yeats" from *W. B. Auden: Collected Poems*, edited by Edward Mendelson. Copyright 1940 and renewed 1968 by W. H. Auden. Reprinted with the permission of Random House, Inc. and Faber and Faber, Ltd. Robinson Jeffers, excerpts from "Love the Wild Swan," from *The Selected Poetry of Robinson Jeffers*. Copyright 1935 and 1963 by Donnan Jeffers and Garth Jeffers. Reprinted with the permission of Random House, Inc.

Jim Harrison
Excerpts from "In Interims: Outlyer," "Sketch for a Job Application Blank," "The Theory and Practice of Rivers," and "Looking Forward to Age" from *The Shape of the Journey: New and Collected Poems*. Copyright © 1998 by Jim Harrison, Reprinted with the permission of Copper Canyon Press, P. O. Box 271, Port Townsend, WA 98368 0271. Excerpts from "First Person Female" from *The New York Times Magazine* (May 16, 1999). Copyright © 1999 by Jim Harrison. Reprinted with permission. Excerpts from *Dalva*. Copyright © 1988 by Jim Harrison. Reprinted with the permission of Dutton Signet, a division of Penguin Putnam Inc. Patrick Smith and Robert DeMott, excerpts from an unpublished interview (August 28–30, 1990, Leelanau, Mich.). Reprinted with the permission of Robert DeMott.

Shelby Hearon
Excerpts from *A Prince of a Fellow*. Reprinted with the permission of the author and Texas Christian University Press.

Editorial and Production Staff

Managing Editors
AMANDA MATERNE
ANNA SHEETS NESBITT

Copyeditors
BARBARA C. BIGELOW
GRETCHEN GORDON
GINA MISIROGLU
MELISSA A. DOBSON
MICHAEL L. LEVINE
PAMELA PARKINSON
KEN WACHSBERGER

Proofreaders
BARBARA C. BIGELOW
GRETCHEN GORDON
JOSEPH C. TARDIFF

Indexer
KATHARYN DUNHAM

Publisher
KAREN DAY

List of Subjects

Introduction

Between 1959 and 1972, ninety-seven American writers were treated in a series of elegantly written, compact yet comprehensive pamphlets by critics of considerable stature. These were called the Minnesota Pamphlets on American Writers, and each installment surveyed the life and work of a single author, focusing on major works and putting these works into useful biographical and historical contexts. Not surprisingly, these monographs attracted a devoted following, and the series proved invaluable to a generation of students and teachers. The idea of reprinting these essays occurred to Charles Scribner Jr. (1921–1995), who himself admired the series a great deal. The reprints appeared in four volumes entitled *American Writers: A Collection of Literary Biographies* (1974).

Since then, seven supplements have appeared, covering hundreds of American writers: poets, novelists, playwrights, essayists, and autobiographers. The idea has been consistent: to provide clear-eyed, critically astute, and informative essays aimed at the general reader. These essays often rise to a high level of craft and vision, but they are meant to introduce a writer of some importance in the history of American literature and to provide a sense of the scope and nature of the career under review. A certain amount of helpful biographical information is also provided.

The critics who contributed articles to this supplement are all professionals: teachers, scholars, and writers. As anyone glancing through this particular supplement will notice, they are held to the highest standards of writing and scholarship. Each essay concludes with a select bibliography of work by and about the author under discussion; the bibliographies are meant to direct those who want to pursue the subject further.

This volume is mostly about contemporary writers, many of whom have received little sustained attention from critics. For example, T. C. Boyle, Jim Harrison, Shelby Hearon, Bobbie Ann Mason, Cormac McCarthy, Gloria Naylor, Paul Theroux, and Oscar Hijuelos have been written about in the review pages of newspapers and magazines, but their work has yet to attract significant scholarship. The essays included here constitute a beginning.

The poets included here, such as Charles Simic, Gary Snyder, and Joseph Brodsky, are well known in the poetry world, and their work has in each case been honored with major literary prizes (Brodsky, indeed, won the Nobel Prize for Literature, while Simic and Snyder have both won Pulitzers), but the real work of assimilation, of discovering the true place of each writer in the larger traditions of American poetry, has only begun in each case. These poets are written about by critics who are themselves established poets, and the depth and eloquence of their essays should be obvious even to casual readers.

The reader will also find essays here on several writers from earlier periods, such as Harper Lee, William Maxwell, Thomas Merton and May Sarton, subjects who for various reasons were neglected in previous volumes and supplements. It is, in fact, a goal of the American Writers Series to double back, as necessary, to classic writers. One recent supplement (1997), for example, revisits major authors from the earlier volumes. The reason for this, of course, is that scholarship continues to grow and change on these figures, and they often look very different in the light of decades of new criticism.

American drama and criticism have, in the past, been somewhat neglected by this series. But the major contemporary playwright August Wilson is treated here. Two significant literary and cultural critics—Alfred Kazin and Norman Podhoretz—are also considered.

A glance at the table of contents of Supplement VIII reveals an eclectic and interesting collection of American authors from a wide range of ethnic, social, and cultural backgrounds. The critics who contributed to this col-

lection likewise represent a range of backgrounds and critical approaches, although the baseline for inclusion was that each essay should be accessible to the non-specialist reader or beginning student without sacrificing critical sophistication—a difficult assignment, but well met by our critics.

The work of culture involves the continuous assessment and reassessment of major texts produced by its writers, and our belief is that this supplement performs a useful service, providing substantial introductions to American writers who matter to readers, and who will be read well into the next century.

—*JAY PARINI*

Contributors

Kathryn Brewer. Professor at the University of South Carolina, Aiken, specializing in African American literature and American literature. State Chair for the National Association of African American Studies Conference. GLORIA NAYLOR

Laurie Champion. Assistant Professor of English at San Diego State University, Imperial Valley. Author of essays on American literature that have appeared in such journals as *Southern Literary Journal, Southern Quarterly, Mississippi Quarterly, Studies in Short Fiction,* and *Journal of the Short Story in English.* Editor (with Bruce A. Glasrud) of *African American West: A Century of Short Stories* and editor of *The Critical Response to Mark Twain's Huckleberry Finn, The Critical Response to Eudora Welty's Fiction,* and *American Women Writers, 1900–1945: A Bio-Bibliographical Critical Sourcebook.* HARPER LEE

Keith Clark. English professor at George Mason University, Fairfax. Author of essays on William Faulkner, Ernest J. Gaines, Lorraine Hansberry, and Ann Petry in such journals as *African American Review, Callaloo,* and the *Faulkner Journal.* Author of *Re-situating the Subject: Masculinity and Community in James Baldwin, Ernest Gaines, and August Wilson* and editor of *Contemporary Black Men's Fiction and Drama,* both forthcoming from the University of Illinois Press. AUGUST WILSON

George Core. Editor of the *Sewanee Review* since 1973. Editor of seven books, chiefly on American literature, and a frequent contributor to periodicals. His essays include one on Malcolm Cowley in the American Writers series. WILLIAM MAXWELL

Patricia Dwyer. Associate Professor of English and Director for Assessment of Student Learn-ing at Shepherd College. Author of "This is the House That Elizabeth Built: Memory, Place, and Desire in the Poetry and Art of Elizabeth Bishop," in *Division of the Heart: Elizabeth Bishop's Art of Place and Memory,* forthcoming from Gasperau Press, and numerous paper presentations on Bishop, most recently at Elizabeth Bishop conferences in Nova Scotia and Ouro Preto, Brazil. MAY SARTON

Robert Faggen. Associate Professor of Litera-ture at Claremont McKenna College. Author of *Robert Frost and the Challenge of Darwin* and editor of *The Cambridge Companion to Robert Frost, Striving Towards Being: The Letters of Thomas Merton and Czeslaw Milosz, Selected Poems of E. A. Robinson,* and *Robert Frost: Early Poems.* He is currently preparing an edi-tion of the notebooks of Robert Frost for Har-vard University Press. JOSEPH BRODSKY

Brian Henry. Assistant Professor of English at the University of Georgia. Author of *Astronaut,* a collection of poetry, and numerous reviews and essays that have appeared in such journals as the *Times Literary Supplement, The Kenyon Review, Boston Review, The Yale Review,* and *The Antioch Review.* Editor of *Verse* and Verse Press. CHARLES SIMIC

Laban Carrick Hill. Professor of literature at several institutions, including Columbia Univer-sity and St. Michaels College. Author of more than twenty books, including a cultural history of the Harlem Renaissance. BOBBIE ANN MASON

Tyler Hoffman. Assistant Professor of English and Codirector of the American Studies Program at Rutgers University, Camden. Associate editor of the *Robert Frost Review* and author of *Robert Frost and the Politics of Poetry,* which is forthcoming from the University Press of New England, and articles on Walt Whitman, Emily Dickinson, Frost, and Thom Gunn. He is currently at work on a book about American public poetry and the performance of culture from Whitman through the rap-meets-poetry scene. GARY SNYDER

Paul Johnston. American literature professor at the State University of New York College, Plattsburgh. He has published articles on Nathaniel Hawthorne and James Fenimore Cooper, as well as on Shakespeare and literary theory. His teaching and research focuses on spirituality in American literature. THOMAS MERTON

James Lee. Emeritus Professor of English at the University of North Texas and Acquistions Consultant for TCU Press. Author of many articles, reviews, and books, including *Classics of Texas Fiction* and *Texas, My Texas.* Founding editor of the learned journal *Studies in the Novel* and coeditor of the anthology *New Texas.* SHELBY HEARON

Liesel Litzenburger. Writer-in-residence at the New College of the University of South Florida. She has taught writing at the University of Michigan and at the Interlochen Arts Academy. Author of a collection of short stories, *Now You Love Me.* PAUL THEROUX

Marybeth McMahon. Student of Alfred Kazin at the Graduate Center of the City University of New York, where she earned her Ph.D. in 1999. She teaches writing at Georgetown University and is working on a book about Willa Cather's later novels. ALFRED KAZIN

Sanford Pinsker. Shadek Professor of Humanities at Franklin and Marshall College. Author of *The Catcher in the Rye: Innocence under Pressure, Jewish-American Fiction, Understanding Joseph Heller,* and numerous articles, reviews, poems, and stories. NORMAN PODHORETZ

Patrick A. Smith. Writer and an adjunct professor of English at Florida State University. Author of a collection of essays on the fiction of Jim Harrison (forthcoming from Michigan State University Press) and *The Thematic Guide to the Short Story* (forthcoming from Greenwood Press). JIM HARRISON

Victor Strandberg. Professor of English at Duke University. Author of essays and books on numerous American writers. His publications include *The Poetic Vision of Robert Penn Warren; A Faulkner Overview: Six Perspectives; Religious Psychology in American Literature: A Study in the Relevance of William James;* and *Greek Mind/Jewish Soul: The Conflicted Art of Cynthia Ozick.* CORMAC MCCARTHY

Pauls Toutonghi. Poet and fiction writer who has published his work in various periodicals. Recipient of an NFAA grant for his novel, *Burnt Sugar Waltz,* and of the Zoetrope Magazine Short Fiction Prize for his story, "Still-Life." T. C. BOYLE

Joseph M. Viera. Assistant Professor of English at Nazareth College who specializes in Latino and Latina literature, especially Cuban American literature. Author of a full-length critical volume on Oscar Hijuelos, *Understanding Oscar Hijuelos,* which is forthcoming from the University of South Carolina Press. OSCAR HIJUELOS

SUPPLEMENT VIII
T. C. Boyle to August Wilson

T. C. Boyle

1948–

AT THE BEGINNING of Thomas Coraghessan Boyle's first novel, *Water Music* (1981), the reader is greeted by the clarion of his authorial voice. "Where historical fact proved a barrier to the exigencies of invention," he writes, "I have, with full knowledge and clear conscience, reshaped it to fit my purposes." This is Boyle at the pinnacle of his power and conceit; the "Apologia," as he chooses to call it, demonstrates the humor intrinsic to his writing. For unlike many authors within our written heritage, who utilize the idea of Apology as a straightforward explication of motives and means, Boyle's paragraph amounts to a sly and surreptitious wink. Boyle uses the Apologia to explain historical inaccuracies which may exist within his text. He also weighs in on the seminal argument of the writer of historical fiction: it is better to tell a good story, he implies, than a historically accurate one, or, in his words, "fiction instead of faction."

Born to Tom and Rosemary Boyle on December 2, 1948 in Peekskill, New York, Thomas John Boyle changed his middle name to the more elegant and difficult to pronounce Coraghessan at the age of seventeen. He received a dual B.A. in history and English from the State University of New York at Potsdam and attended the University of Iowa Writers' Workshop, where he completed his M.F.A. and Ph.D. in 1974 and 1977, respectively. At the turn of the twenty-first century he was teaching at the University of Southern California. Though Boyle originally intended to study music, he enrolled instead in a creative writing class as an undergraduate. His early story, "The OD and Hepatitis Railroad or Bust," was published in 1972 in the *North American Review*. This suc-

cess encouraged Boyle to apply to the University of Iowa Writers' Workshop, where he would write much of the short fiction in his first collection, *Descent of Man* (1979).

Beginning with these earliest stories and continuing in his novels later on, Boyle's work touches on a range of thematic elements. *Descent of Man* includes stories that focus on such topics as a parody of heavyweight boxing, the planning of the Second International Dada Fair, Maoist China in the 1960s, and the Temperance Movement on the American Frontier during the Gilded Age. Settings for his novels include Harvey Kellogg's Battle Creek Sanitarium in Michigan, eighteenth-century Edinburgh, and a contemporary American artists' retreat. While this is partially emblematic of Hegel's "disintegrated consciousness," the departure from the provincial, localized settings which characterize novelists of the past such as Faulkner or Austen, it is also a testament to the strength and variety of Boyle's intellect. Such variety demonstrates his ability to graft his own experiences and ideas onto characters from numerous time periods and geographic locations. This is perhaps most obvious in his novel, *East Is East* (1990), which dramatizes the possibilities of an interloper within the secluded milieu of a modern-day writers' colony.

EAST IS EAST

Hiro Tanaka is five foot ten, close to two hundred pounds. He is half Japanese—his father American, his mother a member of the Yamato race. When *East Is East* begins, he is Third Cook aboard the *Tokachi-maru,* a Japanese-registered freighter bound for the east coast of the United States. Well-mannered and inoffensive, Hiro—an orphaned disciple of the poets Jōchō and Mishima—is possessed of an idealized, pop-culture-fed conception of American life. "If his own society was closed," Boyle writes, "the American was wide open—he knew it, he'd seen the films, read the books, listened to the LPs—and anyone could do anything he pleased there." Labeled an outcast in his own society, a society where mixed race is seen as imperfection, Hiro believes that in America he will find tolerance for his own diverse parentage. "In America," Boyle narrates, his voice borrowing heavily from the internal workings of Hiro's mind, "you could be one part Negro, two parts Serbo-Croatian and three parts Eskimo and walk down the street with your head held high." The hero of this book, then—and here Boyle uses his humorist's love for creating puns from his characters' names—is the quintessential "immigrant coming to America," a variation on the classic dramatic theme of displacement.

Nearing the end of his lengthy and interminable voyage with an unfriendly crew, Hiro becomes embroiled in an argument with his immediate superiors, the First and Second Cooks on the ship. They argue over the proper preparation of *nishiki tamago,* an appetizer that food-loving Hiro has learned to prepare by heart. His superiors decide that his technique is incorrect and they insult his mixed heritage; the three men end up on the floor, grappling with each other, locked in a vicious struggle. For his part in the altercation, Hiro finds himself in solitary confinement. Realizing that he will be unable to disembark upon reaching America, he resolves to escape, to clutch his beloved books of poetry to his chest and leap overboard. In crafting his plan, he often refers to the poets he respects, drawing direct life instruction from their words.

Yet if Hiro hopes that the teachings of these poets will help to guide him through "the great

American cities . . . the City of Brotherly Love, the Big Apple, Beantown," he is soon disappointed. Barely living, he washes up in a caricature of the Deep South. Tupelo Island is rural, swampy, and isolated. The roads are single lane, "tar-bubbled blacktop"; the natural environment is wild. "He wandered aimlessly, his feet battered and bleeding, mosquitoes and ticks and chiggers and gnats drawing yet more blood, venomous reptiles lying in wait for him." In describing it, Boyle applies the humorist's most trustworthy device: he exaggerates everything, makes it monumental, dramatic. "He knew [little] about the wilderness of America. He knew only that it was vast and untamed and seething with bear, lion, wolf and crocodile." Aristotle has said that comedy must focus on the ridiculous and the exaggerated, presenting a *comic mask* that entertains and amuses. Here, Boyle presents this dictum in its utmost degree, displaying the ludicrous in order to advance the comic development of both character and plot.

Hiro is linguistically stranded. He is the modern individual, isolated behind a barrier of language in a setting which is as hostile to his survival as the crew of *Tokachi-maru.* Instead of finding himself surrounded by people who choose to dismiss his cultural origin as valueless, he is surrounded by those who misinterpret or cannot understand it. After a few days on the island, living as a vagrant, eating roots and sour berries, Hiro stumbles upon Thanatopsis House, a colony of artists located in a remote corner of Tupelo. Here Hiro befriends Ruth Dershowitz, a largely unknown young author who is dating the son of the colony's director.

Thanatopsis serves as Boyle's vehicle for a parody of contemporary writers' conferences, his chance to skewer the eccentric personalities of the colony's denizens. "At breakfast, it was thought, artists of a certain temperament required an absolute and meditative silence. . . . Others, of course, needed just the opposite— conviviality, uproar, crippling gossip, lame jokes and a whiff of the sour morning breath of their fellow artists. . . ." Each of the residents is a stereotypical construction, from the "celebrated punk sculptress with the staved-in eyes and skin so pale she looked three days dead" to Peter Anserine, a writer, who each day "hack[s] and snort[s] surreptitiously over his food and the book—always European, and never in translation—that seemed attached to him like some sort of growth." For Ruth, Hiro acts as a distraction from the petty jealousies intrinsic to life at Thanatopsis. He also serves as her inspiration.

The owners of the Japanese brig *Tokachimaru,* however, have informed immigration that Hiro has jumped ship. Along with reports that he is armed, dangerous, and amok, his status as an illegal alien brings the Immigration and Naturalization Service (INS) to Tupelo Island to seek him out. Eventually they catch him, but only after Boyle has developed the love between Hiro and Ruth. Facing deportation, imprisoned in an INS jail cell, Hiro disembowels himself with a spoon. "What was it Jōchō had said?—In a fifty-fifty life or death crisis, simply settle it by choosing immediate death." Hiro embraces the heritage of ritual suicide within his own culture, freeing himself from the constraints of his imprisonment. This decision has been foreshadowed, in a way, by the entire book's preoccupation with death and dying, with its consideration of poets from a tradition which prizes suicide and self-negation. Hiro's self gradually takes shape, molded by his actions and interactions within the American milieu. His suicide constitutes a painstaking trajectory of character development that works to counter some contemporary critical arguments which have assaulted Boyle's fiction for a perceived "lack of depth" in character. Albert Mobilio's piece in the *New York Times Book Review* is a good example of this critical tack; he ravages this aspect of Boyle's work, calling Boyle's characters "about as deep as the page on which we meet them." The difficulties of this procla-

mation are evident when a character such as Hiro Tanaka is considered. Though the moment of his death seems to be an abrupt decision, the path to this end demands gradual development and depth of feeling, both of which are given careful attention throughout *East Is East.*

WATER MUSIC

Perhaps this critical trend can be seen simply as a response to the criticism, generally positive, that greeted Boyle's earlier novels. *Water Music* follows the saga of explorer Mungo Park and London confidence man Ned Rise, who leave England in 1795 in search for the origin of the Niger River. Their goal is financial windfall and fame—instead, they find anonymous death and failure as they are overwhelmed by the hostility of the land into which they have come. As in *East Is East,* Boyle revisits the theme of isolation—linguistic or otherwise—which haunts much of his work. Once again, race predicates this isolation; the European explorer ventures beyond the confines of his continent, entering a society in which his white skin marks him as an outsider and foreign man. "Here too he was white: white as sheets and blizzards. Ali and his circle were astonished all over again. 'His mother dipped him in milk,' someone said. 'Count his fingers and his toes.'" Because of his foreign appearance, the very fact of his humanity is called into question, an occasion which recalls Franz Kafka's *Metamorphosis,* a story which Boyle has cited as crucial to his own development as a writer.

Though the character of Mungo Park is based on an eighteenth-century Scottish explorer by the same name, Boyle's secondary protagonist, Ned Rise, is purely fictitious. Separated for a majority of the novel, the two characters meet when Rise's imprisonment in a work colony intersects with Park's expedition. Park drafts Rise to accompany him as hired labor; this can be seen as Boyle's deferral to the exigencies of plot. Until this point, it is important to note, Rise's character has served as the book's primary infusion of sexual energy. A minor figure in the criminal world of London, Rise subsists on the profits from a burlesque and sex show that he has organized. "For the Blood What's Board with Patience . . . Titillation . . . Come to the Voyeer's Ball . . . The Vole's Head. 8 P.M. . . . Tonight." He also engineers schemes to sell Thames River roe as Russian caviar, regularly satiates his fetish for unlaundered women's underclothes, and engages in a corpse-stealing endeavor with one of his acquaintances. In Rise, Boyle plumbs the depths of marginality, providing a marked contrast for the landed aristocracy, which comprises the other sections of *Water Music.*

Indeed, the marginality of this text—the joy with which it explores the seamy and the grotesque—resembles the larger portion of Boyle's body of work. His works linger in the most fecund and unexpected parts of the landscapes that they explore: the gutters, the backrooms, the hidden and the faceless. Georges Bataille's notion of the taboo as the most compelling and important force in our society clearly animates Boyle's work. In *Water Music,* Boyle compiles an impressive vocabulary of taboo, presenting a long list of perversions and abusive habits. "He'd . . . eaten offal, witnessed perversion, theft, arson, and worse." Like theatre, where everything must be exaggerated and vividly animated, the characters of Boyle's fictions are outrageous and flamboyant. This is pantomime in words, a drama of the obscene and the nearly historical, a mimicry.

This desire to present a voluptuous body of living leads to much of the humor of *Water Music.* Perhaps the single most remarkable example of this is Boyle's recipe for Baked Camel (Stuffed) which appears in the early segments of Park's story. The recipe includes an ingredient list ("500 dates, 200 plover eggs, 20 two-pound carp") and directions for cooking: "Scale carp and stuff with shelled eggs and dates. Season bustards and stuff with stuffed carp. Stuff bustards into sheep and stuffed sheep into camel. Bake two days. Serve with rice." As an actual document, historically correct, the recipe is useless. It has no antecedent in fact, and comes wholly from Boyle's imagination. Yet here, as in much of his work, laughter leads to a sense of immersion, an engagement with the text, an appreciation. The reader's willingness to laugh leads to an understanding of the breadth of Boyle's reach. He has made comedy from the most disparate of elements; he has brought vaudeville to the Moroccan desert.

This breadth must be, of course, compared with another sort of exploration—the journey undertaken by Joseph Conrad in *Heart of Darkness.* Boyle's book is, in many ways, a postcolonial, and tangentially postmodern, antithesis to books such as *Heart of Darkness* or Graham Greene's *A Burnt-Out Case.* In his important essay, "Impressionism and Symbolism in *Heart of Darkness,*" which appeared in the 1988 Norton edition of *Heart of Darkness,* Ian Watt notes that Conrad's work strives to link a greater, symbolic conceptualism to the small, linguistic text. This is the mission of modernism in many senses—the attempt to represent the ways in which the individual's conception of the whole has been shattered. The project of imperialism is seen as just that—a project, a concerted effort to extend the domain of Western culture, which was seen as possessing a quantitative and significant worth. In Boyle, postmodern dissatisfaction with history has been applied to colonialism's cultural mission. The culture which is being disseminated here comes from a false and corrupted source. It is a culture of sham, of scheme, of trickery and vain personal self-interest. Boyle's characters explore notions of cultural depth in a horizontal rather than vertical manner. They have no greater, sublime mission which they serve. They seek to touch on entertainment, on the interesting moment in space, rather than in linear, correspondence-laden time.

RIVEN ROCK

It is important to note, however, that Boyle does not exclusively pursue one type of exploration within his novellic oeuvre. Vertical exploration perhaps best defines the path that Boyle chooses in *Riven Rock* (1998), a novel which is by far his least humorous, most overtly serious work. The genesis of the book is the true story of Stanley McCormick, whose father Cyrus invented the wheat reaper, one of the most important components of the mechanization of American agriculture in the post–Civil War era. Stanley inherits a fortune from his father, whose patents have grossed millions of dollars, and is raised in the upper echelons of Gilded Age society. Here he gradually develops maniacal sexual deviance, a complex that shatters his emotional stability and induces severe schizophrenia. He is unable to consummate his marriage to his wife, and is moved to destructive rage by the very thought of her existence. In this state, Stanley is barricaded into his family's Santa Barbara mansion, where he stays for the remainder of his life. Much of the book focuses on his wife, Katherine Dexter, and her attempts to save both Stanley's mental health and their precarious, legally threatened marriage.

Though *Water Music* includes excerpts from what ostensibly are Mungo Park's journal entries, *Riven Rock* attempts to give the reader an even greater amount of access into the interior workings of its characters. Boyle includes several lengthy and italicized sections, page-long digressions which purport to illustrate the mad patterning of Stanley's thoughts. They lack punctuation or standard syntax, rambling in a wild and consistently neurotic manner. "Stanley knew what was going on he might have been sick but he wasn't retarded and he wasn't blind or dead either and it was the women the women yet again because they weren't content to sit at lunch with him or . . ." These passages recollect, in their way, Virginia Woolf's presentation of Septimus Smith in *Mrs. Dalloway*. Like Septimus, Stanley has dropped his use of regular speech; to him, thought is an unceasing flow of ideas and images, a torrent which cannot be arrested or subdued when it surges out of control. Stanley McCormick is the quintessential isolated individual, isolated not only physically but also emotionally. His madness has divorced his mind from itself, splintered his thoughts into a rabble of competing voices.

Linguists and speculative psychologists ranging from Michel Foucault to Jacques Lacan have engaged in the dialectic of mad language. Of their various theories, Boyle is perhaps in closest agreement with Foucault, with the idea that the language of madness "strangles itself before it reaches articulation." Critics have noted that Stanley's voice lacks the imaginative zest of Woolf's Septimus, whose neurotic ramblings are peppered with didactic statements regarding what he perceives as a lack of truth in the world, or his personalized conceptions of the nature of joy and beauty. "The novel's promise of intellectual and emotional exploration," writes D. M. Thomas in the *New York Times Book Review*, "is not fulfilled." Though this is possibly a result of Boyle's allegiance to the historical character of McCormick, Stanley's thoughts lack philosophic weight or insight into the theory of how to present the language of the insane. They are, however, highly useful elements of contrast, as members of a series of contrasts that mark the body of Boyle's work.

Perhaps most noticeable among these is the constant juxtaposition of rich and poor, of the polar economic groups of American society. Stanley is, of course, tremendously wealthy. His family owns numerous homes and properties, he has a constantly changing wardrobe of fine clothes, he travels to Paris as a child, making the lengthy voyage in the first-class cabin of a luxury cruise liner. His attendants, however, one of whom serves as the narrator for a substantial part of the book, have nothing. "They were on a mission now . . . they were going to make him well. And when he was well he was going to reward them and then they'd have their orange groves and their bungalows and all the rest. That was it, that was what it was all about." Surrounded by affluence, they serve the rich but gain nothing for themselves. Exposed to the worst of Stanley's violent ravings, they ultimately fail to profit, as the entirety of his estate passes into the hands of his wife.

However, in Boyle's version of the story behind *Riven Rock*, Katherine McCormick is not motivated by the desire for monetary gain. A socialite whose family originates in Boston, she has sufficient, independent means, and even without Stanley's support, she is able to spend her life crusading for the issues she passionately supports: women's rights, widespread access to birth control, elevated living conditions for the mentally ill. Katherine McCormick is, in many ways, emblematic of the larger scope of Boyle's modern female characters. Sexually liberated, they seek to define their own physical narrative, to exert ultimate control of their bodies, even if this is against the prevalent mores of their time.

Katherine takes the money and sacrifices her personal wealth for what she sees as the edification of larger society.

> She sold the estate to pay the inheritance taxes and she took what was left to seed the causes and institutions she believed in—MIT, the League of Women Voters, the Santa Barbara Art Museum and Dr. Gregory Pincus, an old friend . . . who developed a little yellow progesterone-based pill that would free women forever from sexual constraint.

Nonetheless, like most of Boyle's women—who are never the protagonists in any of his longer works—Katherine orbits, however elliptically,

about a center of love and emotional concern. Despite having ample opportunity to desert Stanley, she remains his wife, loyal to his impaired mind, hopeful that he will recover. The grim coda to the novel—in which Boyle asserts that because Stanley died in captivity, still haunted by his illness, Katherine's ultimate desire remained unfulfilled—serves to prioritize her ambitions and life choices.

This relentless severity is perhaps part of the reason that critics took a more negative approach to *Riven Rock* than to his earlier, more comic works in general, which had many positive reviews. Tragedy, not comedy, is the work's primary agent; it is, in many ways, Boyle's darkest and least humorous book. Wherever the ridiculous appears, its levity is tainted by the specter of insanity, by the idea that Stanley's health has been ruined, that he will not recuperate.

THE ROAD TO WELLVILLE

Boyle previously explored many of these themes—the issues of physical and mental health—in *The Road to Wellville* (1993), his earlier historical comedy, published five years before *Riven Rock* and set in the same time period. Wellville is based on the life and times of Harvey Kellogg, the originator of Kellogg's cornflakes and the curator of the Battle Creek Sanitarium. The book, which was made into a motion picture released in 1994, moves with a grandly cinematic scope, presenting issues similar to those raised in *Riven Rock*, yet treating these same issues with humor and sardonic wit.

Deluged by excess and American prosperity, the gentry of the country's new industrial behemoth flee to Battle Creek for therapeutic respite from their indulgent way of life.

> [It] was a sybaritic window, a blow-by-blow chronicle of excess and indulgence. . . . Bender

had ordered shell fish in his room, or he'd descended to the [bar] to entertain in state, risen to his suite with coq au vin . . . sent out for three pairs of shoes and six shirt fronts, ordered a carriage, cut flowers, personalized linen. . . .

Wellville follows a husband and wife—William and Eleanor Lightbody—who are making this journey, traveling by rail from their home in Peekskill, New York, to the health spa in Michigan. Their ailment is contemporary society; the burdens of modernity—with its technological stress, drug use, and religious breakdown—have become too heavy to bear. Eleanor has had an unhealthy pregnancy; she goes to Battle Creek in the hopes that the spa can save her baby. William, however, is a reluctant patient, a skeptic who comes only at the behest of his wife.

Here is the crux of much of Boyle's fiction: the journey, the travelogue, the passage which precludes free will. More often than not, this journey is to a place of isolation and entrapment. The individual will respond in a variety of ways; often, by the conclusion of the book, the isolation will be allayed by an act of tragedy and partial redemption. While Hiro Tanaka kills himself and Stanley McCormick remains unable to rejoin society, Wellville has a more cataclysmic conclusion. Battle Creek burns to the ground, freeing the Lightbodys to return to their home in upstate New York. Here Boyle seems to be positing a larger kind of entrapment, the entrapment within a mortality that characterizes the human condition. Unwillingness to accept the inevitability of death, of course, is endemic to most of the characters at Battle Creek. They live with the American dream of immortality. Kellogg, of course, plays into their desires. "By preaching dietary restraint and the simple life, he eased overweight housewives and dyspeptic businessmen along the path to enlightenment . . . they came to subdue their afflictions with a good long pious round of pampering, abstention, and rest." Recognizing both the futil-

ity of the desire to escape from death, as well as the ridiculous nature of all of Battle Creek's attempts to overcome it, William wants to escape this arrangement as quickly as he can. Like Roquentin in Jean-Paul Sartre's *Nausea,* however, his captivity must drag on for an interminable amount of time.

While he is there, William offers a pragmatic approach to the fanaticism at the sanitarium. It is through his eyes that the fanaticism of the patients and doctors becomes comedic. Unless Eleanor imposes them, he accepts few of Kellogg's recommended lifestyle modifications: the doses of inhaled radium, the water-immersion treatments, the constant enemas. At least subconsciously, William recognizes that Kellogg's true adversary is death, and that the battle being fought at Battle Creek is sure to end in loss. William recognizes this, sees it with the detachment that befits a modern man. He is skeptical, sardonic, and marginally accepting of his wife's desire to be at the spa. Because of his love for her, he allows Eleanor to lead him from place to place, controlling even the specifics of his diet. "'But I don't eat meat,' Will protested. 'My wife won't let me. It's been nothing but Graham gems, parsnips, and tomato toast for the last six months.'" Their marriage embodies ideas of empowerment. Eleanor is, much like Katherine McCormick, a crusader for women's rights and assertiveness. She moves against the body of a society whose attitudes towards gender-based equality have not advanced beyond the most rudimentary stages. In the initial stages of the book, William allows his love for her to supersede his desire to leave the spa.

Eleanor's desire to come to the spa arises from a Kierkegaardian desire to become, to develop. If, as Søren Kierkegaard writes, "the self, every moment it exists, is in a process of becoming . . . and not to be oneself is exactly despair . . . ," then the patients at Battle Creek are at the nadir of their despair. They have come to the sanitarium consciously to change the ways in which they live, a process that accentuates their awareness of journey, of the progress from an unreformed to a reformed state. Yet because of the very substance of human nature, even the most significant amount of change is not permanent, and the patients of Battle Creek are aware of this at some level. In order to believe in the actuality of their change, of the alteration of their health to the better, they must be guided with the apparatus of mass hallucination. It is with this that Kellogg is so adept. Taking his cue from Kiekegaard's dictum that "in the life of the spirit there is no standing still," he dazzles his patients with a constant deluge of the unfamiliar and captivating. Even the most basic and common forms of human interaction—eating, sleeping, resting—become new, productive, and, above all, conscious.

BUDDING PROSPECTS: A PASTORAL

Boyle's other work, the fight against this despair—against this inability of the self to be content, to be itself—takes on varying forms. In *Budding Prospects: A Pastoral* (1984), he explores the same theme: the modern individual's fight against the overwhelming force of despair. This is his only extended work written in the first person; and unlike his short stories in which a first-person narrative normally means a heightened sense of irony, this work adopts a fairly earnest tone. *Budding Prospects* focuses on the travails of first-person narrator Felix Nasmyth and his two acquaintances, Gesh and Phil, as they try to cultivate a marijuana farm in Humboldt County, California. While their hope—that they will each gain close to $200,000 from their efforts—initially seems to be quite different than the hopes of the Americans who migrated to Battle Creek, Boyle ultimately reveals the similarity between the ambitions of the two groups.

While the patients at the sanitarium believe that they will escape mortality through better living and health, Gesh, Phil, and Felix believe that they will escape mortality through indulging their sense of pleasure with bacchanalian fervor. They are driven by the hope for money, and by the knowledge that with this money they will sate their lust for alcohol, drugs, and prostitutes.

> Half a million dollars. It was as if the head of NASA [National Aeronautics and Space Administration] had asked me if I wanted to be the first man to walk on Mars. . . . There were risks involved, sure, but that was what made the project so enticing—the frisson, the audacity, the monumental pissing in the face of society.

While Felix is perhaps partially motivated by revolutionary zeal, his first thought is of his monetary future. He has other reasons for agreeing to raise the *cannabis sativa*—a lack of anything better to do, the desire to overcome a past that is fraught with unfinished projects—but material well-being is his first priority. As with any character in Boyle whose ambitions are beyond the realm of the possible, Felix finds himself disappointed. After a series of mistakes and unexpected problems, the crop is harvested and amounts to almost nothing; the three would-be entrepreneurs are left to skulk back to their previous lives—bitter, medicated, and one year older.

As usual, Boyle's characters enjoy flaunting conventional or objective morality. Their attitudes towards any sort of restrictions on their behavior can frequently be summed up by Felix' dictum that, "Certainly, like any other solid citizen with inalienable rights, I broke laws regularly." Throughout Boyle's short stories and his first novel, *Water Music,* the notion of objectivity has been nothing but a humorous idea. Boyle has his characters argue that truth is something that people exploit, that the imaginative lie is much more interesting and valuable. In *Budding Prospects* conventional sexuality is initially dismissed. "The hole was neatly cut, edges smoothed . . . and some sad joker had scrawled *Abandon hope all ye who enter here* just above it. . . . What is lust, I thought. . . . What is flesh? . . . I unfastened my zipper, found that I had an erection and penetrated the wall." Felix has taken leave of the cannabis farm and sought relief in the city; the isolation has transformed him into a being who doubts even the physical fact of his existence.

In this case, *"What is flesh?"* can be read as a contraction of the larger form, "What is flesh in the face of subjectivity?" To a greater extent as they become more intellectually developed, Boyle's characters are oppressed by the idea of their own inconsequence. As Martin Heidegger writes in *Being and Time,* "What oppresses us is not this or that, nor is it everything objectively present together as a sum, but the *possibility* of things at hand in general, that is, the world itself." The very fact of existence torments all of Boyle's characters, warps them into an existential furor that plays itself out in various ways: drug use, madness, lust for worldly goods. Felix echoes Heidegger when he says: "A cavern was opening up inside of me, a pit, a chasm in which I could hear the faint reverberations . . . of all the sad, grasping, multifarious generations as they plunged into the everlasting gloom." Felix's despair over his own failings, and over the fact that even his failings will ultimately amount to nothing, overwhelms him immediately prior to the book's conclusion.

It would be a disservice to Boyle's intent in *Budding Prospects* to say that he ends with the sadness of failure and despair. Felix survives the scheme and continues along with the business of his living. With the final paragraph of the work, he is on his way to find a woman with whom he has fallen in love. He leaves Southern California for her home in the northern part of the state, confident of "a long rainy winter ahead. . . ." He hopes to "break some new ground, and maybe even—if things went

well—to plant a little seed." Well known for his charisma and outgoing candor in interviews, Boyle has confronted these ideas directly. "Comedy is my mode of dealing with tragedy and despair," Boyle has said, stressing that he composes his work with the hope of enlivening and enlightening, in search of what he terms the "rush of pure joy and connection." Instead of slipping into pathos, Boyle's characters often turn to some sort of redemptive action, a flourish of light or humor which blunts the inevitability—or nature—of their own demise. They flaunt contemporary society and engage themselves in social issues to the extent that they dismiss them; they survive to live, despite both their tragic and comedic existence.

THE TORTILLA CURTAIN

Boyle elaborates his take on the problems of contemporary society more fully in his most politically motivated novel, *The Tortilla Curtain* (1995). This work opens with an impact; an affluent yuppie runs down a Mexican immigrant with his Acura. Delaney Mossbacher initially feels remorse and shock at the accident. He is an affluent yuppie who lives in the suburbs of Los Angeles, a self-proclaimed "liberal humanist," a modern, enlightened, successful professional with an "unblemished driving record and a freshly waxed Japanese car with personalized plates." That he has hit the Mexican—Cándido, a poor squatter who camps in the area behind Delaney's gated community—torments him, causes him great guilt. When his friends suggest that the immigrant is at fault, that the Hispanic community is the source of many of Southern California's problems, Delaney is quick to disagree. "Do you realize what you're saying? Immigrants are the lifeblood of this country—we're a nation of immigrants—and neither of us would be standing here today if it wasn't." His voice is strident, opinionated, outspoken.

Delaney will be the work's primary tragic figure, however, as Boyle chronicles the evolution of his viewpoint from a broad-based love for human endeavor to a narrow-minded xenophobia. After a series of thefts in his neighborhood, the homeowner's council, with his gradually growing support, decides to build a wall around the perimeter of the development's homes. Arroyo Blanco (White Stream) becomes emblematic of exclusion and suburban racism. Though the housing development has devastated the ecosystem of the canyon beyond repair, Delaney and his fellow suburbanites are outraged when a wildfire ravages the remainder of the once-wild landscape. They blame the fire on the homeless Mexican immigrants who are camping outside of their wall. Delaney's is chief among the angry voices; he accuses two men of starting the fire, and brings criminal proceedings against them even though they may be innocent. "He was excited now beyond caring—somebody had to pay for this—and so what if he hadn't actually seen the man lying there drunk in his filthy sleeping bag. It was close enough, wasn't it?" He has been transformed; he has become vindictive and fearful, a caricature in his bottomless anger.

Delaney also makes his living as a nature writer, a touch of irony that Boyle cannot resist; his position in the suburban sprawl, as well as his consumerist lifestyle, feed into the destruction of the natural world that he naively espouses. "They were walking hand in hand, Kyra in her Stanford windbreaker, Delaney in a lightweight Gore-Tex backcountry jacket he'd got through the Sierra Club." They are innocent to the point of the ridiculous, monogrammed wanderers in a natural landscape that they cannot understand. While Delaney admires nature from a distance, and becomes vindictive when he perceives that its remnants are under attack, Cándido, the Mexican immigrant, must live his life in its wilderness. Boyle follows the stories of his two protagonists separately. While Delaney struggles with his emotions and gradually becomes more conservative and dogmatic,

Cándido's pregnant wife is forced to give birth in the ravine behind Arroyo Blanco, surrounded by the detritus and trash of the suburban development, nothing separating her body from the ground except a soiled, stolen, plastic tarp.

It is this tarp, along with the barely edible dog food that Cándido has also pilfered from Delaney, that once again reunite Boyle's polar characters. Delaney is outraged that his possessions have been taken; he tracks the thief to a stream in the woods that still dot the canyon floor. As Delaney reaches the place where Cándido sleeps with his wife and newborn—reaches it with a gun in his hand, ready to exact his own version of vigilante justice—a part of the canyon wall sheers off and begins to slide. The flash flood separates the mother from her infant, separates the father from the mother. Nature has been burdened by erosion and pollution; it strikes back with a cataclysmic vengeance. In the roar of mud and swollen creek water, Cándido struggles to make it to safety, clambering up onto the white tile roof of the United States Post Office. His wife survives as well, but his child dies, and even as he is realizing this, even as he is cursing his luck and nature and the discrimination he has met in America, he sees Delaney's hand emerge from the torrent, grasping for life. "When he saw the white face surge up out of the black swirl of the current and the white hand grasping at the tiles, he reached down and took hold of it." The social commentary implicit in a work such as this—with the hypocrisies of its powerful characters, and the altruistic, earnest struggles of its powerless characters—resulted in wide critical acclaim and notice, with *The Tortilla Curtain* receiving comparisons to John Steinbeck's works, and winning the Prix Médicis Étranger in France.

WORLD'S END AND *FRIEND OF THE EARTH*

This pattern—two disparate stories converging into one at the conclusion of a work—is a pattern that Boyle has used several times, most notably in his novel *World's End* (1987). A sprawling, Dickensian text set over the course of four centuries, *World's End* won the PEN/Faulkner Award in 1988, catapulting Boyle to international renown as a writer. Its title is a reference to Upton Sinclair's pulpy novel by the same name, a novel which concludes in a moment of complete subjugation before the forces of history and time. Boyle's version of *World's End* follows this notion of historical inevitability through four generations of Van Brunts, Van Warts, and Cranes, families of Dutch ancestry inhabiting the Peterskill region of upstate New York, where Boyle himself was born. The intricacy of Boyle's plot defies capsulization, as he tackles a host of issues ranging from colonial plunder of Native American lands, to the ways in which generations tend to repeat the mistakes of their forbears, to the nature of existential philosophy when applied to the modern American individual.

The plot focuses on a peasant's rebellion of the late seventeenth century and the two men who were executed for leading it: Jeremy Mohonk, a Native American, and Cadwallader Crane, a fey intellectual who works in the local school. After weeks of hiding from the rule of law, their co-conspirator—Wouter Van Brunt—betrays them. Because of his treachery, his life is spared; he survives to become the progenitor of a long line of Van Brunts, all of whom are cursed by the lingering residue of his betrayal. As if they are genetically programmed to do so, his descendants methodically betray those closest to them. They leave the ones they love, they treat their children badly, they destroy any attempts at political rebellion that their friends try to foment. The last of this line, Walter Van Brunt, is the novel's protagonist in the twentieth century.

Set in 1968, the story line has its requisite personal and political dynamic. Walter leaves his young wife Jessica who, along with Tom Crane (direct progeny of the betrayed Cad-

wallader), is attempting to operate the sloop *Arcadia*. The *Arcadia* is an antiwar boat cruising the Hudson River; it pulls into various ports and, with the help of its young and rebellious crew, spreads the antiwar gospel. Walter, of course, is drawn to the ship without knowing why. On the final night of its run, a subzero winter evening during which the vessel has docked and the entire crew is having a farewell party inside, Walter drives his car through an intensifying blizzard to reach the *Arcadia*'s mooring. Though he has partially unraveled the skein of predestination that is pulling him towards a final act of betrayal, he still cuts the boat adrift and watches it meander out into the river, presumably to run aground and sink. Hypothermic and dying, Walter only partly realizes what he has done; the cold numbs him and he falls asleep in the snow, where he will be found weeks later, a preserved and ice-bound corpse.

The degree to which Boyle has engaged academic ideas about the nature of history is open to debate. Walter makes continual references to Meursualt, the focal character in Albert Camus's *The Stranger*. The work would seemingly indicate agreement with the notion that the existentially cognizant individual frees himself from the weight of history. Matters of life and death are only important to those who delude themselves into accepting the despair that goes along with the notion that their own lives, or the lives of others, have any weight or importance. Walter Van Brunt has taken an introductory philosophy course at the state university. He consciously flaunts the misplaced and strangely warped influence that Friedrich Nietzsche, Sartre, and Camus have had on his thinking. It is in this way that he ends the curse of history's weight and the burden of the past; he applies academic principles of being and nothingness to his own, localized life. He dies as the purely rational individual, purely isolated from the rest of society.

This broader society works as the close focus of Boyle's novel, *A Friend of the Earth* (2000). *Friend of the Earth* is the only of Boyle's works set in the future: much of the episodic text unfolds in 2025, when environmental degradation has prompted dire ecological consequences on a beleaguered and overcrowded earth. Population has exploded, peaking at more than ten billion, and most of the world's species have become extinct. The protagonist of the story is an aging marginal with a history suspiciously like Boyle's own. Tyronne O'Shaugnessy Tierwater was born in Peterskill, New York, is roughly the same age as Boyle will be in 2025, and is marked with many of the characteristics that necessarily haunt a writer's solitary labor: isolation, heroic and single-minded effort, inevitable failure before the demands of time.

The book is, of course, a plea for the environment. Boyle is arguing against modern American patterns of consumption, which he attacks as mindlessly self-centered, destructive, and the greatest single threat to life as we know it in this world. Following predictions of population and weather dynamics that are actually fairly conservative, Boyle sees the world in 2025 as one wracked by "unrelenting meteorological cataclysm," baking heat, and massive death from mosquito-borne epidemics. "There isn't going to be anything left of the place if the weather doesn't let up," writes Boyle. "The storms are stacked up out over the Pacific like pool balls on a billiard table and not a pocket in sight." To say, however, that *A Friend of the Earth* is solely a work of serious contemplative prognostication is to miss much of its energy. This energy, as one would expect given the body of Boyle's previous work, comes in the form of an ironic wit and a broad satire of modern sensibilities, a satire which has always been favorably received within the critical world.

Ty Tierwater's story is concerned with—and here the reader should remember Benjamin's assertion that the writer's primary sense of authority comes from death—the love affairs and personal tragedies that inevitably mark a seventy-five-year life. Consumed by his own life even in the face of ecological holocaust, Tierwater is nonetheless more cognizant of the impending global collapse than most of American society. The second epigraph to the novel, a quote from Tom Waits—"The earth died screaming / While I lay dreaming"—summons visions of the lush life of the contemporary mall, filled with its droves of shoppers, purchasing and purchasing without a thought for the context of their actions. In 2025 Tierwater manages a doomed wildlife refuge for a multimillionaire pop star. The book shuffles back and forth between the late 1980s and this "present day." In 1989 we are presented with the story of Tierwater's daughter, who dies as a martyr for the environmental cause, murdered by agents of a timber corporation against which she is protesting. While many of Boyle's novels compel the reader forward with a sense of personal tragedy, *A Friend of the Earth* also attracts with the idea of global catastrophe. The reader turns the pages to search out any sense of global redemption which, the reader eventually finds, does not come.

DESCENT OF MAN

While much of Boyle's longer fiction develops the theme of the isolation of the individual within society, *A Friend of the Earth*'s affinity is for the public sector, an affinity that spills over into his shorter writing. His shorter pieces are, almost uniformly, more concerned with public affairs, with questions of interaction rather than questions of inner evaluation. Boyle earned his reputation as a satirist with his work in the middle and late 1970s, when he was able to place stories in a roster of the most prestigious fiction-publishing magazines in the country: *The New Yorker,* the *Atlantic Monthly, Esquire, Epoch,* and *Harper's,* among others. His steady rise to prominence came partly on the strengths of his shorter works, which were lauded by critics as intelligent, savvy, quick-witted, and informed of the literary tradition of Western society. His collection, *Descent of Man,* met with a tumult of acclaim, garnering reviews in a host of periodicals both in the United States and Europe, with critics such as Larry McCaffery applauding Boyle's "feel for human passions and sensuous, evocative prose" in the *New York Times Book Review.*

Perhaps the most telling of the works in the collection is the story, "The Second Swimming," which appeared in the *Paris Review* in 1976. Set against the backdrop of the Cultural Revolution in China, the work binds several short, disparate strands of plot beneath one arc of absurdity. It is Mao's birthday, and he has decided to reward his faithful countrymen by taking a swim in a frozen river by wending his way through the capital and immersing himself in the frigid winter water. Interjected into the path of the piece are several excerpts of text, mock-ups of essays similar to those published by the Maoist regime during the height of its persecutions. Entitled "Fighting Leprosy With Revolutionary Optimism" and "Assisting More Deaf-Mutes to Sing 'The East Is Red,'" these passages provide the reader with a significant dose of ironic absurdity.

> Chang Chiu-chu of the Kunghui Commune found one day that the great toe of his left foot had become leprous. . . . Chang went to Kao Fei-fu, a revolutionary machinist of the commune . . . [who] recalled to Chang the Chairman's words: "If you want to know the taste of a pear, you must change the pear by eating it yourself. . . ."

The passage goes on to say that Chang was cured and was, thanks to Chairman Mao's wisdom, able to return to the paddies.

As the story opens, Chang is on his way to the capital, to present Mao with a pig upon his birthday as a token of thanks for the rather dubious restoration of his health. His toe is, of course, in great pain, and as he walks his condition worsens. Boyle relates Chang's journey with great attention to the comic possibilities; the humor of it lurks somewhere behind the text, and is intermingled with a very real sadness and awareness of the possibility of suffering. Boyle himself has commented on this effect, present in much of his writing. "I do feel that the tragic and poignant can be made even more powerful, more affecting, if the writer takes the reader by surprise, that is, puts him or her into a comic universe and then introduces the grimmest sort of reality." The sorrows of the individuals of this piece are rendered to the smallest detail; other strands of the plot enforce even further the deprivations and betrayals associated with the regime of Mao. But in the work's center stands the grandly pompous, dangerous, and appealing figure, comically immersing himself in the freezing water, bending the familiar image of Jesus wading into the River Jordan. Thousands of loyal supporters follow Mao to the river, jump into its dirty currents simply to have the same experience as their leader. In a way, this motion mimics the feelings experienced by Boyle's readers. Not knowing exactly why or because of what oddly compelling force, they are rushed into the worlds that his characters inhabit. The water shocks; the prose is startling and enlivening; the sum of life's emotions move through the language, numinous and elusive, a *masque en scène,* almost grotesque.

Flannery O'Connor's influence can be felt deep within these stories. Her worlds—in which common things are gradually betrayed as perverse, strange, and unexpectedly resonant—hang behind these works, coloring them, giving them tint, body, accentuation. It is as if Boyle's characters are figures submerged in a glass of water: they bend and intensify with each change in perspective, rising out of the backdrop, which is language and the fictional form, which is writing as it has been practiced over the past two hundred years by James Joyce and Nikolay Gogol, Kafka and O'Connor. How else to explain a story such as "Descent of Man," the title piece of the collection, a story that appeared in the *Paris Review* in 1974? "I was living with a woman who suddenly began to stink," it begins, and already the normal questions of love, of relationships and modern love, have been subverted, subverted in a nontraditional way. The woman in question, the narrator's girlfriend, works as a scientist at a primate lab. Over the course of her work there, she falls in love with a chimpanzee, who becomes all but human, his capabilities exaggerated in the most dramatic of ways. Visiting his girlfriend at the lab only days before she leaves him, the narrator is mocked by the chimpanzee. "Then he broke into a snicker, turned to Jane and juggled out an impossible series of gestures. Jane laughed. . . . 'Is he trying to say something?' I asked. 'Oh, potpie,' she said, 'it was nothing— just a little quote from Yeats.'" The Yeats-quoting chimpanzee, then, must take his place next to the other denizens of Boyle's mad, modern American world.

Into this tiny ball of text, Boyle fits classical allusions (the girlfriend leaves the narrator, taking her framed Rousseau reproductions with her, a reference which points to the consciousness-based experiments that the lab doctors have been performing) as well as pop-culture references. (The girlfriend's name, humorously, is Jane, a nod, along with an epigraph that is attributed to Johnny Weissmuller, to the Tarzan films of the early Hollywood era.) This versatility, of course, has been noted by critics, and has provoked a scattering of comparisons to Thomas Pynchon and Tom Robbins. "The rapid-fire modulation between high and low culture . . . ," adds McCaffery, "display[s] a vibrant sensibility fully engaged with American society—and with the wonder and joy that defiantly remain a part of our culture as well." Though Boyle frequently strays

outside America for his subject matter, "Second Swimming" and *Water Music* being good examples of this movement, he is perhaps sharpest when acutely diagramming the dilemmas and interesting portions of our national experience.

Boyle's most anthologized story, and also the title story to his collection, *Greasy Lake* (1985), is a story of this nature, an evocation of middle-class adolescent rebellion in 1960s America. Its protagonists are college-aged proto-punks, citizens of pampered suburban homes and inheritors of their parents' worldly possessions.

> When we wheeled our parents' whining station wagons out into the street we left a patch of rubber half a block long. We drank gin and grape juice, Tango, Thunderbird, and Bali Hai. We were nineteen. We were bad. We read André Gide and struck elaborate poses to show that we didn't give a shit about anything.

The vogue is French nihilism and, driven by a text-inspired sense of bravado, three friends head up to a local lake to seek out some type of adventure. The lake is a point of convocation for the marginal characters of Boyle's fictitious upstate New York town; after the inevitable fight in which the first-person protagonist nearly murders a man, knocking him unconscious with a tire iron in the height of rage, he and his friends flee into the woods.

The denouement of the piece comes with the realization—unspoken by the protagonist or his friends—that these are just children, that their pretensions of toughness are simply that: pretensions and not actualities. Their quest is for some unimpeachable sense of cool, for the perception that they are separated from the bulk of society and, by extension, from their own mortality. Max Apple's assessment of Boyle in the *New York Times Book Review* as a writer whose "characters are in search of the differences between man and beast . . . between plundered and hero" partially applies here. Madly searching for the thing that differentiates them from the sweaty mass of society, the three friends are similar to many of Boyle's characters. Yet in a story like "Greasy Lake," Boyle refutes the argument that is raised by so many of his critics, refutes the notion that the short story as he practices it is often reduced to the joke, to the experiment in humor and linguistic agility. "Greasy Lake" has a powerful interior realization, one that is not articulated, and in this it is reminiscent of the conclusion of James Joyce's "Araby," where the narrator realizes that he is a "creature driven and derided by vanity." Through the crucible of their experiences at the lake, where they are exposed to the messy realities of the "Ur-crime" that they have tried to commit, the three boys realize that they are adolescents. It is to Boyle's credit that none of this is vocalized but merely implied; the writer's work goes on far beneath the surface of the story.

Critics searching through the body of Boyle's short fiction for concerted, painstaking artistic effort have focused on the piece, "Stones in My Passway, Hellhounds on My Trail," a story that is also included in the *Greasy Lake* collection. This is a work of historical fiction; its protagonist is Robert Johnson, the legendary blues guitarist, who died under suspicious circumstances at the age of twenty-four. In Boyle's version of his death, Johnson's appetites are what kill him. Johnson is playing a set at the House Party Club in Dallas, and has spent the time between sets making love to a woman behind the building. The proprietor's daughter, however, is in love with him. Jealous of his affairs with other women, she poisons him with roach powder, adding it to the eggs and beans that she has cooked. Johnson dies with a fierce pain ripping through his stomach, realizing only as he loses consciousness that he has been poisoned. In the French-language edition of Boyle's collected fiction, the stories are grouped into three categories—"Love," "Death," and "Everything in Between." "Stones in My Passway, Hellhounds on My Trail," then, is grouped with the other "Death" stories—with a group of fictions that can be at times tremendously lyrical and serious. "Robert's dream is thick with the thighs of women, the liquid image of songs sung and songs to come, bright wire wheels and sloping fenders . . . and the road, the road spinning out like string from a spool, like veins, blood and heart, distance without end, without horizon." Much of the story is written expressly to bring the reader to this passage. Here, Boyle uses death as a means to meditate on the simple and poetic image of a life lived with dangerous passion and vigor, lived in a concussive and unfolding, constant motion.

This is not unexpected from a novelist who lists, among his antecedents, Kafka, Jorge Luis Borges, Kazuo Ishiguro, and Raymond Carver. While Carver's reserved style is dissimilar to Boyle's flamboyant prose, Boyle has clearly learned the techniques that Carver espoused: layering, attention to smallness, implication. His roots are in humor; like Borges, he will try to make you laugh with the most absurd of stories. This is evidenced in a work such as "Zapatos," which appeared in Boyle's third collection, *If the River Was Whiskey* (1989). "Zapatos" focuses on a nameless, nearly Latin American nation in which a man orchestrates a complex ploy to overcome his government's import-export duties on Italian shoes. Yet within this work there is the deeper playfulness of the writer who refuses to be entirely straightforward, who flaunts conventional notions of reason or understandability. This is a realism that has been suffused with a surprising, narcotic depth. "Zapatos" is also a consideration of the corruption of government; once the man has made his fortune, he feels more comfortable with the regulations his country places on commerce, regulations which seemed unfair when he was struggling. Human nature, Boyle argues, is temperamental, unpredictable, and disloyal. In

Boyle's work, laughter is a means of accessing this secondary meaning. It functions as a vehicle of conduct, a point of connection.

While a comic writer's chief goal must be the application of a veneer of life to the difficult specifics of death and dying, Boyle lingers in the more appropriate domain of the tragedian. The point of connection in his work is often with the fact of mortality, and this death obsession raises itself through the surface of the work many times. In *The 100 Faces of Death, Part IV,* a piece from Boyle's collection of stories, *Without a Hero* (1994), a friend of the first-person narrator is obsessed with death in all of its forms and incarnations. He forces the narrator to watch the *Faces of Death* video series, a franchise of videotapes containing the actual moments of death of hundreds of individuals around the world. This experience traumatizes the narrator, who is overwhelmed by feelings of disgust and sorrow. Time elapses, and several years later the narrator's friend is killed in a violent accident. In his memory, the narrator rents the *Faces of Death* tape. Its first victim, a magician named Renaldo who fails to escape from his own performance, becomes the object of the narrator's displaced compassion. "I waited till the moment came for him to drop the straw. Poor Renaldo. I froze it right there." Because of the horror of dying, and because of the fact that this particular man's death has been captured on tape and watched by an endless series of drunken revelers, the narrator halts the tape in a way in which life cannot be halted.

This is the writer's greatest act of arrogance: the complete control of time, character, and vocabulary. Throughout the body of his work, Boyle never relinquishes control of his subject matter, marshalling towards the exact conclusion that he wishes to reach. In his more recent work—work that includes a novel such as *A Friend of the Earth*—this control has extended to matters of time and place, to the location of his stories in a Gnostic prediction of the world's future. While Boyle has had his share of negative criticism—mostly directed towards the postmodern sense of superficiality that characterizes some of his texts—much of the critical, and popular, response to his work has been positive. His unflinching willingness to consider crucial questions and his dedication to a prose that seeks to eliminate borders even as it entertains place him at the forefront of our modern American novelists. With an ironic humor and a flair for performance, Boyle dedicates himself to an aesthetic that fully confronts the confusing and disjunctive matter of postmodern experience. His critical heritage, currently accruing in papers presented at national and international universities, will be written long into the twenty-first century.

Selected Bibliography

WORKS OF T. C. BOYLE

NOVELS
Water Music. Boston: Little, Brown, 1981.
Budding Prospects: A Pastoral. New York: Viking, 1984.
World's End. New York: Viking, 1987.
East Is East. New York: Viking, 1991.
The Road to Wellville. New York: Viking, 1993.
The Tortilla Curtain. New York: Viking, 1995.
Riven Rock. New York: Viking, 1998.
A Friend of the Earth. New York: Viking, 2000.

SHORT STORY COLLECTIONS
Descent of Man. Boston: Little, Brown, 1979.
Greasy Lake and Other Stories. New York: Viking, 1985.
If the River Was Whiskey. New York: Viking, 1990.
Without a Hero. New York: Viking, 1994.
T. C. Boyle Stories. New York: Viking, 1998.

CRITICAL AND BIOGRAPHICAL STUDIES
Apple, Max. "Characters in Search of a Difference."

New York Times Book Review, April 1, 1979, pp. 14, 39.

Gorra, Michael. "Dope Farmer in Search of Roots." *New York Times Book Review,* July 1, 1984, p. 18.

Heidegger, Martin. *Being and Time.* Edited by Joan Stambaugh. Albany, N.Y.: State University of New York Press, 1997.

Kearns, Katherine. "*Descent of Man*: A Review." *Carolina Quarterly* 31:103–105 (fall 1979).

McCaffery, Larry. "Lusty Dreamers in the Suburban Jungle." *New York Times Book Review,* June 9, 1985, pp. 15–16.

Mobilio, Albert. "Have You Hugged a Tree Today?" *New York Times Book Review,* October 8, 2000, p. 24.

Stille, Alexander. "*Descent of Man*: A Review." *Nation,* April 7, 1979, p. 377.

Thomas, D. M. "Men Who Love Too Much." *New York Times Book Review,* February 8, 1998, p. 8.

Tolson, Jay. "Mungo Park and Swirling Sentences." *Washington Post Book World,* February 7, 1982, p. 10.

FILM BASED ON THE WORK OF T. C. BOYLE
The Road to Wellville. Screenplay by Alan Parker. Directed by Alan Parker. Columbia, 1994.

—PAULS TOUTONGHI

Joseph Brodsky

1940–1996

JOSEPH BRODSKY DIED at his home in Brooklyn, New York, on January 28, 1996—a date that is strangely significant. January 28 was also the date of the death of the Irish poet William Butler Yeats some fifty-seven years earlier. Both men were poets who had achieved international recognition. Both had received the Nobel Prize for literature. But the bridge between Brodsky and Yeats was built back in 1965, when Brodsky was only twenty-five years old. In that year, the Leningrad-born writer was living in state-imposed internal exile in Siberia.

The year 1965 was also the year that T. S. Eliot died. Word of Eliot's death did not reach the exiled Brodsky for a week, but when it did, it inspired him to write in twenty-four hours "Verses on the Death of T. S. Eliot," one of his first elegies, a genre to which he would make many great contributions. The Russian poet's connection to Yeats, however, has much more to do with poetic form than content and also says a great deal about Brodsky's relations with his poetic predecessors and influences. Brodsky's elegy to Eliot was modeled explicitly on W. H. Auden's "In Memory of W. B. Yeats." By imitating Auden's poem, Brodsky was defining important aspects of the relationship of his life to his poetic vision.

While in exile within the Soviet Union, Brodsky was drawn to the works of Eliot. Eliot was an expatriate, an American who had become an English citizen. He was a man who, as many critics have noted, lived in a condition of permanent psychological wandering and exile. And his influences were fragments drawn from diverse cultures (Dante, French symbolism, Hindu poetry) that step far outside the bounds of American and English traditions.

Yeats was an Irish nationalist who wrote in English, and Auden was an English poet who had emigrated to the United States. The figure of the wanderer and exile would come to define Brodsky himself as he reached outside of the confines of the Soviet Union and even the traditions of Russian verse into the English (as well as other major literatures) to remake and redefine Russian poetry. Eventually, the Soviet Union would cast him out, an exile, never to return. Exile and elegiac dialogue with the voices of the past came to define much of Brodsky's poetry as he found freedom in a strange combination of departures and attachments. These are qualities that have helped make him not only a Russian but a Russian-American poet, a wanderer in the wilderness of freedom.

Joseph Brodsky (in Russian: Iosif Alexsandrovich Brodskii) was born in Leningrad on May 24, 1940. His parents, both Russian Jews, lived in a small apartment, "a room and a half." His father, Alexander, was a photojournalist who served in the navy during World War II, then served as curator of the photography department in Saint Petersburg's Navy Museum. In 1950, Alexander Brodskii's career in the Soviet Navy was curtailed because of a Stalinist decree that no Jew could rise higher than a commander's rank. Brodsky's mother, Maria, worked as a German-Russian interpreter in Soviet prisoner-of-war camps and later as a clerk and a bookkeeper. As a child, Brodsky lived through the German blockade of his city.

Brodsky attended public schools in Leningrad until eighth grade and then, as he once wrote, walked through gates of the school never to return. Sickened by Soviet indoctrination, he became an autodidact. He worked briefly as a milling machine operator and as a hospital morgue attendant. He applied for admission to the submarine academy but was rejected because he was Jewish. His passion for learning and his intellectual independence defined his work for the rest of his life. Brodsky read widely in Russian; he also became a scholar of both Western literature and Eastern (and especially Buddhist and Confucian) literature. He became especially learned in Russian philosophy and classical philosophy and literature. Of particular importance to him were the writings of Lev Shestov, an existentialist. Brodsky did not have a religious upbringing, and his interest in the Hebrew Bible and New Testament, often providing the subject matter for his poems, did not surface until the early 1960s.

Brodsky's outrage at the Soviet state began when the government ended the Hungarian uprising of 1956. A result of these repressive events was the cultural movement known as "Polish October." Brodsky, with the help of a woman who was studying at Leningrad University, mastered Polish and was brought into a tradition of Polish writers who would also have an enormous impact on his development. In particular were the hard-chiseled, distant, and ironic poems of Zbigniew Herbert and the philosophically rich work of a writer already in exile, Czeslaw Milosz. Brodsky described Milosz's "Treatise on Poetry" as a starting point for him; its section "The Spirit of History," defined an important problem for him—the use of poetry as a way out of the delusions of historical necessity and of nationalist and totalitarian worldviews.

SELF-SCHOOLED IN POETRY

In his teens Brodsky worked at jobs in Leningrad factories and laboratories. He joined geological expeditions to the Far North (White Sea region, 1957), the Far East (1958), and the South (Caspian Sea region, 1959) as part of a geological team looking for uranium. One member of the group showed him a volume of poetry glorifying the profession of geology and, in a competitive spirit, Brodsky felt he wanted to and could do better: this sparked the composition of his first poems. In January 1959 Brodsky gave his first poetry reading. Over the next several years he worked at translating works from Polish and from other languages that he did not know but made use of transliterations.

Of great importance at this early stage was Brodsky's friendship with Anna Akhmatova (1889–1966), one of the first major literary figures to recognize his talent. She dedicated a volume of poetry to him in 1963, when he was being harassed by the Soviet authorities: "To Joseph Brodsky, whose poems seem to me to be magical." Akhmatova also introduced Brodsky to important English and American poetry, especially the works of Robert Frost. Akhmatova's description in her great poem "Requiem" of the split between actual human suffering and a writer's depiction of it became an inspiration to the poet's own explorations of the tensions between desire and language.

Soviet authorities had already nabbed Brodsky twice before he was arrested and imprisoned in 1964 and tried for "social parasitism." He had not committed any particular political offense, but his commitment to poetry and his energy and independence of mind made him someone of whom the Soviet authorities were suspicious as a potential threat. Brodsky was never a dissident nor a dissident poet. As his mentor and friend Milosz put it: "He considered it beneath his dignity to quarrel with the state." Brodsky's arrest was part of a general crackdown instigated by Soviet premier Nikita Khrushchev between 1958 and 1964 to consolidate Soviet power. Brodsky's trial has become a legendary instance of near-political theater. Decades later, when asked what he had done wrong, Brodsky would respond, "It still beats me what made them so angry. I suppose it was that I was neither pro-Soviet nor anti-Soviet. I was simply a-Soviet. They are used to dealing with either-or situations. In a system like that a human being is either a slave or an enemy. And if you are not part of the system, you are regarded as an enemy." Brodsky viewed poetry as inherently threatening both to the state and the status quo. As he wrote in an introduction to a collection of Osip Mandelstam's poetry, "A poet gets into trouble because of his linguistic, and, by implication, his psychological superiority, rather than his politics. A song is a form of linguistic disobedience, and its sound casts its doubt on more than a concrete political system: it questions the entire existential order. And the number of adversaries grows proportionally." The Soviets charged him with composing pieces that did not conform to their standards of "literary works." The focal point of the trial came when Brodsky responded to questions about his claim to be a poet:

JUDGE: But in general what is your specialty?
BRODSKY: I'm a poet-translator.
JUDGE: And who said that you were a poet? Who included you among the ranks of the poets?
BRODSKY: No one. (Unsolicited) And who included me among the ranks of the human race?
JUDGE: Did you study this?
BRODSKY: What?
JUDGE: To be a poet? You did not finish high school where they prepare . . . where they teach . . .
BRODSKY: I didn't think you could get this from school.
JUDGE: How, then?
BRODSKY: I think that it . . . comes from God . . .

Brodsky was ordered to undergo a psychiatric examination, from which it was determined that he had "psychopathic traits." During his evaluation, Brodsky was tranquilized and tortured. One particularly bizarre form of torture involved his being dipped in an ice bath, then wrapped in a wet towel and placed next to a heater; as the heat dried the towel, it created a tourniquet effect, cutting into his flesh.

Brodsky was sentenced to five years of hard labor in the Far North, despite support from prominent Soviet intellectuals including Akhmatova and composer Dmitri Shostakovich. Brodsky worked primarily on a state farm in the isolated village of Norinskaia, near the Arctic Circle. There he contended with the hard farm labor (including cleaning stables) as well as an extremely harsh climate. But the isolation provided Brodsky with a great deal of time for reading and writing. In this internal exile, he mastered literary English. Using a Russian-English dictionary, he made literal translations of poems by Dylan Thomas, Auden, Eliot, Yeats, and Wallace Stevens. Brodsky was released after serving twenty-two months of his term, largely because of the political turmoil brewing in the Soviet Union after Khrushchev's ouster.

FORCED TO LEAVE THE SOVIET UNION

When Brodsky returned to Leningrad in 1965, a volume of his poetry had been published in Russian in the United States. He had no hand in the selection or preparation of the volume, which included juvenilia. The texts were unreliable and contained numerous errors, but the volume did contain two important early poems: the "Great Elegy for John Donne," and the untranslated "Isaac and Abraham." Only four of Brodsky's poems made it into print in the Soviet Union between 1961 and 1987. Publication of the first volume of poetry supervised by the poet himself came in 1970 with *Ostanovka v pustyne* (A halt in the wilderness).

Eventually, Brodsky's unwillingness to work within the realm of state-sanctioned ideas of literature led to his departure from his homeland. On May 10, 1972, Soviet security officials "invited" him to leave, to accept "an invitation to Israel." It was clear that this was a threat, not a choice. If he stayed in the Soviet Union, he would face imprisonment or worse. Brodsky was allowed to spend his thirty-second birthday with his parents, then was flown to Vienna on June 4. In Vienna, Brodsky was met by Carl R. Proffer, a publisher and professor of Russian language and literature at the University of Michigan. Proffer introduced Brodsky to Auden, who was spending his summers in Vienna. Auden wrote a warm foreword to the first major edition of Brodsky's work to appear in English, *Selected Poems,* translated by George Kline. A position of poet-in-residence was arranged for Brodsky at the University of Michigan, and he became a U.S. citizen on October 11, 1977.

A longtime resident of New York's Greenwich Village, Brodsky taught at various points at Queens College, Columbia University, and New York University. He became a professor of literature and was Five College Professor at Mount Holyoke (Amherst, Smith, Mt. Holyoke, Hampshire, and the University of Massachusetts), and he taught courses on both Russian poetry and American and contemporary world poetry. Brodsky was an extraordinarily gifted, inspiring, and demanding teacher: he provided his students with long lists of books they needed to read, insisted that they memorize poems, and focused class discussion on the details of a given poet's works. As Brodsky wrote in his introduction to an English-language edition of Mandelstam's poems, "the mother of all Muses was Mnemosyne, the Muse of Memory, and a poem (be it a short one or an epic) must be memorized in order to survive." Yale University awarded him an honorary degree in 1978. *A Part of Speech,* a second collection of Brodsky's poetry from the late 1960s to the late 1970s, was published by Farrar, Straus & Giroux in 1980, followed by a volume of his essays, *Less than One* (1986) and another volume of poems, *To Urania* (1988). In 1987, at age of forty-seven, Brodsky received the Nobel Prize for literature.

The Soviet-born poet also became an important figure in encouraging American public education in poetry, and he viewed the development of literary taste as the supreme weapon against cheap rhetoric and demagoguery. Appointed poet laureate of the United States in 1991, Brodsky argued that the American government should make poetry available to the public and subsidize the general distribution of volumes of major American poets' works. In addition to giving dozens of readings throughout the world, Brodsky loved to travel in summers and early fall to his beloved Venice, to Rome, and to Sweden. He married Maria Sozzani in 1990, and they had one child, a daughter. A chronic heart condition of uncertain origins plagued him throughout his life. There has been some speculation that he had contracted rheumatic fever in his youth, although the condition was most likely misdiagnosed. Brodsky had three bypass operations in his lifetime but never gave up chain smoking unfiltered cigarettes. On January 28, 1996, he died of a heart attack at his home in Brooklyn Heights, New York. A memorial service was held at the Cathedral of St. John the Divine in New York City and attended by hundreds. Poets Yevgeny Rein and Czeslaw Milosz as well as dancer Mikhail Barishnakov read poems at his funeral service. Brodsky's remains were kept in a mausoleum in New York for year and then transferred to Venice for burial.

THE POETRY

At the core of Brodsky's life and art lie the twin themes of exile and estrangement, and his works meditate on the true meaning of the term "exile." Brodsky's poetry attempts to embody in the fierce rhythms of his lyric language the acceleration of time and escape from the confines of space. For Brodsky, immortality was but ubiquity in time. Brodsky treated exile with ironic detachment, often adopting mythic personae in his handling of theme. In Brodsky's hands, exile became the condition of modern man seeking freedom from all forms of coercion and rootedness. Through the form of the elegy, the poet regarded exile as an expression of the soul's estrangement from the body.

From the moment he left school, Brodsky conceived of his life and thought in terms of departures—a way of liberating himself from suffocation. He also considered estrangement as a form of witness in which the poet-observer stands outside or watches the predicament of the moment and considers a return to an ancient and perhaps purer source, much the way his mentor Auden dreamed of underground streams and white landscapes in "In Praise of Limestone." If there is a return in Brodsky's work, it is very often not to God or to a spiritual world but to a kind of materiality that includes language. As he wrote in his introduction to Mandelstam's poetry, "Art is not a better, but an alternative existence; it is not an attempt to escape reality but the opposite, an attempt to animate it. It is the spirit seeking flesh but finding words." The theme of the wandering Jew as well as the birth and Passion of Christ recur throughout his work, though he remains equivocal and silent on the Resurrection.

In the "Great Elegy for John Donne" (1963), Brodsky steps outside the tradition of his own poetry into the realm of English metaphysical poetry. He works within the ancient tradition of pastoral elegy, a genre in which one poet mourns the death of another. In choosing to mourn figures far outside the cultural world in which he was raised, Brodsky liberated himself from the confines of time, nationalism, and political obsessions, though he had less of the nostalgia for a world culture that characterized the "Acmeist" movement of early twentieth-century Russian poetry. Elegy offered him the possibility of creating a monument in language, or *tombeau,* that both acknowledges the literary forebear and asserts how he will carry on in a new way. In mourning Donne, Brodsky imagines with great intensity the "sleep" of death

and the way all things disappear with that sleep. But, of course, sleep portends awakening. The sleeping Donne is confronted not by Christ or St. Paul but by the thin voice of his own soul wandering and projecting his life back to him. Brodsky provides in this poem the image of the shroud as a figure of the work of art, stitched with needle and thread but tattered, as a bar against complete annihilation. And, as often occurs in Brodsky's works, the image of the star appears as both a harbinger of the Messiah and as pure materiality cast in beautiful form and taking its place in the vast firmament:

> Whatever millstone these swift waters turn
> will grind the same coarse grain in this one world.
> For though our life may be a thing to share,
> who is there in this world to share our death?
> Man's garment gapes with holes. It can be torn,
> by him who will, at this edge or at that.
> It falls to shreds and is made whole again.
> Once more it's rent. And only the far sky,
> in darkness, brings the healing needle home.
> Sleep, John Donne, sleep. Sleep soundly, do not fret
> your soul. As for your coat, it's torn; all limp
> it hangs. But see, there from the clouds will shine
> that Star which made your world endure till now.

It could be asked at this point whether "that Star" is a sign of the apocalypse or of the Second Coming or just some possibility of a future. Brodsky returned to the figure of the star frequently throughout his career. One of his first Christmas poems, entitled "1 January 1965" (because January 6 is Christmas on the Russian Orthodox calendar, and in the Soviet Union gifts are usually exchanged on New Year's Day), he meditates on the way the Star of the Nativity is an absence, not a presence:

> The Wise Men will unlearn your name.
> Above your head no star will flame.
> One weary sound will be the same—
> the hoarse roar of the gale.
> The shadows fall from your tired eyes
> as your lone bedside candle dies,

for here the calendar breeds nights
till stores of candles fail.

The poem was most likely inspired by the long nights and loneliness he experienced in internal exile in the Far North. Speaking of himself, but also of humanity in the twentieth century, he muses about belatedness: "It's clear that you are now too old / to trust in good Saint Nick; / that it's too late for miracles." Still, his stance avoids nihilism or morbidity. The possibility of joy resides in a revelation of life: "But suddenly, lifting your eyes / to heaven's light, you realize: / your *life* is a sheer gift."

Brodsky's use of biblical, and particularly Christian, themes raise questions about the nature of his religious vision. The poet maintained no formal religious allegiances. Robert Hass aptly summarizes a fair impression of Brodsky's vision: "Nothing is Brodsky's theme, the struggle of consciousness against the horror and boredom of things." Of course, "nothing" is a complicated subject; in Buddhism it is the ground of being, and Brodsky read deeply in Eastern philosophy in his early years. He also read works by the Russian existentialist Lev Shestov, who defended the seeking of faith and meaning against stoic acceptance of a spiritless, material universe. Against the sense of necessity of ancient Athenian rationality, Shestov proposed the ceaseless striving for transcendence of Jerusalem, but without certainty or comfort. Brodsky loved what he called "the terror of uncertainty" and placed it on a higher plane than the catharsis and moral certainty of tragedy. An early poem entitled "A Halt in the Desert" (1966) reveals a mind caught between Athens and Jerusalem, desiring the best qualities of both and fearing the possibility of tyranny in finding a utopia in either:

Tonight I stare out through the black window
and think about that point to which we've come,
and then I ask myself: from which are we
now more remote—the world of ancient Greece,

or Orthodoxy? Which is closer now?
What lies ahead? Does a new epoch wait
for us? And, if it does, what duty do we owe?—
What sacrifices must we make for it?

Brodsky's is a rhetorically less inflated, more conversational response to the apocalyptic vision of Yeats's "Second Coming," in which "somewhere in the sands of the desert / A shape with lion body and the head of a man, . . . / Slouches towards Bethlehem to be born." (His numerous Nativity poems address this "slouching" beast's identity.)

In his early poetry and in his works composed just prior to and following his expulsion from the Soviet Union, Brodsky extends the pastoral elegy to include a variety of mythological and historical figures. Sometimes his use of classical stories masks a contemporary personal predicament but also enables it to suggest something more universal. One early example of his masterful handling of classical myth is "Aeneas and Dido" (1969). The story of Aeneas's leaving Dido must have suggested to the peregrine Brodsky the precarious relationship between intimate desires and heroic endeavors. In the poem, pursuit of something distant and remote—whether Aeneas's pursuit of a distant shore or Dido's pursuit of the sculpture-like Aeneas—is a tragedy of time and movement, space and motionless.

The great man stared out through the open
    window;
but her entire world ended at the border
of his broad Grecian tunic, whose abundance
of folds had the fixed, frozen look of seawaves
long since immobilized.

Dido's suicide becomes transformed into a vision of the destruction of her city, almost as a figure for the way all fixed entities will crumble into ruins:

Dido stood
alone before the bonfire which her soldiers

had kindled by the city walls, and there—
as in a vision trembling between flame
and smoke—she watched great Carthage silently
crumble to ash,

long ages before Cato's prophecy.

At the center of the poem is the sadness of the sea as a consuming figure; the line "The sea became a sea of shining tears" presents a mirror image of both their losses.

Brodsky's creation of masks and his use of classical figures to mask his own predicament became more apparent in works written in the late winter of 1972, when the poet was threatened with permanent exile. Brodsky had fathered a son, Andrei, who was born October 9, 1967. The child's mother, whom Brodsky never married, is addressed as M. B. in dozens of poems. One of the most moving of these poems is "Odysseus to Telemachus" (1972). Tortured by a separation from his son that will probably never have a happy resolution, the modern Odysseus suffers the fate of the wanderer: "To a wanderer the faces of all islands resemble one another." His sense of history is also numb: "I can't remember how the war came out." But the conclusion is particularly grim, as the heroic world of Homer is invaded by the urban world of Sophocles: ". . . away from me / you are quite safe from all Oedipal passions, / and your dreams, my Telemachus, are blameless." It is a disturbing view of human relationships, one in which exile may actually be a better alternative than family or home.

This horrifying sense of death as the basis of understanding between parent and child also underlies *Nature Morte* (1971), a poem that sees the whole world as beginning and ending with death and dead matter—a veritable "still life." Brodsky demythologizes the iconography of death and renders it inescapably ordinary and human: "Scythe, skull, and skeleton—an absurd pack of lies. / Rather: 'Death, when it comes / will have your own two eyes.'" The conclusion

has the crucified Christ answering his mother's questions about the future:

> Mary now speaks to Christ:
> "Are you my son?—or God?
> You are nailed to the cross.
> Where lies my homeward road?
>
> How can I close my eyes,
> uncertain and afraid?
> Are you dead?—or alive?
> Are you my son?—or God?"
>
> Christ speaks to her in turn:
> "Whether dead or alive,
> woman, it's all the same—
> son or God, I am thine."

Love and death, divine and human, sacred and profane are collapsed into an uncertain and dark future in which Brodsky is both son and mother.

The companion poem to *Nature Morte—Nunc Dimittis* (1972)—also views the separation of parent and child through the mythic lens of the story of the Passion of Christ, particularly the Crucifixion. The story takes place at the moment of the transition from the Old to the New Testament, as the Christ child is presented at the temple. Brodsky takes on the role of the older Simeon, departing for the outer dark and light of a post-Christian world. Some biographical readings of this poem indicate that the Anna of the poem also refers to Anna Akhmatova; the poem, in part, is an elegy for the anniversary of her death. But Brodsky also sees himself as Simeon and the Nativity as a moment of birth that simultaneously signals separation, wandering, and death:

> He went forth to die. It was not the loud din
> of streets that he faced when he flung the door wide,
> but rather the deaf-and-dumb fields of death's kingdom.
> He strode through a space that was no longer solid.

The "form of the Child" held in memory is a torch but one "to light up the path that leads into death's realm." Brodsky becomes a light to death.

METAPHOR IN BRODSKY'S POEMS

Inspired by Donne, Brodsky became an inheritor of the English metaphysical tradition, and a number of his poems display a deftness with elaborate metaphoric conceits, a lifting of ordinary experience with highly philosophical and conceptual preoccupations. In the love poems "Six Years Later" and "A Song to No Music," the geometric triangle becomes a transcendent figure both of love and betrayal. "The Butterfly" is written in stanzas that themselves take the form of a butterfly; the butterfly's death becomes a figure for art as flesh becomes the word. It is a meditation that echoes the theodicy of William Blake's poem "The Tiger": Brodsky draws parallels between God and creation on the one hand and the artist and his subject matter on the other. He also gives relentless trial to the possibility that all our constructs are mere tautologies, vicious circles of thought and jokes played by the artist on himself.

Brodsky's experience in a state psychiatric ward was no doubt part of the inspiration for the existential and somewhat absurd vision of "From Gorbunov and Gorchakov," composed between 1965 and 1968. Gorbunov and Gorchakov are both patients in an insane asylum near Leningrad. They have a series of conversations about their dreams and about the madhouse. It is a mad Platonic and even pastoral dialogue stood on its head. Instead of Arcadia, we are in an asylum. Gorbunov's name means "hunchback," and he is also an introspective and philosophical character who devotes his time to thinking about love and suffering. His dreams are filled with images of chanterelles and of the sea. He is also religious and makes numerous references to the Passion story. Gorchakov sees the world in empirical terms. He states that

"existence determines consciousness," whereas Gorbunov argues the reverse: "Consciousness determines existence." They are mirror images of each other speculating in a void. Indeed, the difficulty of determining one voice from another in the digressive dialogue portion of the poem suggests that this dialogue represents one mind split in two, projecting its tautology onto the void. Both men fear solitude and above all silence. Gorchakov betrays Gorbunov and, in turn, may be allowed release for Easter. He becomes a kind of Judas to a martyred Gorbunov. In Canto 10, a dialogue between the two men erupts in a kind of unified chorus to silence that concludes:

> "Silence is the present for the men
> who lived before us. And, procuress-like,
> silence gathers all together in
> itself, admitted by the speech-filled present. Life
> is but a conversation in the face
> of silence." "Gestures, quarrels, men incensed."
> "A twilight talking to a murky close."
> "With walls that stand like arguments against."

During the late 1960s, Brodsky developed the form and theme of "Gorbunov and Gorchakov" in a play entitled *Marbles* (first published in Russian in 1984). A Platonic dialogue in the form of a double anachronism (the action takes place two centuries after our era), the play is set in a prison cell that provides for the three unities of classical drama—those of time, place, and action—but is truly "an oasis of horror in a desert of boredom." *Marbles* is also a mad dialogue between the two inmates, Publius and Tullius, and the title suggests the game of marbles, as they both lose their marbles while contemplating the possibility of transcendence embodied in the marble busts of the great classical poets.

In the poetry Brodsky wrote in the years immediately following his exile from 1974 to 1976 (collected in *A Part of Speech,* 1980), an odd variety of historical figures become masques for his own predicament: Dante, Mary Queen of Scots, and Marshal Georgy Zhukov. "Twenty Sonnets on Mary Queen of Scots" finds the poet declaring his love for the exiled and eventually executed queen, whose plight, he declares, has no cause other than her beauty. "On the Death of Zhukov" (1974) makes a poignant analogy between the gifts of victory and freedom brought by a great military leader and those brought by a great poet. Heroism and triumph are followed by dishonor and exile. Brodsky admired the nobility of military heroes, and the rhythm of the poem suggests the same interrupted beat of a military funeral march found in a similar elegy by the eighteenth-century Russian poet Derzhavin.

Because of his exile from his beloved Florence, Dante has become the patron saint of all modern poets of exile, and Brodsky invokes him strikingly at the end of "The Funeral of Bobò" (1972) an otherwise bitter meditation on death and annihilation:

You were all things, Bobò. But your decease
has changed you. You are nothing; you are not;
or, rather, you are a clot of emptiness—
which also, come to think of it, is a lot.

The bemused and often absurd notion of emptiness is balanced in the concluding quatrain with the appearance of Dante:

Now Thursday. I believe in emptiness.
There, it's like hell, but shittier, I've heard.
And the new Dante, pregnant with his message,
bends to the empty page and writes a word.

Death gives way to emptiness, which suddenly gives way to the poet giving birth to a meditation on death that promises life through language. In "December in Florence," the speaker observes the tension between the great city of the fourteenth century and the modern one and cryptically draws a parallel between his own exile from Leningrad and Dante's exile from Florence. It is a highly compressed meditation on the continuity and survival of the past into the present through language that echoes the poetry of not only Dante but also Akhmatova, Mandelstam (one of the most important influences on Brodsky), and Robert Lowell.

EMBRACING AMERICA

"Lullaby of Cape Cod" is regarded as one of Brodsky's most important poems from the mid-1970s, as he was adopting the United States and strengthening his bond with the English language. Its inspiration has been shown by David Bethea to be in part Mandelstam and also Lowell, underscoring his commitment to both national traditions. Brodsky meditates on displacement and feels for all his wandering "that I know / what the globe itself must feel: / there's nowhere to go." But his attitude toward the United States at this point is somewhat ironic when he states, "I write from an Empire whose enormous flanks / extend beneath the sea." That "Empire" is both the Soviet Union of his birth and his adopted country. Brodsky levels the sense of superiority that one nation may comfortably feel over another. His vision is one of endurance and survival, not of despair. He displays a willingness to go forward and embraces the connection in American literary consciousness between natural history, survival, and Protestantism. Cape Cod becomes not only a place but a verbal icon that is ironically part of the Darwinian world and Christian iconology:

Preserve these words against a time of cold,
a day of fear: man survives like a fish,
stranded, beached, but intent
on adapting itself to some deep, cellular wish,
wriggling toward bushes, forming hinged leg-
    struts, then
to depart (leaving a track like the scrawl of a pen)
for the interior, the heart of a continent.

"Lullaby of Cape Cod" echoes both the success and the troubles that have surrounded Brodsky's reputation in the United States and the English-speaking world. Robert Hass, in a review entitled "Lost in Translation," wrote: "Reading *A Part of Speech* is like wandering through the ruins of what has been reported to be a noble building." He cited as an example the failed translation of a line from "Lullaby of Cape Cod": "Therefore, sleep well. Sweet dreams. Knit up that sleeve. / Sleep as those only do who have gone pee-pee." Hass summarizes the difficulties of translating Russian poetry into English as being due in part to the possibilities of flexible word order of an inflected language. Some of the difficulty, he added, has to do with the relative freshness of highly formal, metrical verse in Russian, a tradition that has become somewhat more stale in English and associated with a stodgy conservatism. Hass admitted, though, that certain translators of Brodsky's poems had achieved great success, specifically Derek Walcott in his version of "Letters from the Ming Dynasty," Richard Wilbur in his version of "Six Years Later" and "The Funeral of Bobò," and George Kline in his version of *Nunc Dimittis*. In conclusion, Hass suggested that Brodsky "sounds something like Robert Lowell when Lowell is sounding like Byron."

Brodsky adhered strictly to rules of craftsmanship that extend back to eighteenth-century Russian verse. He worked in and experimented in a variety of genres: ode, lyrical poem, elegy, and verse narrative. He combined slang with elaborate figurative diction in phrases that extend over lines and even stanzas intended to be sung as much as recited. All of these qualities made translation of his works extremely difficult, even with help of highly accomplished American poets. But, to many, his power came through in English, even if almost all admit that reading the translations should ultimately inspire readers to learn Russian.

Derek Walcott, who collaborated with Brodsky on his translations, described Brodsky's English versions not as mere translations but as recreations—interlinear translations, really, through a series of transformations that lead eventually to transfiguration. Walcott also defended the difficulties of Brodsky's English: "If some critic of Brodsky's work says 'this isn't English,' the critic is right in the wrong way. He is right in the historical, the grammatical sense, by which I do not mean grammatical errors, but a given grammatical tone. This is not 'plain American, which dogs and cats can read,' the barbarous . . . boast of the poet as mass thinker, as monosyllabic despot; but the same critic, in earlier epochs, might have said the same thing about Donne, Milton, Browning, Hopkins." Walcott defends Brodsky's cultivated difficulty in English as fitting his metaphysical turns of mind.

TO URANIA

To Urania is the most unified volume in theme and tone of the three Brodsky collections published in English. (The Russian version, with slightly different contents, was published as *Uraniia* by Ardis Press in Ann Arbor, Michigan, in 1987.) It was the first volume in which he translated most of the poems himself. These poems were composed from 1974 to 1985, the first decade or so after his arrival and settling in the United States. An exuberant desire for cosmic oblivion pervades the entire book. Its opening poem, "May 24, 1980," begins with wild gratitude: "Broken eggs make me grieve; the omelette, though, makes me vomit. / Yet until brown clay has been crammed down my larynx, / only gratitude will be gushing from it." No cliché, especially the Stalinist cliché that you need to break some eggs in order to make an omelette, can stop his voice, his throat.

The Muse of these poems is Urania, one of nine classical muses and the patron of astronomy. She takes Brodsky beyond history to the arctic of his soul and of the universe. In "Lithuanian Nocturne" (1974), Brodsky celebrates his friendship with poet and Lithuanian exile Thomas Venclova. He is aware that Lithuania was invaded and absorbed by Poland, Russia, and the Soviet Union and, as such, is a place that has struggled to maintain its islandlike independence in the far north of Central Europe; its native language is also non-Slavic in a Slavic region. The apotheosis of the poem is not Lithuania nor any homeland but the rare air of space addressed to Urania: "Muse of dots lost in space! Muse of things one makes out / through a telescope only! Muse of subtraction / But without remainders! Of zeroes, in short." His "little aria" seeks "the viewpoint / of air, / of pure air! . . . / It is our 'homeward'! That town / which all syllables long / to return to." The ancient theme of *per aspera ad astra* (the difficult path to the stars) becomes completely materialized in a vision that "the firmament's a chorus of highly pitched vocal / atoms, alias souls."

Homeland is everywhere and nowhere in this volume, something to be escaped on the rocket of lyric without the hope of return, at least to a single home. And Brodsky is everywhere seeking the infinite and the invisible as he does in "Roman Elegies": "The more invisible something is, / the more certain it's been around, / and the more obviously it's everywhere. . . ." This wandering is in evidence from the titles of many of the poems in *To Urania*: "A Polar Explorer," "Lithuanian Nocturne," "North Baltic," "The Berlin Wall Tune," "Dutch Mistress," "Allenby Road," "The New Jules Verne," "Café Trieste: San Francisco," "Near Alexandria," "Roman Elegies," "Venetian Stanzas," "Kellomäki," "Belfast Tune," and "In Italy." In "Venetian Stanzas," Brodsky celebrates the elusive, jumbled, bric-a-brac landscape of a city that became an intersection of Western and Eastern culture. Later, Brodsky turned his

fascination with Venice into an extended essay in English entitled *Watermark*. The inescapable presence of water in the city attracts Brodsky as a symbol of time and of eternity:

> I always adhered to the idea that God is time, or at least his spirit is. . . . I always thought that if the Spirit of God moved upon the face of the water, the water was bound to reflect it. . . . I am looking for either a cloud or the crest of a wave hitting the shore at midnight. That, to me, is time coming out of water, and I stare at the lace-like pattern it puts on the shore. . . . This is the way, and in my case why, I set my eyes on this city.

The title poem of *To Urania* also scans vast landscapes and eventually concludes with a similar image of water as lace, an erotic gesture to this muse of infinitude that governs time and movement: "And still farther east, steam dreadnoughts or cruisers, / and the expanse grows blue like lace underwear."

One of the most poignant lyrics of the book, "The Hawk's Cry in Autumn," is set against the landscape of a New England winter. Brodsky imagines the hawk soaring to an "astronomically objective hell" but still "swelling notes in ripples across the blue vault of space / whose lack of echo spells, especially in October, / an apotheosis of pure sound." To the innocent delight of observing children, the hawk's flight is also its death, showering upon them feathers like snow. The work of art in creating becomes a flight outward with no hope of return.

LESS THAN ONE

Though Brodsky had developed something of a following and a reputation in his adopted country by the mid-1980s, his works were not very well known in the United States at that point, in large part because of the innate difficulty of his poetry, made that much greater by the challenge of translation. The publication of *Less Than One,* a collection of essays, brought him much wider public acclaim. It received the 1986 National Book Critics Circle Award for criticism. Many of the qualities that make Brodsky's poetry great are also present in his prose—grand eloquence and quirky, unpredictable, off-handed observation and commentary in the midst of great, unusual erudition. Comprised of essays primarily of tribute to other poets—Marina Tsvetayeva, Anna Akhmatova, Eugenio Montale, Dmitri Platonov, and W. H. Auden—the volume demonstrates in prose form Brodsky's ability to transform the genre of the pastoral elegy into a study of metaphysics, language, religion, and politics.

Brodsky's great autobiographical theme of exile and estrangement pervades *Less Than One.* Two major essays are devoted to Auden: a fifty-two-page reading of Auden's "September 1, 1939" and "To Please a Shadow." Both essays were written in English, and in "To Please a Shadow" we learn why Brodsky learned English: "My desire to write in English had nothing to do with any sense of confidence, contentment, or comfort; it was simply a desire to please a shadow. . . . Somehow I thought that he might like it better if I made myself clear to him in English." Brodsky's devotion to this master reflects his unwillingness to submit to sentimental attachments to his own native language, or at least his willingness to escape nostalgia and recognize its limitations. The continual estrangement from himself and his willingness to look at himself and others from another or "higher plane of regard" (a phrase borrowed from Robert Frost that he used often) is another aspect of this tribute. His focus on Auden is related to the condition of exile; Auden's "September 1, 1939" was written after the poet had left England to live in the United States while the Nazis were invading Poland. Auden had demonstrated to Brodsky how to escape the confines of history while also acknowledging the shame and guilt of having done so. Brodsky's elaborate reading of the poem is a genre of explication rarely found, or possible, within the ordinary confines of professional literary criticism, and this kind of devotion creates its own message. Poetry and the possibilities of language precede and transcend time and history, and they are greater than time and history. In reading Auden's "In Memory of W. B. Yeats," Brodsky recalls the importance of the lines: "Time . . . worships language and forgives / Everyone by whom it lives." A poet for Brodsky is "simply the [one] by whom the language lives." There is also an ethical imperative for Brodsky in Auden's anti-heroic stance: in his handling of his own self-exile, Brodsky admits and accepts his own insignificance.

Brodsky provides a seventy-two page reading of Marina Tsvetayeva's poem "Novogodnee" ("New Year's Greetings"), a poem that itself is an elegy to her friend Rainer Maria Rilke. Brodsky sees the poem as Tsvetayeva's creating with Rilke a triangle in time, of which "eternity" is but a fraction. His portrait of her technical and metrical precision and her balancing of visionary language and ordinary diction can also be seen as mirroring Brodsky's own poetics. These unabashed and almost baroque studies of individual poems assume that language is the basis of perception and of civilization and that poetry is the highest embodiment of language. Brodsky reinvents the Shelleyan dictum that poets are the unacknowledged legislators of the world.

Brodsky refuses, however, to be cast as an aesthete seeking simply to exempt himself from the world, from time, and from change. One of the most complex and powerful essays in *Less Than One* is "Flight from Byzantium." Its title recalls Yeats's "Sailing to Byzantium." Byzantium (the modern Istanbul) housed the Platonic academy until the fifteenth century and was the capital of Eastern (Greek) Christianity. For Yeats, it was the place of eternity, a paradise without growth or change that would be ideal for the aging artist. Brodsky sees Byzantium as the failure to accept change and to force a type of monotheism upon the world. He rejects, then, any nostalgia for the East, even as he rejects any "Rome" as merely a stop on the endless passage of time into infinitude. The linear principle of continual "departure" and an "irresponsible" attitude toward the icons of the past, something Brodsky sees embodied in Aeneas's onward journey, complicates Brodsky's tremendous attachment to his ancient and modern predecessors. Brodsky's enemy is nostalgia, and his attachments are personal and individual rather than political and national.

Brodsky's essays avoid political attacks on totalitarian government. His main line of attack against the annihilating forces of history, politics, and evil in general derives from a love of the baroque excesses of individual eccentricity. In "A Commencement Address," (given at Williams College in 1984), Brodsky turns an incident in his own youth into a parable. While in a Soviet prison camp, he and his fellow inmates were forced to partake in grueling lumber-chopping competitions, often a contest of guards against prisoners. On one occasion, Brodsky (though he does not name himself) kept chopping long after the competition had ended and everyone else was in a state of exhaustion. This seemingly insane act actually resulted in an end to all further calls for wood-chopping competitions. The victory came by making evil appear absurd through excess that, in its own way, transformed and transcended it.

ON GRIEF AND REASON

Brodsky's second collection of essays, *On Grief and Reason* (1995), contains further meditations on the aim and craft of poetry, again in the form of devoted readings of the works of great poets. The title essay is the most detailed study of Robert Frost's "Home Burial" since Randall Jarrell's pioneering essay forty years earlier. In addition, there are long, intricate studies of

Rilke's poem on Orpheus and Eurydice and Thomas Hardy's "The Convergence of the Twain." The entire collection is a study of the nature of elegy as the pursuit of both the inanimate and the infinite and about the limits of emotion in poetry. Brodsky's premises about the relation of language to culture and poetry are delineated in one of the first essays in the volume, his Nobel lecture entitled "Uncommon Visage" (1987). The author assumes that language is not the instrument of the poet but that the poet is "language's means toward the continuation of its existence." He further states: "The one who writes a poem writes it above all because verse writing is an extraordinary accelerator of consciousness, of thinking, of comprehending the universe." In another essay on creativity entitled "A Cat's Meow" (1995), Brodsky asserts that "language is . . . the inanimate's first line of information about itself released to the animate. . . . Language is a diluted aspect of matter. By manipulating it into a harmony or, for that matter, disharmony, a poet—by and large unwittingly—negotiates himself into the domain of pure matter—or, if you will, of pure time."

In the essay "Altra Ego" (1990), Brodsky describes his idea of the Muse: "The Muse . . . is not an alternative to the beloved but precedes her." (The "beloved" here is the subject of the poem.) And the Muse drives the poet to comprehend what is ultimately infinite and ungraspable. Brodsky's version of Frost's "Home Burial" reveals both what he learned from Frost and what Brodsky projected back into his work. He reads the Frost poem as a "dark pastoral," a dialogue between two irreconcilable voices that drive each other to extremes. The inspiration of Virgil's *Eclogues* is apparent in the works of both writers. Brodsky sees the Frost poem as an expanded or dramatic love poem and elegy. The man, a type of Pygmalion, attempts to understand and control his wife, Amy, a type of Galatea (Brodsky's own "Galatea Encore" reminds us of the importance of the story in his own poetic mythology). Amy's refusal to conform renders her a gateway to the intractable and to the infinite. Each drives the other into a dramatic corner that ends in an uncertain conclusion, a near-bursting of the bounds of emotion and argument. At the core of this conversation is the ultimate muse, the "Life Force," that drives Frost and his readers to a higher plane of regard, an estrangement from his own language and into a new realm.

In "Wooing the Inanimate" (1994)—Brodsky's reading of Hardy's "Convergence of the Twain" and of the elegies written for Emma Hardy—Brodsky sees Hardy's poetic monument as a dramatic figure of discovering the infinite through the passionate pursuit of the inanimate. He argues that in the conclusion of "My Last Drive," Hardy redefines the genres of funeral elegy and love poetry. Emma Hardy, an embodiment of the Immanent Will in "The Convergence of the Twain" (written two weeks after the sinking of the Titanic in the early morning hours of April 15, 1912), invades the poet's memory, challenges his humanity, and redefines love as cold indifference.

Brodsky's "Ninety Years Later" (1994) praises Rilke's 1904 poem "Orpheus, Eurydice, Hermes" for the vision of infinity and dissipation embodied in the depiction of Eurydice: "She was already loosened like long hair, / and given far and wide like fallen rain, / and dealt out like a manifold supply." The interpenetration of language and matter in continual metamorphosis is praised throughout the book. Brodsky's own metamorphosis occurs through continual dialogue with memory and the authors of the recent and deep past.

SO FORTH

"A Footnote to Weather Forecasts" (1986), one of the poems in Brodsky's last collection, *So Forth* (1996), echoes his hatred of monotony. A

vision of the future, really an afterlife, "is a panacea / against anything prone to repetition." The great variety of lyrics in the volume reflect the poet's meditations on his own annihilation. Of the more than sixty poems in the collection, twenty-three were actually written in English. All but seven of those written in Russian were translated by Brodsky himself, without collaboration. Brodsky's style, at this point, has evolved to imitate both later Auden and Frost: the Auden of "September 1, 1939" and the Frost of "Directive" and, later, the kind of witty, philosophical poems of "In the Clearing." Brodsky's facility in English, so in evidence in his essays, has been questioned here. His rhymes can be seen as either witty or forced as his words become intelligent doggerel, as in "Song of Welcome" (1992):

Here's your paycheck, here's your rent.
Money is nature's fifth element.
Welcome to every cent.

Here's your swarm and your huge beehive.
Welcome to the place with its roughly five
billion like you alive.

Welcome to the phone book that stars your name.
Digits are democracy's secret aim.
Welcome to your claim to fame.

The colloquial tone and phrasing, combined with the somewhat prophetic though awkward formality, has a chilling effect. A cosmic perspective of human meaninglessness invades the optimism of late twentieth-century democracy. Brodsky's penchant for verbal play is also in evidence in the colloquial and ironic use of "stars" as a verb. In this book, as in his first over forty years earlier, the "star" is also a cosmic symbol of material power and indifference that will outlast individuals and mankind:

And here are your stars which appear still keen
on shining as though you had never been.
They might have a point, old bean.

Brodsky faces his own annihilation, the possibility of disappearing into the landscape or back into the material world. In "At a Lecture" (1994), he puns (or actually literalizes) the idea of "self-effacement" and makes more figurative the idea of his "reflection," a transformation of his solipsistic and narcissistic self into the more lasting monuments of poetry, statues, or more humbly, furniture:

> Once you know the future, you can make it come
> earlier. The way it's done by statues or by one's
>   furniture.
> Self-effacement is not a virtue
> but a necessity, recognized most often
> toward evening. Though numerically it is easier
> not to be me than not to be you. As the swan
>   confessed
> to the lake: I don't like myself. But you are
> welcome to my reflection.

The concluding figure of the swans alludes to Robinson Jeffers's dialogue with a hypothetical self-pitying version of himself, "Love the Wild Swan." It begins "I hate my verses, every line, every word," yet ends with the self-deprecating but stoic resolution:

> Better bullets than yours would miss the white
>   breast,
> Better mirrors than yours would crack in the flame.
> Does it matter whether you hate your . . . self? At
>   least
> Love your eyes that can see, your mind that can
> Hear the music, the thunder of the wings. Love
>   the wild swan.

The poems in *So Forth* explore the notion of self-effacement—how one is to handle one's own demise with neither heroic grandeur nor pity. Brodsky's aim, then, is highly moral, even if his presentation of life and hope is decidedly grim. "An Admonition" (1986), a meditative poem reminiscent of Robert Frost's "Directive," presents the figure of the man halting in the wilderness; his "job" is to bear witness to the frightening emptiness:

> When you stand on an empty stony plateau alone
> under the fathomless dome of Asia in whose blue-
>   ness an airplane
> or an angel sometimes whips up its starch or
>   star—
> when you shudder at how infinitesimally small
>   you are,
> remember: space that appears to need nothing does
> crave, as a matter of fact, an outside gaze,
> a criterion of emptiness—of its depth and scope.
> And it's only you who can do the job.

This "outside gaze," a perspective on the present cast from the distant future, has been present in Brodsky's poetry from the very beginning, from the presence of John Donne's soul returning and addressing his dead body. In those early poems, as has been noted, Brodsky played heavily on theme of the Nativity. In "Star of the Nativity" (1987), he writes, "A child was born in a cave in order to save the world." From his perspective, everything is enormous: "He was but a dot, and a dot was the star." That perspective is suddenly reversed in the third stanza, when the past becomes the unblinking terror of the future:

> Keenly, without blinking, through pallid, stray
> clouds, upon the child in the manger, from far
>   away—
> from the depth of the universe, from its opposite
>   end—the star
> was looking into the cave. And that was the
>   Father's stare.

The beginning and end of life returns to itself in cold indifference. The collection's title poem, "So Forth" (1989), suggests the monotony of life prone to cycles of repetition (as if to say "so on and so forth") but also urges the spirit to go forth into the distance where new life, figured in the egg, eternally defies the aim of the seeker.

Selected Bibliography

WORKS OF JOSEPH BRODSKY

POETRY

Ostanovka v pustyne (A halt in the wilderness). New York: Chekhov Publishing Company, 1970. Rev. ed., Ann Arbor, Mich.: Ardis, 1989. Reissued, St. Petersburg: Pushkin Fund, 2000.

Joseph Brodsky: Selected Poems. Trans. by George L. Kline. Foreword by W. H. Auden. New York: Harper & Row, 1973.

Konets prekrasnoi epokhi (End of a beautiful era). Ann Arbor, Mich.: Ardis, 1977. Reissued, St. Petersburg: Pushkin Fund, 2000.

Chast' rechi. Ann Arbor, Mich.: Ardis, 1977. Reissued, St. Petersburg: Pushkin Fund, 2000. Trans. by the author and various translators as *A Part of Speech.* New York: Farrar, Straus & Giroux, 1980. (Contents of the English-language volume differ from *Chast' rechi.*)

Novye stansy k Avguste (New stanzas for Augusta). Ann Arbor, Mich.: Ardis, 1983. Reissued, St. Petersburg: Pushkin Fund, 2000.

Uraniia. Ann Arbor, Mich.: Ardis, 1984. Reissued, St. Petersburg: Pushkin Fund, 2000. Trans. by multiple translators as *To Urania.* New York: Farrar, Straus & Giroux, 1988. (Contents of the English-language volume differ from *Uraniia.*)

Chast' rechi: Izbrannye stikhi 1962–1989 (A part of speech: selected poems). Moscow: Khudozhestvennaia literatura, 1990. (Authorized selected poems.)

Sochineniia Iosifa Brodskogo (The works of Joseph Brodsky). Vol. I–IV. St. Petersburg: Pushkin Fund, 1992–1996. Rev. ed., 1997–1998. Vol. V, 1999. Vol. VI, 2000. Vol. VII, forthcoming.

Rozhdestvenskii stikhi. Moscow: Nezavisimaia Gazeta, 1992. Second ed., 1996. Trans. by multiple translators as *Nativity Poems,* forthcoming.

Peizazh s navodneniem (View with a flood). Dana Point, Calif.: Ardis, 1996.

So Forth. New York: Farrar, Straus & Giroux, 1996.

Joseph Brodsky: Collected Poems in English. New York: Farrar, Straus & Giroux, 2000.

Iosif Brodskii: Stikhotvoreniia I poemy. Edited by Lev L. Loseff. St. Petersburg: Novaia Biblioteka Poeta, Akademichesky Proekt, 2000.

Selected Poems, 1962–1972. Trans. by George L. Kline, forthcoming.

Uncollected Poems, 1972–1996. Trans. by multiple translators, forthcoming.

CHILDREN'S BOOKS

Discovery. Illustrated by Vladimir Radunsky. New York: Farrar, Straus & Giroux, 1999.

The Emperor. Illustrated by Vladimir Radunsky, forthcoming.

ESSAYS

Introduction to *Osip Mandelstam: 50 Poems,* by Osip Mandelstam. New York: Persea Books, 1977.

Less Than One. New York: Farrar, Straus & Giroux, 1986.

Watermark. New York: Farrar, Straus & Giroux, 1992.

On Grief and Reason. New York: Farrar, Straus & Giroux, 1995. Title essay reprinted in *Homage to Robert Frost: Joseph Brodsky, Seamus Heany, Derek Walcott.* New York: Farrar, Straus & Giroux, 1996.

PLAYS

Mramor. Ann Arbor, Mich.: Ardis, 1984. Trans. by Alan Myers and the author as *Marbles: A Play in Three Acts.* In *Comparative Criticism.* Vol. 7. Cambridge University Press, 1985. Reissued, New York: Farrar, Straus & Giroux, 1989.

Democracy! Act I trans. by Alan Myers in *Granta* 30 (winter 1990). Act II trans. by the author in *Partisan Review,* spring 1993. Rev. ed. of Act II published in *Performing Arts Journal* XVIII (1996). (The Russian original appears in *Sochineniia Iosifa Brodskogo.*)

ANTHOLOGIES

Modern Russian Poets on Poetry: Blok, Mandelstam, Pasternak, Mayakovsky, Gumilev, Tsvetaeva. Editor, with Carl Proffer. Trans. by Alexander Golubov. Ann Arbor, Mich.: Ardis, 1976.

An Age Ago: A Selection of Nineteenth-Century Russian Poetry. Editor, with Alan Myers. Trans. by Alan Myers. New York: Farrar, Straus & Giroux, 1988.

CRITICAL AND BIOGRAPHICAL STUDIES

Bethea, David M. *Joseph Brodsky and the Creation of Exile*. Princeton, N.J.: Princeton University Press, 1994.

Birkerts, Sven. "The Arts of Poetry XXVIII: Joseph Brodsky." *Paris Review* 83:82–126 (spring 1982).

Haas, Robert, ed. "Lost in Translation." In *Twentieth-Century Pleasures: Prose on Poetry*. New York: Ecco Press, 1984. Pp. 134–141.

Husarska, Anna. "A Talk with Joseph Brodskij." *New Leader,* December 14, 1987, pp. 8–11.

Kline, George L. "A Poet's Map of His Poem." *Vogue,* September 1973, pp. 228, 230.

———. "Iosif Brodsky." In *Columbia Dictionary of Modern European Literature.* Edited by Jean-Albert Bédé and William B. Edgerton. New York: Columbia University Press, 1980. Pp. 121–122.

Kline, George L., and Richard D. Sylvester. "Iosif Aleksandrovich Brodskii." In *Modern Encyclopedia of Russian and Soviet Literature* 3:129–137 (1979).

Loseff, L. V., ed. *Poetika Brodskogo*. Tenafly, N.J.: Hermitage, 1986.

Loseff, Lev, and Valentina Polukhina. *Brodsky's Poetics and Aesthetics.* London: Macmillan, 1990.

———. *Joseph Brodsky: The Art of a Poem.* New York: St. Martin's Press, 1999.

Milosz, Czeslaw. "A Struggle against Suffocation." *New York Review of Books,* August 14, 1980, p. 23.

Proffer, Carl R. "A Stop in the Madhouse: Brodsky's 'Gorbunov and Gorchakov.'" *Russian Literature TriQuarterly* 1:342–351 (1971).

Sylvester, Richard D. "The Poem as Scapegoat: An Introduction to Joseph Brodsky's 'Halt in the Wilderness.'" *Texas Studies in Literature and Language* 17:303–325 (1975).

Vail, Petr. *Peresechennaia mestnost: Puteshestviia s kommentariiami.* Moscow: Nezavisimaia Gazeta, 1995.

Verheul, Kees. "Iosif Brodsky's 'Aeneas and Dido.'" *Russian Literature TriQuarterly* 6:490–501 (1973).

Vishniak, Vladimir. "Joseph Brodsky and Mary Stuart." Working paper no. 4, Alexander Herzen Centre for Soviet, Slavic and East European Studies, Department of Russian Studies, University of Manchester, Manchester, England, April 1994.

Walcott, Derek. "Magic Industry." *New York Review of Books,* November 24, 1988, pp. 35–38.

—ROBERT FAGGEN

Jim Harrison

1937–

"MY INTEREST IS in what I call the 'art' novel, which has never been a market-driven genre," Jim Harrison wrote in *American Literary History*. Not surprisingly, Harrison, the outwardly gruff Michigander who has shaped a lifelong passion for poetry into a career as a fiction writer, essayist, and screenwriter, maintains his distance from the mainstream of American letters. Despite a large group of actors, directors, artists, and writers whom Harrison numbers among his friends, he separates himself from the glitz and glamour of Hollywood as well, spending as little time as possible on the "Dream Coasts" (his phrase for New York and Los Angeles). He prefers driving tens of thousands of miles on the blue highways of America, particularly after the completion of difficult projects. His public appearances, aside from rare book-tour stops and speaking obligations, are limited to out-of-the-way bars or hunting and fishing rendezvous with friends and family. A notable exception is that he often travels to France in support of his books, where he is revered as an icon of American literature and where *The Road Home,* his 1998 follow-up to *Dalva* (1988), went to number two on the best-seller list, something that his work has never accomplished in the United States. His novella collection, *The Beast God Forgot to Invent,* was first published in France in early 2000.

Undoubtedly, Harrison's unwillingness to place himself in the literary spotlight has affected the reception of all his work, but most notably the fiction. Despite a recent, if hard-won, critical acceptance of his work, much of Harrison's early fiction, influenced profoundly by his work exclusively as a poet in the 1960s,

was disregarded as too experimental in style and form to garner a solid mainstream audience.

In fact, Harrison was a poet with a bright future, winning National Endowment for the Arts grants and a Guggenheim Fellowship in the late 1960s, long before he penned his first novel. He draws little distinction between the two forms, instead always seeing the poetry in the fiction that he writes. It is Harrison's fiction that has received more attention. The body of work the author has published since his debut novel in 1971 exhibits an astounding range of genres, protagonists, settings, and themes: from novel to novella; comic picaro to strong female; wilderness to city to a wasteland somewhere between; food to sex to alcohol to psychosis. Harrison's fiction hauntingly echoes William Faulkner's sense of mortality in *As I Lay Dying*: survive, and feel life at every moment, in every sinew of your being; once you're dead, you'll stay dead a long time.

THE BURGEONING POET

James Thomas Harrison was born in Grayling, Michigan, on December 11, 1937, to Winfield Sprague Harrison and Norma Olivia (Wahlgren) Harrison. He was the second of five children. A brother, John, shares the author's passion for books and literature and was longtime director of libraries at the University of Arkansas, Fayetteville. Harrison has spent his adult life living and writing in northern Michigan, both on the Leelanau Peninsula and in a remote cabin on the state's Upper Peninsula; he winters in a home in Patagonia, Arizona. His penchant for immersing himself into topics by researching and experiencing them is legendary in literary circles; in an age of word processors and Internet searches for information he relies on a capacious memory and a legal pad for the writing of his manuscripts. Harrison's fiction-writing career was nearly derailed before it began when the only copy of the manuscript for his first novel, which Harrison typed and sent to his brother John, was lost in the mail for several weeks during a postal strike. According to Harrison, John was fortunate to find the manuscript buried under tons of undelivered mail.

Typically, the stories that he writes have fermented in his mind for several years before they see the light of day. By the time those stories find their way to the published page, they have changed little from the manuscript (Harrison claims that the copyediting for his most popular novella, *Legends of the Fall,* consisted of changing one word from the manuscript stage to the finished product). The granary where he writes in Leelanau is littered with esoteric books on subjects ranging from dam building to Native American history to comprehensive tomes on the flora and fauna of North America. The wall in front of his desk is covered with pictures that recall many of Harrison's characters and his favorite historical figures, and hanging from one of the rafters is a collection of objects with totemic importance for the author, including a pinecone from the forest where one of Harrison's poet-idols, the thirty-eight-year-old Spanish writer Federico García Lorca, was murdered and the compass that his friend the author Doug Peacock carried with him in Vietnam.

Harrison comes by his passion for nature and a curiosity for objects honestly. His father worked as a state agricultural agent in Michigan and encouraged the young Jim to hone his observation skills, a trait that would become vital in all of Harrison's future work. The author's parents encouraged him to read, and the writing life seemed as likely as any for a young man of Harrison's native curiosity and imagination. After receiving a typewriter as a gift from his father, Harrison began writing poetry, because of what he perceived as a short attention span; the poetic form fit nicely into the restless young man's personality.

Harrison received a B.A. degree from Michigan State University in 1960, the same year that he married Linda King. The couple has two daughters, Jamie, who has settled in Montana and has published several mystery novels, and Anna. A defining event for the young Harrison was the deaths of his father and sister, who were killed by a drunken driver in 1962. He poignantly recalls the episode, which influenced the twenty-four-year-old writer's views on the ethereality of life and the permanence of death, in the poem "In Interims: Outlyer": "And if my sister hadn't died in an auto wreck / and had been taken by the injuns / I would have something to do: / go into the mountains and get her back." Images of death, and often more poignantly the anticipation of death in life, appear throughout the author's fiction as well; Harrison's characters, realizing simultaneously the finality and the banality of death, are often hard-charging and impetuous.

Harrison received an M.A. in literature from Michigan State in 1965, the same year he published *Plain Song,* a poetry collection helped to publication by the late Denise Levertov, an early influence who became a mentor to the aspiring writer. The author's poetry prefigures much of what comes later in the fiction, as it focuses on natural themes and personal relationships filtered through the perceptions of a budding romantic. "Poem," the first in the collection, simply states Harrison's relationship to nature: "Form is the woods." The most widely quoted poem of the collection is "Sketch for a Job-Application Blank," in which Harrison describes a childhood accident that rendered him sightless in his left eye: "My left eye is blind and jogs like / a milky sparrow in its socket. . . / O my youth was happy and I was never lonely / though my friends called me 'pig eye' / and the teachers thought me loony." The image, as with so many of his personal experiences, surfaces repeatedly in Harrison's fiction, sometimes as an overt reference to the incident but more often as the metaphorical blindness of his characters to their surroundings.

Plain Song was a watershed for Harrison, whose college career was unremarkable. Harrison often discusses his disdain for the regimentation of university curricula, or what he considers academic hoop-jumping, recalling that the writers whom he admires most, including Sherwood Anderson, Hart Crane, Arthur Rimbaud, Garía Lorca, and Faulkner, were writers of the first rank despite a conspicuous lack of "higher education." Despite his early success as a poet, which provided ample opportunity for him to make a life in the academy, Harrison has resolutely distanced himself by choice, eschewing the strictures of academia for the relative freedom, if financial uncertainty, of the independent writer. Harrison's disdain for the academy is evident in his fiction; for example, in the novella *I Forgot to Go to Spain* (2000) the protagonist recalls, "We all met at Rico's apartment in the East Village, a fearsome place when I had lived there from 1969 to 1972, soon after gaining my flight from the porch and my M.F.A., similar experiences in the long run. The M.F.A. replaced the B.A. in English as the zenith of valueless degrees."

Almost as if to prove his point, Harrison had a brief and unfulfilling career as a writing teacher at the State University of New York at Stony Brook, where he taught for less than two years; he claims that when he left Stony Brook to return to Michigan, the only thing he took with him was a trunk full of student papers, which he had neither graded nor returned. Despite a period of several years when the young Harrison supported a family on less than $10,000 annually, he realized that his best

chance for becoming an artist, his love for Gauguin notwithstanding, was to become a writer, the profession in which he could use the vast imagination cultivated by his parents.

In 1968, in response to his desire to advance writing as creative expression, Harrison took his writing one step further when he and his longtime friend and fellow Michigan State alumnus Dan Gerber founded *Sumac,* a literary magazine that featured work from some of America's finest established and up-and-coming writers and poets, including Galway Kinnell, Charles Simic, Louis Simpson, Gary Snyder, Hayden Carruth, Denise Levertov, Ezra Pound, James Tate, and William Kittredge. In 1997 the journal received renewed critical attention when a collection of work originally featured in the nine-issue run was edited by Joseph Bednarik and published by Michigan State University Press.

Harrison has had time to write fiction and poetry in part because of his prolific work in writing screenplays and essays, a conscious decision to write for a living in the absence of academic support. In all, he has sold seventeen screenplays, including *Carried Away,* an adaptation of his novel *Farmer, Cold Feet,* which he co-wrote with Thomas McGuane, and adaptations of *Revenge* and *Legends of the Fall,* by far his most popular work. He is also a contributor of essays to an eclectic variety of magazines and journals, including *Sports Illustrated, Sports Afield, Outside, Smart, Men's Journal, Antaeus,* the *Psychoanalytic Review,* and *Esquire,* where a monthly food column that ran for more than two years in the early 1990s offers an intimate glimpse into the author's passion for food and drink.

INFLUENCES

Harrison's imagination and his own experiences intertwine to act as fictional touchstones. The author's connection to the natural world—

fueled by his father's own passion for nature—and the author's immersion in some of the country's wildest places is apparent in all of his fiction. He is an avid sportsman whose closest hunting and fishing friends include writers, artists, and literati McGuane (with whom Harrison maintained a twenty-five-year letter-writing relationship), Russell Chatham, and Guy de la Valdéne.

Harrison is obsessed with describing the details of human experience. More than one reviewer has commented on his passion, and critics of his fiction agree that Harrison's fiction works best when it reaches a middle ground between sensuality and violence, which is tempered with an often dark, blunt comic impulse. Reinforcing themes of alienation and lost identity in all of Harrison's fiction is the shape of the narratives themselves, which are often autobiographical at the same time that they draw on the author's vast knowledge of American—especially Native American—history.

A literary omnivore with a voracious appetite for the world around him, Harrison has been influenced by the work of Henry David Thoreau, Mark Twain, Ernest Hemingway, Faulkner, Rainer Maria Rilke, Sergey Yesenin, Rimbaud, James Joyce, Knut Hamsun, Colette, André Gide, Günter Grass, and a host of other American and international writers. The literary is a common thread in Harrison's fiction, seamlessly connecting one theme to the next. *Wolf* (1971), Harrison's first novel, follows the young Swanson as he traverses the Upper Peninsula wilderness in an attempt to transcend the banality of society, while recalling and reconstituting his reality in terms of the books he has read. The protagonist of the novella *Beige Dolorosa* (1994) is a retired English professor who realizes that the vast wealth of literary knowledge he possesses is ineffective in helping him to cope with a debilitating neurological disease and the embarrassment of university politics. In the protagonist's coming to grips with a life in books and his own mortality, Harrison offers a sense of the urgent acceptance with which he documents his own world.

Harrison's characters also study and emulate philosophers, writers, composers, and great works from Søren Kierkegaard to Saul Bellow to Beethoven to the Bible, but those characters are unique amalgams of everything the author has read or experienced. Because of such varied literary and life experiences, Harrison and his characters shun what the author calls a "mono-ethic," the desire for individuals to all have homogenous experiences, a concept Harrison described in an interview with Patrick Smith and Robert DeMott as "amazing, in a political sense . . . with all the diversity, to want some kind of unanimity." Harrison argues that our literary characters are neither believable nor wholly human: "Most of the people who eat chicken, beef, or pork have never known an actual chicken, an actual pig, or an actual cow."

Harrison's work, especially his fiction, has received a lukewarm reception by the academy, not because the work is not "literary" enough, but in part because many scholars have detected an underlying misogynism in it. Harrison vehemently denies the claim, as it stems from a facile comparison of Harrison's work to that of Hemingway, a connection that Harrison no longer finds flattering; in fact, he goes out of his way to separate himself from Hemingway's legacy. Harrison responds to such criticism in his essay "First Person Female," where he recalls that the men in his family, "though they fished and hunted strenuously, would never describe these particular activities as 'manly.' That idea seemed to derive from writers of city origin like the tortured Hemingway, who, though a very great writer, seemed to suffer from a prolonged struggle with his manhood. Faulkner was a bit more nonchalant and colorful on the subject, what with his lifelong fascination with the 'pelvic mysteries of the swamps.'" Despite the fact that Harrison's most highly acclaimed fiction is written from a woman's point of view, a narrative voice driven by his writing poetry, the distinction between "macho" fiction and fiction written from and through a man's experiences is an important one to make.

In his profound identification with poet John Keats's "Negative Capability," the ability to reconcile the contradictions inherent in any narrative without succumbing to the brutalizing force of reason, Harrison finds the complex narrative voice that synthesizes aspects of both fiction and poetry. His unease with closure is, as he writes in "First Person Female," "the capacity a poem or novel must have to keep afloat a thousand contradictory people and questions in order to create the parallel universe of art," which is key in understanding the author's creative impulse. Harrison has harbored the idea since first reading Keats seriously as a teenager and told Smith and DeMott that "the hairs on my neck rose when I read about the 'Negative Capability,' because that's obviously what a novelist has to have more than anything else. The best example of this is Shakespeare or Dostoyevsky—that's what their work is. Nothing human is alien to them. Nothing can't be examined. They never limit themselves to sexual neuroses like many Americans."

The limitations that Harrison sees in contemporary American literature manifest themselves through the critics' insistence on classifying Harrison's work, particularly his fiction, in order to package the author's ideas for mass consumption. In an explanation of the ghazals published in his third book of poems, *Outlyer and Ghazals* (1971), Harrison posits that, in order to maintain the integrity of the artistic vision, a writer must not:

try to bury a horse in a human coffin, no matter how much you loved the horse, or stick some mute, lovely butterfly or luna moth in a damp cavern. I hate to use the word, but form must be an 'organic' revelation of content or the poem,

however otherwise lively, will strike us false or merely tricky, an exercise in wit, crochet, pale embroidery.

For Harrison, the theory that he espouses for poetry is equally true in all writing. In the same way that the form of the poem depends upon a personal context, Harrison avoids formulaic writing, instead relying on the mode of expression that best suits the content of the narrative and his own vision.

While the fiction and the poetry are front and center in Harrison's repertoire, his nonfiction is a testing ground for much of the material that makes its way into the author's creative work. *Just before Dark: Collected Nonfiction* (1991), a collection of Harrison's essays culled from the journals and magazines to which Harrison has contributed, offers valuable insights into the creative mind of the author. Those essays contain kernels of ideas for the poems, the novels, the novellas, vignettes, and philosophical meanderings. "Fording and Dread," for example, offers a cogent discussion of the author's philosophy of writing and describes Harrison's passion for writing as a way of reconciling the beauty of literature with the unbearably brief movement of a life through time, "the limitless ambition of the young writer, whose vast, starry, nineteen-year-old nights must come down to the middle-aged man in the northern night listening for more howls, trying to learn what he is with neither compassion nor self laceration, treasuring that autumnal sensuality of one who has given his life's blood to train his soul, brain and senses to the utmost." The essay is the expression of the author's memory and his ability to articulate that experience—sometimes the single, tenuous thread between existence and nonexistence for Harrison and his characters.

WOLF: A FALSE MEMOIR

That ability to synthesize autobiography and imagination suited Harrison well when he wrote

Wolf, after a hunting accident left the author bedridden and his friend and hunting partner Thomas McGuane suggested that the exercise would make the lengthy convalescence more sufferable. Perhaps in response to his confinement—and certainly in remembering some of the adventures of his early adulthood, specifically a cross-country hitchhiking expedition to California after his high school graduation in 1956—Harrison's first fiction describes both the perceived need for freedom of movement and its consequences on a ravaged American landscape. Carol Severin Swanson, the book's protagonist, travels the country from 1956 to 1960, but the novel is written "from the vantage of the present—it is a false memoir at that and not even chronological and its author is a self-antiquated thirty-three, a juncture when literary souls turn around and look backward." Like the Zen that Harrison's characters intermittently practice (or that Harrison himself relates in a collection of Zen poems, *After Ikkyu and Other Poems* [1996]), the complexities and contradictions of time have little effect on the protagonist. Instead, he acts on instinct and has little concern for others.

The novel reiterates the claims for the individual that Ralph Waldo Emerson, Thoreau, and Walt Whitman espouse, ways of life in which one becomes one's own authority apart from the consensus of mainstream society. The narrative recalls Jack Kerouac and his Beat counterparts in the decades after World War II, although Harrison is less romantic than the Beats, instead viewing Americans' increasing mobility as a cause of the rapid disappearance of wilderness from the American landscape. The result is a rough-hewn, quasi-autobiographical statement on the virtues of the last great place in the American wilderness and a treatise on the profound influence of geography and place in our lives.

Wolf bridges the gap between the author's notions of fiction and poetry, in the process blending the two to his needs. The subtitle of the novel, "A False Memoir," suggests that Harrison is experimenting with the constraints of a genre that is new to him. The phrase "A False Memoir" also hints at the play between autobiography and fiction that characterizes much of Harrison's later work. For Harrison, the connection between autobiography and storytelling is inherent in the process of writing; the two are inseparable and form a synergy that allows Harrison to create characters who are often only barely under control.

A GOOD DAY TO DIE

At no point in Harrison's fiction is that connection more important to the action of a novel, or more overtly violent, than in *A Good Day to Die* (1973), in which the two male protagonists, the alcoholic narrator and Tim, a disaffected Vietnam vet, experience the alienation endemic to the social-protest novel. Around this time, Harrison and friends, including McGuane, de la Valdéne, Peter Fonda, Jimmy Buffett, Hunter S. Thompson, Richard Brautigan, and others began making annual trips to Key West, Florida, to fish for tarpon and discuss literature and film. The reveries reached a pinnacle in 1974, when de la Valdéne hired French videographers to film the short feature *Tarpon,* a documentary that included the principals fly-fishing for tarpon and philosophizing about literature and life; the film was scored by Buffett. These experiences clearly influenced Harrison's early fiction.

Although Harrison's second novel received little of the critical acclaim awarded to Edward Abbey's *The Monkey Wrench Gang* (1975), it predates Abbey's better-known work by two years. The two novels deal with similar themes. Harrison's trio of protagonists decide early in their acquaintanceship to destroy a dam that blocks some of the country's best trout fishing. The setting and characterization of the first scene, in which the unnamed narrator is double-anchored off Cudjoe Key, Florida, with a woman he did not know the night before, are important, as the narrative's frenetic action takes place in a haze of drugs, alcohol, sexual fantasy, and escapism. The lifestyles and themes that Harrison covers in his first novel are not uncommon to the late 1960s and early 1970s, especially in the novels of Harrison's friends and contemporaries, such as McGuane's *The Sporting Club* (1969), Dan Wakefield's *Going All the Way* (1970), and Richard Brautigan's *Trout Fishing in America* (1967), among others.

The narrator's alienation from "acceptable" society underpins the protagonists' actions throughout the story. Although the narrator suggests a previous home life and some stability—typical allusions in the lives of Harrison's characters, even if the reality is invariably much different—his plan is to spend several weeks in the Keys before he heads back north. His life is a struggle for balance between the reality of mainstream society and the release of drugs and alcohol, fishing, and women.

The origin of the narrator's hatred for the damming of rivers is simple enough: fishing is the only contact point for his otherwise free floating experiences, and the serenity of the stream and the one-on-one parrying with the trout erase for a time the narrator's problems. The narrator's dependence on the trout stream has defined his adult life. His fear of anxiety attacks prevents him from feeling safe except "in three minimal areas of Michigan, Montana and Key West," even though he reluctantly, and without apparent reason, agrees to travel west with newfound compatriots Tim and Sylvia toward the manifestation of their final violent act against society.

The act of destruction is doomed from the outset. The narrator incessantly and unsuccessfully monitors his emotions as signposts to action or inaction, but Tim is unpredictably violent and disinterested in similar self-examination. Although the plan to blow up a dam—any dam,

as it turns out—moves inexorably toward its climax from the time that the narrator meets Tim, that plan is nebulous at best. Even the participants are unsure of the dam's existence, and the narrator's conception of the Canyon is based on a cartoon-like recollection of Evel Knievel's attempt at rocketing across the Snake River. Unlike Knievel's own stars-and-stripes effort, however, the tale is without heroes, and the storyteller's inability to distinguish the reality of a luckless, drug-addled trio's actions from the fantasy of the stereotypically intrepid and righteous hero merely signals the extent to which the protagonists have lost touch with society.

As with Carol Severin Swanson's search for an elusive (and perhaps illusory) wolf in Harrison's first novel, in which the search becomes symbolic of self and repeated attempts at ordering the past, the narrator of *A Good Day to Die* can only order his memories in terms of place. The final place is a dam in Idaho, a point in the narrator's reality that can be manipulated and destroyed so that the narrator may reconnect to the physical world. The simple, brutal act of destruction is motivated, finally, by the possibility of closure that the narrator's past has never afforded him. His willingness to carry out the plan speaks more to a Calvinistic predestination for the failure of the plan than to any impulse for wanton destruction or a desire for ecological conservation, a thought that crosses the protagonists' minds when they first meet but is left in the dust and confusion of the narrative's violent conclusion.

The theme that underpins the protagonists' journey—that of the essential inhumanity with which Americans have handled the "Indian Question" (as Harrison later presents it in *Legends of the Fall* [1979], *Dalva,* and *The Road Home*)—is important to Harrison's fiction. The protagonists' association with Native American culture, though, is nearly comic in its absurdity. The trio compare their plight to that of the Nez

Percé, who entered battle with the war cry of their beloved Chief Joseph: "Take courage, this is a good day to die." The Nez Percé were driven from their homeland and slaughtered; that the protagonists compare themselves to the Nez Percé is bitterly ironic. The narrator's life has become one of rapid dissipation and decay; instead of becoming heroes by gaining perceived vengeance on society, the three protagonists have been seduced by a culture that, by the time of the novel's publication, was being exposed as escapist and exhibitionist by Harrison and others.

FARMER

Harrison's third novel, *Farmer* (1976), is a more optimistic work that focuses on a specific area of northern Michigan. In writing the narrative from a number of different perspectives, Harrison describes the parochial culture with which he is so familiar. Joseph Lundgren, the novel's protagonist, dreams of visiting the ocean. Joseph's imagining other places, however, is out of place in his culture, since only Joseph, of the novel's characters, fully understands the intricate relationship of the land to its people.

The protagonist sees the unique character of the land and the effect that it has on the families who choose to live in an area that is by turns beautiful and inhospitable, and even though he is restless enough to change the course of his life by having an affair with one of his students, an eighteen-year-old girl named Catherine, he balks at the thought that the immutable landscape should change in order to suit him. Joseph "despised the farms near town that had been bought up by the managerial class of the sheet metal company in the county seat," and he knows that if the town were to become incorporated, "the farm houses would be modernized and false shutters added. Sometimes white board fences would be built and the outbuildings painted a bright red. Maybe they were trying to

make it resemble Kentucky or New England." The marginal lives that the people make for themselves go through phases of boom and bust, and the landscape of the lives of Joseph's neighbors are intertwined with one another; most of his neighbors feel little need to untangle those ties.

Joseph's desire to visit the ocean is kindled by his affair and by the memory of his friend Orin, a pilot who was killed in Korea. Only by reconciling himself with Orin's death and the love of Orin's widow, Rosalee, can Joseph finally realize his dream. In the last passage of the narrative, in which Joseph finally accepts Rosalee as his partner, Harrison brings the story full circle. The two prepare to fulfill Joseph's dream, and Joseph realizes that he does not have to alienate himself from the place with which he is so familiar, as he thought he must. To travel away from home, Joseph knows, is not to repudiate home, but to reaffirm it. The dreamlike quality of the understated finale echoes the cycle of seasons that dictates the lives of the inhabitants of Joseph's culture. With its evocation of the permanence of nature and the resilience of the Midwestern spirit, the circular narrative gives the novel a closure unique in the body of Harrison's fiction.

The novel has been deemed "regional" because it describes in great detail the lives of the people of northern Michigan, set off from the milieu of the "big city." Harrison balks at such classification, rather viewing a work on its own merits—as either literature or not literature. For Harrison, the rubric "regional literature" is the result of the continued belief of writers and critics in New York City and Los Angeles that the most creative and original intellectual thought comes out of the city, despite the inability of many of those writers to create three-dimensional characters. More important than pigeonholing the narrative is the marked contrast that *Farmer* makes from the first two novels in its affirmation of the power of a particular place, the familiar place that renews itself and heals its inhabitants through its simply stated every-dayness. The novel is a strong statement of the dichotomy of life and death that delves deep into existence and finally—for the first time in Harrison's fiction—readily affirms life.

LEGENDS OF THE FALL

Harrison's penchant for drawing bigger-than-life characters as he does in *Wolf* and *A Good Day to Die* continues with *Legends of the Fall,* a collection of novellas that would give Harrison the popular acclaim that his poetry and his first works of fiction predicted for the author. As a writer living for nearly two decades without the safety net of palatable alternative employment—he survived in the 1960s by working at a number of construction jobs—Harrison was overwhelmed by the success of the collection, which was made possible by the financial support of his friend, actor Jack Nicholson. Harrison has only to say about the success that had been so long in coming that "I didn't know how to handle it. I behaved badly," as quoted in a *Detroit News* article by Ruth Pollack Coughlin.

The first two novellas, *Revenge,* which would later become a film starring Kevin Costner, and *The Man Who Gave Up His Name* are often neglected in the collection; nonetheless, they stand on their own as examples of Harrison's flexibility as a fiction writer. *Revenge,* on the one hand, is a genre piece that details the battle between Cochran, a fighter pilot, and Tiburón, the head of an organized crime family, for the attentions of Miryea, Tiburón's beautiful mistress. *The Man Who Gave Up His Name,* one of Harrison's most imaginative pieces, is a story of loss and restoration in which the protagonist, Nordstrom, not unlike *Warlock* later, gives up his life as an executive to become a cook in a Florida restaurant, where he can dance to his heart's content.

Still, the title story has received nearly all of the collection's critical attention. *Legends of the Fall* succinctly portrays the immediate effect of several myth-making events of the late nineteenth and early twentieth centuries—the Indian Wars, World War I, Prohibition, the Great Depression, and the advent of the automobile—on a wealthy Montana plains family. The result is a lean and taut expression of the life of a man who straddles two distinct epochs in America's consciousness, one that still condones, and perhaps admires, the actions of the myth figure, and one that has thrown off the romantic veil of innocence that spawned the American myth in the first place.

Harrison based the novella on a reading of the journal of Colonel William Ludlow, his wife's great-grandfather, and the narrative began to take shape when Harrison set the novella in the wide-open expanses of Montana rather than Michigan. In the narrative, Harrison codifies a western mythos that becomes increasingly untenable in the aftermath of World War I. The themes of alienation and fragmentation that Harrison treats in the novella are not unlike those that one sees throughout his fiction.

One of the narrative's overarching themes, and one that is repeated in *Dalva* and *The Road Home,* comes from the author's interest in Native American history. Harrison insists that we are bound by a "soul history," a notion that he formed in part from his reading of Swiss psychologist Carl Jung, who developed the concept of the "collective unconscious." Harrison defines his term in the essay "Poetry as Survival," collected in *Just before Dark*: "Our nation has a soul history, not as immediately verifiable as the artifacts of the Smithsonian, whose presence we sense in public affairs right down to [Ronald Reagan's] use of the word 'preservation,' or his cinema-tainted reference to oil-rich Indians." In detailing Americans' essential lack of historical perspective, Harrison dismisses romantic notions of cowboys and

Indians and focuses on the destructive chains of events that comprise America's history in its dealings with Native Americans. Those events would be played out in greater detail in the *Dalva* novels for two decades after the publication of *Legends of the Fall.*

WARLOCK

The diversity of Harrison's themes, and his ability to present an eclectic mix of characters and situations, is nowhere better illustrated than in Harrison's preoccupation with eating and drinking in *Warlock* (1981). The narrative is part detective-fiction spoof and part serious novel that takes on the image of the dispossessed, alienated man, images that Harrison would return to most conspicuously in his fourth novella collection *The Beast God Forgot to Invent.* Images of food and drink are pervasive in *Warlock,* and they create a thematic continuity in the novel. Harrison's attention to consumption forms a backdrop against which the protagonist lives out his life in search of the perfect meal. The imagery is derived in part from the author's own reputation as a gastronome. (Harrison, in the middle of one of his more extravagant feeding frenzies, once braced himself against the running board of a limousine to pull the director Orson Welles out of a car in front of Elaine's restaurant in New York City.) The novel also concerns the intimate connection Harrison draws between writing and the preparation and consumption of food perhaps best described in his essay "Consciousness and Dining," from *Just before Dark*: "Curiously, in both writing and cooking you're a dead duck if you don't love the process. When you short-circuit or jump start the process in either, you end up with an imitation of your own or someone else's best effects." For Harrison, food and drink are therapeutic for the body and the spirit and symbolic of a society's health or an individual's state of mind. While Harrison's observations can be playful, his skillful weaving of food imagery with the abstract, philosophical aspects of the narrative gives the preparation and consumption of food and drink an importance more often associated with French literature than American literature.

The evolution of the protagonist through a series of improbable, life-altering events is accompanied by detailed descriptions of meals that denote success (or, more likely, defeat) for the protagonist Johnny Lundgren ("Warlock") in repeated attempts at reconciling himself with his wife and regaining his fragile psychic and physical balance. The result, consistent with Harrison's working within the contradictions inherent in the complex societies that he constructs, is neither heroic nor tragic, but disarmingly ambivalent. Harrison divides Warlock's quixotic quest into three parts, each of which details the protagonist's increasing psychic fragmentation, his lack of direction and discretion, brought on by ennui, and his uncanny knack for the failed relationship. The novel's quirky appeal comes from its use of dark comedy; Harrison proves himself one of the few writers skillful and brazen enough to risk combining farce with "serious literature."

Despite Harrison's attempt at implementing characteristics of the farce and a literary style with some obvious ironic overtones, the author insists in the preface that the novel "is an attempt at a comic novel not ruled by Irony, who drags her tired ass, making us snicker cynically rather than laugh out loud," and that it "aims to draw its energies from more primary colors, say from the dance that is *A Midsummer Night's Dream* to those two archfools Don Quixote and Walter Mitty, with the definite modification of a venal Quixote and a gluttonous, horny Mitty."

SUNDOG

In his novel *Sundog* (1984), the story of Robert Corvus Strang, Harrison details the life of a man who must deal with his own physical and psychic alienation from society through introspection and his lifelong relationship with water. Harrison's fascination with water is apparent in the narrative—to research dams for the novel, Harrison was given a guided tour through a dam by Senator Bill Bradley—and the imagery that pervades *Sundog* is crystallized in the title poem of *The Theory and Practice of Rivers and Other Poems* (1986), a limited edition collection published two years after *Sundog*. In the long poem describing his own relationship to the natural world, Harrison uses water as metaphor for the journeys of life:

> The rivers of my life:
> moving looms of light,
> anchored beneath the log
> at night I can see the moon
> up through the water
>
> .   .   .   .
>
> It is not so much that I got
> there from here, which is everyone's
> story: but the shape
> of the voyage, how it pushed
> outward in every direction
> until it stopped . . .

In the same way that Harrison describes "The rivers of my life," Strang's own life moves through a series of eddies and currents that lead him to a fateful decision to entrust his life to the water by physically entering it.

Although Harrison's portrayal of the self-aware, philosophical, and intelligent Strang differs markedly from the psychotic energy of the protagonists in *A Good Day to Die,* the complex love triangle between the narrative's three major characters has prompted some critics to question Harrison's ability to create convincing relationships. Despite Harrison's assertion that Strang is a conglomeration of the characters he has known and about whom he is comfortable writing, especially in his personal relationships, some reviewers have found Strang's character diffuse and unbelievable. That Strang has

elicited such varied responses from critics supports the author's contention that his characters often are denigrated because they do not fit the preconceived notions that readers on the "Dream Coasts" have for their literature. In an interview with Kay Bonetti, Harrison recounted that the impulse to create Strang "came out of my conviction that the American literary novel as opposed to a more commercial kind of novel tends to ignore about seven-eighths of the people. The literary novel often concentrates itself upon people in New York or Los Angeles, academic and scientific communities. People don't write about the Strangs of the world because they don't know any of them."

The narrative is noteworthy for its three distinct voices—Strang, the narrator, and an underlying narrative text that unifies the plot and moves the story along to it conclusion—which describe a tangled ménage à trios between Strang, his ex-wife's niece Eulia, and the narrator, perhaps Harrison himself. The unifying theme in the narrative, as in *A Good Day to Die,* is the dam image, a symbol of man's tenuous control over nature and his desire to impose order on nature. Strang, much as the narrator and Tim in *A Good Day to Die,* devotes his life to the dams initially through happenstance, although Strang's lifelong attention to the art of dam building contrasts the short-lived need for destruction that ruins the lives of the three protagonists in the earlier novel.

In an effort to restrain himself from becoming too deeply involved in Strang's profoundly personal history, the narrator rearranges his notions of reality, insisting that "this is not my story, and I will keep my intrusions to a minimum." The narrator keeps his promise only intermittently, although his own insights are important to the story's form in terms of both the relationships between Strang and Eulia, and the narrator's own understanding of the caprices of a vanishing and increasingly unpopular American idealism. Harrison illustrates that idealism through Strang's dogged determination to continue his work as a builder of dams despite the limitations brought on by a near-fatal herbal remedy that he took to cure his lifelong epilepsy.

DALVA AND THE ROAD HOME

The notion of "soul history" that underpins *Legends of the Fall* comes fully formed in Harrison's most critically acclaimed novels, *Dalva* and *The Road Home,* related books written a decade apart (*Dalva* itself being nearly a decade removed from *Legends of the Fall*). Both detail the lives of the Northridge family. Dalva, the one-eighth Native American ancestor of John Wesley Northridge, searches for her son, Nelse, whom she gave up for adoption when she gave birth out of wedlock at sixteen. Northridge, a missionary and adventurer who sides with the Indians in the time around the Civil War and during the Indian conflicts, keeps diaries of his journeys and his contact with the Native Americans. In Dalva's present, more than a century later, Michael, a Stanford historian, tries to salvage his career by reconstructing a history based on the diaries. While Dalva's own story is written as a legacy to her son, whom she finds eventually and with whom she continues the relationship in *The Road Home,* the overarching theme of the narrative is the way in which the history of people long since dead comes to life and changes the present.

Dalva is divided into three different narrative voices—Dalva's, Michael's, and Northridge's—which combine Harrison's poetic sensibility with an unblinking eye for the less palatable events of history. Harrison's narrative technique, with its many digressions and its scrupulous attention to the details of history, creates the impression of suspended time and implies the complexity of reconstructing a family's history from the diaries that Northridge leaves behind. The novel shifts from Northridge's own en-tanglement in the "Indian Problem" to Michael's personal dilemmas to Dalva's force of spirit, from first-person accounts of the Civil War and its aftermath to Michael's not original notion that he is part of the first generation in which "we get to know all of the world's bad news at once." For Harrison, the sources of history can come from any place at any time. In that sense, history is not unlike fiction; indeed, Harrison implies that the two are relentlessly intertwined.

Dalva's character, Harrison told Smith and DeMott, is a conglomeration of the women he has met, the kinds of women who are too often ignored in fiction. "Dalva—and I think that's probably the attraction of a lot of women to Dalva—I had known a lot of inordinately strong women in my life, but I had very rarely seen them in fiction, even women's fiction where there's of course a great deal of whining just like the contemporary male middle-class novel. As I call it, 'nifty guys at loose ends.'" In "First Person Female," Harrison writes that he tends "to think of art as essentially androgynous and that gender is biological rather than a philosophical system. . . . On an almost absurd level I thought once that since I'm blind in my left eye, I'm missing half of life—and if I'm writing only as a man, I'm cut in half again. Being down to a scant quarter isn't enough to sustain my life."

Like Herman Melville's Ishmael (the protagonist introduces herself with "My name is Dalva"), Dalva is the controller of her narrative, the only character suited to reconstruct her family's tale. She has at her command memories of her childhood in Nebraska, memories of Duane Stone Horse, her dead lover and the father of her son, memories of her grandfather and great-grandfather—all histories that have come down to her through both firsthand experiences and the family's oral traditions. For Dalva, the practice of writing diaries not only orders her thoughts, it also allows her to generate new perspectives on her own life by synthesizing past events and her felt sense of where they will take her in the present. "Everyone in the history of my family was a letter writer, a diary keeper," recalls Dalva. "It's as if they thought they'd disappear if they didn't put themselves on paper. For a while in my twenties I stopped the habit but it made my thinking boringly recurrent. I resumed the practice so I could get rid of the thoughts and information, leaving room for something new." Importantly, the writing is also an identity-forming exercise. Dalva, because of her status as the keeper of the family's history, is necessarily the strongest character in the narrative, and her task requires a vision and balance that none of the other characters exhibits; in protecting the integrity of her family's history, she continuously makes space for new experiences by writing out the old ones, a process that makes linear time irrelevant for her. The narrative is a history-within-a-history, each successive paragraph a further accretion of the Northridge family's soul history, which finally divulges to the characters, especially Dalva, the information that allows the protagonist to find her lost son in a staid and simple reunion. Dalva's character is abstruse, even enigmatic.

In *The Road Home,* the prequel/sequel to *Dalva,* Harrison reiterates the connectedness of family through the generations and the generations' connectedness to nature. He also exhibits a profound sense of the ways that history informs all actions in the present and time eventually annihilates the present in making it past. Harrison's realization of the implications of time's passing manifests itself in a poem from *The Theory and Practice of Rivers,* "Looking Forward to Age." In the poem, Harrison anticipates his own mellowing and his ability to write the images that encompass death, the most human of all events, at the same time that they imply a simple and contented continuation of the spirit:

I will walk down to a marina
on a hot day and not go out to sea.

I will go to bed and get up early,
and carry too much cash in my wallet.

On Memorial Day I will visit the graves
of all those who died in my novels.

If I have become famous I'll wear a green
janitor's suit and row a wooden boat.

The narrative in which Harrison's mature vision comes to fruition is divided into five parts— Dalva's grandfather John Wesley Northridge; Nelse, Dalva's son; Naomi, Dalva's mother; Paul, Dalva's uncle (and perhaps the father of her lover Duane Stone Horse); and Dalva herself—each an integral part of the Northridge clan's history.

The result is a harmonious mixing of points of view punctuated by seemingly disparate stories that all intertwine to form the narrative. John Wesley Northridge, the son of the family's journal keeper, muses that "It is easy to forget that in the main we die only seven times more slowly than our dogs." His story forms a crucial link between the history of the family's record keeper and the future of the family, Nelse, who has fallen in love with J. M., an exotic dancer whom he has met in Nebraska. Northridge's life is one of nearly unbearable love and loss, a theme that permeates the story, with Nelse's own attempts at wooing J. M. and Dalva's extended recollection of her short-lived affair with Duane and his suicide off the Florida Keys. Northridge, who in his youth was a passionate artist and devotee of Keats (like Harrison himself), first loved Willow, a young Native American girl, but was forced to stop pursuing her by her family and the moral code of the day.

In his awakening sexuality, Northridge realizes that the romantic notions of the artist are fabricated, that "It is largely misunderstood that the first forays of a young man or young woman into the world of arts and literature, the making of them, are utterly comic and full of misadventures, rather than most of the dour and melancholy renditions that are made public." In fact, even though Northridge realizes that the world of the artist is a largely illusory one, he cannot dispel all of his romantic notions. His subsequent love affairs, especially one with the sister of the woman who would eventually be his wife, are life-altering experiences that haunt him until his death. Near the end of his life, Northridge recalls telling his father, the diarist, *John Keats was the greatest man in the history of the world,"* adding: "I rather like Keats's notion of 'negative capability' where one cherishes and nurtures the thousands of contradictory ideas in one's head, rather than trying to reduce them to functional piths and gists."

Nelse, who has gone in search of his birth mother, exhibits many of the Northridge's characteristics. He is a naturalist and a headstrong young man, an "enviable *nomad*" who settles down with a young, married stripper. The interviews that Harrison did in support of the novel offer a glimpse into the mind of a writer who accepts the passing of time at the same time that he works to understand the impulses that drive him to continue writing. In writing Nelse's character, Harrison admitted that the difficulty he had recreating Nelse's frenetic energy nearly thirty years after he penned Swanson's foray into the wilderness in *Wolf* was a matter of age, a mellowing in Harrison that forced him to research the anger of a man in his early thirties by interviewing such men, not by recalling his own anger.

In the process of searching for his mother, Nelse establishes a relationship with his grandmother, Naomi, under the pretense of doing a phenological (bird migration) survey of her property along the Niobrara River in Nebraska. Between Nelse's search for his mother and Dalva's own narrative, Naomi and Paul both reinforce and call into question the history of the family. While Naomi has remained a widow since the death of her husband in Korea, Paul wonders if he is the father of Duane Stone Horse. Both surmise that Dalva and her lover were, in fact, half-siblings. Predictably, the question remains unanswered—after all, the narrative focuses on the reunion of Dalva and her son. The scene from the conclusion of *Dalva* is replayed, and Nelse and Dalva form the relationship about which Dalva has dreamed for her entire adulthood. Dalva, who suffers from ovarian cancer, retraces her lover's trail to the coast and ends her life, loaded down by the totems of her past: "I've quickly packed my bag with Niobrara stone, the piece of hammock, and the belt I will take with me on my long voyage downward. Nothing else but my body and the fresh pill I had just taken. I send a kiss and a good bye to those I love so much. Naomi, Paul, Lundquist, Nelse, and J. M. I hope I am going to join my lover."

Dalva's death, much as the lives and deaths of all of Harrison's characters, offers a bittersweet closure to a life and places before the reader the unanswerable and unutterable question implicit in all of Harrison's fiction: What is the nature of truth in the course of a short life spent always searching, paradoxically, for ways to live—and die—with as much dignity as we can muster? The ending of the novel is both a signal of the maturation of Harrison's vision and a starting point for what will follow.

THE WOMAN LIT BY FIREFLIES

Despite Harrison's success as a novelist and the reception of *Legends of the Fall,* his later novellas remain relatively unexplored by critics. In 1990 Harrison published *The Woman Lit by Fireflies,* a three-novella collection that, in addition to his writing six versions of two screenplays at the same time, tested the limits of Harrison's resiliency as a writer. The collection's title story describes the dissolution of a woman's marriage to an aging radical who daily becomes more conservative and more concerned with the fluctuation of the stock market (he listens to tapes called *Tracking the Blues* on long car trips) than he is with his relationship with his wife. *Sunset Limited* and the first appearance of Brown Dog in the story of the same name round out the collection.

The introspective title story illuminates the diversity of Harrison's style, although *Sunset Limited* has received criticism as a slick screenplay-like effort. Harrison wrote the story when he imagined what it would be like if one of his group of friends—Chatham, McGuane, or de la Valdéne—were stranded in South America. *The Woman Lit by Fireflies* and *Brown Dog* (the first novella in a trilogy that ends with the novella *Westward Ho* in *The Beast God Forgot to Invent*) have been more roundly accepted as works typical of Harrison's talent and vision, although the two novellas have little in common. Critics have generally praised Harrison for his willingness to tackle the issue of psychological abuse from a woman's point of view and see the protagonist of *The Woman Lit by Fireflies* as a logical progression from the strength of Dalva's character. Clare, who spends a night in an Iowa cornfield remembering the deaths of her friend, Zilpha, and her beloved dog, Sammy, and having imagined conversations with her daughter, Laura, dreams of living out her life in Paris. The displacement that she feels in the field that night is replaced by the magic of her favorite place.

JULIP

Like *The Woman Lit by Fireflies, Julip* (1994) contains three stories that, on the surface, have little in common, and the title story is told from a woman's point of view. *The Seven-Ounce Man,* Brown Dog's second appearance, continues the character's misadventures with the law and his attempts at preserving Native American history and his own sense of place within a

society that repeatedly shuns him. *The Beige Dolorosa,* a response to Harrison's own disavowal of the academy thirty years before, shows Phillip Caulkins, a middle-aged academic, trying to reorder his life after the threat of a bogus sexual-discrimination suit and the more frightening prospect of a degenerative neurological disorder.

The title story details the life of a young dog breeder who has affairs with three men who are stalked by her brother when she allows herself to be seduced by all of them. Julip, who holds control over the older men as a result of her sexuality, convinces the men to testify on behalf of her brother Bobby, the shooter, in order to have him moved from Raiford Prison to a mental hospital, where he can receive the attention that he needs. As in his previous attempts at delineating the female psyche, Harrison immerses himself fully in the character of Julip. The difference in tone between Julip and some of Harrison's earlier attempts at writing from a woman's perspective (Julip is more sexual than either Dalva or Clare, and the story is more plot-driven than either of the previous efforts) can be attributed to Harrison's view at the time of writing *Julip* that, as with the difficulty he admitted in writing the young Nelse in *The Road Home,* he and his contemporaries have aged as mysterious and sexually appealing young women remain the same.

THE BEAST GOD FORGOT TO INVENT

The Beast God Forgot to Invent, also a collection of three novellas, contains exclusively male voices that circumscribe the characters' conflict with a banal society. The themes that he treats in the stories are not new for Harrison, although the collection carries a more acerbic tone throughout and the comedy is a bit darker than that in much of the earlier fiction. The title story details the last days of Joe Lacort, who has been seriously injured in a motorcycle accident and cannot remember anything except the immediate present. Lacort's protector Norman Arnz, who sees the world through Joe's eyes, follows both the tracks of Joe's mind and the visible tracks that allow him to keep an eye on Lacort in the Upper Peninsula wilderness. Lacort, Arnz reports, is able to define himself only in terms of his relationship with the wilderness and has "ever so slight an aura around him now in my mind that must resemble the origin of some primitive religion. I just recalled one late June dawn when he arrived quite literally covered with mosquito and blackfly bites, muddy clothes, quite eager to show me the one-hundred-thirty-seven water sounds he had logged in his notebook. What was I to make of this?" Because of his infirmity, Lacort attracts women who want to take care of him; still, he repeatedly escapes society to act out his newfound innocence on nature and to record his own sightings of a three-form chimera that haunts the wilderness of his mind (or, perhaps, the "real" wilderness).

Arnz, who analyzes his own life in terms of Joe's, recalls that he went to college at Northwestern and "though it has an excellent scholastic reputation this fact did not reduce the torpor I felt as a student. . . . I am scarcely interesting even to myself. I am the personification of Modern Man, the toy buyer who tries to thrive at the crossroads of his boredom." Harrison's portrayal of the doomed Joe, who drowns after swimming thirty miles into frigid Lake Superior to rescue his dog, Marcia, is sympathetic toward Joe—the story is written by Arnz as a deposition to the coroner who is investigating Joe's case—and symbolic on several levels. The title of the story is a reference both to Joe's belief that he can see a beast in the wilderness that no one else has ever seen and that Joe is unique in his predicament and his response to the life that has been taken suddenly from him. The characters that surround him are no less lost in their own society, increasing the chaos that arises from such a simple premise.

Westward Ho is a similar treatise on the venality of American culture and society. In the story, Brown Dog searches for Lone Marten, the titular head of a group of Native Americans who try to protect a Michigan burial ground from university excavators. Marten has stolen a bearskin rug that Brown Dog's uncle Delmore has given him, and in the process of retrieving it the protagonist becomes a chauffeur for the big-shot Hollywood screenwriter Bob Duluth, who is connected to Brown Dog by his own run-ins with the law and serendipity; the two seemingly disparate souls become close through their misadventures, and Brown Dog recovers his bearskin rug. Along the way, Brown Dog is seduced by an aspiring French actress named Sandrine and has to break into the fortress-like home of Hollywood's most powerful producer to retrieve the bearskin.

Brown Dog's reward for fulfilling the improbable mission is a ride home from the Minneapolis airport with Uncle Delmore, the responsibility of helping to raise the children of his ex-love Rose, and, perhaps most importantly, the opportunity to immerse himself once more in his beloved wilderness. When Delmore pulls the car over on the way back to the Upper Peninsula, the sight of his homeland nearly overwhelms Brown Dog, who "half stumbled down through a grove of poplar, cedar and birch to the lake where he knelt in the muddy reeds and rinsed his face in the cold water. On the way back up the hill he took a longer route through the woods, half-dancing through the trees like a circus bear just learning his ungainly steps."

I Forgot to Go to Spain recalls *The Man Who Gave Up His Name* in its evocation of midlife ennui and unfulfilled dreams. The protagonist is a wealthy author who has made his mark writing "Bioprobes," best-selling one-hundred-page biographies on famous people. Despite his wealth, the author regrets never having fulfilled his one remaining dream, to visit Spain; his effort to finally visit the country is nearly derailed by a dinner with the wife to whom he was married for only nine days and the French mistress, Claire, who lives in Paris on the allowance that he provides.

The writing that the protagonist does, distilled from research that his sister gives him and for which he pays her a six-figure salary, mirrors the popular writing that Harrison disregards as a symptom of a throwaway society. Several times in the novella, the protagonist mentions the relative worthlessness of his M.F.A. degree, and he sees the work that he does (more than three dozen of the "Bioprobes" over a thirty-year period) as nothing more than a product to be consumed by a public too happy to be spoon-fed infotainment. The last project that he has taken on—and which he vows, finally, to leave unfinished so that he can fulfill his dream—is, ironically, a biography of Michael Eisner, the president of Disney.

The view of the protagonist in the present as a man who has largely wasted his talents and energy by working himself into a rut is contrasted to his recalling a planned trip to Spain when he was nineteen. The reverie is prompted by his sleeping with a young graduate theology student. The protagonist recalls himself as a young romantic (perhaps not unlike Harrison himself) who "planned on talking my way into spending a night in Miguel Hernandez's jail cell, wherever that was. The grim walls would inculcate me with the spirit of his poetry." The plan never comes to fruition, and the protagonist is left to become highly successful, in one way, as a writer at the same time he laments choosing a path that has thwarted his passion.

The three novellas in the collection hinge upon the regret that the protagonists feel—at being incapable of helping those in need, at leaving the sacred places that have informed their lives, and at never having visited those places that might, through the realization of dreams, become sacred. More often than in any

other of his fiction, Harrison reiterates his disdain for the vacuity of American culture and poses an increased attention to the life of the mind as the only solution. Still, all three stories, far from becoming the elegies to "Modern Man" that they seem upon first reading to be, are redeemed by the indomitable spirit of place.

CONCLUSION

Despite the different points of view and themes that Harrison offers in his short works, the novellas in all four collections are held together tightly by one of the many threads that run throughout his fiction: the characters are all linked by their essential inability to function within the constraints of a society that has become alien to them—either through their own machinations, or at the hands of someone who represents that society. His characters, then—both male and female—are not unlike Harrison himself.

In "A Natural History of Some Poems" in *Just before Dark,* Harrison muses that "It is possible to tread water until you are unable to do anything else." Indeed, after consistent production of fiction and poetry over nearly four decades, Harrison remains prolific. In 1998 he published simultaneously *The Road Home* and *The Shape of the Journey,* his collected works in addition to the long poem *Geo-Bestiary,* which reinforces Harrison's views on man's relationship to nature, ecological preservation, and the shifting shape of life (as in so much of Harrison's work, in lengthy discussions couched in metaphors of rivers and water). Harrison's roots in poetry allow him to use those images to craft fiction that is at once spare, dense, and, above all, vital. He has become perhaps America's most prominent writer of the novella, and all of his writing—fiction, poetry, and nonfiction—is important in the body of American literature for the multiplicity of its themes and the diversity of its voices, as well as

Harrison's unique expression of the human condition and a keen sense of the natural world, through and against which his characters play out their lives.

Selected Bibliography

WORKS OF JIM HARRISON

FICTION

Wolf: A False Memoir. New York: Simon & Schuster, 1971.

A Good Day to Die. New York: Simon & Schuster, 1973.

Farmer. New York: Viking Press, 1976.

Legends of the Fall. New York: Delta/Seymour Lawrence, 1979.

Warlock. New York: Delta/Seymour Lawrence, 1981.

Sundog: The Story of an American Foreman, Robert Corvus Strang. New York: E. P. Dutton/Seymour Lawrence, 1984.

Dalva. New York: E. P. Dutton/ Seymour Lawrence, 1988.

The Woman Lit by Fireflies. Boston: Houghton Mifflin/Seymour Lawrence, 1990.

Julip. Boston: Houghton Mifflin/Seymour Lawrence, 1994.

The Road Home. New York: Atlantic Monthly Press, 1998.

The Beast God Forgot to Invent. New York: Atlantic Monthly Press, 2000.

POETRY

Plain Song. New York: W. W. Norton, 1965.

Walking. Cambridge, Mass.: Pym Randall Press, 1967. (100 numbered and 20 signed and lettered copies.)

Locations. New York: W. W. Norton, 1968.

Stony Brook Holographs. Stony Brook, N.Y.: Stony Brook Poets Foundation, 1968.

Outlyer and Ghazals. New York: Simon & Schuster, 1971.

Letters to Yesenin. Fremont, Mich.: Sumac Press, 1973. (1,000 softcover, 100 numbered, and 26 lettered hardbound copies.)

Returning to Earth. Berkeley, Calif: Ithaca House, 1977.

Letters to Yesenin and Returning to Earth. Los Angeles: Sumac Poetry Series Center Publications, 1979.

Selected and New Poems, 1961–1981. New York: Delacorte/Seymour Lawrence, 1981.

The Theory and Practice of Rivers and Other Poems. Seattle: Winn Books, 1986. (A signed limited edition.)

The Theory and Practice of Rivers and New Poems. Livingston, Mont.: Clark City Press, 1989.

After Ikkyu and Other Poems. Boston: Shambhala, 1996.

The Shape of the Journey: New and Collected Poems. Port Townsend, Wash.: Copper Canyon Press, 1998.

OTHER WORKS

Cold Feet. Screenplay by Tom McGuane and Jim Harrison. Directed by Robert Dornhelm. Avenue Pictures, 1990.

Revenge. Screenplay by Jim Harrison and Jeffrey Fiskin. Directed by Tony Scott. Columbia, 1990.

Just before Dark: Collected Nonfiction. Livingston, Mont.: Clark City Press, 1991. Reprint, New York: Houghton Mifflin, 1992.

Wolf. Screenplay by Jim Harrison and Wesley Strick. Directed by Mike Nichols. Columbia, 1994.

The Boy Who Ran into the Woods. New York: Atlantic Monthly Press, 2000.

SELECTED ARTICLES AND ESSAYS

"Grim Reapers of the Land's Bounty." *Sports Illustrated,* October 11, 1971, pp. 38–40ff.

"To Each His Own Chills and Thrills." *Sports Illustrated,* February 7, 1972, pp. 30–34.

"Old Faithful and Mysterious." *Sports Illustrated,* February 14, 1972, pp. 68–72ff.

"Where the Chase Is the Song of Hound and Horn." *Sports Illustrated,* March 20, 1972, pp. 64–69ff.

"Machine with Two Pistons." *Sports Illustrated,* August 27, 1973, pp. 36–38ff.

"Fishing." *Sports Illustrated,* October 14, 1974, p. 98ff.

"Marching to a Different Drummer." *Sports Illustrated,* November 4, 1974, pp. 38–40ff.

"Salvation in the Keys." *Esquire,* June 1976, pp. 152–153.

"A River Never Sleeps." *Esquire,* August 1976, p. 6.

"Not at All Like Up Home in Michigan." *Sports Illustrated,* October 25, 1976, pp. 54–56ff.

"Advertisement." *New York Times Book Review,* September 19, 1982, p. 35.

"The Revenge Symposium." *Esquire,* May 1983, p. 88.

"Sporting Food." *Smart Magazine,* 1989–1990. (Total run of ten columns.)

Preface to *Russell Chatham: One Hundred Paintings.* Livingston, Mont.: Clark City Press, 1990.

Introduction to *Mem-ka-weh: Dawning of the Grand Traverse Band of Ottawa and Chippewa Indians,* by George Weeks. Traverse City, Mich.: Village Press, 1991.

"The Raw and the Cooked." *Esquire,* 1991–1993. (A monthly column.)

"Great Poems Make Good Prayers." *Esquire,* October 1993, pp. 146–147.

"Pie in the Sky." *Esquire Sportsman* 2, no. 2:33–34 (fall–winter 1993).

"The Beginner's Mind." In *Heart of the Land: Essays on Last Great Places.* Edited by Joseph Barbato and Lisa Weinerman. New York: Pantheon Books, 1995. Pp. 136–150.

"Squaw Gulch." In *Who's Writing This: Notations on the Authorial I with Self-Portraits.* Edited by Daniel Halpern. Hopewell, N.J.: The Ecco Press, 1995.

Foreword to *Diggin' in & Piggin' Out: The Truth about Food and Men,* by Roger Welsch. New York: HarperCollins, 1997.

"First Person Female." *New York Times Magazine,* May 16, 1999, pp. 100–101.

"Eating French: Time for Some Deep Thinking about Real Food." *Men's Journal,* November 1999, pp. 72, 74, 76, 78.

JOURNALS, CORRESPONDENCE, AND MANUSCRIPTS

The primary archive of Harrison's work, including his twenty-five-year correspondence with writer and friend Thomas McGuane, and a large collection of first editions, small-run articles and interviews, and ephemera, is housed at Michigan State University in East Lansing, Michigan.

CRITICAL AND BIOGRAPHICAL STUDIES

Colonnese, Tom. "Jim Harrison: A Checklist." *Bulletin of Bibliography* 39, no. 3:132–135 (September 1982).

Fergus, Jim. "The Sporting Club." *Outside,* March 1989, pp. 40–44, 112–117.

Iyer, Pico. "Romancing the Home." *The Nation,* June 23, 1984, pp. 767–770.

Matthieussent, Brice. *Jim Harrison, de A à W.* Paris: C. Bourgois, 1995.

McClintock, James I. "Dalva: Jim Harrison's 'Twin Sister.'" *The Journal of Men's Studies* 63:319–330 (spring 1998).

Prescott, Peter S. "The Macho Mystique." *Newsweek,* July 9, 1979, p. 72.

Reilly, Edward. *Jim Harrison.* New York: Twayne Publishers, 1996.

Roberson, William H. "'A Good Day to Live': The Prose Works of Jim Harrison." *Great Lakes Review* 9, no. 1:29–37 (1983).

———. "The Macho Mistake: The Misrepresentation of Jim Harrison's Fiction." *Critique* 29, no. 4:233–244 (summer 1988).

Torrey, Beef. "Collecting Jim Harrison: 'Untrammeled Renegade Genius.'" *Firsts: The Book Collector's Magazine,* May 1999, pp. 38–47.

SELECTED INTERVIEWS

Bednarik, Joseph. "On Becoming a Tree: Talking with Jim Harrison." *Silverfish Review* 20:24–37 (spring 1991).

———. "A Conversation with Jim Harrison." *Northwest Review* 33, no. 2:106–118 (1995).

Bonetti, Kay. "An Interview with Jim Harrison." *Missouri Review* 8, no. 3:65–86 (1985).

Coates, Joseph. "Bedrock Americana: Jim Harrison Speaks of Worlds Where Nature and Spirit Are One." *Chicago Tribune,* August 12, 1990, pp. 14:1+.

Elliott, Ira, and Marty Sommerness. "Jim Harrison: A Good Day for Talking: An Interview with the

Author of *Wolf* and *Farmer.*" *October Chronicle,* October 29, 1976, unpaginated. 8 pages.

Fergus, Jim. "The Art of Fiction CIV: Jim Harrison." *Paris Review* 30:52–97 (1988).

Harrison, Jim. *American Literary History* 2, no. 2: 274–276 (summer 1999).

Nuwer, Hank. "The Man Whose Soul Is Not for Sale: Jim Harrison." *Rendezvous: Journal of Arts and Letters* 21, no. 1:26–42 (fall 1985).

Reed, Julia. "After seven acclaimed novels, Jim Harrison is finding it harder to elude fame." *Vogue,* September 1989, pp. 502, 506, 510.

Skwira, Gregory. "Words from the Woods." *Detroit,* March 25, 1984, pp. 8–9, 11, 13–15, 16, 18–19.

Smith, Patrick A., and Robert J. DeMott. Unpublished interview, August 28–30, 1997. Leelanau, Michigan.

Smith, Wendy. "PW Interview: Jim Harrison." *Publisher's Weekly,* August 3, 1990, pp. 59–60.

Walker, Casey. "What I'm Thinking about for Two Hours." *Wild Duck Review* 3, no. 2:3–6 (April 1997).

FILMS BASED ON THE WORKS OF JIM HARRISON

Carried Away. Screenplay by Ed Jones and Dale Herd. Directed by Bruno Barreto. Fine Line, 1996.

Legends of the Fall. Screenplay by Susan Shilliday and Bill Wittliff. Directed by Edward Zwick. Tri-Star, 1994.

—PATRICK A. SMITH

Shelby Hearon

1931–

IN AN INTERVIEW with James Ward Lee and in several introductions and commentaries, Shelby Hearon has insisted that her novels deal with the disguises we wear as we struggle to understand our various worlds. There is no doubt that disguises—and other deceptions—play large thematic roles in her works, but the author also explores a number of other themes: appearance versus reality, free will versus determinism, rivalry between mothers and daughters, and the struggle of women to free themselves from traditional roles. Hearon is also concerned with the role of the artist and the way women use art to realize their full potential. But no matter what the particular themes or plots, almost all of Hearon's novels focus on the lives that women lead in the modern world. One notable exception is *Five Hundred Scorpions,* her only novel featuring a man (named Paul Sinclair) as the protagonist, but even in that book, there is a great deal of emphasis on the women who surround him. None of this is to say that Shelby Hearon wears blinders where male characters are concerned, nor is it true that she engages in male bashing. It is just that she knows the roles of women, has worked to understand them, and depicts them in her works with great sensitivity.

Shelby Reed Hearon was born in Marion, Kentucky, on January 18, 1931, to Charles Reed and Evelyn Roberts Reed. Her androgynous name, Shelby, comes from an ancestor who was a governor of Kentucky, but despite her Bluegrass State roots and her early years there, she spent much of her life in Texas, the setting of many of her novels. Charles Reed was a geologist, so the Hearon family followed him as he prospected for gold in the mountains of north

Georgia, oil in Texas, and fluorspar in Kentucky. While the family was still in Kentucky, the Reeds took Shelby out of the local public high school, which lacked a college preparatory curriculum, and sent her to the Sayre School, a Presbyterian girls' school in Lexington. There she studied Latin and Greek and learned to circumvent the strictures of the private school with its emphasis on ladylike behavior and the avoidance of "the appearance of evil." Then, in 1947, when Shelby was sixteen, the Reeds moved to Austin, Texas, where Charles was doing seismic work for the oil industry, and where Shelby was to remain for thirty-seven years.

ALL THINGS TO ALL PEOPLE

In Austin, Shelby Hearon was an outstanding student. She finished high in her class, bore up under her androgynous name, and won the state extemporaneous writing contest—the news headline read "Austin Boy Wins Ready-Writing." (Years later, when she was turned down for a Guggenheim Fellowship, her letter of rejection said, "Mr. Hearon, your work was given every consideration.") At the University of Texas, Hearon was accepted into the Plan II honors program and graduated—with honors—in 1953. That same year she married Robert Hearon, her high school sweetheart. In a marriage that lasted until their divorce in 1976, Shelby and Robert Hearon became the parents of two children: Anne and Reed.

During her years with Bob, Shelby Hearon lived the life of an Austin attorney's wife typical of the time: she was active in her local Parent-Teacher Association, volunteered for

Planned Parenthood, and was a member of the Junior League. She became president of all three organizations and was one of Austin's outstanding young matrons. As she told the interviewer Elizabeth Bennett of the *Houston Post* in 1975, "I was Betty Crocker in the kitchen, Brigitte Bardot in the bedroom and Dr. Spock—or I guess it's Montessori now—with the children. At least I thought I was in all those roles in the middle-class picture I've just drawn for you."

It was out of this mother–homemaker–civic matron life that she began writing her first novel, *Armadillo in the Grass* (1968). The publication of *Armadillo* did not change her life immediately, for she continued her full-time wife and mother roles for another eight years; however, she knew that she would never be the same person once she made her start as an artist. Fifteen years after the publication of *Armadillo,* she wrote in the introduction to a second edition, "It is the one you broke your past for, the one you turned and went the other way to get to." Her turning began with *Armadillo* and continued with *The Second Dune* (1973), *Hannah's House* (1975), and *Now and Another Time* (1976). In 1976 she sought a divorce from Robert Hearon, her husband of twenty-three years.

As Hearon wrote in the introduction to her fifth novel, *A Prince of a Fellow* (1978), "When I began the novel . . . I was, for the first time, a woman living alone. I was in a rented apartment with rented furniture high in the treetops above Barton Creek (near Austin, Texas)." By the time the novel was finished, she was living in a farmhouse west of Austin and writing of a "world where nothing was what it seemed, where every face and voice masked a different identity, where even the past dissembled and deceived, and the very dead refused to stay put."

The fifteen novels and seventeen stories she wrote between 1968 and 2000 brought her many awards and honors, as well as a steadily growing reputation as an artist of serious intent. Two

of her novels—*The Second Dune* and *A Prince of a Fellow*—won awards from the Texas Institute of Letters, and five of her stories won the National Endowment for the Arts/PEN short story prize. In addition, she has received awards, grants, and fellowships from the John Simon Guggenheim Foundation, the National Endowment for the Arts, and the American Academy of Arts and Letters. Hearon was the recipient of an Ingram Merrill grant and, in 1993, was named a distinguished alumna of the University of Texas at Austin. She has been a visiting writer and a workshop faculty member at some sixteen universities, including Middlebury, the University of Massachusetts at Amherst, the University of Miami, Colgate, and the University of Illinois at Chicago.

Hearon is principally a novelist. Though she has written short stories, reviews, and essays, she does not consider them the chief business of her writing. Therefore, this article will discuss only the novels.

ARMADILLO IN THE GRASS

Shelby Hearon's first novel, *Armadillo in the Grass,* mirrors the life that Hearon—as wife, mother, and emerging artist—was living in the 1960s. PTA and Junior League only go so far in satisfying an intellectual person's thirst for identity and status. As Clara Blue's friend Sarah says in *Armadillo,* "Women must have devised their social life as a prevention for madness." Like Clara Blue, the Shelby Hearon of teas and Planned Parenthood meetings needed an artistic outlet, so when her children were of school age, Shelby spent five years writing and rewriting the book that she "broke [her] past for." The novel was accepted by Knopf and condensed in *McCall's* in August 1968. Hearon had embarked on a career of writing that would take her through fifteen novels and a number of other works. With that first novel, she began casting aside the life "of the ordinary housewife." As one of her characters says in *Armadillo in the Grass,* "If your husband idealizes you at a moment in the past, and your children are too lost in themselves to know you are there, who is there to see you?"

Since 1968, more and more people "see" Shelby Hearon as a writer of sensitive and provocative novels. The Shelby Hearon that we read at the end of the twentieth century had her fictional beginnings almost forty years earlier. But like Clara Blue, she had a long way to go before she found her true voice as a writer. In many ways, *Armadillo in the Grass* is an apprentice novel. There is a naïveté in the voice of Clara, the first-person narrator, and the plot lacks the sophistication evident in later Hearon novels. Things come too easily and quickly for Clara; it is almost as if the author is in a hurry to get her character launched. For example, in a year, Clara learns to sculpt in several media, becomes accomplished in her field, and even wins a prize. Nevertheless, the author is an acute observer of the natural world Clara glories in, and she demonstrates quick and sure touches as she depicts the upper-middle-class social world of Clara and her family. Hearon is also quite at home describing the anatomy of the animals Clara sculpts and the way an artist handles her material. And even though the reader is aware of the speed with which the book rushes toward Clara's success, there is a sense that Clara's story—at least as she has lived it so far—is complete.

Armadillo in the Grass takes a year of Clara Blue's life and follows her from mother, wife, and amateur naturalist to budding artist. Clara's husband, Archer Anslow Blue, a professor of history, gives her a twenty-five-pound block of clay and challenges her to reproduce the animals she sees in her yard when she is tending her children and observing nature in the hills around Austin. Clara persuades the sculptor Locke Smith (Hearon may be going a little too far with the locksmith/unlocking pun) to take her on as a student, and in the course of her study she falls in love with Locke the way patients sometimes fall in love with their analysts. Nothing, however, comes of her crush. Shortly after she professes her love for him and after he has discerned her talent, Locke tells Clara that if he takes her into his arms, she "will wake up at 6 a.m. tomorrow a culturette." We know, as Locke does, that there is more to Clara than the bored homemaker who embarks on an affair and a life of dilettantism. Locke leaves Austin, and Clara is on her way to realizing herself as an artist.

While *Armadillo in the Grass* is not a fully accomplished novel, it is satisfying in showing a woman in crisis in a time and place that seem real. Hearon has written more than once that her books all start with a sense of place. She says, in fact, that she often spends four months or more coming to know any new place she is writing about. Because of Hearon's accurate rendering of place, we are able to feel ourselves in a world of real things and real people. In *Armadillo,* life in a university city, life among the intellectual classes, life with a husband and two small sons in a semibucolic setting adds to the theme of the frustrated homemaker seeking the same kind of intellectual status that the privileged males knew in Austin in the 1960s. And, as in all Hearon's writings, the style is clear and sure and fits the themes and characters of the novel. Hearon knows how to capture a moment, how to create a fictional picture, how to render a slice of modern urban life.

RECURRING MOTHER-DAUGHTER THEME

Hearon has mentioned several times that her novels seem to come in pairs. Although this is not always the case, it is true of *The Second Dune,* the novel that followed *Armadillo.* The themes are complementary in that the central figures are women struggling to find themselves in a world of men. *The Second Dune,* published by Knopf in 1973 and condensed in *Redbook* magazine in June of that year, won the best novel award of the Texas Institute of Letters, an organization for which Hearon would later serve as president. In *Dune,* we see for the first time Hearon's handling of the mother-daughter motif. In the novel, the central character, Ellen Marshall, is a woman searching for meaning for herself and her four-year-old daughter, Eleanor—always called Ellen Nor by herself and Ellen. Learning to be a woman is still a work-in-progress for Ellen. The traditional way of learning how to be a woman seems outmoded in the modern era. In an earlier time, mothers taught daughters "to look across the gulf to men and count ourselves only as they counted us. We learned to take our hearts and wrap them in ribboned boxes to be raffled at socials to the dark one on the right. . . . Although we thus learned early to tune our ears to the language of men, it is from female to female that the Word is passed." And while Ellen is trying to learn another language, the new language of women, she hopes to be able to pass it to her daughter— and maybe to her husband and son.

Before Ellen married John Marshall, they had a rather hole-and-corner affair while she was still married to Franklin Hawkins, the father of Frank, Jr., now twelve and resentful of John and Ellen—and Ellen Nor, his half-sister. Ellen's life with Franklin was that of the traditional Austin matron of the 1960s—the role that Shelby Hearon mastered before she began her first novel. Franklin was so much the unreconstructed male that Ellen felt the need—in an emblematic scene—to make an appointment at his office in the bank to announce that she has been having an affair and wants a divorce. And so she escapes to John and finds that while things are better with him, she still has to find her way to total womanhood on her own. "The trouble is that happily-ever-after is a country run by husbands. . . . My conviction is that girls who know the right spells to cast can get out of their own towers without waiting for some pass-

ing prince." As Ellen looks backward to the world she inhabited with Franklin and toward the present and future with John, she is ever aware that her destiny is still in her own hands. This is one of the themes that runs through every Shelby Hearon novel: everyone is pretty much on her own, old rules don't serve, "princes of fellows" rarely are what they seem, and the lives of women have to be reinvented by women, who often have to disguise themselves as wives and mothers and daughters and tower-bound princesses.

The mother-daughter motif is the strongest element in Hearon's third novel, the outstanding *Hannah's House,* published by Doubleday in 1975. *Hannah's House* focuses on the lives of Beverly Foster and her daughter, Hannah—and on the failure of each to take the full measure of the other. Beverly, a woman of great humor and irony, always signed her school papers "Bananas Foster" and has gone through life thinking of herself as "Bananas." Her daughter, on the other hand, has no sense of humor, no sense of fun, no feel for irony. The house of the title refers to the yellow stucco house in Austin that Beverly has to buy to launch Hannah on her life as a sorority girl, engaged debutante, starry-eyed bride. Hannah is the perfect picture of the vapid University of Texas sorority girl of the 1970s. She does all the right things—pledge parties, teas, and football games with her fiancé, the stultifying Eugene. What Beverly "Bananas" Foster buys is a living room suitable for Hannah's launching. She goes about her role as sorority-girl mother in the most ironic way, for Bev is a hippie who works for HEXPOP (Halt Exponential Population Growth), has a college professor lover, and in no way fits in with Hannah's life. She is happily divorced from Hannah's father, the CPA ("Certified Public Asshole"), and is very much in synch with the bohemian life of Austin of the 1960s and 1970s.

Beverly tries to please Hannah and steel herself for the upcoming marriage, but her sisters take over some of the more unpleasant chores as the wedding approaches. After all, they are more like Hannah than Beverly is. Bev is startled when she learns that Hannah has ordered her life to please Bev, to be the kind of daughter that Beverly can be proud of. Suddenly things are not at all what they seem. For the moment, the disguises are dropped and the ironic Bev is touched as Hannah dissolves into tears and says, "Nothing I ever did, not ever, was what you wanted, Mother." Hannah flees up the stairs and Bev says to herself, "For nineteen years I have worked to make a girl who for nineteen years has worked to please her mother. I bury my head . . . and weep for all of us everywhere who breed ourselves into families, for all of us everywhere who are never enough for one another." In the end Hannah marries Eugene and Bev marries Ben, her lover. The book ends with Bev thinking, "It is important to leave behind in this yellow stucco house the image of one singular and separate life." Hers? Or Hannah's?

Hannah's House is Hearon's first completely satisfactory novel: the plot works perfectly, the characters of Hannah and Bev are both fully realized, and the life in a world of do-gooders, professors, sorority girls, and hippies is perfectly captured. And what is most refreshing, the humor shines through, even in the most serious parts of the story. Hearon proved her ability to handle irony without savagery. The themes that inform all of Hearon's novels are evident in *Hannah's House*. Bev's "Bananas" disguise as an ironic and sharp-tongued modern bohemian protects her essential vulnerability; Hannah's disguise as an airhead is assumed to please her mother, her aunts, her grandmother, and the world of the perfect coed. Things are definitely not what they seem in Hearon's third novel.

TANGLED RELATIONSHIPS

The following year—1976, the year of Shelby's divorce from Robert Hearon—saw the publica-

tion of Hearon's most confusing and in many ways least satisfactory novel, *Now and Another Time*. The novel traces two—sometimes three—generations and explores the impact of family dynamics on children. It begins in 1934 in East Texas (the "another time" of the title) and concludes in Austin, Houston, and the Texas Hill Country (in the part entitled "Now"). In the first third of the novel we meet two couples: Mary and Albert Allen and Tom and Frances Henderson; in the second part of the novel we follow the relationships of their offspring, Julia Allen and Jim Henderson, who grew up together. Julia is now married to Hardin Chambers, and Jim Henderson is married to a woman named Jo. Hardin Chambers and Jim are law partners. All through college Jim and Julia are pals, almost brother and sister: Julia introduces Jo to Jim, and he finds Hardin for her. They deny their true feelings for years in much the same way their parents did. In "another time," Mary Allen and Tom Henderson, her doctor, almost had an affair—should have had one, it turns out. In the second two-thirds of the novel, Julia and Jim Henderson complete the cycle that almost began with their parents. Late in the novel, in Houston, Jim and Julia come together for the lovemaking that should have happened years before. In a bittersweet ending, Jim and Julia resume their previous lives. But, if we may echo part of a line from the lovers in the movie *Casablanca*, "they will always have Houston." Hardin is confirmed for the state supreme court, and Jim takes over the law firm that Hardin had run for so long. For at least a brief moment Jim and Julia lived out the legacy bequeathed by their parents in "another time."

Yet there is much more going on in the novel than the Jim-Julia story. Their parents, their children, the passing of time, the shifting of place, and the mixing of themes all make for a novel with a confusing plot, and there are too many characters for the reader ever to know one well. Perhaps the theme announced on the cover of the mass-market paperback signals one of the book's weaknesses: "inherited passions and recurring dreams" may sound a little too much like a soap opera for some readers.

CHARACTER AS "SURROGATE"

If *Now and Another Time* is not sharply focused and always clear, Hearon's next novel is. *A Prince of a Fellow* is the story of Avery Krause, a "frizzy-haired, washed out princess looking for a prince. Some ordinary prince on a limping horse, to carry me off to his leaking, rented castle. . . . No one special; after all, I am nothing fancy." At thirty, Avery may be hoping to find a prince, but she gets only frogs. "You never learned. Each time you shut your eyes convinced the frog you kissed would turn. If not this one, then the next one. Green, bloated bastards all of them puckering up those slimy lips in fraud."

Avery runs a radio talk show on "Pasture Radio," a tiny station out in the Texas Hill Country town of Prince Solms (a disguise for New Braunfels, the most German of all the Texas German towns). She is having an unsatisfactory affair with the mayor of San Antonio, a king of frogs, who spends much of the time he is with Avery talking about his wife and sons. Before him, she had been enamored of another fraud, an actor back in Kentucky where she was a drama teacher. He said his name was Charles Henry David, but Avery says, "To his delight, people could never remember whether he was Charles David or David Charles. I called him Henry; I never knew his real name." Avery, as a drama teacher, "presented illusions as real," and she is not too surprised that the actor does the same to her. Once again, things are not what they seem; everyone is in disguise. Her job on "Pasture Radio" fits her illusionary world perfectly, for the listening audience has to imagine the people they hear. On the air, Avery is a princess if her hearers want her to be. For the Germans of Prince Solms, Avery Krause is pure German; but, in reality, she says, "I am, rather, as my mamma is, a Swede sitting like a burr in the saddle of a large German family." The radio news is read to the largely German settlement by Otto, who has a heavy Teutonic accent. Otto is really "a forty-five-year-old Mexican with a Pancho Villa mustache, who works afternoons (out of his lederhosen and into his stiff black suit) as the cemetery sexton."

A Prince of a Fellow is the first novel Hearon wrote after her divorce from Robert Hearon. Part of what she hoped to do in the novel, she stated in an introduction to the Texas Christian University Press reprint, was to "learn a sense of optimism in meeting strangers, an easy toughness in taking care of myself. If all fiction is wish fulfillment, I was sending out a surrogate to test the waters, to take the knocks and teach me how." Avery is a perfect surrogate for a woman making her way without guidance from a mother, a sister, or a husband and family. Avery has a mother, but her mother is obsessed with thwarting the German uncles of her late husband—with Otto Ramirez's help she even moves Avery's father from the German section of the cemetery to lie among the Swedes of her family. So Avery is pretty much free to make her own mistakes, to kiss frogs in the hope that one will turn into a prince.

She may well have found her prince in Gruene Albrecht, a Czech writer. Of course it turns out that Gruene Albrecht is really Billy Wayne Albrecht, a German whose father beat his mother to death and who is contemplating suicide when Avery rides to his rescue at the end of the novel. Apart from the disguises worn by Billy Wayne, Avery, and Otto, there is the grand disguise worn by Queen Esther of the Missionary Baptist Church, who is, in reality, Jane Brown, a local woman educated in the East and fired from the Prince Solms schools during integration. Jane/Esther went back East and earned a national reputation before returning to

Texas to become Queen Esther in the church and a commentator on Avery's "Pasture Radio" show.

Everyone in *A Prince of a Fellow* has a disguise—Willy Vlasic, the congressman from the region who "dyes his hair and stuffs his jockey strap"; the uxorious but wandering mayor of San Antonio; Avery's Swedish mother; and Avery, the prince maker. Hearon says in the introduction to the reprint that, as she was adapting to her new life in a German farmhouse west of Austin, she was "leaving behind between hardcovers the world where nothing was what it seemed, where every face and voice masked a very different identity, where even the past dissembled and deceived, where even the very dead refused to stay put. Leaving behind the first novel to employ my fascination with disguise: *A Prince of a Fellow*." During this time of transition from wife and mother to *femme sole,* Hearon took on the contract job of helping to write former Congresswoman Barbara Jordan's autobiography.

PAINTED DRESSES AND AFTERNOON OF A FAUN

Hearon's next book, *Painted Dresses* (1981), is one of her most highly regarded works. It is the parallel story of Nell Woodward, the painter of dresses, and Nick Clark, a scientist dedicated to disproving the idea of scientific determinism, an idea foisted off on him by his family of scientists. Nell and Nick do not meet until well into the novel, and their love story takes place only toward the end. But each character is searching for meaning—one in art, one in science. Each is pondering the matters of free will and predestination, of choice versus determinism. In her search, Nell divorces her husband and leaves her son behind to go to Santa Fe and become a painter. Nick struggles in a loveless marriage after his mean-spirited brother tricks him into marrying one of his castoffs and experiments

with rats in an attempt to disprove a predetermined life. Nell is exercising her free will in leaving her family and painting the dresses that lead to her success as an artist. Her paintings are all versions of her at various stages of life. Nell might be hard-pressed to explain their symbolic meanings, but she sees intuitively that their emptiness is a sign that she has not yet filled the dresses that represent passages in her life. As Nick says when he sees her paintings at the end of the novel, "I expected paintings; instead, they are you."

There is much more to this novel than the simple story of Nick and Nell in love. Hearon questions Darwinian and Lamarckian biology and Presbyterian determinism; she probes her recurring themes of appearance versus reality and the disguises we wear to get us through life—or to hide from ourselves. And in this novel Hearon creates a number of memorable minor characters: Nick's parents and his evil brother; his wife, the sluttish Virginia; Nell's mother and sister; and the alcoholic Max. But most of all, Hearon has created a believable story of two people who, after a long time, find each other. Nell realizes that it took all those hard years for them to get together, and she tells Nick, "I know we had to have been there to be here. But I wish we hadn't stayed there so long." The novel is dedicated to Bill Lucas, the philosophy professor Shelby Hearon married in 1981, the year of the novel's publication. She and Lucas met in 1978, while he was working toward a Ph.D. in philosophy at the University of Texas. After their marriage they moved to White Plains, New York, where Lucas took a job at Manhattanville College.

Following her pattern of novels in pairs, Shelby Hearon's seventh novel, *Afternoon of a Faun* (1983), complements *Painted Dresses* in that it presents us with characters in pairs whose relationships are made clear only as the novel nears completion. First we meet Jeanetta, who is about to learn, on her fifteenth birthday, that

Finis and Betty Mayfield of Paducah, Kentucky, adopted her immediately after her birth. Up to now, Jeanetta has led the charmed life of a Barbie doll. Her parents dote on her, and Betty considers her daughter almost a little sister. The knowledge that she is not the biological child of the Mayfields is devastating to Jeanetta, for she is ill prepared to accept that things are not what they seem.

The person paired with Jeanetta as a central figure is Harry James, a disturbed young homosexual whose do-gooder parents unthinkingly gave him the name of a celebrity bandleader and left him to shift for himself as they pursued liberal causes. The Jameses both look like Rose Kennedy and are always referred to as the Rose Ks by Harry, now in disguise as Harry Roncevaux. He meets the third pair, Ebie and Danny Wister, a childless couple from Kentucky who are on holiday in Aspen. Ebie is pregnant and tells Harry that she had a daughter who died at the age of four. Harry "takes up" with the Wisters and follows them back to Paducah, where Ebie has her baby, puts it up for adoption, and leaves for her father's home in Louisiana. The father, as eccentric as any character in this novel of eccentrics, lives as a recluse in one room of a decaying southern mansion and runs a network of tax protestors. Ebie dies in a fire there, Danny marries Louise (an old lover), and Harry moves on again to Bennington College. Fifteen years pass and Harry meets Jeanetta, a student in a summer music camp, and figures out that she is the child of Danny and Ebie. Harry then invites Danny up to pick his daughter out of the assembled musicians at a concert. Danny zeroes in on the wrong girl, is sure that she is his daughter but does not want to meet her, and goes away. What Harry learns is that one never really knows who one's parents are—"not the ones who had you or the ones you adopted, could pick you out of a crowd. They could pass you on the street and never know that you were theirs. Anybody else could be more kin."

Afternoon of a Faun has problems with plot, for things are too stretched out; for instance, we almost forget about Jeanetta before she reappears late in the novel. We also have trouble figuring out what is really taking place with Ebie and Danny, with Harry and Danny, and with Harry and Danny and Ebie. And finally there are the strange interludes when Ebie is back in Louisiana. But, as is the case with many of Hearon's novels, the gems are to be found in the details, the small scenes, the depictions of ordinary life: Finis Mayfield spouting quotations from the Masonic sacred books; Harry's eccentricities; Jeanetta's airhead postures; the Rose Ks off saving the onion growers and the lettuce pickers; the lunacy of Ebie's father and the tax protestors. All these elements do not make for a unified plot, but they do produce some great scenes along the way.

PLOT AND CHARACTER IN *GROUP THERAPY*

After her marriage to Bill Lucas and her move to New York, Hearon, not surprisingly, set her next novel partly in Texas and partly in New York. Hearon is preoccupied with place and with people on the move in search of themselves. New York is new ground for Hearon and provides her with a fresh venue to make her own. In *Group Therapy* (1984), Lutie Sayre, the main character and narrator, moves from Austin to take a job not far from where Hearon and Bill Lucas were living in Westchester County. Lutie is a familiar Hearon character. She is naive, canny, intuitive, and smart. A sociologist with a degree from the University of Texas, Lutie, ever the naïf, rents a trailer and moves her furniture to New York because she has an interview at Vassar. When she says "Yes, ma'am" to the chair of sociology interviewing her, she is turned down for that job and has to take a temporary position at the State University of New York at Purchase. In characteristic fashion, Lutie begins building a nest there. As one of her self-help projects, she makes trips into New York City to take part in Joe Donaldson's group therapy sessions. She and Joe fall in love, and Lutie finds herself providing her own informal group therapy for Joe and his two sons.

Lutie, a sociologist with a specialty in matrilineal descent, understands Joe and his boys, but she has never come to terms with certain issues involving herself, her mother, and the two eccentric aunts she visits in Savannah, Georgia, halfway through the novel. All are obsessed with keeping up appearances: the mother is wedded to the University of Texas and virtually "married" to Dr. Pinter, the administrator she works for at the university. Her aunt in Savannah denies to Lutie and the world that her clergyman husband shot himself and insists that he died of overwork because of an integration issue in the church. (The Rutledges, two sisters who are chief benefactors of the church, more or less drove Lutie's uncle to suicide, but since they help provide for Lutie's aunt, they must be deferred to.) All of these "therapies" help Lutie to see herself more clearly and to recognize what Joe told her early on: nobody changes but we can find better ways to be who we are. In the final scene Lutie notes that even though nobody changes, "you had to make provisions for the fact that they changed *in relation to you.*" Lutie and Joe understand each other better, and there is hope that they will make a success of their "group."

Group Therapy has a more unified and coherent plot than some of Hearon's other novels, and the character of Lutie is fully developed. The scenes in Joe's sessions where patients are asked to come in costumes which represent who they think they are or who they want to be offers clever commentary on the theme of disguises. Several of Shelby Hearon's other themes are nicely explored in *Group Therapy*: things are not what they seem—in Austin, in Savannah, in New York. Her mother has no idea how she has hidden herself in her work with Pinter; the sisters fail to see the real nature of the Rutledges or the suicide of the Reverend Mr. McCall; and Lutie never understands her marriage to the feckless Dabney. Nothing was what it seemed. There is also the matter of familial—specifically matrilineal—determinism. Is one predestined by genetic makeup, or is one able to free oneself from some imagined destiny? All in all, *Group Therapy* is a satisfying novel, stylistically and thematically, and the characters are well drawn.

LITERARY DEPARTURES

The next two novels, *A Small Town* (1985) and *Five Hundred Scorpions* (1987), represent departures from Hearon's usual plots, but many of her favorite themes are still explored. *A Small Town* is different from Hearon's other novels in that it is essentially the story of a small Missouri town. Much of the history of Venice, Missouri, where the great earthquake of 1811 took place, is seen through the eyes of Alma van der Linden, who goes from little girl to mature woman in the course of the story. Alma's life is strange even by small-town standards. Her grandfather and his brother, both physicians, live at opposite ends of town and don't speak. Her father and mother barely speak, and she suspects her father of having a mistress—she even goes so far as to follow him and spy on him for days. As a teenager, Alma seduces the high school principal, marries him after his divorce from the town librarian, and bears two children. When a visiting scientist comes to town for an extended study of the seismology of the region, Alma begins an affair with him and is found out by her now-adolescent children.

There is much plot movement in *A Small Town,* and this brief summary barely tells the full story. The novel features a myriad of characters, dark secrets held and revealed, even a murder. Everything that can happen to Venice happens—except the predicted quake that might rend the Mississippi River asunder as the great New Madrid quake did in the early nineteenth century. But a massive emotional quake is just under the surface of Venice, and the novel resonates with all the shock waves. As in most of Hearon's novels, it is the journey—not the arrival—that matters. And along the way in *A Small Town,* we get a great deal. Even if many of the characters are not fully developed— Alma's mother, Neva; Hydrangea Pickens; the twins named Reba and Sheba; Alma's older sisters, Gloria and Greta; Louis Le Croix, Alma's husband; and the adulterous geologist, Dyer—they are such sketches as good fiction is made of. And the scenes of the novel are equally arresting, even if some of them are not fully fixed in the overall story line. Yet, despite, the stuttering of the plot, *A Small Town* is a very satisfying novel. The themes that Hearon treats so often—the effect of earlier generations on later, the question of free will versus determinism, the act of putting on disguises to protect our inner selves from an outer world, and the sometimes disastrous relationships between mothers and daughters—are handled here in an intelligent way. Alma is a full character, and even though the others are not, what we see through her eyes tells us the stories of a small town.

Five Hundred Scorpions hardly seems like a Shelby Hearon novel at all. Set mostly in Mexico on a scientific study, the novel has as its main character Paul Sinclair, a lawyer from Virginia who pulls up stakes and slips away from his wife and two sons almost under cover of darkness to join the Tepoztlan project. He literally sneaks away from home by leaving some cryptic notes to his family and disappearing into the heart of the Mexican jungle with a pair of female anthropologists whose goal is to show that the woman-centered culture of the region destroys the men.

The person who recommends Paul to Dr. Helena Guttman is Paul's old college nemesis, Todd Stedman. Todd had been expelled from Princeton over a minor cheating scandal, and it turns out that the person who turned him in was his friend Paul Sinclair. Now it is payback time, and Todd hopes Paul will be ruined by the Mexican experience and that Paul's wife, Peggy, will fall into his arms. Todd's attempt to seduce Peggy and render Paul a cuckold neatly plays against what is going on in Mexico, where all the men in Tepoztlan seem to be cuckolds at the same time they are cuckolding others. Paul's role in Mexico is to get close to the men and study the sexual mores of the males of the village, though he is never told the full import of the study by the two female anthropologists. Further, his own hopes to seduce the alluring Dr. Guttman are as unrealized as are Todd's to seduce Peggy.

When the huge earthquake hits Mexico City and Tepoztlan, all the five hundred species of scorpions of the region are unleashed. Paul is bitten and almost dies, and Peggy comes to the rescue. Nothing between them is resolved, but at least Paul has had his fill of adventure and may have survived the midlife crisis that sent him south of the border. The characters peopling this novel are well drawn, and the exotic setting is, as is the case with all Hearon's novels, carefully rendered and realistic. The theme that so often governs all others in Hearon's work— things are not what they seem—is layered and re-layered in this novel of treachery, disguise, and mystery. Mexican culture is a mystery to the anthropologists, to Paul, and, it would seem, to many of the local people. Though a real departure from Hearon's usual concerns, *Five Hundred Scorpions* is a success structurally, stylistically, and thematically.

OWNING JOLENE: SIGNATURE HEARON

Owning Jolene (1989), winner of an American Academy of Arts and Letters Literary Award, finds Hearon on familiar ground again. Set largely in San Antonio and centered on the life of a smart young woman narrator, *Owning Jolene* is among the best of Hearon's novels: sentimental, ironic, affecting. It is also Hearon's funniest novel partly because Jolene spends her early life being kidnapped by her parents in the most imaginative and fanciful ways. Her father, Turk Jackson, who sells oil-field equipment, wants Jolene to have a normal life, so he keeps snatching her from her mother, Midge, who wants anything but. When Turk has Jolene, Midge Temple perpetrates her kidnappings in an array of disguises—once dressing up as an exterminator. Midge always takes Jolene to some Texas suburb, sets herself up as a piano teacher, and tries to hide in plain sight. Then Turk tracks them down and takes Jolene away. At one point, when the parents reach a time of stasis, Jolene spends several years with an uncle and aunt, a pair of con artists cut from the same bolt of cloth as her mother.

In her late teenage years, Jolene escapes from her family and strikes out on her own. She begins a love affair with a well-known painter and becomes his favorite model. The lover is Henry Wozencrantz (but in true Hearon fashion he is a victim of disguise, for his mother raised him as Henry Kraft and only later did he discover who he really is). Jolene longs for anonymity, but Henry paints her nude, and she ends up as the featured subject in a successful show in San Antonio that becomes the subject of a *Newsweek* feature—Jolene is even on the magazine's cover.

Despite everything done to make her otherwise, Jolene is an honest and sensible young woman. She finally takes charge of her life and decides that she is the one to "own" Jolene. She also provides commentary on the ability to exercise free will and not be a victim of familial determinism. Jolene may be a little too canny for one so young, but she is a youthful version of the women Hearon admires and who take

their lives in hand and win out against serious odds. The many disguises of the novel are typical Hearon, for once again we see how life is a series of masks that we wear to make our way to sanity.

NOVELS OF THE 1990s

Owning Jolene was followed in 1991 with *Hug Dancing,* another Hearon novel about a woman breaking the ties that have bound her and striking out in another direction. The novel opens with *"They lived happily ever after"* and ends with *"Once upon a time."* In between, we witness the courtship and marriage of Cile Tate and Drew Williams. Of course, Cile has a husband and Drew a wife, and the disentangling of the two marriages is as much a part of the story as the entangling of their lives. Cile is married to a Presbyterian minister, a man of predestination and determinism and a discounter of free will in this life, or at least in Cile's. When she tells him that she is leaving him for Drew, he announces it from the pulpit of his church before she can tell her teenage daughters or alert anyone in the congregation. A mean trick played by a mean man, a man who has his eye on a member of the congregation and who is in her bed—or she his—before Cile's footprints are out of the yard.

Drew is married to a Dallas socialite named Mary Virginia and is the father of two sons, also teenagers. Cile becomes friends with Drew's mother, Lila Beth Williams. Lila Beth introduces Cile to her daughter-in-law, Mary Virginia (who goes by the nickname "Emvee"). Cile and Emvee meet weekly so their children can play—or whatever teens do. When Cile finally meets Emvee's husband, Drew, she is startled to recognize him as her old high school sweetheart, then going by the name of Andy. (Mary Virginia made him change his name because she couldn't bear to be married to someone sharing a name with the singer Andy

Williams.) Drew and Cile begin a love affair almost immediately, and after many slips and struggles manage to marry and "live happily ever after."

The novel takes place in Waco, Texas, the citadel of Texas Baptists, where Baylor University has long prohibited "hug dancing" as the first step on the way to fornication. Though the main characters in the novel are Presbyterians—as Hearon is—there is a strong overlay of Baptist disapproval as Cile and Drew move from marriage to adultery to marriage. For a time, Drew gets cold feet, but love prevails in the end. Admittedly a romantic story, *Hug Dancing* is more, for we meet some of Hearon's best-drawn characters, we have a plot that is tight, and there is much to think about as the novel moves toward "Once upon a time."

Hearon immersed herself in the Waco, Texas, environment to prepare for this book. She moved there for a time; she subscribed to the Waco newspaper—it was in the *Tribune-Herald* that she first heard the term "hug dancing"—and she dug into the town until she had it to a T. Texans who know Waco and who are acquainted with the Baptist worldview will feel at home in the pages of *Hug Dancing,* for Hearon paints a perfect picture of the small southern city on the Brazos.

Life Estates (1994), Hearon's thirteenth novel, is the parallel story of two friends, both widows in their fifties who are in the process of adapting to life without husbands. Sarah Rankin and her husband, Nolan, had already moved into separate rooms before his death, and Sarah had begun to create a separate life for herself by establishing a wallpaper shop (Rooms of One's Own). Her friend Harriet is widowed when her husband, Knox Calhoun, crashes his car into a tree. Harriet's life was centered on her marriage—"It seems like I spent all day getting ready for him to come home in the evening." But Sarah confesses that she didn't really take to marriage: "It was the institution that rubbed me the wrong way." Sarah also suffered because Nolan's ideas about sexual pleasure were rudimentary and self-centered.

The working title of this novel was "Friends for Life," but *Life Estates* may better describe what the novel is about. Each of the widows has a life estate in her husband's will, with the estate passing to the children on her death—a normal way of doing things in the legal world. But, as Sarah points out, "Life is a life estate," something we are granted temporarily and that passes on to others when we die. The novel is about mortality, for Harriet learns that she has a tumor in her chest, and Sarah learns from her doctor-lover that her friend for life has but a short time to live. Harriet dies, and Sarah finds happiness—another life estate—with Will, her late husband's physician. (Years before, Will had refused to treat Sarah, for he knew even then that his attraction was too strong; now, all these years later, they are free to live out their "life estate.")

Set partly in Mineral Springs, South Carolina, and partly in East Texas, *Life Estates* is one of the few Hearon novels that doesn't have the strong sense of place. The plot is clear and well ordered, though, with flashbacks that fill us in on the early lives of Harriet and Sarah—when they were in school together, when they went swimming in their Rose Marie Reid swimsuits, and when they reveled in their "girlhood of corsages." Now widows with children, they look back over life and are willing to admit how many of their girlhood expectations were never fulfilled. Harriet learns shortly before Knox dies that he had a lover. In one of the funny scenes in this otherwise sad novel, she discovers that the other woman is actually a country club friend. At a dance, Harriet confronts the woman, who runs from the room in tears. Harriet follows her to the powder room in a fury and pulls out the gun she has bought to protect her from the crime wave that she imagines is sweeping East Texas. Her friends run into the restroom, see her drawn gun, and all pull out their own guns: "Jo . . . spied the gun in my bag . . . and pulled out a big .38 from her satin purse. And then every single member of [the] Birthday Club opened her bag and all of us had guns! We had ourselves an arsenal—five .38s, six .22s and one Tec-9." No blood is shed, but Madge, the other woman, moves to Houston.

Life Estates is a sad and serious novel that lacks the humor so often found in Shelby Hearon's fiction. But, as in all Hearon's novels, we get an intimate look at appearance versus reality: the two women characters, on the surface, have perfect married lives, perfect children, perfect "life estates." Because reality is so different from dreams, most of us are forced to wear masks. Will, Sarah's lover, wore his disguise as mere family friend for years until he and Sarah could come together. Harriet, who had no proper disguise, confronted ugliness and death without a hedge against reality.

The year *Life Estates* was published (1994), Shelby Hearon was divorced from Billy Joe Lucas, her husband of eighteen years. The following year, 1995, she married William Halpern, a cardiovascular physiologist, and went to live in Burlington, Vermont, where Halpern taught at the university's medical school. Whether Hearon's marriage to a cardiovascular specialist encouraged her to write a novel about a heart transplant is not clear, but it is likely that Bill Halpern was helpful to her in some of the research she did for *Footprints* (1996), a novel about a transplant and about the effect such surgery can have on the donor families and the recipients. Part of Hearon's research for *Footprints* involved her witnessing such an operation in Houston.

The novel opens at a barbecue in Texas, where recipients and donor families meet. A white couple, Nan Mayhall and her husband, Douglas, are there because their daughter's heart is now in the chest of a black minister from Texas. Nan is reluctant to be celebrating this

event, but Douglas feels himself in the presence of their daughter Bethany when he sees the Reverend Calvin C. Clayton. One of the struggles between Douglas and Nan is the amount of grief each feels for the daughter who was killed in a car wreck at twenty-two. Because Nan doesn't take great pleasure in meeting Calvin C. Clayton, Douglas thinks he is the only one who misses their daughter. Douglas, a professor at an Ivy League university, is an eminent brain researcher. Nan, who stopped short of a doctorate in paleontology to be a "married woman," is clearly a minor character in her husband's orbit. Even though he often introduces her to colleagues as "a naturalist in her own right," it is clear that her research and her interests are secondary.

As the novel opens, Nan finds herself, at forty-nine, playing a minor role in the eyes of all who see her. She has borne two children: Bert, a son in the dangerous profession of cave diving, and the late Bethany. She is a faculty wife to a distinguished husband who has already had one affair and is on the verge of another. The second affair, with an English professor who "empathizes" over the loss of Bethany, is serious because Douglas thinks the younger woman can get pregnant and provide some sort of replacement for his dead daughter. When Doug's stepmother warns Nan that Doug "is going to want to start over," Nan calls him on the phone and screams "IF YOU MAKE A BABY, I SWEAR I'LL COME UP THERE AND TEAR YOUR ARMS LOOSE FROM YOUR BODY AND BEAT YOU SENSELESS WITH THEM. DO YOU HEAR ME?"

Later, when Bert is feared killed or injured in a scuba diving accident, the full measure of Doug's grief is made clear. When Bert dismisses himself as "the one who survived," Doug erupts and tells them about his own life as the one who survived when his brother Walter was killed. Doug's father tried to wipe out all trace of Walter Mayhall and make Doug the focus of all his protective efforts. Doug was "the one who lived," and he found the burden almost intolerable. Doug tells Nan and Bert:

> I had nothing left of my brother. They stripped the premises and burned his memory to ash. Now your mother is trying to do the same thing to your sister. I mention that I've talked to the preacher who's got her heart . . . and your mother moves the length of the East Coast in order not to hear me. If I say *Bethany*, if I even say my girl's name, your mother starts in about something that's been dead since before the mind of man. Digging up some creature nobody would give a fuck about if it wasn't deader than history.

In the final chapter the Reverend Clayton dies, and with him goes Bethany's heart. After Clayton's death, Douglas says, "YOU DIDN'T EVEN THINK OF BETHANY." Nan replies, "Our daughter was already gone, Douglas. She died Thanksgiving day." The novel ends on a sad but reconciliatory note as Doug and Nan drive west of Houston to the ranch on which Doug was raised. Things will never be the same for either of them with Bethany gone, but they understand "the heart transplants of parenting"—and themselves—a little better than they did.

Footprints is a sharply focused novel that creates in Nan a character we can understand and sympathize with. Her story is the story of the educated and intelligent woman who relegates herself to a secondary role as a part of her family obligations. But she never dismisses herself as many capable women have done, nor does she ever give up her own independence even when almost overwhelmed by the faculty world in which she finds herself. In most ways she is a typical Shelby Hearon woman. Like the author herself, Nan is thirsty for knowledge and eager to exercise her mind. We know her—and her creator—by the time we are finished with this novel.

ELLA IN BLOOM

Hearon's fifteenth novel, *Ella in Bloom* (2000), is the story of a forty-nine-year-old woman still trying to please her mother. Ella Hopkins lives in the New Orleans suburb of Metairie, Louisiana, and writes her mother back in Austin, Texas, about the wonders of her rose garden, about her life of teas and country clubs. Ella has created the perfect garden around her perfect small house with its brick fence laden with roses. Ella's roses are not the unofficial roses of the common rose gardens, but odd specimens from Denmark and England and far-flung lands of the Rising Sun. Her letters home read like pages from the Smith and Hawken garden catalogs. But the whole world Ella creates for her mother is make-believe. She and her gawky but brilliant and talented daughter live in a run-down shack in Old Metairie with a yard that is usually a swamp. Ella barely makes a living as a plant sitter and caretaker for rich people on vacation. She is an expert on roses but has none. The roses she invents for her mother come from what she learns from Henry Legrand, the rosarian of a local tourist attraction.

Ella ran away from home as a late teen with the no-good but attractive Buddy Marshall, who, we learn late in the novel, first slept with Ella's perfect sister Terry. Terry married R. Rufus Hall, an up-and-coming young Austin lawyer who fitted her mother's notion of the ideal husband for her favorite daughter. Rufus (or Red as he is known to himself and Ella) was the man Ella was closest to in her teen years. But Red/Rufus married the perfect Terry, and the happy pair is living in a plush section of Austin with two fine sons. Still, one must remember Hearon's main themes: things are not what they seem, and we are all in disguise. Terry starts an affair with Skip Rowland, a West Texas rancher who is a double for Buddy Marshall, and is killed when her chartered plane crashes on a visit to him. At the funeral and at Ella's mother's birthday party later, we learn how little Ella has meant to her mother. But Ella wins in the end when she and Red become lovers and decide to live happily ever after—and this time things *are* what they seem.

Along the way, we meet a couple of Hearon's best characters. Ella is rounded and believable. She is Lutie Sayre, Jolene Temple/Jackson, and Avery Krause come to maturity. She is Bananas Foster of another time. She is the character Shelby Hearon has been working toward all these years. Ella's daughter, Robin (who has renamed herself Birdie), is Jolene and Lutie and Avery in an early stage—and she will turn out to be her mother someday. But not Agatha Hopkins, the grandmother who lives in a world of her own devising, one as false as the world of Ella's letters. Not only are the characterizations rich, but the settings are up to Hearon's high standards. Waterlogged Metairie comes alive; the house Ella and Birdie live in is real to us; and the rose gardens—real and imaginary—emit "odors savors sweet."

The world and life of Shelby Hearon in all its permutations is to be found in the pages of her novels. The band of intelligent women we meet in her works are extensions of the intellectual and intelligent Shelby Hearon, the star student who never forsook learning. We also see the Shelby Hearon who has weathered the emotional turmoil of life in our times.

Selected Bibliography

WORKS OF SHELBY HEARON

NOVELS
Armadillo in the Grass. New York: Knopf, 1968.
The Second Dune. New York: Knopf, 1973.
Hannah's House. Garden City, N.Y.: Doubleday, 1975.
Now and Another Time. Garden City, N.Y.: Doubleday, 1976.
A Prince of a Fellow. Garden City, N.Y.: Doubleday, 1978.
Painted Dresses. New York: Atheneum, 1981.
Afternoon of a Faun. New York: Atheneum, 1983.
Group Therapy. New York: Atheneum, 1984.
A Small Town. New York: Atheneum, 1985.
Five Hundred Scorpions. New York: Atheneum, 1987.
Owning Jolene. New York: Knopf, 1989.
Hug Dancing. New York: Knopf, 1991.
Life Estates. New York: Knopf, 1994.
Footprints. New York: Knopf, 1996.
Ella in Bloom. New York: Knopf, 2000.

SHORT STORIES
"The British Museum." *Southwest Review* 71 (1986).
"Dry Run." *Cosmopolitan,* November 1987.
"Bazaars in Zanzibar." *Mississippi Review* 15 (1987).
"Improvisations." *Cosmopolitan,* April 1988.
"Hall of Mirrors." *Southwest Review* 78 (1993).
"Distressed Passenger." *Southern Review* 39 (1994).
"Good News." *Shenandoah* 43 (1994).
"A Most Unusual Wedding." *Redbook,* June 1996.

CRITICAL AND BIOGRAPHICAL STUDIES
Bennett, Patrick. "Shelby Hearon: Time, Sex, and God." *Talking with Texas Writers: Twelve Interviews.* College Station: Texas A&M University Press, 1980. Pp. 111–134.

———. "Laura Furman, Beverly Lowry, and Shelby Hearon." *Texas Women Writers: Tradition of Their Own.* Edited by Sylvia Ann Grider and Lou Halsell Rodenberger. College Station: Texas A&M University Press, 1997. Pp. 148–159.

Lee, James Ward. Unpublished interview with Shelby Hearon, March 7, 2000.

Lynn, Sandra. "Texas, Women, Fiction." *Pawn Review* 4:2–17 (1980–1981).

Marshall, Carol. "The Fairy Tale and the Frontier: Images of Women in Texas Fiction." In *The Texas Literary Tradition.* Austin: University of Texas College of Liberal Arts, 1983. Pp. 195–206.

Rodenberger, Lou. "Shelby Hearon, Beverly Lowry, and Sarah Bird." *Updating the Literary West.* Edited by Thomas J. Lyon. Fort Worth: Texas Christian University Press, 1997. Pp. 600–607.

—*JAMES WARD LEE*

Oscar Hijuelos
1951–

CELEBRATED AS ONE of America's most gifted contemporary writers, Oscar Hijuelos established his literary reputation only seven years after the publication of his first novel, *Our House in the Last World* (1983), a classic immigration story. His second novel, *The Mambo Kings Play Songs of Love* (1989), won the 1990 Pulitzer Prize, securing Hijuelos's place in American letters and making the Cuban American writer the first U.S. Latino to win the highly coveted award for fiction. Commenting on the book's reception in *Confluencia,* literary scholar Juan Bruce-Novoa observed that *The Mambo Kings Play Songs of Love* represents "a major step in U.S. Latinos' progress from the margins into the mainstream."

While some of Hijuelos's prominence is based on the novel's recognition as a literary masterpiece, the writer's more mainstream popularity is due in large part to the box-office success of the 1992 film adaptation titled *The Mambo Kings.* Soon after the book's release in 1989, *The Mambo Kings Play Songs of Love* became the obsession of the New York City art gallery owner Arne Glimcher, who paid an astonishing $250,000 for the option rights. Making his directorial debut, Glimcher turned the novel into a feature film released by Warner Brothers. Focusing only on the first half of the novel, the movie depicts the story of the Castillo brothers, who in the film emigrate from Cuba to New York City in 1952 to pursue their dream of becoming famous musicians. According to Glimcher, as quoted in *Magill's Survey of Cinema,* the brothers symbolize "the last moment of innocence in America."

Opening in February 1992, Glimcher's film *The Mambo Kings* received mixed reviews. *Entertainment Weekly* called it "a tinsel-edged dream of a movie," having "a romantic fatalism that borders—agreeably—on kitsch." Film critic Gene Shalit called the film "a scorcher" and a "hot movie" due to its "hot music, hot romance." *Time*'s Richard Corliss concurred, claiming that by watching *The Mambo Kings* "for two bouncy hours, whether you are a gas pumper in Omaha or an art dealer looking for new canvases to conquer, you can be a Cuban in love."

Several reviewers castigated the film's quality, seeing beyond the romanticization and "hotness." Writing for the *Boston Globe,* Michael Bowen concluded that the film "reduced the book's marvelous texture to one-dimensional stereotypes," making it seem like "an Elvis film with a Latin beat." Enrique Fernández, writing for the *New York Times,* assessed the film's shortcomings, decrying Hollywood's historical representation and treatment of Hispanic characters on the silver screen:

> Latin characters remain mostly "hot." In Hollywood film, that mirror of the American imagination, Latinos turn up as fiery gang members *(West Side Story),* hot-tempered bandits (any [Sam] Peckinpah film), smoldering playboys (usually played by Ricardo Montalban or Cesar Romero) or purveyors of the mambo, the rhumba and the steamy lambada.

Fernández also asserted that while Latinos are soon expected to comprise the largest minority group in the United States, they and their cultures are still perceived as "other," marginal people living on the fringes of mainstream Anglo-American society.

Contrary to form, the film version of *Mambo Kings* negatively affected the novel's sales. Ruth Leibman, manager of a New York City bookstore, criticized Hijuelos's publisher for substituting a picture of Armand Assante and Antonio Banderas, the film's stars, for the original dust jacket design when it reprinted the novel in paperback. Referring to its effect on sales, Leibman said the new cover "was like putting a razor to a balloon," reported Martha Guevara in the *St. Louis Post-Dispatch*. Despite these mixed reviews, however, the film's success brought Hijuelos further publicity, thus drawing much attention to the Latino population in America.

Hispanic fiction has not always enjoyed this kind of global attention. Before *Mambo Kings,* U.S. Latino writers generally found it difficult, if not impossible, to convince the New York publishing world of the burgeoning interest in their creative works. Consequently, these writers turned to smaller, usually academic, presses—particularly the University of Houston's Arte Público Press and the University of Arizona's Bilingual Review Press—which recognized the rapidly growing audience for Latino literature. "Considering the often virulent attacks launched by Hispanics on mainstream publishers for ignoring Latino writers," wrote Bruce-Novoa, *The Mambo Kings Play Songs of Love* "marked a long anticipated breakthrough for this group." As such, critics and reviewers attribute the widespread popularity and ever-growing demand for Latino literature, in part, to Hijuelos, for placing Hispanic characters upon the literary stage. Along with Cuban American writer Cristina García, whose literary fiction has also been well received and critically acclaimed, Hijuelos—much like other ethnic American writers—has granted an international reading community with a portal into his world, breathing life into, and thus validating, the lives of U.S. Latino characters, many of whom are fashioned directly from the author's own milieu.

GROWING UP CUBAN AMERICAN

Born in New York on August 24, 1951, the second son of working-class Cuban immigrants, Oscar Hijuelos was raised in New York City and has lived there ever since. Pascual and Magdalena Hijuelos strove to build a better, more prosperous, life than the one destined to them under the dictatorship of Cuba's then-leader, Fulgencio Batista. The family rented a cramped apartment in a tenement building on 118th Street on the city's Upper West Side, an eclectic neighborhood, bordering Spanish Harlem and Columbia University. In this diverse mixture of residents—a multicultural environment shared by Hispanics, African Americans, Irish, Jews, as well as affluent intellectuals who were chiefly Columbia students and faculty—young Hijuelos lived with his older brother, Joseph, and his Spanish-speaking parents.

Upon his arrival in the United States, Hijuelos's father Pascual was determined to attain the elusive American Dream, that promise of economic and political freedom for which the country is renowned. Unfortunately, there were many obstacles in Pascual's path: not only was he unable to speak English, but he lacked any skills that could lead to gainful employment. Although he had inherited a modest sum of money after his own father's death, Pascual "was unprepared for what came [in the United States]," says Hijuelos, the writer, as quoted by Dinitia Smith in *New York* magazine. "He pissed away his inheritance. He was very generous, trusting to a fault. Occasionally, he liked to drink too much. Then he lamented his life decisions." As a consequence, Pascual took a low-paying job as a hotel dishwasher and, eventually, a cook at the Biltmore Hotel—a position he maintained until his death of a heart attack in 1968, the year in which Oscar turned seventeen. Working additional jobs to support his family until his death, Pascual grew disillusioned by his lot in America, becoming an alcoholic, which interfered severely in his relationship with his sons. When asked about his home life as a child, Hijuelos told Lydia Chavez in the *Los Angeles Times Magazine,* "We were the classic dysfunctional family"; but even though "the fights between his parents were ceaseless," he admitted, there was always "a lot of affection in my household and that makes a big difference."

The writer's mother, Magdalena Hijuelos, descended from a family that originated from Barcelona and Majorca and owned factories in Cuba until her father lost his fortune. Like the women of her time, faithful to her traditional Cuban culture, Magdalena never worked outside the home. Instead, she relegated herself to her family's demands in America, performing her domestic chores, all despite a penchant for literature, poetry in particular, and a dream of one day becoming a teacher. In her spare time, Magdalena clandestinely wrote poetry. Her unfulfilled dreams partly fueled the great disappointment Oscar Hijuelos sensed during his early family life. While growing up in a complex familial environment in a neighborhood with a thriving drug scene and escalating gang violence, Hijuelos dreamed of becoming a cartoonist. The locale of his childhood fed Hijuelos's creative imagination, providing him with fertile inspiration for the many characters who now occupy the pages of his fiction.

Because he was raised in a Spanish-speaking home, Hijuelos believes that he lived between two worlds: the Old, representing the Cuban, and the New, representing America. Understandably, Hijuelos has struggled to reconcile his own identity as a Cuban American, a theme that is realized in much of his fiction.

Hijuelos attended grammar school at Corpus Christi in the city and high school at Cardinal Hayes in the Bronx. While admitting that he had absolutely no aspirations of becoming a writer while growing up, he credits his then girlfriend with exposing him to literature when she gave him a book by the writer Donald Bar-thelme. After graduating from Brandeis High School in Manhattan, Hijuelos attended Bronx Community College for a year before transferring to City College at the City University of New York, where he not only majored in English as a creative writer, earning a B.A. in 1975, but also received an M.A. in English in 1976. During his time at CUNY, Hijuelos was mentored and nurtured as a fledgling writer by three prominent literary figures: Susan Sontag, Frederic Tuten, and Donald Barthelme especially. Hijuelos recalls being curious—and impressed—when he learned that the author of the book his friend had given him (his future mentor, Barthelme, a short-fiction writer who frequently wrote for *The New Yorker*) taught at City College. Hijuelos told Josh Getlin in a 1990 interview for the *Los Angeles Times*:

> One day, I went up into the offices looking for him. . . . I looked into one room and there's a scholarly looking guy by a typewriter, and I asked him if he was Donald Barthelme. He said no, he was William Burroughs. I walked down the hall and asked another man if *he* was Barthelme, and he said his name was Joseph Heller. Finally I found the man.

At CUNY, Hijuelos—inspired by Barthelme's appreciation for the English language—began to write fiction, turning to his own life and surroundings for inspiration. In the interview with Getlin, the author explained: "I . . . wanted contact back with the roots because I had been out there, in the mainstream world, long enough to feel the chill. American culture was just so anonymous, it rarely gets into depth, it's a very surface thing. But I realized that I could get on a freedom train and write about Cuba." His first novel, the autobiographical *Our House in the Last World* (1983), was the product of his master's degree program in creative writing at City College. Through the story, Hijuelos weaves, almost seamlessly, his development as a second-generation Cuban American with his social and cultural commentary on the world around him.

OUR HOUSE IN THE LAST WORLD

Frederic Tuten, director of CUNY's creative writing program, remembers his former student Hijuelos as ambitious, disciplined, and dedicated. Originally, Hijuelos focused on playwriting, but "nothing sold." While working at Transportation Display, Inc., a New York City firm that creates advertisements for subways and buses, Hijuelos began to write short stories, harvesting his vivid memories of growing up bicultural.

Our House in the Last World—which Hijuelos has called "private and intimate"—chronicles the formation of a second-generation Cuban American through what critics and reviewers have termed a classic immigration novel or an "immigrant memoir." Such novels, explained Gustavo Pérez Firmat in his book *Life on the Hyphen: The Cuban-American Way,* typically trace a character's permanent migration to and adaptation to another country. *Our House* focuses on the processes of emigration and adaptation to the United States: isolation, alienation, disillusionment, and assimilation.

Hijuelos's "sacred mission" as a writer is to portray characters who "don't fit in" or who don't comply with America's stereotypes of Latinos. Much of his work addresses what the writer calls "second-classness," the combination of growing up Latino and poor. Because of his ethnicity, Hijuelos believes that he was "always feeling the need to try harder," noted Jerome Weeks in the *Dallas Morning News.* The result: an inadequacy and marginalization within America's mainstream culture that contributed to the writer's frustrations and anger at the world: "I had so much tension in me as a kid," Hijuelos recalled in the interview with Getlin. "If you're raised in a certain way, you're used to public clinics and feelings of second-classness."

With its focus on the Santinio family, *Our House* tells the story of Alejo and Mercedes Santinio, a young Cuban couple who, shortly after their marriage, emigrate to New York in search of the American Dream. The novel's narrative is presented in the third person, through the point of view of Hector, the Santinio's second son and presumably Hijuelos's alter ego. Organized into fourteen chapters—chronologically spanning from 1929 to 1975—the novel opens in Cuba with Hector's mother, Mercedes Sorrea, the daughter of a Spanish aristocrat, Teodoro, who involves himself in the Cuban political process and loses his wealth. Devastated and suffering from "worry and depression," Teodoro dies, leaving his wife and daughters to deal with his financial burdens.

Mercedes sits for an entrance exam to a teachers' school, but unable to stop thinking about her dead father, "she couldn't answer the questions or decipher the numbers on the pages." Settling for a simple life with her mother, Mercedes becomes a ticket attendant at the local movie house. There she meets Alejo Santinio, who "was not a handsome man. Nor did he look particularly Cuban or Spanish."

Befriending and manipulating Alejo's mother, Doña Isabel, Mercedes implies that rumors are circulating that she is pregnant. Doña Isabel orders her son to marry Mercedes, and at first the couple seems happy. Having inherited five thousand dollars from his father, Alejo becomes impatient with life in their small Cuban town: "All he knew was that he wanted to leave San Pedro and head out into the world, to break away from the small town life he sometimes found so boring." In 1943, with World War II continuing in Europe, Alejo talks Mercedes into migrating to the United States, where his sister Margarita lives with her husband. Disturbed by the prospect of leaving her homeland, Mercedes finally acquiesces only because it will distance her husband from his evil sister Buita, who hates Mercedes for marrying Alejo. Once in New York, the couple settles into Alejo's sister's small apartment, located "between the sinister reaches of Harlem and the shadow of the University." In the same neighborhood where Hijuelos grew up, the Santinios begin their new life in America. This move, however, is criticized by the novel's skeptical narrator:

> But who gave thought to the fact that they spoke no English? Who considered the differences between doing business in a small Cuban town and in America? Or that they would need plans, connections? . . . Or that Mercedes would be unhappy with fear and loneliness, or that they would miss the very things that so bored them now? Alejo? He thought only that he would have more excitement and fun, perhaps more opportunity, and that he would escape the midday lethargy, the sleepiness of humid, heavy-aired, Cuban afternoons.

This accusatory tone becomes the running commentary in the novel. Referring to this authorial intrusion, reviewers have found Hijuelos's criticism of his family—his father, in particular—harsh. Hijuelos responded in the *Los Angeles Times Magazine* interview: *Our House* was a way "to come to terms with my father's experience. I was walking around with a lot of anger and needed to climb out of an emotionally charged atmosphere."

At first the Santinios enjoy New York. But Alejo, who remains hopeful of attaining his dreams, proves to be a poor financial administrator. For all of her unworldliness and continued mourning of her father's death, Mercedes realizes that the Santinio family is being left behind as boarders from Cuba come and go. Alejo is impervious to their success, unaware that others who were in their situation have prospered.

Mercedes' isolation from the successful Cuban immigrants is further exacerbated by the arrival of Alejo's sister Buita, who immediately moves into the family's already crowded apart-ment and takes control. Alienated in exile, Mercedes "defer[s] to Buita because she [is] afraid of being left alone in this new country where she did not know the language." Meanwhile, Alejo becomes increasingly isolated from Mercedes, whom he perceives as unsupportive and nagging. She retreats to her dreams. A frustrated Alejo abandons the home for days.

Although the marriage remains nominally intact, Alejo's isolation and alienation are further compounded by his inability to bring his dreams to fruition. He blames Mercedes for his problems, longing for the way things used to be: "In Cuba, they know how to raise children so that the man doesn't get involved, but in the small apartments of New York, you see the kids all the time."

Hector's narrative begins what Pérez Firmat calls "life on the hyphen." Readers first learn of the family when Horacio, the Santinios' elder son, is nine. In the summer of 1954, Mercedes travels with her sons to Cuba. Horacio, possessing none of the family's romanticism, is an uneasy hybrid with a strong sense of American independence. He is irreverent of his ancestry, eschewing his mother's idealization of her father. Instead, he wishes he could have met his grandfather Teodoro Sorrea, "not the saint Mercedes always made him to be, but a dude who almost made a fortune off that tax-skimming scheme," a con artist, he thought. Horacio sees "the clogged-with-shit stone toilets that were made tolerable only by the strong fragrances of the fruit trees and blossoms. Cuba," for Horacio, "was in the nineteenth century—okay, a nice place," he says, "and not anything more."

Upon the family's return to the United States, Horacio's life with his family becomes more hellish as he serves as a punching bag for his drunkard father. Unable to bear his home life, Horacio leaves for the U.S. Air Force, becoming "a few lines of scribble on blue airmail paper, first from Biloxi, Mississippi, and then from London, England." When he returns from his military assignment, the narrator records a total metamorphosis: "He had returned from England a complete European . . . very far from the gutter and insecurity he had left behind." While it appears that Horacio has succeeded in distancing himself from his culture, his family, his past, upon Alejo's death, the reader sees that Horacio has succeeded in creating a bicultural identity. He rejects the bad elements of his childhood and embraces the good. At the funeral, Horacio shows a surprising empathy for Alejo. Upon observing the coffin, he states, "At least he won't be suffering anymore. You won't see him yelling or crying anymore. No more work for him. Now he's resting."

Horacio's brother, Hector, however, finds no resolution. The younger son is overprotected by Mercedes, and the family's problems are compounded when, after visiting Cuba, Hector becomes ill with a mysterious virus from exposure to *"microbios"* or germs. While Hector finds paradise in Cuba, this is marred by his realization that he does not look Cuban. Hector, who wants nothing more than to become *un cubano* (a Cuban man), feels alienated from his culture by his light skin and blond hair—the fundamental theme of a novel that constantly questions what comprises one's identity.

Upon their return to New York, Mercedes denies reality, only taking Hector to the hospital after Horacio finds him urinating blood. The doctors conclude that Hector is suffering from a terrible infection and needs to be sent away to a children's hospital in Connecticut. His long convalescence not only cures him of his illness but strips him of his Cuban identity. Completely isolated from his family, from his Cuban roots, Hector is forced to speak only English. A nurse locks him up in a closet for hours at a time, refusing to let him out until he communicates his needs in English. "Day after day," writes Hijuelos, the nurse "badgered him with the same punishments and repeated phrases. In time she made him suspicious of Spanish. Spanish words

drifted inside him, he dreamed in Spanish, but English began whooshing inside. English forced its way through him, splitting his skin."

This episode in Hector's life is based on Hijuelos's own experiences as a child, which, as Getlin noted, mark what would become a "long process of assimilation into the larger American culture." Hijuelos believes that the experience left him "introspective" and "creative" since he became "accustomed to spending an inordinate amount of time alone," according to Lauren Picker in *Newsday*. For Hector the dominant struggle becomes the search for an identity. Is he Cuban or is he American? Upon his return, Alejo disdains his son's loss of Spanish, his loss of Cubanness. Hector's struggle for an identity is augmented by the fact that he and his father are "like twins, separated by age, with the same eyes, faces, bodies. Except Alejo was from another world— *Cubano, Cubano.*"

Hector's isolation becomes manifold. In his quest for self, he turns to his mother's nemesis, Buita, who encourages him to visit her in Miami. Her home is everything his tenement in New York City is not: beautiful, luxurious, and enticing, complete with swimming pool. Hector finds Miami healing: "He wanted to be cured of his sense of illness: inadequacy, stupidity, obesity, ignorance. He wanted to go to bed and wake up a Cuban in the Havana of 1922 . . . but he would settle for Miami." Hector's utopia is short-lived, however, when he discovers that he cannot "pass," that he is stared at by Miami's Cuban exiles, who suspect him as an out-of-place American tourist. When he sits in a cafeteria filled with Spanish-speaking Cubans, the waitress approaches him and speaks English. When Hector addresses her in Spanish, she responds, "you speak good Spanish, for an American." Hector is disheartened and returns to New York. His assimilation is uneasy at best: he moves into his own apartment (though in his mother's neighborhood) and enrolls in college to become a writer. His personal cultural struggles are never resolved. He must continue to balance himself on Pérez Firmat's hyphen, walking a tightrope between not being Cuban enough yet not being American either.

For Hijuelos, *Our House* clearly foreshadows his eminence as a contemporary American writer. Critics and reviews have extolled the novel's virtues. Writing for the *New York Times Book Review*, Edith Milton concluded:

> What gives *Our House in the Last World* its aura of affections and gentleness is its people; they are members of the family, irritating, predictable and ours. Their insanities are touching and somehow genial. And as they decline from hope to resignation, from romance to nagging, they are not just material for a literary exercise but the subject of a loving and deeply felt tribute.

In the *Straits Times*, Claire Tham praised Hijuelos's novel, particularly the "latter segments, where the intensely visceral quality of his writing imparts a searing vividness to the most ordinary actions, and confers on his characters, ordinary, resilient people whose lives might not otherwise be deemed worthy of being told, a certain epic stature."

Not only did Hijuelos receive accolades for *Our House,* but it brought him two prestigious awards: a grant from the National Endowment for the Arts and a Rome Fellowship in literature from the American Academy and Institute of Arts and Letters. The latter prize supported him for a year in Italy as he worked on his second novel and became fascinated with archeology.

THE MAMBO KINGS PLAY SONGS OF LOVE

While in Italy, Hijuelos developed ideas for a second novel, which he researched methodically upon his return to New York. Although publishers wanted him to write a second novel similar to his first, the writer refused because he wanted

to expand his range of subjects. Fascinated with "basements, boiler rooms, and cement back yards," as Getlin put it, Hijuelos again turned to his own experiences and background, this time concentrating on family members who had been musicians in Cuba. He specifically remembered an uncle, Pedro Telleria, a building contractor in Miami, who had once been a member of Xavier Cugat's band in the 1930s. As a young boy visiting Miami, Hijuelos recalled how his uncle would take him into his garage to show his nephew "photos of himself in Cuba in the good days, playing music," wrote Wil Haygood in an interview with the writer for the *Boston Globe,* "and the words coming from the uncle landed in the nephew's ear like good music itself, stories about Cuban musicians and Desi Arnaz and what it meant to play with Cugat." Coincidentally, Hijuelos learned that the elevator attendant in his New York City apartment building had also been a musician, recording several albums in his native Dominican Republic, where he was "something of a star." These two former musicians, the middle-aged building attendant and his uncle with the photos on his garage wall, became the focus of the author's imagination.

Of his interest in Latin music from the 1940s, the writer revealed to Peter Watrous in the *New York Times*: "When I hear certain songs, Nelo Sosa's *'Cuchero para el Tren,'* for example, I hear Havana as it was in 1942." Commenting on his writing process in the 1990 interview with Getlin, Hijuelos remarked: "The music began taking over. I became fascinated by the lives of people who had this great talent, but then took different directions when they bumped into tougher realities here in America."

As his ideas materialized, Hijuelos created the two central characters of *The Mambo Kings Play Songs of Love,* the brothers Cesar and Nestor Castillo, Cuban musicians who emigrate to the United States in 1949. While the Castillo brothers do not achieve the universal stardom they had envisioned, they do enjoy a moment in the national spotlight, appearing briefly on the *I Love Lucy Show* as Ricky Ricardo's singing cousins from Cuba. Hijuelos's inclusion of America's beloved comedic couple, Ricky and Lucy Ricardo, into the novel's plot proved nothing short of genius. Joseph Coates noted in the *Chicago Tribune*: "This apparently trivial 24 minutes of entertainment, reprised throughout the book, becomes the mythical hinge of a considerable epic. And it is Hijuelos's achievement to make clear both the silliness and seriousness of this consummately American apotheosis: the Great Appearance on National TV."

Instead of using a conventional narrative structure, Hijuelos organized the *Mambo Kings* into four main sections: an introduction and conclusion to frame the narrative, and two major chapters. The prologue and epilogue are both narrated in the first person by Eugenio Castillo, the son of the younger Mambo King, Nestor Castillo. The remaining sections of the novel, which are named after the two sides of a record, "Side A: In the Hotel Splendour 1980" and "Side B: Sometime later in the night in the Hotel Splendour," recount the tale of the Mambo Kings from 1949 to 1980. Hijuelos's intent was to mimic the sensations one experiences when listening to music: "The formal idea was sort of like having a record going round and round," revealed Hijuelos in an interview for *Publishers Weekly*. "You know how sometimes when you listen to music and the song cuts off and you're into another feeling? I wanted to move atmospherically. I saw the chapters as different songs."

The novel's prologue opens with Eugenio, who discovers a rerun episode of the *I Love Lucy* show in which his dead father, Nestor, and his uncle, Cesar, make a guest appearance. Eager to share the experience, Eugenio runs to uncle Cesar's nearby apartment to find the aging Mambo King drunk and passed out. After helping his uncle to the couch, Eugenio watches intently as he witnesses what he calls the resurrection of his dead father on the screen: "For me, my father's gentle rapping on Ricky Ricardo's door has always been a call from the beyond, as in Dracula films, or films of the walking dead, in which spirits ooze out from behind tombstones and through the cracked windows and rotted floors of gloomy antique halls." Eugenio's six-page introduction ends, and the first major section of the novel, the larger "Side A," begins.

In "Side A: In the Hotel Splendour 1980," the narrative point of view shifts to the third person, focusing on Cesar, now a defeated man in his sixties, who has checked into the seedy Hotel Splendour, where, as a younger man, he had experienced many of the best times in his life—almost all sexual exploits with women. He is determined to end his suffering over the loss of his dear brother, Nestor, his deteriorating heart condition, and his deep depression. He has been "suffering from bad dreams, [and he] saw apparitions, felt cursed, and, despite all the women he took to bed, found his life of bachelorhood solitary and wearisome." With him, Cesar has a suitcase filled with old letters; photographs of his earlier, happier, days with Nestor, as well as his heyday as the Mambo King; and several records of his band, Mambo Kings. With this suitcase, Cesar also brings a substantial amount of whiskey, which he will use to end his life. As Cesar relives his past, readers become privy to the novel's principal theme: memory. "Hijuelos has created a story, both structurally and thematically, of remembrance," wrote Bob Shacochis in his *Washington Post Book World* review of the novel, noting that "the frame is significant, for perhaps no one has a more self-destructive memory than the exile, blinded by nostalgia, incapacitated by homesickness, motivated by regrets." The remainder of the novel is a series of Cesar's flashbacks, nostalgic remembrances that are conjured while the dying

Mambo King listens to one of his band's records from the 1950s, "The Mambo Kings Play Songs of Love."

Cesar's first of many flashbacks readily establishes his characterization in the novel: "He would have given anything to have the physical virtuosity now that he did when he was thirty-six and first brought Miss Mambo [Vanna Vane] up those stairs and into the [hotel] room. He used to live for that moment when he could strip a woman down on a bed." Ironically, Cesar's thoughts are interrupted when he hears a young couple entering an adjoining room, presumably for a sexual encounter.

Establishing memory as the novel's governing structure, the rest of "Side A" and the entirety of "Side B"—an equally developed part of the novel, subtitled, "Sometime later in the night in the Hotel Splendour"—are filled with more of Cesar's nostalgic recollections of his life. The novel now focuses on the function of memory for Cesar's beloved brother, Nestor, who refused to release the past. Instead he chose an obsessive—and romantic—longing for his Cuban love, María. Hijuelos writes of Nestor:

> He was the man plagued with memory . . . the man with the delusion that the composition of a song about María would bring her back. He was the man who wrote twenty-two different versions of "Bella María de Mi Alma," . . . "Beautiful María of My Soul," a song of love, that night when they drew the attention and interest of their fellow Cuban Desi Arnaz.

It is in the last section of "Side B," in a short chapter entitled, "Toward the end, while listening to the wistful 'Beautiful María of My Soul,'" that Cesar dies. After a memory sequence of the countless women he has loved in his life, Cesar passes away, and the following morning he is found with "a tranquil smile on his face."

Returning to Eugenio as the first-person narrator, *Mambo Kings* ends with a short epilogue.

At least a year has passed since Cesar's death, and Eugenio, who has traveled to Los Angeles on vacation, visits Desi Arnaz at his Belmont estate. There, Desi—now donning blue overalls and sporting a full head of white hair—welcomes Eugenio, showing him around his home. Eugenio observes the many framed pictures of Desi and Lucy with famous actors, including a photograph of Desi with Nestor and Cesar, taken when the Castillos made their guest appearance on *I Love Lucy*. Reminiscing about the Castillos, Desi remembers the brothers as "good songwriters," and he even sings part of "Beautiful María of My Soul." After being invited to stay in Arnaz's guest bedroom, Eugenio is left alone in the living room while Arnaz makes some phone calls: "Sitting in Desi Arnaz's living room, I remembered the episode of the *I Love Lucy* show . . . except it now seemed to be playing itself out right before me. I blinked my eyes and my father and uncle were sitting on the couch opposite me." In this scene of magical realism that has been likened to the technique of Gabriel García Márquez, Eugenio is reunited with his dead father. The resurrection is complete. Eugenio narrates: "I walked over and sat on the couch and wrapped my arms around my father. Expected to find air, but hit on solid flesh." The Tropicana nightclub then appears before Eugenio, allowing him to finally gain closure on his relationship with his father as he experiences the episode of *I Love Lucy* in which his father and uncle sing their hit, "Beautiful María of My Soul."

Upon its publication in 1989, *Mambo Kings* was an instant success. Michiko Kakutani of the *New York Times* wrote: "By turns street-smart and lyrical, impassioned and reflective, *The Mambo Kings Play Songs of Love* is a rich and provocative book—a moving portrait of a man, his family, a community and a time." Grace Edwards-Yearwood, writing in the *Los Angeles Times,* called the novel "a pleasure to read" and Hijuelos "a writer of considerable talent."

More critical of the novel, Charles Solomon asserted in the *Los Angeles Times*: "Some of Hijuelos's recurring descriptions suggest the prose equivalent of refrains, but like the songs of the Mambo Kings, they go on a bit too long, and the reader tires of . . . the veritable Frederick's catalogue of feminine undergarments; and enough 'members' to populate a good-sized lodge." Indeed, some reviewers found the book sexually overcharged, and others noted that the female characters were depicted only as sexual objects. In an interview with Dinitia Smith for *New York* magazine, Hijuelos elaborates:

> The sex in *Mambo Kings* was obviously done with a wink. Anyone taking it seriously doesn't have a sense of humor. . . . I wrote the kind of book that would make me chuckle. Life is not all death and taxes. To impose a value system on Cesar that did not exist in his time is to distort the portrait. Cesar was like a Bacchus to me, a mythical figure. He loved women and their virtues. I would never impose on women the way Cesar would.

Despite these criticisms, the Latin American writer to whom Hijuelos has been compared often, the venerable García Márquez, told Hijuelos that he wished he had written the novel— perhaps the greatest complement any contemporary writer could hope to receive.

That *Mambo Kings* achieved great commercial, as well as critical, acclaim is an understatement. In an interview with *Publishers Weekly,* Nicolás Kanellos of Arte Público Press explained that the novel marked the first time in American literary history "that a major publisher invested in a Latino writer and put his book at the top of the list." Indeed, Farrar, Straus & Giroux, the novel's publisher, ordered a first printing of 40,000 copies and aggressively promoted the book with a $50,000 publicity campaign—unknown for the debut of any work by a U.S. Latino. In addition, 135,000 copies of the paperback edition were printed, and the novel was translated into 30 languages.

Aside from being a finalist for both the National Book Critics Circle Award and the National Book Award, *Mambo Kings* was awarded the 1990 Pulitzer Prize. Hijuelos was "stunned" when he got a phone call from Roger Straus, his publisher, announcing that he had won the Pulitzer. Unaware that he was even nominated for the prize, Hijuelos immediately thought of his father Pascual's struggles in the United States, and only after that did he consider the "historical implications" of his being the first U.S. Latino to win the Pulitzer for fiction. Ironically, Hijuelos was presented with the prize at a ceremony at Columbia University's Low Library, located just a few blocks from his childhood home.

When the film version of the novel was produced, Hijuelos diplomatically admitted that he "liked the idea" of the film but "felt it had some problems scriptwise," reported Smith. While the film further contributed to Hijuelos's mainstream popularity, it changed the writer's lifestyle little. Hijuelos only upgraded his one-bedroom apartment to a two-bedroom in the same building and he purchased a washer and dryer.

THE FOURTEEN SISTERS OF EMILIO MONTEZ O'BRIEN

In a conversation with George Plimpton for *USA Today* in March of 1993, Hijuelos explained what an imposition his newly acquired celebrity had become to his writing life: "I'm a shy person and becoming the focus of so much attention threw me out of whack for a while and made writing more difficult. . . . It's paralyzing." Surprised and overwhelmed by the colossal success of *Mambo Kings,* Hijuelos carefully pondered his next work. Supported by a prestigious Guggenheim Fellowship, he published a near epic (484 pages long) titled *The Fourteen Sisters of Emilio Montez O'Brien.* This book, together with his two previous novels, form a trilogy, providing readers "an acquaintance with a general stream of at least a certain aspect of Cuban history and certainly the history of those pre-Castro Cubans who interacted with America," commented Picker in *Newsday.* The three novels, according to Hijuelos, function like "a triptych, a compendium of the feelings I have about my background and notions like identity," he told Plimpton.

Fourteen Sisters depicts Cuban American life, but it constitutes a major departure from what has been regarded as Hijuelos's very "macho" *Mambo Kings.* Hijuelos told *New York Times* contributor Susannah Hunnewell that, while visiting a friend in Pennsylvania, he had a dream of "a house filled with women," prompting him to write about a "world in which women were very powerful."

In an interview with Katie Davis of National Public Radio, Hijuelos described how he prepared to write about women. He began by researching pregnancy and its effects, which got him thinking about menstruation and how the monthly cycle serves to remind women of their physicality, making them more aware of themselves on various levels—emotionally, psychologically, and physically: "I think it leads to . . . the idea that women are more introspective and more sensitive. That's not to get pretentious," says the writer, "but, it made me feel very sympathetic with what women must go through all the time."

In *Fourteen Sisters,* Hijuelos employs a vastly different setting from the urban Spanish Harlem of *Our House* and *Mambo Kings.* Wanting to write "about this other America [he had] never really participated in," explained Smith, Hijuelos laid his tale in the pastoral setting of Cobbleton, Pennsylvania, an invented, quaint, small town at the turn of the twentieth century—a locale based on his recollections of a rare family trip to Lancaster County, Pennsylvania, when he was younger. This radical shift in setting was also part of the writer's intent to "do something

different," or to "push the envelope" in regard to what people had come to expect from him.

By 1993 Hijuelos was heralded as *the* greatest "Hispanic" writer, and he began to feel that he was being stereotyped by not simply being called an "American" writer, which he prefers. In an interview with Robert Dominguez for the *New York Daily News,* Hijuelos further explained:

> There are other things going on in my books that have a lot more to do with the general world. I don't think it's pigeonholing me, but I do think it's an oversimplification of work that's much more complicated. *Mambo Kings* has been translated into 27 or 28 languages, and it's got to have a universal element beyond the cha-cha-cha.

Despite the vast contrast between his third novel and his earlier works, his publisher predicted success, printing 75,000 copies initially; in addition, the bidding for the rights to the paperback edition began at $400,000.

Organized into five major chapters, each with various subsections, *Fourteen Sisters,* Hijuelos's "love letter to women," spans almost the entirety of the twentieth century. The novel chronicles the lives of Nelson O'Brien, an Irish immigrant who, after the death of his sister, Kate, in 1898, travels to Cuba to photograph the Spanish-American War. There, he meets and marries the aristocratic Mariela Montez and takes her to the United States, where the couple settlés in the small Pennsylvania town of Cobbleton. Nelson works as a portrait photographer, eventually purchasing and running the Jewel Box Movie Theatre. Mariela, who never stops longing for her Cuban homeland, refuses to learn English or to assimilate into her small Pennsylvania town. Nevertheless, the Montez O'Briens build a humongous family, adding a new child to their fast-growing clan every couple of years until they have fourteen daughters and one son, Emilio, the novel's title character.

While the book depicts the family drama of its many characters, *Fourteen Sisters* concentrates primarily on the eldest child, Margarita, and the youngest child, Emilio, both of whom function as the novel's protagonists. In the hundred years covered by the narrative, readers learn about the Montez O'Briens as they navigate their way through the changing times and current events. Margarita—never to have children of her own—serves as a second mother to her fourteen sisters and brother. When she finally leaves her home, it is to marry a wealthy, but deranged, Lester Thompson, who does not deserve her affection. Realizing that Lester has married her only to enact revenge on his WASP family and is incapable of loving her, Margarita eventually returns to her familial home.

Emilio, the sole male child, is haunted by the femininity that pervades the Montez O'Brien home. Like his father, who retreats to his bottles of Dr. Arnold's Relaxation Heightener, "a dark, syrupy liquid which came in a curvaceous amber bottle and whose ingredients were . . . sugar, Persian tar, honey, Arabian and Persian opiates and other miracle tonics," Emilio eventually turns to alcohol. A decent actor in second-rate films (who hangs out with Errol Flynn) and a carouser after his return from serving in World War II in Italy, Emilio is almost driven to ruin. Devastated by the loss of his wife and daughter, he returns to the feminine comforts of the Montez O'Brien home, where he is healed.

Comparing Hijuelos to García Márquez, Michiko Kakutani of the *New York Times Book Review* raved about the novel, calling it "a family saga, one of those commodious, emotionally generous books that immerse us in a well-upholstered fictional world," and concluded that readers finish the novel "the way one finishes a long letter from a beloved family member, eager for all the news not to end." Marie Arana-Ward, writing in the *Washington Post Book World,* applauded Hijuelos as "remarkable . . . for the breadth of his soul, the depth of his humanity, and for the precision of his gauge on the rising sensibilities of his time."

While the novel was generally well received, *Fourteen Sisters* generated a fair amount of negative criticism, making it Hijuelos's least successful work to date. For some reviewers, the novel was weakened by its many characters, and several critics noted that, at best, Hijuelos was able to give only a running list of traits that described each of the characters. Others complained that the novel was too long, that it lacked judicious editing, that Hijuelos overwrote. The novel's often quoted opening passage reveals the controversy:

> The house in which the fourteen sisters of Emilio Montez O'Brien lived radiated femininity. Men who passed by the white picket fence—the postman, the rag seller, the iceman—were sometimes startled by a strong scent of flowers, as if perfume had been poured onto the floorboards and ground. And when the door to the house—a rickety, many-roomed Victorian affair some few miles outside the small Pennsylvania town of Cobbleton, with teetering beams and rain-soaked clapboard façade (with gables, rusted hinges, and a fetid outhouse on a foundation that tended to creak during heavy rains, a roof that leaked, and with splintering surfaces everywhere)—when their door opened on the world, the power of these females, even the smallest infants, nearly molecular in its adamancy, slipped out and had its transforming effect upon men. Over the years a thick maple tree, standing out in the yard, had been the scene of numerous accidents: men were thrown from their horses or, begoggled and yet blinded by what they may have taken as the sun, skidded their Model Ts, their Packards, their sporty sedans off the road into a ditch, axles bent and crankcases hissing steam.

This passage illustrates the controversial attention to detail that some reviewers praised but others found overwriting. Arana-Ward, while lauding the novel, observed that it is not problem-free: "Hijuelos's tone can be mannered, even starchy, as if he were reaching too consciously to construct a novel of another time and place. His prose is vaguely foreign in its tonality at times, not pretentious but theatrical, as if he were reading aloud in an ancestral salon." Other reviewers commented that *Fourteen Sisters* lacks plot. And finally, several commentators—particularly, Sven Birkerts for the *New Republic*—observed that Hijuelos was trying too hard to write like the great Latin American masters, particularly García Márquez: "The line between influence and imitation has been crossed. It is as if Hijuelos were writing the scene not like but as García Márquez. The displacement ultimately undermines the artistic authority of the novel."

MR. IVES' CHRISTMAS

Only two years after the publication of his third novel, Hijuelos released *Mr. Ives' Christmas* (1995), a work that has been heralded as his best. This time Hijuelos's book did not feature a Hispanic protagonist. Uninterested in how critics and reviewers have come to categorize his writings, Hijuelos stated that each of his novels flowed into the next: *Mambo Kings* led to *Fourteen Sisters,* and the Christmas scenes in that book led to his writing *Mr. Ives' Christmas.* He was inspired to write the novel when his religious beliefs were derided by a college professor at a cocktail party. Raised in the Roman Catholic faith, Hijuelos believes in a supreme being, a God; in fact, he distrusts atheists: "They are like tone-deaf," he told David Gonzalez in a piece for the *New York Times.* "They hear a piano being played and they only hear 'thunka-thunk.' There is this wild jazz going on called religion and some people don't have the chops." *Mr. Ives' Christmas*—which *Time* magazine contributor Gina Bellafante hailed as a "moving meditation on the spiritual life" and a tribute "to religious piety, unfailing modesty and moral rectitude"—moves further away from the theme of ethnic identity, a topic that dominates much of Hijuelos's earlier works.

Organized into seven chapters, some of which contain several short subsections, and told in a third-person narrative, *Mr. Ives' Christmas* centers on Edward Ives, a dark-featured foundling of unknown parentage or heritage, who is cared for by nuns in an orphanage in New York City during the first few years of his life. When he is adopted, his father, a foundling himself, not only raises Ives but instills in the young boy a genuine love for the Catholic faith, a religion he practices devoutly throughout his life. As an adult, Ives attends the Arts Students League, where he meets his future spouse, the beautiful Annie MacGuire, who poses as a nude subject for the group of aspiring artists. The couple court, fall in love, and marry, producing two children, a son and later a daughter. Ives works as a successful professional illustrator for an advertising agency on Madison Avenue, while Annie is an English teacher.

This seemingly ordinary tale of a seemingly ordinary man and his family turns tragic, however, when, just days before Christmas of 1967, Ives' seventeen-year-old son, Robert—six months short of entering a Franciscan seminary, where he would devote his life to the priesthood—is pointlessly killed at close range by Danny Gomez, a Puerto Rican hoodlum, outside the neighborhood Catholic church. Robert had been talking to a friend after choir practice when he was gunned down. Hijuelos writes:

> Then this other kid, a brawny teenager in an army jacket, came walking along, jitterbugging, his stride so exagerrated [sic] and dancelike that Robert could not prevent his blue eyes from widening or his forehead from crinkling at the humorous affectation. Finding it amusing, he began to smile in a friendly, well-intended way, and, just like that, the teenager said something that Robert did not quite have the time to digest, and then pulled out his pistol and fired three shots, *pop, pop, pop.*

This incident galvanizes the novel's plot, as Ives grapples with his deep faith in Catholicism, struggling to comprehend how his God could permit such a senseless act of violence. Ives' best friend and Robert's godfather, Luis—a Cuban American character much like Alejo Santinio from Hijuelos's first novel—believes firmly in a system of justice based on "an eye for an eye." Outraged by the murder, he offers to hire a hitman to exact revenge upon Robert's killer. Ives disapproves, however, and takes the "high road," as Hijuelos has called it, fighting his feelings of anger toward his son's killer. Instead, Ives is determined to "trust in God and cling to the path of righteousness."

In an attempt to help his son's killer gain forgiveness for his destructive act, Ives develops a written communication with Gomez, who is serving time in prison for the murder. Ives even aids in the man's education, sending him books and instructional material that will help teach him to read. In time, however, Ives realizes that this gesture, as well as his other volunteer work in the community, is making him feel greater resentment. Unable to cease grieving, Ives continues mourning his son's loss for years; his wife, Annie, urges Ives to move away from the dark past, but Ives cannot. He is plagued with chronic insomnia and a severe skin condition, the result of his scratching, until one night when he dreams of his son, "Robert, as he might have been at forty-three years of age: a grown man in choristers' white-and-black robes, handsome, serenely wise, wading waist high in the water" of a stream. Robert takes hold of his father's hands, noticing the cuts: "'Pop, why do you keep doing this to yourself?' Then, bending, his hands cupped, his son scooped out a handful of water, and this he poured over his father's head, and then he brought up some more and washed his limbs with that water; and then he was gone." The following morning, Ives cannot find a trace of his cuts. In the end, through his son's visitation in a dream, Ives has been cured and can finally begin to make peace with Robert's death.

The novel earned glowing reviews from readers and critics alike. "This is a magnificently sad and enchanting novel, a celebration, ultimately, of giving and of grace," wrote Donna Seaman for *Booklist.* "The shortest of [his] recent novels, *Mr. Ives's Christmas* is . . . both the deepest and the best," observed Jack Miles in the *New York Times.* Perhaps Kakutani—also praising the book in a 1995 review—best captures the brilliance of Hijuelos's fourth novel:

It is Mr. Hijuelos's achievement in this novel that he has made religious faith, that most mysterious and private of emotions, a truly palpable passion: not the sunny, epiphanic sort of faith advertised by preachers, but a more mundane, hard-won sort of faith, a faith tested by death and loss and daily reaffirmed, however haltingly, by myriad small choices and acts.

EMPRESS OF THE SPLENDID SEASON

Contemplating his next book, Hijuelos thought about his days as a teenager, when he worked as a messenger, delivering packages to wealthy New Yorkers at posh addresses—people who lived in opulently appointed apartments, filled with luxuries the young writer could never have imagined from his home in Spanish Harlem. Hijuelos was struck by the cleaning women he met, mostly kind blacks and Latinas, who toiled day in and day out to make the lives of the rich clean and comfortable. What he remembered most, years later, was the "invisibility" of these women: "There's a whole core of decent people out there who just work and help make the world go round," he told Dan Cryer in *Newsday.* Interested in the "kind of person who's basically invisible to most people," Hijuelos imagined his next protagonist, Lydia España, the Cuban American cleaning woman at the center of his fifth novel, *Empress of the Splendid Season* (1999). "Even the most ordinary people in life, the unglamorous, the typical people," noted Hijuelos in a conversation with Jane Henderson for the *St. Louis Post-Dispatch,* "have rich inner lives. I look around and I bring a little of that out."

With its third-person narrative, *Empress*—which Hijuelos has called "a Cinderella tale in reverse that works out all right"—traces the lives of its lead character, Lydia, from her origins in Cuba to her subsequent life as a housekeeper for the rich in New York City. After his success with *Ives,* Hijuelos returned to his roots by writing a fifth novel reminiscent of his first, with its portraiture of immigrant life in the United States—characters seeking the American Dream. Like Mercedes Santinio, Lydia descends from an aristocratic Cuban heritage and leaves her island nation in the 1940s. And, as with Mercedes, there is scandal involved in a romantic relationship. This time, however, it is much more serious as the daughter, Lydia, shames her family when she is caught by her father, the small town's mayor, in a compromising situation with an older man. This incident results in her banishment from her home. She is sent to New York, where she struggles to exist.

In New York City, Lydia meets the debonair Raul España, a waiter and also a Cuban immigrant. The couple marry and produce two children: Alicia and Rico. Hijuelos again illustrates the struggles of living in two cultures through the España children, who eschew the ethnic heritage their parents force upon them, striving to assimilate into the dominant, mainstream culture. To support her young children and her ailing husband, Lydia—whose "English was adequate but not good enough for the Woolworth's store manager to hire her, nor for the Macy's personnel department"—resigns herself to working as a housekeeper. Hijuelos writes:

In 1957 when her beloved husband, Raul, had fallen ill, Lydia España went to work, cleaning the apartments of New Yorkers much better off than herself. She took up that occupation because Raul, with jobs in two restaurants, had waited on so many tables, for so many hours, and had snuck so many drinks from the bar and smoked so many cigarettes, that his taut heart had nearly bust, half killing him one night at the age of forty-one. (Lydia imagined the heart muscles all twisted like a much used table rag.) She went to work because, aside from their own children, her husband had a second little family to look after in Cuba (the devil!) and because, among other reasons involving the vicissitudes of making money, they were suddenly "poor."

This passage, the novel's opening paragraph, illustrates the similarities between this narrator and the narrator in *Our House*: both are less-than-objective observers who are critical of the husbands in the novels. Raul España and Alejo Santinio are characterized with many similar traits and are held accountable for their failure to attain any kind of material success in the United States. But while *Empress* does share similarities with Hijuelos's earlier work—*Our House* in particular—it nevertheless showcases the talents of a more mature, more seasoned author, as evidenced in the novel's compassionate narrative voice—a significant development that indicates Hijuelos's growth as a bicultural individual in America.

The remainder of *Empress* chronicles Lydia's daily life as she cleans apartments. One of her principal and most liked clients is the benevolent Mr. Osprey, an affluent international lawyer, who rescues Rico from his Harlem surroundings when the boy gets into trouble after hanging out with the "wrong" crowd. Osprey generously subsidizes the boy's education at a prestigious prep school in New England, the same school from which Osprey, himself, and his sons graduated. Rico's life is changed forever, distancing him from his uneducated, immigrant parents. After prep school, Rico wins a scholarship to an Ivy League university and eventually becomes a successful New York psychologist whose patients include "businessmen . . . and wives distressed by the perturbations of age." For Rico, life as a second-generation Cuban American is alienating, comprised of unfulfilled longings for the Cuba his parents remember and of daily demands placed on him by mainstream American culture. It is not surprising that Hijuelos—who has achieved a privileged place in mainstream America—identifies with this character: "Rico is part of me in the sense that a part of me feels cut off and detached from the dense humanity that I came from. Fortunately, I can really put it to good use in my work," he told Cryer.

Alicia, the Españas' first child, also rebels against her traditional Cuban upbringing, joining her American counterparts in the rapidly changing social culture of the 1960s. When compared with Rico, Alicia is even further distanced from her Cuban parents and their culture. After her "hippy" phase, Alicia settles into a traditional American lifestyle: she marries the Anglo-American Douglas Johnson, moves to upstate New York, and produces two children who—to Lydia's dismay—speak nothing but English, further underscoring the great divide that exists between generations. For both Alicia and Rico, their Cuban ethnicity, as one reviewer has put it, "is something they simply hope to outgrow," foreshadowing the near extinction of Cuban American culture.

As the novel moves toward its conclusion, Lydia suffers the loss of her husband, and the years begin to take their toll on the aging cleaning woman. Like Mercedes in *Our House,* Lydia feels alienated and lonely in her old age. In the final chapter of the novel, "A Postscript," the narrative point of view is fixed on Rico, who is in the middle of a therapy session with a patient (a young woman "suffering from loneliness . . . recounting her travails with men"). Rico's mind accidentally drifts to a childhood experience when he, his sister, and his mother spotted the actor James Mason coming out of the St. Regis Hotel. Rico remembers how starstruck, even flirtatious, his mother had been as she unsuccessfully tried to get the actor's attention. Musing over what could have been, Rico's thoughts are captured by Hijuelos:

> Wouldn't it have been nice, Rico used to think, even when his patients were relating certain intimacies to him, had someone like James Mason materialized at the door, waving his beautifully manicured hands about the room and changing everything; getting rid of the heartaches, the concerns about health, the bills, and the anxieties, and spreading before them the promise of a wondrous future, that piece of Heaven, like the ones they saw in the pretty magazines and television commercials; to let them forget themselves in the diversions of earthly pleasures.

This ending also reinforces one of Hijuelos's recurring themes: memory. In fact, the author told *Boston Globe* contributor John Koch that he feels "more a part of that past world than [he does] of the present," and even in his fifth novel Hijuelos's work is dependent on his own familial and cultural history.

For the most part, *Empress* was well received by reviewers, although it did not escape criticism. *Los Angeles Times* reviewer Scott Bradfield praised Hijuelos for being "a natural storyteller and moralist" and for accomplishing "for Cuban-Americans what Richard Wright and James Baldwin achieved for African-Americans, Philip Roth for Jews and David Leavitt for homosexuals: He has brought them into the mainstream of attention." However, Bradfield also pointed out that "too often, Hijuelos alienates his reader by generalizing about the rich and the poor." Perhaps the most critical has been Kakutani, who, in the *New York Times,* lambasted the novel for seeming "like a tired reworking of old material."

However, most reviewers have applauded the *Empress.* In an article for the *National Review,* Mark Falcoff called it "a delicious, voyeuristic look into the lives of those millions of Spanish-speaking people who have come to this country enticed" by the American Dream. Robin Nesbitt, writing for *Library Journal,* observed that *Empress* "intermingles time periods, life histories, and social classes to create an intriguing look at family, wealth, and race in modern America." *Publishers Weekly* praised Hijuelos's use of realism, which "penetrates the lives behind the humble tenements and massive university buildings." Further, Barbara Mujica, writing in *Americas,* noted that "Hijuelos avoids cloying ethnicity, creating characters who are both distinctly Cuban and universal," and instead "transcends stereotypes and cliches, creating characters who speak to us on a profoundly human level."

Selected Bibliography

WORKS OF OSCAR HIJUELOS

NOVELS
Our House in the Last World. New York: Persea, 1983.
The Mambo Kings Play Songs of Love. New York: Farrar, Straus & Giroux, 1989.
The Fourteen Sisters of Emilio Montez O'Brien. New York: Farrar, Straus & Giroux, 1993.
Mr. Ives' Christmas. New York: HarperCollins, 1995.
Empress of the Splendid Season. New York: Harper-Flamingo, 1999.

CRITICAL AND BIOGRAPHICAL STUDIES
Arana-Ward, Marie. "When Men and Women Were Many." *Washington Post Book World,* March 14, 1993, pp. 1,10. (Review of *The Fourteen Sisters of Emilio Montez O'Brien.*)

Bellafante, Gina. "Book of Virtue: Oscar Hijuelos Creates That Literary Rarity, a Good Man." *Time,* November 27, 1995, p. 98. (Review of *Mr. Ives' Christmas.*)

Birkerts, Sven. Review of *The Fourteen Sisters of Emilio Montez O'Brien. New Republic,* March 22, 1993, pp. 38–41.

Bowen, Michael. "Sizzling Score Not Enough to Save *Mambo Kings*." *Boston Globe,* September 4, 1992.

Bradfield, Scott. "Dreams Die Hard." *Los Angeles Times Book Review,* March 7, 1999, p.3. (Review of *Empress of the Splendid Season.*)

Bruce-Novoa, Juan. "Hijuelos' *Mambo Kings*: Reading from Divergent Traditions." *Confluencia* 10, no. 2:11-22 (1995).

Chavez, Lydia. "Cuban Riffs & Songs of Love: For Novelist Oscar Hijuelos, the Raw Sex and Swagger of *Mambo Kings* Give Way to the Allure of the Feminine—and a New Case of Nerves." *Los Angeles Times Magazine,* April 18, 1993, p. 22.

Coates, Joseph. "When Cuban Musicians Dream the American Dream." *Chicago Tribune Book World,* August 13, 1989, pp. 6–7.

Corliss, Richard. "Arne Glimcher, Ole!: A Manhattan Art Dealer Turns Movie Director, Bringing the Sounds of Cuban Americans to Exuberant Screen Life." *Time,* March 9, 1992, p. 66.

Cryer, Dan. "Of Mambo Kings & Cleaning Women." *Newsday,* February 15, 1999.

Dominguez, Robert. "West Side Storyteller: Novelist and Native Son Oscar Hijuelos Chronicles Cuban-American Experience." *New York Daily News Online* (http://www.nydn.com), February 23, 1999.

Edwards-Yearwood, Grace. "Dancing to the Cuban Beat." *Los Angeles Times Book Review,* September 3, 1989, pp. 1, 10. (Review of *The Mambo Kings Play Songs of Love.*)

Elias, Amy. "Oscar Hijuelos's *The Mambo Kings Play Songs of Love,* Ishmael Reed's *Mumbo Jumbo,* and Robert Coover's *The Public Burning*." *Critique* 41, no. 2:115-28 (2000).

Falcoff, Mark. Review of *Empress of the Splendid Season. National Review,* February 22, 1999, p. 50.

Fein, Esther B. "Oscar Hijuelos's Unease, Worldly and Otherwise." *New York Times,* April 1, 1993, p. B2.

Fernández, Enrique. "Americans Twice Over." *Review* 32:43-44 (1984).

———. "Spitfires, Latin Lovers, Mambo Kings." *New York Times on the Web* (http://www.nytimes.com), April 19, 1992.

Getlin, Josh. "The Prize and the Passion: Cuban-American Author of Pulsating *Mambo Kings* Treasures His Roots and a Pulitzer." *Los Angeles Times,* April 16, 1990, p. E1.

Gonzalez, David. "Townie Brings a Tale of Faith to Seminary." *New York Times,* September 21, 1996, p. 21.

Guevara, Martha. "Just Nothing Like Reading a Movie: Films Pump Up Sales of Treasures of World Literature." *St. Louis Post-Dispatch,* August 22, 1993.

Haygood, Wil. "Beat Author." *Boston Globe,* November 18, 1990, p. 21.

Henderson, Jane. "Writer Oscar Hijuelos Makes a St. Louis Stop." *St. Louis Post-Dispatch,* January 26, 2000, p. E3.

Hunnewell, Susannah. "A House Filled with Women." *New York Times Book Review,* March 7, 1993, p. 6.

Kakutani, Michiko. "Cuban Immigrants in the 50s of Desi and Lucy." *New York Times,* August 4, 1989, p. B4. (Review of *The Mambo Kings Play Songs of Love.*)

———. "From Macho Mambo World to a Softer One of Sisters." *New York Times,* March 2, 1993, p. B2. (Review of *The Fourteen Sisters of Emilio Montez O'Brien.*)

———. "A Test of Faith for a Father Who Longs for Grace." *New York Times,* November 28, 1995, p. B2. (Review of *Mr. Ives' Christmas.*)

———. "Unlike *Mambo Kings,* An Empress Tidies Up." *New York Times,* February 5, 1999, p. E45. (Review of *Empress of the Splendid Season.*)

Kauffmann, Stanley. *"The Mambo Kings." New Republic,* March 30, 1992, p. 26.

Koch, John. "Oscar Hijuelos: The Interview." *Boston Globe Magazine,* March 28, 1999, p. 10.

Mallon, Thomas. "Ripening in Pennsylvania." *New York Times Book Review,* March 7, 1993, p. 6. (Review of *The Fourteen Sisters of Emilio Montez O'Brien.*)

Miles, Jack. "The Ghost of a Christmas Past." *New York Times Book Review,* December 3, 1995, p. 9. (Review of *Mr. Ives' Christmas.*)

Milton, Edith. "Newcomers in New York." *New York Times Book Review,* May 15, 1983, p. 12. (Review of *Our House in the Last World.*)

Mujica, Barbara. Review of *Empress of the Splendid Season. Americas,* August 1999, pp. 62–63.

Muller, Gilbert H. *New Strangers in Paradise: The Immigrant Experience and Contemporary American Fiction.* Lexington: University Press of Kentucky, 1999.

Nesbitt, Robin. Review of *Empress of the Splendid Season. Library Journal,* January 1999, p. 150.

Pérez Firmat, Gustavo. "Rum-Rump-and-Rumba." In his *Life on the Hyphen: The Cuban-American Way.* Austin: University Press of Texas, 1994. Pp. 136–153.

Picker, Lauren. "Talking with Oscar Hijuelos: Literary Cross-Dressing." *Newsday,* April 4, 1993.

Plimpton, George. "A Reluctant 'Mambo King.'" *USA Today,* March 14, 1993, p. 14.

Publishers Weekly, December 14, 1998, p. 56. (Review of *Empress of the Splendid Season.*)

Seaman, Donna. Review of *Mr. Ives' Christmas. Booklist,* October 1, 1995.

Shacochis, Bob. "The Music of Exile and Regret." *Washington Post Book World,* August 20, 1989, pp. 1–2. (Review of *The Mambo Kings Play Songs of Love.*)

Sheppard, R. Z. "Hail Cesar." *Time,* August 14, 1989, p. 68. (Review of *The Mambo Kings Play Songs of Love.*)

Smith, Dinitia. "'Sisters' Act: Oscar Hijuelos, Mr. Mambo Kings Plays a Different Song of Love." *New York Magazine,* March 1, 1993, pp. 46–51.

Solomon, Charles. Review of *The Mambo Kings Play Songs of Love. Los Angeles Times Book Review,* August 19, 1990, p. 10.

Tham, Claire. "Heartbreak in New York." *Straits Times,* September 12, 1992.

Watrous, Peter. "Evoking When Mambo Was King." *New York Times,* September 11, 1989, p. C17.

Weeks, Jerome. "Part Comedy, Part Tragedy, All-Engrossing: Cuban-American Hijuelos' Sensibility Begins with Hyphen." *Dallas Morning News,* February 14, 1998.

INTERVIEW

Davies, Katie. "Oscar Hijuelos Discusses Latest Novel." *All Things Considered.* National Public Radio, April 10, 1993.

Siegel, Robert. "Oscar Hijuelos: Author's New Book *Mr. Ives' Christmas.*" *All Things Considered.* National Public Radio, December 23, 1995.

FILM BASED ON THE WORK OF OSCAR HIJUELOS
The Mambo Kings. Screenplay by Cynthia Cidre and Oscar Hijuelos. Directed by Arne Glimcher. Warner Bros., 1992.

—JOSEPH M. VIERA

Alfred Kazin

1915–1998

THE ONLY SON of poor Jewish immigrants in Brooklyn, New York, Alfred Kazin was born June 5, 1915. At the time of his death, he was one of the nation's most eminent literary critics. Coming of age in the 1930s, Kazin achieved lasting recognition with the groundbreaking study of modern American literature, *On Native Grounds: An Interpretation of Modern American Prose Literature,* in 1942. The author of nine books of literary criticism and commentary, four autobiographical works, and hundreds of essays, reviews, and articles, Kazin was a critic of prodigious powers whose passionate feeling for literature and intensely original yet highly accessible insights characterize his prose.

During his early years, Kazin was closely associated with the New York Intellectuals, a group of writers and critics largely of working-class and Jewish backgrounds who started out between the two world wars and who allied themselves politically and critically with some form of marxism or socialism. He shared with this group an abiding interest in examining the cultural foundations of literature; and following Edmund Wilson, the New York Intellectuals' primary model, Kazin wrote about literature from a sociological, historical, and aesthetic perspective.

While Kazin's critical style was deeply influenced by Wilson, and though he shared with prominent New York Intellectuals like Lionel Trilling and Irving Howe a deep respect for the moral and aesthetic value of literature, he came to eschew what he saw as the narrowing political orthodoxy of neoconservatives like Nathan Glazer, Irving Kristol, and Norman Podhoretz. A sometimes scalding critic of American materialism and capitalism's lust for wealth,

especially during President Ronald Reagan's administration, Kazin nevertheless was not a political activist and staunchly declared himself a political radical who was no ideologue. "To be a critic," he stressed, "nothing else is so important as the ability to stand one's ground alone."

During a lifetime of writing, Kazin more than stood his own ground. He explored with rare fervor literature's simultaneously radical and traditional urge to search for a higher truth and to struggle with overwhelming forces—historical, political, economic, moral, and spiritual. Unique among his peers, Kazin achieved a distinctly rhapsodic style of celebratory appreciation, an ability to connect with the individual mind of the artist whose work he examined, and a singular capacity to uncover and to teach students what he called "literary genius"—a feature of great literature that could be brought to light, he maintained, but never wholly contained by his or any critic's efforts.

MEMOIR

Perhaps the best way to understand Kazin is first and foremost as a writer—one fiercely engaged in a struggle to understand the world, himself, and all the writers in it with words, "mere words," to steer his course. The critical lamp he used to illuminate literature he regularly turned on himself. The dedicated keeper of a journal almost continuously from 1933 until his death, he was someone for whom "writing was everything"—a phrase of T. S. Eliot that Kazin enthusiastically settled on for the title of one of his later books. In the first of three memoirs, *A*

93

Walker in the City (1951), Kazin delves into his own beginnings as the son of Eastern European Jewish immigrants, Charles Kazin and Gita Fagelman Kazin. The book could easily be called *One Writer's Beginnings,* and it stands, along with Eudora Welty's stirring memoir of that title, among the best personal reminiscences by a writer of the twentieth century.

Widely praised upon its publication, *A Walker* evokes vividly, in sometimes heartbreakingly poignant detail, Kazin's boyhood in the largely poor and Jewish Brownsville section of Brooklyn in the 1920s. If the subject of the book is a boy's coming of age and awakening to his own identity, it is also the story of a boy coming to terms with his *sensibility*—in this case, the sensibility of an artist in the Jamesian sense, "a person upon whom nothing is lost." The world of Brownsville and Manhattan, which beckons like the Promised Land in the writer's imagination, is not evoked through the building up of external detail so much as through the intense feeling woven into every observation. Kazin the man records the tender impressions of the boy as he both sees *and* feels the world. Through the lens of his own lonely attachment, Kazin evokes his father's solitary apartness as he cleans his hands after a day of housepainting; his mother's duty-bound existence as dressmaker and caretaker of her small family; the near comic but gruelingly desperate desire of Sophie, the Kazins' live-in cousin, for a husband.

Coincident with his discovery of the terrible aloneness of those near to him, especially his parents, is a deeper isolation underlying this lyrical but haunting book—an isolation Kazin chiefly associates with being a Jew. God, he notes memorably, was "our oldest habit" and a source of infinite restlessness. Being a Jew, for Kazin, involves a deeply dual experience; it means belonging, but it also means living outside of the streaming pulse of non-Jewish life that perpetually beckons. Mingled with the "stale smell of the synagogue" and the "loveless intimacy" he feels with those who frequent it is the sense of pressing alienation from all things not Jewish. Perhaps the most striking element of Kazin's boyhood existence and the one he most strongly associated with his Jewishness throughout his autobiographical writing is the sense of lonely yearning. It is a yearning to grasp history born of his mother's fearful past in tsarist Russia, a yearning to embrace the present—*to be*—that stems from his desire to "redeem the constant anxiety" of his parents' lives. It is a yearning for expression, rich and unfettered, born of a family where intimate conversation between his parents is as inconceivable as a dinner out. In one of the book's greatest achievements, language itself appears a powerful emanation of Kazin's identity as a Jew—each word straining to capture the isolation he inhabits while simultaneously seeking to shatter it.

Loneliness is indeed a central feature of this book. Although Kazin was not an only child—he has a younger sister, Pearl—she barely figures in *A Walker.* In fact, it seems her presence would have disrupted the book's inescapably solitary spell. Companionship with Pearl is not possible for the author in a book devoted to the relentless singularity of his journey. So much is discovered while alone and within himself—the beauty of the city streets while playing "one o' cat by myself in the sleepy twilight"; the play of light falling through a store window; the soft warmth of summer; the forbidden mystery of sex mingled in the sounds of a dark cellar. Discoveries of the self and the world are the fruit of solitary occupations—of walking and reading, in particular. The little red volumes of *The World's Greatest Selected Short Stories* appear as necessary to his existence as putting one foot in front of the other. Throughout this memoir, the solitude of walking recapitulates the solitude of thought and the solitude of writing itself.

While solitude and loneliness are clearly features of *A Walker,* the book captures an exhilaration at the pulse and variety of life that is characteristic of all Kazin's memoir writing and critical commentary on American culture. There is, for example, a certain unmistakable relish in the description of the earnest Jewish mother's cry to her son to "Fix yourself!"; in the memorably suggestive name of the painters' union boss, Jake the Bum; and in the dramatic distinctness of New York street names—Pitkin, Sutter, Belmont, Kosciusko, DeKalb. Though Kazin records again and again his own feeling of sadness amid the bustle of people, he also conveys his attachment to all he sees. Again, it is the attachment of a writer, and many sections of this book have a novelistic power. The boy's unexpected encounter with an erstwhile neighbor, Mrs. Solovey, the cultured but lonely wife of a druggist, and their impromptu French lesson is memorable because of Kazin's deep sympathy for her. The two seem to share an unspoken and imperceptible feeling about language, about the everyday fragility of existence that makes their fleeting connection possible. When Mrs. Solovey asks insistently *en Français* why the boy prefers summer, and he stumbles to explain he likes "*la chaud . . .* the warmth . . . the evenness," she stares at him silently, "in gratitude." It is, for a moment, the gratitude of mutual understanding.

Voices and characters come alive in this book to evoke memorably a distant time and place—the Jewish immigrant neighborhood of Brownsville with its gas lamps and bakeries and the noisy hum of human striving. But it is also a portrait tinged with melancholy, consciously revealing and battling life's fleeting nature. The desperately poor Soloveys' business crumbles, and they drift away obscurely; the gas lamps are long gone, as are "the ratty little wooden tenements" and the corner drugstore, already in the late 1940s when Kazin was writing the book. Only language and Kazin's fierce attachment to it can combat life's irrevocable tran-

sience and the constant threat that the past will slip away forever. Only language and Kazin's attachment to literature, to "lonely Americans" like Emily Dickinson and Walt Whitman, can quell his sense of forever being on the outside.

In *A Walker in the City,* Kazin redeems the lost world of his poor beginnings, but he also locates the launching point of his journey as a writer. (He designates the book's four parts "chapters of the journey.") That journey truly begins at the book's conclusion, when Kazin discovers a connection between himself and "the shape and color of time in the streets of New York" and a bond with those American writers of the nineteenth century—"fellow aliens"—whom he sought most of his life to understand and to celebrate. Dedicated to his son Michael, and written in the harrowing shadow of the Holocaust, *A Walker in the City* is one writer's attempt to recover the past in order to bear the present and imagine the future. In its evocation of the early-twentieth-century struggle of Jewish immigrant families to find a foothold in America and in its quality of quiet jubilation and searching aloneness, it is a singularly powerful, distinctly American book.

Over the course of the next twenty-seven years, Kazin published two more memoirs—*Starting Out in the Thirties* (1965) and *New York Jew* (1978)—that chronicle the twists and turns of his tumultuous personal life and his rise as a literary journalist, critic, and leading interpreter of American literature. Although not as highly acclaimed as *A Walker in the City,* both books were well received by critics and commentators, including Edmund Wilson who praised *Starting Out* in a letter to its author.

While *A Walker* explores the awakening of a boy to his life as a writer, *Starting Out in the Thirties* is about inhabiting that life. Written when the author was in his mid-forties, the book reveals a writer well seasoned by his experience as a critic, editor, and literary journalist. Kazin's reflections, though charged by a characteristic sense of wonder about everything and everyone he encounters, are less inward, more outspoken, and flushed with a speed and excitement suggestive of the acceleration and turbulence of both personal and historic events.

The book recalls Kazin's years attending City College, where he earned a B.S.S. in 1935, and Columbia University, where he received an M.A. in 1938. During this time, Kazin began publishing reviews and critical commentary in the *New Republic, Scribner's,* and the *New York Times,* among other venues, and he details his early encounters with fellow writers, including most notably Malcolm Cowley and Edmund Wilson, who profoundly influenced him. While recalling his launch into the world of literary journalism, Kazin also outlines features of his political perspective and literary interests, casting these in relation to fellow writers. Kazin's underlying need to distinguish himself from those radical socialists and Marxists (especially those whose allegiance to Stalin was unwavering) is captured in an early declaration in the book: "I was a literary radical, indifferent to economics, suspicious of organization, planning, Marxist solemnity and intellectual system-building; it was the rebels of literature, the great wrestlers-with-God, Thor with his mighty hammer, the poets of unlimited spiritual freedom whom I loved." Kazin associates his literary aims with a kind of independent or radical desire for freedom; the literature he is most passionate about is the work of writers seeking liberation from economic, social, and religious forces. The working-class writers of the 1930s in particular—including James T. Farrell, Robert Cantwell, and Clifford Odets—attract Kazin's interest because of their attempt to capture meaning amid a time of "endless storm" and social crisis, when Franco, Mussolini, and Hitler threatened not only world peace, but the moral imagination. Writing, for Kazin, is now in part an escape from a meaninglessness constantly imposed by the threat and disorder of war. "I looked to literature," Kazin emphasizes, "for strong social argument, intellectual power, human liberation."

Clearly influenced by older, established critics like Cowley and Wilson, Kazin records his part in a shared literary and cultural tradition, which unites writers as divergent in their views as V. F. Calverton, Sidney Hook, Granville Hicks, and Philip Rahv. He shares with these writers a spirit of revolution and literary crusade carried forth in the literary pages of the *New Republic, Partisan Review,* and the *New Masses,* among other periodicals. His portrait of Cowley, in particular, has the fervor of an admiring sympathy. Cowley, Kazin writes, "heard the bell of literary history sounding the moment" wherever he moved or ate, and his many articles breathed "intellectual fight," inspiring readers with unassailable clarity and distinct authority.

However, just as Kazin elucidates his early entry into a literary fraternity of sorts, *Starting Out* also records his strong antipathy, especially in the wake of the Nazi-Soviet pact and the Moscow trials, toward those writers whom he sees as part of the "cult of Stalin," stubborn ideologues, who lack moral imagination and are insensible to human suffering. Although Kazin declares his youthful "trust in the righteousness of history," that trust is deeply and irrevocably shaken when he learns of Hitler's non-aggression pact with Stalin and recalls screaming "No!" at the radio. If history debunked the hope for the liberation of humanity of an earlier generation of writers, it also ignited a destructive skepticism, which Kazin captures in his portrait of Mary McCarthy. McCarthy's "wholly destructive critical mind" is objectionable to Kazin in part because it suggests humanity is not to be saved, so much as despised.

In this atmosphere of political turmoil and strained hopes for the future in the late 1930s, Kazin worked daily at the New York Public Library on his first book of criticism, *On Native Grounds,* at the suggestion of Columbia's Carl

Van Doren. He was also writing reviews fairly regularly and teaching college courses to make ends meet. Despite his near meteoric rise into a literary society that found him meeting James T. Farrell and Nathaniel West, and on adjoining beach towels with Edmund Wilson by 1940, Kazin records the persistent loneliness that runs like a dark leitmotif through his life. Compelling passages detailing further his life in Brownsville, his parents, and his cousin Sophie's disastrous pursuit of love make up vivid parts of this book. For Kazin, writing is "a path to the outside world." Marriage, however, becomes a refuge from a loneliness rooted in his life as a Jew and among his family. In 1938, when Kazin meets Natasha (Asya Dohn) and within two weeks marries her, he seems to be marrying a romantic and literary ideal rather than a person. Enraptured by her "Russian face, the Russian name, the Russian blouse . . . the Russian devotion to causes," he admits what he can only admit in hindsight—that he hardly knows the heart within the woman. The first of four marriages, the marriage to Asya is at once part of the ecstasy and hopefulness of Kazin's literary rise during this period.

Focusing primarily on the 1930s, *Starting Out* recalls Kazin's engagement with a literary world charged by the social and political tumult of the Great Depression, as well as a political idealism and "spirit of youthful crusading" among writers. Its closing note, "Epilogue 1945," provides an important frame for the book, suggesting with haunting abruptness that the energy and hopefulness amid the "lean and angry" years of the 1930s were unsustainable for Kazin after the war, and that the country, in its newly attained economic and military strength, had changed (and fallen) unalterably.

In the book's final section, Kazin reflects on two newsreels—one viewed in 1940, the other in 1945—and registers a desperate change within him and the nation. The first heralds, through a display of the large-scale production of arms, the end of the depression and a new age of "boundless technical power." The second features "an enormous pile of bodies, piled up like cordwood" and the ghostlike stare of survivors at Belsen, the newly liberated concentration camp. The spectacle of human horror—of genocide, of lives so decimated and close to death they are mere "sticks" on the screen—is more than the author or the audience can bear. People in the theater cough, some laugh. Kazin's memoir ends. The final note is important, for it suggests that Kazin the writer measures his own past as well as the nation's through the immeasurable impact of a dual horror. The country has risen out of the depression, but it has done so by dedicating itself to unstoppable arms production and by accepting as "sacrifice to progress" the cost of so many dead.

Kazin's third and longest memoir, *New York Jew,* covers more than thirty years of his life experiences, observations, and events. With torrential energy and often in impassioned prose, Kazin relays an extraordinary amount of material. The book's first sentence sets the breathless pace of the memoir and recounts three transforming events from which the rest of Kazin's account (and life) springs: "One dreamlike week in 1942 I published my first book, *On Native Grounds,* became an editor of the *New Republic,* and with my wife, Natasha, moved into a little apartment on Twenty-fourth Street and Lexington." With the publication of *On Native Grounds,* Kazin received immediate recognition as a critic of the first order. That same year, he was appointed literary editor of a leading periodical and moved to Manhattan—a move that signals Kazin's personal triumph over his humble Brownsville beginnings and the poverty and lonely despair of his parents. But this book is not a story of simple triumph or of life at the top of the New York literary world; it is a record of Kazin's continuing evolution as a writer and his continuing struggle to find meaning in a world torn by the war and the accelerating materialism in its wake. It also chronicles the author's search for a deeper understanding of his identity as a New York Jew—one whose legacy is limitless possibility as well as alienation and suffering.

In *New York Jew,* the past for Kazin represents both a burden and liberation. Writing and researching his "literary and intellectual history," *On Native Grounds,* in the New York Public Library is recalled as an exhilarating journey that involves making discoveries of the literary past and finding his place in the present. In the works of William Dean Howells, Henry James, Stephen Crane, Theodore Dreiser, and others, Kazin recalls exploring the explosive changes at the end of the nineteenth century, of writers coming to terms with surging numbers of immigrants, America's increasing wealth, and the loneliness of the individual amid so much power and energy. At the same time, he celebrates the thrill of intellectual freedom he experiences with his beloved friend, the historian Richard Hofstadter, in that most democratic of buildings, the public library. As if reciting a sacred prayer, Kazin notes the library's hours: "OPEN EVERY DAY OF THE YEAR 9 A.M.–10 P.M., MONDAY–SATURDAY. 1–10 SUNDAY." Writing the book for this son of poor immigrants is a kind of hymn to democratic freedom at the same time that it is an opportunity to explore the limits of that freedom for himself and writers of an earlier age.

Catapulted into the literary world with the success of *On Native Grounds,* Kazin recalls in *New York Jew* his subsequent engagement with a host of notable figures, including Delmore Schwartz, Alfred Stieglitz, Lionel Trilling, Robert Frost, Hannah Arendt, Henri Cartier-Bresson, and Saul Bellow, as well as President John F. Kennedy. As in *Starting Out,* vivid portraits are features of this book, yet the "close-ups" are even more searching and intense. Many times it is as if Kazin is writing a review of the personality and intelligence of those he meets. The result is frequently captivating, while the sheer range of figures is sometimes dizzying. It is easy to imagine many readers in 1978 beginning this book by thumbing through the pages of the index for names mentioned.

Many descriptions significantly reveal Kazin seizing the chance to position himself within the literary critical tradition of which he is now a part. Van Wyck Brooks, for example, appears outdated in both his manner of dress and style of criticism. Kazin claims that for Brooks, who is recalled besporting a white suit and debonair grace, the nineteenth century was a "golden age without social struggle, without killing, war, monopoly, without religious turmoil, without American power lust." Kazin notes further that Brooks's "strategy" as a critic, unlike his own, "made every writer charming and reduced every book to fitting quotations." In his rendering of Brooks, Kazin appears very much the eager member of a new generation of writers who seeks to surpass his ancestor and discover new ways to examine how literature is affected by and how it struggles with the tumultuous political and historical changes of its time. The passage underscores once again that literature, for Kazin the historicist critic, exists within history, not outside it.

So comfortable is Kazin as prominent critic and writer by the late 1970s, he freely takes issue with everyone and everything he wishes—even with his much admired predecessor Edmund Wilson. In a no-holds-barred manner characteristic of Kazin's writing in the 1960s and 1970s, Wilson is called to account for his stubborn isolationism during the war years; he also appears, as Kazin notes, "full of prejudices formed by a more sheltered and complacent America than mine." Although tougher by far than Brooks is, Wilson's perspective appears limited by the eccentricities of his personality and his own moment in history. But descriptions of Wilson are overwhelmingly admiring and sometimes capture a more self-effacing and vulnerable Kazin.

One of the most memorable encounters between Kazin and Wilson depicted in the book comes when the eminent critic summons Kazin to meet with him after publication of *On Native Grounds*. The evening turns out, to Kazin's horror, not to be a celebration of his achievement, but an occasion to roast it. Wilson and his then-wife Mary McCarthy both take part in unrestrained railing against the young writer's work. The shock of the event wears off, as Kazin recounts, only when Wilson walks him to the subway in the rain, pondering with him a scene from James Joyce's *Ulysses*. The moment, recounted by Kazin with touching and incisive detail, suggests the young writer's initiation into Wilson's and a wider literary universe. In being criticized for his criticism, Kazin experiences a kind of rite of passage; arguing and discussing literature and history with Wilson, as with Hofstadter and later Hannah Arendt, becomes a privilege of friendship, as well as a key means of furthering his evolution as a writer.

No single person in Kazin's life, however, is as influential as the single event of the war. With it, Kazin notes, a nightmare begins that brings "everything else into question," a nightmare that will haunt him "until my last breath." Once again, Kazin registers the dire impact of the Holocaust, quoting in full a 1943 letter of Shmuel Ziegelboim, a Polish Jew in exile in London, to Poland's president and prime minister. In it Ziegelboim, whose wife and daughter were killed by the Nazis, warns of the "ruthless cruelty" of the Germans, who "are now murdering the few remaining Jews in Poland." Written just prior to his suicide, Ziegelboim's letter cries out not just to the Polish government but to the world to prevent the certain annihilation of the remaining Jews; it is a cry for liberation that resounds in Kazin for the rest of his life and one that deepens his search in literature for a hopeful vision of humanity.

At least some of Kazin's anxiety about the unfolding horror of the war is registered in his fierce industry during the war years, which brought new opportunities for him as a writer. The 1940s find Kazin serving as literary editor and later contributing editor of the *New Republic*, then working for Henry Luce's magazine, *Fortune*, in the Time-Life Building, and traveling to England to cover the final year of the war. These years also include travel to the Huntington Library in California to prepare an edition of William Blake's poetry and a short stint of teaching at Black Mountain College in North Carolina. Impressions of these experiences—including reflections on the Hollywood quality of Luce's world, Blake's *The Marriage of Heaven and Hell*, and the sense at war's end of American navy men being "lifted above the rest of humanity by being . . . American"—are intriguing parts of the narrative.

Just as Kazin's literary world was expanding, however, his first marriage, built more on the fantasy of assuaging loneliness than on reality, was fast disintegrating, and it ended just prior to his leaving for England on the *SS Hart Crane* in "the dead of winter," 1945. The "intensely gentle" Natasha clearly cannot compete with the outspoken and fascinating personalities Kazin encounters through his literary work. In "peace-astonished" London, while on line at the army post office on Duke Street, Kazin meets Louise (Caroline Bookman), whom he marries in 1947 in another dreamy glow of hope and expectation. Once back in New York in a studio on Pineapple Street in Brooklyn Heights, Kazin struggles with his sense of unease with Louise and in the postwar world around him. Recounting writing *A Walker in the City*, Kazin recalls his characteristic thrill at all he sees and remembers—his Brownsville past, the Brooklyn Bridge, the "triumphant, glossy" city—along with his growing detachment from it: "I had suddenly gone from a world in which everyone and everything I loved seemed a more gracious extension of myself to one where I felt suspended in the clear cold light of some unending detachment." Although cast in relation to Louise, Kazin makes clear, his is a detachment that others feel as well.

In a fast-changing world, Kazin feels himself—along with other old liberals and fellow Jews—living "at the edge of the abyss created in modern culture, in all our cultured minds, by the extermination of the Jews." While Kazin notes some former radicals like Sidney Hook sought shelter in a new conservatism, he clearly cannot tolerate complicity with the fevered anticommunism of the time. Among European intellectuals who flocked to New York after the war, Hannah Arendt is the brightest in the constellation for Kazin, and it is her fierce struggle to understand the Germans' attempt to systematically annihilate the Jews that draws Kazin to her: "It was for the *direction* of her thinking that I loved her, for the personal insistencies she gained from her comprehension of the European catastrophe." Kazin notes that writers as various as Robert Lowell, Randall Jarrell, and Mary McCarthy gleaned from Arendt "intellectual courage before the moral terror the war had willed to us."

Shortly after the birth of their son Tim (Michael) in 1950, Kazin's second marriage collapsed. Back on Pineapple Street, he again resumed writing *A Walker* and met his soon-to-be third wife, Beth (the novelist Ann Birstein), whom he married in 1952. The early years with Beth are recalled by Kazin as years of great personal and literary activity, including travel to Cologne for a teaching appointment, to a Fulbright conference in Cambridge, a lectureship at Harvard, teaching at Smith, and the birth of his daughter Rachel (Cathrael).

Yet the tumult of personal discontent does not abate. The early thrill of Beth's contrasting personality becomes an agony of marital opposition ("I was hopelessly one self. Beth the novelist included so many selves . . ."). With Beth, Kazin appears perpetually caught in a rainstorm without an umbrella—perpetually without the equipment to understand her or to save their embattled love for each other. (This marriage too ends in divorce the same year *New York Jew* is published, 1978.)

In part capturing the fast-paced and perhaps internal frenzy of this time, Kazin's book accelerates madly through the 1950s and 1960s and into the 1970s, interspersed with vivid commentary on Robert Frost at Amherst (he "had emotions as well as genius"); an aging Edmund Wilson and his study of the Civil War, *Patriotic Gore*; a fleet of Kennedy administration luminaries at the beach on Cape Cod; the war in Vietnam; and his young radical son at the Chicago Convention in 1968. The speed does not detract from the acuteness of Kazin's observations, however, but lends to the closing chapters of this book an intensity and desperation to make sense of it all. Contemplating the raw power of New York City in the book's final scene, Kazin's narrative gives way to a painful yearning. While at a party high above Lincoln Center amid a cacophony of voices in conversation that quickly becomes a babble of chaos, Kazin turns to admire a blazing red sunset over New Jersey. His rapture seems at least in part to be about wishing so much natural beauty could counter the "mass and volume, money and power" of the city that constantly threaten to overwhelm him. In the final lines of the book, Kazin writes pleadingly, "I want to love again. I want my God back. I will never give up until it is too late to expect you." *New York Jew* ends the way it begins with a chapter entitled "Words," and the author's longing for language to recover a lost past and unfold the meaning of his ever-fragile place in the present.

CRITICISM

Kazin's prominence as a literary critic began with publication of his first book, *On Native*

Grounds, a massive study of modern American literature begun in 1938 and completed in 1942, with the help of a Guggenheim Fellowship (awarded in 1940). With its publication, the twenty-seven-year-old author was widely celebrated not just for his critical aptitude, but for the ambitious scope of his subject—the prose works of American writers from the 1890s to the 1940s. In his first book of literary criticism, Kazin consciously set out to work in the tradition of Van Wyck Brooks and Edmund Wilson, viewing literature from a historical as well as an aesthetic perspective. However, Kazin was also clearly a pioneer intent on carving out new literary territory and delving more deeply into the tumultuous effects of what he called "the country's power" on the literary imagination.

At the time of the book's publication, no single, book-length study of the rise of the modern in American literature existed. The most prominent studies of American literature (still a fledgling field at American universities) focused on writers of an earlier period, most notably Brooks's *The Flowering of New England, 1815–1865* (1936) and Perry Miller's *The Puritans* (1938). Wilson's *Axel's Castle: A Study in the Imaginative Literature of 1870–1930* (1931), which examined both American and European symbolist and avant-garde authors, offered Kazin perhaps the best model for his book. Wilson's ability to weave politics and history in this study, as in his literary journalism, no doubt deeply influenced Kazin's critical method in *On Native Grounds* and its author's attempt to explore literature in relation to the political, intellectual, and cultural history of its time. However, even as Kazin sought to emulate Wilson's role as "literary radical," he set out to explore more thoroughly than any critic had before him the connection between the nation's rise as a dominant world power and its literature during a crucial fifty-year period from the end of the nineteenth century to just before the Second World War. In shaping a historical

context for this period, Kazin was boldly advancing into largely unexplored terrain and setting a powerful precedent for the many historicist critics of American literature who came after him. One of the great achievements of the book is Kazin's ability to examine history not as "background" for the literary artists of the period, but as the atmosphere they breathe; along with Wilson, Kazin advanced the critical method of viewing American writers embedded in the historical and cultural scene.

Arranged chronologically, *On Native Grounds* comprises three sections or stages in the development of the nation's literature: "The Search for Reality (1890–1917)" focuses on the years just prior to World War I and the rise in realist literature; "The Great Liberation (1918–1929)" focuses on the years just after the war and the writers of the 1920s, who according to Kazin form "the most abundant spectacle of successive creativity in our literary history"; and "The Literature of Crisis (1930–1940)" focuses on the literature of the 1930s in light of competing political perspectives during the Great Depression and a time of impending war. Compared to writers of an earlier genteel tradition, the writers featured in *On Native Grounds,* including Howells, Theodore Dreiser, Frank Norris, John Dos Passos, Willa Cather, F. Scott Fitzgerald, and Ernest Hemingway, make up a turbulent, rising force in Kazin's analysis. It is the turbulence—the feisty urge to oppose convention, to seek meaning in a world that threatens it—that most interests Kazin in this book.

In his study, Kazin characterizes the "modern" as a tension between the individual and a fast-changing world in the grips of industrial capitalism. Alienation is a key concept for Kazin, as he views writers struggling to combat or express a modern and American sense of "terrible estrangement . . . a nameless yearning for a world no one ever really possessed." That Kazin sees this struggle as noble reflects his own hopeful attitude toward literature—an attitude rooted in the exigencies of his own time. During the late 1930s, Kazin viewed literature as a moral force and believed—more fervently than he could after the war—in the "*necessary connection between literature and social criticism.*" Reflecting on this hopeful quality of *On Native Grounds* in the 1982 preface to the fortieth anniversary edition, Kazin wistfully notes that "the 'modern' spirit that was my subject, the 'modern' hope in every field of intellectual endeavor from which my book had arisen, closed in on itself with the war, and after the war became an academic matter." *On Native Grounds* is very much a book of the 1930s in its spirit of hopefulness, its focus on political and social history, and its simultaneous opposition to a purely ideological view of literature.

While it captures the presiding spirit and concerns of its time, *On Native Grounds* remains a pioneering work of American literary criticism. Many of the book's features are now so much a part of literary analysis, it is difficult to conceive their originality. In discussing the works of Howells in relation to the Haymarket riots, of Dreiser and the muckrakers in light of the presidency of Franklin D. Roosevelt, of Cather in relation to the transcontinental railroad, for example, Kazin offers an important and lasting illustration of the use of history in the examination of literature. In addition, although studies of American modernism have chiefly come to focus on the innovations of poets like T. S. Eliot and Wallace Stevens, not on American realists like Howells and Henry James or naturalists like Dreiser and Norris, Kazin's understanding of the "modern" American sensibility—as one fraught by a sense of perpetual alienation and loss in a world of ever-increasing possibility—remains a vital part of modernist criticism.

Another source of the book's enduring quality is Kazin's ability to explain individual writers and their work in clear and passionate

language. Kazin's criticism and commentary from his first book to his last, more than fifty years later, is distinct in American literary criticism for its readability and for the characteristic sense of wonder and enthusiasm which the author brought to all his subjects. While literary critics came in Kazin's lifetime to employ a sometimes highly technical and theoretical language adopted from other disciplines like anthropology and philosophy, Kazin never abandoned his impassioned journalistic style which sought to *reach* its audience and relied on strongly declarative sentences and the quoting of key passages from the texts being examined. A steadfast believer in literature's moral power, Kazin did not believe in purely academic or scholarly analysis for its own sake and objected to the use of literature as an ideological tool. *On Native Grounds* stands as a masterpiece of style as well as an important introduction to American prose writing of the late nineteenth and early twentieth centuries.

In the decades following the publication of *On Native Grounds,* Kazin continued to make his mark as a leading American literary critic, his reviews and commentary appearing regularly in major newspapers and periodicals. His prodigious output during the 1950s, 1960s, and 1970s includes two collections of essays, *The Inmost Leaf: A Selection of Essays* (1955) and *Contemporaries* (1962), and a book-length study of twentieth-century American prose writers, *Bright Book of Life: American Novelists and Storytellers from Hemingway to Mailer* (1973). Much of the material in these books had appeared previously in other venues, including the *New Republic, The New Yorker,* the *New York Review of Books,* and the *New York Times.* Perhaps because of the wide-ranging subjects of these books, they were not as well received as his first critical study, though they were recognized as serious contributions to literary debate and criticism. Each contains gems of observation and critical insight on a range of writers that should not be overlooked in a review of Kazin's work.

The Inmost Leaf, which takes its title from a phrase of Herman Melville in a letter to Nathaniel Hawthorne, focuses on European and American writers, including Joyce, Marcel Proust, Blake, Henry David Thoreau, Fitzgerald, Melville, Franz Kafka, and others. What draws Kazin to this diverse group of writers is their furious will to struggle with an overwhelming power—be it whale or God or society's obsession with money. The artist as Melvillean "isolato," one apart from yet bound to the world, continues to fascinate Kazin, who brings the individual peculiarities of each writer's vision to beaming light. One of the best (and longest) essays in the collection is "An Introduction to William Blake," reprinted from *The Portable Blake,* a volume edited by Kazin in 1946. Requisite reading for anyone interested in Blake, it is also a stunning example of Kazin's energetic and passionate style, of his forceful enthusiasm for discovering through *his* writing what it means to read and appreciate poetry.

One of many revelations this essay offers is Kazin's pairing of William Blake and Ludwig van Beethoven. Set beside each other, the unlikely match makes perfect sense as Kazin notes the composer and poet's shared "artistic independence and universality." He writes, "What is nearest and first in both men is so strong a sense of their own identity that they are always reaching beyond man's conception of his powers." The unexpected insight becomes, however, not the thesis for a comparative essay, but the launching pad for Kazin's look at Blake's grand poetic designs, at his "unappeasable longing for the absolute integration of man . . . with the universe." In the subtlest of twists in this essay, Blake's search for "integration," his pursuit of "the highest flights of his own imagination," connects him not only to the great composer, but reveals his relevance to the contemporary reader. With an eye always on the

ever-increasing power and wealth of modern America, Kazin celebrates Blake's singular struggle against "the false materialism of the age to find his way back to perfect human sight." One of the most striking effects of Kazin's essay is that through its searching reflections and the energetic pulse of careful observation, it becomes one with Blake's "impassioned rejection of all that is . . . self-limiting in modern thought." As is evident in most all of Kazin's writing, part of its power comes from the sense that the literature examined is not only profound, but *necessary* to existence.

Contemporaries, a collection of more than seventy short essays and critical commentary on "the modern spirit in literature," offers far more heterogeneous fare. Dedicated to Edmund Wilson, it is arranged in nine loosely connecting groups of essays. Focusing chiefly on American prose writers from Emerson to Saul Bellow, Kazin also includes somewhat abbreviated considerations of modern literature in Europe and Russia, and a multi-essay reflection on Sigmund Freud and the influence of psychoanalysis. The collection's two final sections, "The Puzzle of Modern Society" and "The Critic's Task" (condensed in a single, abridged section entitled "History" in the revised second edition), include reflections on the political scene of the late 1950s and early 1960s, and on the writer's role in journalism and academe.

These two sections are especially noteworthy for their outspoken attacks on "the cult of art" and the pursuit of pleasure in modern culture. Even as art appreciation expands in the postwar years, Kazin maintains a compelling impatience with those who see art as an attainable form of salvation. "An honest sense of the limits of art," he notes, would allow us "a more grateful sense of its power." Superficial ideas and "false sophistication" of thought are frequently derided by Kazin, who continually advises his readers to appreciate the mystery of literature and the complexity of the world of ideas.

A highlight of the final section is Kazin's essay on President John F. Kennedy, "The President and Other Intellectuals." In it, Kazin notes Kennedy's considerable "charm for some of the most interesting minds of the United States," including the famously anti–New Deal (anti-liberal) Robert Frost, and the tough-minded Murray Kempton and Walter Lippmann. Hardly a hymn to Kennedy's charisma, however, the essay refuses to adopt a purely admiring stance. Kazin suggests that Kennedy's reputation as an intellectual has more to do with his "cultivation of the high brow world as an executive taste and Presidential style," rather than the president's own intellectual pursuits. While somehow managing not to undercut Kennedy's power to lead and pausing to point out the president's ability to act independently and subvert convention in decision making, Kazin nevertheless emphasizes the highly manipulated *image* of the president as tireless thinker: "Never in any administration have we been told so constantly how little sleep the President gets." As Kazin sees it, Kennedy's intellectual quality has more to do with misguided public perception than reality. Taking the highly charismatic national leader to task for what seems like a schoolboy's ambition to look smart, Kazin grants only "would-be intellectual" status to the man famous for surrounding himself with "brains." In this essay, Kazin reveals how much he could not—and would not—be seduced by the power he felt it his role to understand critically and disinterestedly. Given the appreciable glamour attached to those poets, historians, and scholars who in some way touched or became part of the Kennedy circle, Kazin's objectivity is all the more impressive.

Among the wide-ranging essays on literature in *Contemporaries,* several pieces reveal Kazin's deepening interest in American writers whose "feeling for language" and struggle with God distinguished their work. Essays on Melville, Dickinson, and Faulkner are among the best in the book and still pose enduring questions about the work of these writers. The short essay on Dickinson, "Called Back," effectively links the poet's curious and innovative style with her struggle for belief. The short phrase that gives the essay its title was written in a letter by the poet just prior to her death, and is just the kind of small detail that Kazin enjoys scrutinizing to make a simple, but large point. In this instance, Kazin notes shrewdly that no one who reads very far into the more than 1,700 poems in Johnson's edition "can miss the fact that Emily Dickinson was not sure of what being 'called back' could mean." It is Kazin's grasp of Dickinson's uncertainty in relation to the Almighty, her "constant wariness of the gods" in her poetry that makes this brief essay worth reading more than forty years after it was written.

Yet attention to language is not all that Kazin brings to the works discussed in this book. He clearly believes that the critical method of the New Critics—with its focus on language, technique, and style—is severely limited because of its neglect of history. The burden of history, of the past, remains an ever-present preoccupation of Kazin. In "William Faulkner: The Stillness of *Light in August,*" Kazin is at his best registering the weight of the past within a specific work of art. For him, Faulkner's protagonist, Joe Christmas, is just as much an emblem of "the race-mad South," as he is of the "Calvinist obsession of the elect." He is a prisoner of his own history *and* the nation's, but he is more than that as well. He is "an incarnation not only of the 'race problem' in America, but of the condition of man." In this essay, Kazin convincingly suggests that the greatness of Faulkner's novel resides in its effort to capture a meaning—an understanding of history—that can never be fully attained.

A little more than a decade after *Contemporaries,* Kazin published *Bright Book of Life* (1973), in which he expands his view of the modern and examines twentieth-century American novelists and storytellers from Hemingway to Thomas Pynchon. Chapter titles (for example, "Faulkner to Percy" and "Capote to Mailer") suggest a progression or single line of development, but the chapters themselves belie this suggestion. Kazin's primary interest is not how one writer leads to another, but how each writer's individual modern qualities are distinct from another's. Style is a central concern of Kazin, who never fails to bring to light its relation to history and culture. A unifying force of this book is, in fact, the critic's sense of each writer taking part in a shared struggle to understand and combat the forces of history—past and present. Hemingway's preoccupation with precision of feeling, with consciousness itself, for example, is seen by Kazin as a means of conquering what the writer called the "shapelessness," "the panorama of futility and anarchy that is contemporary history." Faulkner's novels, on the other hand, reveal according to Kazin not "a triumph *over* experience," but the "struggle of language to find support for the mind in its everlasting struggle with the past."

Throughout this collection, Kazin weaves aesthetic observation with historical analysis. But there is a growing tension between the two, especially in the book's later chapters, when Kazin views the literary imagination as increasingly threatened "by the fury of public events and technological change." In examining the work of Truman Capote and Ralph Ellison, for instance, Kazin explores the troubling sense of history as "accident" and the novel as a futile struggle against an inherently "absurd" American reality. Vladamir Nabokov's fiction is distinguished for Kazin in its attempt not to recapture the past or convey reality, but to create an "antiworld" in which fiction *is* the longed-for reality. Too brief to offer a definitive or comprehensive examination of the modern American novel, *Bright Book of Life* nevertheless offers an insightful look at what Stephen

Crane called the "unmistakable" quality of a writer's work. It also illustrates Kazin's own growing anxiety about the ability of the modern novelist to adequately depict the vast and rapidly changing American scene.

In his next book of criticism, *An American Procession: The Major American Writers from 1830–1930—the Crucial Century* (1984), Kazin embarked on yet another journey to trace the evolution of an American literary tradition. While this book overlaps the fifty-year period covered in *On Native Grounds, An American Procession* is more intensely focused on a declared set of major writers and is, in its control and concentration of subject matter, the work of a mature writer and critic. While no longer tinged with Kazin's earlier hopeful sense of literature as liberation from a corrupt and powerful world, the study nevertheless suggests literature's enduring transformative power. During a time when literary criticism was fast becoming an academic profession and increasingly divorced from the interests of a general reader, Kazin almost defiantly maintains his journalistic and readable style while also diving deeply into the biographical and historical complexities of each writer's life and work. The result is a richly textured and compelling work of criticism that remains requisite reading for anyone interested in the period.

Largely well received by leading critics, including Richard Ellman and Denis Donoghue, *An American Procession* reveals Kazin at his most passionate and insightful. In his study, Kazin separates the century into two periods and groups of writers: the first is before the Civil War and includes "the transcendental idealists," Emerson, Thoreau, and Whitman, and "the great romancers," Hawthorne, Edgar Allan Poe, and Melville; the second follows the First World War and includes the modernist writers Eliot, Ezra Pound, Hemingway, Dos Passos, Fitzgerald, Edmund Wilson, and Kenneth Burke.

What makes these groupings so convincing is Kazin's ability to detail the similarities of writers, while not forcing them into a mindless continuum or strictly linear progression. While he focuses on the way each writer constructs or battles with the notion of self in society, he takes care and obvious pleasure in elucidating each writer's distinctness as an artist. For instance, Melville is seen as restless counterweight to Emerson and a far more despairing challenger of prevailing notions of power and self. Emerson's "infinitude of the private mind" is in Kazin's view entirely suspect in Melville's fictional world of contradiction and paradox, even as both writers are possessed by a will to test the limits of the imagination.

As is typical in Kazin's work, the chapters that most resound are those that deal with the great wrestlers with ideas about the self, society, and the Almighty; in this book, those on Melville and Dickinson are especially noteworthy. The slippery question of what in these writers' works is peculiarly American is addressed by Kazin with clarity and shrewdness. In *Moby-Dick,* Kazin notes that the confrontation "between Nature—as it was in the beginning, without man, God's world alone—and man, forever and uselessly dashing himself against it" is part of a supremely American nineteenth-century experience, "for it connects the still-present 'wilderness,' the ferocity of brute creation, with the anxiously searching mind that has lost its father in heaven." It is in identifying this "anxiously searching" quality of the mind of the American writer that Kazin is so memorable and forceful as a critic of American literature. In no other critic's work but Kazin's could one make the leap so nimbly from Melville to Dickinson and understand the two as literary compatriots who share a common turbulence and restlessness of spirit, an always pressing need to pursue an inscrutable and unseen God. *An American Procession* remains an invaluable guide to the uniquely American

quality of the major writers discussed. It also offers critical insight into the peculiarities of their style and its relation to their individual struggles to conquer the unconquerable questions of existence.

The 1980s were a particularly productive decade for Kazin, who published two more books during this period. *A Writer's America: Landscape in Literature* (1988) offers a close and probing look at landscape's influence on American writers from Thomas Jefferson to the early twentieth century. A somewhat underappreciated work, it registers with keen insight the inexorable impact of the land on the American mind and imagination. While not a comprehensive study, it covers a large territory of writers and thinkers with depth and precision. Much like the early naturalists he writes of, Kazin explores the American sense of space with a striking fearlessness and independence of mind, pausing to examine with freshness and enthusiasm whatever captures his interest along the way. At least some of the "recurrent thrill of discovery"—which Kazin observes in imaginations as divergent as Emerson and Melville, Audubon and Hemingway—is recaptiulated in his own rhapsodic and lyrical style. In *Our New York: A Personal Vision in Words and Photographs* (1989) Kazin's reflections on his native city are set beside contemporary photographs by David Finn. Like Finn's black and white photographs, Kazin's text embraces the dark contrasts of life in the city, rising to celebrate the lofty inspiration of the Brooklyn Bridge and descending to despair over the poverty and hopelessness of those who live on the streets. But here the harsh disparities of the city (its super rich and grossly underprivileged; its intoxication and incivility) appear less to ignite Kazin's imagination, as they do in the memoirs, than to spark a somewhat bitter helplessness. Part reflections on his coming of age, part journalistic observations of the city and its inhabitants in more recent years, part commentary on Finn's work, this book lacks the focused intensity and freshness of his unalloyed earlier writings of self-discovery in the city he so clearly loves.

In 1983 Kazin married his fourth wife, the writer Judith Dunford, whom he once claimed he felt so deeply about that she was "the only woman I had any right to marry." Built on a mutual devotion that lasted until Kazin's death in 1998, this marriage afforded Kazin a new sense of personal stability and happiness even as his health began to fail during these years. Three of Kazin's books written during this period are dedicated to Dunford.

This period also found Kazin continuing to reap recognition and distinction for his work. In 1982 Kazin received the Hubbell Medal from the Modern Language Association and in 1987 he was appointed (the Phi Beta Kappa) orator at Harvard, where he later returned to deliver the distinguished William E. Massey Sr. Lectures in the History of American Civilization in 1994 (reproduced in *Writing Was Everything*). In 1991 he delivered the Emmy Parrish Lectures in American Studies at Baylor University, and in 1996 he was awarded the first Lifetime Achievement Award in Literary Criticism by the Truman Capote Literary Trust. A member of the American Academy of Arts and Letters and the American Academy of Arts and Sciences, Kazin also received honorary degrees from Adelphi University (1964), the University of New Haven (1974), Hebrew Union College (1981), State University of New York (1987), Long Island University (1989), and American University (1995).

After teaching at institutions as various as Smith College, the State University of New York at Stony Brook, and the University of Notre Dame throughout his early life, Kazin also settled into a more permanent academic home in 1973 at Hunter College of the City University of New York and shortly thereafter at the City University of New York's Graduate Center, where he was appointed distinguished professor of English and taught for more than fifteen years. During the 1980s and 1990s, Kazin also held distinguished visiting professorships at Cornell, George Mason, and Brown universities. Although his influence as professor was less profound than as writer, he was a dedicated if often fiery teacher who sought to inspire his students with the passion he felt for literature. In the classroom, he was much like Melville's white whale—fierce and inscrutable, while at the same time possessed of "a mighty mildness of repose," a gentle solicitude for anyone who wished to learn. While he mentored a relatively small number of Ph.D. students, he left an indelible impression on generations of students across the United States.

In his later years, Kazin was fond of describing himself in Ford Maddox Ford's words as "an old man mad about literature." The phrase was apt for more than one reason, as it captured his relentless passion for reading and seeking knowledge through a tireless appreciation of literature. But it also suggested his fury at what he saw as the commodification of literature and its increasing use for ideological purposes, especially in the Academy. As literary criticism expanded widely in the 1960s through the 1980s to embrace new methods of analysis, including those built on poststructuralism, deconstruction, feminism, gay and lesbian studies, and African American studies, Kazin insisted on a method that remained fixed on an understanding of the text through its historical underpinnings and a close examination of a writer's style as, it conveyed the fundamental struggle to express a particular self at a particular time through a particular artistic medium. Criticism that featured the critic and his or her political preoccupations over and above the artist had little interest for Kazin, who held to a deep conviction that his role was not only to search out the truths of an artist's work but always to seek new ways to appreciate it. Happily ignoring the risk of being dismissed as "old-fashioned" by younger critics, Kazin continued to write about writers whose work he believed endured because of a quality that had little to do with the writer's gender, race, or sexuality, but everything to do with a genius for language, a passion for ideas, and a determination to understand history and one's place in it.

Of the three books Kazin produced in the 1990s, his last and final book of literary criticism, *God and the American Writer* (1997), focuses on writers Kazin had written about for more than fifty years, including Melville, Hawthorne, Dickinson, Abraham Lincoln, and Faulkner. It is dedicated to Richard Hofstadter, "an absent friend." With this work Kazin seems to recall consciously his attachment to an earlier time and his steadfast interest in unlocking the mystery of America's literary tradition through the writers who first formed it. While in this book Kazin does not embark on new literary territory, he sheds new light on the nation's religious history and the struggles with belief of more than a dozen American writers. Written while Kazin was battling prostate cancer and nearing the end of his life, the book expresses in its driving and passionate sentences an astonishingly persistent literary curiosity, as well as an underlying personal urgency to address issues relating to life and death, spirit and belief.

Covering the same period and many of the same writers as in *An American Procession,* Kazin proves in this book that part of what makes the writers examined great is the fact that there is always more to glean and learn from their work—always more, that is, for one capable, as Kazin clearly is, of looking ever deeper into the work and rereading with care. This book displays Kazin's lifelong ability to get under the very skin of an author, to interpret and appreciate a work of art from inside its creator. Here is Kazin on *The Scarlet Letter*:

Only in a work of art, of the intensest emotions, did there surface his own long struggle with his

ancestors. Hawthorne is all over his book, loving Hester and chastising her, hating Chillingworth and despising Dimmesdale, using little Pearl to say the commonplaces of freedom that no one else dared to say—all the while affirming and subverting the standards of an age he profoundly distrusted.

Reading Hawthorne means for Kazin understanding the shadow the past cast on him as well as his uncomfortable relation to the present. What distinguishes Kazin's insight is his obvious pleasure at having the chance to discover it; literature throughout this book is a gift through which he has the chance to grapple with a greater mystery.

In *God and the American Writer,* Kazin offers new insight into Emerson: "He built on the infinite as if it were within the reach of a single sentence"; Melville: "The style [of *Moby-Dick*] is . . . sharpest in its despair, taking us where no one wants to go"; and Dickinson: "Even her punctuation—dashes between words, dashes marking off one line from another, the dashes enabling her (and the reader) to breathe—can remind us, as only the greatest poets do, of our inner despair of words, mere words, crying out against the silence of the universe." Yet one of the highlights of this book is the chapter on Abraham Lincoln, "The Almighty Has His Own Purposes." In it, Kazin examines with an infectious wonder the "literary genius" not of a great American novelist or poet, but of the president of the United States.

Kazin views Lincoln as the nexus of both tremendous historical and religious shifts. He notes that America's "age of *belief* reaches its culmination in the second inaugural." This striking claim is made vivid in Kazin's close reading of Lincoln's address. In each sentence Kazin ties language to a historical significance unthought of by the New Critics who came before him and unimaginable for the new historicist critics who came after him. This is Kazin at his best—awestruck, bold, and idiosyncratic:

Lincoln's God was born of war. It would not have survived without him, since only Lincoln understood Him. Lincoln had nothing to say about Jesus as redeemer and intervener in this life. What was personal to Lincoln was a sense of divinity wrested from the many contradictions in human effort. God came to him through a certain exhaustion. Faith was still deep and intense enough to allow doubt and survive it. The sense of Providence during the Civil War—there was still no alternative—was of a kind we cannot now fully take in.

Through Kazin, we have the chance to understand a sense of the Almighty we might otherwise not recognize. At the same time, we are invited to understand the moral value not just of leadership but of language itself. The chapter on Lincoln in this extraordinarily powerful last book reveals Kazin as both master critic and literary crusader intent on illuminating history and literature and investing it with a rare saving grace.

Alfred Kazin died on his eighty-third birthday on June 5, 1998, in New York City. In his more than sixty years of writing, he was among the first critics to bring much-needed perspective to the literary tradition in America, and he helped to shape both literary taste and understanding among a broad readership in the United States and abroad. As a tireless chronicler of his life in his memoirs and journals, he sought to understand himself and the world during a time of unprecedented global conflict and change. In his love of language, mastery of technique, and profound sense of wonder, he was a writer of the highest rank.

Selected Bibliography

WORKS OF ALFRED KAZIN

BOOKS

On Native Grounds: An Interpretation of Modern American Prose Literature. New York: Reynal & Hitchcock, 1942. Rev. ed., San Diego: Harcourt Brace Jovanovich, 1982. (The 1982 edition features a new preface by the author.)

A Walker in the City. New York: Harcourt Brace, 1951.

The Inmost Leaf: A Selection of Essays. New York: Harcourt Brace, 1955.

Contemporaries. Boston: Little, Brown and Co., 1962. Rev. ed., New York: Horizon Press, 1982. (The 1982 edition features several additional selections, including a new introductory chapter, "To Be a Critic." It excises several pieces from the 1962 edition.)

Starting Out in the Thirties. Boston: Little, Brown, 1965. Reprint, New York: Vintage, 1980.

Bright Book of Life: American Novelists and Storytellers from Hemingway to Mailer. Boston: Little, Brown, 1973. Reprint, Notre Dame: University of Notre Dame Press, 1980.

New York Jew. New York: Knopf, 1978.

An American Procession: The Major American Writers from 1830–1930—the Crucial Century. New York: Knopf, 1984.

A Writer's America: Landscape in Literature. New York: Knopf, 1988.

Our New York: A Personal Vision in Words and Photographs. Photographs by David Finn. New York: Harper & Row, 1989.

Writing Was Everything. Cambridge: Harvard University Press, 1995. (Printing of the William E. Massey Sr. Lectures in the History of American Civilization delivered by Kazin in 1994.)

A Lifetime Burning in Every Moment: From the Journals of Alfred Kazin. New York: HarperCollins, 1997.

God and the American Writer. New York: Knopf, 1997.

ARTICLES

"In Every Voice, in Every Ban." *New Republic,* January 10, 1944, pp. 44–46. (A response to the suicide of Shmuel Ziegelboim in London as protest to Jewish genocide in Germany.)

"Radicals and Intellectuals." *New York Review of Books,* May 20, 1965, p. 3. (A review of Christopher Lasch's *The New Radicalism in America, 1889–1963: The Intellectual as a Social Type.*)

"On Perry Miller." *New York Review of Books,* November 25, 1965, p. 10.

"The Jew as Modern Writer." *Commentary* 41:37–41 (April 1966).

"History as LBJ." *New York Review of Books,* December 1, 1966, p. 3. (A review of Rowland Evans's and Robert Novak's *Lyndon B. Johnson: The Exercise of Power.*)

"Josephine Herbst (1897–1969)." *New York Review of Books,* March 27, 1969, p. 19.

"The Confidence of FDR." *New York Review of Books,* May 20, 1971, p. 3. (A review of James MacGregor Burns's *Roosevelt: The Soldier of Freedom.*)

"Displaced Person." *New York Review of Books,* December 30, 1971, p. 3. (A review of V. S. Naipaul's *In a Free State.*)

"'The Giant Killer': Drink and the American Writer." *Commentary* 61:44–50 (March 1976).

"A Meditation on Keats." *American Scholar* 46:109–115 (1976).

"Restoring *Sister Carrie.*" *New York Review of Books,* February 19, 1981, pp. 12–14.

"Woman in Dark Times." *New York Review of Books,* June 24, 1982, pp. 3–4, 6. (A review of Elisabeth Young-Bruehl's *Hannah Arendt: For Love of the World.*)

"The Fascination and Terror of Ezra Pound." *New York Review of Books,* March 13, 1986, pp. 16–24.

"In Washington." *New York Review of Books,* May 29, 1986, pp. 11–18.

"Fallen Creatures." *New York Review of Books,* November 5, 1987, p. 12. (A review of Richard Ford's *Rock Springs: Stories.*)

"The Past Breaks Out." In *Inventing the Truth: The Art and Craft of Memoir.* Edited by William Zinsser. Boston: Houghton Mifflin, 1987. Pp. 61–81.

"A Forever Amazing Writer." *New York Times Book Review,* December 10, 1989, pp. 3–4, 39. (A review of the Library of America's two volumes of Abraham Lincoln's writings: *Abraham Lincoln: Speeches and Writings 1832–1858* and *Abraham Lincoln: Speeches and Writings 1859–1865.*)

"The Art of *Call It Sleep.*" *New York Review of Books,* October 10, 1991, pp. 15–18.

"Cry, the Beloved Country." *Forbes,* September 14, 1992, pp. 140–141, 144, 149–150, 154, 156.

"*Howards End* Revisited." *Partisan Review* 59:29–43 (winter 1992).

"Jews." *New Yorker,* March 7, 1994, pp. 62–73.

"A Jew on Horseback." *New York Review of Books,* June 22, 1995, pp. 4, 6. (A review of Isaak Babel's *1920 Diary* and *Collected Stories.*)

"The Long Voyage Home." *New York Review of Books,* November 20, 1997, pp. 18–19. (A review of Charles Frazier's *Cold Mountain.*)

"Laughter in the Dark." *New York Review of Books,* April 23, 1998, pp. 4–8. (A review of Isaac Bashevis Singer's *Shadows on the Hudson* and Janet Hadda's *Isaac Bashevis Singer: A Life.*)

"River Morning." *New Republic,* May 11, 1998, p. 40.

OTHER WORKS

The Portable Blake. Edited with an introduction by Alfred Kazin. New York: Viking, 1946. (Kazin's introduction is reprinted in *The Inmost Leaf.* New York: Harcourt Brace, 1955.)

F. Scott Fitzgerald: The Man and His Work. Edited with an essay by Alfred Kazin. Cleveland: World, 1951.

The Stature of Theodore Dreiser: A Critical Study of the Man and His Work. Edited by Alfred Kazin and Charles Shapiro, with an introduction and essay by Alfred Kazin. Bloomington: Indiana University Press, 1955.

Moby-Dick, by Herman Melville. Edited with an introduction by Alfred Kazin. Boston: Houghton Mifflin, 1956.

Emerson: A Modern Anthology. Edited with an introduction by Alfred Kazin and Daniel Aaron. Boston: Houghton Mifflin, 1959.

The Works of Anne Frank. Edited with an introduction by Alfred Kazin and Ann Birstein. New York: Doubleday, 1959.

Sister Carrie, by Theodore Dreiser. Edited with an introduction by Alfred Kazin. New York: Dell, 1960.

The Financier, by Theodore Dreiser. Edited with an introduction by Alfred Kazin. New York: Dell, 1961.

The Open Form: Essays for Our Time. Edited with an essay by Alfred Kazin. New York: Harcourt, Brace & World, 1961.

Selected Short Stories, by Nathaniel Hawthorne. Edited with an introduction by Alfred Kazin. New York: Fawcett, 1966.

Writers at Work: The Paris Review Interviews. Third series. Introduction by Alfred Kazin. New York: Viking, 1967.

The Ambassadors, by Henry James. Edited with an introduction by Alfred Kazin. New York: Bantam, 1969.

CRITICAL AND BIOGRAPHICAL STUDIES

Adams, Robert M. "A Self-Made Man." *New York Review of Books,* October 5, 1995, p. 23. (A review of Alfred Kazin's *Writing Was Everything.*)

Alter, Robert. "The Education of Alfred Kazin." *Commentary* 65:44–51 (June 1978).

———. *"A Lifetime Burning in Every Moment: From the Journals of Alfred Kazin." New Republic,* August 12, 1998, pp. 35–36.

Cook, Richard. "The Journals of Alfred Kazin." *American Literary History* 2, no. 2:242–250 (summer 1990).

Delbanco, Andrew. *"A Writer's America: Landscape in Literature." New Republic,* January 30, 1989, pp. 36–38.

———. "On Alfred Kazin (1915–1998)." *New York Review of Books,* July 16, 1998, p. 22.

Dickstein, Morris. *Double Agent: The Critic and Society.* New York: Oxford University Press, 1992. (Of special interest: pp.106-109; pp. 151-160.)

Donoghue, Denis. "The Return of the Native." *New York Review of Books,* July 19, 1984, pp. 32–34. (A review of Alfred Kazin's *An American Procession.*)

Stone, Robert. "American Apostle." *New York Review of Books,* March 26, 1998, pp. 25–28. (A review of Alfred Kazin's *God and the American Writer.*)

Wilentz, Sean. "He Heard America Singing." *New York Times Book Review,* July 19, 1998, p. 31.

Ziff, Larzer. *"American Procession." American Literature* 57:322–324 (May 1985).

—MARYBETH McMAHON

Harper Lee

1926–

NELLE HARPER LEE was born on April 28, 1926, in Monroeville, Alabama. Her parents, Amasa Coleman Lee and Francis Finch Lee, had three children, of which Nelle was the youngest. Her father and her sister, Alice, practiced law together in Monroeville. Lee received her early education in the Monroeville public schools, then attended Huntington College for a brief period in 1944 and 1945. She studied law at the University of Alabama from 1945 to 1950, including a year spent in England as an exchange student at Oxford University. In 1950 Lee moved to New York City and was employed as an airline reservation clerk. In the city, Lee presented a literary agent with manuscripts of two essays and three short stories. One of the short stories was eventually expanded into the novel *To Kill a Mockingbird*.

A SINGLE NOVEL

Lee's only novel, *To Kill a Mockingbird*, was first published in 1960 by Lippincott, during the time of the civil rights movement. It remained on the best-seller lists for over eighty weeks, was published as a *Reader's Digest* Condensed Book, and was chosen as Literary Guild and Book-of-the-Month selections. For *To Kill a Mockingbird*, Lee was awarded the Pulitzer Prize in 1961 (making her the first woman since 1942 to win the Pulitzer), the Alabama Library Association Award (1961), the Brotherhood Award of the National Conference of Christians and Jews (1961), and the *Bestsellers* magazine's Paperback of the Year Award (1962). *To Kill a Mockingbird* was also a success internationally; it was chosen as a British Book Society Top

Book of the Year and has been translated into many languages.

After the success of *To Kill a Mockingbird*, Lee returned to Monroeville. She received honorary doctorates from Holyoke College and the University of Alabama in 1962 and 1990, respectively. In 1961 her essay, "Love—In Other Words," appeared in *Vogue* and her essay, "Christmas to Me," appeared in *McCall's*. As the twenty-first century began, Lee was living in New York City and returning to Monroeville during the winters to stay with her sister, Alice. Her reclusiveness was well known; she consistently refused interviews and awards in order to maintain her privacy.

To Kill a Mockingbird shows the atrocities of discrimination and bias based on ethnicity. Although the novel is told in rather simplistic terms, providing almost a morality tale of right versus wrong with very little middle ground at the surface level, it is still considered a classic. *To Kill a Mockingbird* is set in the small community of Maycomb, Alabama, during the mid-1930s.

The novel is narrated by Jean Louise Finch, who is nicknamed "Scout." The beginning of the novel describes Scout, her brother Jem Finch, and their father, Atticus Finch, who is a widowed attorney. Early on, the novel reveals the adventures of Jem, Scout, and a boy named Dill (Charles Baker Harris), who spends summers with his aunt, a neighbor of the Finches. Some of the children's adventures indirectly involve Arthur "Boo" Radley, an outcast and a recluse who lives near the Finches. The children imagine stories about Boo and perform pranks, such as daring each other to touch Boo's front door. When Boo was a teenager his father had locked him in the house as punishment for a minor offense, and town gossip maintains that Boo is insane. After the characters are introduced and the setting is established, the major subject of the novel is revealed. Scout learns that her father is defending Tom Robinson, a black man accused of raping Mayella Ewell, a poor, white, young woman. Atticus explains to Scout that although the town may not support him in his efforts to acquit Tom, he looks forward to defending Tom. During the trial, it becomes clear that Bob Ewell, Mayella's father, is guilty of assaulting her and has accused Tom of raping her in order to evade accusation for his own assault of Mayella. Even though Atticus provides substantial evidence that Tom is innocent, the jury convicts him. Although Atticus tries to assure Tom that he will win an appeal, Tom is shot while attempting to escape from prison. One sub-plot of the novel concerns Boo, who places treats in a tree for Jem and Scout and who eventually protects Scout by killing Bob Ewell, who poses a threat to Scout in his determination to seek revenge upon Atticus for publicly accusing him of assaulting Mayella.

Early in the novel, readers are introduced to some of the residents of Maycomb, many of whom represent stereotypical residents of small southern towns. Scout implies the narrow-minded attitudes of Maycomb County residents as she explains why their perspectives never change:

> Although Maycomb was ignored during the War between the States, Reconstruction rule and economic ruin forced the town to grow. It grew inward. New people so rarely settled there, the same families married the same families until the members of the community looked faintly alike. Occasionally someone would return from Montgomery or Mobile with an outsider, but the result caused only a ripple in the quiet stream of family resemblance. Things were more or less the same during my early years.

There was indeed a caste system in Maycomb, but to my mind it worked this way: the older citizens, the present generation of people who had lived side by side for years and years, were utterly predictable to one another: they took for granted attitudes, character shadings, even gestures, as having been repeated in each generation and refined by time. Thus the dicta No Crawford Minds His Own Business, Every Third Merriweather Is Morbid, The Truth Is Not in the Delafields, All the Bufords Walk Like That, were simply guides to daily living: never take a check from a Delafield without a discreet call to the bank; Miss Maudie Atkinson's shoulder stoops because she was a Buford; if Mrs. Grace Merriweather sips gin out of Lydia E. Pinkham bottles it's nothing unusual—her mother did the same.

Indicative of Maycomb County's propensity to stereotype and generalize, individuals are categorized as members of specific families. Maycomb's habit of defining individuals as members of particular families demonstrates the narrow-mindedness of the residents of Maycomb and helps to explain why Atticus' defense of Tom causes Jem and Scout ridicule from the community. Although most people in Maycomb attribute to members of a family the same characteristics, Lee clearly denies such generalizations, for Atticus and Aunt Alexandra, his sister, do not have much in common. While Atticus adheres to strong internal ethics and does not try to conform to the expectations of others, Aunt Alexandra is obsessed with her social position and tries to impress others.

Lee establishes the residents of Maycomb and their attitudes to provide a foil for the attitudes and the morals that Atticus teaches his children. The first eight chapters of the novel describe various actions of the people who live in Maycomb. The main plot development involving Tom's pending trial is not introduced until chapter nine. Tom's case serves to illustrate the bigoted attitude of Maycomb and the community's unwillingness to change their views. Atticus proves Tom's innocence, but the community knows that to admit Bob Ewell is lying, they must believe a black man instead of a white man. Maycomb residents are not willing to forgo stereotypical notions of African Americans even when evidence clearly contradicts their views based on race and social hierarchy.

Two poor families, the Ewells and the Cunninghams, are introduced early in the novel. This provides the character development necessary for readers to judge future events. On the first day of school, during class, a "cootie" jumps out of Burris Ewell's hair, and he is described as unclean and ill-mannered. His father, Bob Ewell, is described as "contentious." When Burris curses at Miss Caroline Fisher, the teacher, a fellow student comments that Burris does not represent Maycomb's manners. Like the Ewells, the Cunninghams are part of the poor white social class; however, the Cunninghams are portrayed as honest, proud, and independent. Scout recounts the time Mr. Cunningham paid legal fees to Atticus with commodities such as wood and turnip greens. When she tells Miss Caroline that another student, Walter (Walter Cunningham Jr.), is a Cunningham, she assumes Miss Caroline understands the social standings of the individual members of the community.

Near the end of the novel, Atticus tells Jem that one of the Cunninghams (presumably Walter Cunningham Sr.) served on Tom's jury and originally argued for an acquittal. Atticus explains that although Tom was doomed to a guilty verdict, he nevertheless achieved a minor success because it took the jury a few hours rather than the expected few minutes to convict Tom. Even though Cunningham eventually votes for a guilty verdict, Atticus explains to Jem that he was the only man on the jury who expressed some uncertainty about Tom's guilt. Atticus notices a slight progress in the community's attitude because at least one man feels disturbed about convicting an innocent

black man. He tells Jem, "There's a faint difference between a man who's going to convict and a man who's a little disturbed in his mind." In the end, as Atticus explains to Jem, "something came between them and reason," and Tom was convicted. Discrimination transcends rational thought, a lesson Atticus tries to teach his children.

The Finches' neighbor, Miss Maudie Atkinson, also recognizes the slight progress made by Atticus in his fight against ethnic discrimination. After Tom's conviction, Miss Maudie tells Jem and Scout that she sat on her porch during the trial, waiting to hear the verdict. While waiting, she reminded herself that Atticus "won't win, he can't win, but he's the only man in these parts who can keep a jury out so long in a case like that." She implies that because the jury did not convict Tom without at least some discussion, Atticus helps Maycomb make "a step—it's just a baby-step, but it's a step." Miss Maudie also tells Aunt Alexandra that by choosing Atticus to defend Tom, Maycomb pays Atticus the highest compliment of trusting him to make morally virtuous decisions. Aunt Alexandra wonders which segment of the Maycomb County community Miss Maudie thinks is trusting Atticus, and Miss Maudie says, "The handful of people in this town who say that fair play is not marked White Only; the handful of people who say a fair trial is for everybody."

As a result of the trial, Atticus may have inspired Miss Maudie to fight for ethnic equality. Earlier in the novel, Miss Maudie says rumors that Boo is crazy are "three-fourths colored folks and one-fourth S. Crawford." Throughout *To Kill a Mockingbird*, Stephanie Crawford is portrayed as the stereotypical small-town gossip, and Miss Maudie's accusations about her support the idea expounded in the novel that gossip is malicious; however, Miss Maudie also blames the "colored folks" for the rumors about Boo, an accusation clearly contradicted in the novel. Early in the novel, Miss

Maudie recognizes the hypocrisy of Mr. Nathan Radley's "foot washing Baptist" views that enable him to justify his discrimination against his brother Boo. Ironically, when she accuses colored folks of gossiping about Boo, she simultaneously exposes her own hypocrisy. Even though she supports Atticus at the end of the novel, it is not clear whether she is completely free from her own biased views.

Throughout the novel, Scout becomes increasingly aware that discrimination is wrong. At the end of the novel, she realizes she misjudged Boo, and after Tom's trial, she appears more socially conscious. Near the beginning of the novel, she and Jem build a snowman. Jem builds the base of the snowman out of dirt, and Scout says, "I ain't ever heard of a nigger snowman." Apparently, Atticus has not yet convinced her that the word "nigger" is a derogatory term she should not use. Later, when Scout's classmate, Cecil Jacobs, ridicules her because her "Daddy defends niggers," Scout asks Atticus if Cecil's comment is true. "Don't say nigger, Scout. That's common," Atticus tells her. Atticus explains to Scout that defending Tom is a privilege, not a punishment. Atticus believes that moral righteousness begins in the home, and that if he does not practice morality, he cannot teach it to his children. He also says, "simply by the nature of the work, every lawyer gets at least one case in his lifetime that affects him personally. This one's mine, I guess." Atticus gains Scout's respect, and the next day she goes to school and feels noble in her decision to walk away from Cecil's ridicule. Even though Cecil calls her a coward, she feels noble for not avenging the insult against Atticus, for she knows she betrays Atticus if she fights Cecil.

When Bob Ewell is on the witness stand during the trial, Scout observes that "all the little man on the witness stand had that made him any better than his nearest neighbors was, that if scrubbed with lye soap in very hot water, his skin was white." Scout's comment is loaded with obvious racially biased overtones. Later, when the prosecuting attorney, Mr. Gilmer, cross-examines Tom, Scout goes outside the courthouse with Dill. Dill tells Scout that Atticus did not humiliate and condescend to Mayella, the victim, the way Mr. Gilmer humiliates and condescends to Tom. Scout replies, "Well, Dill, after all he's just a Negro." To Scout's comment, Dill replies, "I don't care one speck. It ain't right, somehow it ain't right to do 'em that way. Hasn't anybody got any business talkin' like that—it just makes me sick." The discussion between Dill and Scout suggests that because Dill does not live in Maycomb County, he is not infected with its "usual disease."

Prior to meeting Mr. Dolphus Raymond, a wealthy member of the community, Scout believes the rumors that suggest he is an evil man who drinks too much. Mr. Raymond explains to Scout and Dill that he only pretends to walk around in a drunken stupor. Mr. Raymond says that when Dill gets older, he won't "cry about the simple hell people give other people—without even thinking. Cry about the hell white people give colored folks, without even stopping to think that they're people, too." Immediately after Mr. Raymond's comment, Scout says, "Atticus says cheatin' a colored man is ten times worse than cheatin' a white man. . . . Says it's the worst thing you can do." During this scene Scout begins to understand and change her biased views against both Tom and Mr. Raymond. Because she realizes that Mr. Raymond is not the man Maycomb invents, she also begins to understand that Maycomb's views about others are incorrect as well.

After Scout meets Mr. Raymond, she returns to the courthouse and hears the portion of Atticus' speech that epitomizes the faulty reasoning of racism. Atticus says that Tom's conviction rests on the faulty assumption

that *all* Negroes lie, that *all* Negroes are basically immoral beings, that *all* Negro men are not to be trusted around our women, an assumption one associates with the minds of their caliber.

Which, gentlemen, we know is in itself a lie as black as Tom Robinson's skin, a lie I do not have to point out to you. You know the truth, and the truth is this: some Negroes lie, some Negroes are immoral, some Negro men are not to be trusted around women—black or white. But this is a truth that applies to the human race and to no particular race of men. There is not a person in this courtroom who has never told a lie, who has never done an immoral thing, and there is no man living who has never looked upon a woman without desire.

Here, Atticus presents the underlying issue in Tom's trial. Since Scout respects Atticus' views, she learns more than the jury about Tom's case.

SYMBOLISM AND PRINCIPAL THEMES

The title *To Kill a Mockingbird* alludes to the atrocities of bias against Tom and Boo. The significance of killing a mockingbird is first explained in chapter ten, immediately following the chapter that introduces Tom. Here, Scout recalls that when Atticus gave air rifles to Jem and her, he instructed, "I'd rather you shot at tin cans in the back yard, but I know you'll go after birds. Shoot all the bluejays you want, if you can hit 'em, but remember it's a sin to kill a mockingbird." Furthermore, Scout recalls, "That was the only time I ever heard Atticus say it was a sin to do something. . . ." Scout asks Miss Maudie about shooting mockingbirds, and she tells Scout that Atticus is correct: "Mockingbirds don't do one thing but make music for us to enjoy. They don't eat up people's gardens, don't nest in corncribs, they don't do one thing but sing their hearts out for us. That's why it's a sin to kill a mockingbird." Atticus and Miss Maudie's points are that it is morally wrong to harm those who do not harm others. The inequity of cruelty is one of the major motifs depicted in *To Kill a Mockingbird,* for Atticus teaches his children not to be cruel.

Symbolic of mockingbirds, Tom and Boo are unjustly persecuted. Like the mockingbirds whom Miss Maudie describes as singing for the pleasure of others, Tom brings pleasure to Mayella, whom he has befriended by providing companionship and help with chores. Ironically, Tom's good deeds toward Mayella eventually lead to his death. Mr. Underwood, the publisher of the local newspaper, prints an editorial in which he says that killing Tom is like "the senseless slaughter of songbirds by hunters and children. . . ," explicitly comparing the innocent Tom's death with the death of innocent mockingbirds. Scout realizes that although it may appear that Tom is given a fair trial, "in the secret court of men's hearts Atticus had no case. Tom was a dead man the minute Mayella Ewell opened her mouth." Scout understands that, despite evidence of the contrary, the white jury will believe a white person instead of a black person.

Boo is also a symbolic mockingbird, but unlike Tom, who is completely innocent, Boo is imprisoned for committing a minor offense. According to legend, when he was a youth, Boo and a group of other teenaged boys committed a childhood prank that entailed locking a courthouse official in an outhouse. Instead of attending the state school where the other boys were sent, Boo's father kept him locked inside his own house. The town rumor is that after fifteen years locked in the house, Boo stabbed his father in the leg with a pair of scissors. For this crime, Boo was locked in the basement of the courthouse. Obviously, the punishment is excessive, making Boo a victim of his father's injustice. When Boo's father dies, Boo's brother, Nathan, comes to live with him and leaves him locked indoors.

Just as Tom performs kind deeds for Mayella, Boo performs kind deeds for Jem and Scout. When Jem, Scout, and Dill run from the Radley house because they see the shadow of a man wearing a hat, Jem leaves his pants on a fence.

When Jem goes back for his "breeches," he finds them "folded across the fence . . . like they were expectin' me." Later, Jem realizes that Boo had sewn his pants and left them on the fence.

The gifts Boo places in the tree's knothole for Jem and Scout epitomize his generosity. Scout and Jem write a letter to thank whoever gives the prizes to them, but when they go to put the letter in the knothole, they discover the hole has been filled with cement. Jem asks Nathan if he filled up the hole and Nathan says, "Yes. . . . You plug 'em with cement when they're sick." After confining Boo to the courthouse basement, his father says it is "all right to shut him up," much like Nathan's closing of the tree's knothole.

In addition to more subtle comparisons of Boo with a mockingbird, Scout makes the comparison directly. Atticus does not hesitate to protect Boo, who risks his life to protect Scout and Jem. Heck Tate, Maycomb's sheriff, dramatically demonstrates how Bob Ewell stabbed himself, by holding a knife to himself and falling. When Atticus assures Scout that Bob Ewell killed himself, Scout understands fully the morality at work. She says to prosecute Boo would "be sort of like shootin' a mockingbird, wouldn't it?" Obviously, Scout understands the broad implications of Atticus' explanation that it is a sin to kill mockingbirds.

Throughout the novel, the protection of innocent people parallels the protection of mockingbirds. In the novel the term "cover-up" is often used to describe protecting another person or oneself. After the dispersal of the mob that appears at the courthouse to harass Atticus, he realizes that Mr. Underwood has sat in a nearby building with a shotgun, witnessing the entire disturbance. As Atticus is leaving, Mr. Underwood looks down from the window and says, "Had you covered all the time, Atticus." At the end of the novel, Scout feels embarrassed when

she is introduced to Boo because she has played pranks on him and mocked him. Not wanting Boo to know she is embarrassed, she runs to Jem's bed and says, "I tried to cover up by covering Jem up." Boo protects Jem when he sews Jem's pants and leaves them on the fence. When Miss Maudie's house burns during the middle of a cold night, the neighbors evacuate their homes because they fear the fire may spread. Scout shivers in the cold, and Boo puts a blanket around her. Boo literally covers up Scout and both literally and metaphorically comforts her. Atticus says, "Someday, maybe, Scout can thank [Boo] for covering her up." Not wanting Nathan or the neighbors to know Boo left his house, Atticus suggests they should not tell anyone Boo covered up Scout or that Boo sewed Jem's pants. He tells Jem they should keep it "to ourselves." Scout repays Boo for covering her when at the end of the novel she covers for him by pretending that she believes that Boo did not kill Bob Ewell. Ironically, throughout *To Kill a Mockingbird*, people who perform moral deeds frequently need protection. Most of the people in Maycomb County live according to a morality that does not protect the innocent, making it necessary for the innocent people to defend each other. Frequently, the virtuous have to violate Maycomb County's unethical rules to protect themselves and others from injustice.

Witnessing the events involving Tom and Boo becomes an initiation experience for Scout, Jem, and Dill. The adult Scout, Jean Louise Finch, narrates *To Kill a Mockingbird*, telling the story many years after the events have occurred. Events are told from the adult Jean Louise's point of view, but the younger Jean Louise, Scout, is a character in the novel. Scout, Jem, and Dill lose their innocence when they witness the atrocity of discrimination against Tom and when they understand their own and Maycomb County's discrimination against Boo.

The development of the children is often denoted by overt references to their ages and other signifiers that mark the passage of time. For the framework of *To Kill a Mockingbird,* Lee uses a circular structure that involves time. The opening and closing passages of the novel work as enveloping frames for the narrative proper. The novel opens with a reference to Scout and Jem's age: "When he was nearly thirteen, my brother Jem got his arm badly broken at the elbow. . . . Jem, who was four years my senior. . . ." After establishing a reference point that involves time, the narrator briefly summarizes events that have occurred generations before this reference point. The narrative quickly moves forward from a description of the time in which Simon Finch, the first of Scout's ancestors to come to America, had settled at Finch's Landing, which is near Maycomb County, to when Scout was two years old.

As in the enveloping frame that begins the novel, in the narrative proper, Lee often refers to the children's ages to establish a new time frame. She allows readers to follow easily the chronology of events and simultaneously draws attention to the children's development. The narrative proper begins, "When I was almost six and Jem was nearly ten, our summertime boundaries . . . ," establishing the chronologically ordered sequence of the narrative proper and defining textual boundaries. Readers assume the plot will reveal events that lead to Jem's broken arm, three years later. When Jem and Scout first meet Dill, Jem asks him his age. Dill says, "Goin' on seven. . . . I'm little but I'm old."

Frequently, references to the children's ages mark the beginning of a new chapter, establishing a new setting and a forward movement in time. Chapter three opens during the beginning of Scout's first year of school. Jem prevents her from fighting Walter because she is "bigger'n he is." Scout argues, "He's as old as you, nearly." The second paragraph of chapter seven marks a new school year: "School started. The second grade . . ." The beginning of the chapter establishes Scout's promotion from the first to the second grade. On the first page of chapter eight, Scout says that Mrs. Radley has died, and Atticus visits her family. Jem tells Scout to ask Atticus if he saw Boo when he visited the Radleys, and Scout says, "You ask him, you're the oldest."

Chapter nine establishes Scout's further development. Scout, who is still in the second grade, is ridiculed by Cecil. She says that Cecil's mockery marks "the beginning of a rather thin time for Jem and me. . . . I was far too old and too big for such childish things." Chapter eleven begins: "When we were small, Jem and I confined our activities to the southern neighborhood, but when I was well into the second grade . . . ," thus establishing Jem and Scout's development further. On the first page of chapter thirteen, Aunt Alexandra says, "Jem's growing up now and you are too." On the first page of chapter fourteen, Scout says, "As we grew older, Jem and I thought it generous to allow Atticus thirty minutes to himself after supper." The second paragraph of chapter fifteen establishes that "Jem had outgrown the treehouse." In the third paragraph of chapter sixteen, Scout says, "for once he [Jem] didn't remind me that people nearly nine years old didn't do things like that."

Chapters seventeen through twenty-five, in which Tom's trial and death are portrayed, reveal the children's awareness of ethnic discrimination. Their psychological maturation is portrayed indirectly as the result of their increased awareness of injustice. Chapter twenty-six begins with another reference to time: "School started. . . . Jem was in the seventh grade . . . I was now in the third grade." Jem and Scout enter their new class ranks with a deeper understanding of humanity than they had in earlier school grades.

References are also made to the ages of other characters, suggesting that the human life span is an important issue in *To Kill a Mockingbird.* Chapter ten begins, "Atticus was feeble: he was nearly fifty. . . . I asked him why he was so old. . . . He was much older than the parents of our school contemporaries." Atticus is "too old" to play football with Jem, "too old" to fight Bob Ewell, and his "age was beginning to show." When Mrs. Dubose is introduced, Scout recalls, "She was very old." In the second paragraph of chapter nineteen, readers are told that "Tom was twenty-five years of age." When Judge Taylor asks Mayella her age, she answers, "Nineteen-and-a-half."

The missionary circle, a Maycomb County women's Christian group, listens to Mrs. Merriweather, a member of the group, describe the Mrunas, an African tribe. "They put the women out in huts when their time came . . . they subjected children to terrible ordeals when they were thirteen." Mrs. Merriweather's report includes a description of the Mruna custom of outcasting the elderly. Her report also alludes to the Mruna initiation rituals. Although it is not physically painful, Jem is going through an initiation into his social system, an initiation that is emotionally painful. Obviously, the characters' ages are significant. References to the ages of characters not only offer readers more description of the people involved, but they also help develop the maturation theme throughout the novel.

While many chapters open with references to physical ages, other chapters begin with references to particular times, intervals marked by seasons, months, or hours. Moreover, these time qualifiers are frequently combined, serving both to establish a new time period and to emphasize time as motif. The narrative proper begins in the first chapter, when Scout tells how old she and Jem are when the unfolding events occur. In the first paragraph of the narrative proper, "summertime" and "days" are used as time references. The first paragraph of chapter four includes the following words used to denote time: "first," "end," "year," "years," "time," "twelve years." Chapter eight opens, "For reasons unfathomable to the most experienced prophets in Maycomb County, autumn turned to winter that year. We had two weeks of the coldest weather since 1885." The second paragraph of chapter twenty-four begins, "August was on the brink of September." On the first pages of chapters twenty-five, twenty-seven, and twenty-eight, references are made to specific months of the year: "September had come," "By the middle of October," and "The weather was unusually warm for the last day of October." The maturation theme is developed more acutely with Lee's portrayal of the changing seasons, symbolic of growth.

Lee often acknowledges Jem and Scout's or only Scout's particular grade in school, frequently near the beginning of a chapter. For example, chapter twenty-six opens, "School started. . . . Jem was in the seventh grade. . . . I was now in the third grade." Scout's first school year ends at the beginning of chapter four, and again references to the passing of time abound. The second paragraph of chapter four begins, "As the year passed, [I was] released from school thirty minutes before Jem, who had to stay until three o'clock." Attending school brings about changes in Scout's attitude, suggesting she experiences social growth. Although Scout is too young to understand what causes her social change, she recognizes that her "first year of school had wrought a great change" in her relationship with Calpurnia, the black woman who cooks for the Finches. Instead of provoking Calpurnia as she does before she starts school, Scout tries to appease her. Consequently, Scout notices that Calpurnia's attitude toward her mellows.

Summer is frequently associated with Dill's visits to Maycomb, tying the experience theme to the changing of seasons. When Dill visits, adventures occur, adventures that develop into experiences that lead to maturity. The second paragraph of the narrative proper begins, "That was the summer Dill came to us," establishing a clear time frame for the beginning of the plot. Chapter two opens: "Dill left us early in September. . . . We saw him off on the five o'clock bus. . . . I would be starting to school in a week. . . . Hours of wintertime had found me in the treehouse. . . ." The first two paragraphs of chapter two mark the end of summer and the end of Scout and Jem's initial adventures with Dill. Scout begins school, an event that marks a new experience and a new season. Early in chapter four, the ending of the school year is marked by the beginning of summer and the prospect of Dill's return: "Summer was on the way. . . . Summer was our best season . . . summer was Dill. The authorities released us early the last day of school." Dill's departure marks the end of the summer following Scout's first year of school. The first sentence of chapter six orients readers to another new time frame: "This was his [Dill's] last night in Maycomb. . . . We'll see him next summer." A reference to the moon, symbolic of time change, occurs on the first page of chapter six: "A gigantic moon was rising behind Miss Maudie's pecan trees." In the beginning of part two, on the first page of chapter twelve, Dill is associated with summer again: "Summer came and Dill was not there." The first paragraph of chapter twenty-four ends with the word "today," and the second paragraph begins, "August was on the brink of September. Dill would be leaving for Meridian tomorrow; today . . ."

At the end of *To Kill a Mockingbird,* Scout summarizes the experiences that she, Dill, and Jem share throughout the novel. In her summary, she uses the most acute portrayal of seasons as representative of the changes in time frames. Returning from walking Boo home, Scout thinks:

> Daylight . . . in my mind, the night faded. It was daytime and the neighborhood was busy. . . . It was summertime, and two children scampered down toward a man approaching in the distance. The man waved, and the children raced each other to him.
>
> It was still summertime, and the children came closer. A boy trudged down the sidewalk dragging a fishingpole behind him. A man stood waiting with his hands on his hips. Summertime, and his children played in the front yard with their friend, enacting a strange little drama of their own invention.
>
> It was fall, and his children fought on the sidewalk in front of Mrs. Dubose's. The boy helped his sister to her feet, and they made their way home. Fall, and his children trotted to and fro around the corner, the day's woes and triumphs on their faces. They stopped at an oak tree, delighted, puzzled, apprehensive.
>
> Winter, and his children shivered at the front gate, silhouetted against a blazing house. Winter, and a man walked into the street, dropped his glasses, and shot a dog.
>
> Summer, and he watched his children's heart break. Autumn again, and Boo's children needed him.

In this passage, as in earlier passages that identify particular seasons, seasons represent the children's emotional growth, maturity that results from childhood experiences.

Near the end of the novel, Scout understands she will become a woman someday. She says, "There was no doubt about it, I must soon enter this world, where on its surface fragrant ladies rocked slowly, fanned gently, and drank cool water." Scout will physically join the world of the missionary circle; however, because of Atticus' influence, she seems unlikely to absorb the conventional values the women in Aunt Alexandra's social groups share. Scout recognizes that she is "more at home in my father's world" and describes the moral virtues of people such as Atticus, Tate, and Jem, who are not hypocrites. At the very end of the novel, Scout recognizes a major lesson her father teaches: "Atticus was right. One time he said you never really know a man until you stand in his shoes and walk around in them. Just standing on the Radley porch was enough." Indeed, the experiences Scout summarizes have taught her the major message Atticus proclaims throughout the novel.

Scout, Jem, and Dill are portrayed as belonging to various developmental stages of life, with an emphasis on their maturation. After Tom's death, Scout notices Jem enters another stage of development. Jem prevents Scout from mashing a bug, and she says that his new compassion for insects must reflect "a part of the stage he was going through." Jem tells her she should not kill the insect because it is not hurting anyone, and she says, "Reckon you're at the stage now where you don't kill flies and mosquitoes. . . ." Jem is mature enough to understand the parallels between killing innocent insects, killing mockingbirds, and killing Tom. Atticus points out to Uncle Jack that Scout's use of bad language reflects her particular developmental stage. Atticus says, "Bad language is a stage all children go through, and it dies with time when they learn they're not attracting attention with it. Jem's getting older and she follows his example a good bit now." Atticus recognizes that Jem is in a later developmental stage than Scout, and he knows Jem sets examples for Scout. Although not explicitly referred to as a developmental stage, when Dill runs away from home and comes to stay with the Finches because he feels he cannot communicate with his parents, he acts in a manner specific to a childhood stage. Jem tells Atticus that Dill has come to their house, even though Scout tells Jem that he is a traitor for informing Atticus that Dill has run away from home. Scout is one year younger than Dill, and Dill and Scout are clearly in a earlier developmental stage that Jem, who, of the three children, responds to Dill's running away from home in the most mature manner.

While Scout and Dill's developments are portrayed primarily as a story about childhood experience, Jem is portrayed as maturing from one developmental stage to a more mature developmental stage as an initiation story patterned in the *bildungsroman* tradition. The two major divisions in the novel begin with references to Jem's age. Part one opens telling us Jem "was nearly thirteen"; part two opens, "Jem was twelve." The novel is structured according to Jem's age, making initiation a major motif of the work both structurally and thematically. On the first page of chapter twelve, Calpurnia notes that Jem is "just about Mister Jem now. . . . Mister Jem's growin' up," and Scout says that "I ain't big enough" to beat up Jem. Shortly after Jem realizes that Boo has sewn his pants, he acts moodily, suggesting he feels remorse for having played pranks on Boo. He tells Scout that "it was not until one reached the sixth grade that one learned anything of value."

When Jem discovers that the knothole in which Boo places gifts has been filled with cement, he remains "deep in thought" and cries later that evening. Jem is mature enough to understand that Boo has been denied the pleasure of giving gifts to Jem and Scout. A few chapters after he empathizes with Boo, Jem destroys Mrs. Dubose's camellia bush, an incident that occurs "the day after Jem's twelfth birthday." It is an immature act, but Jem does it out of rage because he understands the significance of the insults about Atticus defending Tom that Mrs. Dubose shouts at Scout and Jem. Scout does not react to her insults as strongly as Jem because she is too young to understand the magnitude of Mrs. Dubose's offense. Jem is mature enough to understand Mrs. Dubose's mockery, yet not mature enough to react against her in an adult fashion.

After establishing Jem's age as twelve at the beginning of part two, Scout says:

> He was difficult to live with, inconsistent, moody. His appetite was appalling, and he told me so many times to stop pestering him. . . . Overnight, it seemed, Jem had acquired an alien set of values

and was trying to impose them on me. . . . In addition to Jem's newly developed characteristics, he had acquired a maddening air of wisdom.

Obviously, Jem is in the process of abandoning the childhood world in which Scout still firmly belongs.

Jem even changes physically, the most tangible evidence of his maturation. Scout observes that Jem's hair changes, wondering when it will "look like a man's" hair. She notices "his eyebrows were becoming heavier," and "a new slimness about his body. He was growing taller." Jem shows Scout the hair on his chest and tells her that he also has hair under his arms. The physical descriptions are given immediately prior to Jem's advice to Scout that she should not let Aunt Alexandra irritate her. Scout recalls that not too long ago, Jem advised her not to irritate Aunt Alexandra. That earlier time, Jem's advice involved telling Scout to respect her elders, an attitude suggesting that Jem then believed that people should obey rules without considering their validity. The change in Jem's advice reflects his more mature attitude, his understanding that Aunt Alexandra tends to irritate others, and his growing inclination toward a belief in situational, internal ethics.

Miss Maudie notices Jem's development from a child to an adolescent, for she bakes only two small cakes, one for Scout and one for Dill. She cuts a slice from the big cake, the adults' cake, for Jem. On the other hand, while serving Jem a slice from the adults' cake, she tells Jem that he is "not old enough to appreciate what I said" about Atticus' defense of Tom. Jem recognizes that he is too old to eat from the children's cake, yet not old enough to understand adult concepts completely, for he "was staring at his half-eaten cake. 'It's like bein' a caterpillar in a cocoon, that's what it is,' he says." The half-eaten cake symbolizes Jem's state of feeling half adult, half child. Of course, the caterpillar symbolizes that although Jem has not completely entered the adult world, he clearly no longer is a child.

During the developmental stage in which Jem stands neither as child nor adult, he seems to reach a high level of maturity. Immediately after the trial, Jem faces Atticus and says, "It ain't right, Atticus." Whereas Atticus is the adult who distinguishes right from wrong, Jem now assumes the role of a person mature and wise enough to recognize inequity. Jem, however, is only mature enough to understand the injustice done to Tom and depends on Atticus' wisdom to explain why Tom is convicted. He asks Atticus, "How could they do it, how could they?" Miss Stephanie and Aunt Alexandra gossip about Tom's death in front of Jem, agreeing that "he's old enough to listen." After Tom's death, even Aunt Alexandra recognizes that Jem is mature enough to hear adult conversations.

Shortly after Tom's conviction, Jem assumes adult responsibilities. Typically, parents express concern for their children's safety, but in an act of role reversal, Jem says that he fears Bob Ewell will harm Atticus because Atticus interrogated him on the witness stand during Tom's trial. Also, Jem escorts Scout to the Halloween party because Atticus is unable to attend, thus assuming Atticus' paternal role. While walking to the pageant, Jem treats Scout paternally. Among other fatherly deeds, he carries her costume, helps her when she trips, provides her with instructions for walking in the dark, and gives her money. Of course, Jem's most protective and paternal action toward Scout is his attempt to protect her from Bob Ewell, who has threatened to hurt Scout in order to gain revenge against Atticus.

Dill and Scout will progress in the same manner as Jem, eventually becoming adults who share Atticus' morals and compassion for humanity. References to time, seasons, months, and ages are used to reveal the children's maturation; moreover, the tree, a traditional symbol for growth, becomes one of most powerful symbols in *To Kill a Mockingbird,* representing, among other ideas, the development of

Scout, Dill, and Jem. The children's development consists of both physical and psychological growth, including heightened awareness of ethics and morals, the most significant involving their discovery that bias is unethical. Interestingly enough, the title *To Kill a Mockingbird* suggests the opposite: it becomes an imperative statement that instructs us not to kill mockingbirds.

CRITICAL RECEPTION

Primarily because *To Kill a Mockingbird* made a strong statement against ethnic bias when it was first published during the civil rights struggle, it initially received mostly favorable critical acclaim. While most reviewers praised the novel unequivocally, others presented mixed reviews. Most of the critics giving mixed reviews offered general praise for the novel, citing only minor problems in a story they otherwise considered outstanding. Almost all reviewers agreed that Lee portrays the South superbly, but they disagreed about the point of view and plot.

In favorable reviews of *To Kill a Mockingbird,* Herbert Mitgang, Katherine Gauss Jackson, and the reviewers for *Time* and the *Times Literary Supplement* compare *To Kill a Mockingbird* with the Carson McCullers classic *The Member of the Wedding.* Reviewers Leo R. Ward, Keith Waterhouse, and Malcolm Bradbury commend Lee's portrayal of the South. Ward, in *Commonweal,* notes the quiet and complete introduction the novel gives "of seeing and feeling and acting in the Deep South." Waterhouse, a British novelist writing for the *New Statesman,* says, "Lee does well what so many American writers do appallingly: she paints a true and lively picture of life in an American small town. And she gives freshness to a stock situation." *Punch* reviewer Bradbury notes that Lee understands the American South and succeeds as a novelist because of her ability to confirm that "intel-

ligence and decency are positive values." Richard Sullivan and Robert W. Henderson cite the narration and point of view among the novel's strengths. The reviewer for *The New Yorker* comments, "Lee is a skilled, unpretentious, and totally ingenuous writer who slides unconcernedly and irresistibly back and forth between being sentimental, tough, melodramatic, acute, and funny. . . ." The critic for *Kirkus Review* says the incidents portrayed in the novel blend together to provide "an attractive starchiness that keeps this southern picture pert and provocative." James B. McMillan, writing for the *Alabama Review,* notes that Lee combines point of view, characterization, and plot to create a "fine, fresh novel."

While many initial reviewers praised *To Kill a Mockingbird* without reservation, others offered mixed opinions. Some initial reviewers faulted the novel for its problematical point of view or its melodramatic plot. Others regarded the point of view as one of the novel's strengths, while citing other weaknesses. Among critics who offered mixed opinions, most agreed that one of the novel's strengths is Lee's ability to portray the South realistically. For example, Granville Hicks, in a review published in *Saturday Review,* notes that although Lee shows impressive "insight into Southern mores," the conclusion of the novel is "melodramatic" and the point of view problematical. Similarly, *Atlantic Monthly* reviewer Phoebe Adams suggests that the first-person narration from the point of view of a young girl with an educated adult prose style is "frankly and completely impossible." On the other hand, in his review for the *San Francisco Chronicle,* George McMichael praises Lee's use of point of view. He says, "Best of all, Harper Lee has wisely and effectively employed the piercing accuracy of a child's unalloyed vision of the adult world."

Mixed admiration for *To Kill a Mockingbird* was expressed in reviews published in the *New York Times Book Review,* the *Christian Century,*

Booklist, and the *New York Herald Tribune Book Review.* Frank H. Lyell, writing for the *New York Times Book Review,* asserts that "Lee writes with gentle affection, rich humor and deep understanding of small-town family life in Alabama." He praises the "quietly and logically" developed plot and commends Lee's "level-headed plea for interracial understanding." However, Lyell also notes that Scout's style often "has a processed, homogenized, impersonal flatness quite out of keeping with the narrator's gay, impulsive approach to life in youth." In the *Christian Century,* Elizabeth Lee Haselden says *To Kill a Mockingbird* "is a good book, not a great one; an interesting book, but not a compelling one." She says Lee's novel does not allow readers to identify with characters, fails to portray characters' inner struggles, and does not depict compassion for humanity. Conversely, the *Booklist* reviewer concludes, "Despite a melodramatic climax and traces of sermonizing, the characters and locale are depicted with insight and a rare blend of wit and compassion." Harding Lemay, writing for the *New York Herald Tribune Book Review,* says that Lee fails in her attempt to merge "two dominant themes of contemporary Southern fiction—the recollection of childhood among village eccentrics and the spirit-corroding shame of the civilized white Southerner in the treatment of the Negro." He adds that although her attempt to blend these two themes "fails to produce a novel of stature, or even of original insight, it does provide an exercise in easy, graceful writing and some genuinely moving and mildly humorous excursions into the transient world of childhood. . . . The two worlds remain solitary in spite of Miss Lee's grace of writing and honorable decency of intent."

Some initial reviewers of *To Kill a Mockingbird* included an interview with Harper Lee along with their assessments. Early interviews with Lee appeared in reviews published in *Newsweek, Life,* and the *Christian Science Monitor.* The *Newsweek* reviewer says Lee describes herself as a "'journeyman writer' by trade and a 'Whig' by private conviction," noting that Lee says she believes "'in Catholic emancipation and the repeal of the Corn Laws.'" In *Life* the reviewer asserts, "Despite a solemn theme, Miss Lee writes with a wry compassion that makes her novel soar." In the companion interview, Lee stands in a courthouse in Monroeville, Alabama, and describes the courthouse: "The trial was a composite of all trials in the world—some in the South. But the courthouse was this one. My father's a lawyer, so I grew up in this room, and mostly I watched him from here." In this interview, Lee also acknowledges that her own father is the model for Atticus: "My father is one of the few men I've known who has genuine humility, and it lends him to natural dignity. He has absolutely no ego drive, and so he is one of the most beloved men in this part of the state." Joseph Deitch, writing for the *Christian Science Monitor,* refers to Lee as "a gifted new American writer." He quotes Lee as saying that a writer "should write about what he knows and write truthfully." In addition, Lee reveals in the interview, "Writing is the only thing that has made me completely happy. . . . Writing is the hardest thing in the world for me." Deitch says Lee's favorite writers include Charles Lamb, Robert Louis Stevenson, Jane Austen, and Thomas Love Peacock.

Following its initial success, *To Kill a Mockingbird* has come to be seen as a literary masterpiece. In 1963 Popular Library published a paperback edition of *To Kill a Mockingbird,* which reached its ninety-fourth printing in 1974. As of 1982 *To Kill a Mockingbird* had sold over fifteen million copies, and the novel has never been out of print since its original publication in 1960. In 1995 a thirty-fifth anniversary edition of *To Kill a Mockingbird* was published by HarperCollins. That edition was widely reviewed, and in some ways sparked opportunities for the novel to be reevaluated from a more recent perspective. Although the thirty-fifth anniversary edition was marketed as including a foreword by Harper Lee, it consists merely of a paragraph, in which she says "I loathe Introductions."

Although it is considered a classic American novel, *To Kill a Mockingbird* has received very little attention from literary critics. Of the seven or eight critical studies concerned with this novel, many consider it in broader contexts. Jill May's essay, "Censors As Critics: *To Kill a Mockingbird* As a Case Study," uses *To Kill a Mockingbird* as a case study of censorship of young adult literature, and her essay is as much about that as it is about *To Kill a Mockingbird*. Likewise, in "Discovering Theme and Structure in the Novel," Edgar H. Schuster uses *To Kill a Mockingbird* to illustrate broader points. He discusses ways to identify literary elements such as theme and character in novels, analyzing *To Kill a Mockingbird* to demonstrate effective ways to interpret literature.

Fred Erisman, in "Literature and Place: Varieties of Regional Experience" and "The Romantic Regionalism of Harper Lee," discusses *To Kill a Mockingbird* as a regional novel. In "Literature and Place," he analyzes Sarah Orne Jewett's *The Country of the Pointed Firs,* Robert Penn Warren's *All the King's Men,* and *To Kill a Mockingbird* to exemplify how regional literature invites readers to appreciate the ways that setting affects plot. In "The Romantic Regionalism of Harper Lee," Erisman focuses on *To Kill a Mockingbird,* describing Maycomb as "a microcosm of the South" and arguing that "Lee presents an Emersonian view of Southern romanticism."

Some critics compare *To Kill a Mockingbird* with other literary works. In "*To Kill a Mockingbird*: Harper Lee's Tragic Vision," R. A. Dave suggests that the characters in *To Kill a Mockingbird* constitute a microcosm of humanity, illustrating similarities between the ways in which Lee and Walt Whitman portray the mockingbird myth. In his essay review "Keen Scalpel on Racial Ills," Edwin Bruell compares *To Kill a Mockingbird* with Alan Paton's *Cry, the Beloved Country.* He says both novels offer insights into contemporary social and personal problems, citing the "powers of compassion and understanding" as major similarities between the works. In "*Store* and *Mockingbird*: Two Pulitzer Novels about Alabama," William T. Going compares *To Kill a Mockingbird* with T. S. Stribling's *The Store.* He notes similarities such as locale, characterization, symbolism, and theme and concludes that *To Kill a Mockingbird* reflects Alabama history more acutely than Stribling's historical novel.

In "The Secret Courts of Men's Hearts: Code and Law in Harper Lee's *To Kill a Mockingbird*," Claudia Durst Johnson examines ways *To Kill a Mockingbird* portrays "the law in its broadest sense: familial, communal, and regional codes. . . . The codes that motivate people in this Alabama community promote destruction as often as they prevent it."

Johnson's seminal 1994 study, *To Kill a Mockingbird: Threatening Boundaries,* the first full-length treatment of the novel, analyzes it from a historical perspective. Johnson points out the significance of events such as the Great Depression and the famous Scottsboro trial that occurred during the 1930s, the setting Lee uses in *To Kill a Mockingbird.* She also discusses the significance of the violence surrounding desegregation in Alabama and across the nation during the civil rights movement. "Readings," the second section of *To Kill a Mockingbird: Threatening Boundaries,* consists of five analytical readings of the novel. While all of the chapters provide innovative insights about *To Kill a Mockingbird,* chapter five, "The Gothic Tradition," is arguably the strongest chapter in her book. In it Johnson places *To Kill a Mockingbird* in the Gothic tradition, examining issues such as architecture, family, sexual roles, and taboos.

Johnson also wrote a second full-length study of *To Kill a Mockingbird*, called *Understanding To Kill a Mockingbird: A Student Casebook to Issues, Sources, and Documents* (1994). This study includes historical documents such as court transcripts, newspaper articles, interviews, and excerpts from literary texts. Johnson provides commentary and analysis, placing *To Kill a Mockingbird* in its historical context. She also explains developments such as the Scottsboro trials and the civil rights movement; she considers it relevant to know the social climate at the time of *To Kill a Mockingbird* and at the time in which Lee wrote the novel.

As Johnson notes, much of the criticism of *To Kill a Mockingbird* has been written by those in the legal profession, practicing lawyers and professors of law. Much of their criticism concerns the legal ramifications of segregation and the personal ethical code Atticus represents as a practicing attorney. Frequently, attorneys cite Atticus as a moral hero, a role model for an attorney who practices a professional code of ethics. For example, professors of law Thomas L. Shaffer and Timothy L. Hall offer full-length essays about Atticus Finch. In "The Moral Theology of Atticus Finch," Shaffer attributes Atticus' heroism to his respect for truth. He argues that Atticus reflects truth through personal, political, professional, and courageous deeds. In "Moral Character, the Practice of Law, and Legal Education," Hall discusses "ethics in terms of character," presenting Atticus as a lawyer-hero who exhibits a strong sense of character and uses his personal character to morally resolve ethical dilemmas.

Later criticism of *To Kill a Mockingbird* written primarily from a legal perspective is collected in a 1994 special issue of *Alabama Law Review* entitled *Symposium: To Kill a Mockingbird*. The special issue includes an introduction and five essays written by scholars of law and Johnson's "Without Tradition and within Reason: Judge Horton and Atticus Finch in Court," an essay written from a literary perspective. The issue also contains a commentary that discusses late-twentieth-century segregation issues in Alabama's institutions of higher education.

In "Without Tradition and within Reason: Judge Horton and Atticus Finch in Court," Johnson argues that the use of reason by Atticus runs against convention in a society typically motivated by emotion, and that as a result, Atticus' character reflects a level of civilization that is more refined than that of other members of his community. She attributes Atticus' display of refined civilization to his use of reason to make decisions, his ability to acknowledge the written word, and his strength to resist community values.

Johnson's article begins with a brief overview of the continuing debate concerning Atticus' status as a heroic role model for lawyers. "Finch," she notes, "the small-town lawyer who had been accused by his townspeople in 1935 of excessive love of black people, was in 1992 being charged with racism." Johnson explains that in his 1992 article published in *Legal Times*, Monroe H. Freedman "challenged the wisdom of upholding Harper Lee's character as a moral lawyer and a worthy model on the grounds that Finch operated as a state legislator and community leader in a segregated society." Legal scholars defended Atticus in subsequent articles published in *Legal Times*. Responding to the debate initiated by his essay, Freedman acknowledges in a second essay published in the same journal that the controversy started when he suggested that Atticus excuses the Ku Klux Klan and mobs and defends Tom out of "an elitist sense of noblesse oblige" instead of human compassion or genuine concern for social justice.

Freedman continues the debate in an article in the *Alabama Law Review*'s *Symposium: To Kill a Mockingbird,* titled "Atticus Finch—Right and Wrong." Freedman denies accusations that he applies "presentism" (applying present standards to the past) in his criticism of Atticus. Freedman maintains that he examines Atticus according to the standards of the setting of *To Kill a Mockingbird,* thus judging Atticus from moral standards relevant in the 1930s instead of looking at Atticus from a contemporary point of view. Freedman also demonstrates how some critics rewrite *To Kill a Mockingbird* "to create a mythologized hero." Freedman's most interesting argument against Atticus as hero involves an examination of Atticus' statement to Scout that he hoped Scout would never have to take a case such as defending Tom. Arguing against Timothy Hall's attack on Freedman's earlier assessment of Atticus, Freedman notes, "Forget about 'working on the front lines for the NAACP.' Here is a man who does not voluntarily use his legal training and skills—not once, ever—to make the slightest change in the pervasive social injustice of his own town."

Symposium: To Kill a Mockingbird also includes articles by professors of law Bryan K. Fair, Thomas L. Shaffer, and Calvin Woodard. In "Using Parrots to Kill Mockingbirds: Yet Another Racial Prosecution and Wrongful Conviction in Maycomb," Fair relates Tom's conviction to contemporary convictions of innocent people, focusing on racial discrimination in today's criminal justice system. Shaffer, in "Growing Up Good in Maycomb," examines *To Kill a Mockingbird* in terms of the virtues Scout, Jem, and Dill learn as children, relating moral lessons to faith and religion. And in "Listening to the Mockingbird," Woodard assesses *To Kill a Mockingbird* in terms of the South's justice system and examines the mockingbird as a symbol for the region.

One of the most astute essays written about *To Kill a Mockingbird,* Teresa Godwin Phelps's "The Margins of Maycomb: A Rereading of *To Kill a Mockingbird,*" offers "marginalization" as another social disease in Maycomb. Questioning the underlying ethical message of *To Kill a Mockingbird,* she analyzes Jem's "four kinds of folks." Phelps points out the stereotypical roles Calpurnia and Tom represent and raises questions concerning Maycomb's acceptance of the Ewells not attending school and the community's willingness to ignore the abuse and poverty inflicted upon the Ewell children. Phelps says the novel reinforces the status quo of its characters' distinct social classes, discouraging them from questioning their social standing.

Subsequently, the *Southern Quarterly* presented three essays about the novel: Carolyn Jones's "Atticus Finch and the Mad Dog: Harper Lee's *To Kill a Mockingbird,*" Diann L. Baecker's "Telling It in Black and White: The Importance of the Africanist Presence in *To Kill a Mockingbird,*" and Laurie Champion's "'When You Finally See Them': The Unconquered Eye in *To Kill a Mockingbird.*" Jones demonstrates that "the call for critical reflection on the self, the rule of compassion, and the law that it is a sin to kill a mockingbird," three elements of Atticus' heroism, are revealed during "scenes in which he confronts mad dogs." Baecker focuses on the African American characters in *To Kill a Mockingbird* to examine both the ways in which the novel depicts race-related issues and the ways in which the identity of all the residents of Maycomb County are influenced by an Africanist presence. Champion argues that *To Kill a Mockingbird* is primarily a story about perception, the ability to see clearly. She points out ways that various types of eye and light imagery form a structure that supports Emersonian transcendentalism.

A film adaptation of *To Kill a Mockingbird,* directed by Robert Mulligan and written by Horton Foote, was released in 1962. It was nominated for eight Academy Awards, receiving three: best actor for Gregory Peck's performance as Atticus, best screenplay for Horton Foote's adaptation, and best black-and-white art direction-set direction.

Initially, the film adaptation received favorable reviews. Many reviewers praised Mulligan's direction of the film, Foote's adaptation of the novel, and the actors' performances, especially Gregory Peck's performance as Atticus. Other reviewers commented on the film's success in capturing the mood and atmosphere of the novel. Most reviewers found the film's point of view successful, while others regarded it as disruptive to the film's theme. The *Variety* reviewer calls *To Kill a Mockingbird* a "major film achievement. . . . A significant, captivating and memorable picture that ranks with the best in recent years." On the other hand, the *Time* critic says that the film "has nothing very profound to say about the South and its problems. Sometimes, in fact, its side-porch sociology is simply fatuous: the Negro is just too goody-good to be true, and Peck, though he is generally excellent, lays it on a bit thick at times—he seems to imagine himself the Abe Lincoln of Alabama."

Two critical studies that compare the film to the novel appeared in the 1990s. Colin Nicholson, writing in *Cinema and Fiction,* discusses ways the film adaptation creates Scout's point of view and creates visual images to compress ideas expressed in the novel. Nicholson says that both novel and film are "sentimentalised narratives," which help "to create the conditions for a tidily 'happy' ending, an ending that further suggests that problems have been raised which the authoress, and following her the director Robert Mulligan, cannot finally resolve." Nicholson concludes that the happy ending of both book and film ignores the severity of "serious moral and social issues." Instead, it works to suppress the very truth the entire plot has exposed. Another recent comparison of the novel with the film is Dean Shakelford's "The Female Voice in *To Kill a Mockingbird*: Narrative Strategies in Film and Novel." Shakelford argues that the film adaptation compromises the emphasis the novel places on Scout's "growing

distance from her provincial Southern society and her identification with her father, a symbol of the empowered."

Despite the unusual fact that Harper Lee has published only one novel, *To Kill a Mockingbird* has remained commercially successful for over forty years and has received remarkable critical acclaim in terms of awards and fame for the author. Perhaps Lee has always had a single message to offer readers, and as she says in the foreword to the thirty-fifth anniversary edition of the novel, "*Mockingbird* still says what it has to say. . . ." When an author has written a novel that impacts readers for over forty years and that continues to disseminate the author's message, perhaps there is no need to continue to write.

Selected Bibliography

WORKS OF HARPER LEE
To Kill a Mockingbird. New York: J.B. Lippincott, 1960.
"Love—In Other Words." *Vogue,* April 15, 1961, pp. 64–65.
"Christmas to Me." *McCall's,* December 1961, p. 63.

CRITICAL AND BIOGRAPHICAL STUDIES

BOOKS
Bloom, Harold, ed. *To Kill a Mockingbird.* Modern Critical Interpretations Series. Philadelphia: Chelsea House, 1999.
Johnson, Claudia Durst. *To Kill a Mockingbird: Threatening Boundaries.* New York: Twayne, 1994.
———. *Understanding To Kill a Mockingbird: A Student Casebook to Issues, Sources, and Documents.* Westport, Conn.: Greenwood, 1994.

ARTICLES OR BOOK SECTIONS
Altman, Dorothy Jewell. "Harper Lee." In *Dictionary of Literary Biography: American Novelists Since*

World War I. Second Series. Volume 6. Edited by James E. Kibler Jr. Detroit: Gale, 1980. Pp. 180-183.

Ayer, John D. "Narrative in the Moral Theology of Tom Shaffer." *Journal of Legal Education* 40:173–193 (1990).

Baecker, Diann L. "Telling It in Black and White: The Importance of the Africanist Presence in *To Kill a Mockingbird*." *Southern Quarterly* 36:124–132 (spring 1998).

Barge, R. Mason. "Fictional Characters, Fictional Ethics." *Legal Times,* March 9, 1992, p. 23.

Blackwell, Louise. "Harper Lee." In *Southern Writers: A Biographical Dictionary*. Edited by Joseph M. Flora and Louis D. Rubin Jr. Baton Rouge: Louisiana State University Press, 1979. Pp. 276–277.

Champion, Laurie. "'When You Finally See Them': The Unconquered Eye in *To Kill a Mockingbird*." *Southern Quarterly* 37:127–136 (winter 1999).

D'Alemberte, Talbot. "Remembering Atticus Finch's *Pro Bono* Legacy." *Legal Times,* April 6, 1992, p. 26.

Dave, R. A. "*To Kill a Mockingbird*: Harper Lee's Tragic Vision." In *Indian Studies in American Fiction*. Edited by M. K. Naik. Dharwar, India: Karnatak University, 1974. Pp. 311–323.

Erisman, Fred. "The Romantic Regionalism of Harper Lee." *Alabama Review* 26:122–136 (April 1973).

———. "Literature and Place: Varieties of Regional Experience." *Journal of Regional Cultures* 1, no. 2:144–153 (1981).

Fair, Bryan K. "Using Parrots to Kill Mockingbirds: Yet Another Racial Prosecution and Wrongful Conviction in Maycomb." *Alabama Law Review* 45:403–472 (1994).

Ford, Nick Aaron. "Battle of the Books: A Critical Survey of Significant Books by and about Negroes Published in 1960." *Phylon* 22:119–134 (summer 1961).

Freedman, Monroe H. "Atticus Finch, Esq., R.I.P." *Legal Times,* February 24, 1992, pp. 20–21.

———. "Finch: The Lawyer Mythologized." *Legal Times,* May 18, 1992, p. 25.

———. "Atticus Finch—Right and Wrong." *Alabama Law Review* 45:473–482 (1994).

Going, William T. "*Store* and *Mockingbird*: Two Pulitzer Novels about Alabama." In his *Essays on Alabama Literature*. Birmingham: University of Alabama Press, 1975. Pp. 9–31.

Hall, Timothy L. "Moral Character, the Practice of Law, and Legal Education." *Mississippi Law Journal* 60:511–554 (1990).

Hoff, Timothy. "Influences on Harper Lee: An Introduction to the Symposium." *Alabama Law Review* 45:389–401 (1994).

Johnson, Claudia Durst. "The Secret Courts of Men's Hearts: Code and Law in Harper Lee's *To Kill a Mockingbird*." *Studies in American Fiction* 2:129–139 (1991).

———. "Without Tradition and within Reason: Judge Horton and Atticus Finch in Court." *Alabama Law Review* 45:483–510 (1994).

Jones, Carolyn. "Atticus Finch and the Mad Dog: Harper Lee's *To Kill a Mockingbird*." *Southern Quarterly* 34:53–63 (summer 1996).

Margolick, David. "To Attack a Lawyer in *To Kill a Mockingbird*: An Iconoclast Takes Aim at a Hero." *New York Times,* February 28, 1992, p. B7.

May, Jill P. "Censors As Critics: *To Kill a Mockingbird* As a Case Study." In *Cross-Culturalism in Children's Literature: Selected Papers from the Children's Literature Association*. Edited by Susan R. Gannon and Ruth Anne Thompson. New York: Pace University Press, 1988. Pp. 91–95.

McDonald. W. U. "Harper Lee's College Writings." *American Notes and Queries* 6:131–132 (May 1968).

Nicholson, Colin. "Hollywood and Race: *To Kill a Mockingbird*." In *Cinema and Fiction: New Modes of Adapting, 1950–1990*. Edited by John Orr and Colin Nicholson. Edinburgh: Edinburgh University Press, 1992. Pp. 151–159.

Phelps, Teresa Godwin. "The Margins of Maycomb: A Rereading of *To Kill a Mockingbird*." *Alabama Law Review* 45:511–530 (1994).

Schuster, Edgar H. "Discovering Theme and Structure in the Novel." *English Journal* 52:506–511 (October 1963).

Shaffer, Thomas L. "The Moral Theology of Atticus Finch." *University of Pittsburgh Law Review* 42:181–224 (1981).

———."Christian Lawyer Stories and American Legal Ethics." *Mercer Law Review* 33:877–901 (1982).

————. "Growing Up Good in Maycomb." *Alabama Law Review* 45:531–561 (1994).

Shakelford, Dean. "The Female Voice in *To Kill a Mockingbird*: Narrative Strategies in Film and Novel." *Mississippi Quarterly* 50:101–113 (winter 1996–1997).

Woodard, Calvin. "Listening to the Mockingbird." *Alabama Law Review* 45:563–584 (1994).

SELECTED REVIEWS

"About Life and Little Girls." *Time*, August 1, 1960, pp. 70–71.

Adams, Phoebe. "Summer Reading." *Atlantic Monthly*, August 1960, pp. 98–99.

"Boo Radley Comes Out." *Time*, February 22, 1963, p. 93.

Bradbury, Malcolm. "New Fiction." *Punch*, October 26, 1960, pp. 611–612.

Bruell, Edwin. "Keen Scalpel on Racial Ills." *English Journal* 53:658–661 (1964).

Crowther, Bosley. "*To Kill a Mockingbird*." *New York Times*, February 15, 1963, p. 10.

Deitch, Joseph. "Harper Lee: Novelist of the South." *Christian Science Monitor*, October 3, 1961, p. 6.

"Fiction: Three to Make Ready." *Kirkus Review*, May 1, 1960, p. 360.

"First Novel: Mocking Bird Call." *Newsweek*, January 9, 1961, p. 83.

Haselden, Elizabeth Lee. "We Aren't in It." *Christian Century*, May 24, 1961, p. 655.

Henderson, Robert W. "Lee, Harper. *To Kill a Mockingbird*." *School Library Journal*, May 15, 1960, p. 44.

Hicks, Granville. "Three at the Outset." *Saturday Review*, July 23, 1960, pp. 15–16.

Jackson, Katherine Gauss. "Books in Brief." *Harper's Magazine*, August, 1960, p. 101.

Kauffmann, Stanley. "Good Feelings and Bad Spirits." *New Republic*, February 2, 1963, pp. 30–31.

"Lee, Harper." *Booklist*, September 1, 1960, p. 23.

Lemay, Harding. "Children Play; Adults Betray." *New York Herald Tribune Book Review*, July 10, 1960, p. 5.

"Literary Laurels for a Novice." *Life*, May 26, 1961, pp. 78A–78B.

Lyell, Frank H. "One-Taxi Town." *New York Times Book Review*, July 10, 1960, pp. 5, 18.

McMichael, George. "*To Kill a Mockingbird*." *San Francisco Chronicle*, July 31, 1960, p. 23.

McMillan, James B. "*To Kill a Mockingbird*." *Alabama Review*, July 1961, p. 233.

Mitgang, Herbert. "Books of the Times." *New York Times*, July 13, 1960, p. 33.

"Sheer Purgatory." *Times Literary Supplement*, October 28, 1960, p. 697.

Sullivan, Richard. "Engrossing First Novel of Rare Excellence." *Chicago Sunday Tribune Magazine of Books*, July 17, 1960, p. 15.

"*To Kill a Mockingbird*." *The New Yorker*, September 10, 1960, pp. 203–204.

"*To Kill a Mockingbird*." *Variety*, December 12, 1962, p. 6.

Ward, Leo R. "*To Kill a Mockingbird*." *Commonweal*, December 9, 1960, p. 289.

Waterhouse, Keith. "New Novels." *New Statesman*, October 15, 1960, p. 580.

FILM BASED ON THE WORK OF HARPER LEE

To Kill a Mockingbird. Screenplay by Horton Foote. Directed by Robert Mulligan. Universal Pictures, 1962.

—*LAURIE CHAMPION*

Bobbie Ann Mason

1940–

*I*N THE PREFACE to her 1975 book of criticism *The Girl Sleuth: A Feminist Guide,* Bobbie Ann Mason writes of Vladimir Nabokov's famous literary creation, "Lolita must have read Nancy Drew and the Bobbsey Twins. We all did." This statement could be the philosophers' stone for Mason. According to her, the girl detective series books teach that "the American dream is the desire to absorb, know, and conquer everything, to go everywhere and to do it all." No one can escape such messages of popular culture, not even twelve-year-old Lolita, whose illicit sexual relationship sets her adrift from American culture. For Mason, Nancy Drew and the Bobbsey Twins offer a world that is ultimately knowable and manageable. That is why these books end so happily. "Sloppy emotions and meaningful moralities are shunned in favor of zestful pursuits. . . . The books themselves are fictional nests, escapes from the cruel real landscape," Mason writes. The characters in Mason's own fiction are deeply influenced by the works of popular culture and use them as maps to achieving the "good life," only to find their markings inadequate.

Consequently, like Nabokov's *Lolita,* Mason's fiction exposes the faults and destructiveness of American culture, while her characters attempt to control and impose meaning on an existence characterized by irrationality. Much like Nabokov, the subject of her graduate dissertation, Mason casts her eye on a world in which people are as emotionally marginalized as Humbert Humbert and Lolita, and live within a world where fantasy never adds up with reality. In *Shiloh and Other Stories* a man leaves his wife to become a cowboy out West; in *Spence + Lila* a woman whose identity is centered on her

feminine capacity to nurture is stricken with breast cancer and must have a mastectomy; *In Country* has a seventeen-year-old girl going on a quest to solve the mystery of her dead father only to learn that he was just a kid not much different from herself. But unlike Nabokov, whose characters are privileged—educated and upper class—Mason's stories contain distinctly rural, working-class people who are attempting to adjust to an increasingly modernized South. As they come up against the intoxicating allure of American consumerism and the kind of smart, sophisticated representation portrayed in magazines, books, and the movies, they find that the tools and skills they learned on the farm do not translate to the world at large. These people have learned to take what comes— drought, insects, cattle disease, dead dogs—but off the farm they discover that they must now take their lives into their own hands. Many of Mason's characters are unable to do this. Instead, they are left dangling between the security of their familiar lives and the desire for change and independence that is marketed so appealingly. Ironically, these characters, perhaps foolishly, find hope amid this indeterminacy, in their very survival.

BACKGROUND

The theme of accommodation was bred in Mason from an early age. She was born May 1, 1940, in Mayfield, Kentucky. Her parents, Wilburn Arnett and Christianna (Lee) Mason, believed that their firstborn would be a boy and did not have an alternate girl's name picked out; they named their daughter Bobbie Ann, a feminization of Robert. At the time, Mason's parents did not have a home of their own. They worked and lived on her paternal grandparents' small farm, which was located along a critical artery of rural America. Mason describes its location in her memoir *Clear Springs* (1999):

> The farm is one field to the east of the railroad track that used to connect New Orleans with Chicago. The track runs beside Highway 45, an old U.S. route that unites Chicago with Mobile, Alabama. Highway 45 goes past Camp Beauregard, a Civil War encampment and cemetery, and leads toward Shiloh, a Civil War battlefield, and continues to Tupelo, Mississippi, where Elvis Presley was born.

When looking at a map of this region east of the Mississippi River, it is worth noting that Highway 45 runs parallel to the more famous Highway 49, where at the crossroads of Highway 61, legend has it that Robert Johnson sold his soul to the devil and became the greatest blues guitarist ever. Highway 49, which is west of 45, has become a familiar monument for African Americans and aficionados of the blues. For Mason, Highway 45 plays an equally essential cultural role because it crosses the important historical locations that defined the world in which she grew up and which she came to write about.

The Mason family is the product of western Kentucky and the inspiration for Mason's fiction, with respect not only to the geography of her stories but also to their characters, plots, and themes. Samuel Mason, her great-great-great-grandfather, was one of the Cumberland pioneers. Four of his ten children settled on Panther Creek, at Clear Springs, Kentucky, when it was part of the Jackson Purchase. All of Mason's immediate family are from this area. In 1920 Mason's grandfather, Robert Lee Mason, bought a fifty-three-acre farm for five thousand dollars, eight miles down the road from the original family homestead, and moved there with his new wife, Ethel (Arnett) Mason, and young son Wilburn. The land was cleared and fertile, and only a mile from the town of Mayfield. Wilburn was an only child, and the expectation was that he would remain on the farm as an adult and inherit it when Robert and Ethel died. In May 1936, when Christy Lee, Bobbie Ann's mother, was not yet seventeen, she eloped with Wilburn and moved to the family farm. Christy had grown up with an aunt after her mother died in childbirth and her father abandoned the family. Marrying Wilburn was both an escape from the difficult circumstances she had known and an opportunity to create the kind of family life that she had missed as a child. The marriage took Wilburn's parents by surprise, but they quickly included Christy into the family. Four years later Bobbie Ann, their first grandchild, was born.

Farm life in western Kentucky at this time was harsh. Mason's family made their own clothes, grew nearly everything they ate, and lived an essentially isolated life. Bobbie Ann spent her first years playing alone or with grownups. The outside world, however, began to make inroads into their rural life when Bobbie Ann was still very young. Her father was drafted into the U.S. Navy during World War II and spent much of the war loading ammunition in the belly of a destroyer in the Pacific theater. This introduction to a larger, more diverse world interested Bobbie Ann's mother more than it did her father, who was happy to return to farming after the war. Christy Mason got a glimpse of a more exciting and sophisticated life through her husband's war experience. In the introduction to *Clear Springs* Mason writes about her mother, "If she'd had the chance, she might have busted out to the big city years before I dreamed of doing so. . . . But she remained caught in a household dominated by my cautious, worried, tight-stitched grandmother."

Nevertheless, Christy Mason's desires did not go unnoticed by her daughter, who grew up intensely sensitive to the divide between her life on the farm and life in town. Her first contact with the "big city" was nearby May-field, population eight thousand, when after the war her mother took a job at the Merit Clothing Company as a seamstress. Bobbie Ann and her younger sister, Janice Kaye, who was born in 1944, were enrolled in a day care for Merit workers. Bobbie Ann felt out of place with the town children because she had had little exposure to other kids, and eventually she and Janice returned home to their grandmother's care. Kindergarten, too, was an unsuitable environment for her: Bobbie Ann lasted a day. The following year, she attended the Cuba School along the Tennessee border, where she encountered a gifted first-grade teacher who stressed creativity and the arts, even transforming the class into a marching band for the high school basketball team. "I played tissue-and-comb. . . . Mama made me a majorette outfit—a satin skirt with a gold-trimmed weskit, and a tall hat with tassels," Mason writes in *Clear Springs*. In this kind of environment Mason thrived and got a taste of the exotic world outside her family's fifty-three acres. By the end of the year her teacher recommended she skip a grade.

The next year, however, Mason was subjected to the arbitrariness of this larger world when two weeks into the school year her principal announced a new rule—no grade skipping. In spite of her disappointment at being put back into second grade, Mason enjoyed school, recalling in her memoir that she "delighted in the new books each fall, the intricate puzzles of words and numbers in the workbooks, the surprises from the larger world that appeared in the *Weekly Reader.*" Her parents encouraged her interests. "Somehow, my family allowed dreams—even those they'd given up for themselves. They prized learning. Mama had quit school in the tenth grade, but she always regretted it, and she wanted me to get an education so I could have the chances she missed. Daddy was always reading paperbacks. . . . Granny . . . had wanted to be a teacher." Still, Mason was

confused by the contradictions presented by school, as when a grammar book instructed against use of the word "ain't," a word that everyone she knew used—including her teacher. When the books that her parents and teachers prized suggested that her world was wrong, Mason began to develop a sense that her life was somehow deficient.

Around this time Mason became enamored with the girl detective series, including the Bobbsey Twins and Nancy Drew. These books fueled Mason's feelings about the inadequacy of her home and the magnificence of the outside world. In *The Girl Sleuth* Mason describes this period:

> I read them all: Nancy Drew, Judy Bolton, Beverly Gray, Kay Tracey, the Dana Girls, Vicki Barr, Cherry Ames. I was an authority on each of them. But they were also *my* authorities, the source of my dreams. The ideas I derived from them and carried to adulthood (you only have to imagine me lugging these dreams on the train to New York City when I left college) were that the art of living was to be like a girl detective and that New York was the center of the universe. A girl detective was a sort of tourist out to see the world and solve its mysteries, bringing back souvenirs of the solutions, little picture postcard proofs of adventure, the real life.

During these years Mason was often sick and whiled away many a day reading. In the span of her tenth and eleventh years she had three stays in the hospital for pneumonia and a middle-ear infection. These times were like vacations for her. She was allowed to have ice cream and milkshakes every day. Her parents bought her books to read. She found the farm dreary and ordinary, while the hospital seemed remarkable. She loved being sick. It was her first opportunity to be taken out of her home and into "the real life."

In her early adolescence Mason became interested in writing. She wanted to write books just like the mystery books she loved. In *Clear*

Springs she recalls her early thoughts about writing.

> I asked Granny, "How does a writer think up a whole book? Does she just make it up as she goes along?" Granny allowed as how Laura Lee Hope, the Bobbsey author, got the plot all worked out in her mind beforehand. She made plans. She didn't just write the first thing that came into her head. I studied on this idea for some time. . . . I didn't follow Granny's advice. . . . The pleasure of writing was discovering what might pop out of my mind unbidden.

Her first stories involved a pair of detective twins, Sue and Jean Carson, whose father was a famous detective. "Jean was grimly mature, with a boyfriend," Mason explains in *Clear Springs*. "She wanted to be a nurse. Sue, the more ambitious twin, was more like me; she wanted to be an airline hostess." Mason pursued her interest in writing in other ways as well. In the back of a magazine she saw an ad for an institute called the Famous Writers' School and mailed in the aptitude test. The school replied that she had great talent and should sign up for their correspondence course immediately. Mason innocently took this response as a confirmation of her ambition to become a writer, but she could not afford to take the course. After several letters from the school, Mason replied that she didn't have the money to become a famous writer. She was only eleven years old. The correspondence school stopped writing.

Life on the farm involved backbreaking work and endurance. Mason did not want to be like her grandmother, hulling beans in a hot kitchen when she was fifty years old. She listened to the radio and imagined a life not haunted by crop failure. She yearned for an existence not so dependent on nature. For her, farmers did not take initiative. They reacted to whatever presented itself. Consequently, she and her family ate each meal as if they didn't know where their next meal might come from. This type of life was especially hard on women. Mason wit-

nessed her grandmother suffer from severe depression over the years. Granny Mason was hospitalized in Memphis in 1950 and committed to the state mental hospital for a period of several months in the early 1960s. Her grandmother received shock treatments and was prescribed Thorazine for the rest of her life.

Mason's mother, on the other hand, was torn between her sense of responsibility toward the farm and her own interests. In the summer before Bobbie Ann entered high school in 1954 and two years after her sister LaNelle was born, Mason's mother was offered an opportunity to manage a restaurant on the highway across the train tracks. Both enjoyed the experience immensely, but it was short lived. Mason's grandfather made it clear that her mother had to give up the restaurant job. "I thought I saw a little fire go out of her then. . . . But my own flame was burning brighter. I had had a glimpse of life outside the farm, and I wanted it." In high school, after Mason's brother Don was born in 1957, she and her mother became active fans of a Kentucky singing quartet, the Hilltoppers. The two of them traveled all over the region to Hilltoppers performances. Mason became the president of the Hilltoppers fan club and wrote the bimonthly newsletter. She was paid ten dollars a week for expenses and fifteen dollars a week in salary. She saved all of the money for college. As her attention moved beyond the farm, she also worked as a soda jerk at the Rexall drugstore in Mayfield and continued to read widely.

COLLEGE AND WRITING CAREER

When it came time for college, Mason initially wanted to apply to Duke University to study parapsychology with Dr. J. B. Rhine, but her English teacher, who considered this program an unacceptable academic pursuit, refused to write her a letter of recommendation. Instead, Mason entered the University of Kentucky as a math major, as her teacher insisted. Once in college, however, Mason's academic interests proved wide ranging. "Indiscriminately I sampled etymology, existentialism, the theater of the absurd, Shakespeare, French symbolists, realism, naturalism, logic, Jack Kerouac. Dada and surrealism followed my Rimbaud period," she writes in *Clear Springs*. She ended up an English major and wrote for the campus newspaper. In the summers she wrote the society column in the local Mayfield newspaper. During one semester at college, *Life* magazine hired her to write a weekly promotional column for the student newspaper that previewed the coming week's issue of the magazine. All of these efforts were meant to help her reach her goal of moving to the big city and the sophisticated world that she had first read about in the Bobbsey Twins and Nancy Drew. "I figured I would go to a city. I would not work outdoors. I would work in an office or a store. I couldn't imagine that anybody would pay me to read or write the kind of books I cared about," she writes in *Clear Springs*. In spite of these feelings, Mason's college experience centered increasingly around her creative writing classes, where she distinguished herself in fiction writing. Her writing professor, Robert Hazel, was a figure in the mode of F. Scott Fitzgerald, whom Mason described in her memoir as her "literary hero" at that time. Hazel lectured his students on the nobility of the literary vocation and the purity of the artistic endeavor. Though this appealed to Mason, she did not feel that her rural background equipped her for such a pursuit.

After graduating from the University of Kentucky in 1962, Mason traveled to New York City and checked in to the Taft Hotel in Times Square. In her first weeks in New York, she applied for a number of secretarial, clerical, and writing jobs. She ultimately landed a job as a writer for Ideal Publishing Company, which published the fan magazines *Movie Stars, Movie Life,* and *TV Star Parade.* During the next year

Mason wrote features on such teen stars as Fabian, Annette Funicello, and Ann-Margret, and discovered how commercial publishing functioned. She recalls in *Clear Springs*:

> The editor would buy a set of photos from a traveling salesman. The pictures could be of young TV stars Susan and Dan walking on the beach together. The editor would dream up an idea about these pictures, based on something in the news— their new TV series, perhaps. Then she would write a provocative headline: "The Scary Secret Susan Shared with Dan on a Lonely Beach." The art department would create a layout, placing the photos and sizing them, with the provocative headline, space for subheads, and a block of lines designated for the copy—usually only a couple of paragraphs.

Mason was only marginally interested in her work. In fact, she didn't want to work at all. She wanted to study literature at New York University or Columbia. In her free time she would write. "I filled up pages with Thomas Wolfe–inspired meditations," she recalled in *Clear Springs*. While working at these fan magazines, however, Mason found herself attracted to the letters that came into the office from readers all over the country. Mason found their naïveté unsettling. "Most of the letters were from people like those back home, people I knew who watched images on the screen and often confused the actor and the role. . . . I could see stories in these letters, like something I imagined writing one day—stories of disappointment and desire."

At the beginning of 1963 Mason renewed her friendship with her former creative writing teacher Robert Hazel, who had taken a teaching position at New York University. Through Hazel, she met many poets and artists and attended lectures on such topics as French painting and Federico García Lorca at the New School. Still, she felt a certain discomfort with the literary world. As she wrote in *Clear Springs*: "At my job, I was exploiting the kind of people who romanticized the movies, but Bob Hazel exalted the very kind of people who loved the movies and TV—farm folks, laborers, working people—while condemning what they felt. My parents were at home watching *Gunsmoke*. Bob Hazel would have sneered." As a result, Mason's sense of herself as a writer was full of conflict because she felt hurt personally by Hazel's ironic stance. She wanted the life of an author, but the subjects she felt compelled to write about were perceived as inappropriate by people she respected. At this time even though she was only beginning to come to terms with this friction, she was slowly moving toward a solution. First, she decided to relocate. "I knew I shouldn't be building a career based on TV stars. . . . [I]t was trees I needed." She enrolled at Harpur College in Binghamton, New York, for graduate studies in English. The year at Harpur was tense and uncomfortable. The school was small and its faculty was made up of traditionalist professors with whom Mason could not establish a dialogue. Because she felt out of place, she transferred to the larger, more diverse University of Connecticut at the end of the year. This environment posed other problems, as she recalled in *Clear Springs*:

In Connecticut, I found myself wading into a maelstrom. Everything—even the worth of literary study—was in question. The growing youth rebellion against middle-class values gathered me up and whipped me around like a wind ripping into sheets on the clothesline. I had aspired my whole life toward such amenities as central heat and running hot water, and suddenly they were the wrong goals.

The more Mason waded into graduate studies, the more she realized how large the divide was between her country ways and aspirations and what sophisticated intellectuals prized. She was repeatedly derided by her peers as "middle class" for such trivial crimes as shopping with Green Stamps. Fortunately, these conflicts hardened Mason's resolve instead of shattering

it. She had learned growing up on a farm how to endure through drought, pestilence, and illness as well as how to survive as an outsider. This stubborn trait led her to return to what she knew—the land. Even her dissertation, on a novel famous for its high aestheticism and literary artifice, Mason called "an exercise in seeing the landscape." In a 1991 interview with Bonnie Lyons and Bill Oliver, Mason described her affinity with Nabokov:

I think his extraordinary childhood allowed him to indulge a child's way of seeing that's up close and particular. What I admire about Nabokov's work are his details and his seizing on the tiniest things. He thought these were the essence of reality, things you wouldn't notice necessarily. Nabokov said that the literal meaning is so much more important than what people find underlying it. He was much more interested in the pattern of the butterfly wing than in anything about symbolism or life on the wing or whatever butterflies are supposed to represent.

This renewed sensitivity to the particular paralleled Mason's involvement in the back-to-the-land movement. When she married her classmate Roger Rawlings on April 12, 1969, they set up house on a farm in rural Connecticut. Describing this time, Mason writes in *Clear Springs*, "I was ready to hoe." She also began working on a novel. "It was a story about the Beatles, in experimental, psychedelic, Donald Barthelme–inspired prose. A VW busload of hippies travel cross-country from California to see the Beatles at Shea Stadium. It was Jack Kerouac in reverse, through a mirror fractured by sound. Actually, it was sillier than that. But I was hopeful." The novel was never finished, but Mason did receive her doctorate in literature in 1972. Her dissertation was published in 1974 as *Nabokov's Garden: A Guide to Ada*.

With Mason's return to the land came a desire to go home to Kentucky, but neither she nor Rawlings could find teaching jobs there. Instead, they settled in northern Pennsylvania, where Mason became an assistant professor in the English department of Mansfield State College. She and Rawlings bought an old farm and planted a garden. Mason began writing another novel and completed her critical study of juvenile literature, *The Girl Sleuth*. This study was a labor of love for Mason because after spending most of the previous decade studying canonical literature she was finally able to return to a type of writing that nurtured her earliest interest in books. In this study she examined a side of herself that went unrecognized by graduate schools. In her introduction to the book Mason explained its significance:

> Histories of children's literature have systematically ignored the existence of series books. Critics of children's literature have dismissed them as bad habits. Elementary education textbooks used in colleges have made only passing reference to them. [Reading and analyzing these books] acknowledges significant textures of our real (if sometimes embarassedly hidden) lives.

With this book Mason went public with her affirmation of popular culture, her belief that there is literary and critical value to the books that have traditionally been shunned by academic and literary critics. This sense of value extended in Mason's conception to the people who read such books and watch popular films and TV programs such as *Gunsmoke*. Eventually, this realization would become the basis of Mason's fiction.

With *The Girl Sleuth* Mason finally understood that while she had been running away from her past to discover something of merit to write about, she had ignored the very material that was essential to her development as a writer. She describes this sudden insight in *Clear Springs*:

> By this time, I had become a writer—belatedly, after many twists and turns while I looked over my shoulder at my childhood dreams and shook

my head to get out the nightmare residue from my journey north. I had discovered that I could draw on my true sources in order to write fiction. How could I have failed to recognize them? They had claimed me all along. So much of the culture that I had thought made me inferior turned out to be my wellspring. And my mother was my chief inspiration.

In 1978 Mason began writing short stories seriously and started to send them to *The New Yorker*. In a 1989 interview with Marianne Walker in the *Louisville Courier-Journal*, Mason talked about her early efforts to be published:

> The twentieth story I sent to *The New Yorker* was accepted. The first story I sent was the second one I wrote when I started writing in 1978. I got a little note saying "Sorry" with editor Roger Angell's initials. And then the second story I sent, I got a letter from him. I kept sending stories and kept getting letters from him, encouraging rejection letters. And so then it got very exciting because he had taken an interest in my writing and the other editors there were also taking an interest. I felt very privileged and encouraged. . . . The one exciting stage in that progression was about mid-point, after I had sent in about ten stories with those self-addressed envelopes. The next letter said, "In the future, don't bother sending return envelopes." I knew then that someday it was very possible that I would make it.

SHILOH AND OTHER STORIES

The stories that appeared in *The New Yorker* and the *Atlantic Monthly* were collected and published by Harper and Row in 1982 under the title *Shiloh and Other Stories*. The accomplishment of this book arises out of Mason's courage to return to the people and circumstances that she had abandoned after high school. Mason described it differently in *Clear Springs*: "One reason to fashion a story is to lift a grudge." The writing of these stories was a way for Mason to exorcise the sense of betrayal she felt from the "real life" that she had been trying to live up to for the past twenty years. And the overwhelming success she received reinforced the choice she made. In his *New York Times* review of the book, Anatole Broyard wrote, "*Shiloh and Other Stories* reminds us that even in 1982 we still have a regional literature that describes people and places almost unimaginably different from ourselves and the big cities we live in." Yet there is a strange familiarity about the circumstances of these characters. They suffer from the common maladies of contemporary life—divorce, unemployment, illness, natural disaster.

In the title story, Leroy Moffitt returns home from the hospital after being injured in an accident in his tractor trailer to discover that his wife, Norma Jean, is not the person he married. She's become independent, enrolling in night classes at the local community college and transforming herself into a fitness nut. On the advice of Norma Jean's mother the couple takes a trip to the Civil War battlefield Shiloh. As it turns out, the historical significance of the battlefield is lost on them. As they move through the park looking at plaques that dot the countryside, Leroy has difficulty seeing Shiloh as a battlefield. He seems to think it should look like a golf course or park. Leroy tries to distract himself from Norma Jean's desire for a divorce by focusing on the site before him. What Norma Jean has said, however, cannot be fully blotted out. Amid the confusion of his pain, Leroy gets tangled in the two pasts—his and Norma Jean's and the war's.

> Leroy takes a lungful of smoke and closes his eyes as Norma Jean's words sink in. He tries to focus on the fact that thirty-five hundred soldiers died on the grounds around him. He can only think of that war as a board game with plastic soldiers. Leroy almost smiles, as he compares the Confederates' daring attack on the Union camps and Virgil Mathis's raid on the bowling alley. General Grant, drunk and furious, shoved the Southerners back to Corinth, where Mabel and Jet Beasley were married years later, when Mabel was still thin and good-looking. The next day, Mabel and Jet visited the battleground, and then Norma Jean was born, and then she married Leroy and they had a baby, which they lost, and now Leroy and Norma Jean are here at the same battleground. Leroy knows he is leaving out a lot. He is leaving out the insides of history. History was always just names and dates to him. . . . And the real inner workings of a marriage, like most of history, have escaped him.

Leroy's isolation from the past is so great that he cannot grasp the implications not only of his failed marriage, but also of the larger fabric of history. He is unable to change in such a degree as to have any sense of understanding. Instead he runs back to what he knows in the present moment—his failed marriage and the woman who has no use for him. In the end, everything has "escaped him."

Leroy's realization that he is "leaving out the insides of history" represents a core theme in Mason's work. Her characters are no longer defined by such southern milestones as the Civil War but they have not found a new code of conduct. They are stuck in between, and it is the point of convergence of past and present that Mason limns. The other stories in this collection center around this transitional landscape, where corner grocery stores are being transformed into convenience stores and the town square is being replaced by strip malls on the highway. In "The Climber," Dolores faces the uncertainty of being tested for breast cancer while her husband, Glenn, employs a tree service to cut down a magnificent tulip tree in their yard to make room for a workshop he wants to build. This story offers a strange kind of sacrifice for convenience and pleasure as represented in the objects that Glenn plans to build—picnic tables. Mason, however, refuses to reduce the story to the simple moralizations characteristic of traditional southern literature. In this story, as in the others, the tension between tradition and the modern present does not carry significant weight for the characters, because the present is so overwhelming that the past has no power. Instead, "The Climber" seems to coalesce around the corresponding loss of the tulip tree and the potential loss of Dolores's identity as a woman. Mason refuses to suggest anything more than the notion that what has been known is no longer known, or is no longer correct. Dolores expresses this sentiment near the end of the story after hearing a song on the radio. "The Oak Ridge Boys used to be a gospel quartet when Dolores was a child. Now, inexplicably, they are a group of young men with blow-dried hair, singing country-rock songs about love." Like Leroy in "Shiloh," Dolores is unable to understand the implications of a change in format. Nevertheless, she does find an answer that is as hermetic as the world around her seems. When she receives the benign diagnosis of fibrocystic disease and is told by her doctor that she will have to avoid foods containing caffeine, she feels let down. "Dolores will have to resist chocolate cake. Somehow, this is a welcome guide for living, something certain—particular and silly. Yet somehow she feels cheated." And Dolores *is* cheated because the answers she is able to discover are as banal as the picnic tables her husband plans to build.

In "A New-Wave Format" Mason attempts to replace the failed historical perspective rooted in the Old South with a newer historical perspective—the late 1960s and early 1970s. By having Edwin Creech, a forty-three-year-old bus driver who transports mentally disabled adults, use the music of Janis Joplin, the Doors, the Rolling Stones, and others as a vehicle for self discovery, Mason makes it possible for a character to achieve a vision of self and history that promises fulfillment. Edwin says to his live-in girlfriend Sabrina, "I feel like I've had a developmental disability and it suddenly went away. Something like if Freddie Johnson learned to read. That's how I feel." This story is unusual in this collection as well as in Mason's other

work because typically when her characters gain a larger perspective it does not suggest that growth will occur. Like Sandra in "Offerings" and Nancy in "Nancy Culpepper," people might discover the connection they have to their home, but it is only momentary, like the sudden flash of a lightning bug in the dark.

Shiloh and Other Stories was recognized in a year when women writers made a near sweep of the various literary prizes in America. In 1983 Cynthia Ozick, Mason, Anne Tyler, and Alice Walker received four of the National Book Critics Circle's five nominations for fiction. Alice Walker won the Pulitzer Prize for her novel *The Color Purple* and Marsha Norman a Pulitzer for her play *'Night, Mother.* Walker also won the American Book Award for fiction and Mason received the PEN/Hemingway Award for the year's best first fiction. But these accolades have not spared Mason criticism. Reviewers have complained that the narrative arc in her stories is repetitious because each story exists in the same transitional fluidity of social dislocation. But what these critics overlook is that Mason traces this dislocation in a myriad of ways—divorce, separation, adult children moving back home with their parents. The stories cannot be reduced to a simple thematic concern, but rather the subject matter is revealed to have strikingly different manifestations. In an article in the *New York Times,* Michiko Kakutani observes that in their similarities the stories possess "the texture and density of a finely crafted novel—though not interlinked, the stories worked together like episodes in a Robert Altman movie, fitting snugly, side by side, to give one an extended glimpse of a specific world."

As well, critics have faulted Mason for lingering on the minutiae of her characters' shallow lives. Such critical witticisms as "K Mart realism," "hick chic," "Diet-Pepsi minimalism," and "post-Vietnam, post-literary, postmodernist blue-collar neo-early-Hemingwayism" have been used to describe her style. Whatever these characterizations mean, they do not take into account the essential narrative strategy that Mason employs with respect to the poor, rural, and undereducated. Through the details of her stories, most of which come directly from her own or her family's experience, she is authenticating the culture that she feels represents most of America, but is ignored at the very least and more often ridiculed. "The characters in my world don't have the guidance or perspective to know that there might be this *other* view of television or malls. They're in that world and they like television fine, thank you. And they love the malls, and I don't judge them for it. When they go to the shopping mall, and many of them go just to window shop, they're looking at deliverance from a hard way of life," Mason told Mervyn Rothstein in a 1988 interview. Other marginalized groups, such as participants in the black arts movement and the feminist movement, have used the tactic of unconditional inclusion successfully. What makes Mason different is that she is not writing about any single racial or gender group but working-class white culture. Mason's feminist and academic credentials offered a framework for constructing a validating hegemony for the culture in which she grew up. This recontextualization makes Mason's fiction as socially radical as any.

IN COUNTRY

While Mason was forty before she published her first story, her second book, *In Country,* appeared in 1985, just three years after *Shiloh and Other Stories* was published. The novel expands on her first collection by returning to its geographical and spiritual milieu and once again exploring the historical dislocations wrought on ordinary, blue-collar people, this time in the larger cultural context of the Vietnam War. The book tracks seventeen-year-old Samantha (Sam)

Hughes's quest to come to terms with the war that killed her father and to discover a relationship with the father she has never known. It is also a book that builds on *Shiloh*'s authenticating strategy. Without question Mason's first collection was a form of coming out. The stories publicly exposed her deep affinity with the kind of rural, noncollege-educated, blue-collar people that the educated elite—of whom as a young woman she so desperately wanted to be apart— scorn. *In Country* seems to reach deeper and more personally into Mason's disillusionment with the American dream by undermining the kind of literature that she cherished as a girl but came to distrust as an adult—juvenile detective fiction. In this way the novel is an antidote to the Nancy Drew paradigm. In *The Girl Sleuth* Mason aptly describes Nancy's world.

Much of Nancy's popularity . . . comes from the appeal of her high-class advantages. She has everything a girl could want—a mere given for the privilege of sleuthing, Nancy-style. She lives, with her understanding and trusting Dad, in a comfortable, tree-shaded Colonial brick home with a circular drive—the affluent American version of fairyland. Her lovely home is located in exclusive River Heights, a city which is variously Eastern and mid-Western, Nancy has an endless wardrobe (with numerous "sports dresses," whatever those are), a dependable and worshipful boyfriend, and her own car. She gets to go anywhere in the world she wishes and she doesn't have to go to school. And for all her privileges, she is utterly unspoiled and charming. She is independent, brilliant, poised, courageous, kind, attractive, gracious, well-to-do—i.e., free, white, and sixteen.

Sam of *In Country* might be seen as the anti-Nancy. She is poor, fatherless, and lives in a house with a crumbling foundation. She wants a car, but her only prospect is a run-down, rusting VW bug. Her wardrobe consists of jeans and T-shirts. She has just graduated from high school, and she is unsure whether she wants to go to college. Essentially, Sam is in a kind of transitional space between childhood and adulthood without the guidance that she needs to negotiate this territory. Her only role model is her Uncle Emmett, who is so damaged by the Vietnam War that he is unable to work, perhaps suffering from the effects of being poisoned during the war with Agent Orange. Her mother has, in essence, abandoned her by moving to Lexington, Kentucky, the big city compared with Hopewell, with her new husband and baby. As Mason describes Sam's state in part one of *In Country,* "She's in limbo, stationed right in the center of this enormous amount of energy." In a sense Sam is an orphan at the beginning of the novel, and she is out to solve a mystery—the mystery of her dead father; but unlike such pursuits in the Nancy Drew books, Sam's quest is not so much an adventure or lark but is essential to her development as a person.

Mason's novel is unique in its denial of the traditional war bildungsroman, which is male centered. Instead, Mason sends Sam on a quest to validate her identity in a way that Bruce Springsteen's lyrics cannot. Set in the summer of 1984, the novel is textured with the rhythms and songs of that summer's blockbuster album, Springsteen's *Born in the U.S.A.* As a counterpoint to Sam's search, the music reminds us of how superficial our lives can be. It is only by reading her father's battlefield diary, awakening to her uncle's deep grief, sleeping with a Vietnam vet, and spending the night out in the wilderness that she comes to recognize that there are things in the world more authentic than video games and television. In this sense the novel is a rite-of-passage story that navigates the traditional phases of the genre—from separation to isolation to integration.

Interestingly, like Edwin Creech in "A New-Wave Format," Sam focuses her attention on the 1960s and 1970s in order to define herself and her heritage but she explores deeper than Edwin, who only finds the promise of fulfillment, not the actual experience thereof. In contrast, Sam examines the era's most disturb-

ing historical event, the Vietnam War, and comes out of her experience with a larger vision, as is clear in the final scene of the novel, when Sam, her uncle, and her paternal grandmother visit the Vietnam War Memorial in Washington, D. C.:

> Sam flips through the directory and finds "Hughes." She wants to see her father's name there too. She runs down the row of Hughes names. There were so many Hughes boys killed, names she doesn't know. His name is there, and she gazes at it for a moment. Then suddenly her own name leaps out at her. . . .
>
> SAM A HUGHES. It is the first on a line. It is down low enough to touch. She touches her own name. How odd it feels, as though all the names in America have been used to decorate this wall.

Through this simple recognition of her own name, Sam finds the link to the past and to her father for which she has been searching. In moments such as this Mason is able to uncover the mystery behind the dislocation her characters feel. This resolution is anchored in the notion that we are all alike, and thus equal—in both happiness and devastation.

SPENCE + LILA

In *Shiloh and Other Stories* Mason explores the lives of a kind of middle generation, people who grew up in the Old South but must live in the New South, a place where the old certainties of family and religion are no longer dominant, a place where farms have been blacktopped over to make way for malls, subdivisions, and fast-food outlets. Cut off from their roots, these characters drift aimlessly. In *In Country* Mason looked at a child of this middle generation and the legacy of dislocation she inherited. In her next book, the short novel *Spence + Lila* (1988), Mason examines a late-middle-aged farm couple, married almost all their lives, as they face the crisis of Lila's breast cancer and heart disease. The chapters alternate between Lila's perspective and Spence's as if this couple has been together so long that their views are almost interchangeable. The significance of their predicament is relayed in a narrative that seems almost a eulogy for the kind of existence these folks have lived: "She and Spence have spent a lifetime growing things together." Lila, who has birthed, mothered, and harvested three children—Nancy, Cat, and Lee—and countless gardens, is faced with the loss of one of her immense breasts.

> "I think they're going to take this breast off," Lila says, placing her hand under her right breast.
>
> "You've always been so proud of those," Cat says, reaching to touch the top of Lila's breast lightly.
>
> "My big jugs," Lila says, smiling. "I raised three younguns on these. I guess they're give out now." She can't say what she feels—that the last thing she would have expected was to be attacked by disease in the very place she felt strongest. It seemed to suggest some basic failing, like the rotten core of a dying tree.

In this novel it appears that everything that "felt strongest" is under attack. Spence and Lila still plant soybeans and corn, but more out of a sense of obligation than need. Their neighbors have given up the family farm or taken loans only to go under; some are reduced to growing marijuana in between rows of corn to bring in a little extra cash. Their children are unable or unwilling to partake of their legacy. Nancy, vaguely feminist, has moved north to Boston and started a family of her own; Cat is a bookworm with no real connection to the earth; and Lee has a factory job and is stuck in mortgage slavery. These children subsist on junk food and are so estranged from nature that they go to Mister Sun, a tanning salon, every chance they get. An industrial park has been erected next to their farm and has chased the songbirds away. An industrial spill has killed all the fish in the lake. There is an apocalyptic feel to this barren landscape. The symbols of regeneration are being destroyed. As a result, this couple's experience and knowledge are of things that are of no use in the face of such a modern scourge as cancer.

At the hospital, Spence and Lila seem not simply out of place, but overwhelmed by the high-tech medicine, while their daughters, especially Nancy, are sufficiently comfortable to challenge authority. When the doctor explains the procedure to Lila, Nancy responds aggressively.

> "How small would the lump have to be for you to recommend a lumpectomy instead?" Nancy asks the doctor.
>
> "Infinitesimal," he says. "It's better to get it all out and be sure. This way is more certain."
>
> "Well, more and more doctors are recommending lumpectomies instead of mastectomies," Nancy argues. "What I'm asking is, what is the dividing line? How large should the lump be for the mastectomy to be preferable?"
>
> Lila sees Spence cringe. Nancy has always asked questions and done things differently, just to be contrary.

After the operation Lila cannot understand what is happening to her.

> Lila feels as though she has been left out in a field for the buzzards. The nurses are in at all hours, making no special effort to be quiet—a nurse who checks dressings, another one who changes dressings, a nurse with blood-thinner shots three times a day, a nurse with breathing-machine treatments, various nurses' aides who check temperature and blood pressure, the cleaning woman, the mail lady, the priest and nuns from the hospital, the girls who fill the water jugs, the woman who brings the meal trays, the candy stripers selling toiletries and candy and magazines from a cart. Lila can't keep track of all the nurses who come to check her drainage tube—squirting the murky fluid out of the plastic collection bottle, measuring the fluid intake and output, writing on charts.

While Lila's daughters seem so competent in the hospital, they are of no use keeping up with their mother's responsibility in the garden. They pick the corn too late in the day, so that its sweetness is gone after freezing. In cleaning the house, they rearrange everything.

The novel ends with Lila back on the farm and in her garden. "Lila's hands are full of vegetables, and she cradles them in her left arm. Beads of sweat have popped out on her forehead. She's smiling. 'Look at that pumpkin, would you!' she cries, pointing. 'That's going to be the biggest one we ever had! Well, I'll say!' She lets out a big laugh. 'That's going to be one for Cinderella.'" This ending is bittersweet, because while Lila does survive her operation and return to her home, the circumstances of their lives have not changed. With this ironic reference to Cinderella, Mason reminds the reader that Spence and Lila's lives can never be a fairy tale, that no matter how big the pumpkin grows it won't carry them off into happiness.

Some critics have found in *Spence + Lila* a withered sensibility. And indeed, the spare descriptions and plot offer a difficult soil for growth. Frank Conroy delivered this assessment in the *New York Times Book Review*: "What happens in this novel is we end up watching Bobbie Ann Mason being moved by a love story. She seems to know something about these people that isn't there in the text; she knows, in any event, more than us, and even though we trust her, we feel to some extent abandoned. We feel uneasy, forced to peer around the author to catch quick glimpses of her characters." As a result, readers can feel as dislocated as the characters, limited in their ability to truly enter this imagined world. Still, there are wonderful moments in the novel, including a brilliantly rendered description of a ride Spence takes in his neighbor's crop duster. The narrative also displays Mason's superb ear for the plain, direct dialogue of western Kentucky, the poetry of its terse idiom.

LOVE LIFE

In Mason's next book, *Love Life* (1989), she returns to the short story form that earned *Shiloh and Other Stories* high critical praise. At first glance, the fifteen stories collected here appear to be a further exercise in claiming the value and authenticity of her entrapped and dislocated characters. Mason refuses to judge or look deeply inside them. Instead, she presents in an almost anthropological way what she knows, rather than what she thinks. In this way Mason's power is in the wholeness of the collection. *Love Life* shows Mason to be not so much a great short story writer as a genius of the art of the short story collection. By picking up her pen every twenty pages or so, Mason is able to reveal the textures and contradictions of this region in a way that clearly could not be understood in a more linear and cohesive narrative. In her review of the collection in the *New York Times,* novelist Lorrie Moore wrote, "There is depth here, in the way the word is used to describe armies and sports teams: an accumulation, a supply. When one story is finished, a similar one rushes in to fill its place. There is also profundity. Ms. Mason dips her pen in the same ink, over and over, because her knowledge of the landlocked Middle America she writes about—most of it centered in Kentucky and Tennessee—is endless and huge."

The collection begins with the title story, in which another rootless woman, Jenny, returns to her family's hometown to take care of her spinster aunt Opal, a retired high school teacher. While Jenny is trying to settle down, her aunt watches MTV and longs to bust loose. This story seems to be a meditation on happiness and love.

Opal laughs. "I was talking to Ella Mae Smith the other day—she's a retired geography teacher?—and she said, 'I've got twelve great-great-grandchildren, and when we get together I say, "Law me, look what I started!"'" Opal mimics

Ella Mae Smith, giving her a mindless, chirpy tone of voice. "Why, I'd have to use quadratic equations to count up all the people that woman has caused," she goes on. "All with a streak of her petty narrow-mindedness in them. I don't call that a contribution to the world." Opal laughs and sips from her glass of schnapps. "What about you, Jenny? Are you ever going to get married?"

"Marriage is outdated. I don't know anybody who's married and happy."

Opal names three schoolteachers she has known who have been married for decades.

"But are they happy?"

"Oh, foot, Jenny! What you're saying is why are *you* not married and why are *you* not happy. . . ."

The story finally coalesces around the tension between settling down and running wild. Somehow, the people in these stories always want to be someplace else. In "Midnight Magic" a man named Steve leads a kind of rootless and hedonistic existence, but envies a friend who is getting married. He is attracted to all the traditions, even if the traditional "something blue" turns out to be the bride's tinted contact lenses. In "Piano Fingers" a deliveryman fantasizes about writing a television show featuring "an ordinary guy who drives a delivery van" and solves neighborhood crimes. "Sorghum" follows a bright young woman who relieves the coarseness of her marriage by taking up with an attractive electronics-store owner from Memphis.

In these stories, the old truism "The grass is always greener on the other side of the fence" might be replaced with "The grass is always greener when seen on TV." In "Airwaves," for example, a woman compares the sexual techniques of her estranged boyfriend to that of men discussed on *The Phil Donahue Show*; she later explains that any sort of reconciliation between her and her former partner is out of the question. "It would never work," she says. "We don't like the same TV shows anymore." Mason's stories resonate with the kind of wholeness of

place that James Joyce's *Dubliners* contains, but her sensibility has a distinctly contemporary texture, her focus moving in and out of homes and lives with the eerie flatness and saturated colors of videotape. Her stories are so evocative of a particular place and time that eventually they may require the kind of annotation needed by present-day readers for an understanding of medieval literature. A mere decade after they were written, these stories seemed to display a historical remoteness in their references to television programs like *The Phil Donahue Show*. As the decades pass, a reader's cultural literacy changes, and references to Michael Jackson as the "King of Pop," and mentions of other cultural icons, consumer items, and trademarks, might not have the immediacy they did in the 1980s. It will be interesting to observe how time changes the way Mason's stories are read.

FEATHER CROWNS

In her fiction, Mason has dealt with characters of her parents' generation and of her own and that which followed. Thus, it seems fitting that with her next novel, *Feather Crowns,* Mason would step further back into the past, to her grandparents' generation, to locate the seeds of contemporary malaise, of dislocation, only to discover that this former time was not much different from the present. Set in the years from 1900 to 1963, the historical novel *Feather Crowns* begins at the turn of the twentieth century, a time of great change and uncertainty. Like the products of the New South featured in her stories, the characters in this novel are longing for emotional connection and yearning for a place where apparently contradictory states—security and freedom, safety and independence—exist.

The people of Hopewell, Kentucky—the same setting as *In Country*—live in the shadow of Civil War devastation and twentieth century anxiety. The novel centers on a young mother, Christie Wheeler, who lives in the suffocating presence of her husband's extended family. She feels trapped and utterly ordinary until the winter of 1900, when something extraordinary happens to change her life forever: she gives birth to quintuplets. Suddenly, she and her children are celebrities. Her husband's Uncle Wad then tries to exploit the babies for profit, while strangers come from all over to see and hold them. Christie watches as these people stand in her home and criticize her furniture and child-rearing abilities. At the same time, a flood of baby clothes, baby food, and letters arrive at the Wheeler home, giving Christie her first look at a world beyond Hopewell.

Shortly after this, her quintuplets suddenly die. These deaths ensure Christie's alienation from her past. Mourning her lost children, she decides that she cannot continue to live in Hopewell. She feels a need to purge herself of her grief and to do that she must leave the Wheeler home, but this is not possible until a freak show hustler offers Christie a hundred dollars a week to tour the country with her dead babies—grotesquely preserved and housed in a glass case. The potential freedom the money offers gives Christie a hope that she and her husband can build a new life far from Hopewell. Instead, they trek a long, strange journey across the United States in the company of the margins of society—freaks, con men, and medicine men. In the end they seem to trade one kind of bondage for another.

The novel's closing section, a monologue in which Christie tries to make sense of her long life, is set in 1963 on her ninetieth birthday. In these pages Christie reaches an accommodation wherein she clearly does not regret what has happened to her.

> When you're old, you feel so wise sometimes, it seems like you've learnt everything you need to know before you die. But it don't stop you from wanting to repeat ever day, from here to eternity.

> Just the simple pleasures—coffee and bacon-and-eggs in the morning; the sunrise, which I *never* miss; finding a bird feather on the porch step; or hearing a bull bawling to his cows; seeing a pair of kittens tangled up a-playing; seeing roses bloom on the trellis once again, from the same rosebush I started in 1897; finding a fresh egg that's still got a sticky spot. Do you know what I mean?

Christie's method for coping with the unexpected is to find meaning in the simple offerings of everyday life, and Mason's body of work might be seen as a tribute to this ethos.

CONVERGENCE OF LIFE AND ART

Mason's 1999 memoir, *Clear Springs,* tells her own story, much of which was revealed previously in her fiction. This book essentially exposes Mason as a writer not only of fiction but of a hybrid of fact and fiction, a metafiction in which the details and stories come from her own experience. One might describe Mason's fiction as an inversion of New Journalism. Instead of imagining conversations, events, and actions that might have happened and asking the reader to believe that they are real, Mason records events and conversations that did happen and drapes them in a fictional veil. In *Clear Springs* readers learn countless details, such as the fact that Mason's father drove a bus for the mentally handicapped, like her character Edwin Creech does in "A New-Wave Format." This multilayered narrative spans three generations— that of Bobbie Ann Mason, her parents, and grandparents—the same three generations that *Shiloh, In Country, Spence + Lila,* and *Love Life* cover. In these pages Mason reveals a true American odyssey of growing up on the farm, moving to the big city, and finally returning home, and explains how the conflicts between her Old South heritage and the rootless society that issued from it led her to writing fiction.

While writing *Clear Springs,* Mason gathered seventeen of her stories from *Shiloh* and *Love*

Life into a collection of stories, *Midnight Magic: Selected Stories of Bobbie Ann Mason* (1998). Together with her memoir, this book gives readers a clear picture of Mason's vision. At the beginning of the twenty-first century, it remained to be seen whether Mason had exhausted as a creative source the small, isolated region of America that she has written about, and where she might travel next to send back her "picture postcard proofs of adventure, the real life."

Selected Bibliography

WORKS OF BOBBIE ANN MASON

FICTION

Shiloh and Other Stories. New York: Harper and Row, 1982; Lexington: University Press of Kentucky, 1995.

In Country: A Novel. New York: Harper and Row, 1985. Film version directed by Norman Jewison, 1989.

Spence + Lila. New York: Harper and Row, 1988.

Love Life: Stories. New York: Harper and Row, 1989.

Feather Crowns: A Novel. New York: HarperCollins, 1993.

Midnight Magic: Selected Stories of Bobbie Ann Mason. Hopewell, N.J.: Ecco, 1998.

NONFICTION

Nabokov's Garden: A Guide to Ada. Ann Arbor, Mich.: Ardis, 1974.

The Girl Sleuth: A Feminist Guide. Old Westbury, N.Y.: Feminist Press, 1975; Athens: University of Georgia Press, 1995.

Clear Springs: A Memoir. New York: Random House, 1999.

CRITICAL AND BIOGRAPHICAL STUDIES

Barnes, Linda A. "The Freak Endures: The Southern Grotesque from Flannery O'Connor to Bobbie Ann Mason." In *Since Flannery O'Connor: Essays on the Contemporary American Short Story.* Edited by Loren Logsden and Charles W. Mayer. Macomb: Western Illinois University Press, 1987. Pp. 133–141.

Barth, John. "A Few Words about Minimalism." *New York Times,* December 28, 1986, p. 1.

Blais, Ellen A. "Gender Issues in Bobbie Ann Mason's *In Country*." *South Atlantic Review* 56:107–118 (May 1991).

Blythe, Hal, and Charlie Sweet. "The Ambiguous Grail Quest in 'Shiloh.'" *Studies in Short Fiction* 32:223–226 (September 1995).

Booth, David. "Sam's Quest, Emmett's Wound: Grail Motifs in Bobbie Ann Mason's Portrait of America after Vietnam." *Southern Literary Journal* 23:98–109 (spring 1991).

Broyard, Anatole. Review of *Shiloh and Other Stories. New York Times,* November 23, 1982, p. C14.

———. "Reading and Writing: Country Fiction." *New York Times,* December 19, 1982, sec. 7, p. 31.

Chambers, Andrea. "Bobbie Ann Mason's *In Country* Evokes the Soul of Kentucky and the Sadness of Vietnam." *People Weekly* 24:127–129 (October 28, 1985).

Conarroe, Joel. "Winning Her Father's War." *New York Times Book Review,* September 15, 1985, p. 7. (Review of *In Country*.)

Conroy, Frank. "The Family at Her Bedside." *New York Times,* June 26, 1988, p. 7. (Review of *Lila + Spence.*)

De Vries, Hilary. "Mining the Vagaries of Rural America." *Christian Science Monitor,* November 20, 1985, p. 28.

Dwyer, June. "New Roles, New History, and New Patriotism: Bobbie Ann Mason's *In Country*." *Modern Language Studies* 22:72–78 (spring 1992).

Fine, Laura. "Going Nowhere Slow: The Post-South World of Bobbie Ann Mason." *Southern Literary Journal* 32:87–97 (fall 1999).

Flora, Joseph M., and Robert Bain, eds. "Bobbie Ann Mason." In their *Contemporary Fiction Writers of the South: A Bio-Bibliographical Sourcebook.* Westport, Conn.: Greenwood Press, 1993. Pp. 275–285.

Gardner, Marilyn. "Bestseller, Bobbie Ann Mason's First Novel." *Christian Science Monitor,* September 6, 1985, p. B2.

Gholson, Craig. "Bobbie Ann Mason." *BOMB* 28:40–43 (summer 1989).

Havens, Lila. "Residents and Transients: An Interview with Bobbie Ann Mason." *Crazyhorse* 29:87–104 (fall 1985).

Hill, Dorothy C. "An Interview with Bobbie Ann Mason." *Southern Quarterly* 31:85–118 (fall 1992).

Humphreys, Josephine. "Her Old Kentucky Home." *New York Times,* May 30, 1999, p. 5.

Jersild, Devon. "The World of Bobbie Ann Mason." *Kenyon Review* 11:163–169 (summer 1989).

Kakutani, Michiko. Review of *In Country. New York Times,* September 4, 1985, p. C20.

———. "Struggle and Hope in the New South." *New York Times,* June 11, 1988, p. 18. (Review of *Spence + Lila.*)

———. "Watching TV and Being Rootless in the South." *New York Times,* March 3, 1989, p. 35.

Kinney, Katherine. "'Humping the Boonies': Sex, Combat, and the Female in Bobbie Ann Mason's *In Country.*" In *Fourteen Landing Zones: Approaches to Vietnam War Literature.* Edited by Philip K. Jason. Iowa City: University of Iowa Press, 1991. Pp. 38–48.

Kirby, Jack T. "'Redneck' Discourse." In his *The Countercultural South.* Athens: University of Georgia Press, 1995.

Kling, Vincent. "A Conversation with Bobbie Ann Mason." *Four Quarters* 4:17–22 (spring 1990).

Krasteva, Yonka. "The South and the West in Bobbie Ann Mason's *In Country.*" *Southern Literary Journal* 26:77–90 (spring 1994).

———. "The Significance of the Closed Frontier in Bobbie Ann Mason's *In Country.*" *Bells* (Barcelona, Spain) 7:83–93 (1996).

Krist, Gary. "Fiction Chronicle." *Hudson Review* 42:125–132 (spring 1989). (Includes a review of *Spence + Lila.*)

Limon, John. "Family Likeness: War in Women's Words." In his *Writing After War: American War Fiction from Realism to Postmodernism.* New York: Oxford University Press, 1994.

Lupack, Barbara T., ed. "History as Her-Story: Adapting Bobbie Ann Mason's *In Country* to Film." In her *Vision/Re-vision: Adapting Contemporary American Fiction by Women to Film.* Bowling Green, Ohio: Bowling Green State University Popular Press, 1996. Pp. 159–192.

Lyons, Bonnie, and Bill Oliver. "An Interview with Bobbie Ann Mason." *Contemporary Literature* 32:449–470 (winter 1991).

McCorkle, Jill. "Love, Death and Other Mysteries." *Washington Post,* July 1, 1988, p. B8.

Moore, Lorrie. "What Li'l Abner Said." *New York Times Book Review,* March 12, 1989, p. 7.

Nussbaum, Paul. "Recreation of Western Kentucky." *Los Angeles Times,* November 29, 1985, p. 6.

Pichaske, David R., ed. *Late Harvest: Rural American Writing.* New York: Paragon, 1991.

Pollack, Harriet. "From *Shiloh* to *In Country* to *Feather Crowns*: Bobbie Ann Mason, Women's History, and Southern Fiction." *Southern Literary Journal* 28:95–116 (spring 1996).

Quammen, David. "Plain Folks and Puzzling Changes." *New York Times,* November 21, 1982, p. 7.

Rothstein, Mervyn. "Homegrown Fiction: Bobbie Ann Mason Blends Springsteen and Nabokov." *New York Times Magazine,* May 15, 1988, pp. 50, 98–99, 101, 108.

Ryan, Barbara T. "Decentered Authority in Bobbie Ann Mason's *In Country.*" *Critique* 31:199–200 (spring 1990).

Walker, Marianne. "Bobbie Ann Mason: In Her Own Words." *Louisville (Kentucky) Courier-Journal,* January 29, 1989, p. 4.

Wilhelm, Albert E. "Making Over or Making Off: The Problem of Identity in Bobbie Ann Mason's Short Fiction." *Southern Literary Journal* 18:76–82 (1986).

Willis, Meredith Sue. "Stories with a Sense of Place." *Washington Post Book World,* March 26, 1989, p. 11.

—*LABAN HILL*

William Maxwell

1908–2000

*T*HE AMERICAN SHORT story writer, novelist, and editor William Maxwell was born in Lincoln, Illinois, on August 16, 1908. He lived in Lincoln until 1923, when the Maxwell family moved to Chicago, where he completed high school. Maxwell attended the University of Illinois as an undergraduate, earning his B.A. in 1930. After a year in graduate school at Harvard, he returned to the University of Illinois to teach freshman English and to take occasional graduate courses. In 1933 he moved to New York City. After halfhearted efforts at working elsewhere, Maxwell settled down to what turned out to be a forty-year career at *The New Yorker* as an editor, which was punctuated by two brief periods during which he tried his hand as a full-time writer. Never having been a fast writer or one who wrote well under pressure, as did his colleague A. J. Liebling, he returned to the magazine on each occasion—insinuated himself back on to the staff, as he put it.

Maxwell died on July 31, 2000, at the age of ninety-one. His beloved wife, Emily, had passed away just eight days earlier. In the preface to his short-story collection *All the Days and Nights: The Collected Stories* (1995) Maxwell writes: "When we were first married [back in 1945], after we had gone to bed I would tell [Emily] a story in the dark. They came from I had no idea where. Sometimes I fell asleep in the middle of a story and she would shake me and say 'What happened next?' and I would struggle up through layers of oblivion and tell her."

Daniel Menaker, in a memorial tribute to his old friend and colleague, stresses these aspects of Maxwell: "the perduring influence of his parents; his spare, sure sense of narrative; his concern about decorum and its chronic destruction by love and hate; his capacity for blunt honesty; and the openness and trust of his friendship."

This modest man—he was often quoted as saying of his craft, "I've never known what I was doing"—stands as one of the best of *The New Yorker*'s editors, apart from the people who founded and shaped it—Harold Ross, William Shawn, Wolcott Gibbs, and Katharine Sergeant Angell (who hired Maxwell in 1934). The Ross-Shawn era continued until 1987, ten years after Maxwell retired. Throughout the late 1980s and the 1990s Maxwell wrote only rarely for *The New Yorker.* Anyone who studies the history of this magazine, particularly its fiction, will recognize Maxwell's genius as an editor of fiction, especially the short story. "Maxwell would develop intimate relationships," Ben Yagoda has written in *About Town: "The New Yorker" and the World It Made,* with "Sylvia Townsend Warner, Frank O'Connor, Eudora Welty, John Cheever, Mavis Gallant, John Updike, Larry Woiwode—and they would come to think of him as a true collaborator." To that list could be added John O'Hara, Nancy Hale, J. D. Salinger, Shirley Hazzard, Harold Brodkey, and still others. Yagoda also points out that Maxwell was "the first *New Yorker* fiction editor who was a serious writer in his own right." Because of this, "he understood their struggles, shared in their triumphs, and agonized over rejections." He was especially close, as the reader will see, to Sylvia Townsend Warner and Frank O'Connor.

"IMAGINATION'S HOME"

For most of his mature life Maxwell lived in an apartment on East 86th Street in New York City and in a house nearby in Westchester County, but as he often said—and as is obvious—the Middle West was his "imagination's home." Most of his fiction and all of his novels except *The Château* (1961) are set in the American Midwest. And the American couple in *The Château* is from Illinois. The best of Maxwell's novels are laid in Illinois. Some of Maxwell's best short stories unfold in New York City, but, as the author himself has remarked in an interview with Kay Bonetti for the *Missouri Review,* "I've always lived in New York City a very circumscribed life and tried to lead the life I would have if I'd lived in Lincoln [Illinois]. This was not a particularly conscious determination, it's just that I grew up in a small town and it marked me for life. . . . I'm so deeply attached to home." It is no surprise then that Maxwell's fiction is deeply autobiographical, that it turns around domestic relationships in general and the family in particular, and that the action is punctuated with uncannily accurate descriptions of not only people but dogs, cats, and horses.

Anyone seriously engaged by William Maxwell will want to read his idiosyncratic family history, *Ancestors* (1971), a lively combination of oral history (including tall tales), history proper (especially church history and local history), reminiscence, and fiction. This book cries out for a preface but does not have one. Some forty pages into his narrative, Maxwell writes this wonderful explanation: "I have to get out an imaginary telescope and fiddle with the lens until I see something that interests me. . . . If the telescope is focused properly, ideas are caught in it as well as people."

The general subject of *Ancestors* is Maxwell's family as far back as he could trace it; the theme involves how the family turned from being daft on religion (especially the form of Protestant-

ism known as the Disciples of Christ or the Campbellite church) to being concerned mainly with money. It is a familiar story in the United States—of how an overpowering concern with spiritual matters changes to an equally powerful concern with material things. Maxwell, an admitted nonbeliever in matters of a religious nature, including a belief in God, uses his father as his chief exemplar. By the time the elder William Maxwell died at the age of eighty, he was more nearly an advocate of the Rotary Club than of his family's church (in which many of his ancestors had been preachers), and he was buried by an Episcopal priest whom he had met at the Rotary Club.

The young William Maxwell worshiped his mother, as any reader of his fiction will know. His were household, not churchly, gods. So the house on Ninth Street in Lincoln, where he spent much of his childhood, was "a world in itself." And the house and his mother were so closely akin in his mind, as he tells us in *Ancestors,* that he did not distinguish between the animate presence of the lady of the house and the inanimate house over which she presided with considerable grace and style. "The house," as he puts it, "was the outward reflection of a very happy marriage."

Of Lincoln, the author writes: "Every person was exceptional in some way. . . . I wonder that so small a place could hold so much character." And of these souls, he adds: "You could be eccentric and still not be socially ostracized. You could even be dishonest. But you could not be openly immoral." Now comes an even more telling remark: "Men and women alike appeared to accept with equanimity the circumstances (on the whole, commonplace and unchanging) of their lives in a way that no one seems able to do now anywhere." Then the author makes a sharp distinction about his hometown and Winesburg, Ohio: "I am aware that Sherwood Anderson writing about a similar though smaller place saw it quite differently. I believe in Winesburg, Ohio, but I also believe in what I remember." There are no grotesques in Maxwell's world. In referring to the characters in Maxwell's stories as "being exactly life-size," Brooke Allen, writing in the *New Criterion,* secures her related point this way: "Small-town eccentricity has been a sadly overworked theme in American writing, and by keeping his characters on a human scale Maxwell has made them living beings who never approach the grotesque."

FIRST NOVEL

William Maxwell's first novel, *Bright Center of Heaven,* written in 1934 when the author was in his early twenties, appeared in the midst of the Great Depression. Harper & Brothers accepted the work for publication but had no money to promote it; Maxwell's editor said: "Now we must pray." The entire first printing of 1,000 copies sold quickly, but only one hundred or so copies of the second printing sold. Maxwell never allowed it to be reprinted.

The author voiced misgivings about the novel, especially the ending and the distinguished black man who provides a comic version of the intruder plot by visiting the pocket society that has gathered around Mrs. West on her farm in Wisconsin. Mrs. West, a widow, is in straitened circumstances owing to the depression and to her own improvident ways. She has an assorted group of boarders, chiefly artists, many of whom are parasites, in addition to her children and her servants to feed and otherwise to care for. Most of them, while pleasant enough and by no means intractable, are of little help to her. All of them tend to be self-centered and impractical.

One of the novel's earliest critics, Theodore Purdy, wrote in the *Saturday Review of Literature* that *Bright Center of Heaven* is "an admirable satiric comedy, bittersweet in flavor, yet always humorous"; and this judgment is entirely right. The satire is directed plainly toward the impractical natures of the various people at Meadowland, which in some ways is a utopian community like that satirized by Nathaniel Hawthorne in *The Blithedale Romance.* Maxwell himself has said that Meadowland is a farm more nearly like that in Anton Chekhov's *Cherry Orchard* than "an ordinary farm." Certainly any reader with the faintest knowledge of farming will realize it is not a working farm, but the rural backdrop provides a setting for a version of pastoral comedy.

Despite Maxwell's misgivings, *Bright Center of Heaven* possesses a considerable interest all its own, especially for anyone interested in first novels. In many respects it is a tour de force, a narrative that carries the reader swiftly through the unfolding action. It also "provides a useful introduction to the Maxwell oeuvre," as Bruce Bawer has observed.

One of this author's most distinctive virtues appears immediately in this novel—the sure way in which he introduces and delineates a large cast of characters. Consider one of them, Nigel, a young actress. She provides the romantic interest in the novel. Nigel is having an affair with a middle-aged man named Paul; but the older of Mrs. West's sons is unaware of this relationship and is head over heels in love with Nigel—besotted with her. When we first meet her, she is idly wondering whether she is pregnant. She thinks to herself: "If I could only say to Susan casually, *Susan, I think I'm going to have a child. . . .* The very thought of the relief it would bring made her light-headed, but she was afraid to do it. There were too many years between them, and Susan's babies had arrived properly, with the sanction of the Church and the state." She hangs fire: "She could not tell Susan; and until she was certain of it she could not tell Paul. He would grieve so. He would blame himself so terribly for ruining her career. Poor darling." The brilliance of this little sequence results from Maxwell's presenting what could have been an interior monologue as an imagined dialogue—a conversation. Hence we get not picture but scene and learn about all three characters at once.

Bright Center of Heaven, like any other good novel, depends upon a succession of such good scenes—some, like this one, little more than snapshots, others developed in detail. A little later in the action Nigel and Thorn (the older of Mrs. West's sons) meet. Maxwell describes Thorn's feelings through metaphor: "As a swollen stream bearing dead logs and brush . . . overleaps its banks and floods the wide defenseless fields, higher and higher the feeling rose. Thorn's heart grew wild with fear. . . . Thorn was too excited to speak." When he recovers himself, he tells Nigel how his father died of pneumonia in middle age.

Now the author changes the limited point of view to Paul, who writes to his friend Jerry Carson. In this letter Paul describes life at Meadowland, presenting exact accounts of not only the unreal life there but of the quaint characters living at the farm. *"There is Bascomb West from Philadelphia, a strange young man, full of whimsical conversation."* He turns to Josefa Marchand, *"a young pianist. Very forceful and masculine and genuinely gifted, I believe, though the milk of human kindness is not in her."* And so on. Then he continues: *"The seventh boarder is coming this afternoon—a negro chap. . . . Come to think of it, Susan met him through you. . . . If things go badly, we shall hold you responsible."* We have now heard various references to Jefferson Hunter, "only one of innumerable flies preserved in the amber of his Aunt Susan's conversation," as the whimsical Bascomb has thought to himself, "grinning at the idea of a Negro at Meadowlands, and speculating upon the difficult situation which his Aunt Amelia's prejudices would almost certainly construct for her." Nigel, learning of the stranger's impending visit from Thorn, has created another mental image: "Very likely there would be race riots at Meadowland before nightfall, and Amelia coming down to dinner in a Confederate flag, with a picture of Robert E. Lee pinned on her bosom." (Amelia, who has been on a diet of weak tea and cottage cheese for years and who is a bundle of prejudices, is a wonderfully comic figure.)

All this is in keeping with the satirical temper of the novel, which is gentle and comical, never strident or bitter, even after Mr. Hunter arrives. When he does, nothing spectacular occurs. There is a long sequence in which the action unfolds through his perspective: "He was in a strange country. He didn't know who was friend and who was enemy." Whitey, Mrs. West's younger son, shows Mr. Hunter the farm:

> He was pleased with the cleanness of the farm. Each building was spotlessly white, with green trellises—so neat and orderly. Yet taken all together they seemed to present a special kind of chaos. . . . What of the effort that must be exerted to establish order over so many domains. That in itself must be rather a nightmare, a confusion springing from order.

Of his hostess, he wonders: "What connection there was between this disorderly order and the mind of Mrs. West, who was so charming, so like an angel." Mrs. West unwittingly brings pandemonium in her wake.

During the late supper, the day reaches its climax. Hunter grows exasperated with most of the people there: "So far as he could tell, these seven people had no meaning beyond themselves. . . . They did not express the life of the nation. They had no visible work. They were all drones and winter would find them dead." He continues to think to himself: "If they weren't all mad, then their conduct was inexcusable." As we remember the depression era, we are inclined to side with Hunter.

Now he and Paul (a former teacher) become involved in an argument. Mrs. West has talked about her pioneer forbears. Mr. Hunter declares, "The pioneer was guilty of the great sin against nature." Paul retorts: "What, pray tell, was that?" Mr. Hunter replies: "The great sin against nature is taking more than you need." And so the guest turns into a critic of the West family and its whole history; and in going on to advocate the greatness of the black race, he loses all sense of proportion and becomes rude and hectoring. Soon thereafter he decides to bolt and enlists Whitey to take him in the night to the train station. And we see no more of the guest who has caused such a stir in this strange closed society.

Jefferson Hunter, as Maxwell and others have said, is a stereotyped character (the Educated Negro) who never comes fully to life. His display of temper isn't accounted for, and having vented his spleen (for little reason), he leaves. As the American writer Zona Gale told the young Maxwell, he needed another scene in the novel; and, in recounting her response, he admitted she was right. Had Maxwell provided that scene, Hunter might have then become a round character who passes E. M. Forster's test in *Aspects of the Novel*—"being capable of surprising in a convincing way." Forster explains: "If it does not convince, it is a flat pretending to be round. It has the incalculability of life about it—life within the pages of a book." On that rock the flatness of Hunter's character (which should not be a stereotype)—the vessel of this novel—founders. Sylvia Townsend Warner, in musing over a character of her own like Hunter, who doesn't come to life, provides an exact description of the difficulty in *Bright Center of Heaven* in a letter written thirty years after the novel appeared: "The characters one deprives of their development can weigh on one's conscience, can't they?" Maxwell, alas, did not revise this novel as he did three of the five that were to follow it.

All the same *Bright Center of Heaven* ends on a moving note as the author returns to the mind of Mrs. West: "She gave herself up to the remembrance of her dead marriage. But it was only for a short while; she was much too alive to sleep with ghosts."

In his essay "Reading," W. H. Auden states: "Some books are undeservedly forgotten; none are undeservedly remembered." I think that applies to *Bright Center of Heaven,* a memorable novel despite Maxwell's misgivings about Jefferson Hunter, about the missing scene, and about its being too derivative of Virginia Woolf's *To the Lighthouse* and other unspecified sources. I wish the author had provided that missing scene and had the novel reissued. In any case, Maxwell, for whatever reasons, never wrote anything so comic afterward—so lighthearted, so droll and amusing, so funny.

A SHORT NOVEL

They Came Like Swallows (1937), Maxwell's second novel, was revised by him in 1959 for the new Vintage edition (1960), and that revision was reprinted by David Godine, along with several other titles by Maxwell, in the 1980s and early 1990s. In 1997 the novel was again reprinted, with a new preface, by the Modern Library.

The title derives from W. B. Yeats's poem "Coole Park" (1929), about the great house called Coole Park, Lady Gregory (its owner), and the house's distinguished history, especially its guests, among them the Irish playwright J. M. Synge, Lady Gregory's nephew Captain John Shawe-Taylor, the art dealer Sir Hugh Lane, and Yeats himself. (Synge, Shawe-Taylor, and Lane all died young.)

They came like swallows and like swallows went,
And yet a woman's powerful character
Could keep a swallow to its first intent;
And half a dozen in formation there,
That seemed to whirl upon a compass-point,
Found certainty upon the dreaming air. . . .

The swallow as controlling image in this novel of course alludes to Maxwell's mother—her loss and yet her continuing presence as a living memory. The symbolism of the swallow for Yeats appears more fully in "Coole Park and Ballylee" than in "Coole Park" itself:

> Another emblem there! That stormy white
> But seems a concentration of the sky:
> And, like the soul, it sails into the sight
> And in the morning's gone, no man knows why;
> And is so lovely that it sets to right
> What knowledge or its lack had set awry. . . .

Through the image of the swallow sailing on the dreaming air, Maxwell creates the poetry of this artful yet simple novel. The careful reader will remember the epigraph from "Coole Park" when he or she comes to the scene about the bird trapped in the house.

When *They Came Like Swallows* was first published by Harper & Brothers, it was loosely set in twelve-point Janson type with lots of leading, which yielded only about 250 words per page. The handsome original edition, which was chosen as a Book-of-the-Month Club selection, ran to 267 pages. But the paperback version, although slightly augmented by the author in his revision, is 100 pages shorter, only about 30 pages longer than *So Long, See You Tomorrow* (1980). Maxwell, among his other accomplishments, is a master of the short novel; and he stands in the company of Herman Melville (*Benito Cereno* and *Billy Budd*), Henry James (*Washington Square* and *Daisy Miller*), Glenway Wescott (*The Pilgrim Hawk*), and Katherine Anne Porter (*Pale Horse, Pale Rider* and *Noon Wine*) so far as this mode, a very demanding one, is concerned.

Henry James praises "the beautiful and blest *nouvelle*" (the short novel) as our ideal, relishing the form for its shapeliness and its "strong brevity and lucidity." No one ever casually wrote a good short novel: the form in some ways is more demanding than the short story and less forgiving of lapses and errors. Maxwell edited an important instance of the short novel

when he secured John O'Hara's "Imagine Kissing Pete" for *The New Yorker*, then one of the longest pieces of fiction ever published in that magazine.

One may view the long story as running in the neighborhood of 8,000 to 20,000 words, and the short novel ranging in length from 20,000 to 50,000 or 60,000 words. The length varies considerably. In his introduction to *Great American Short Novels*, the editor William Phillips, in pondering the nature of this form, notes that he cannot say "how much of [the felicities of the short novel] is due to a kind of instinctive recognition of the fitness of the form to the spontaneities or the compulsions or the lack of cultural stamina, so characteristic of the native tradition." He adds: "The fact is . . . that these traits of social as well as literary life in America have been realized in what might be called the *illuminations* of the *nouvelle*. So remarkable a novel, for example, as *The Great Gatsby* has the quality of an incomplete vision."

The mode—and its illuminations—is natural to the fiction of William Maxwell and constitutes his principal form. He instinctively knew how to work out the economy of *They Came Like Swallows* and *So Long, See You Tomorrow* so that a book-length fiction, not a long part of a book that would have to be pieced out with other fiction, would ensue. With seeming ease and great sureness he accomplishes what James calls "the complicated thing with a strong brevity and lucidity" that arrives, "on behalf of multiplicity, at a certain science of control." This accomplishment, as any real writer knows, is no mean feat.

If the technical mode of *They Came Like Swallows* is the short novel, its genre is comedy. But this is not the comedy that we associate with obvious quick humor. The novel is written in a darker tone than *Bright Center of Heaven*. No one reading *They Came Like Swallows* will guffaw at any point in the action, which is often somber, sometimes shattering. The comedy in the novel entails the pattern of healing and reconciliation occurring in the Morison family after the sudden and unexpected death of Mrs. Morison from Spanish influenza. The story is set soon after the end of World War I amid the euphoria that event brought.

Even now many people do not realize the devastating effects of this worldwide eruption of influenza, which killed far more people in the United States than were lost by the American Expeditionary Force in Europe in 1917–1918. There was little defense against this flu, as the novel makes plain; there was also little or nothing in the way of effective medicine for those who contracted it. Mrs. Morison, having been weakened by giving birth to her third son only a few days before she died, had little chance to recover.

Katherine Anne Porter, who takes up the same general subject in *Pale Horse, Pale Rider* (1936), shows how quickly the flu struck and carried off its victims. Her protagonist, Miranda, who catches the flu, is nursed by Adam, her fiancé, who is a soldier. Adam contracts the flu from Miranda and then dies as she is recovering. This story, like Maxwell's, is deeply autobiographical. But Maxwell presents *They Came Like Swallows* as a realistic novel with the roving point of view, whereas *Pale Horse, Pale Rider* often has the dreamlike and allegorical quality that runs through American romance, not realism. Porter writes:

Almost with no warning at all, she floated into the darkness . . . and she saw Adam transfixed by a flight of . . . singing arrows that struck him in the heart and passed shrilly cutting their path through the leaves. Adam fell straight back before her eyes, and rose again unwounded and alive; another flight of arrows loosed from the invisible bow struck him again and he fell, and yet he was there before her untouched in a perpetual death and resurrection. She threw herself before him, angrily and selfishly she interposed between him and the track of the arrow, crying, No, no, like a child cheated in a game. It's my turn now, why must you always

be the one to die? . . . And he lay dead, and she still lived.

In the Morison family it is Elizabeth who dies. Her husband and their sons all recover. When Robert, the oldest, hears the news (at the end of book 2), this is how he reacts: "His head roared grandly like the shell in the parlor. He reached out for the weights, the cone-shaped weights of the cuckoo clock, and clung to them, swaying, until space formed and the earth was solid under his feet." Robert, who is still weak from the flu, reacts in much the same way as Miranda when she is in the throes of her illness and fears for Adam. Maxwell, in the revised version of his novel, perhaps feeling this passage was too poetic and sentimental, struck it out.

In explaining his work on the revision in a letter written to Frank O'Connor (collected in *The Happiness of Getting It Down Right*, 1996), Maxwell says this: "There was nothing I could do short of rewriting it out of existence, except here and there to do the small detail work that pulls a character back into recognizable human focus, and to restore a grand scene that I mistakenly deleted, in which I was impertinent to my father." This scene occurs at the end of chapter 10 of book 1 and should be compared with the original.

My comparison of *They Came Like Swallows* with *Pale Horse, Pale Rider* results not only from the commonality of the subject and the time but the fact, to repeat, that both are deeply autobiographical. Miss Porter, like Maxwell's mother, contracted the flu; but she, like Miranda, survived only to learn that her fiancé had died.

They Came Like Swallows, perhaps the most purely autobiographical of Maxwell's novels, demonstrates what he has remarked in an interview with John Seabrook and George Plimpton for the *Paris Review*: "True autobiography is very different from anything I've ever written. Edmund Gosse's *Father and Son* has a candor which comes from the intention of the writer to hand over his life. If the writer is really candid then it's good autobiography, and if he's not, then it's nothing at all." He refines this point: "I don't feel that my stories, though they appear to be autobiographical, represent an intention to hand over the whole of my life. They are fragments in which I am a character along with all the others. They're written from a considerable distance. I never feel exposed by them in any way."

So, even though in some respects Maxwell never got over the death of his mother when he was a lad of eight, he did not believe that in writing about it he was confessing anything profoundly intimate and private. In telling of his early life in the preface to *All the Days and Nights: The Collected Stories,* he strikes a different emphasis when he reveals his youthful desire to "go to sea, so that I would have something to write about." In recalling his comical experience about a schooner marooned in port, he says of its captain, "He had no idea when the beautiful tall-masted ship would leave its berth." "I had no idea," Maxwell adds, "that three-quarters of the material I would need for the rest of my writing life was already at my disposal." Flannery O'Connor, in writing of the same matter, observes that anyone who has survived childhood has more than enough to write about. "If you can't make something out of a little experience, you probably won't be able to make it out of a lot," she says. "The writer's business is to contemplate experience, not to be submerged in it." Maxwell, the evidence shows, wholly agreed with her.

They Came Like Swallows has the elegant simplicity of the plain style at its best; and the prose is modulated to reflect the post of observation. First comes that of Peter (or Bunny) Morison, who is only eight when the action unfolds: "For a moment he was outside in the rain. He was wet and shining. His mind bent from the wind. He detached a wet leaf." Then Bunny quits daydreaming of being outside and returns to the scene within the comfortable house: "Always when he and his mother were alone, the library seemed intimate and familiar. . . . The vermilion leaves and yellow leaves folding and unfolding upon the curtains depended utterly upon his mother. Without her they had no movement and no color."

In part 2 of the novel, entitled "Robert," Bunny's older brother is the viewpoint character. Robert, being five years older than Bunny and in his early teens, naturally registers life in a more complicated key than Bunny, a timid and withdrawn child who is wildly imaginative. Here is Robert, after he has climbed on the roof of the house, daydreaming about recovering his leg (lost in a freak accident): "On the whole it would do," he thinks. He returns to the real world, looking down on his aunt, Irene: "The sky all around him had lost its brightness and some of its color. And the heat had gone out of the tin roof, when he put his hands against it. Like an explorer long out of touch with the world, he advanced to the edge and looked down. Irene was there in the garden, alone." Later, after he has fallen asleep while reading a romantic saga, *The Scottish Chiefs,* Irene tells him to go to bed.

> With shapes of men and horses moving beside him, Robert made his way up the stairs to the sewing-room, undressed, and got into bed. For the first time he perceived how still the house was, how full of waiting. When he was little, he used to be afraid of the dark. He used to think that unnameable things were about to spring at him from behind doors. . . . He was not afraid any longer.

The house is "full of waiting" because Bunny is sick with the Spanish influenza and is threatened by death. Later, of course, his mother succumbs to it. By then Robert himself has sickened but has nearly recovered.

Robert, who has an accurate idea of how influenza threatens his parents (who are hospitalized together out of town), is not so astonished and overwhelmed by his mother's death as is Bunny; but her death leads Robert to remember his grandfather's death by mischance and then to dream of his own accident. Upon awaking, he strongly feels his mother's ghostly presence: "He was not afraid now. His mother was there, and she was not going away just yet." He tries to say goodnight to her, "but no words came." And then he thinks: "There was too great a distance between them." This is one of the most moving passages in a novel that often rises to poetry in the depth of feeling that is conveyed. Maxwell himself said that he believed that emotion should play a stronger part in fiction than idea; but, as he suggested, "abstract thinking" sometimes has a role in his work.

But thinking does not offer the boys' father, James Morison, any solace. He is not a reflective man. Deeply in love with his wife and happily satisfied, until her death, with his general domestic situation, he has no defenses against the ravages of mortality. Here he is in the beginning throes of his grief: "In the long run it was a mistake to have children. James did not understand them. He never knew what was going on in their minds. But that was Elizabeth's doing, after all. It was she who had wanted them." Later, after Bunny and Robert have misbehaved, James wonders if it were his fault that Elizabeth caught influenza as they went by train to a special hospital for her to deliver her child: "James set about to deal with the image that obsessed him. With so much sickness, with the epidemic everywhere it stood to reason that someone with influenza might have been on that interurban." Finally, as the funeral is about to begin, James, seeing his dead wife with "a bunch of purple violets" in her lifeless hands, experiences this revelation: "It was Elizabeth who had determined the shape that his life should take, from the very first moment that he saw her. And she had altered that shape daily by the sound of her voice, and by her hair, and

by her eyes which were so large and dark. And by her wisdom and by her love." *They Came Like Swallows* has run its course, and it ends on exactly the right note of finality. Its poetry arises from the grief and pity within the action but is not contained or circumscribed by them.

The rippling effect of joy overwhelmed by sadness is orchestrated through the structure of the novel by its roving point of view. The author himself describes the emotive unfolding of the story in beautiful terms. "The metaphor for *They Came Like Swallows*," Maxwell told Bonetti, "was a stone thrown into a pond making a circle, and then you throw a second stone and it makes a circle inside the first circle, as it's getting bigger, and then you throw another stone inside those other two. I made the novel on that structure." There are striking parallels between Maxwell's statement and Yeats's prose draft of his poem "Coole Park": "Address the swallows fluttering in their dream like circles. . . . A circle ever returning unto itself." Maxwell could have read only the final poem before he wrote his fine novel. The prose draft was not available.

THE FOLDED LEAF AND *TIME WILL DARKEN IT*

"In *The Folded Leaf* I saw myself walking across flat territory, such as you'd find in eastern Colorado, toward the mountains. . . . So I just kept getting closer to the mountains by creating scenes," Maxwell told Bonetti. At the end of this novel Lymie Peters sees himself in a desert valley surrounded by foothills with mountains in the distance.

The Folded Leaf (1945) has proved to be one of Maxwell's most durable novels. In the late 1990s it was reprinted in England as a Harvill paperback. Any informed reader, looking at the curve of this author's long and distinguished career, would perceive that Maxwell, in publishing this novel and *Time Will Darken It* (1948) in a three-year period, had reached his peak as a novelist. Although Maxwell continued to publish regularly until his death, he did not achieve the late harvest that one associates with some of the greatest artists: Shakespeare, Beethoven, Yeats. Minor writers rarely have this kind of efflorescence late in their careers, finding a new and rich way into their material as Shakespeare does in, say, *The Tempest*. That axiom would apply, in particular, to writers such as Maxwell, who remain more or less confined to their own experiences as providing material for their work. Yet those experiences are, after all, what motivated him to write in the first place. "I didn't want the things that I loved, and remembered, to go down to oblivion. The only way to avoid that is to write about them," he states in the interview with Bonetti.

The Folded Leaf derives directly from Maxwell's boyhood and early manhood in Chicago. Of it, his favorite novel, Maxwell said in a *Paris Review* interview: "the whole of my youth is in it." This novel takes us through a ten-year period after his mother's death, indeed through college; *The Château* limns four months when he was first married and living in France; in *So Long, See You Tomorrow* Maxwell returns to his early life in Lincoln, Illinois. Some critics consider *The Folded Leaf* autobiography, not fiction; while relying upon the materials of autobiography, it is clearly fiction. No sane critic would argue otherwise.

"Autobiography is simply the facts," Maxwell declares in the *Paris Review*; "but imagination is the landscape in which the facts take place, and the way that everything moves." The writer, whether he is deliberately drawing upon his own past or not, must find the characters and the themes and plot within his material and develop his story through them, especially the element of character. In his conversation with Bonetti, speaking of his use of actual people, Maxwell admits: "Sometimes I suffered the torments of the damned about describing real people. . . . But in this struggle, the artist won out. There

was a point at which I would not give up something which I knew was right aesthetically."

Looking at that issue from another perspective, Maxwell comments in the *Paris Review*: "In *The Folded Leaf,* the man who owned the antique shop bore a considerable resemblance to John Moser, who was the movie critic at *The New Yorker.* Nothing that John ever said is in that book, but I felt a certain security at the beginning of the identification. Then I forgot about Moser entirely, because the person in the book sprang to life." That character, Alfred Dehner, is not only a dealer in antiques but a landlord, letting rooms on the second floor of the spacious house where his shop and living quarters are located. Dehner rents Lymie Peters and Spud Latham a room, lying to them about the previous rent. Later he hires one of their mutual friends to manage the rooming operation, and this character, Richard Reinhart, plays an important role as the friendship begins to unravel. Dehner is a minor but essential character who takes off as the action develops, as Maxwell admitted. This is the kind of fictive development in *The Folded Leaf* that Maxwell describes thus: "The parts I invented seem so real to me I have quite a lot of trouble convincing myself they never really happened." The related observations by the author cover the complicated relation between fact and fiction, autobiography and imagination, and memory and invention and show, as Maxwell points out in the *Paris Review,* that autobiography is not "just the raw material for fiction." Since Maxwell is a singularly autobiographical author, I explore this matter in detail.

A novel of initiation, *The Folded Leaf* has many virtues that make it more successful than the usual novel written in this mode, in which a boy makes his way into manhood. Perhaps the most distinctive aspect of Maxwell's novel is the way that he juxtaposes the lives of Lymie and Spud, both lonely boys whose relations with their fathers are strained. And they both have come to Chicago unwillingly, having been dispossessed of the small towns in which they grew up and experienced days largely halcyon. When we first see Spud in his new habitat, he is so miserable that he leaves his parents' apartment in a huff and goes to a park to pick a fight, one that is prolonged and that he nearly loses. Earlier Spud has saved another miserable stranger, Lymie, from drowning in a pool filled with battling boys who are playing water polo. Throughout most of the action, Spud, an amateur boxer, continues to train and fight until he breaks a wrist. During this time Lymie acts as Spud's batman as well as being his faithful friend. As critics have pointed out, the portrait of this friendship never falls into sentimentality—although there is plenty of sentiment, as in the scene when Lymie, against his deepest instinct, goes to Spud's house for supper and is accepted as a member of Spud Latham's family. Mrs. Latham immediately realizes that something is troubling Lymie and soon learns that he is an only child who has lost his mother. Mrs. Latham worries about this thin, undernourished boy and perceives that his regimen of living in seedy hotels and eating in cheap restaurants with his father has resulted in his near-emaciation.

Immediately after this affecting scene Maxwell presents another that is moving in a different but equally intense way. Mr. Peters takes Lymie to the cemetery where Mrs. Peters is buried. We learn that Lymie's mother has been dead five years and that Lymie and his father visit her grave on the anniversary of her death each year; we also find that Lymie had a sister who died four days after her birth. Mr. Peters, who is bursting with clichés and saws, opines to Lymie: "You get out of life just what you put into it," while darkly thinking "there was a definite connection between Lymie's absent-mindedness and the fact that he seemed to gravitate toward whatever was artistic and

impractical." Never are father and son, always wary around each other, even this close again, including after Lymie's failed attempt at suicide. We learn then, late in the novel, that Mr. Peters is more upset by Lymie's not leaving him a note before he made that attempt than about his having tried to kill himself. "I didn't think about it," Lymie says to his father. "With that one remark the distance which had always been between them stretched out and became a vast tract, a desert country." In the meantime, Spud has grown no closer to his father. There is a vast gulf between fathers and sons in middle-class America in the 1920s. There is love but not understanding. But love and understanding exist within the tight circle that Lymie and Spud and Sally (Spud's girl) and their friends have made.

The Folded Leaf, which nearly founders when Lymie impulsively tries to kill himself after the gulf opens up between him and Spud (after Spud becomes jealous of the friendship between Lymie and Sally), regains its sureness of touch in the closing pages. Then the author presents a lyric evocation of the desert in chapter 58, telling us that "reality is almost never perceived through one of the senses alone" and that "the desert is the natural dwelling place" of people like Lymie "who have stopped justifying and explaining, stopped trying to account for themselves or their actions, stopped hoping that someone will come along and love them and so make sense of their lives."

Lymie, marooned in the desert of his hospital room, is truly alone and forlorn. But he is now visited by Reinhard and Spud, and he begins to return to the human community as he is starting to recover. Maxwell now gives us one of his most philosophical statements about the human condition (and Lymie's part in it):

The truth is that Lymie had never wanted to die, never at any time. The truth is nothing like as simple or as straightforward a thing as Lymie believed it to be. It masquerades in inversions and paradoxes, is easier to get at in a lie than in an honest statement. If pursued, the truth withdraws, puts on one false face after another, and finally goes underground, where it can only be got at in the complex, agonizing absurdity of dreams.

At this point, for Lymie, "the world began to take on its own true size." The novel speeds to its conclusion, and Lymie, Spud, and Sally are reconciled—but nothing among them will ever be quite the same.

In *The Folded Leaf,* at least on the face of it, Maxwell is often writing in the vein of social realism that characterizes much American fiction of the 1920s and later. But a good deal more is going on, as Edmund Wilson observes in a blurb for the novel: "With careful, unobtrusive art, Mr. Maxwell has made us feel all the coldness and hardness and darkness of Chicago, the prosaic surface of existence which seems to stretch about one like asphalt or ice. But there are moments when the author breaks way into a kind of poetic reverie that shows he is able to find a way out."

William Maxwell's novels are principally comedies of manners. On occasion he approaches tragedy, especially in *Time Will Darken It* and *So Long, See You Tomorrow*; but finally his fiction stresses redemption, especially as the novels end with the restoration of order, not in death or in disorder.

Time Will Darken It (1948) centers on the chaos that envelopes the King family during an overly long visit from relatives. Late in the novel, the protagonist, Austin King, wanders through his hometown in despair. In this brilliant sequence Maxwell limns the center of the town: a saloon, the pool hall, "a row of shabby houses nearby," the hotel, "the hackstand next door," the livery stable, various stores, the barber shop, the lumberyard, "Giovanni's confectionary and moviedrome," the telephone building, the jail, the park, the building where

his law office is, and, most important, the railway station.

In a metaphoric passage superbly executed by the author, Austin sees himself as swimming toward a locomotive's headlight when in fact he is thinking of flinging himself on the tracks as the "through train from St. Louis" arrives. Were the train not late, we are led to believe, Austin King might have killed himself. "I felt the most terrible sadness because it was not the way I expect to die," he thinks. Then: "I let go, knowing . . . that I would never escape from this trap alive. I came to the surface again, without struggling, and saw the two lights on the last car of the train getting smaller and smaller." Austin now returns to the world of his obligations, going back to the hospital to await the arrival of his second child. Earlier in the evening he visited Nora Potter, who became furious with him, and in his frustration he thinks: "It was the last show of that kind he would ever put on." But Austin changes his mind and is restored to his senses. The Potters finally return to Mississippi, taking the wounded Nora with them.

The Potters' first visit to Draperville generates the action of *Time Will Darken It.* This is a variation of the archetypal situation in which an intruder enters a closed society, an instance of which we witnessed in *Bright Center of Heaven.* Here is how *Time Will Darken It* begins:

> In order to pay off an old debt that someone else had contracted, Austin King had said yes when he knew he ought to have said no, and now at five o'clock of a July afternoon he saw the grinning face of trouble everywhere he turned. The house was full of strangers from Mississippi; within an hour the friends and neighbours he had invited to an evening party would begin ringing the doorbell; and his wife (whom he loved) was not speaking to him.

The stage is set for "the grinning face of trouble" as the drama unfolds.

In the course of the apparently meandering action, which is filled with reversals and other surprises, the Kings' marriage is threatened by Nora Potter's obsessive fascination with Austin; Austin nearly loses his law practice in consequence of allowing her to read law in his office; his wife Martha's health is adversely affected as her pregnancy is complicated; Austin decides he must make good on the bad investments his friends and acquaintances make in the Potters' plantation in Mississippi; Nora is scarred physically and emotionally; and practically everyone involved in the action proper is changed for the worse. Even the Beach "girls," the middle-aged spinster daughters of the widowed Mrs. Beach who start the kindergarten where Nora works and is injured, will never be the same. "We've had our chance and missed it," Lucy Beach says.

Paralleling the lives of the Kings and the Potters—in addition to those of their next-door neighbors, the Beaches—are the lives of the Kings' cook and maid, Rachel, and her irregular family, and of Miss Ewing, the office manager and secretary at the law offices of Holborn and King. Of the two women, Rachel experiences the more demanding tribulations when her common-law husband unexpectedly appears and mistreats her and her children. Miss Ewing, who knows everything except how to deal with the disruptive force in the law office, Miss Potter, finds herself unable to work and becomes mad or nearly so. She steals money from the petty-cash fund for no reason, and she spreads the inaccurate rumor that Miss Potter and Mr. King are having an affair. What goes on in the lives of Rachel and Miss Ewing—who have only the Kings in common—complements and fortifies the main action.

It is no happenstance that Maxwell, a master of the domestic world, chose Martha's cook and maid, Rachel, and Austin's secretary, Miss Ewing, as means of illustrating his main plot through complementary minor plots. And what goes on in the Potter family mirrors the King family in some ways. When the Potters, includ-

ing the willful Nora, finally leave, we realize that the Kings, their harried hosts, have narrowly escaped bankruptcy, the stillbirth of their son, the collapse of Austin's law practice, and Austin's death by his own hand, all of which would have meant a more intense and tragic cast for this fiction.

The author himself did not allude to such terms of art as tragedy and comedy, plot and subplot, theme and symbolism. Instead he describes writing *Time Will Darken It* in the *Paris Review* as writing a drama: "I found the book was proceeding by set conversations, rather like a play." He notes: "When I started a new chapter I asked myself who hadn't talked to whom lately." This comic explanation accounts for the course of the action dealing with a large cast of characters (Maxwell's most numerous) and for the roving point of view as the omniscient author shifts the fictive perspective from one character or group to another and from scene to summary.

One of the most striking features of *Time Will Darken It* is that Maxwell often skirts presenting what another writer, dramatizing a turning point, would depict as a scene rather than summarize. The most brilliant instance of such a throwaway technique occurs toward the end of part 5, when Nora is endeavoring to keep the children warm at the kindergarten. The coal in the stove hasn't started fully with kindling and newspaper: "The fire, rebuilt, burned feebly. . . . The children stood around, all bundled up and shivering. In the hall closet, while she was rummaging for more paper, Nora found a can of kerosene." In the next chapter, through the apparently aimless conversation of a bridge club, we learn what happened. The Potters, parents and son, have again arrived in town. "Austin met them at the train. . . . Nora was conscious. She knew them." Another voice: "They're staying with the kin; the way they did before." A third voice: "I wouldn't have had any of them in my house if I had been Martha." Here we get a brilliant synoptic account not only of Nora's accident but of how the community feels about Nora (including her supposed affair with Austin), Martha, and the mystery of what occurred at the kindergarten. "With only the word of four-year-old children to go on, I don't suppose we'll ever know," another bridge player says.

Maxwell employs the same technique when Rachel leaves her brutal common-law husband, Everitt; and, more important, when Austin dutifully visits Nora in the hospital. That scene, which has been prepared carefully by Austin's thinking that he must go, no matter how much agony it causes, is not presented by the author except through Austin's brief painful memories of the event when Nora becomes furious with him.

Toward the end of *Time Will Darken It,* Mary Caroline Link, a homely girl with a crush on the handsome Potter boy, Nora's younger brother, asks her mother whether certain married couples are in love. Finally she importunes her mother: "Are Mr. and Mrs. King in love?" Mrs. Link, distracted and exasperated, replies: "I don't know, dear." She adds: "I suppose they are. How can you tell?" This is the kind of communal conversation that takes place at the bridge club: it represents not only the community's point of view but the reader's as well. *Time Will Darken It,* like *Bright Center of Heaven,* is a novel adumbrating the complicated aspects of love, particularly within the family, that are affected by the corrosive power of time.

William Maxwell's fiction is written in a fluid prose that sometimes rises to a bright indicative poetry: "The roads runs straight with death and old age intersecting at right angles, and the harvest is stored in cemeteries." Ultimately we are carried into death on the flood of time. Such metaphors punctuate and color the action as the inexorable movement of time is revealed in the shifting patterns of light and dark and of the seasons' turning. The reader who would understand Maxwell fully must attend to his metaphors.

Shakespeare might have struck the phrase "Time will darken it"; instead Maxwell did. What Shakespeare did write about the power of time includes this passage from *First Part of King Henry IV* (act 5, scene 4):

> But thought's the slave of life, and life time's
> fool;
> And time, that takes survey of all the world,
> Must have a stop.

John Donne, in his "Sun Rising," writes poetry equally apt for this context:

> Love, all alike, no season knows nor clime,
> Nor hours, days, months, which are the rags of
> time.

In writing of Sylvia Townsend Warner in his introduction to *Four in Hand: A Quartet of Novels* (1986), Maxwell declares: "Miss Townsend Warner could tell a story, she could create characters that had the breath of life in them, she had a sense of subject, imagination, irony and wit." And, he continues in his letters, "she saw the world with a clear eye and she had a flawless prose style." Everything in this passage applies to Maxwell himself, who as Townsend Warner's literary executor edited these novels as well as a selection of her letters published in 1982. ("Dear William, I think of you so often. You might turn round in the street and see my anxious ghost looking after you"— October 27, 1962.)

THE CHÂTEAU: A NOVEL OF "DISPLACED PERSONS"

The list of novelistic virtues that Maxwell supplies appears in abundance in *Time Will Darken It,* as we have seen. That novel, as Alec Wilkinson points out in a *New Yorker* article titled "An American Original: Learning from a Literary Master," is his least autobiographical, "the only one of his novels that is almost entirely imagined." In contrast, *The Château* (1961) is markedly autobiographical. When the first draft was finished, Maxwell worried that he had written only a travel diary. Frank O'Connor volunteered to read "the whole mess," a "good-sized grocery carton" nearly filled with manuscript. He traced the outlines for two novels, which Maxwell then rewrote as one. O'Connor seemed to like each of the two parts equally well. Of the part of the action dealing with the young American couple he writes: "I saw inescapably one perfect novel. . . . No novelist before you had ever realised that the itinerary of an American couple in France was a novel in itself." He continues: "Then I realised that wasn't what you intended at all, and started to get involved in the Viennot circle. . . . Then the second novel began to possess me." O'Connor concludes: "You're like Hamlet, following the ghost, and as Horatio I can only stand back and wonder. The novel you see isn't either of the novels I see: the proof of that is that the really great scenes move from one part of the stage to the other." This is first-rate criticism, and O'Connor realizes that the draft, with its two lines of action, is unfinished.

In the interview with Bonetti, Maxwell describes his reaction: O'Connor "didn't assume that it was a travel diary at all. . . . A great weight fell off my shoulders. I thought, 'If it's two novels, anybody can make them into one.' So I did." In the published novel the reader can still find the shadowy second novel involving "the Viennot circle," as O'Connor calls it. Had Maxwell used this as his principal plot, I believe *The Château* would have been stronger. But other critics, including Elizabeth Bowen, seem to think otherwise. Bowen, writing in the *Reporter,* praises the scenes taking place in the château as "some of its most formidable": "the spellbinding monotony of the château, the masks of its inmates, transient or hereditary, portrayed in a mood of ironic comedy, combine

to build up a maximum suspense." She finds the novel successful on the whole, saying that few novels "have such romantic authority as *The Château,* fewer still so adult in vitality, so alight with humor."

Maxwell, in one of his few obiter dicta about writing, notes in *Four in Hand*: "The material of a novel—the *action*—is an experience which the novelist lives through and is permanently affected by." Maxwell clearly believed that the author can live through that experience in fact or in imagination. When autobiography is involved, the question is whether the author permits the experience as originally lived to enable him or her to find an appropriate plot. *The Château,* as it stands, is almost plotless aside from the peregrinations of the newly married couple in France—chiefly at the château itself (in a village near Blois) and later in Paris. The title announces the controlling image, which is the principal place (Paris aside) where the action unfolds. O'Connor suggested what might have been a better title—*Displaced Persons.* The Americans are not the only displaced characters in the novel: a Canadian, three Germans, and still others suffer, in one degree or another, some sense of cultural displacement.

The novel is built on a series of scenes, usually occurring in interiors (the château, various restaurants and hotels, an apartment, a cathedral) that alternate with the panorama of the wider world, especially the countryside. As Percy Lubbock, following James, declares in *The Craft of Fiction,* the scene should come first in importance: "To the scene, therefore, all other effects will appear to be subordinated." Scenes inevitably turn upon character and its revelation. And character is often revealed through dialogue, the principal constituent of scene.

In the scenes unfolding in *The Château,* we see the couple from the American Midwest, Barbara and Harold Rhodes, trying to understand the patois and idiom of their French hosts, especially Mme. Vienot and her circle. As the action continues, Barbara and Harold shed some of their awkward innocence and become more sophisticated in the ways of the world, especially in the ways of postwar France; nevertheless, many of the scenes turn upon misunderstanding, the misunderstanding that results from a clash of cultures caused by an imperfect awareness of foreign customs and a defective sense of language. From this persistent misunderstanding, of things being slightly askew, springs a gentle comedy of manners. Maxwell himself has pointed out that in the fiction of Henry James (especially in the international novels) the action takes on a moral cast; but in *The Château* the action involves social, not moral, dilemmas; yet in every case manners are involved. In this novel the author makes the telling point that there is a considerable difference in the manners of France and the United States, even though the table manners are the same. Harold perceives this cultural fact as he realizes a new acquaintance, a Frenchman, has been offended by Harold's calling him an acrobat and by Barbara's saying that his mother is *hors de siècle* (living in the wrong era). In trying to compliment the man, they each have unwittingly offended and alienated him. Conversation, foundering at this cultural divide, grinds to a halt. This kind of misunderstanding often occurs, partly because Barbara and Harold haven't worked hard on their French before becoming part of the first wave of American tourists in postwar France.

The French for their part see both the Nazis and their American conquerors as invaders. The nation is still obsessed by memories of the German occupation. The result is caught perfectly in Harold's remark to his wife: "Do I imagine it, or is it true that when they speak of the Nazis . . . the very next sentence is invariably some quite disconnected remark about Americans?" (Later Harold thinks to himself: "There were no Germans in the forest now, but would it ever be free of them?") In such ways Maxwell registers exactly the tenor of France in the late 1940s. Practically every aspect of daily life is covered, including allusions to French politics, even a snapshot of Charles De Gaulle. In this kind of general exchange we see the complexion of French life. Barbara speaks to Harold:

BARBARA: Did you hear her say "I like your American custom of not shaking hands in the morning?"

HAROLD: They shake hands at breakfast?

BARBARA: Apparently.

The succession of chapters devoted to Paris in the middle of the novel, chapters 13 through 16, shows Maxwell at his most resourceful. First he describes, in lyrical prose, the sleeping city. Then he focuses his camera on our young American couple as though they were strangers to us:

The sleepers, both in one bed, were turned toward each other. . . . Shortly afterward they turned away from each other, as if to demonstrate that in marriage there is no real resting place. Now love is gathered like great long-stemmed summer flowers, now the lovers withdraw from one another to nourish secretly a secret life.

Next Maxwell presents one of his dazzling dreams, done so artfully we do not know which lover is having the dream: all we know is that the woman in it may be accused of murder and that she wants to hide some papers before she may come under suspicion. (Later the dream comes to life in a news story reported in the Paris papers.) Now we return to the mundane waking world: "We're back in Paris." Barbara and Harold try to decide whether or not to stay with Eugène Cestre in his wonderful apartment. They stay, and the day passes quietly, culminating as Eugène drives the couple through the city late that night, hurtling through the streets.

The next day begins suddenly. A water pipe has burst, and the apartment, especially the kitchen, is flooded. For a long time Harold fears the damage is his fault or Barbara's. Finally he has the kind of revelation that characterizes Maxwell at his best: "The discovery that it was not their fault had come too late. They had had so much time to feel they were to blame that they might just as well have been."

They go back to sleep, only to be awakened by the unexpected appearance of three down-at-the-heels Germans caught in the coils of French bureaucracy. They are tired and hungry, so Barbara serves them breakfast, giving them food she and Harold bought the day before. One of them, who hasn't seen an orange in twelve years, saves his. Barbara and Harold, after deciding to buy the Germans some oranges, have this comical exchange:

BARBARA: Do you think they were Nazis?

HAROLD: No, of course not. How could they have been? Probably they never even heard of Hitler.

Our American cousins continue to be sweetly—and daftly—innocent.

Barbara and Harold now go to visit Eugène's cousin, Sabine, whom they have met at the château. She serves them supper, and the conversation with Sabine and her friend, a man, at first goes beautifully: "The four-sided conversation moved like a piece of music." Then Barbara and Harold, having had too much wine and having become overly comfortable, commit faux-pas in trying to compliment the young man, who is discomfited at hearing his mother is living in the wrong era (Barbara meant to say she is charmingly old-fashioned) and that the man himself is an acrobat (this "compliment" by Harold falls flat), as we have seen.

The next day the Rhodes find themselves trapped in bureaucratic snafus comparable to what has caught the Germans. They have immense difficulty in securing gasoline coupons for their host and in getting visas to Austria. Eugène's directions to them prove all wrong.

Later the dinner arranged by him goes awkwardly. The next day their difficulties continue as Barbara loses her umbrella and Mme. Straus, another friend from the château, fails to appear as scheduled.

These matters are examples of what Frank O'Connor calls counterpointing, and in this letter (late October 1958) he warns Maxwell not to overdo it. But Maxwell is too lavish in his use of parallelism to compare and contrast these displaced persons. The novel would be better were it fifty to one hundred pages shorter.

O'Connor claims that *The Château* is not a novel as Jane Austen or Ivan Turgenev understood the form. And it is not the novel as it was written by Kingsley Amis, Iris Murdoch, and John Updike in the 1960s, as Miranda Seymour points out in a *Times Literary Supplement* review of the new Harvill reprint. It is something close to what Maxwell tried to avoid writing—a travel diary. In any case, whether or not a reader likes the form he created, that form is something new that grows naturally out of the experience; and it, including the long epilogue in which all the loose ends are tied up, is right for this occasion, except the matter of proportion. There is too much detail; there are too many scenes. All the same, as Seymour suggests, "it is hard not to see it as a work of genius."

SO LONG, SEE YOU TOMORROW

So Long, See You Tomorrow (1980), winner of the American Book Award, was William Maxwell's sixth and last novel. Technically it is his most accomplished. Much of it unfolds through the medium of reminiscence, and for that and other reasons some critics have taken it to be autobiography, not fiction. In *Touching the World* (1992), Paul John Eakin, taking the word "memoir" (in the first paragraph of chapter 2) with utmost seriousness, proceeds to consider Maxwell's novel as a new form of autobiography to be measured by the fancy term "referential aesthetic." Nevertheless Eakin presents a fine critical account of *So Long, See You Tomorrow.*

Within a few months of the novel's publication, Walter Sullivan reviewed it in the *Sewanee Review,* calling it "a small jewel of a book" that is "a consummate success." "The novel is so soundly conceived and so brilliantly executed—I know of no narrative which has a structure quite like the one Maxwell employs—that theme cannot be separated from method." Of that brilliant performance, he concludes that this work "deserves the attention of all who are interested in learning more about the way fiction works."

Alec Wilkinson to some extent adjudicates the matter of genre. "An autobiographical writer," he declares in "An American Original," "is often trying to deliver himself from an experience that haunts him." Maxwell directly describes that event in his life, his mother's death, in *They Came Like Swallows,* as we know. In *So Long, See You Tomorrow,* according to Wilkinson, Maxwell's "way of treating it is more oblique—what he is writing about really is his mother's absence from the family and the permanent shadow such deprivation cast over the household. In the narrative the consequences of his mother's death are combined with the description and aftermath of the murder of a tenant farmer by his lover's husband."

The method, as Sullivan observes, is contrapuntal—what Maxwell and O'Connor, in speaking of *The Château,* call counterpoint. *So Long, See You Tomorrow,* which is brilliantly successful, is a cardinal instance of what James calls the "shapely nouvelle" at its finest, perfectly executed.

James is a continuing presence in Maxwell's fiction, as this remark to Wilkinson suggests: "Henry James said 'Dramatize, dramatize, dramatize,' not 'Generalize, generalize, generalize.'" The result is the scenic exactness we have seen in Maxwell—the succession of scenes artfully interpolated within the narrative flow of the action that alternates as it establishes time and place through the larger action. Overall, the economy of means in *So Long, See You Tomorrow* is astonishing.

In this novel Maxwell uses the first-person narrative voice, never before utilized in his previous novels. When younger, he admitted, in writing in the first person he tended to become too garrulous and to focus the action on the narrator, himself. "The answer," he observes, "is to treat oneself as an outside person, as a character, who is therefore manageable. And also not the center of the action and of attention, but somewhat on the side."

Eakin does not seem to take into account the possibility that the first-person narrator speaking in the first four and one-half chapters and the coda (chapter 9) is not the self Maxwell would be were he writing straight autobiography. "We're so many selves, a whole cast of characters," Maxwell told Bonetti. "Now I'm one person, now I'm another." The narrator who reports the aforementioned chapters is not to be found in Maxwell's previous novels, nor in his family chronicle, *Ancestors.*

In musing about the special problems that *So Long, See You Tomorrow* posed for him, Maxwell comments in the *Paris Review*: "The first-person character has to be a character and not just a narrative device. So I used myself as the 'I' and the result was two stories, my own and Cletus Smith's, and I knew they had to be structurally combined, but how?" By chance he read a letter from the Swiss artist Alberto Giacometti to the French painter Henri Matisse describing how the former "came to do a certain piece of sculpture" and found his answer.

Early in the novel Maxwell develops a wonderful analogy between the house that is being built for the narrator's family and the sculpture by Giacometti. "I seem to remember that I went to the new house one winter day and saw snow descending through the attic to the upstairs bedroom," he begins. He then turns over the possibilities and admits that the memory may be that caught in a photograph, not an event he witnessed. The narrator continues: "Before the stairway was in, there was a gaping hole in the center of the house. . . . One day I looked down through this hole and saw Cletus Smith standing on a pile of lumber looking at me. . . . We climbed up another ladder and walked along horizontal two-by-sixes with our arms outstretched, teetering like circus acrobats on the high wire."

Late in the novel, once the story is fully told and the narrator is mulling over its consequences, he says, looking back at Cletus' agonizing half life after his parents are separated: "He can never go to that school again. He walks in the Palace at 4 A.M. In that strange blue light. With his arms outstretched, like an acrobat on the high wire. And with no net to catch him if he falls." We—narrator and reader—don't know what happened to Cletus. All we know is that his friendship with the narrator is fractured, as was the friendship between Cletus' father, Clarence Smith, and his best friend, Lloyd Wilson.

In "The New House" (chapter 3), the narrator describes not only the scaffolding of the new house but Giacometti's *Palace at 4 A.M.* in the Metropolitan Museum of Art, and he compares the two structures through implicit analogy. We thus see a work in progress that symbolizes the possibilities of life. By comparing the two structures Maxwell is able to join the story of his early life with the narrative in which the collapse of the Smith and Wilson families—culminating in the murder of Wilson and the suicide of Smith—is recounted. The image of the acrobat on the high wire is perfect because it captures not only Cletus' position as he teeters over the unforgiving ground of the real world but reminds us of how his father committed suicide in the gravel pond, drowning himself and accomplishing by force of will what the investigating officer said was impossible. The image of the acrobat combines the various im-

ages in the novel—the gravel pit, Giacometti's sculpture, and the framework of the house—and it is the controlling image for both lines of the narrative. Maxwell has the skill of a poet in developing imagery to reveal and complement character and theme. His performance in *So Long, See You Tomorrow* is acrobatic.

THE SHORT WORKS

Maxwell wrote four books of stories, all of which were published after *The Château,* which shows that he was principally a novelist. Although the earliest of the stories in the fourth volume, *All the Days and Nights: The Collected Stories* (1995), appeared in the late 1930s and the early 1940s, most of them were published serially in the 1960s, 1970s, and 1980s.

It is easy to see the relation of many of the stories to Maxwell's novels. "The Holy Terror" (1986) can be taken as an epilogue to *They Came Like Swallows.* "What Every Boy Should Know" (1954), "The Front and the Back Parts of the House" (1991), and "A Final Report" (1963) are complements to *Time Will Darken It.* "The Pilgrimage" (1953), with a few changes, could be a sequence within *The Château,* as could "The Gardens of Mont-Saint-Michel" (1969); and "The French Scarecrow" (1956) may be seen as an epilogue to the same novel. "The Trojan Women" (1952) stands as a prologue to *So Long, See You Tomorrow.* And so on. The stories laid in New York City, such as "Over by the River" (1974; the only long story in the book), "Haller's Second Home" (1941), and "The Thistles in Sweden" (1976; probably the best story in the book) are easily identified. Maxwell writes nearly as well about Manhattan and about New England as he does the country of his imagination—central Illinois.

It is not possible in this essay to examine a large number of the twenty-three stories and the twenty-one improvisations (fables or short stories) appearing in *All the Days and Nights.* Anyone interested in the modern American short story, especially at *The New Yorker,* will want to read them all and to study some of them for their technical accomplishment. Any editor forging a substantial anthology of the American short story should include Maxwell.

In response to a question posed by Bonetti—"Did you ever worry about borrowing from writers whose manuscripts you've read?" (at *The New Yorker*), Maxwell said: "There was nobody who was at all like me as a writer. I'm sure that my sense of how to write well was tremendously sharpened by working with such writers. So it was not a problem. It was a great help." His stories, most of which appeared in *The New Yorker,* are written in the modes, tones, and voices one associates with that magazine; but they are not derivative or mechanical.

Maxwell has pointed out that *The New Yorker*'s stories in the days of the editors Harold Ross and William Shawn proceeded sentence by sentence, having the economy and tightness of poetry. Every sentence counts, and the narrative proceeds clearly from beginning to end so that the reader doesn't have to double back for information. Therefore, as Maxwell put it, he tried to write "sentences that [wouldn't] be like sand castles."

Let us consider some representative passages. First come two scenes from "Over by the River":

> And when the policeman got back to his post a woman in a long red coat was going through the trash basket directly across the street from him. She was harmless. He saw her night after night. And in a minute she would cross over and tell him about the doctor at Bellevue who said she probably dreamed that somebody picked the lock of her door while she was out buying coffee and stole her mother's gold thimble.

This bag woman reappears later in the action:

> Walking the dog at seven-fifteen on a winter morning, he suddenly stopped and said to himself, "Oh God, somebody's been murdered." . . . Somebody in a long red coat. . . . How could she sleep on cold stone, with nothing over her? "Can I help you?" His voice sounded strange and hollow. There was no answer. The red coat did not stir. Then he saw the canvas bag crammed with the fruit of her night's scavenging, and backed down the steps.

Let us now consider the opening and closing paragraphs of "The French Scarecrow":

> Driving past the Fishers' house on his way out to the public road, Gerald Martin said to himself absentmindedly, "There's Edmund working in his garden," before he realized that it was a scarecrow. And two nights later he woke up sweating from a dream, a nightmare, which he related next day, lying tense on his analyst's couch. . . .

> Edmund . . . carried the dummy outside, removed the hat and then the head, unbuttoned the shirt, removed the straw that filled it and the trousers, and threw it in the compost pile. The hat, the head, the shirt and trousers, the gloves that were the hands, he rolled into a bundle and put away. . . . The two crossed sticks reminded him of the comfort that Mrs. Ryan, who was a devout Catholic, had and that he did not have. The hum of the vacuum cleaner overhead in the living room, the sad song of a mechanical universe, was all the reassurance he could hope for, and it left so much (it left the scarecrow, for example) completely unexplained and unaccounted for.

"The French Scarecrow" embodies a brilliant instance of how an author can employ a controlling image to reveal action and to embody theme. Consider, in contrast, another kind of ending from another story in *All the Days and Nights,* in its way as good as the conclusion of "The French Scarecrow." An American couple is staying in a hotel in a French village. It has been a long and often trying day.

> "I suppose Périgueux really isn't the kind of town that would support a movie theater," Ray said.

"That's it," Ellen said. "Here, when people want to relax and enjoy themselves, they have an apéritif, they walk up and down in the evening air, they dance in the street, the way people used to do before there were any movies. It's another civilization entirely from anything we're accustomed to. Another world."

They went back into the bedroom and closed the shutters. A few minutes later, some more people emerged from the movie theater, and some more, and some more, and then a great crowd came streaming out and, walking gravely, like people taking part in a religious procession, fanned out across the open square.

This story, "The Pilgrimage," about American innocents abroad who think themselves extraordinarily sophisticated, comes to its droll climax as the action ends.

I have held my commentary to a minimum to allow the reader to perceive the exact nuances of Maxwell's style—the natural idiom of the dialogue, the simple and precise diction, the artful variation in syntax, with most of the sentences in natural order but an occasional inversion and periodic sentence. There are no sand castles here.

"In presenting to Maxwell in 1995 the Gold Medal for Fiction of the American Academy of Arts and Letters," Wilkinson tells us, "Joseph Mitchell said, 'William Maxwell's principal theme, like James Joyce's, is the sadness that often exists at the heart of a family. . . . He is as aware as any novelist who ever lived of what human beings are capable of.'" Perhaps I have presented too sunny an account of Maxwell's writing, especially his fiction; and so I quote this passage from "My Father's Friends" (in *All the Days and Nights*). The narrator, who is Maxwell, recalls one of his father's friends, a cranky and outspoken man, and his sweet wife, who became a surrogate mother to Maxwell and then died young herself. On his own, at thirteen or fourteen, he goes to visit her in the hospital:

She saw me, but it was as if she were looking at somebody she had never seen before. Since then, I have watched beloved animals dying. The withdrawal, into some part of themselves that only they know about. . . . I skittered down the steps and got on my bicycle and rode away from the hospital feeling I had made a mistake. I had and I hadn't. She was in no condition to receive visitors, but I had acquired an important item of knowledge—dying is something people have to live through, and while they are doing it, unless you are much closer to them than I was to her, you have little or no claim on them.

Anyone who takes William Maxwell to be a sentimentalist should look at this passage and others like it. In Maxwell there is a flinty knowledge about the worst that life can offer, the knowledge that lies behind this remark to Nancy Hale in a letter written to her in May 1941: "Whenever I read anything of yours . . . , I am convinced against a mountain of evidence to the contrary that there is such a thing as the human heart."

"READING IS RAPTURE"

In *The Outermost Dream: Essays and Reviews* (1989), Maxwell has collected the best of his occasional journalism. These pieces, published from 1956 through 1987, are devoted to prose nonfiction—"diaries, memoirs, published correspondence, biography and autobiography" which, as he observes in the preface, "do not spring from prestidigitation or require a long apprenticeship." Some of the writers involved, it is clear, Maxwell had read and admired for years before he wrote about some aspect of their lives or work. These would include Katharine and E. B. White, V. S. Pritchett, Frank O'Connor, Eudora Welty, Louise Bogan, and Sylvia Townsend Warner. The others, it would appear, he took up for the given occasion and probably include Karen Blixen (Isak Dinesen), E. M. Forster, Colette, Byron, Edith Nesbit, Samuel Butler, and several more.

Anyone interested in Maxwell and his connection with *The New Yorker* will take up the book eagerly, for the first list includes many authors with whom he worked in one way or another. One of the most distinguished of these is O'Connor. Maxwell has written not only "The Duke's Child," collected here, but "Frank O'Connor and *The New Yorker*," which is reprinted in a remarkable collection of letters between himself and O'Connor entitled *The Happiness of Getting It Down Right* (edited by Michael Steinman, 1996). The latter piece on O'Connor concludes thus: "When I think of him I hear his voice, I see his extraordinary face, I remember the affectionate and amused expression in his eyes, the kingly turn of his head, the beautiful smile. In speaking of him I cannot bring myself to use the past tense."

This, of course, is not literary criticism of the usual sort. What Maxwell did in writing about the careers of other artists was to present a combination of reminiscence, appreciation, biography, history, and a good deal else, including whimsy. Maxwell viewed each book on its own terms, generally writing about it and its maker because they had touched him in a way at once singular and profound. So he quotes this remark by Francis Kilvert: "Life appears to me such a curious and wonderful thing that it almost seems a pity that even such a humble and uneventful life as mine should pass altogether away without some such record as this." Maxwell so thoroughly agreed with that sentiment he might have written it himself, as is the case with this sentence struck by Kilvert: "I feel as if life is a dream from which at any moment I may awake."

Maxwell was especially good at presenting a subject in a dazzlingly clear light through the means of a strong narrative and exactly chosen representative details. He also quoted exceptionally well. Here is a passage from "V. S. Pritchett's Apprenticeship" (1972) to prove my points: "Suddenly, in his early thirties, his life changed completely. His writing improved and his talent began to be recognized. And, emerging from a period of emotional bankruptcy, he fell deeply in love and married again. This second, ecstatically happy marriage he keeps in his closed fist, like a boy with a prized marble. 'There is, I am sure,' he says, 'a direct connection between passionate love and the firing of the creative power of the mind.'"

And so Maxwell carries us through the wonderful experience of what he calls the "rapture of reading." "It stands to reason," he explains in "Mr. Forster's Pageant" (1961), "that a book one reads with rapture must have been written with it." In the prefatory note he writes: "Reading is rapture (or if it isn't, I put the book down meaning to go on with it later, and escape out the side door). A felicitously turned sentence can induce it. Or a description. Or unexpected behavior. . . . Or dialogue that carries with it the unconscious flowering of character." His infectious idea is elaborated through his examples. In *The Outermost Dream* the reader often has the feeling in experiencing Maxwell's excitement about a particular artist that "reading is rapture." What he says about these figures and their lives and art is remarkable: "They tell us what happened—what people said and did and wore and ate and hoped for and were afraid of, and in detail after often unimaginable detail they refresh our idea of existence and hold oblivion at arm's length." This is criticism with a heart and a soul, with the blood and marrow of life itself. It possesses what William Maxwell insists all good writing must have—"the breath of life."

Selected Bibliography

WORKS OF WILLIAM MAXWELL

NOVELS AND SHORT STORIES
Bright Center of Heaven. New York: Harper & Brothers, 1934.

They Came Like Swallows. New York: Harper & Brothers, 1937. Rev. ed., New York: Vintage, 1960. New York: Modern Library, 1997. (Contains an introduction by Maxwell.)

The Folded Leaf. New York: Harper & Brothers, 1945. Rev. ed., New York: Vintage, 1959. New ed., New York: Vintage International, 1996.

Time Will Darken It. New York: Harper & Brothers, 1948. Rev. ed., New York: Vintage, 1962. Reprinted as *Time Will Darken It: A Novel.* Boston: D. R. Godine, 1983. New ed., New York: Vintage International, 1997.

The Château. New York: Knopf, 1961. Reprint, Boston: D. R. Godine, 1985. New ed., New York: Vintage International, 1995.

The Old Man at the Railroad Crossing and Other Tales. New York: Knopf, 1966.

Over by the River and Other Stories. New York: Knopf, 1977.

So Long, See You Tomorrow. New York: Knopf, 1980. New ed., New York: Vintage International, 1996.

Five Tales: Written for His Family on Special Occasions and Printed to Celebrate His Eightieth Birthday, 16 August 1988. Omaha, Nebr.: Cummington Press, 1988.

Billie Dyer and Other Stories. New York: Knopf, 1992.

Time Will Darken It; The Château; So Long, See You Tomorrow. New York: Quality Paperback Book Club, 1992. (Contains a preface by the author.)

All the Days and Nights: The Collected Stories. New York: Knopf, 1995.

OTHER WORKS

The Heavenly Tenants. Pictures by Ilonka Karasz. New York: Harper & Brothers, 1946. (Children's book.)

Ancestors. New York: Knopf, 1971. Reprinted as *Ancestors: A Family History.* Boston: D. R. Godine, 1985. New ed., New York: Vintage International, 1995.

The Outermost Dream: Essays and Reviews. New York: Knopf, 1989.

Mrs. Donald's Dog Bun and His Home Away from Home. Illustrated by James Stevenson. New York: Knopf, 1995. (Children's book.)

The Happiness of Getting It Down Right: Letters of Frank O'Connor and William Maxwell 1945–1966. Edited by Michael Steinman. New York: Knopf, 1996.

The Element of Lavishness: Letters of Sylvia Townsend Warner and William Maxwell, 1938–1978. Edited by Michael Steinman. Washington, D.C.: Counterpoint, 2001.

WORKS EDITED

The Garden and the Wilderness, by Charles Pratt. New York: Horizon Press, 1980.

Letters, by Sylvia Townsend Warner. New York: Viking, 1982.

Four in Hand: A Quartet of Novels, by Sylvia Townsend Warner. New York: Norton, 1986. (Contains an introduction by Maxwell.)

CRITICAL AND BIOGRAPHICAL STUDIES
Allen, Brooke. "Intimations of Mortality." *New Criterion* 13, no. 5:62–67 (January 1995).

Auden, W. H. *The Dyer's Hand and Other Essays.* New York: Random House, 1962. Pp. 2–12.

Bawer, Bruce. *The Aspect of Eternity: Essays.* St. Paul: Graywolf Press, 1993. Pp. 178–198.

Bell, Pearl K. "Book of Laughter and Remembering." *New Republic,* May 4, 1992, pp. 38–40.

Bonetti, Kay. "An Interview with William Maxwell." *Missouri Review* 19, no. 1:79–98 (1996) and 19, no. 2:83–95 (1996).

Bowen, Elizabeth. "Second Home." *Reporter,* May 25, 1961, pp. 54–55.

Eakin, Paul John. *Touching the World: Reference in Autobiography.* Princeton, N.J.: Princeton University Press, 1992. Pp. 40–50.

Forster, E. M. *Aspects of the Novel.* New York: Harcourt, Brace & Company, 1927.

Gill, Brendan. *Here at "The New Yorker."* New York: Random House, 1975.

Ginsberg, Harvey. "A Modest, Scrupulous, Happy Man." *New York Times Book Review,* January 22, 1995, p. 3. (Interview.)

Hampton, Wilborn. "William Maxwell, 91, Dies." *New York Times,* August 1, 2000.

Lubbock, Percy. *The Craft of Fiction.* New York: Scribners, 1921.

Menaker, Daniel. "The Gentle Realist." *New York Times Book Review,* October 15, 2000, p. 39.

O'Connor, Flannery. *Mystery and Manners: Occasional Prose.* Edited by Sally and Robert Fitzgerald. New York: Farrar, Straus & Giroux, 1969.

Phillips, Robert. "Making Sense of What Takes Place." *Hudson Review* 65:491–493 (autumn 1992).

Phillips, William, ed. *Great American Short Novels.* New York: Dial Press, 1946. (Contains an introduction by Phillips, pp. vii–xiv, and *Pale Horse, Pale Rider* by Katherine Anne Porter, pp. 577–624.)

Ross, Walter W. "William Maxwell." In *Dictionary of Literary Biography Yearbook.* Detroit: Gale Research, 1980. Pp. 260–266.

Seabrook, John, and George Plimpton. "The Art of Fiction: William Maxwell." *Paris Review* 85:106–139 (1982).

Seymour, Miranda. "A Young Man with Money and a Wife." *Times Literary Supplement,* April 7, 2000, p. 28.

Sullivan, Walter. "The Feckless Present, the Unredeemed Past." *Sewanee Review* 88:439–441 (summer 1980).

Thurber, James. *The Years with Ross.* Boston: Little, Brown, 1959.

Tolson, Jay. "So Long, Mr. Maxwell." *U.S. News and World Report,* August 14, 2000, p. 10. (Obituary.)

Wilkinson, Alec. "An American Original: Learning from a Literary Master." *The New Yorker,* December 27, 1999, pp. 68–75.

Yagoda, Ben. *About Town: "The New Yorker" and the World It Made.* New York: Scribners, 2000.

Yeats, William Butler. *The Collected Poems of W. B. Yeats: Definitive Edition, with the Author's Final Revisions.* New York: Macmillan, 1956.

—GEORGE CORE

Cormac McCarthy

1933–

CHARLES JOSEPH McCARTHY Jr. was born in Providence, Rhode Island, on July 20, 1933. (He later changed Charles to Cormac, after an Irish king.) After the age of four, he grew up near Knoxville, Tennessee, as the third of six children of Charles Joseph and Gladys McGrail McCarthy—parents affluent enough to afford maids. A graduate of Catholic secondary schools, McCarthy in the 1950s twice attended the University of Tennessee at Knoxville without getting a degree, putting in a four-year stint with the U.S. Air Force between times. At about age twenty-three, while stationed in Alaska, he discovered his affinity for literature, reading "a lot of books very quickly," as he recalled, including such lifelong favorites as works by Herman Melville, William Faulkner, and Fyodor Dostoyevsky.

In 1961 McCarthy married a college friend, Lee Holleman, with whom he had a son, Cullen; they divorced in 1964. The following year he obtained a fellowship from the American Academy of Arts and Letters and the William Faulkner Foundation Award that paid for a trip to Europe, which led to his marriage in 1966 to an English pop singer named Anne DeLisle. After sojourning in Europe for a year, they moved to Tennessee and lived in what she called "total poverty" near Knoxville. In 1977 McCarthy separated from his wife (they divorced in 1978) and moved to El Paso, Texas, where—despite winning a MacArthur fellowship ("genius grant") of $236,000 in 1981—he lived in quasi-primitive fashion in a tiny cottage, cutting his own hair, eating meals in cafeterias or off a hot plate, and doing his wash at the laundromat. There, after placing his first four novels within

a hundred-mile radius of Knoxville, he has set his last four novels in the vast borderland territory of the great American Southwest. He has, in addition, written several screenplays and a play, *The Stonemason* (1994), which reflects his experience of working with a southern black family for several months.

McCarthy's first five novels, through *Blood Meridian* (1985), attained a total sales of only about fifteen thousand copies despite garnering many favorable reviews, but in 1992 *All the Pretty Horses* proved a breakthrough novel, selling over 500,000 copies in two years and bringing about the republication of all his earlier novels in Vintage editions. (Its film version, directed by Billy Bob Thornton and starring Matt Damon and Penelope Cruz, was released in the fall of 2000.) With the completion of his Border Trilogy—*All the Pretty Horses, The Crossing* (1994), and *Cities of the Plain* (1998)—McCarthy has established himself as one of the major American novelists of the later twentieth century.

THE ORCHARD KEEPER

The Orchard Keeper (1965), McCarthy's first published novel, begins in the vein of a mystery story. Its plot line starts with the killing, in self-defense, of a vagrant hitchhiker by an outlaw and bootlegger named Marion Sylder, who deposits the corpse in a vat once used for insecticide in the orchard of the book's title. Dramatic possibilities open up when we realize that the victim was the father of Sylder's close friend John Wesley Rattner, an adolescent boy whose mother swears him to avenge his father's death. But neither Sylder nor the boy ever realizes that the dead man is the lost father, whose bones remain anonymously rotting in the pit year after year. In the end the plot of *The Orchard Keeper* proves subordinate to the book's mood and theme. The true subject of McCarthy's first novel, which was to be enunciated prominently in all the later ones, is the nostalgic sense of an old way of life passing into oblivion.

In support of that theme, at the outset the orchard of the title is being swallowed back into the primal wilderness of the Tennessee mountains where the orchard keeper, Arthur Ownby, has spent nearly ninety years living off the land with utmost simplicity. His eventual arrest and imprisonment for violent resistance to law officers marks the end of such Daniel Boone–like independence, and with his capture the whole roster of country characters, including Marion Sylder and John Wesley Rattner, also experience the passing of their indigenous way of life centered on hunting, fishing, and total immersion in nature. In his closing paragraph, McCarthy editorializes about these country people: "They are gone now. Fled, banished in death or exile, lost, undone. . . . No avatar, no scion, no vestige of that people remains."

Another recurring feature that characterizes this first novel is McCarthy's reverence toward the rural landscape for its wild fauna and flora, its majestically passing seasons, and the sustenance it furnishes for its hardy native population. By contrast, young Rattner's only trip to the city shows it in a bad light, as the boy gapes at an evangelist "screaming incoherently and brandishing a tattered Bible" on a street corner while the market next door displays "meat white-spotted and trichinella-ridden . . . tottering up from moats of watery blood, a tray of brains, unidentifiable gobbets of flesh scattered here and there."

Probably the most distinctive characteristic of this first novel is McCarthy's masterly command of style in both dialect/dialogue and expository prose. Appropriately for its Faulkner Award (for a first novel), *The Orchard Keeper* recalls Faulkner's extended cadences but still evinces a verbal originality and precision that has earned praise from other major authors, such as Robert Penn Warren and Saul Bellow. A brief sample will serve to illustrate the point as McCarthy describes:

> shacks strewn about the valley in unlikely places, squatting over their gullied purlieus like great brooding animals rigid with constipation. . . . They were rented to families of gaunt hollow-eyed and dark-skinned people . . . [who] came and went, unencumbered as migratory birds, each succeeding family a replica of the one before and only the names on the mailboxes altered, the new ones lettered crudely in above a rack of paint smears that obliterated the former inhabitants back into the anonymity from which they sprang.

Prefiguring McCarthy's style in all his later novels is his penchant for words rarely found in even his most sophisticated reader's vocabulary: "murrhined," "esotery," "verspertine," "ciborium," "spodomantic." Perhaps, as the critic Mark Winchell surmises, this college dropout gains a measure of satisfaction in sending English professors scurrying to their dictionaries.

OUTER DARK

In his second novel, *Outer Dark* (1968), McCarthy again sets his cast of characters in his beloved landscape of rural Appalachia, but here he chooses a turn-of-the-twentieth-century time setting and uproots his people from their local environment. The story begins with the birth of a child to Culla and Rinthy Holme, a brother and sister living in an isolated backwoods cabin. To hide their shame, he abandons the baby on a mat of moss in the deep woods, but it is rescued by an itinerant tinker who hears the infant wailing. Thereafter the pursuit of the child by its mother, which in turn spurs the pursuit of her by her brother, introduces two new features that recur in all of McCarthy's later books: the "on the road" plot line and the obligatory great chase scene. Through the latter motif, he reinvigorates his earlier mode of character development, investing his two main characters with prodigious reserves of endurance and resourcefulness against an appalling degree of hardship and danger. Meanwhile, his "on the road" gambit permits him to develop a remarkably vivid and individualized set of minor characters with whom the brother or sister consorts during their epic journeys. The dialect and dialogue among such country people is one of McCarthy's finest ongoing achievements.

Although McCarthy's fundamental stance is that of naturalistic realism, the central mode of twentieth-century literature, he also resorts powerfully to surrealistic instances of dream imagery, of ghostly emanations from the past, and of quasi-miraculous action in the present. In *Outer Dark* the great chase motif offers the prime example of these effects, beginning with Culla Holme's nightmare of being assaulted by a mob and continuing through his book-long ordeal of being menaced and hunted for crimes he did not commit, much in the fashion of an Alfred Hitchcock movie. By far the most evil and mysterious of Holme's antagonists are the trio of drifters who kill at random a number of people they happen across, including as the book ends the lost infant and the tinker who expropriated him. These graphic murders, along with several victims of lynching who are seen hanging in trees, foreshadow the obsession with bloody violence that has become associated with McCarthy's work, especially after its culmination in *Blood Meridian*.

The fact that we never see the interior minds of these killers, but only their actions, apparently figures into the book's title, which the narrative mentions only once—when the sister surreptitiously leaves her brother sleeping in the night: ". . . she waited again at the front door with it open, poised between the maw of the dead and loveless house and the outer dark." Although the "inner dark," or human capacity for committing appalling acts of evil, is surely one of McCarthy's most compelling subjects, he appears at this point to find it inexplicable and therefore describable only through its actions and effects, not its interior chemistry. Another possible use of the title, some critics say, is the biblical reference to "outer darkness" in this book's title—the realm into which unregenerate sinners will be cast and therefore an appropriate link with Culla Holme's homeless and hopeless wanderings.

CHILD OF GOD

The title phrase *Child of God* (1973) makes an innocent appearance early in this novel when McCarthy tells his readers that his main character is "a child of God much like yourself perhaps." By the end of this tale of serial murder and multiple necrophilia, however, McCarthy's portrayal of a psychopathic pervert turns "child of God" and "much like yourself" into decidedly problematic phrases, all the more so when he suggests that Lester Ballard's derangement—initially set off by the forced sale of his home at auction—has a theological grounding: "You might have said he was half right who thought himself so grievous a case against the gods."

Along with McCarthy's new interest in the interior psychology of evil—or "inner dark"—*Child of God* exhibits several other innovative features. One is the use of multiple narrators, with chapters narrated in the third person (presumably McCarthy himself) interspersed with chapters narrated by inhabitants of the local Appalachian community. The latter technique, though sometimes digressive, represents a Faulknerian strain reminiscent of the interwoven monologues of *As I Lay Dying* and the local color tradition that Faulkner deployed in *The Hamlet*. The other new feature of note is McCarthy's increasing focus on technical competence as a prime virtue in a largely chaotic environment. In this novel the main instance of this motif is the four-page discourse describing in close detail the blacksmith's work refurbishing an old axe blade. Lester Ballard likewise displays such high competence in handling a rifle that he is banned from shooting for prizes at the town fair.

The plot line of *Child of God* follows a gradual spiral of degradation, beginning with Ballard intruding voyeuristically upon a pair of youths having sex in a parked car at night. Later in part 1 he is accused, falsely, of raping a drunken slattern he encounters on the roadway, and spends a week in prison as his punishment. Meanwhile, the local narrators fill in details that might exculpate Ballard's actions, such as his father's suicide and mother's disappearance when the boy was nine or ten, the violent blow on the head he received when he tried to stop the sale of his home at auction, and his comradeship with an amoral old dumpkeeper who sexually assaults one of his own nine daughters.

Part 2 begins with Ballard coming across a pair of young people in the act of coition in a vehicle one morning. After discovering that they are dead, by carbon monoxide apparently, he takes their money and fornicates with the girl's corpse, which he then hauls off to his remote cabin for additional usage of that sort. Next, after being rebuffed by the daughter of his dumpkeeper friend, he shoots the girl and burns his friend's house down as a cover. Finally, after his own cabin burns down with the abducted girl's body in it, he stashes the bodies of seven later victims in the cavern where he takes refuge, a place that could symbolize the "inner dark" of his own being.

In part 3, Ballard is captured (wearing a wig made of a young woman's scalp) and incarcer-ated in a mental hospital at last, but not without a heroic effort on his part to maintain his life of savage freedom. During his great chase scene, Ballard's crossing of a flooded river evokes a curiously sympathetic editorial from McCarthy's narrator, indicating the author's view that society is more blameworthy than the murderer they seek to apprehend: "He could not swim, but how would you drown him? . . . You could say that he's sustained by his fellow men, like you. Has peopled the shore with them calling to him. . . . But they want this man's life. He has heard them in the night seeking him with lanterns and cries of execration." Whatever else one may think of this excursion into either evil or psychic illness—McCarthy himself seems to favor the latter interpretation—*Child of God* undoubtedly exhibits a growing mastery of literary technique and a distinctly original portrayal of his grand theme: the relationship between a conventional community and its transgressors.

SUTTREE

Suttree (1979), McCarthy's longest and most static novel, comprises the author's farewell to Knoxville. That the divorce was mutual may be inferred from some of the reviews—for example, J. Z. Howard's "'A Masterpiece of Filth': Portrait of Knoxville Forgets to Be Fair" (*Memphis Press-Scimitar,* January 20, 1979). Rumored to be about twenty years in the making, *Suttree* appears to date back to the countercultural rebellions of the beatnik 1950s and flower child 1960s—the time of the author's ne'er-do-well youth. Emphatically renouncing the material comforts of bourgeois society (like McCarthy himself in real life), its two main characters, Cornelius Suttree and Gene Harrogate, inhabit the city's derelict underworld in close association with the petty criminals, prostitutes, alcoholics, bums, and demented outcasts who make up the surprisingly cohesive and mutually supportive McAnally Flats community. It is, McCarthy says, "a world within the world. In these alien reaches . . . that the righteous see from carriage and car another life dreams. Ill-shapen or black or deranged, fugitive of all order, strangers in everyland."

The good-natured comradeship of these fellows can be inferred from McCarthy's nomenclature: Abednego Jones, Nigger (also known as Nig), Gatemouth, Trippin through the Dew (a gay man), Jabbo, Bungalow, Oceanfrog, Cabbage, Bucket, the Indian, Harry the Horse, the Jellyroll Kid, Flop, Smokehouse, Worm, Big Frig, and even a horse named Golgotha. A striking feature of this community is its total detachment from the larger social environment. Though the time setting is 1951, there is no mention of the Cold War (with Joseph Stalin newly in possession of the bomb), the Korean War, President Harry S Truman, McCarthyism, or any other salient topic of the time. Nor does Suttree have any meaningful connection with his blood kin: he does gladly accept an envelope from home with a $300 check enclosed, but he destroys the attached letter from his mother without reading it. (No explanation of his mother's offense is ever given.) And though at midpoint in the novel we learn that Suttree is a father, his only visit to his abandoned wife and child (to attend the latter's funeral) leaves no subsequent mark or reference. So the Knoxville demiworld serves as his only real family.

The two main characters begin their friendship in prison, where Suttree is serving time for participating (while drunk) in robbing a drugstore and Harrogate has been incarcerated at age eighteen for sneaking into a farmer's field, night after night, so as to enjoy carnal intercourse with watermelons that he expertly cores for the purpose. As with the foregoing list of characters' names, episodes of this sort apparently express McCarthy's "subtle obsession with uniqueness" that is part of any artist's calling. Harrogate's uniqueness carries over to other episodes, such as poisoning scores of bats so as

to collect a bounty from the city, attempting to rob a bank by setting off dynamite in an underground tunnel (which results in a huge surge of sewage nearly drowning him), and wearing a shirt "fashioned from an enormous pair of striped drawers, his neck stuck through the ripped seam of the crotch, his arms hanging from the capacious legholes like sticks." Suttree's uniqueness, as so often in McCarthy's fiction, pertains largely to his resourcefulness, not only in earning his livelihood via trotline fishing or surviving a week in the mountains without food or shelter in the winter, but also in helping others. He rescues Harrogate from the sewage spill, for example, by spending four days searching through the pitch-black limestone caverns that underlie Knoxville.

Like Ernest Hemingway, McCarthy is severely limited in his portrayals of women. Most of the women in *Suttree* come under the generic category of "whores," one of whom supports Suttree for a time with her illicit earnings until a violent quarrel ends their cohabitation. The only other sustained erotic relationship of Suttree's involves his "whore's" opposite counterpart, a virginal country girl whose desperate state of poverty does not preclude her having "perfect teeth, [and] skin completely flawless, not so much as a mole." This highly idealized love affair poses a threat to Suttree's independence in light of their many couplings without contraception, but the chance of Suttree having to confront an excruciating responsibility is nullified by a convenient happenstance: one midnight as Suttree sneaks down to the riverside for a bit of stargazing, a landslide kills his sweetheart back at their campsite. Again like Hemingway, McCarthy is not a writer much inclined to contemplate the tiresome responsibilities of domestic life, and, as in *A Farewell to Arms,* only the death of the beloved can solve the problem.

Although weak on plot and depth of characterization, *Suttree* exhibits its author's strengths in enhanced measure. With respect to his large and varied cast of characters, McCarthy's ear for dialect and dialogue achieves perfect pitch in this novel. As usual, his style often shimmers with precise and original imagery, even (or especially) when the focus is least promising. Here is Harrogate's submersion in subterranean sewage, for example, occurring in total darkness: "Coming toward him was a soft near soundless mass. Sucking over the stones. Seeking him out. . . . Its breath washed over him in a putrid stench. . . . He was engulfed feet first in a slowly moving wall of sewage, a lava neap of liquid shit and toiletpaper from a breached main." Elsewhere Suttree sustains an erection: "Out of a pinwheel of brown taffy his medusa beckoned." Or Suttree encounters a beggar whose "lower face hung in sagging wattles like a great scrotum." There are also the deceased in their underground caskets, "the deathwear stained with carrion." And sometimes there are more attractive images: "a sole star to the north . . . like a molten spike that tethered fast the Small Bear to the turning firmament." And though he eschews the biting social criticism of a Charles Dickens or Faulkner, McCarthy can attain a powerful tone of protest when moved to do so, as when he recalls his Catholic boyhood: "This kingdom of fear and ashes. Like the child that sat in these selfsame bones so many black Fridays in terror of his sins. Vice-ridden child, heart rotten with fear."

In the end a new expressway runs through the McAnally neighborhood and destroys its community of colorful paupers. Portending this end is the illness that nearly kills Suttree in the closing pages, an episode that allows McCarthy to work one of his strongest suits—a surrealistic fantasy of Joycean proportions that accompanies Suttree's delirium. Afterward, Suttree is born again, as it were, free to leave Knoxville while taking with him "for talisman the simple human heart within him." He would not go alone. McCarthy's own participation in this maneuver is evident in the book's final paragraph, where a metaphor of hunter and hound stands for the artist hungrily pursuing the whole of reality, both urban and rural: "Somewhere in the gray wood by the river is the huntsman and in the brooming corn and in the castellated press of cities. His work lies all wheres and his hounds tire not." As it turned out, "all wheres" was to become El Paso, Texas, where Cormac McCarthy took up residence while writing his next four novels, set in the vast badlands surrounding the borders of the American/Mexican Southwest.

BLOOD MERIDIAN

Considered a great novel by many eminent critics (for example, Harold Bloom), *Blood Meridian; or, The Evening Redness in the West* stands as Cormac McCarthy's masterpiece, a potential American classic by reason of its unique features of characterization, style, and theme. Adapted from an actual episode dating from the late 1840s, when the Mexican government paid American mercenaries a bounty for the scalps of Indians, the plot of *Blood Meridian* is wholly "on the road" as it follows its band of vagabond killers through countless episodes of slaughter and mayhem. What prevents these episodes from an effect of tiresome repetition is the startling gruesomeness of each instance, told with riveting attention to detail. Three examples should suffice—with a warning that this is adult fare not for the weak of stomach. The first describes the only black in the party responding to a racial taunt by slicing off his fellow mercenary's head:

Two thick ropes of dark blood and two slender rose like snakes from the stump of his neck and arched hissing into the fire. The head rolled to the left and came to rest at the ex-priest's feet where it lay with eyes aghast. . . . [The] columnar arches of blood slowly subsided until just the neck bubbled gently like a stew and then that too was stilled. He was sat as before save headless, drenched in blood, the cigarillo still between his fingers, leaning toward the dark and smoking grotto in the flames where his life had gone.

The second example shows the aftermath of an Apache action:

[The mercenaries] found the lost scouts hanging head downward from the limbs of a blackened paloverde tree. They were skewered through the cords of their heels with sharpened shuttles of green wood and hung gray and naked above the dead ashes of the coals where they'd been roasted until their heads had charred and the brains bubbled in the skulls and steam sang from their noseholes.

For readers who are sated with murder, McCarthy's original imagination can present other objects of interest, such as this figure who gets abducted into the mercenaries' band:

They passed behind a wagonsheet where within a crude cage of paloverde poles crouched a naked imbecile. The floor of the cage was littered with filth and trodden food and flies clambered about everywhere. The idiot was small and misshapen and his face was smeared with feces and he sat peering at them with dull hostility silently chewing a turd.

There is no question that episodes like these will rivet a reader's attention, but do they serve a purpose beyond mere entertainment or, at best, morbid satire concerning human behavior? There are two reasons to think so: first, McCarthy's remarkably vivid, masterly style, both in expository prose and in the give-and-take of his characters' dialogue; and second, the intellectual power that permeates some of that dialogue. In his three epigraphs to this novel, McCarthy indicates his intellectual seriousness by citing Paul Valery ("Finally, you fear blood more and more") and Jacob Boehme ("death and dying are the very life of the darkness") along with a news item concerning "a 300,000-

year-old fossil skull [that] . . . shows evidence of having been scalped."

Beyond its loosely episodic format, *Blood Meridian* takes its design from the relationship between its two main characters: "the kid" (never otherwise named) and "the judge" (sometimes called Judge Holden). That relationship begins when the fourteen-year-old kid—in whom "broods already a taste for mindless violence"—joins a band of scalp-hunters led by the judge and a man named Glanton. It ends, after Glanton's violent death two hundred pages later, with the judge killing the kid (now forty-three years old) for no apparent reason.

The mystery of the judge's motive appears to be a key to the novel's meaning. Although some reviewers evoke the names of Melville and Faulkner, the most likely candidate for McCarthy's mentor is probably Friedrich Nietzsche, whose rejection of conventional morality in favor of a naturalistic superman seems to anticipate the judge's character. (The judge says, for example: "Moral law is an invention of mankind for the disenfranchisement of the powerful in favor of the weak.") The first sign of the judge's superhuman status is his prodigious resourcefulness, both physical and mental. A seven-foot giant capable of tossing an anvil across a room, the judge also enjoys intellectual eminence to dwarf all other McCarthy protagonists. Besides his verbal elegance in English, he converses in Latin, German, Dutch, Spanish, and several Indian dialects. True to his moniker, he is learned in the law as well as avidly interested in archeology, geology, chemistry, astronomy, literature, philosophy, religion, and the graphic arts. In his practical affairs, he is an accomplished cook, musician, and bon vivant, utterly without peer even among McCarthy's most notable masters of Darwinian survival.

The judge's leading Nietzschean characteristic is his independent thinking. Unlike his fellow adventurers who join the killing game only for the money, the judge thoroughly enjoys his business and takes care to justify his work philosophically. Like Hemingway, the judge seems to feel that the power to inflict death imparts a godlike sense of superiority over it. ("A great killer must love to kill," Hemingway wrote in *Death in the Afternoon,* adding: "when a man is still in rebellion against death he has pleasure in taking to himself one of the Godlike attributes: that of giving it. This is one of the most profound feelings in those men who enjoy killing.") At times the judge's callousness seems adventitious, as when he dandles an Apache child on his lap before scalping him, but his final and most significant murder—of the kid—occurs within a penumbra of significant speech. As in Nietzsche's *The Birth of Tragedy,* the judge's talk evokes the Dionysian motif of the dance. As he lines up the unsuspecting kid for a blood sacrifice, he queries, "What man would not be a dancer if he could. . . . It's a great thing, the dance." The kid's disdain—"I aint studyin no dance"—fails to derail the judge's five-page discourse that culminates in his claim, "Only that man who has offered up himself entire to the blood of war, who has been to the floor of the pit and seen horror in the round and learned at last that it speaks to his inmost heart, only that man can dance."

After killing the kid in the outhouse, the judge does indeed dance as the novel ends—"dancing and fiddling at once. His feet are light and nimble. He never sleeps. He says that he will never die. He dances in light and in shadow and he is a great favorite. He never sleeps, the judge. He is dancing, dancing. He says that he will never die." Whether evoking the dance of Shiva, the Hindu god of time and death, or T. S. Eliot's round dance in *Four Quartets,* or the Dionysian frenzy in *The Bacchae* of Euripides—as various critics have argued—the judge remains the most original, prodigious, and enigmatic character in McCarthy's extraordinary pantheon, a figure to place beside Captain Ahab or Thomas Sutpen.

ALL THE PRETTY HORSES

After *Blood Meridian,* McCarthy went on using the American Southwest setting in the Border Trilogy. The first of these books, which became a best-seller and winner of the National Book Award and the National Book Critics Circle Award, was *All the Pretty Horses.* Among the reasons for its popularity are a quasi-mythic plot line based on Western Romance and "on the road" traditions, and the pristine virtues of its hero, John Grady Cole, on whom McCarthy bestows a devotion to ethical principles that totally contrasts with the demonic amorality of Judge Holden in *Blood Meridian.*

All the Pretty Horses is organized in four sections. Part 1 begins with the dissolution of John Grady Cole's family, shown in the funeral of his grandfather, the divorce of his parents, and the sale of the family ranch. With little more than the clothes on his back and his grandfather's advice in his ears—"He never give up. . . . He was the one told me not to"—Cole hits the road with his somewhat older buddy, Lacey Rawlins, in search of his destiny. Although the setting is mid-twentieth century, the two youths choose to ride horses from their Texas town into Mexico, where they soon fall in with another adolescent wayfarer, Jimmy Blevins, who is also on horseback. When Blevins gets into trouble (some Mexicans take his horse), Cole displays the code of honor that appears to be Cormac McCarthy's center of interest: "I cant [sic] do it," he says to Lacey's query whether they should "just leave him [Blevins]."

As part 1 ends, they do leave Blevins—but only at Blevins's insistence after retrieving his horse—and Cole and Rawlins ride on several hundred miles until they get work at the eleven-thousand-acre Purisima ranch. Part 2 is about love and work, the latter involving the taming of wild horses and the former involving a passionate romance with the hacienda owner's daughter. Part 3 renders the punishment for Cole's indiscretion—a sojourn in a Mexican prison where he and Rawlins are nearly murdered by other prisoners. Freed through the influence of his sweetheart's great aunt, Rawlins goes back home to Texas while Cole follows his honor code back to the Purisima ranch out of devotion to his true love and his horse. In part 4, he loses the girl but regains not only his horse but those of Rawlins and Blevins. Here McCarthy's gift for fantastic yet engrossing narrative is most on display as Cole endures a harrowing chase scene involving a corrupt Mexican police chief that he kidnaps. After his return to Texas, his honor code holds to the end as he looks up Rawlins so as to return his horse and tries in vain to do likewise with Blevins's horse.

The theme of *All the Pretty Horses* resolves rather easily into a handful of precepts related to Cole's honor code. After the initial "never give up" injunction laid down by his grandfather, Cole goes on to articulate the male preference for deeds over words (to the quip "Everything's talk isnt it? [sic]" he answers "Not everything"); to assert the undomesticated core of his personality ("he contemplated the wildness about him, the wildness within"); to affirm his unyielding will power ("all I know to do is stick"); and to define his final stance of continued questing (to Rawlins's query "Where is your country?" Cole answers, "I don't know. . . . I don't know where it is").

As a teenager, Cole cannot carry the whole burden of McCarthy's philosophical thought, so the task typically falls to mature onlookers. One of these figures is an old man named Luis, who frames what might be Cormac McCarthy's reason for seldom analyzing his people in any depth: "He said that among men there was no such communion as among horses and the notion that men can be understood at all was probably an illusion." The other voice of wisdom in this novel belongs to the girlfriend's great aunt

in the Hacienda Purisima. In her fourteen-page conversation with Cole she delivers a number of insights and speculations that are relevant to McCarthy's fiction at large, including perhaps most importantly the conflict between fate and free will. On one hand, she says, "The question for me was always whether that shape we see in our lives was there from the beginning or whether these random events are only called a pattern after the fact. . . . Do you believe in fate?" On the other hand, she says, "At some point we cannot escape naming responsibility. It's in our nature."

As always, McCarthy's distinctive style merits attention. Not surprisingly, in *All the Pretty Horses* the Hemingway influence sometimes goes to excess, as in the following excerpt: "Antonio regarded the stallion with great reverence and great love and he called him caballo padre and like John Grady he would talk to the horse and often make promises to him and he never lied to the horse." At his memorable best, however, McCarthy converts his mentor's style into a tour de force of original imagination. The following (abbreviated) excerpt demonstrates why many readers find McCarthy comparable in the best sense with William Faulkner.

> In the evening he saddled his horse and rode out west from the house. . . . At the hour he'd always choose when the shadows were long and the ancient road was shaped before him in the rose and canted light like a dream of the past where the painted ponies and the riders of that lost nation came down out of the north with their faces chalked and their long hair plaited and each armed for war which was their life . . . and above all the low chant of their traveling song which the riders sang as they rode, nation and ghost of nation passing in a soft chorale across that mineral waste to darkness bearing lost to all history and all remembrance like a grail the sum of their secular and transitory and violent lives.

THE CROSSING

The Crossing, the second novel in the Border Trilogy, resembles *All the Pretty Horses* in its four-part structure and in its focus on the superhuman exploits of a teenage boy. In part 1, a 125-page segment, McCarthy writes in the tradition of Faulkner's *The Bear* as sixteen-year-old Billy Parham tries to save the life of a pregnant wolf by making an epic run with the creature from his New Mexico hometown into the mountains of central Mexico where he plans to release it. In a typical editorial passage, McCarthy portrays Homo sapiens as the world's most savage creature, "come pale and naked and alien to slaughter all [the wolf's] clan and kin and rout them from their house. A god insatiable whom no ceding could appease nor any measure of blood." In the end the boy is forced to shoot the wolf to end its brutal torment at the hands of dogfight enthusiasts who have expropriated it.

Part 2 begins with the wolf's burial in the wild mountains, then follows Billy's ride home to confront the shocking discovery that his parents have been murdered by horse thieves. (The suspicion that the killers are Indians furnishes the main link between this plot and part 1, which began with a ten-page encounter between Billy and a sinister Indian drifter.) After he snatches his younger brother Boyd from his foster home, the two boys head back into Mexico in search of the stolen horses and, if possible, revenge. By this time Billy's difference from ordinary domestic folk is pronounced enough to summon forth an eccentric editorial outburst from the author: "When he walked out into the sun and untied the horse from the parking meter people passing in the street turned to look at him. Something in off the wild mesas, something out of the past. . . . In that outlandish figure they beheld what they envied most and what they most reviled. If their hearts went out to him it was yet true that for very small cause they might also have killed him."

Many unlikely coincidences characterize the plot. Later in part 2, for example, the boys spot one of their stolen horses, by chance, in the street of a Mexican village, as they would do several times again in other times and places. And as part 2 ends, the boys execute a harrowingly dangerous rescue of a girl in distress from two men who apparently intend to rape and kill her. ("[One of them] said if [girls] were old enough to bleed [that is, menstruate] they were old enough to butcher.")

Part 3 of *The Crossing* is probably McCarthy's closest approximation of a Clint Eastwood movie. Here the two Parham brothers encounter all three of their stolen horses on a country road, take them at gunpoint from the two young Mexicans who are tending them, only to lose them again to a gang of riflemen summoned by those two Mexicans, and then regain them yet again by besting these enemies with an astounding display of courage and resourcefulness. In the aftermath, Boyd is nearly shot dead, but is saved in the book's great chase scene when the horse carrying the two boys, with the pursuing riflemen barely a hundred yards behind, unloads its wounded rider on a chance truck that passes this way, driven by sympathetic field workers. Both truck and horse then speed quickly out of harm's reach, and after a medic attends Boyd's wound, the two boys are reunited with the girl they had rescued. Part 3 ends with Boyd riding off with the girl, leaving Billy mystified about their whereabouts. Perhaps it is a foreshadowing of this isolation that leads Billy, earlier in part 3, to talk to his horse: "When he'd said all he knew to say he told it stories. He told it stories in spanish [sic] that his grandmother had told him as a child and when he'd told all of those he could remember he sang to it."

The deus ex machina of the passing truck has many parallels in the feminae ex machina who come to Billy's rescue as repeatedly, on timely occasions, Mexican women (or sometimes men) take him in, furnish food to him and his horse, and somehow fend off the dangers stirred up by his hostile encounters elsewhere. A sojourn of this sort precedes the beginning of part 4, where Billy's return to America evokes from a border guard the astounding information that the country has entered World War II. A good patriot, Billy tries three times to join the army but is thrice rejected because of a heart murmur, which leaves him ethically free to undertake his third and last foray into Mexico, this time in search of his missing younger brother.

With his own country's West declining now into bourgeois homogeneity, Billy must ply the code of the (Old) West, if he is to do so at all, in this south of the border setting, and so part 4 begins with an eight-page battle of the bottle in a Mexican saloon. After a drunken Mexican repeatedly refuses to drink the booze that Billy buys for the house, Billy takes in a draught of the Mexican's liquor, spits it on the floor, and calls it "stinkin catpiss." Somehow he finesses the danger of this little display of machismo: "Then it all passed. He . . . turned and walked out the door." The book ends with Billy, after discovering that Boyd is dead (having himself killed two men), retrieving his brother's bones from a Mexican cemetery, bringing them back to America, and burying them in their native soil. The singular loneliness of the vagabond adventurer suffuses the closing vignette: a twenty-year-old bereft not only of brother, parents, and home, but of any viable culture too. Unsuited for his contemporary society, and with his proper milieu (the Old West) having died away, he sits in the empty road and weeps as a cold wind blows.

Clearly, the plot line of *The Crossing,* filling an essentially realistic novel with extraordinary coincidences and superhuman exploits, is not the reason for the book's appeal to a sophisticated reading audience. Nor are the main characters drawn deeply to engage our psychological intelligence: McCarthy, in this work, is no Faulkner, Henry James, or even Mark Twain.

Nonetheless, the novel's blurbs attest to some rare magic at work: "a miracle in prose" (*New York Times*), "a soul-shaking novel" (*Washington Post*), "mythic and unforgettably grand" (*Boston Globe*), "[perhaps] the first great western" (*Village Voice*).

Perhaps one reason for these appraisals of *The Crossing* is the extraordinary inventiveness of its digressions. Throughout the Border Trilogy, McCarthy's use of teenage protagonists calls forth a series of older, deeply experienced mentors to whom the boys give respectful attention. Some of McCarthy's best writing permeates these digressive interludes, which comprise his best claim to the status of philosophical novelist.

In *The Crossing* there are three major episodes of this sort, all of them relevant to McCarthy's own fiction. The first might be called the former priest's tale, a twenty-one-page tour de force about God, fate, and art. Among its memorable aphorisms are comments about storytelling: "For this world also which seems to us a thing of stone and flower and blood is not a thing at all but is a tale . . . and the tale has no abode or place of being except in the telling only and there it lives and makes its home. . . . Of the telling there is no end." Hence the importance of the artist: "If the world was a tale who but the witness could give it life? Where else could it have its being?" The second major digressive episode is the blind man's tale, a twenty-page segment that features the most gruesome violence in the novel (in telling how the man became blind) and some further aphorisms related to his blindness: "He said that the world was sentient to its core and secret and black beyond men's imagining and that its nature did not reside in what could be seen or not seen." And finally, there is the gypsy's tale, a thirteen-page digression that bears out the limitations of the artist's genre: "We seek some witness but the world will not provide one. . . . It is the history that each man makes alone." This absence of narrative, in turn, is what makes photographs so poignant: ". . . as the kinfolk in their fading stills could have no value save in another's heart so it was with that heart also in another's in a terrible and endless attrition and of any other value there was none. . . . In their images they had thought to find some small immortality but oblivion cannot be appeased."

CITIES OF THE PLAIN

In concluding the Border Trilogy, McCarthy undertakes to unify the three books by having the two heroes of the earlier novels join forces in the last one. In *Cities of the Plain* (1998), the story begins with John Grady Cole and Billy Parham enjoying the pleasures of a whorehouse as fellow ranch hands. This concession to modern realism, however, soon gives way to old-fashioned romance as Cole falls passionately in love with a beautiful Mexican teenager who had been sold into sex slavery by her impoverished family. His effort to rescue this girl, strongly abetted by Parham, is the main plot line of this last book, which delays its harrowing climax by devoting many pages to workaday activities on the ranch.

No longer teenagers, Cole and Parham are fully formed men in their late twenties now, and their culture has changed too. As Parham says, "This country ain't the same. Nor anything in it. The war changed everthing [sic]." One change is that they rely more on motor vehicles than on horses to go about. More ominously, the threat to their way of life is epitomized in the Pentagon's plan to expropriate the ranch where they work, evidently for use in atomic tests like the one in the book's last two pages. But in part 1, Parham and Cole, who is called "the all-american cowboy" by his comrades, ply their trade in the old style among the cattle and horses of the back country while waiting for the romance to ensue. In part 2, Cole sends Parham to the Mexican brothel to buy the girl's freedom, but Eduardo, the brothel's master, proves unwilling to make a deal. Nonetheless, Cole refurbishes a decrepit cottage as a home for his hoped-for bride. Part 3 delays the love story with a long episode in which the cowboys kill a band of wild dogs that have been eating calves from their herd. When the romance resumes, it takes a tragic turn wherein Cole's effort to bring the girl to him causes her murder by Eduardo. In part 4 the narrative concludes with Eduardo and Cole engaged in a knife fight that is fatal to both participants, and Parham is later seen "coming up the street all dark with blood bearing in his arms the dead body of his friend."

In *Cities of the Plain* McCarthy continues to ply his central themes of change, loss, and the struggle of art against oblivion. A mute instance of these issues is relayed via the millennium-old Indian petroglyphs that thrice appear as "ancient pictographs among the rocks, engravings of animals and moons and men and lost hieroglyphics whose meaning no man would ever know." Another unspoken version of the theme is "a knowing deep in the bone that beauty and loss are one," a variation of which occurs to an aged Mexican: "How frail is the memory of loved ones. . . . how those voices and those memories grow faint and faint until what was flesh and blood is no more than echo and shadow. In the end perhaps not even that." And when asked by Cole what is "the hardest lesson" of life, old Mr. Johnson replies, "It's just that when things are gone they're gone. They aint comin back."

The question of what the lost past meant, if anything, evokes McCarthy's other central theme of this book and others. Earlier, Cole had evoked a sense of determinism in describing his love for the girl: "There's some things you dont decide. Decidin had nothin to do with it." Even while loving her in a hotel room, he "thought about his life and . . . wondered for all his will and all his intent how much of it was his own doing." Given the untutored state of his two cowboys, even as older men, McCarthy must once again resort to older wisdom purveyors to develop this theme. One of those wise men, surprisingly, is the villainous pimp-cum-murderer Eduardo, who carries on an elegant discourse with both cowboys in turn. To Parham he speaks of men's capacity for delusion: "Men have in their minds a picture of how the world will be. How they will be in that world. . . . but there is one world that will never be and that is the world they dream of." To Cole, all through their fatal knife fight, Eduardo philosophizes shrewdly: "In his dying perhaps the suitor will see that it was his hunger for mysteries that has undone him. . . . Your kind cannot bear that the world be ordinary."

The most unlikely yet significant of these wisdom purveyors is reserved for the thirty-page epilogue that concludes both *Cities of the Plain* and the Border Trilogy. Here Billy Parham, now seventy-eight years old and utterly pauperized, offers to share his remaining crackers with another vagrant wanderer taking shelter under an interstate highway bridge. In the stranger's richly textured discourse about the need for a meaningful design in one's life and one's inability to find it, the role of storytelling emerges as the one viable mode of imagining a design. What the stranger's story (here parsed as a traveler's dream) reveals is the inevitability of whatever pattern unfolds through a lifetime: "Its shape was forced in the void at the onset and all talk of what might otherwise have been is senseless for there is no otherwise. . . . The probability of the actual is absolute. That we may imagine alternate histories means nothing at all." To judge by the epilogue, McCarthy's long dialectic between fate and free will is moving toward a deterministic closure.

DRAMA

In the tradition of American novelists—like Henry James, F. Scott Fitzgerald, Faulkner and Hemingway, Carson McCullers, Robert Penn Warren, John Updike, Joyce Carol Oates, and Reynolds Price—Cormac McCarthy succumbed to the urge to become a playwright, with (like all of the above) uncertain success. Broadcast on PBS television in January 1977, *The Gardener's Son* (1976) was based, like so much else in McCarthy's work, on an actual historical episode in South Carolina during the Reconstruction years. The main plot features a murder committed by a poor, crippled white youth against the superintendent of a cotton mill for uncertain reasons. The youth's death sentence rendered by a majority-black jury may be their response to the unjustified hanging of black suspects by white juries—an indication of the moral ambiguity often found in McCarthy's writing.

McCarthy's play, *The Stonemason,* set in 1971 in Louisville, Kentucky, seems designed to remedy the near-total lack of conventional family life in the eight novels. Gathering under one roof the four generations of a black family, the five-act play follows the efforts of Ben Telfair to emulate his centenarian grandfather's high example regarding work and family responsibility. Here for once McCarthy does portray a set of strong conventional females—Ben's mother, wife, and sister—but the dramatic thrust of the play remains focused on the males. In the end, the noble Telfair heritage appears ruined by the suicide of Ben's father, Big Ben, on account of shady business dealings, along with the death by drug overdose of Ben's nephew and the departure of his sister. But there is in Ben's familial loss an affirmation of the human bond—the sense, not often found in McCarthy's fiction, that "we cannot save ourselves unless we save all ourselves." There is even a positive theology in the play, in that the foregoing insight comes via a "God of all being . . . whom the firmament itself has not power to puzzle." But though an interesting departure, *The Stonemason* lacks the heft and force to counteract the burden of human dysfunction in the larger opus. A fair judgment of McCarthy's oeuvre must finally rest on his major work, the eight novels.

JUDGMENT

Although McCarthy's novels are often compared to those of Melville and Faulkner, he evinces neither Melville's rare breadth of intellectual inquiry nor Faulkner's vast range of in-depth character portraits. While Melville explored the possibilities of belief in *Moby-Dick,* aligning Christianity with Starbuck, fatalism with Stubb, hedonism with Flask, a perverse Transcendentalism with Ahab, and noble savage attributes with Queequeg, McCarthy's main characters—*Blood Meridian*'s Judge Holden excepted—have no intellectual life. Some of his minor characters in their wisdom-giver roles do promulgate the author's original thinking, but his books at large comprise an epic of survival featuring physical strength, stoic endurance, and practical ingenuity. Likewise, McCarthy never approaches Faulkner's vast range of in-depth character portraits construed across every divide of class, race, gender, and intelligence. Unlike Faulkner, McCarthy never creates an upper- or middle-class character of interest, rarely portrays women outside the category of "whores," and reduces domestic life to the circuit of absentee husbands and fathers like Suttree and Glanton. His virtually all-male cast is not only socially independent but crucially free of having dependents. What McCarthy shares with Melville and Faulkner is, literally, more style than substance—a precision and vivacity of language that is indeed worthy of those forebears.

Instead of philosophical or social criticism, McCarthy's eight novels appear to construct a composite portrait of the American male, equally capable of noble or savagely brutal behavior. Whether noble (John Grady Cole) or villainous (Judge Holden), whether sane (Suttree) or mad (Lester Ballard), McCarthy's

American male exhibits vast reserves of courage, endurance, and technical know-how. Regarding this last point, Eric Hoffer, the immigrant longshoreman turned social philosopher, told a television audience circa 1970 that the most distinctive feature of American society, making it different from any other in the world, is the "diffusion of competence" among its population. The average American might thus be expected to ply a broad variety of skills, from playing a guitar to using a computer to fixing his own plumbing or automobile.

Hoffer's insight provides a key to the novels of Cormac McCarthy. As with Hemingway, practical mastery of a craft or tactic equates with moral rectitude in McCarthy's portrayals, supplanting conventional notions of good and evil. In *All the Pretty Horses,* for example, John Grady Cole not only proves himself able to break any wild horse in four days flat, he also wins the passionate love of his sweetheart across boundaries of language (English, Spanish), culture (American, Mexican), family (her hostile father and aunt), and social stature (rich girl, poor boy). In the climactic chase scene Cole successfully eludes a Mexican posse while simultaneously riding herd on a kidnapped hostage (a thuggish police captain) and coping with a hemorrhaging bullet wound, for which he cauterizes himself with a pistol butt heated red-hot, howling with pain. Not a bad show for a lad of sixteen.

In *Blood Meridian,* McCarthy raises this ideal of American competence to mythic dimensions. Here, the judge, like his historical counterpart, displays fluency in several languages (English, Spanish, Latin, Dutch, German, several Indian dialects), proficiency in philosophy and the arts (he can play a violin), a grounding in the law (hence his moniker "the judge"), an avid interest in the natural sciences, and miraculous powers of crisis management. In his case the great chase episode features an ultimate climax: as the Indian pursuers close in on his exhausted little band, the judge scrapes some chemicals together—saltpeter from this cave, sulfur from that ledge, urine from himself and his men—and presto! he produces enough gunpowder to effect their survival. This is American competence writ large.

Ultimately, McCarthy's gift is singular—no one else writes as he does—but narrow. With his focus on a limited range of human interests and behavior, often expressed in gruesome violence and set against an exotic cultural and/or geographical terrain, McCarthy evinces a sensibility that is both Gothic-Romantic and essentially adolescent. Like American writers from James Fenimore Cooper to Twain to Hemingway, McCarthy places his characters on the road (after clearing away the entanglements of family ties) to test their individual capacities as modern versions of knights errant from the Middle Ages. Though capable of bonding with other men, whether Suttree's community of the down and out or Glanton's band of killers, McCarthy's typical male is uninterested in the larger conventional society in which he lives, espousing instead an old-fashioned self-reliance and the more "natural" way of life obtained before the complexities of modern times ruined it.

Among the critics of McCarthy one area of universal agreement stands out, along with one fundamental area of controversy. Virtually all readers agree that McCarthy is a brilliant master of style in every category, whether dialogue or exposition, plain speech or prose poetry, in lyric mode or baroque. They disagree, however, about how to judge the morbidity, freakishness, and "taste for mindless violence" (to quote the opening paragraph of *Blood Meridian*) that so largely define McCarthy's fictional world, raising the corollary question of why the writer fails to give any account (apart from implicit condemnation) of the familiar world most of us live in. Even his most benign novel, *Suttree,* depicts savage beatings, rotting corpses, and

"lives running out like something foul, night-soil from a cesspipe." What's more, the author's notorious reclusiveness—giving no interviews, public readings, or written manifestos about his work (letters, forewords)—obliges the works to speak for themselves. Predictably, the result has been a rich but conflicting range of interpretations. Do these books indicate the author's nihilism? His moral revulsion against nihilism? His exuberant primitivism? His existential rebellion against conformity? His critique—or, via satire, endorsement—of modern/Christian/capitalist/ postmodern society? His Oedipal obsessions? His theory of entertainment? All of the above?

Upon the answer depends, in large part, the resolution of the final question about Cormac McCarthy: the question of his status among his contemporaries, which ranges, depending on the critic, from "the greatest living American author" (so says Steven Shaviro in Edwin T. Arnold's and Dianne C. Luce's *Perspectives on Cormac McCarthy*) to "a major literary talent [who renders] an extremely narrow vision of the human condition and almost no vision at all of the subtler complexities of human feeling and thought," according to John W. Aldridge's fine overview of the McCarthy oeuvre in *The Atlantic Monthly.* Regarding the first five novels, Mark Winchell renders ambivalent praise, calling McCarthy "a master craftsman with the courage of his perversions" in *The Southern Review.* Winchell contrasts rather than compares McCarthy with Faulkner, finding in the latter "a moral center . . . that judges the evil and depravity of the world," whereas "In McCarthy's universe that moral center either doesn't exist or cannot hold." Denis Donoghue also notes "McCarthy's refusal to bring in a moral verdict on the characters and actions of the book *[Blood Meridian]*" in his essay collection, *The Practice of Reading* (1998), but he ascribes this stance to the author's philosophical sophistication. Like Nietzsche, Donoghue says, McCarthy proposes a worldview beyond good and evil, preferring instead to portray what Lionel Trilling—speaking of modern literature at large—called "the canonization of the primal, non-ethical energies."

In the end, the choices are so wide-ranging—with McCarthy variously described as a Gnostic nihilist, a satirist, a voice of social protest, an apostle of perversity, a Gaelic atavar, a neo-Nietzschean philosopher, or just an Alfred Hitchcock in prose—that he becomes finally unjudgeable, beyond any consensus of interpretation. Even so, Cormac McCarthy has vindicated his talent with a remarkably original, substantial, and vividly written shelf of novels, arguably including one classic work, *Blood Meridian*. What W. H. Auden said of William Butler Yeats—"Time worships language and forgives / Everyone by whom it lives"—may prove even more relevant to Cormac McCarthy than to Yeats, and even more crucial.

Selected Bibliography

WORKS OF CORMAC McCARTHY

The Orchard Keeper. New York: Random House, 1965. Reprint, New York: Vintage, 1993.

Outer Dark. New York: Random House, 1968. Reprint, New York: Vintage, 1993.

Child of God. New York: Random House, 1973. Reprint, New York: Vintage, 1993.

Suttree. New York: Random House, 1979. Reprint, New York: Vintage, 1992.

Blood Meridian; or, The Evening Redness in the West. New York: Random House, 1985. Reprint, New York: Vintage, 1992.

All the Pretty Horses. New York: Alfred A. Knopf, 1992.

The Stonemason: A Play in Five Acts. Hopewell, N.J.: Ecco Press, 1994.

The Crossing. New York: Alfred A. Knopf, 1994.

Cities of the Plain. New York: Alfred A. Knopf, 1998.

Note: McCarthy's unpublished screenplay, *Whales and Men,* is deposited in the Albert B. Alkek Library at Southwest Texas State University, according to an essay by James D. Lilley entitled "Of Whales and Men: The Dynamics of Cormac McCarthy's Environmental Imagination" (*Southern Quarterly* 38, no. 2:111–122 [winter 2000]).

CRITICAL AND BIOGRAPHICAL STUDIES

Aldridge, John W. "Cormac McCarthy's Bizarre Genius." *The Atlantic Monthly* 274, no. 2:89 (August 1994).

Arnold, Edwin T. "Blood & Grace: The Fiction of Cormac McCarthy." *Commonweal* 121:11–16 (November 4, 1994).

———. "Cormac McCarthy's *The Stonemason*: The Unmaking of a Play." *Southern Quarterly* 33:117–129 (winter–spring 1995).

———. "Horseman, Ride On." *World & I,* October 1998, pp. 259–267.

Arnold, Edwin T., and Dianne C. Luce, eds. *Perspectives on Cormac McCarthy.* Jackson: University Press of Mississippi, 1993. (This collection of essays includes a very useful introduction and bibliography by the two editors.)

Bartlett, Andrew. "From Voyeurism to Archaeology: Cormac McCarthy's *Child of God.*" *Southern Literary Journal* 24:3–15 (fall 1991).

Bell, Vereen M. *The Achievement of Cormac McCarthy.* Baton Rouge: Louisiana University Press, 1988. (A major McCarthy criticism that includes an astute analysis of the first five novels. This book figures to remain a permanently valuable staple of McCarthy studies.)

Brickman, Barbara Jane. "Imposition and Resistance in Cormac McCarthy's *The Orchard Keeper.*" *Southern Quarterly* 38, no.2:123–134 (winter 2000).

Campbell, Neil. "'Beyond Reckoning': Cormac McCarthy's Version of the West in *Blood Meridian; or, the Evening Redness in the West.*" *Critique* 39, no. 1:55–64 (fall 1997).

Chollier, Christine. "'I aint come back rich, that's for sure' or The Questioning of Market Economies in Cormac McCarthy's Novels." *Southwestern American Literature* 25, no. 1:43–49 (fall 1999).

Daugherty, Leo. "Gravers False and True: *Blood Meridian* as Gnostic Tragedy." *Southern Quarterly*

30:122–133 (summer 1992). Reprinted in *Perspectives on Cormac McCarthy*. Rev. ed. edited by Edwin T. Arnold and Dianne C. Luce. Jackson: University Press of Mississippi, 1999. Pp. 159–174.

Ditsky, John. "Further into Darkness: The Novels of Cormac McCarthy." *Hollins Critic* 18:1–11 (April 1981). (Includes portions of a letter from McCarthy to Ditsky.)

Donoghue, Denis. "Teaching *Blood Meridian*." In *The Practice of Reading*. New Haven: Yale University Press, 1998. Pp. 258–277.

Hall, Wade, and Rick Wallach, eds. *Sacred Violence: A Reader's Companion to Cormac McCarthy*. El Paso: Texas Western Press, 1995. (A collection of eighteen essays presented at the First Conference on Cormac McCarthy at Bellarmine College in October 1993. This rich and diverse book relates McCarthy to such classic sources as Dante, John Milton, Gnosticism, Hindu myth [the dance of Shiva], and the Bible; to American writers Nathaniel Hawthorne, Ralph Waldo Emerson, T. S. Eliot, and Flannery O'Connor; and to figures from the recent zeitgeist, including Albert Camus, Jacques Derrida, Michel Foucault, Marc-Antoine Girard, Roland Barthes, Mikhail Bakhtin, and Gilles Deleuze.)

Hunt, Alex. "Right and False Suns: Cormac McCarthy's *The Crossing* and the Advent of the Atomic Age." *Southwestern American Literature* 23, no. 2:31–37 (spring 1998).

Jarrett, Robert L. *Cormac McCarthy*. New York: Twayne Publishers, 1997. (Defines McCarthy against the southern tradition embodied in Faulkner and reads *Blood Meridian* and the Border Trilogy novels as postmodern revisions of the traditional Western novel [questioning manifest destiny] and Romantic [quest-driven] fiction.)

Josyph, Peter. "Older Professions: The Fourth Wall of *The Stonemason*." *Southern Quarterly* 36, no. 1:137–144 (fall 1997).

Lilley, James D. "Of Whales and Men: The Dynamics of Cormac McCarthy's Environmental Imagination." *Southern Quarterly* 38, no. 2:111–122 (winter 2000).

Luce, Dianne C. "'When You Wake': John Grady Cole's Heroism in *All the Pretty Horses*." In *Sacred Violence: A Reader's Companion to Cormac McCarthy*. Edited by Wade Hall and Rick Wallach.

El Paso: Texas Western Press, 1995. Pp. 155–167.

———. "The Road and the Matrix: The World as Tale in *The Crossing*." In *Perspectives on Cormac McCarthy*. Revised ed. edited by Edwin T. Arnold and Dianne C. Luce. Jackson: University Press of Mississippi, 1999. Pp. 195–219.

McBride, Molly. "From Mutilation to Penetration: Cycles of Conquest in *Blood Meridian* and *All the Pretty Horses*." *Southwestern American Literature* 25, no. 1:24–34 (fall 1999).

Palmer, Louis H., III. "Southern Gothic and Appalachian Gothic: A Comparative Look at Flannery O'Connor and Cormac McCarthy." *Journal of the Appalachian Studies Association* 3:166–176 (1991).

Peebles, Stacey. "'Lo fantástico': The Influence of Borges and Cortázar on the Epilogue of *Cities of the Plain*." *Southwestern American Literature* 25, no. 1:105–109 (fall 1999).

Phillips, Dana. "History and the Ugly Facts of Cormac McCarthy's *Blood Meridian*." *American Literature* 68:433–460 (June 1996).

Pitts, Jonathan. "Writing On: *Blood Meridian* as Devisionary Western." *Western American Literature* 33, no. 1:7–25 (spring 1998).

Priola, Marty. "Chess in the Border Trilogy." *Southwestern American Literature* 25, no. 1:55–57 (fall 1999).

Robisch, S. K. "The Trapper Mystic: Werewolves in *The Crossing*." *Southwestern American Literature* 25, no.1:50–54 (fall 1999).

Schafer, William J. "Cormac McCarthy: The Hard Wages of Original Sin." *Appalachian Journal* 4:105–119 (winter 1977).

Schopen, Bernard A. "'They Rode On': *Blood Meridian* and the Art of Narrative." *Western American Literature* 30:179–194 (summer 1995).

Sepich, John. "The Dance of History in Cormac McCarthy's *Blood Meridian*." *Southern Literary Journal* 24:16–31 (fall 1991).

———. "A 'Bloody Dark Pastryman': Cormac McCarthy's Recipe for Gunpowder and Historical Fiction in *Blood Meridian*." *Mississippi Quarterly* 46:547–563 (fall 1993).

———. *Notes on "Blood Meridian."* Louisville, Ky.: Bellarmine College Press, 1993. (A discussion of the historical sources from which McCarthy drew his account of the scalp-hunters, including the real life figures of John Joel Glanton and Judge Holden.)

Shaw, Patrick W. "The Kid's Fate, the Judge's Guilt: Ramifications of Closure in Cormac McCarthy's *Blood Meridian*." *Southern Literary Journal* 30, no. 1:102–119 (fall 1997).

Shelton, Frank W. "*Suttree* and Suicide." *Southern Quarterly* 29:71–83 (fall 1990).

Southern Quarterly 38, no. 3. (spring 2000). (A special issue on the Border Trilogy.)

Spencer, William C. "Altered States of Consciousness in *Suttree*." *Southern Quarterly* 35:87–92 (winter 1997).

Traber, Daniel S. "'Ruder Forms Survive,' or Slumming for Subjectivity: Self-Marginalization in *Suttree*." *Southern Quarterly* 37, no. 2:33–46 (winter 1999).

Twomey, Jay. "Tempting the Child: The Lyrical Madness of Cormac McCarthy's *Blood Meridian*." *Southern Quarterly* 37, nos. 3–4:255–265 (spring–summer 1999).

Wallace, Garry. "Meeting McCarthy." *Southern Quarterly* 30:134–139 (summer 1992).

Wallach, Rick. "Introduction: The McCarthy Canon Reconsidered." In *Sacred Violence: A Reader's Companion to Cormac McCarthy*. Edited by Wade Hall and Rick Wallach. El Paso: Texas Western Press, 1995. Pp. xv–xx.

———. "Judge Holden, *Blood Meridian*'s Evil Archon." In *Sacred Violence: A Reader's Companion to Cormac McCarthy*. Edited by Wade Hall and Rick Wallach. El Paso: Texas Western Press, 1995. Pp. 125–136.

———. "From *Beowulf* to *Blood Meridian*: Cormac McCarthy's Demystification of the Martial Code." *Southern Quarterly* 36, no. 4:113–120 (summer 1998).

Wegner, John. "Whose Story Is It?: History and Fiction in Cormac McCarthy's *All the Pretty Horses*." *Southern Quarterly* 36, no. 2:103–110 (winter 1998).

———. "'Mexico para los Mexicanos': Revolution, Mexico, and McCarthy's Border Trilogy." *Southwestern American Literature* 25, no. 1:67–73 (fall 1999).

White, Edmund. "Southern Belles Lettres: Cormac McCarthy." In *The Burning Library: Essays*. Edited by David Bergman. New York: Alfred A. Knopf, 1994. Pp. 321–326.

Winchell, Mark Royden. "Inner Dark: or, The Place of Cormac McCarthy." *Southern Review* 26, no. 2:293–309 (April 1990).

Witek, Terri. "'He's Hell When He's Well': Cormac McCarthy's Rhyming Dictions." *Shenandoah* 41:51–66 (fall 1991).

———. "Reeds and Hides: Cormac McCarthy's Domestic Spaces." *Southern Review* 30:136–142 (January 1994).

Woodward, Richard B. "Cormac McCarthy's Venomous Fiction." *New York Times Magazine*, April 19, 1992.

—*VICTOR STRANDBERG*

Thomas Merton

1915–1968

On the last day of January 1915, under the sign of the Water Bearer, in a year of a great war, and down in the shadow of some French mountains on the borders of Spain, I came into the world. Free by nature, in the image of God, I was nevertheless the prisoner of my own violence and my own selfishness, in the image of the world into which I was born. That world was the picture of Hell, full of men like myself, loving God and yet hating Him; born to love Him, living instead in fear and hopeless self-contradictory hungers.

*T*HUS BEGINS ONE of the most remarkable books of the twentieth century, Thomas Merton's *The Seven Storey Mountain* (1948). Many of the traits that make this work remarkable are present in its opening paragraph: Merton's directness, not to be mistaken for simplicity, his stark religious sensibility, his awareness of his own fallen state and that of the world he inhabits, and his belief nevertheless in the beauty inherent in being human.

Remarkable too, yet at the same time representative of his time, are the circumstances and events of Merton's early life, retold in *The Seven Storey Mountain,* an autobiography. The place of Merton's birth in 1915 was the village of Prades, in southern France. His parents were artists. His father, Owen Merton, born in New Zealand, and his mother, Ruth Jenkins Merton, born in Ohio, had met at art school in Paris and had taken up residence in rural France just as World War I was getting under way. Under pressure from the war, the family soon left France, living first in Douglaston, New York, with Ruth's parents, before moving to nearby Flushing.

Neither parent was particularly religious, although each kept some contact with the religions of their childhoods, Ruth with the Quakers and Owen with the Church of England. While in Flushing, Ruth gave birth to a second son, John Paul, before succumbing to stomach cancer in 1921, at the age of thirty-four. During the next twenty years Thomas Merton lived an unsettled life, sometimes with his father, who died of a brain tumor in 1931, sometimes with his grandparents, and sometimes on his own as a student. He moved from Flushing to Bermuda, then back to Douglaston, then back to France, then to England, then finally again to New York as a student at Columbia University, where he enrolled in 1935 after an unsuccessful stint at Cambridge. He graduated from Columbia in 1939 with an MA in English, and in 1940 he took a position teaching English at Saint Bonaventure University, in western New York. The previous year, in November 1939, despite his own worldly, bohemian existence up to that point and the tenor of the intellectual world at that time, he received admittance into the Catholic Church. On December 10, 1941, three days after the attack on Pearl Harbor by Japan, Merton entered the Abbey of Our Lady of Gethsemani, a Trappist monastery in rural Kentucky, where he remained for the rest of his life, until his accidental death by electrocution while on a spiritual pilgrimage to the Far East. During that time, he published more than fifty books and wrote journals, essays, and letters that continued to furnish the reading public with volume after volume in the decades following his death.

Merton's place in American literature is as unusual as was his place in American society. A monk, foreign born of bohemian artist parents, living in a monastery in rural Kentucky, Merton acknowledged the marginal nature of his existence in American life even as he considered himself thoroughly at home in the United States. "I have always had an American outlook and American habits of thought," he explained to a reporter when he traveled to Louisville, Kentucky, in June 1951 to be naturalized as an American citizen. "Naturalization for me is simply a formal affirmation of my love for America and my gratitude toward the land that has always been 'my country.'" When in *The Sign of Jonas* (1953), the journal Merton kept of his early years in the monastery, he wished to account for the energetic life of the monks, he wrote, "Here at Gethsemani we are at the same time Cistercians and Americans. It is in some respects a dangerous combination. Our energy runs away with us. We go out to work like a college football team taking the field." While acknowledging the monks' marginal existence, Merton considered the monastery at Gethsemani to be the center of America and his vocation there to be essential to America's future. Similarly, his writing often consciously challenged the Protestantism of American literary tradition even as he worked within that tradition.

Merton's place in American literature is both enriched and complicated by five distinctive features. These features—his modernism, his Catholicism, his protestantism (with a small *p*), his affinity with Quakerism, his mysticism— must be examined separately in order to obtain an understanding of his work as a whole. His Catholicism is significant because the American literary tradition is essentially Protestant, and not just because the majority of American writers have been Protestant, but because there is something strongly Protestant at the core of American identity. Before considering his Catholicism, however, it is helpful to consider Merton's modernism, which predates and forms the context of his Catholicism. Significant too is the protestant element prevalent in Merton's writing, his philosophical orientation against the prevailing norms of society. This orientation often has affinities in Merton with the specifically Quaker strain of American literature, despite Merton's youthful rejection of his mother's Quakerism. Perhaps most important to many of his readers and admirers since his death is Merton's mysticism, particularly as it is linked to the religions and traditions of the East. It is in this respect that Merton might seem farthest from the core of American society and culture, yet even here he demonstrates strong links to the American literary tradition, a tradition that is itself both a part of American society and culture and at odds with it.

The extent of Merton's written legacy is remarkable. When he entered the monastery he felt at least in part that he was leaving behind his youthful ambition to be a writer. Yet at the time of his death he had published over fifty books and pamphlets, as well as a profusion of articles for magazines and journals. He had kept his own extensive journal and corresponded widely with friends, fellow writers, and fellow religious men and women, and sometimes even with strangers, although the latter usually quickly became his friends. He was a poet, essayist, novelist, spiritual thinker, diarist and memoirist, translator, anthologist, and correspondent. Across these different genres, the paradoxes and challenges, as well as the pleasures, of Merton's mind and life abound.

MERTON AND TWENTIETH-CENTURY MODERNISM

In *The Sign of Jonas* Merton records a visit from the abbot general of his order. Like Merton's other superiors, the abbot general encouraged Merton to continue writing poetry, a practice that Merton had begun before entering the monastery and that he now considered giving up, as writing was not a traditional vocation for monks of Merton's order, the Cistercians, familiarly known as Trappists. The abbot general felt that Merton's writing was important, even though, he admitted, "he did not understand the poems." Such puzzlement might be expected. Merton did not write easily understood devotional verse. His poetry is not immediately inspirational. It is not conventional and it is certainly not sentimental. The same can be said of much of his other writing. Though his prose is often direct, his intentions are rarely simple. The difficulties his writing can present are due to some degree to the nature of his material; mystical experience by definition resists language. But a greater source of the difficulties in Merton's writing is the modern sensibility that both informs and shapes it. For thoughhe lived a life many might regard as medieval, Merton was very much of the twentieth-century.

Merton's associates in the publishing world had no small part in defining twentieth-century letters in America. The editor who accepted the manuscript of *The Seven Storey Mountain* was Robert Giroux, who continued to edit much of Merton's work, first at Harcourt, Brace and Company, then at Farrar, Straus & Giroux, a secular publishing house with high literary standards. Merton's poetry, as well as a good deal of his prose, was published by James Laughlin, whose publishing house, New Directions, also published Baudelaire's *Flowers of Evil*, Franz Kafka's *Amerika*, Ezra Pound's *Cantos*, Tennessee Williams' *A Streetcar Named Desire*, Jean-Paul Sartre's *Nausea*, Jorge Luis Borges' *Labyrinths*, Louis-Ferdinand Celine's *Death on the Installment Plan*, Dylan Thomas' *Portrait of the Artist as a Young Dog*, and William Carlos Williams' *Paterson*. Though this is not the company we expect to find in the devotional section of a bookstore, it is the company of someone who, as Merton said admiringly of Albert Camus, is a cosmopolitan twentieth-century man.

Merton's early poetry takes its form from the poetic world he inherited—the modernism of T. S. Eliot, influenced by the seventeenth-

century metaphysical poets who had come back into vogue at the beginning of the twentieth century. In *The Sign of Jonas* we find Merton sitting in the sun after dinner, on Passion Sunday 1948, reading Eliot's *Four Quartets*. He recalls having read the "East Coker" section before its publication, at a cottage in western New York, where he was spending the summer with college friends, one of whom had a copy of the poem in manuscript. Eliot's poetry, together with that of Eliot's mentor Ezra Pound and his contemporaries William Carlos Williams and Wallace Stevens, did much to remove poetry from the sphere of wide readership enjoyed by such Victorian poets as Tennyson and the Brownings. While the Victorians had written verse easily accessible to the general reader, the moderns turned away from such poetry, finding it sentimental and false. Eliot's poetry remains difficult and puzzling for many readers, yet Merton admired it and wished that he himself could write such verse. Merton had already, in *The Seven Storey Mountain*, expressed his own sensibility and its distance from conventional middle-class values. He describes his love for Saint Thérèse de Lisieux, the nineteenth-century Carmelite nun known familiarly as the Little Flower. Accepting the Little Flower meant, for Merton, suppressing his own natural antipathies toward the sentimental. Saint Thérèse, he explains, had a "taste for utterly oversweet art, and for little candy angels and pastel saints playing with lambs so soft and fuzzy that they literally give people like me the creeps." "She wrote a lot of poems," he continued, "which, no matter how admirable their sentiments, were certainly based on the most mediocre of popular models."

Merton's poetry, exemplified by "After the Night Office—Gethsemani Abbey," written in the first years of his monastic life, is at once deeply spiritual and determinedly unsentimental. It begins in darkness, the darkness of the abbey in the hour after the monks have risen from bed at 2:00 A.M. and met in choir to chant the prayers of matins, the earliest of the daily canonical hours. The poem opens with two images of the coming morning, the first "the grey and frosty time / When barns ride out of the night like ships," and the second "the Brothers, bearing lanterns" who "Sink in the quiet mist" as they begin their work in the barns. But it will not just be the barns that emerge out of the night into light, and not just brother monks who bear light into the darkness. At the poem's close, "the lances of the morning / Fire all their gold against the steeple and the water-tower."

> Returning to the windows of our deep abode of
>   peace,
> Emerging at our conscious doors
> We find our souls all soaked in grace, like
>   Gideon's fleece.

The light of day is also the spiritual light of grace, which emerges out of darkness just as do the barns out of the cover of night and Merton's poems out of the difficulty and obscurity they initially present the reader. Merton recalls that when he and his friends had first read "East Coker" they had not liked it, but reading it again that warm spring afternoon years later he found that he admired it very much. Such is the case with much twentieth-century poetry, including Merton's. The reader has to live with it, let it become familiar, let himself grow into it, before it yields its meaning and its beauty.

The world that Eliot characterized as a wasteland, the world that produced the lost generation of Ernest Hemingway, the world of the trenches and gas and tanks of World War I, was the world that Merton was born into and that he rejected when he entered the monastery. Though he himself did not go to war, his younger brother John Paul was killed in World War II, shot down over the English Channel while returning from a bombing raid against Germany. When Merton, after this war, wrote *The Waters of Siloe* (1949), a history of the Trappists from their origins to the present day, the Abbey at Gethsemani was overcrowded with young men who came to the monastery to change their lives. He begins with two anecdotes, one of a wealthy French industrialist in Paris who turned his back on the cosmopolitan life and the other of a young American returned from the war, where he had "found out at very close quarters what happened to the dead bodies of men left unburied at Okinawa." The world of the twentieth century was a world not of progress but of violence and death and unreality given scope to a degree unsurpassed in human history, the world of Pearl Harbor and the Nazi death camp at Buchenwald and the site of the atomic bomb blast at Hiroshima. The young men who came to the gates of Gethsemani, Merton declared, "have not come to the monastery to escape from the realities of life but to find those realities: they have felt the terrible insufficiency of life in a civilization that is entirely dedicated to the pursuit of shadows."

A commitment to literary modernism is not the only hallmark of the twentieth century we find in Merton's writing. Though he rejected the psychoanalytic theories of Sigmund Freud in his college days, after first embracing them, he remained open to the political, economic, and social principles advocated by Karl Marx, which he had likewise embraced as a student. Soon after becoming a Catholic, if not before, however, he rejected the materialist basis of the solutions proposed by Marxism, preferring instead a spiritual solution grounded in love; he nevertheless remained influenced by the Marxist analysis of the modern condition, particularly as it focuses on modern man's alienation. This interest connected Merton to such mid-twentieth-century thinkers as Herbert Marcuse and Erich Fromm. It was the subject of his last talk, given the morning of his death. In "Marxism and Monastic Perspectives," included as an appendix to *The Asian Journal of Thomas Merton* (1973), Merton observed that the idea of alienation is basically Marxist, and what it means is that man living under certain economic conditions is no longer in possession of the fruits of his life. His life is not his. It is lived according to conditions determined by somebody else. I would say that on this particular point, which is very important indeed in the early Marx, you have a basically Christian idea. Christianity is against alienation. Christianity revolts against an alienated life.

For Merton, the attraction of life in a monastery—in which the monks by their own choice live a self-sufficient existence of meaningful labor, liturgical prayer linked to the hours of the day and the seasons of the year, and direct contemplation of God—was that it was an unalienated life.

Related to his thoughts on alienation is Merton's existentialism, his desire to confront life as it is, rather than as it might be packaged by this or that system of thought. The necessity for authentic life free of illusion appears throughout his work, most forthrightly in *Conjectures of a Guilty Bystander* (1966). This work, like his earlier *Sign of Jonas,* is constructed from his journals, with much editing, rearranging, and augmentation. But whereas *The Sign of Jonas* concentrates on his life as a monk, *Conjectures of a Guilty Bystander* focuses on his life as a citizen of the twentieth century. As he contemplates the discouragements of twentieth-century life—mass murder, racism, empty lives—he focuses not on social solutions but on philosophical responses, which must precede social action in order that that action be effective. To live an authentic life, each man must confront the reality of his own inevitable death. But instead, Merton asserts, man

seeks to forget his inner dread of death by concern with objects, by aimless immersion in public opinion and action. Such a temptation could not be serious if he were not able to persuade himself of the great importance of his concerns, his opinions, and his acts. But certain forms of social

life—particularly the routines of mass society—are so patently artificial and fictitious that it is difficult even for those who are not very intelligent to be completely taken in by them. Hence a general sense of uneasiness, a sense that one has been "had," and a consequent resurgence of anxiety and dread. Yet man seeks to justify his inauthentic existence by the illusion that he remains master of his own destiny and of the world, and by the further illusion that he has almost reached the point where he will have conquered sickness, despair, and even, perhaps, death itself.

It is inauthentic existence, based on a false sense of self, that gave rise, in Merton's existentialist view, to the horrors of the twentieth century, to the mass killing that took place at Auschwitz and Hiroshima in World War II, to the civil rights riots gripping Birmingham and Harlem in the 1950s. The violence of the age was personally present to Merton in the American bombers that flew over the monastery to and from Fort Knox. All of these have their places in Merton's writing. So too do the mundane but still soul-killing realities of modern life. Writing in *Bread in the Wilderness* (1953) of the difficulty that contemporary poets face, Merton observes that

an age, like the one we live in, in which cosmic symbolism has been almost forgotten and submerged under a tidal wave of trademarks, political party buttons, advertising and propaganda slogans and all the rest—is necessarily an age of mass psychosis. A world in which the poet can find practically no material in the common substance of every day life, and in which he is driven crazy in his search for the vital symbols that have been buried alive under a mountain of cultural garbage, can only end up, like ours, in self-destruction.

The 1950s, when Merton wrote this, has been conceived falsely by later generations as a time only of happy days and sock hops. But the 1950s also gave American culture the music of John Coltrane and the early novels and essays of James Baldwin, both admired by Merton. Out of the 1950s came the stand-up comic Lenny Bruce, often arrested for obscenity, who challenged American society and its views on race and sex and war and who read aloud as part of his nightclub act Merton's "A Devout Meditation in Memory of Adolph Eichmann," collected in *Raids of the Unspeakable* (1966). Out of the 1950s came the 1960s, a decade of protest and a widespread questioning of and turning from the norms of American society, questionings and turnings that Merton, within the confines of the Abbey of Gethsemani, had not only anticipated but that he continued to inspire.

MERTON AND CATHOLICISM

In American literary history even more than in American social history, the Catholic is a marginalized figure. The Protestant temper of the Puritans who came to New England in the seventeenth century has been inherited, often unconsciously, by subsequent American writers who have in turn defined American culture and sensibility in essentially Protestant terms. The American emphasis on individualism has its roots in the Protestant Reformation's belief in the individual's right to read and even interpret the Bible individually, in his own language, without the intervention of a priestly caste. The American resistance to hierarchical authority has similar roots in the radical Protestant rejection of the Catholic hierarchy of pope and cardinals and bishops. The nineteenth-century American classics that defined American literature and thought—Nathaniel Hawthorne's *The Scarlet Letter,* Herman Melville's *Moby-Dick,* the essays of Ralph Waldo Emerson and Henry David Thoreau, Mark Twain's *Adventures of Huckleberry Finn,* Kate Chopin's *The Awakening,* the poems of Walt Whitman and Emily Dickinson—explore the individual self independent of or in opposition to any controlling or limiting forces, even in opposition to the universe itself.

Throughout his writing, Merton asserts his Catholicism against this American sensibility, in his rejection of individualism, in his submission to authority, and in his embrace of ceremony, though the American in him struggles with all these things. In *The Seven Storey Mountain* he projects a thoroughly American self, in opposition to the Catholic spirit of the country people of France, where he returned with his father after the death of his mother. He recalls a conversation when he was twelve with an old Catholic couple, the Privats, with whom he boarded while his father was in Paris. "I began to justify Protestantism," Merton writes.

> I gave them the argument that every religion was good: they all led to God, only in different ways, and every man should go according to his own conscience, and settle things according to his own private way of looking at things.
>
> They did not answer me with any argument. They simply looked at one another and shrugged and Monsieur Privat said quietly and sadly: *"Mais c'est impossible."*

Merton's boyish argument is essentially the argument of Emersonian individualism, and the reaction of the old couple is the position Merton himself would come to take. We cannot by our own lights and by our own efforts save our souls, or even discover who we are. Only the help and prayers of others and our own surrender of will to God can save us.

Although he would later come to recognize the validity of some Protestant thought, particularly that of Dietrich Bonhoeffer, the German theologian whose opposition to Adolf Hitler and Nazism led to his imprisonment and execution, Merton remained committed to his rejection of American individualism. He recognized as well the paradox of American individualism: the conformism that unexpectedly results from a continuing need to assert the self when society begins with an emphasis on individual distinction. In "Liturgy and Spiritual Personalism," an essay included in *Seasons of Celebration* (1965), Merton observes:

> We are beginning to understand that we live in a climate of all-embracing conformities. We have become mass-produced automatons. Our lives, our homes, our cities, our thoughts, or perhaps our lack of thoughts, have all taken on an impersonal mask of resigned and monotonous sameness. We who once made such a cult of originality, experiment, personal commitment and individual creativity, now find ourselves among the least individual, the least original and the least personal of all the people on the face of the earth—not excluding the Russians. In this desperate situation, the ideal of individuality has not been laid aside. Rather, it has taken on the features of an obsessive cult. People "express themselves" in ways that grow more and more frantic in proportion as they realize that the individuality and the distinctive difference they are attempting to express no longer exist.

In place of American self-reliance and individualism, Merton embraces a Christian personalism that is rooted in the sacraments and liturgy of Catholicism. In his earliest work of purely spiritual reflection, *Seeds of Contemplation* (1949), Merton rejects the false self we create for ourselves out of misguided individualism, "the man that I want myself to be but who cannot exist, because God does not know anything about him." Our true being, instead, is discovered, paradoxically, in the privacy of the sacraments and the liturgy. "Let us above all remember and admire the discretion, the sobriety and the modesty with which the liturgy protects this personal witness of the individual Christian," Merton writes in "Liturgy and Spiritual Personalism." "We sing alike, we pray alike, we adopt the same attitudes. Yet oddly enough this 'sameness' does not wound our individuality." Rather, because the participant in the liturgy does not have to display his or her individuality, he or she is free to discover it within, "a discovery that respects the hiddenness and incommunicability of each one's personal secret, while paying tribute to his presence in the common celebration."

The liturgy of the Catholic mass, then, is not simply a curtailment of individual freedom imposed from an authoritarian priestly caste. It is a response to mankind's deepest needs. The sense of sin, far from being an agent of an authoritarian system that seeks to control individual lives, is a condition of anguish from which mankind needs rescue. In another essay in *Seasons of Celebration,* "Ash Wednesday," Merton declares that the penitent who presents himself to a priest to receive ashes is not simply one who is convinced of his own sinfulness.

> A sinner, in the way the liturgy understands him, is not a man with a theoretical conviction that violation of the law brings punishment for guilt. A sinner is a drowning man, a sinking ship. The waters are bursting into him on all sides. He is falling apart under the pressure of the storm that has been breaking up his will, and now the waters rush into the hold and he is dragged down. They are closing over his head, and he cries out to God: "the waters are come in even unto my soul."

"Ash Wednesday," Merton concludes, "is for people who know what it means for their soul to be logged with these icy waters: all of us are such people, if only we can realize it."

The sacraments and the liturgy not only rescue us from sin; they similarly rescue us from time and give us joy in nature. Nature itself is good, Merton affirms in "Time and the Liturgy," also included in *Seasons of Celebration,* as is the passage of time, as "the seasons express the rhythm of natural life." But the liturgy adds another dimension, Merton continues, for "Jesus has made this ebb and flow of light and darkness, activity and rest, birth and death, the sign of a higher life, a life we live in Him, a life which knows no decline, and a day which does not fall into darkness." Nature is not, then, as it was for America's Puritan founders, a dark and savage place that needs to be transformed, but rather a world of holiness and beauty, and time is "a sacramental gift in which [man] can allow his freedom to deploy itself in joy."

The discovery of selfhood within the communal life of the Church is not the only paradox prominent in Merton's rejection of American sensibility. Even more striking is Merton's discovery of freedom in obedience. Merton's most famous lines are those he wrote in *The Seven Storey Mountain* of his entry into the monastery at Gethsemani: "So Brother Matthew locked the gate behind me and I was enclosed in the four walls of my new freedom." The explanation of this paradox is to a large extent prosaic: by becoming obedient to a superior, the monk frees himself from decision making, from responsibility and concern. Even this limited application of obedience (the greater obedience is not to this or that superior but to the will of God) did not come easily to Merton, however, and much of the interest in his writing comes from the tension between his desire for obedience and his naturally independent spirit. This tension recurs throughout *The Sign of Jonas,* which begins in the winter of 1946, five years after Merton entered the Abbey of Gethsemani. Yet even after five years of obedience, Merton feels, "I still have my fingers too much in the running of my own life." His desire to live as a hermit, rather than as member of a community of monks, despite his philosophical commitment to community, is the source of much conflict with his superiors. And eventually he has his way: he was granted permission to live in a hermitage on the monastery grounds in the summer of 1965. A rumor that he would leave (or already had left) the monastery for good circulated in Merton's last years, and followed him to Bangkok in December of 1968.

More significant is his struggle with authority over matters of conscience. Is there to be no limit to obedience even when one's superiors—the leaders of society, for instance—are allied with evil, either actively or passively? Merton had already recognized this problem when he came to revise the chapter "Freedom under Obedience" for his *New Seeds of Contemplation,* published in 1962, thirteen years after the original *Seeds of Contemplation.* While he remains committed to his rejection of Emersonian self-reliance ("The most dangerous man in the world is the contemplative who is guided by nobody . . . [who] identifies the will of God with anything that makes him feel, within his own heart, a big, warm, sweet interior glow"), he qualifies this with the observation that "no one can become a saint or a contemplative merely by abandoning himself unintelligently to an oversimplified concept of obedience. Both in the subject and the one commanding him, obedience presupposes a large element of prudence and prudence means responsibility." At this time, Merton's difficulties with his superiors over matters of conscience, specifically their censorship of his writings protesting the atomic bomb, were becoming so acute that he found recourse only in the private circulation of mimeographed letters.

Obedience, finally, is not obedience to that which is contrary to one's own nature, but rather the acceptance of one's place in the world, without trying to remake the world to suit one's will. In December 1966, Merton was visited in his hermitage by the folksinger Joan Baez and her husband, Ira Sandperl. They urged him to leave the monastery so that he could more effectively disseminate his antiwar beliefs. "Someone has to talk to the students and you are the one," they told him in a conversation recorded in his journal, published in the volume *Learning to Love: Exploring Solitude and Freedom* (1997). "I can't fully explain why I don't," Merton comments. "I mean, I can't explain to them. This solitude is God's will for me—it is not just that I 'obey' the authorities and the laws of the Church. There is more to it than that. Here is where my roots are."

MERTON AND THE
SPIRIT OF PROTESTANTISM

Though Merton was explicit in his rejection of Emersonian individualism and self-reliance, he nevertheless felt an affinity with Emerson's most prominent disciple, Thoreau, whom Emerson described as "a protestant *à l'outrance*" (a protestant to the extreme). It is not inappropriate to consider Merton in a similar way, as one in whom the spirit of protest against the norms of society lives. Merton not only read and admired Thoreau, he took as Thoreau's precursors the spiritual thinkers who lived as hermits in the ancient Middle East. These individuals, Merton explains in *The Wisdom of the Desert: Sayings from the Desert Fathers of the Fourth Century* (1960), lived in the desert to free themselves from the busy world of the city, the world of getting and spending, the world of power, the world of oppressors and oppressed. So too did Thoreau turn his back on the dusty road that led to the marketplace. And so too did Merton leave his worldly existence behind when he entered the monastery at Gethsemani.

In "Rain and the Rhinoceros," the first essay of *Raids on the Unspeakable,* Merton gives a picture of himself in his hermitage on a rainy night, toasting a piece of bread at his log fire while oatmeal boils over on his Coleman stove. He reads Philoxenus, a sixth-century hermit, by the light of a gas lantern and listens to the rain, "all that speech pouring down, selling nothing, judging nobody, drenching the thick mulch of dead leaves, soaking the trees, filling the gullies and crannies of the wood with water, washing out the places where men have stripped the hillside!" It is a self-consciously Thoreauvian scene, which Merton explicitly acknowledges: "Thoreau sat in *his* cabin and criticized the railways. I sit in mine and wonder about a world that has, well, progressed." Merton's 1961 book *The Behavior of Titans* includes the essay "Signed Confession of Crimes against the State," in which an imaginary witness confirms

Merton's nonconformist guilt by declaring, "He has come to the wood with his shoes in his hand, and with a book. He has sat with papers and a book. He has done no work." With obvious irony Merton admits, "The very thoughts of a person like me are crimes against the state. All I have to do is think: and immediately I become guilty. In spite of all my efforts to correct this lamentable tendency to subversiveness and intellectual sabotage, I cannot possibly get rid of it."

Merton's affinity with Thoreau is both contradictory and obvious. In a society dominated by Protestant individualism, what better gesture of protest could one make than becoming Catholic? By entering the monastery, Merton shares in Thoreau's rejection of consumer society and at the same time rejects the self-centered society that Thoreau and Emerson represent. In this respect, Merton displays a greater affinity with Hawthorne than with Hawthorne and Thoreau. In Hawthorne's *The Blithedale Romance,* the doomed heroine Zenobia denounces the pretense to utopia of the society around her, crying out, "It's all self, self, nothing but self!" Like Huckleberry Finn, Merton would go barefoot—though unlike Huck, Merton would go barefoot to mass.

Like Thoreau, Merton was attracted to nature for its beauty, its value in and of itself. But also like Thoreau, Merton loved nature as an alternative to mass society. The rhinoceros of "Rain and Rhinoceros" is a reference to a 1959 play by Eugène Ionesco, in which the members of society turn one by one into dull, rampaging animals. His interest in Ionesco speaks to Merton's literary modernism, but at the same time it is in keeping with the tradition of protest against mass society in American literature. Both temperamentally and theologically Merton is an antinomian, one who believes that faith alone is necessary for salvation, that not the law but the heart should be our guide to life. In this he is deeply American; antinomianism appears in American cultural history as early as the 1630s, when Anne Hutchinson was driven from the Boston of her Puritan neighbors for her insistence that not the letter of the law but the spirit of the believer determines man's salvation. Similarly, both Merton and Huck Finn prefer to go without shoes not only for the sheer pleasure of it, but also for the rejection of constricting social norms shoes represent. And thus in Merton we find the paradox of a monk who both argues for obedience to authority as the path to true freedom and who somehow became a sympathetic correspondent with teenaged hippies in the 1960s, a monk who listened to Bob Dylan and the Beatles and who drank beer with Joan Baez when she and her husband visited his hermitage. From the earliest days of his conversion to Catholicism, though, Merton had self-consciously given himself to a counterculture, and thus his emergence as a figure of the era of protest and nonconformism is not so contradictory after all.

MERTON AND THE QUAKER TRADITION

If Catholicism has had a more marginal presence in American literature than the number of Catholics in American society would lead one to expect, the opposite might be said about the Quakers, as members of the Society of Friends are familiarly known. Quakers are now far less a presence in American society than Catholics, yet they occupy a significant place in American literary and cultural history. Just as the Puritan characterized Boston in colonial America, so did the Quaker characterize Philadelphia. When Benjamin Franklin, in his autobiography, comes famously into Philadelphia from Boston as a young man, with nothing but two puffy roles of bread, it is to a Quaker meetinghouse that he first goes (and falls asleep). The qualities of the Quakers—their pacifism, their belief in the brotherhood and equality of all men, their resistance to the demands of society—serve as a foil to Franklin's pragmatism throughout his autobiography. At the same time their ideals form part of the foundation of the society Franklin would help create.

These qualities continued to be associated with the Quakers throughout the eighteenth and nineteenth centuries, and even into Merton's own day in the Quaker refusal to serve in the military in the Vietnam War and in their work for equal rights. In the nineteenth century Frederick Douglass, in his *Narrative of the Life of Frederick Douglass,* hailed the Quaker poet John Greenleaf Whittier as "the slave's poet." Whitman took much of his language, as well as his outlook, from the Quakers. And earlier, in the eighteenth century, the Quaker reformer John Woolman recorded in his *Journal* his own tireless work to end slavery, bring peace to relations with the Indians, and diminish the exploitation of workers, beasts of burden, and natural resources worldwide, producing as he did, it can be argued, the single most spiritual, as well as political, work in American literature.

Though his mother had been a Quaker, Merton's youthful rejection of the Quakers was as adamant as his rejection of all other manifestations of Protestantism in his mid-twenties. Yet in 1964 he wrote a letter ("To a Quaker"), later published in the "Letters in a Time of Crisis" section of *Seeds of Destruction* (1965), in which he declares, "I feel very close indeed to the Friends and I always have." This declaration, if not entirely honest, is consistent with the softening of Merton's initial dismissiveness of Protestantism. But if Merton had not always felt close to Quakerism, he had at least always felt the liberal social tendencies that connected him to the Friends in American cultural history. In the late 1950s and early 1960s these tendencies became manifest in his work, first in his writings against nuclear war and then in his writing on civil rights and in his association with those opposed to the war in Vietnam.

Such concerns may be unexpected in one who has removed himself from acquaintance with the world. But even a monastery has inescapable worldly connections. Bombers of the Strategic Air Command stationed at nearby Fort Knox flew overhead, their bomb-bay doors visible from the ground. "I have seen the SAC plane, with the bomb in it, fly low over me," Merton wrote in *Day of a Stranger* (1981), "and I have looked up out of the woods directly at the closed bay of the metal bird with a scientific egg in its breast. A womb easily and mechanically opened!" Should this womb have opened, the resulting devastation would not have spared the monks at Gethsemani. When Merton traveled to nearby Louisville, the world of whites and blacks, the American civil rights struggle, was visible. When President John F. Kennedy was assassinated, the news was posted on the abbey bulletin board. "The whole thing leaves one bewildered and slightly sick," Merton wrote in his journal. "Sick for the madness, ferocity, stupidity, aimless cruelty that is the mark of so great a part of this country. Essentially the same blind, idiot destructiveness and hate that killed Medgar Evers in Jackson, the Negro children in Birmingham." Merton's rejection of racism and war had been evident early in his life. At the time he made the decision to go to Gethsemani, he had weighed strongly the possibility of going to work at a Catholic mission in Harlem instead. As a student, he had signed pledges of nonviolence and opposition to war. These tendencies only strengthened as he matured.

In Merton's rejection of atomic war, he did not concern himself with America's strategic advantage or disadvantage. Hiroshima and Auschwitz were alike manifestations of the violence and selfishness of the twentieth century. When he wrote, in "A Devout Meditation in Memory of Adolph Eichmann," of the psychiatrist who had found the Nazi SS officer *"perfectly sane,"* and when he wrote in the prose poem *Original Child Bomb: Points for Meditation to Be Scratched on the Walls of a Cave* (1962) of the dropping of the atom bombs on Hiroshima and Nagasaki, Merton was in his view writing of the same thing, of the same tendencies. "We rely on the sane people of the world to preserve it from barbarism, madness, destruction," his "Devout Meditation in Memory of Adolf Eichmann" declares. "And now it begins to dawn on us that it is precisely the sane ones who are the most dangerous."

For Merton, the violence of the twentieth century was first and foremost a spiritual problem. Yet unlike the Quakers, he could not, as a Catholic, simply declare himself to be a pacifist. After all, Saint Augustine had declared in favor of "just war," and the church fathers to whom Merton owed obedience had not repudiated that doctrine. For Merton, this meant reading deeply in Augustine and in other church fathers on military justification. Without declaring all war to be repugnant, Merton easily found himself able to maintain that nuclear response, or indeed any conflict carried out with modern weapons and tactics, did not meet Augustine's standards for just war.

Less easy was the task of getting his thoughts published, as all his writing had to be approved for publication by Church censors who did not necessarily see that such writing was appropriate for one who had the vocation of a monk. Eventually he was granted permission to publish on "peace" rather than on "war," and his essay "The Christian in World Crisis" was included in *Seeds of Destruction,* which also included two long pieces on "Black Revolution" and a tribute to Mohandas Gandhi. Censorship, though, was only one manifestation of the basic problem Merton faced in reconciling his contemplative monasticism with his worldly concerns. Could he play a significant role in the protest against the war in Vietnam without forsaking his vocation? Did he know enough of what was going on in the world to add anything important to the movement for civil rights?

Merton addressed this question directly in "Contemplation in a World of Action." Since the world he was born into is a world not only of violence but selfishness, change can only come about when the self, the will, is abandoned in favor of something greater, "the fullness of personal awareness that comes with a total self-renunciation." In the absence of such self-renunciation, he who would resist the violence of the world, he who "attempts to act and do things for others or for the world," will finally have nothing to offer but "the contagion of his own obsessions, his aggressiveness, his ego-centered ambitions, his delusions about ends and means, his doctrinaire prejudices and ideas." Merton recognized his inability to speak for oppressed others, and he did not pretend to. Rather, he asked those like himself—white liberals, Christians, Americans—to engage in personal reexamination and to recognize the need for letting go of their most cherished sense of self. "We are living through the greatest crisis in the history of man," he continues. "And this crisis is centered precisely in the country that has made a fetish out of action and has lost (or perhaps never had) the sense of contemplation. Far from being irrelevant, prayer, meditation and contemplation are of the utmost importance in America today."

Merton's writing on race was not explicitly aligned with the nonviolence of Martin Luther King Jr., although Merton invariably expressed admiration for King. In a letter to a fellow white priest, included in the letters section of *Seeds of Destruction,* Merton criticizes the white man's complaint that some blacks lacked "patience" in their demands for civil rights: "At the present time the word 'patience' has been used and abused to cover every kind of inaction, foot dragging, double crossing, and political shilly-shallying so that when a person says 'patience' to the Negro now, the Negro simply dismisses his statement as meaningless." Those blacks who dismissed patience at that time were gener-

ally seen, by whites at least, as militant. In a 1968 essay titled "The Answer of Minerva: Pacifism and Resistance in Simone Weil," a review of a biography of the French philosopher and Resistance fighter, Merton distinguished between what Gandhi called the nonviolence of the weak and the nonviolence of the strong, "which opposes evil with serious and positive resistance, in order to overcome evil with good." "Simone Weil," Merton goes on to say, "would apparently have added that if this nonviolence had no hope of success, then evil could be resisted by force. But she hoped for a state of affairs in which human conflict could be re-solved nonviolently rather than by force." American society has faced this dilemma before. John Woolman and other Quakers worked for the end of slavery not through violence but through persuasion. John Greenleaf Whittier had similar hopes in the mid-nineteenth century. But the Puritan way, embodied by the abolition-ist John Brown and approved of by Emerson and Thoreau, among others, and not the Quaker way, finally brought an end to slavery in America.

As Merton's biographer, Michael Mott, has pointed out, much of Merton's own ambivalence is suggested by his comment on Weil. Merton in this as in so many things knew and believed what he considered the Catholic position, in this case the efficacy of love, but he at the same time felt the frustration of the existential reali-ties of the world.

MERTON AND MYSTICISM

In his introduction to *Gandhi on Non-violence,* Merton develops the idea of the West in its encounters with the East as a "one-eyed giant":

The one-eyed giant had science without wisdom, and he broke in upon ancient civilizations which (like the medieval West) had wisdom without sci-ence: wisdom which transcends and unites, wisdom which dwells in body and soul together and which, more by means of myth, of rite, of contemplation, than by scientific experiment, opens the door to a life in which the individual is not lost in the cosmos and in society but found in them. Wisdom which made all life sacred and meaningful—even that which later ages came to call secular and profane.

Published in 1964, this statement had a number of significant meanings. Generally, it called into question the West's sense of superiority over other cultures. More specifically, it challenged the United States' emerging policy of destruction in Vietnam.

At the same time, Merton here links medieval Western Christianity—the roots of his own monastic life—with the religions of the East, and he connects both to a mode of being—mythic, ritualistic, contemplative—that provides a way for man to discover order and significance in his otherwise pointless existence. This way is mysticism, the focus of much of Merton's life after his conversion to Catholicism. There is perhaps no other word more foreign to mainstream American culture than "mysticism," and Merton's attempt to make this concept meaningful for American readers often fell (and continues to fall) on uncomprehending ears.

And yet mysticism is not completely absent from American literature. The Puritans, it is true, were more concerned with clearing the wilderness and planting corn than they were with visionary revelation; they tended to drive out spirit-driven enthusiasts such as Anne Hutchinson. Nor were either the southern planters or the northern Yankees much inclined toward the supernatural, however much they differed in other ways. Yet American literature is not antithetical to mysticism. Merton felt a particular kinship with Emily Dickinson, not only because of her withdrawal from society but also for the mystical element in her poetry. Before Dickinson, in the eighteenth century, there had been Jonathan Edwards, who both tried to open his parishioners up to the abyss and to infuse in them an inward sense of "a divine and supernatural light." John Woolman, too, wrote not just of slaves working in the mines to put silver on the tables of the wealthy, but also of his own mystical visions in which he experienced loss of self and union with the sufferers of the world. (By contrast, Benjamin Franklin, the contemporary of Edwards and Woolman, was in this sense the prototypical pragmatic American, for whom lightning is nothing more than a force to be harnessed to machinery.) Even Emerson and Thoreau had an interest in the religions of the East, and Whitman more than either. In the twentieth century, the beat poets displayed affinities with mysticism, as did Eliot and Pound, and as do many contemporary nature writers, among whose number Merton must be counted.

Like many American nature writers, Merton was drawn to the desert: "The climate in which monastic prayer flowers," he wrote in *The Climate of Monastic Prayer* (1969), "is the desert, where the comfort of man is absent, where the secure routines of man's city offer no support, and where prayer must be sustained by God in the purity of faith. Even though he may live in a community, the monk is bound to explore the inner waste of his own being as a solitary." For Merton the desert is both literal and figurative. It is the place where the desert fathers, the forerunners of Christian monasticism, lived. But more important than the physicality of the desert is its emptiness, for mystical experience begins with an emptying out of the ego-self. Such an emptiness, or "dark night of the soul" in the words of the Spanish mystic Saint John of the Cross, cannot be sustained for long, but it is nevertheless essential. In *Zen and the Birds of Appetite* (1968), a collection of essays written shortly before his death, Merton observes that "the self-centered awareness of the ego is of course a pragmatic psychological reality, but once there has been an inner illumination of pure reality, an awareness of the Divine, the empirical self is seen by comparison to be 'nothing,' that is to say, contingent, evanescent, relatively unreal, real only in relation to its source and end in God." To arrive at interior emptiness, where the presence of God can fill the void, is the goal of mystical experience.

This emptiness, this dark night, is found both in mystical Christianity and in Zen, where it appears as "the Absolute Ground-Consciousness of the Void, in which there are no shores." As mysticism had by the twentieth century been supplanted in the West by "a tradition of stubborn ego-centered practicality," Merton felt that modern Christians could learn much from Zen and from the religions of the East to help them recover their own heritage of mystical communion with God. Merton remained a Christian, however, despite his interest in Zen. Whereas in Zen the focus of mystical experience is simply the Void, in Christianity the focus is Christ, or the Holy Spirit, found within oneself when all else is let go. From this experience of Christ as a reality greater than oneself yet within oneself, there emerges a new man, the individual born again in Christ. There emerges also a new sense of joy, as tormented ego is obliterated, and a new sympathy for the suffering people of the world, as the Christian experiences not just Christ, but Christ on the cross in his own soul.

Mystical experience, Christian or otherwise, is "direct and pure experience . . . liberated from verbal formulas and linguistic preconception." It is in this sense existential; it comes to grips with life itself, not with ideas about life. It is also by definition wordless; once it is put into words it becomes something else, a difficult challenge for the writer who wishes to convey something of the nature of mystical experience. For this reason, Merton does not often attempt to convey his own mystical experience directly. Instead he writes of the history of mysticism, its results, its practitioners. Hoping to provide

an opening to the void, he gives us self-negating paradoxes of the Zen masters, the sayings of the desert fathers, the words of the fourth-century-B.C. Chinese philosopher Chuang-Tzu. Above all, he presents us with his own life, in all its fullness and self-contradictions, his joy and his dread, his search for solitude and for community, his turning from the world and his engagement with it, his renunciation of the self in the full development of his person and spirit.

MERTON AND HIS READERS

Thomas Merton died in Bangkok, Thailand, on December 10, 1968, a few weeks shy of his fifty-fourth birthday. He had traveled to the East to participate in two conferences: an interfaith Spiritual Summit Conference in Calcutta and a meeting of Asian monastics, including some of his own Trappist order, in Bangkok. While in Bangkok, he stepped out of a shower in his hotel room and grasped a fan that had faulty wiring. He died of electrocution. His body was returned to Kentucky by a SAC bomber, carried in the same bay that on other flights carried "the scientific egg" Merton had written about at Gethsemani.

The Thomas Merton who readers know today differs from the Thomas Merton readers knew at the time of his death. In his lifetime, Merton drew on his journals for *The Sign of Jonas, The Secular Journal of Thomas Merton* (1959), and *Conjectures of a Guilty Bystander,* arranging, cutting, revising where necessary to achieve his conceptions for these books. Since his death, a similar volume only incompletely edited by Merton has appeared, *A Vow of Conversation: Journal, 1964–1965* (1988), as have the complete journals, in seven volumes, edited by various hands but presenting the originals as faithfully as possible. More focused selections from his journals, such as those collected in *The Asian Journal,* have also appeared. His letters have been published as well, though these publications by no means exhaust his extant cor-

THOMAS MERTON / 207

respondence. In his lifetime Merton published a handful of books of poetry, generally small, and one slim volume of *Selected Poems* (1959), updated once. Since his death New Directions has published *The Collected Poems of Thomas Merton* (1977), an enormous volume of over one thousand pages, although Merton would have been the first to admit that he did not write a thousand pages of good poetry. Another collection, *The Literary Essays of Thomas Merton* (1981), brings together a great deal of scattered material. Other books bringing together fugitive essays or repackaging previously published matter have likewise appeared.

Thus Merton has become a figure much more fixed in readers' minds since his death. When confronted with such an array of titles, it is difficult for the newcomer to Merton to get a sense of how he seemed to his original readers. Despite his cloistered life, Merton as a writer was always responding, whether to the news of the day or to other writers or to his own evolving feelings. Readers wanted to know what Merton thought of Vatican II, the 1960s Roman Catholic ecumenical council that redefined the nature of the Church, or of the self-immolation of a Buddhist monk protesting the Vietnam War, or of the March on Washington for civil rights. Above all, they wanted to know what he would write next. Merton was for many a friend, a companion in their own spiritual journey, though they knew him only through his books.

But now, since his death, there is no more evolution, no more surprising or challenging turns. His readers may still have questions, as the personal life of this private man continues to be the subject of speculation—Did he have an affair with a nurse in Louisville? Was he planning to leave Gethsemani?—but now the questions and possible answers are all in the past tense. There is, no doubt, yet more writing to be gathered and published or republished in different form, but now the reader does not wait for the next news; rather, he or she is confronted

with a massive body of work to sort out. But where does one begin? And how does one proceed?

From a purely literary point of view, probably no book of Merton's is more successful than the one that brought him fame. Merton may have eventually become a better person than he was when he wrote *The Seven Storey Mountain*—more generous, less certain about matters of spirit—but being a better person does not necessarily make one a better writer. The intensity, the directness, the vivid intelligence of *The Seven Storey Mountain* continue to remind readers of the spiritual urgency of their own lives, whatever those lives might be. *My Argument with the Gestapo: A Macaronic Journal* (1969), Merton's early, premonastic novel, gives a slightly different, though no less vivid, idea of Merton as a young man, as well as suggesting what direction his writing might have taken had he not entered the monastery.

Readers looking for a friend and companion will still respond to the books derived from his journals, and to the journals themselves. Those Merton prepared himself are not simply four installments of a life, however. *The Sign of Jonas* is no doubt the friendliest of the group, as we find Merton going about his daily life and coming to know himself and his vocation more fully. *Conjectures of a Guilty Bystander,* on the other hand, is among his most difficult and challenging books, existential, philosophical, engaged with his reading of the thinkers of the mid-twentieth century and with the questions they shared. His letters often present him at his most relaxed and playful, as well as his most direct and thus most accessible.

Readers with more specific interests will benefit from pursuing them. Merton's thoughts on spiritual life are presented in *No Man Is an Island* (1955); *Seeds of Contemplation; Thoughts in Solitude* (1958); and *The Climate of Monastic Prayer.* Again, these are quite different books, appealing to different sensibilities, though consistent in the experience that produced them. Even the revision, *New Seeds of Contemplation,* differs subtly from its precursor, the earlier book more intense, the latter more circumspect. (Merton's sense of humor flashes through even in so mundane a task as revision. The author's note to the original *Seeds of Contemplation* declares modestly that "these are the kind of thoughts that might have occurred to any Cistercian monk." In *New Seeds* this observation is qualified in the following footnote: "In the twelve years since this was written and published, not a few Cistercians have vehemently denied that these thoughts were either characteristic or worthy of a normal Cistercian, which is perhaps quite true.")

Merton's reflections on the East and Eastern religions can be easily identified by the respective text titles: *Zen and the Birds of Appetite, The Asian Journal of Thomas Merton,* and *The Way of Chuang-Tzu* (1965). Merton's social writing can be found in *Seeds of Destruction* and *Thomas Merton on Peace* (1971). *Ishi Means Man* (1976), on Native Americans, is an excellent example of a small volume produced by an independent press. His writing on monastic or mystical life includes *The Waters of Siloe, The Ascent to Truth* (1951), and *The Silent Life* (1957). *The New Man* (1962) is perhaps Merton's most successfully philosophical book, while *Seasons of Celebration* is his most Catholic. *Raids on the Unspeakable* is perhaps his least Catholic book, but also the one nearest to *The Seven Storey Mountain* in literary quality. *Bread in the Wilderness,* on the Psalms, expresses his sense of poetry with a fullness that his own poetry does not always demonstrate. Of the poetry collections, the *Selected Poems* is by far the more approachable book, while enthusiasts and scholars will eventually want *The Collected Poems.* Merton's later, more experimental poetry—*Cables to the Ace; or, Familiar Liturgies of Misunderstanding* (1968) and *The Geography of Lograire* (1969)—remains difficult, but his earlier poetry, particularly those poems derived from his life at Gethsemani, have

a deserved, if minor, place in twentieth-century American poetry.

The major biography is Michael Mott's *The Seven Mountains of Thomas Merton* (1984). At over six hundred pages, with complete notes and extensive bibliography, it should be the first resource for those who wish to know more about Merton's life. Appreciations, remembrances, critical studies, and tributes continued to appear in remarkable numbers in the decades after his death. At the other end of the spectrum from Mott's exhaustive study is a small essay written by John Howard Griffin, who died before his own biography of Merton could be completed and whose research Mott inherited. "In Search of Thomas Merton" is only eight pages long, but it captures the essence of the man whom so many loved and enjoyed. It is included in *The Thomas Merton Studies Center,* a small volume published by the Merton center at Bellarmine-Ursuline College in Louisville. Griffin, who knew Merton well, reminds the reader of Merton's reason for coming to Gethsemani: "He made the point again and again in journals that he did not come into this solitude and silence of the hermit life 'seeking,' but rather he came here because this is where he believed Christ wanted to find him."

Selected Bibliography

WORKS OF THOMAS MERTON

POETRY

Thirty Poems. Norfolk, Conn.: New Directions, 1944.

A Man in the Divided Sea. Norfolk, Conn.: New Directions, 1946. (Includes *Thirty Poems.*)

Figures for an Apocalypse. Norfolk, Conn.: New Directions, 1948.

The Tears of the Blind Lions. New York: New Directions, 1949.

The Strange Islands. New York: New Directions, 1957.

Selected Poems. New York: New Directions, 1959. (Contains seventy-two poems, with an introduction by Mark Van Doren and "Poetry and Contemplation, A Reappraisal," an essay by Merton.) Revised, 1967. (Contains eighty-eight poems; "Poetry and Contemplation" omitted.)

Original Child Bomb: Points for Meditation to Be Scratched on the Walls of a Cave. New York: New Directions, 1962. (A prose poem.)

Emblems of a Season of Fury. Norfolk, Conn: New Directions, 1963. (Includes thirty-one poems plus translations of thirty-seven poems by Pablo Antonio Cuadra, Raïssa Maritain, Ernesto Cardenal, Jorge Carrera Andrade, César Vallejo, and Alfonso Cortès.)

Cables to the Ace; or, Familiar Liturgies of Misunderstanding. New York: New Directions, 1968.

The Geography of Lograire. New York: New Directions, 1969.

The Collected Poems of Thomas Merton. New York: New Directions, 1977.

PROSE

Exile Ends in Glory: The Life of a Trappistine, Mother M. Berchmans, OCSO. Milwaukee: Bruce, 1948.

The Seven Storey Mountain. New York: Harcourt, Brace, 1948.

Seeds of Contemplation. Norfolk, Conn.: New Directions, 1949.

The Waters of Siloe. New York: Harcourt, Brace, 1949.

What Are These Wounds? The Life of a Cistercian Mystic, Saint Lutgarde of Aywières. Milwaukee: Bruce, 1950.

The Ascent to Truth. New York: Harcourt, Brace, 1951.

The Sign of Jonas. New York: Harcourt, Brace, 1953.

Bread in the Wilderness. New York: New Directions, 1953.

The Last of the Fathers: Saint Bernard of Clairvaux and the Encyclical Letter, Doctor Mellifluus. New York: Harcourt, Brace, 1954.

No Man Is an Island. New York: Harcourt, Brace, 1955.

The Living Bread. New York: Farrar, Straus and Cudahy, 1956.

The Silent Life. New York: Farrar, Straus and Cudahy, 1957.

Thoughts in Solitude. New York: Farrar, Straus and Cudahy, 1958.

The Secular Journal of Thomas Merton. New York: Farrar, Straus and Cudahy, 1959.

Disputed Questions. New York: Farrar, Straus and Cudahy, 1960.

The Wisdom of the Desert: Sayings from the Desert Fathers of the Fourth Century. New York: New Directions, 1960. (Translation with introductory essay by Merton.)

The Behavior of Titans. New York: New Directions, 1961.

The New Man. New York: Farrar, Straus and Cudahy, 1962.

New Seeds of Contemplation. Norfolk, Conn.: New Directions, 1962.

Peace in the Post-Christian Era. Kentucky: Abbey of Gethsemani, 1962.

Life and Holiness. New York: Herder and Herder, 1963.

Seeds of Destruction. New York: Farrar, Straus & Giroux, 1965.

Gandhi on Non-violence. New York: New Directions, 1965. (Edited and with an introduction by Merton.)

The Way of Chuang-Tzu. New York: New Directions, 1965. (Selections from Chuang-Tzu rendered in English by Merton, with an introductory essay.)

Seasons of Celebration. New York: Farrar, Straus & Giroux, 1965.

Conjectures of a Guilty Bystander. Garden City, N.Y.: Doubleday, 1966.

Raids on the Unspeakable. New York: New Directions, 1966.

Mystics and Zen Masters. New York: Farrar, Straus & Giroux, 1967.

Faith and Violence: Christian Teaching and Christian Practice. Notre Dame, Ind.: University of Notre Dame Press, 1968.

Zen and the Birds of Appetite. New York: New Directions, 1968.

My Argument with the Gestapo: A Macaronic Journal. Garden City, N.Y.: Doubleday, 1969. (Novel.)

The Climate of Monastic Prayer. Kalamazoo, Mich.: Cistercian Publications, 1969. (Foreword by Douglas V. Steere.) Reprinted as *Contemplative Prayer,* 1969.

Contemplative Prayer. New York: Herder and Herder, 1969. (Reprint of *The Climate of Monastic Prayer,* 1969.) Reprinted as an Image paperback with an introduction by Thich Nhat Hanh, 1996.

Contemplation in a World of Action. Garden City, N.Y.: Doubleday, 1971.

Opening the Bible. Collegeville, Minn.: Liturgical Press, 1971.

The Thomas Merton Studies Center: Three Essays. Santa Barbara, Calif.: Unicorn, 1971. (Essays by Merton, Monsignor Alfred Horrigan, and John H. Griffin.)

Thomas Merton on Peace. Edited by Gordon C. Zahn. New York: McCall, 1971. Reissued with minor changes (see below) as *The Nonviolent Alternative,* 1980.

The Asian Journal of Thomas Merton. Edited by Naomi Burton, Patrick Hart, and James Laughlin. New York: New Directions, 1973.

Ishi Means Man. Greensboro, N.C.: Unicorn, 1976.

The Monastic Journey. Edited by Patrick Hart. Kansas City: Sheed, Andrews, and McMeel, 1977.

Love and Living. Edited by Naomi Burton Stone and Brother Patrick Hart. New York: Farrar, Straus & Giroux, 1979.

The Nonviolent Alternative. New York: Farrar, Straus & Giroux, 1980. Revised edition of *Thomas Merton on Peace,* 1971. ("Chant to Be Used in Processions around a Site with Furnaces" is omitted.)

Thomas Merton on St. Bernard. Edited by Patrick Hart. Kalamazoo, Mich.: Cistercian Publications, 1980.

Day of a Stranger. Edited by Robert E. Daggy. Salt Lake City, Utah: Gibbs M. Smith, 1981.

Introductions East and West: The Foreign Prefaces of Thomas Merton. Edited by Robert E. Daggy. Greensboro, N.C.: Unicorn, 1981. Reprinted as *Honorable Reader: Reflections on My Work,* 1989.

The Literary Essays of Thomas Merton. Edited by Patrick Hart. New York: New Directions, 1981.

Woods, Shore, Desert: A Notebook, May 1968. Edited by Joel Weishaus. Sante Fe: Museum of New Mexico Press, 1982.

A Vow of Conversation: Journal, 1964–1965. Edited by Naomi Burton Stone. New York: Farrar, Straus & Giroux, 1988.

Thomas Merton in Alaska: The Alaskan Conferences, Journals, and Letters. Edited by Robert E. Daggy. New York: New Directions, 1989.

Honorable Reader: Reflections on My Work. Edited by Robert E. Daggy. New York: Crossroad, 1989. Reprint of *Introductions East and West,* 1981.

The Springs of Contemplation: A Retreat at the Abbey of Gethsemani. Edited by Jane Marie Richardson. New York; Farrar, Straus & Giroux, 1992.

Passion for Peace: The Social Essays. Edited by William H. Shannon. New York: Crossroad, 1997.

JOURNALS AND LETTERS

Run to the Mountain: The Story of a Vocation. Vol. 1 (1939–1941), *The Journals of Thomas Merton.* Edited by Patrick Hart. San Francisco: HarperSanFrancisco, 1995.

Entering the Silence: Becoming a Monk and Writer. Vol. 2 (1941–1952), *The Journals of Thomas Merton.* Edited by Jonathan Montaldo. San Francisco: HarperSanFrancisco, 1996.

A Search for Solitude: Pursuing the Monk's True Life. Vol. 3 (1952–1960), *The Journals of Thomas Merton.* Edited by Lawrence S. Cunningham. San Francisco: HarperSanFrancisco, 1996.

Turning toward the World: The Pivotal Years. Vol. 4 (1960–1963), *The Journals of Thomas Merton.* Edited by Victor A. Kramer. San Francisco: Harper SanFrancisco, 1996.

Dancing in the Water of Life: Seeking Peace in the Hermitage. Vol. 5 (1963–1965), *The Journals of Thomas Merton.* Edited by Robert E. Daggy. San Francisco: HarperSanFrancisco, 1997.

Learning to Love: Exploring Solitude and Freedom. Vol. 6 (1966–1967), *The Journals of Thomas Merton.* Edited by Christine M. Bochen. San Francisco: HarperSanFrancisco, 1997.

The Other Side of the Mountain: The End of the Journey. Vol. 7 (1967–1968), *The Journals of Thomas Merton.* Edited by Partick Hart. San Francisco: HarperSanFrancisco, 1998.

The Intimate Merton: His Life from His Journals. Edited by Patrick Hart and Jonathan Montaldo. San Francisco: HarperSanFrancisco, 1999.

A Catch of Anti-Letters: Letters by Thomas Merton and Robert Lax. Mission, Kans.: Sheed, Andrews, and McMeel, 1978.

The Hidden Ground of Love: The Letters of Thomas Merton on Religious Experience and Social Concerns. Edited by William H. Shannon. New York: Farrar, Straus & Giroux, 1985.

The Road to Joy: The Letters of Thomas Merton to Old and New Friends. Edited by Robert E. Daggy. New York: Farrar, Straus & Giroux, 1989.

The School of Charity: The Letters of Thomas Merton on Religious Renewal and Spiritual Direction. Edited by Patrick Hart. New York: Farrar, Straus & Giroux, 1990.

The Courage for Truth: The Letters of Thomas Merton to Writers. Edited by Christine M. Bochen. New York: Farrar, Straus & Giroux, 1993.

Witness to Freedom: The Letters of Thomas Merton in Times of Crisis. Edited by William H. Shannon. New York: Farrar, Straus & Giroux, 1994.

At Home in the World: The Letters of Thomas Merton and Rosemary Radford Ruether. Edited by Mary Tardiff. Maryknoll, N.Y.: Orbis, 1995.

Striving Toward Being: The Letters of Thomas Merton and Czeslaw Milosz. New York: Farrar, Straus & Giroux, 1996.

Thomas Merton and James Laughlin: Selected Letters. Edited by David D. Cooper. New York: Norton, 1997.

MANUSCRIPTS

The most significant repository of Merton manuscripts, as well as other materials, is the Thomas Merton Studies Center at Bellarmine College, in Louisville, Kentucky. Significant manuscript holdings can also be found at Columbia University and Saint Bonaventure University.

CRITICAL AND BIOGRAPICAL STUDIES

Baker, James Thomas. *Thomas Merton: Social Critic.* Lexington: University Press of Kentucky, 1971.

Carr, Anne E. *A Search for Wisdom and Spirit: Thomas Merton's Theology of the Self.* Notre Dame, Ind.: University of Notre Dame Press, 1988.

Cooper, David D. *Thomas Merton's Art of Denial: The Evolution of a Radical Humanist.* Athens: University of Georgia Press, 1989.

Cunningham, Lawrence S. *Thomas Merton and the Monastic Vision.* Grand Rapids, Mich.: Eerdmans, 1999.

Forest, James. *Living with Wisdom: A Life of Thomas Merton.* Maryknoll, N.Y.: Orbis, 1991.

Furlong, Monica. *Merton: A Biography.* New York: Harper & Row, 1981.

Hart, Patrick, ed. *Thomas Merton: A Monastic Tribute.* New enlarged edition. Kalamazoo: Cistercian Publications, 1983.

————. *The Legacy of Thomas Merton.* Kalamazoo, Mich.: Cistercian Publications, 1986.

Higgins, John J. *Merton's Theology of Prayer.* Spencer, Mass.: Cistercian Publications, 1971.

Higgins, Michael W. *Heretic Blood: The Spiritual Geography of Thomas Merton.* Toronto: Stoddart, 1998.

Inchausti, Robert. *Thomas Merton's American Prophecy.* Albany: State University of New York Press, 1998.

Labrie, Ross. *The Art of Thomas Merton.* Fort Worth: Texas Christian University Press, 1979.

Lentfoehr, Thérèse. *Words and Silence: On the Poetry of Thomas Merton.* New York: New Directions, 1979.

Malits, Elena. *The Solitary Explorer: Thomas Merton's Transforming Journey.* San Francisco: Harper & Row, 1980.

Mott, Michael. *The Seven Mountains of Thomas Merton.* Boston: Houghton Mifflin, 1984. (The authorized biography.)

Padovano, Anthony T. *The Human Journey: Thomas Merton, Symbol of a Century.* Garden City, N.Y.: Doubleday, 1982.

Pennington, M. Basil. *Thomas Merton, Brother Monk: The Quest for True Freedom.* San Francisco: Harper & Row, 1987.

Rice, Edward. *The Man in the Sycamore Tree: The Good Times and Hard Life of Thomas Merton.* Garden City, N.Y.: Doubleday, 1970.

Shannon, William H. *Thomas Merton's Dark Path.* Revised edition, New York: Farrar, Straus & Giroux, 1987.

————. *Silent Lamp: The Thomas Merton Story.* New York: Crossroad, 1992.

————. *"Something of a Rebel": Thomas Merton, His Life and Works: An Introduction.* Cincinnati, Ohio: St. Anthony Messenger Press, 1997.

Twomey, Gerald, ed. *Thomas Merton: Prophet in the Belly of a Paradox.* New York: Paulist, 1978.

Woodcock, George. *Thomas Merton, Monk and Poet: A Critical Study.* New York: Farrar, Straus & Giroux, 1978.

BIBLIOGRAPHIES

The most comprehensive bibliography of both primary and secondary materials is that of Breit and Daggy. For more complete bibliographical information on secondary material since 1986, consult *The Merton Seasonal,* published by the Thomas Merton Studies Center at Bellarmine College. The Burton bibliography, also published by the Thomas Merton Studies Center, is a good guide to both Merton's life and his publications, including books, essays, and poems.

Breit, Marquita E., and Robert E. Daggy. *Thomas Merton: A Comprehensive Bibliography.* New York: Garland, 1986.

Burton, Patricia. *Merton Vade Mecum: A Quick Reference Biographical Handbook.* Louisville, Ky.: Thomas Merton Studies Center, 1999.

Dell'Isola, Frank. *Thomas Merton: A Bibliography.* Rev. ed., Kent, Ohio: Kent State University Press, 1975.

—*PAUL JOHNSTON*

Gloria Naylor

1950–

THE EPIGRAPH TO Gloria Naylor's first novel, *The Women of Brewster Place* (1982)—from Langston Hughes' poem "Harlem"—asks, "What happens to a dream deferred?" And the epigraph to her 1998 novel *The Men of Brewster Place*—from another Hughes poem, "Tell Me"—asks, "Why should it be *my* dream deferred overlong?" These epigraphs frame five interconnected novels that chronicle the history of the African American experience in a society where individual lives are circumscribed by gender, race, and class.

Until she read Toni Morrison's novel *The Bluest Eye* (1970) in 1977, Naylor has said, she did not realize that a voice authenticating her experience as an African American woman existed. Up to that time in her life, she had only read writers who were either male or white. Discovering the existence of a novel like *The Bluest Eye,* Naylor told Toni Morrison, "said to a young black woman struggling to find a mirror of her worth in this society, not only is your story worth telling, but it can be told in words so painstakingly eloquent that it becomes a song."

Naylor's critically acclaimed novels celebrate women's lives, presenting a sense of community, self, courage, determination, and strength among African American women that is based on Naylor's own family background, including the women role models of her early childhood, and is also drawn from the work of African American women writers. These women promote a sense of what Toni Morrison calls "the village," where bloodmothers, othermothers, and community othermothers create a sense of belonging, sharing, and power. Powerless, ab-

sented, and silenced within the larger dominant society, within these communities, the black women promote voices of self-valorization and identity that help them break down the barriers they face, so that, like ebony phoenixes, they can rise out of the ashes of oppression.

EARLY LIFE

The oldest of the three daughters of Alberta McAlpin and Roosevelt Naylor, Gloria Naylor learned her love of books and reading from her mother, who had become an avid reader as an escape from the hard physical labor of being a sharecropper in Robinsville, Mississippi. Denied access to public libraries in the pre–Civil Rights South, Alberta insisted on moving north after she and Roosevelt were married in 1949, in order to enhance their children's chances for freedom and opportunity. Gloria Naylor was born in New York City on January 25, 1950. In 1960, shortly after the death of Naylor's maternal grandfather, Evans McAlpin, she and her family moved into a Harlem apartment building owned by her maternal grandmother, Luecelia McAlpin. The apartment was located on West 119th Street, a street that Naylor includes in her first novel, *The Women of Brewster Place.* Naylor's work also includes many characters based on her Aunt Sadie and Aunt Mae, who symbolize female independence, strength, and courage for her and who served as role models in the way they lived out their dreams.

In 1963, when Gloria was thirteen, the family moved to Queens, then a suburb, where Alberta thought her children would receive a better education. As a child, Naylor would watch

Shakespearean drama in the park, an influence from her early life that appears in all her novels. After she graduated from high school in 1968, Naylor joined the Jehovah's Witnesses and was a minister for them in New York, North Carolina, and Florida, until 1975, when she returned home to enter college. The biblical references in her novels are a direct influence from this experience. She first attended Medgar Evars College as a nursing major and later transferred to Brooklyn College as an English major, where her introduction to Toni Morrison's novel *The Bluest Eye* led to her reading such influential African American women writers as Ntozake Shange, Zora Neale Hurston, Alice Walker, Nikki Giovanni, and Ann Petry. In 1979 her short story "A Life on Beekman Place" was accepted by *Essence* magazine. After graduating from Brooklyn College with a bachelor of arts degree in 1981, Naylor went to Yale University on a scholarship. Her 1985 novel *Linden Hills* originated as her master's thesis at Yale.

The publication of two short stories in *Essence* magazine, "A Life on Beekman Place" (which appeared in 1980) and "Mama Still Loves You" (1982), marked the beginning of Naylor's career as a novelist: these became the "Lucielia Louise Turner" and the "Kiswana Browne" stories in her first novel, *The Women of Brewster Place: A Novel in Seven Stories,* which she finished in 1981 while working as a switchboard operator and attending college. In between these two literary successes Naylor was married and divorced. The success of her novels was as unexpected to her as was the failure of her marriage: she later told Toni Morrison that she had viewed marriage as safe—as "traveled" territory—while writing was "untraveled" territory that was frightening to her.

THE WOMEN OF BREWSTER PLACE

"What happens to a dream deferred?" asks the epigraph to the seven stories that comprise *The Women of Brewster Place.* Gloria Naylor's first novel chronicles the "common lives" and the "common loves," as Naylor calls them, of a community of women whose dreams have all, in one way or another, been deferred. Each of the seven women on Brewster Place, "like an ebony phoenix each in her own time and with her own season," has a story, which the novel frames between dawn and dusk (in chapters so titled) of one day.

The Women of Brewster Place marks the beginning of a series of interconnected novels in which a place or a character in one book is developed into a major character or idea in another book. The idea of interconnectedness is similar to the belief in "women's ways of knowing" that is central to all Naylor's books, beginning with *The Women of Brewster Place.* "Women's ways of knowing" is an African belief that views women as having particular power because they give birth to children, therefore giving life and creating a link between the physical and spiritual worlds according to African ontology. Women carry knowledge, which can be present in either the physical or the spiritual world. This concept is inverted in Western thought, according to Lacanian theory. In Western terms, the man is viewed as having the power and the woman becomes Other because she lacks a phallus and therefore power. Women only "make" others, not themselves, in the phallocentric order. They lack a voice and a presence in patriarchal law. Their ways of speaking must come from outside the phallocentric order, through absence, through renaming, and through silence. And this is what happens in all of Naylor's novels, beginning with *The Women of Brewster Place,* where the stories of the seven women are varying reflections of women's lack of power within the phallocentric order and demonstrate the traditional women's roles that have deferred these women's dreams and brought them to a dead-end street. It is only when they rename themselves and give themselves voice through women's ways of knowing that their dreams can be fulfilled in ways outside patriarchal law.

Brewster Place, a "bastard child" conceived by city officials, at one time was the starting place for various peoples just beginning their lives in the United States. It has seen a first generation of Irish immigrants and a second generation of Mediterranean immigrants. But now Brewster Place is a dead-end street walled off from the rest of the city, home to the "multi-colored 'Afric' children of its old age" who "mill like determined spirits among its decay." These latest residents cling to the street "with a desperate acceptance that whatever was here was better than the starving southern climates they had fled from. Brewster Place knew that unlike its other children, the few who would leave forever were to be the exception rather than the rule, since they came because they had no choice and would remain for the same reason." But on this dead-end street walled off from all possibilities, the ebony phoenixes arise from their ashes not only to tell their own stories but also to promote a strong sense of community, female bonding, and love that endures once they find their own potentials and identities within themselves.

The first story, "Mattie Michael," is the moral center of the novel. Mattie's role is to connect the lives of the community of women of Brewster Place. In this respect she serves as an ancestor figure, a transmitter of culture and inventor of language who connects the past to the present and the future and thereby gives the women around her a sense of clan, heritage, community, tradition, and roots—which in turn allows them to find their voices and gives them a presence within a world defined by patriarchy. Naylor has said that she created Mattie to be just the opposite of William Faulkner's Dilsey in *The Sound and the Fury,* the wise black maid who is nurturing, loving, and strong in defense of the white family for whom she works but who has no sexuality or identity of her own. Like the African Great Mother, Mattie is an earth mother, a creator of life and wisdom. She is the *nommo,* creative potential, who represents, according to Barbara Hill Rigney, "a group consciousness, a history as well as a culture." As an ancestor figure, her relationships are benevolent, instructive, and protective. These qualities promote a positive sense of community and wholeness, but, like Kali from African myth, even though she represents enduring love she can also destroy.

Through flashbacks to her past, Mattie, who was born in Rock Vale, Tennessee, recounts how she ended up on Brewster Place. Mattie's dream is deferred because she looks for her identity outside of herself. Rejected by her father when she becomes pregnant, Mattie loses her home and family, the very qualities associated with women's identity in the rural South. The consequence of her one act of freedom and individuality symbolizes the consequences of breaking the rules for women. The penalty Mattie pays for her one sexual encounter is enough to prevent her from ever exploring her sexuality again; instead she defines her life through her son. In this role she is the creator as well as the destroyer of potential: in order to be a nurturing mother she completely denies her own identity and worth as a woman. And even though she sacrifices for her son, Basil, she protects him so fiercely from the world that she does not allow him to mature and create an identity for himself. Naylor says of Mattie: "I held her accountable for the monster she had created. There were warnings that she was given." Even Miss Eva, the woman who took Mattie in when she was displaced by her father and taught her how to nurture, share, and love, warns her that she is living her life through her son. Thus, when Basil jumps bail (which Mattie has raised) and Mattie loses everything, including her house, she is forced to move to Brewster Place.

Until this point in her life, Mattie's only experience has been within a patriarchal culture in which it is acceptable for men, but not for women, to explore their sexuality and claim their bodies as their own; at the same time, in such a culture, a woman without a man is viewed as nonsexed and is deprived of identity, voice, and power. Mattie responds to the constraints of this patriarchal realm by ignoring her own potential and living through her son. On Brewster Place, however, Mattie learns from Miss Eva to accept the ancestral qualities that define her in relation to a community of blood-mothers, othermothers, and community other-mothers.

The second woman on Brewster Place whose dream is deferred is Etta Mae Johnson, Mattie's childhood friend. Like Mattie, Etta looks outside herself for a voice and an identity, but unlike Mattie, she defines herself through her body. She arrives on Brewster Place as a last resort, and Mattie takes her in. The other women ridicule Eva for her life as a prostitute, which began, she says, when she "found out that America wasn't ready for her yet . . . [so] she took her talents to the street."

Etta's life, as she recounts it, is much the same sort of life captured in the blues of Billie Holiday, with whom Etta feels an affinity. Staying with Mattie has provided a safe haven for Etta, a haven where she has a sense of belonging and community. Nonetheless, she still defines herself through men, despite the fact that this is the means of survival that brought her to the dead end in her life represented by Brewster Place. "Even if someone had bothered to stop and tell her that the universe had expanded for her, just an inch, she wouldn't have known how to shine alone."

Etta agrees to go to church with Mattie, in order to find a suitable man among the church-going widowers and "settled minded men." In church, the congregation sings "Go Down Moses," whose words seem to chronicle the racist and sexist abuses Etta has faced in her life. The words are "as ancient as the origin of their misery, but the tempo had picked up threefold in its evolution from the cotton fields. They were now sung with the frantic determination of a people who realized that the world was swiftly changing but for some mystic, complex reason their burden had not." And neither has Etta's burden changed. As she listens to the words, wondering if she could have survived without being a whore, she slips back into that very role. At the end of the service she manipulates Mattie into introducing her to the Reverend Moreland T. Woods, who she thinks must be different from all the other men she has met in poolrooms, nightclubs, numbers dens, and on a dozen street corners.

In actuality, Woods is a con man. He takes Etta to a sleazy motel for the night, where "his last floundering thrusts into her body . . . bring her back to reality." As she walks back to Mattie's apartment she is broken because she realizes he is no different from the other men she has known. But as she nears the apartment, she hears her Billie Holiday records playing and realizes that Mattie is waiting up for her. "Etta laughed softly to herself as she climbed the steps toward the light and the love and the comfort that awaited her." In Mattie's house she shares real meaning with another human being. She is connected and belongs, something she has never felt before. Her relationship with Mattie helps both women survive within the patriarchal world.

Kiswana Browne, the third voice on Brewster Place, comes to the dead-end street by choice, not out of necessity like Mattie and Etta Mae. A product of the middle-class suburb of Linden Hills (the setting for Naylor's next novel), Kiswana wants to help the women of Brewster Place improve the quality of their lives. But to achieve this goal, she must first learn her own identity. A self-styled black revolutionary who hunts for her African roots, changes her name, kinks her hair, and leaves college because school is "counterrevolutionary," Kiswana has acquired ideals she does not know how to absorb. It is not until a confrontation with her mother over her new name that Kiswana begins to understand her own identity. Disturbed that Kiswana has changed her name, Mrs. Browne relates the story of how she was named for her grandmother, who was Native American. By changing her name, Kiswana denies her own roots and history. She unknowingly has done the same thing to herself that the Yankees did to Mattie's grandfather during the Reconstruction era, when they took away his identity by renaming him.

While talking, both mother and daughter realize they share common characteristics. They both paint their toenails because they are connected to men who are "into feet." As she looks at her mother she stares "at the woman she had been and was to become." She recognizes the connectedness of women's lives that will enable her to better help the tenants on Brewster Place. Through this incident, Kiswana realizes that she is the source of her own power and her own ideals. By accepting her own identity and realizing that "black isn't beautiful and it isn't ugly—black is. It's not kinky hair and it's not straight hair—it just is," Kiswana can help the other women on Brewster Place realize their dreams and their voices. Because she has become a part of the community, Kiswana now has a voice that connects her to her past and her future, and she can share it with the other women to help them understand their heritage and their own self-worth.

The fourth voice, that of Lucielia Louise Turner, presents a woman whose dream is deferred because she tries to construct a conventional nuclear family with a man who physically and psychologically abuses her. Like Mattie and Etta, "Ciel" defines her life through a man who strips her of her identity. Her boyfriend Eugene leaves her for a year, and when he returns, she takes him back because she says that her daughter Serena needs a father. But

when she becomes pregnant with their second child, he threatens to leave her if she does not have an abortion. With two children, he says, "I ain't never gonna have nothin'." After aborting the baby to please Eugene, Ciel is paralyzed by grief, but when Eugene says he is still going to leave her, she begs him to stay—even as she realizes with horror how she has demeaned herself.

As Ciel and Eugene are arguing, Serena is in the kitchen alone and electrocutes herself by playing with a fork in an electric socket. The following scene, in which Mattie arrives to bathe Ciel and cleanse her of her grief, symbolizes the nurturing, mothering, loving bond between women. Mattie, the novels' ancestor figure, rocks Ciel back to psychological health. Her healing presence offers the love and compassion that will allow Ciel to find her own voice without Eugene, to leave Brewster Place and to piece together her life once again.

Cora Lee, the fifth voice on Brewster Place, seems to embody the stereotype of the black woman as single mother or welfare mother. But behind this stereotype is a woman trapped by the genderized notion, absorbed from her parents and from the patriarchal culture around her, that she can only achieve worth and identity through becoming a mother. As a child, Cora Lee has an obsession with acquiring new baby dolls—and when she grows up, she has real babies, by men who are mere "shadows," whose real names she may not know. These men only bring her the "thing that feels good in the night" and makes babies that she can nurture. The problem, however, is that she only takes care of her offspring when they are babies; by the time they are toddlers she loses all interest in them and neglects them. She derives sustenance and power from her children as helpless newborns but cannot translate this into anything meaningful beyond the infant stage.

Kiswana becomes aware of Cora Lee's appalling neglect of her children. She tries to get

Cora Lee involved in her children and interested in the responsibilities of mothering by persuading Cora Lee to take the children to see a Shakespeare play in the park (a direct influence from Naylor's own childhood). The play, which is being produced by Kiswana's boyfriend, is *A Midsummer Night's Dream,* with its famous line: "We are such stuff as dreams are made of." And as she watches the play, Cora Lee does dream— that her children can become professionals and that she can mother and nurture them to adulthood. The vision does not last, however. Ultimately Cora Lee is unable to "see" beyond the only role she knows. Her dreams will be deferred, and she will go back to the old patterns of her life, in which she only knows how to assume identity through mothering infants.

Lorraine and Theresa, the next two voices the reader meets on Brewster Place, are a lesbian couple who have come to Brewster Place, like Kiswana, by choice. But even though they chose to come here, this is also a dead end for them, because Lorraine longs to be accepted by the community of women, "to chat and trade makeup secrets and cake recipes." In trying to fit into this community, she feeds her own belief that somehow there is something wrong with her lifestyle; her own identity is in conflict with the conventions of the dominant society whose acceptance she craves. Theresa, conversely, is happiest in the company of gay friends, and she refuses to work at hiding her sexual orientation.

Despite Lorraine's efforts at becoming part of the community, the other women of Brewster Place do not accept the lesbian couple. Lorraine's only friend on Brewster Place is Ben, the janitor, who is also alienated from the people around him. Ben and Lorraine become family for one another, but after Lorraine is brutally raped, Lorraine kills Ben when he tries to help her. The implication of Lorraine's story is that the women who refused to accept her hold attitudes that are little different from the attitude of the man who rapes her, and that all who have treated Lorraine as Other, outside the embrace of community, have contributed to her sense of alienation and have culpability in the death that results from the rape.

The novel ends with a section titled "Block Party." In this section Mattie has a dream in which all the women join together to bring down the wall that alienates, isolates, and silences them. Her dream of the creative potential of women's ways of knowing—her dream that the potential of women's knowledge will be transmitted through connectedness, traditions, heritage, and roots—finally has a chance of coming true. In the epilogue, "Dusk," the tenants have been evicted, but hope still remains for them because the street is "dying but not dead." The community of women, the "colored daughters of Brewster, spread over the canvas of time, still wake with their dreams misted on the edge of a yawn. . . . They ebb and flow, ebb and flow, but never disappear." They refuse to be defeated as they were when they first came to Brewster Place, because they believe in their power to create their own ways of knowing through their own voices.

Following her graduation from Brooklyn College in 1981, Naylor took the advance she received from *The Women of Brewster Place* to go on trip to Europe. But as a woman traveling alone, she was harassed on the streets. "The freedom that Hemingway and Baldwin experienced I didn't have," she has said. "I resented that; I was bitter that I couldn't have the world like they have the world." The experience influenced her portrayal of women and fueled the feminist perspective that infuses *Linden Hills,* the book she began when she entered Yale the next year. Meanwhile, *The Women of Brewster Place* won the American Book Award in 1983. (In 1989 the book was made into a television movie starring Oprah Winfrey as Mattie Michael.)

LINDEN HILLS

In the epigraph to *Linden Hills,* the novel's narrator asks Grandma Tilson—the ancestor of the women who live on First Crescent Drive in Linden Hills—if she will go to hell when she dies. Grandma Tilson responds that she does not have to wait to die to find hell; hell exists in Linden Hills among the black middle class who have denied their heritage in their quest for money.

Linden Hills is a black suburb modeled on Dante's "Inferno," an allusion that Naylor combines with influences from African American women's literature and the Bible to create an allegory that demonstrates the ways in which the African American middle class has abandoned its identity and values. The nine circles of this suburb parallel the nine descending circles of Dante's Hell; the descending street addresses represent the various ways in which the black middle-class residents of Linden Hills have sold their souls for the "silver mirror" of the epigraph. The inhabitants of Linden Hills have sacrificed the connectedness of heritage, roots, and traditions, values associated with women's ways of knowing (values demonstrated in *The Women of Brewster Place*), for the American dream of materialism.

Naylor begins the novel with a history of the five generations of Nedeed men who created the suburb of Linden Hills, beginning with the original Luther Nedeed, who is able to buy the land only because white people do not value it (a genesis that recalls Toni Morrison's 1973 novel *Sula,* where the worthless land known as the Bottoms is conveyed to black residents as a "nigger joke"). The first five drives in Linden Hills are at the least desirable end of the suburb and parallel the first five circles of Dante's Hell, where the least serious crimes are committed. The last four drives—parallel to the lowest four circles of Hell, reserved for those souls who have committed the most serious offenses—are inhabited by the most prosperous residents of the suburb. All streets descend to the very center of Linden Hills, where Luther Nedeed lives, in a house that is surrounded by a cemetery and a lake.

The first Luther Nedeed arrives from Mississippi to purchase the land that becomes Linden Hills—described only as being "up north"—in 1820. He builds his home in the middle of it and becomes an undertaker because in the North black and white can be buried together. Thus, he beats the white man at his own game, turning worthless land into a "silver mirror." He then returns to Mississippi to marry an octoroon wife. Together they have one son who inherits the business. This pattern is repeated every generation, with each Nedeed male marrying an octoroon wife who has one son. Over five generations this family creates the black suburb that represents middle-class black America's loss of identity, culture, community, and clan.

The reader follows Willie through the nine circles of Linden Hills that starts on First Crescent Drive and ends at Luther Nedeed's house on Tupolo Drive. Just as Virgil guides Dante through the nine circles of the Inferno because he is familiar with them, Lester Tilson, a resident of First Crescent Drive, is Willie's guide through the nine levels of Linden Hills, a journey into self-knowledge for Willie that occurs over the course of four days. It is significant that both Willie and Lester are poets. More importantly, Willie is a high school dropout who does not write down his poetry. Rather, he memorizes it, connecting him with the oral tradition and the roots of African culture that slaves kept alive in the United States when white society denied them the right to read and write. Willie's "ways of knowing," then, are not connected to the white influences.

Willie's first visit is to the home of Ruth and Norman Anderson, who live on Wayne Avenue, a poor neighborhood outside of Linden Hills. Ruth once lived on Fifth Crescent Drive, which parallels the abode of the angry in Dante's Hell. She and her husband are now living in poverty, but their union represents the only relationship in the novel that works. Ruth is a symbol of the biblical Ruth, who is selfless in love, something the residents of Linden Hills do not know or understand. She also serves as a parallel to the Beatrice figure of Dante's "Inferno," the symbol of ideal love. She stays with her husband Norman despite the fact that he cannot work full-time because he has an attack of the "pinks" every spring, a disease that forces him to scrape all the pink from his skin—pink representing everything that is part of the white world. This disease functions as a warning to Willie and Lester of the dangers associated with denying heritage and tradition for the white world of materialism.

As Willie and Lester work their way through the Linden Hills neighborhood doing odd jobs, they are able to contrast the people they meet with the Andersons, who are materially poor but who are connected to one another and have a sense of community and clan. The residents of Linden Hills experience only the emptiness of upward mobility, which strips them of self, culture, and voice. The Andersons represent a sense of community, while the residents of Linden Hills only represent a neighborhood.

The first house Willie and Lester visit is Lester's house on First Crescent Drive. Lester lives here with his mother and sister. First Crescent Drive is the counterpart of the first circle of Dante's Hell, the dwelling place of the unbaptized, who are neither good nor evil. Three generations of Tilson women have lived here: Lester's grandmother, his mother, and his sister, Roxanne. Grandmother Tilson is the voice of community and clan, the Great Mother who warned her neighbors that they were in danger of losing their souls and of "giving up that part of you that lets you know who you are" by renting land from Luther Nedeed. Lester's mother, on the other hand, married into Linden Hills and worked her husband to death in her quest for material success. The daughter, Roxanne, epitomizes those in limbo. She has sold her soul for the "silver mirror": her Ivy League degree, her good job in the white world, her blacking creams and hair straighteners are all symbols of success in pursuit of the white American dream that have stripped her of her own identity.

The next house at which Willie and Lester go to work is Winston Alcott's house on Second Crescent Drive, a parallel with the second level of Dante's Hell, where the carnal sinners live. Winston betrays his lover, David, by marrying a woman he does not love because he wants to achieve status and upward mobility in Linden Hills. Admitting he is gay will deny him access to this dream. Like Paolo and Francesca, the lovers in Dante's second circle who are punished for infidelity by being separated for eternity, David reads poems at Winston's wedding that allude to his infidelity and his selling his soul for the "silver mirror," thus denying his own identity and sexuality.

Willie and Lester next move to Third Crescent Drive, where they clean out the garage for Xavier Donnell, a workaholic who has given up all identity to pursue professional success. He even fears marrying a black woman, because this might interfere with his quest for the "silver mirror." Not only does he give up any connection to other human beings, he tries to become almost nonhuman, portrayed comically in the extent to which he even tries to change the patterns of his own bodily functions.

Next Willie and Lester go to Fourth Crescent Drive, parallel to the fourth circle of Dante's Hell, the place reserved for the greedy, to do chores for Chester Parker, whose wife, Lycentra, has just died. Chester hires Willie and Lester to strip his dead wife's bedroom wallpaper and repaint the room for his next wife. Chester is a betrayer who in his greed cannot wait to bury his wife before acquiring a replacement for her. His Judas-like greed is also pointedly demonstrated at the dinner table, at the wake that is a symbol of Christ's Last Supper.

Fifth Crescent Drive, the last level of upper Hell in Dante's "Inferno," anger, is home to the Reverend Michael T. Hollis. Minister to the Sinai Baptist Church, he is as hollow as its rich interior. Having forgotten that his calling to the ministry was to save souls, he loses his soul to the god of materialism.

Laurel Dumont lives at Sixth Crescent drive, the first of the last three levels of Linden Hills, parallel to lower Hell in the "Inferno." She commits suicide because she has given up her identity for a professional life that isolates her from any connection to family, community, or self. She is afraid to look at herself in mirrors because she has lost all connection to the values associated with community, voice, roots, and heritage.

Daniel Braithwaite lives on the next level of Linden Drive, Tupelo Drive, parallel to the eighth circle of Dante's Hell, the level reserved for frauds. He is a historian who does not present the true identity of the black community but only the false covering created by the Nedeed family. He is unable to connect the past to the present and is thus unable to interpret meaning from events.

Luther Nedeed lives on the last level of Tupelo Drive, and Luther's wife, Willa, is the next voice that leads the reader on the journey into the history of the black middle class's plight. The Nedeed women symbolically represent the mother as Other. They serve no function to the Nedeed men except to produce an heir to the Nedeed plantation community. They are little more than slaves who are treated as property.

When Willa Nedeed gives birth to a son who is white, Luther accuses her of having an affair. He therefore rejects the son as his child and imprisons both the son and Willa in the basement of his house. Nedeed consciously starves

his son, hoping that after he dies Willa will repent her sins and be a "good" Nedeed wife.

While imprisoned in the basement that is also the morgue for Luther's funeral home business, Willa finds documents that teach her the history of the previous Nedeed wives and launch her on a journey into self-knowledge and women's ways of knowing. In trunks in the morgue she finds the Bible of Luwana Packerville Nedeed, the cookbooks and recipes of Evelyn Creton Nedeed, and the photographs of Priscilla McGuire Nedeed that record the silencing and absencing of these women. Because they were not allowed a voice or language within a patriarchal society, they voiced their abuse through women's ways of knowing: diary entries, recipes, photographs, all ways of knowing outside patriarchal interference.

Luwana's journal entries, written between books of the Bible, chronicle her history as a slave. Her husband bought her freedom from the master only to enslave her himself. She was even the property of her son. Creating an alter ego, she recorded her abuse in two voices in these diary entries. One voice wrote to the other about her husband's evil treatment, while the other voice wrote that "nothing . . . is going on in your home that is not repeated in countless other homes around you." With a silver hat pin, she even recorded on her body how many times her husband allowed her to speak—665 times over the course of a year—to say hello in the morning and goodnight in the evening. This should be 720 times, but the 55 times missing equal the days her husband and son were away from home interviewing at schools for the son. Willa notes that there is no 666th time, when she should have said goodbye to her son as he was leaving for school, so her history is unfinished, a blank, just as she was blank in the Nedeed house. Her life serves to represent the absencing of women by patriarchy.

Next Willa discovers Evelyn's recipes. At first these recipes anger Willa, because she thinks the records of Evelyn's canning meant that she enjoyed cooking. What Willa's anger reveals, though, is her complete immersion into patriarchal definitions of her as Other. At this point in her journey she does not realize that she cannot decipher the abuse because she does not know women's ways of knowing. In actuality these canning recipes and the other recipes Willa finds record the gradual silencing and voicelessness of Evelyn by her Nedeed husband that leads to her bulimia, a disease affecting people who have no control over their own lives or identities. Because she cannot live with the absencing any longer, Evelyn finally poisons herself.

As Willa discovers how Evelyn ended her life, she begins to realize that there is a pattern to all these codes of the past Nedeed women, and as she finds the photographs of Priscilla Nedeed, she recognizes that she is also a part of this silencing and absencing. At first Willa thinks the photographs record the growth of Priscilla's son, but in reality they reveal a gradual absencing of her, not only in the photographs but in the family. Her marriage silenced and absenced her just as the other Nedeed women had been silenced and absented.

Willa realizes through the Nedeed women's records of their history that she too has been oppressed by patriarchy. All these years she has defined herself through a man. She married a man "that she didn't love because there was no question of asking for love in return. It had been enough that he needed her." She married him because it was socially unacceptable in patriarchal society to be single at the age of thirty. Subscribing to male assumptions of identity, Willa is the mother as Other until she finds power and strength in the journals, recipes, and photographs of the other Nedeed women. Once she recognizes the abuse and oppression, she refuses to be absenced and silenced. As she examines one photograph, Willa realizes that Priscilla Nedeed used bleach to blot out her own face from the photograph, as a way of representing her lack of power, presence, and voice within patriarchal dominance and control. As she looks at the "gaping hole that was once Priscilla McGuire," Willa begins to touch her own face to assure her own presence.

The depiction of Willa's journey to self-realization and self-knowledge is brilliantly interwoven with the story of Willie's attempt to purchase a camera. He is told by the sales clerk that he cannot use the camera because he has no face. This surreal and nightmarish experience of his own "absence" connects him not only to Willa Nedeed but also to Laurel Dumont, whom the present Luther Nedeed evicts from her residence because her husband is divorcing her. Without a husband, she has no rights to the house or the land in Linden Hills and it reverts back to the Tupelo Reality Corporation. She commits suicide by diving into an empty swimming pool, silencing her role as the voiceless woman. Willie is the one who finds her body, and he also learns that Luther Nedeed watched her suicide and did nothing to prevent it.

Willie next visits Daniel Braithwaite's house. He is the historian in Linden Hills who has only recorded what he sees, but his sight is that of the people in Linden Hills selling bits of themselves to the highest bidder as Grandmother Tilson had warned. The narrative then returns to Willa's discovery of her own face and therefore her own reflection. Gaining strength from this image she picks up her dead son, whom she has wrapped in a bridal veil, and she ascends the twelve steps to the kitchen. In a confrontation with Luther she falls against the fireplace, setting the house on fire. Willie and Lester are working at the house, doing odd jobs for Luther, when the fire breaks out. When Willie runs to get help, no one on Tupelo Drive will come to Luther Nedeed's aid, and both Luther and Willa die in the fire. The narrative therefore ends with the implication that the residents of Linden Hills are no longer willing to help preserve the foundation of control and manipulation at the center of their neighborhood, suggesting that the history of the abuse of Nedeed women may be at an end and offering hope that without the destructive force of Luther Nedeed, the neighborhood may develop into a community exhibiting the qualities associated with the Andersons in the beginning of the novel.

Willie and Lester survive to walk up Tupelo Drive to the light. They are not only connected to one another but Willie is left to record the Nedeed women's ways of knowing through his poetry, thus voicing the real history, culture, heritage, and roots of the black experience in America.

MAMA DAY

Whereas she said she was exorcising demons in her first two novels, in her third novel, *Mama Day* (1988), Naylor said (in an interview with Angels Carabi for *Belles lettres*) that her goal was to write about "the power of love and the power of magic. . . . *Mama* is about the fact that the real basic magic is the unfolding of the human potential and that if we reach inside ourselves we can create miracles." In *Mama Day* Naylor uses three different voices that reveal varying approaches to human potential and the hindrances that deter miracles and growth of the human spirit. The most ambitious of her novels, *Mama Day* is structurally based upon magical realism, which Naylor (in an interview with Kay Bonetti) has said she views as "the line between that which is real and that which is not real."

The novel takes place in Willow Springs, an island community off the coasts of South Carolina and Georgia belonging "in no state," fourteen years after one of the narrators, George, dies. Willow Springs, "an island of soft brown girls, or burnished ebony girls with their flashing teeth against that deep satin skin," symbolizes the qualities of the African concept of *nommo,* the communication, the verbalization,

the potential that creates heritage, roots, culture, connectedness, and voice. It not only celebrates women's ways of knowing, but it also celebrates the heritage of African Americans. Naylor associates that heritage with the all-black community whose residents organize their culture around the remaining spirit of Sapphira Wade, who was brought to the island as a slave by Bascombe Wade and gained her freedom in 1823. *Mama Day* creates its own ways of hearing and seeing African American history, roots, community, and clan, ways of knowing that Naylor associates with being female and black in this novel.

Three voices take the reader on a journey into the history of these ways of knowing. The voice of the community narrates the history of Sapphira Wade to the reader. She gave birth to seven sons in one thousand days, and the seventh son had three girls, Abigail, Miranda (known as "Mama"), and Peace. The narrative then switches to the voices of George and Cocoa, whose common story parallels that of *Romeo and Juliet*'s star-crossed lovers. George's and Cocoa's individual stories reveal the different ways that males and females interpret the world, but more importantly, the stories reveal two different ways of reading human potential and history: the first is associated with white male values, which Cocoa learns from the mainland, while the second is the way of the island, which is associated with women's ways of knowing that are African and matriarchal.

The novel begins with a map of Willow Springs, a family tree of the Day family, and a bill of sale for Sapphira, all ways of defining identity in the white patriarchal world, ways that have also been used to oppress, control, silence, and rename women and African Americans. In *Mama Day,* however, these markers become symbols of identity and voice. The map shows Willow Springs as being the closest point to Africa from the United States, while the family tree gives the Day family a history, a culture, a voice, a heritage, things that were taken away from most African Americans by slavery. A note that follows the family tree and explains the name of the Day family also gives Sapphira Wade spiritual voice: "'God rested on the seventh day and so would she.' Hence, the family's last name." Sapphira becomes the ancestor figure, the Great Mother who creates human potential and history on this island. And as Virginia C. Fowler notes in *Gloria Naylor,* the family tree also links the living members of the Day family with the dead members. This connection is part of the African belief system that holds that the living hear and are guided by the voices of their dead ancestors. Thus, Abigail, Mama Day, and Cocoa are all guided to their human potential through the voices of their ancestor, Sapphira Wade, even though they do not know her name.

The third document, the bill of sale of Sapphira Wade, symbolizes her refusal to be defined by the white system of slavery. Her power, both physical and spiritual, comes from the date—1823—she was deeded the land. From this day on, the numbers eighteen and twenty-three become the ways of knowing that are handed down through the women descendants of Sapphira. She is, as the community narrator tells us, "a true conjure woman." We must learn to read in a different manner, accepting the authority of voices that not only hear but read signs from all the human senses and nature. The voices that narrate *Mama Day,* as Fowler states, "invite us to shed our assumptions about time, about reality, about truth." We are to shed our assumptions based on white male definitions of women and blacks and listen to the rituals of Willow Springs, a place beyond the bridge to the mainland that offers new ways of approaching history, identity, and voice. We must listen to that which is not definable by scientific methods. The difficulty of such a task is demonstrated through the example of Reema's son, who cannot shed his male assumptions based

on the white educational system of the mainland. He has no name, and furthermore, when he writes a book that traces the history of Willow Springs and tries to define the meaning of the numbers eighteen and twenty-three empirically, he fails because he refuses to enter into the world that asks him to suspend logical explanations. Willow Springs, conversely, insists on the "restorative powers for black Americans of the past and of female and African-derived traditions and ways of looking at the world."

The second narrator, George, Cocoa's husband, represents the view of the mainland, the values associated with white patriarchal dominance that will not allow itself to suspend logical means and listen to new ways of hearing. Raised in the Wallace P. Andrews Shelter for Boys, George learns early in his life to base his beliefs on rules and facts. Having no past, he believes only in the present and in that which can be explained by logical, rational, scientific means. He is the direct opposite of Cocoa, who has family, background, tradition, roots, and access to a collective conscience. He does not understand why she describes people in terms of food dishes instead of physically, and he understands the meaning of place only in terms of geography.

George's trip to Willow Springs with Cocoa defines the difference not only between them, but also between Willow Springs' ways of knowledge and the "across the bridge thinking." Thus, George later tells Cocoa of the frustration he felt when he could not find Willow Springs on any map: "I really did want to go," he tells her, "but I wanted to know exactly where I was going." He recognizes that he is entering another world, but he does not understand how to read other ways of viewing events, people, and history. This inability ultimately leads to his death, but at the same time his death has the positive outcome of allowing Cocoa to live and pass on the values associated with women's ways of knowing.

Cocoa, on the other hand, is the narrator associated with the qualities of *nommo*. Born in Willow Springs, Cocoa is a direct descendent of Sapphira Wade. She returns to the island of Willow Springs to learn her identity and work at gaining a connection to the past. The stories she narrates of the island's ancestor figures, Sapphira, Abigail, Peace, and Mama, give voice, tradition, and heritage not only to the Day family but also to African Americans. Her voice narrates incidents to her son by her present marriage fourteen years after George dies. In a conversation with the dead George she learns the history that gives voice and presence to the present and the future.

The story Cocoa tells begins when she meets George in New York. Although she had been considered beautiful on Willow Springs because of her dark skin, in New York she is insecure about her looks, as she unknowingly responds to standards of female beauty defined by the white male culture of urban America. Her history degree from the mainland helps her in her quest for identity on the mainland, but when she returns to Willow Springs, she begins to learn her real history and identity through the stories of her family.

Through Cocoa's voice, Naylor asks the reader to leave George's "real" and rational world to enter the world of human potential associated with the magical realism of Cocoa and Mama Day's world. In a long description of the background of the Day women, Cocoa narrates the importance of linking the past with the present to provide for a future. Cocoa's illness, caused by a hex, provides the vehicle for this connection. In the ensuing quest for ways to cure Cocoa of the hex, the reader learns of Mama Day's powers, powers that are both physical and spiritual, both real and based upon faith. Mama Day transfers these powers to Cocoa, who gives them a voice and a presence that Mama Day could not. Until this happens, there can be no peace for the Day women and

no connection between the spiritual and the human.

Miranda, Abigail, and Peace are the daughters of the seventh son of a seventh son of Sapphira Wade, John-Paul. Peace, the youngest daughter of John-Paul and Ophelia, dies when she drowns in the well on the family's land, the old homestead referred to as the "other place" in the present-day Willow Springs. Her mother subsequently goes increasingly mad. Thus "peace" is taken from the family, which they try to restore from then on. Abigail has three daughters of her own, Peace, Grace, and Hope. Peace dies as an infant before she can be given a crib name, a nickname in African legend that connects the past with the present and the future. Hope gives birth to Willa Prescott, who dies in Linden Hills. Grace, Abigail's second daughter, gives birth to Ophelia, who is nicknamed "the baby girl" after her great-grandmother, but when she refuses to answer to the name, Abigail nicknames her Cocoa. Thus, Cocoa is the last of the Day women, the one who will honor the past and ensure the future by finding the meaning to peace associated with the family name and history.

The history of the family is unraveled through Mama Day's powers. Like her ancestor Sapphira Wade, Mama Day is a conjure woman who reads nature to make her diagnoses and who treats problems by using natural remedies, patterns of healing associated with African societies. She tries never to overstep the bounds of nature. A central image in the book is that of Mama Day's "gifted hands." Mama Day's hands are associated with creation and guidance. Her hands make the quilt she gives to Cocoa and George (for their wedding) that traces Cocoa's history. Her hands also deliver most of the babies born in Willow Springs.

However, when Bernice Duvall takes fertility drugs that infect her ovaries, Mama—the Great Mother figure, the *nommo,* the creative potential, the healer—knows that she must go to the "other place," the Day homestead, to perform rituals that will allow Bernice to conceive a child. The "other place" symbolizes the pain and suffering of the Day family in the past, in particular the death of Peace and the enslavement of Sapphira. But it also symbolizes the important link between the dead ancestors and the living descendants, not just for Cocoa and successive generations of the Day family but for all African Americans. When Cocoa is dying from the spell that has been cast on her, Mama Day instructs George to go to the chicken house on the Day land to bring back whatever he finds that will heal Cocoa. Without realizing it, he brings back the history of Sapphira Wade that gives the family roots, tradition, heritage, voice, and a connection to the past that will transform the present into future generations.

The only time Mama Day uses her powers in magical ways are when mainlanders or evil people try to hurt the islanders. Thus, she creates two lightning storms, one to impress upon the white sheriff who comes looking for moonshiners that there are different ways of reading reality on the island. The other instance in which Mama Day uses her powers to destroy is to put a hex on Ruby, a woman knowledgeable in voodoo, for attempting to kill Cocoa and therefore attempting to destroy the collective consciousness of African Americans that Willow Springs represents.

Cocoa survives to tell her story to her son. At the novel's end she lives in Charleston, South Carolina, a mainland city, but the implication is that now she carries with her the Willow Springs way of reading life and can bring it with her to the mainland. Cocoa's ability to connect past pain and suffering with the present to create a voice that gives her and future generations presence and a collective consciousness is the hope and the peace of the Day family.

BAILEY'S CAFÉ

Bailey's Café (1992), which Naylor also produced as a screenplay, is the fourth book in her series of interconnected novels revealing women's ways of knowing history, tradition, roots, heritage, culture, and voice. Appearing in *Mama Day* as the place near where George was born, Bailey's Café has no rules, restrictions, or codes and is "located" on a street with no name in no particular city. Those who enter the café do so understanding that it is not a café but rather a way station for those looking for a safe place to rest. The indefinite setting and the positioning of the women's stories between two male voices—whom Naylor characterizes only through politics, sports, and religion—indicate yet another definition of women as Other that does not allow them a voice or presence.

Whereas Brewster Place houses those with dreams deferred, Bailey's Café is "a relay for broken dreams," of women branded as whores by patriarchal definition. The café is set between Gabe's pawn shop, which displays "the broken relics of uncountable dreams" in its windows, and Eve's boardinghouse. And just as Brewster Place is on a dead-end street, Bailey's Café is "the last place before the end of the world." Like Willow Springs, though, it is more than it appears to be; it is a place "to take a breather for a while," a place where people can begin to hope again. The owner directs all the women who come here to go to Eve's boardinghouse, the house with the garden in front. If they find the garden, then they are home. Women arrive at Eve's boardinghouse with broken spirits, but here no one judges them. Under Eve's care and guidance, each of her guests is allowed to find her own self-worth and her own potential. Each woman's story has a biblical parallel and relates a different gender-related abuse, yet each woman finds a way to hope or dream and finds dignity within herself, even though society names her whore and therefore Other.

Eve was the first woman to come to Bailey's Café. Thrown out of Pilottown for discovering and enjoying her own sexuality, a discovery allowed men, but not women, Eve has opened a boardinghouse as "a way station" for women whose identities have been defined by their bodies within patriarchal control. A parallel to the biblical Eve, who is thrown out of the garden for sinning, Eve creates her own garden and her own voice that develops the self-worth of each woman who enters her paradise. And that this paradise is outside patriarchal control is evident through the narrator's comment that "there was nowhere on earth for a woman like [her]." The women who come to her boardinghouse plant their own flowers, flowers with a story as different as each woman who plants them. In the middle of the yard the stump of one tree is surrounded by lilies. According to Fowler, these lilies are associated with purity, which overshadows the phallic tree. Eve's refusal to sell any of the lilies and her insistence on creating her own garden of Eden symbolizes her insistence that her sexuality is pure and belongs to her to do with as she wishes, not as patriarchy tells her to. Eve does not pass judgment on the women, having only two rules. She insists that the men who come to visit the women here leave by midnight and that they bring flowers to the women. This teaches the women to accept no less than they deserve. She therefore functions as the *nommo*, the creative potential that allows the reader and the women to develop different ways of knowing and different ways of reading human potential.

The first woman to come to Eve's boardinghouse at the end of the world is Sadie. Her story is so painful that the narrator must tell it for her. Sadie is "the one the coat hanger missed," and as a child she is abused by her mother, who eventually leads her into a life of prostitution. Sadie has been sexually ravaged in every way possible. While the johns are using her body, she dulls the pain of the sexual encounters by dreaming of owning a house with a white picket fence (much like the house of the Dick and Jane reader in Toni Morrison's *The Bluest Eye*). She endures this life of pain and keeps "turning

tricks" in the hope that her mother will love her, but her mother only cares about getting the money from Sadie's tricks to feed her alcoholism. When Sadie goes from her mother's house into a house of prostitution, she meets Daniel, an alcoholic janitor, who speaks to her every night but never calls her by her name. When the bordello closes, he asks her to marry him, still never calling her by name, which symbolizes her lack of identity. Daniel gives her a house, but when he dies his daughters drive Sadie out. In an attempt to save this house, she resorts to selling her body again, and when this fails, she sells herself for the price of a bottle of cheap wine to keep her dream alive. Thus, when she arrives at Eve's and the Ice Man tells her he loves her, Sadie is so broken and alone she is no longer able to respond to a sincere expression of human emotion.

The next woman who lives at Eve's is Esther, who, like her biblical parallel, sacrifices for the good of the people. Sold at the age of twelve by her brother to a man who brutalizes her in the basement of his house, Esther learns the use of "leather-and-metal things." Her abuse is so unspeakable that she is completely alone in the world except for a radio that airs *The Shadow*, a program that consistently features the line, "Who knows what evil lurks in the hearts of men?" The evil she endures in the basement of that house at the hands of patriarchy defines her as Other, making her voiceless and silent.

The next story is that of Mary, nicknamed "Peaches" by her father because she is "yellow and sweet." Her father defines her in terms of patriarchal ideals of physical beauty and thus as an object for men to use. He is glad that boys pursue her and tries to get them to acknowledge their sexual desire for her. He surrounds her with mirrors in her room so she can look at her beauty all day, but the mirrors frighten her. With no identity except for her physical appearance and no idea how to define herself or give herself presence, Peaches eventually takes a bottle cap and scars her face with it.

Jesse Belle, the next woman the reader meets at Eve's, is a parallel to the biblical Jezebel. She comes to Eve's house to overcome her heroin addiction, an addiction she acquires after marrying into an upper-class family that rejects her because she does not belong to this class. It takes Uncle Eli nineteen years to find a reason to alienate her from her husband and son. He finally succeeds when he sees her in a bar with another woman and exposes her homosexuality, even though her husband has known this all along. Not able to cope with the label patriarchy defines her by, Jesse Belle turns to drugs to dull her pain. Eve is nonjudgmental and keeps giving her drugs until Jesse Belle finds her own path to overcoming her drug addiction, and consequently to find the voice to create an identity and a presence for herself.

The novel ends with the birth of Mariam's baby. Mariam is a victim of female circumcision who comes to Brewster Place as a last resort. Here, the women nurture her; at the birth of her son, George, "the world lit up with lights" and all the women were present. Although there is no resolution at the end of the novel, the implication is that "nothing important can happen" without community, and that within the community provided by Eve's boardinghouse the women who come here achieve self-worth and find identity through female ways of knowing the world.

THE MEN OF BREWSTER PLACE

The Men of Brewster Place (1998) returns to the setting of Naylor's first novel. The epigraph this time, however, does not ask "what happens to dreams deferred?" but instead asks why are "my dream[s] deferred overlong?" The seven stories in this novel reveal the life circumstances that influenced the men who seemed to stand

between the women and their dreams in *The Women of Brewster Place.*

Unlike *The Women of Brewster Place,* which opens at dawn, *The Men of Brewster Place* opens at dusk, with only one man hoping that he will triumph against the odds. Ben, the narrator, says that for all the men on Brewster Place "there was always a Her in his story" who positively affected their lives. Unlike the women on Brewster Place, who have a common dream of community, tradition, heritage, and sharing, the men are isolated from one another, and this leaves them unable to be a positive influence in the lives of the women around them.

Ben, the janitor at Brewster Place (who was also a character in *The Women of Brewster Place*), is the novel's first voice. He came to Brewster Place after he could do nothing to stop the rape of his daughter by his white boss. His story introduces the silence, the absencing, and ridicule the black man is forced to endure in the dominant white world. Ben tells three stories that show a variation on the silencing that emasculates the black man. The first story he tells involves his Grandpa Jones, whose ten-year-old sister is beaten, raped, and killed by a white man. At the funeral, when he shouts out against the injustice of his sister's death because no one else will speak out, his mother tells him to shut his mouth and "be a man." Grandpa Jones's story teaches Ben that "being a man" for the black man means being quiet about white abuse of black children and women, creating voicelessness, absencing, and silence for him not only in the white world but in the black world as well. His next story recounts how a black man named Billy worked hard at his job as a bellhop and a shoe-shine man in order to avoid the less-desirable alternatives, such as working in the cotton fields. But because he must be well dressed and clean, his own people accuse him of being an Uncle Tom. Ben's second story shows how he learned that to survive in the white world a black man must accept being hated and alienated from his own people, another way of being silenced and absenced. This silencing is further reinforced in Ben's own life when he is powerless to help his own daughter. When Mr. Clyde rapes her, all Ben can do is sit back and be silent and listen to the white man laugh at him. Ben's voice sets the background for the rest of the stories in *The Men of Brewster Place,* which illustrate variations on the ways that black men are shaped by the silencing, hatred, and ridicule they often endure in the white world.

The next of the novel's voices is that of Brother Jerome, a musician who plays "the black man's blues." His music "plays" the lives of the men of Brewster Place, giving them some common bond even though they do not associate with one another, having learned that being alone is the only safe condition.

Basil, the next voice, is Mattie's son from *The Women of Brewster Place.* In that novel the reader sees Basil as a spoiled child whose mother would do anything to help him. When he is arrested, he runs away for fear of being imprisoned, and by jumping bail he is responsible for his mother's losing her house. In *The Men of Brewster Place,* the reader meets Basil years later, after his mother has died. The reader learns that Basil has spent all these years making the money to pay back his mother, but since he cannot do that, he tries to "find some woman, somewhere, and make her life happy." The woman he chooses, however, turns him in to the police. After he is released from prison six years later, Basil tries to reestablish a bond with his sons, but one is on probation and the other has built a wall around himself. Basil then spends the rest of his days wondering if he could have made a difference. Like his mother, Mattie, his voice is ineffective and absenced. Like Ben, he must remain silent in the dominant society if he wants to survive.

Eugene, the next voice, is the husband of Ciel from *The Women of Brewster Place.* The image

he projected there was one of a man who accepts no responsibility for his actions. Here, however, the reader learns that the reason he kept leaving Ciel was because he could not voice that he was gay. Because he feels responsible for Ciel's pain and for his daughter's death, he spends his days on Brewster Place going to a man who flogs him. Eugene thinks that the floggings will bring some kind of redemption for his part in his family's tragedy. Thus, still not able to speak his sexual identity, Eugene is voiceless and absenced. Again, like Ben, Eugene must remain silent if he is to survive in the dominant society.

The next voice, that of Moreland T. Woods, minister of Sinai Baptist Church, appeared in *The Women of Brewster Place* as a guest minister. Here, as in that novel, he is a slick con artist whose "soul's been greased with Vaseline and nothing much is real." Just as he took advantage of Etta Mae's misfortune for his own satisfaction, here he realizes that the church is a place where men "became somebody, at the least a child of God." He wants to be minister of Canaan Baptist Church because it is a bigger congregation and he wants to use the bigger congregation to support his political career. He does not care about the lives or souls of the people in the church or how he can help them better their lives. He is the one who contributes to the voicelessness of the men here.

The next voice is that of C. C. Baker, the man who raped Lorraine in *The Women of Brewster Place.* He raped her because being a man meant displaying power over whomever he could within the six-foot space between that wall and the ally, the only space he has in the white patriarchy. In this novel, he is being questioned by the police for the murder of his stepbrother. During the interrogation the reader learns that most of his vocabulary is some "variation on the word fuck." Denied money, power, and respect by the larger dominant world, C. C. Baker's type learns that on the street to be a success means raping or murdering. This is the only way he can have a voice.

Abshu, the last voice in *The Men of Brewster Place*, is the boyfriend of Kiswana from *The Women of Brewster Place*. Head of the community center, he tries to provide positive role models for boys so they do not take the route of C. C. Baker to prove their manhood. Abshu is the lone man waiting for the dawn at the end of the novel.

As seen through the portraits of these men, silence is the only code of survival for the black men in Brewster Place, who are forced into isolation by lack of voice in the larger white world. But there is still hope, because even though he walks toward the dawn alone at the end of the novel, Abshu is still "one man against the dawning of the inevitable," and as long as there is one man left, there is hope that there will be communication, voice, and presence for African Americans in the dominant society. And even if the men are still alone, simply the fact that they have told their stories is a beginning for connectedness and community. There is the hope for human potential.

In the 1980s and 1990s Gloria Naylor created a canon of distinctive fiction that captured the stories and the voices of black women by brilliantly weaving elements of the southern agrarian, northern urban, African, African American, and European traditions. In 2000 Naylor's novel *Mama Day* was being made into a movie by her own company, One Way Productions.

Selected Bibliography

WORKS OF GLORIA NAYLOR
The Women of Brewster Place: A Novel in Seven Stories. New York: Viking, 1982.
Linden Hills. New York: Ticknor and Fields, 1985.
Mama Day. New York: Ticknor and Fields, 1988.
Bailey's Café. New York: Harcourt Brace Jovanovich, 1992.

Children of the Night: The Best Short Stories by Black Writers, 1967 to the Present. Edited by Naylor. Boston: Little, Brown, 1995.
The Men of Brewster Place. New York: Hyperion, 1998.

CRITICAL AND BIOGRAPHICAL STUDIES
Baker, Houston A., Jr. *Workings of the Spirit: The Poetics of Afro-American Women's Writing.* Chicago: The University of Chicago Press, 1991.
Bonetti, Kay. "An Interview with Gloria Naylor." New York: American Prose Library, 1988, audiotape.
Carabi, Angels. "Interview with Gloria Naylor." *Belles lettres* 7:36–42 (spring 1992).
Felton, Sharon, and Michelle C. Loris, eds. *The Critical Response to Gloria Naylor.* Westport, Conn.: Greenwood Press, 1997.
Fowler, Virginia C. *Gloria Naylor.* New York: Twayne Publishers, 1996.
Gates, Henry Louis, Jr., and K. A. Appiah, eds. *Gloria Naylor: Critical Perspectives Past and Present.* New York: Amistad Press, 1993.
Harris, Trudier. *The Power of the Porch: The Storyteller's Craft in Zora Neale Hurston, Gloria Naylor, and Randall Kenan.* Athens: The University of Georgia Press, 1996.
Kelley, Margot Anne, ed. *Gloria Naylor's Early Novels.* Gainesville: University Press of Florida, 1999.
Mellard, James M. *Using Lacan: Reading Fiction.* Urbana: University of Illinois Press, 1991.
Stave, Shirley A. *Gloria Naylor: Strategy and Technique, Magic and Myth.* Newark: University of Delaware Press, 2000.
Taylor-Guthrie, Danille. *Conversations with Toni Morrison.* Jackson: University Press of Mississippi, 1994.
Ward, Catherine. "Gothic and Intertextual Constructions in *Linden Hills*." In *Gloria Naylor: Critical Perspectives Past and Present.* Edited by Henry Louis Gates Jr. and K. A. Appiah. New York: Amistad, 1993.
Whitt, Margaret Earley. *Understanding Gloria Naylor.* Columbia: University of South Carolina Press, 1999.

—*KATHRYN BREWER*

Norman Podhoretz

1930–

BEST KNOWN AS the editor of *Commentary* magazine from 1960 to 1995, Norman Podhoretz (Pod-HOR-etz) continues to be an important and controversial neoconservative spokesperson. A left-leaning radical during much of the 1950s and early 1960s, Podhoretz gradually became disenchanted with the New Left during the late 1960s and spent the next decades trying to undo the cultural damage that those of his intellectual circle had unwittingly set into motion. Breaking ranks with former friends was not easy and it did not come without significant professional cost, but Podhoretz embraced his newfound conservatism with courage, unswerving commitment, and, most of all, a tough-minded critique of leftist thought.

A prolific, often brilliant writer of literary essays, reviews, and political-cultural analysis, Podhoretz's work has appeared in the most important magazines of late-twentieth-century America: *Partisan Review, The New Yorker, Esquire, Harper's, New Republic,* and, of course, *Commentary,* the venue with which his name is most associated. His unflinching candor and hard-hitting polemical arguments have not always been appreciated by his political adversaries, but there is little doubt that the chronicle of his intellectual growth is at once the story of life among a certain group of New York intellectuals and how their quarrels about culture ended up affecting the nation as a whole.

When does a person decide to become a literary critic? No doubt the answer varies from critic to critic, but in Podhoretz's case, a passage from *Making It,* his 1968 autobiography, suggests that it occurred when he was a Columbia undergraduate and realized, sadly, that he would never become an important poet:

I had a small talent for verse, yet try as I did for more than two years, there was finally no concealing the fact from myself that as compared with Allen Ginsberg [of *Howl* fame] John Hollander [an important poet now teaching at Yale], and a dozen other Columbia poets of the time, I rated at the most generous estimate a grudging honorable mention. (Even Mark Van Doren, who admired *everyone*'s poetry, clearly thought little of mine: the only B I ever got in English at Columbia was in a creative writing course I took with him.)

Those who have grown tired of Podhoretz's conservative hectoring can only wonder about how different his subsequent career might have been had Professor Van Doren given him the usual, indeed, *expected,* A. As it turned out, the young Podhoretz found lavish praise in other quarters of Columbia's distinguished English department: F. W. Dupee gave him an A+ in a course on contemporary literature and even more extraordinary, Lionel Trilling, a professor known for being suspicious of students with unusually high grades, also gave him an A+ in a course on the British Romantics. Since these professors had large reputations (both appeared regularly in the pages of the prestigious intellectual quarterly *Partisan Review*), their assessments of his talent meant something.

So, the question of what he would do after graduation was answered. He would become "*a literary critic.* An unlikely answer today perhaps [and an even more unlikely one at the present moment], for anyone so ambitious as I was at nineteen, but in the late 1940's . . . nothing could have been more natural for an undergraduate who was doing well in English than to look forward to a career as a critic, while supporting himself, of course, by teaching." Several decades later Podhoretz would revise his ambitions. Literature no longer seemed as important or as exciting as it once did, but the skills he had developed at Columbia could now be applied to the wider cultural landscape. Granted, politics had always been a part of Podhoretz's literary criticism. What had changed, however, was the focus of his ambition. He craved cultural power and the wide influence it would bring; and when he become the editor of *Commentary* magazine at the tender age of thirty, he had a platform that his large ambitions required.

Podhoretz's restless ambition, the principle subject of *Making It,* can best be understood as a series of sea changes (what he called "conversions") that led him further and further from the cramped, impoverished conditions of his Brooklyn childhood. His is yet another case of a man's character becoming his fate. "One of the longest journeys in the world," he insists in *Making It*'s oft-quoted opening sentence, "is the journey from Brooklyn to Manhattan—or at least from certain neighborhoods in Brooklyn to certain parts of Manhattan." What made the journey long was not the literal distance, just as the cost was not merely that of a subway token, but rather what Podhoretz refers to as the "fine-print conditions" in the social contract that lower class youngsters like himself were forced to pay to reap the benefits of upward mobility.

EARLY LIFE

Norman Podhoretz was born on January 16, 1930, to Julius and Helen P. (Woliner) Podhoretz. The family lived in the Brownsville section of Brooklyn, New York, where Julius Podhoretz worked as a milkman. By all the usual measuring rods, Podhoretz's family was lower class, but poverty and the alienation that presumably came with this territory was not a proposition Podhoretz was willing to accept. Indeed, he makes a point (in *Making It*) of dismissing the "whole idea of class as a prissy

triviality." In this regard his adolescence differs sharply from that of an immigrant Jewish son such as Irving Howe (born a decade earlier) who was stamped as a socialist from the tender age of thirteen. Podhoretz, by contrast, remembers no sidewalks filled with the meager goods of the dispossessed, no street corner demonstrations, no uncles hotly debating politics around the kitchen table. Even more significant, he did not number himself among those who wore their "alienation"—both from the parochial and the mainstream—as a badge of honor and who dreamed of a universalism fashioned from Marxist cloth. Podhoretz not only belonged to a different generation but also to a very different situation. As he puts it, "I was not, for all that I wrote poetry and read books, an 'alienated' boy dreaming of escape." As he would later insist in *My Love Affair with America: The Cautionary Tale of a Cheerful Conservative* (2000), he was always aware of how much sheer opportunity was packed into the American dream, and he was always grateful.

Still, when Podhoretz revisits his Brooklyn childhood in *My Love Affair with America,* the fourth volume in his series of autobiographical ruminations, a fuller, more complicated portrait of the pains of immigrant adjustment emerges. As David Brooks points out in a review published in the *Weekly Standard,* a conservative newspaper, "There's been a lot of romantic comedy, by Neil Simon and others, about the sorts of Jewish neighborhoods Podhoretz was leaving. But the Podhoretz home was no sitcom setting. His maternal grandfather was an angry, spiteful man. His great aunt committed suicide." Brooks goes on to make it clear that Podoretz, to his credit, resists the impulse to come off as a self-pitying character, concentrating instead on the ways that his family subtly disguised just how bad things were from the young boy growing up in their cramped quarters.

It was not until he left Brownsville, at nineteen, to spend a summer as a camp counselor in Wisconsin that Podhoretz learned the truth about just how poor his family was. Visiting the sumptuous vacation home of a Columbia classmate, he closes the door of the room he had been sent to and hears:

> . . . a click as the latch snapped firmly into place. At the sound of this click, I burst into tears. Bewildering by my strange reaction, I stood there weeping for a few seconds, and then it came to me that what had caused it was the fact that the doors in our apartment in Brooklyn, thickly encrusted as they had been from repeated painting over the years, could never be snapped shut with that marvelously satisfying click. . . . It took this trivial detail to make me realize fully for the first time in my life that I was poor.

Read from the vantage point of *My Love Affair with America,* much of the material in *Making It* seems as much an exercise in mythmaking as it is an effort at autobiography. Perhaps the two conditions are always inextricably related, but in Podhoretz's case, there are curious internal contradictions. For example, at one point in *Making It* he wants the record of his early life to reflect a pattern of heavy reading such as would explain how and why his brilliant career as an undergraduate English major at Columbia unfolded as it did, but in other spots he comes clean about how unprepared he was when, many years later, he joined the editor Jason Epstein in a publishing venture involving children's literature. He knew virtually nothing about children's literature because he had spent his childhood "mainly reading comic books and a few collections of fairy tales."

In truth, when Podhoretz was thirteen, "making it" was defined by his red satin Cherokees S.A.C. (social-athletic club) jacket: "It had by no means been easy for me [Podhoretz remembers], as a mediocre athlete and a notoriously good student, to win acceptance from a gang which prided itself mainly on its masculinity and its contempt for authority, but once this had

been accomplished, down the drain went any reason I might earlier have had for thinking that life could be better in any other place."

What changes this arithmetic (although some might argue that Podhoretz continued to crave "acceptance" and versions of his red satin gang jacket throughout his life) was a tough, no-nonsense high school English teacher Podhoretz calls Mrs. K. in *Making It,* and then reveals to be Harriet Haft in *My Love Affair with America.* As he came to understand what she was trying to communicate with all her talk about manners, he realized that raw talent was not sufficient. A better class of people was quite willing to admit him to their ranks, but if, and only if, he were willing "to signify by my general deportment that I acknowledged them as *superior* to the class of people among which I happened to have been born. That was the bargain— take it or leave it."

In truth, the pact with a larger America was struck at the moment Podhoretz began his public school training. When a first-grade teacher asked where the young Podhoretz was headed, he presumably replied: "I goink op de stez." Whether or not he actually said these words, which look for all the world as if they were pulled from a page of *Call It Sleep* (1934), Henry Roth's classic novel of Jewish immigrant adjustment on the lower East Side of New York during the early twentieth century, the teacher's response was at once swift and purposeful in the no-nonsense way that public education then defined its duty to those who badly needed *melting*: she "instantly marched me off to the principal's office and had me placed in a remedial-speech class." Remembering that moment more than sixty years later, Podhoretz's gratitude has no bounds, for the remedial-speech class not only shaped him up and pointed him toward the possibilities of a larger, unaccented American speech but, more important in his case, it also gave him a taste of the English language that he would later come to revere in the rhythms of British literature and in the supple American paragraphs he would write as a literary critic and socio-political commentator.

Later, Podhoretz would learn that whenever matters of "art" or "culture" or, as his Columbia professors liked to put it, "the life of the mind" were concerned, versions of the same brutal contract came into play. At Columbia, where he accepted these conditions with "the wildest enthusiasm," Podhoretz left his Cherokees S.A.C. jacket far behind, trading it for the uniform of the club (tweed sports coat, white shirt and tie, gray gabardine slacks) he now eagerly sought to enter. The same modus operandi would apply when he did his postgraduate work at Cambridge University in England and sat at the feet of the distinguished literary critic F. R. Leavis.

At the same time, however, Podhoretz never quite cast off his hard-knock lower-class roots. What he had learned in the turmoil of his home and from Brooklyn's meaner streets remained. The result was an alternating rhythm of accommodation and resistance, one that continued throughout his public life. On a certain level he craved success as defined by those who insisted that one speak, dress, and, most of all, think in acceptable ways while at the same time there was always a part of Podhoretz that was skeptical, if not downright suspicious, of abstractions that did not square with what he knew in his guts. In much the way that a minor character in Saul Bellow's novel, *The Adventures of Augie March* (1953), notes that Augie had "opposition" in him, one could say the same thing about Podhoretz. Curiously enough, he did not warm to Bellow's larky protagonist (he much preferred the brooding, introspective Joseph of Bellow's earlier novel *Dangling Man*, 1944) and wrote a negative review that differed sharply from the warm praise *The Adventures of Augie March* received from other critics. Such opposition, however, got Podhoretz a measure of controversial attention, and this would become a modus operandi as his subsequent career unfolded.

Podhoretz, in short, marched to his own drum from the moment he began to think of himself as a member of the intellectual community. His mother (reduced to a cameo role in *Making It,* but given much wider space in *My Love Affair with America*) would "gaze wistfully at this strange creature, her son, and murmur, 'I should have made him a dentist,' registering thereby her perception that whereas Jewish sons who grow up to be successes in certain occupations remain fixed in an accessible cultural ethos, sons who grow up into literary success are transformed almost beyond recognition and distanced almost beyond a mother's reach." Such are the small-print costs in the brutal contract that cultural success makes with lower-class boys like Podhoretz. But there are also ways in which one's background could be powerfully integrated into the work one did as a cultural critic, and in "My Negro Problem—And Ours" (*Commentary,* February 1963; reprinted in *Doings and Undoings: The Fifties and After in American Writing,* 1964), Podhoretz hit upon a formula that he would use to good effect in his later books.

"MY NEGRO PROBLEM—AND OURS"

If the operative word of the famous *Partisan Review* 1952 symposium, "Our Country, Our Culture," was *our,* thus indicating in a single word that the age of alienation was now over, the operative word in Podhoretz's article was *my.* In announcing that his response to much of the liberal rhetoric inspired by the Civil Rights movement was qualified by existential memories of growing up in Brownsville, he brought a new dimension to the shape a contemporary political essay might take. Here was a voice that made no apologies for the personal thumbprint on virtually every paragraph, and moreover, that insisted on an inextricable relationship between the "my" and the collective "our."

Granted, Podhoretz can hardly claim credit for inventing the personal essay, but his insistence that the truth about race be told with an unblinking candor seemed utterly (and, for some, shockingly) unique at the time. Podhoretz begins "My Negro Problem—And Ours" with an epigraph from James Baldwin whose passionate words about race then carried great authority. Podhoretz goes on to consider two propositions he could never quite understand as a child growing up in an integrated Brooklyn neighborhood: one is that all Jews are rich, and the other is that all Negroes were persecuted: "These ideas had appeared in print; therefore they must be true." But what if one's own experience and the evidence of one's senses suggested quite the opposite? After all, Podhoretz goes on to point out, "I was puzzled to think that Jews were supposed to be rich when the only Jews I knew were poor, and that Negroes were supposed to be persecuted when it was the Negroes who were doing the only persecuting I knew about and doing it, moreover, to *me*."

Podhoretz's older sister, who had joined a left-wing youth organization, was appalled when he expressed such views (she would, as it turned out, hardly be alone in this), but even when she patiently explained the patterns of economic exploitation under which Negroes, as blacks were then called, suffered, he remained unconvinced: "A city boy's world is contained within three or four square blocks, and in my world it was the whites, the Italians and Jews, who feared the Negroes, not the other way around. The Negroes were tougher than we were, more ruthless, and on the whole they were better athletes." Truth to tell, he feared Negroes and, even worse, he hated them.

"My Negro Problem—And Ours" is an effort to understand where this hatred came from and why vestiges of the problem persist not only in himself but also in the collective "our" of his title. If, as Baldwin had eloquently argued,

whites tend to regard all Negroes as "faceless" and therefore as not altogether human, Podhoretz adds an important corollary to the equation: "What Baldwin does *not* tell us," he insists, "is that the principle of facelessness is a two-way street and can operate in both directions with no difficulty at all." Thus, Podhoretz argues, *he* was as faceless in his neighborhood as the Negroes were to him, and "if they hated me because I never looked at them, I must also have hated them for never looking at *me*. To the Negroes, my white skin was enough to define me as the enemy, and in a war it is only the uniform that counts and not the person."

Given the hatred on both sides of the racial divide, Podhoretz worries that efforts at mass integration are doomed to failure, and it is here that his essay moves from what had been a purely personal problem to a hard-hitting consideration of our national situation:

> Thus everywhere we look today in the North, we find the curious phenomenon of white middle-class liberals with no previous personal experience of Negroes—people to whom Negroes have always been faceless in virtue rather than faceless in vice—discovering that their abstract commitment to the cause of Negro rights will not stand the test of a direct confrontation. We find such people fleeing in droves to the suburbs as the Negro population in the inner city grows; and when they stay in the city we find them sending their children to private school rather than to the "integrated" public school in the neighborhood.

Podhoretz takes a special delight in holding the feet of upscale liberals to the fire, but he is even tougher on himself. Envy, for example, played a large part in the assessment of his Negro problem because Negroes were *bad* [read: looser, freer, romantically reckless] in ways that even the baddest little Jewish boy never could be. They were also graceful and athletic. But accounting for his continuing hatred of blacks, however mollified it has been since his childhood days in Brooklyn, is more difficult. As an educated, thoroughly sophisticated Manhattanite, why is it that an "insane rage" wells up in him at the specter of Negro anti-Semitism? Why does he feel a sense of "disgusting prurience" at the sight of a mixed couple? And why does violence stir in him whenever he encounters "that special brand of paranoid touchiness to which many Negroes are prone"?

What person in his right mind would confess such feelings *publicly*? The answer, of course, is Podhoretz, not merely because the result would be an attention-getting essay (although that it surely was), but also because, as the essay's concluding paragraph insists:

> . . . such feelings must be acknowledged as honestly as possible so that they can be controlled and ultimately disregarded in favor of the convictions. It is *wrong* for a man to suffer because of the color of his skin. Besides that clichéd proposition of liberal thought, what argument can stand and be respected? If the arguments are the arguments of feeling, they must be made to yield; and one's own soul is not the worst place to begin working a huge social transformation.

"My Negro Problem—and Ours" was more talked about (and often despised) than it was closely read. Podhoretz would later claim that he was more pleased with this essay than with anything he had written until that point, and that he thought of it as the piece which unlocked his deepest, most authentic *voice,* but these joys were considerably tempered when he found himself being asked to participate on panels as a spokesperson for racist views. Nearly forty years after its initial publication, the essay still retains the power to infuriate some and to strike others as a singular example of moral courage.

DOINGS AND UNDOINGS

Of the twenty-seven essays collected in *Doings and Undoings,* "My Negro Problem—and Ours" is clearly the most controversial, and the most important, followed closely by Podhoretz's famously negative review of Saul Bellow's much-praised breakthrough novel *The Adventures of Augie March* as well as assorted pieces on Norman Mailer whom he admires (to the point of imagining [quite wrongly] that he "discovered" him) and the likes of Philip Roth, John Updike, and the Beats, all of whom he regards as wildly overestimated. Many of the other essays remain tethered to their time and place, largely of interest now as evidence of Podhoretz's early brilliance as a literary-cultural critic.

As the essayist Joseph Epstein once put it, Norman Podhoretz was "*the* coming bright young intellectual in America." Not only was he widely regarded as the best student Lionel Trilling ever had at Columbia and as a particular favorite of F. R. Leavis, who published one of his essays in *Scrutiny* (the influential journal he edited at Cambridge) but Podhoretz also had the enviable distinction of beginning his career as a literary critic *at the top*—writing, in his mid-twenties, for such important magazines as *Harper's, New Leader, The New Yorker, Partisan Review, Reporter,* and *Show.*

What distinguishes Podhoretz's early criticism is an effort, often brilliantly achieved, to relate an aesthetic judgment of an individual book with a consideration of the social or literary condition that surrounds it, and thus to use the book review as a launching pad for his own views about all manner of subjects. By comparison, most other book reviewers, then and now, have decidedly modest goals. Moreover, Podhoretz was a writer who saw book reviewing as a way to unleash paragraphs that readers would admire, and remember. Nor did he shy away from advancing controversial opinions. Here, for example, is what he writes about Saul Bellow's *The Adventures of Augie March*:

> *Augie* was largely the product not of a state of being already achieved, but rather of an effort on Bellow's part to act as though he had already

achieved it. As a test case of the buoyant attitudes of the [postwar] period . . . *Augie* fails—and it fails mainly because its buoyancy is embodied in a character who is curiously untouched by his experience, who never changes or develops, who goes through everything yet undergoes nothing.

Bellow's many admirers were clearly upset by such assessments (as was Bellow himself), and in the close-knit world of the New York intellectuals, Podhoretz's negative review, virtually the only one *The Adventures of Augie March* received, meant that tongues wagged and certain people made it clear, as Podhoretz reports in *Making It,* "We'll get you for that review if it takes ten years." The moment illustrates just how long the memories of the New York intellectual crowd could be (Podhoretz's antagonist was not being hyperbolic; he meant every word he uttered) and how combative their temperaments were. In this hothouse world Podhoretz gave as good as he got: every anti-Podhoretz crack at a literary gathering or damning sentence in public print was stored away for later use.

At least a part of Podhoretz relished the attention that swirled around his young shoulders (the very fact that people now knew his name—and *Podhoretz* is not a particularly easy one to pronounce or remember—was heady stuff), but there were, at the same time, worries about the effect that the controversy he had kicked up would have on his career: "Attention I had wanted? Attention I was getting. But I was nevertheless unsettled by the particular form it was taking. . . . What I had worried about was what such members of the Family [a playful, Mafia-like term Podhoretz used to define those New York intellectuals, many of them Jewish, who shared similar temperaments, literary tastes, and political convictions] as might read my review would think of me." Podhoretz need not have worried (at least as he recounts how the scenario played itself out) because the "Family," down deep, was less enthusiastic about *The Adventures of Augie March* than its "on

record" opinion revealed. *His* paragraphs, by contrast, represented "what they all really thought about *Augie* but were afraid to come out and say."

MAKING IT

Moments like this, and there are dozens of them in *Making It,* partly explain why so many reviewers savaged what would turn out to be the first in a continuing series of Podhoretz memoirs. For his critics, the issue was not only when enough self-justification is enough or when going over the same ground about a contested literary judgment becomes tedious, but also the larger question of when ambition itself becomes indistinguishable from vulgarity. The thesis at the center of Podhoretz's argument is that success has replaced sex as "the dirty little secret" that novelist D. H. Lawrence had once used to characterize the repressed life of post-Victorian England.

But if it is almost universally acknowledged that it is better to be rich than poor, to be a success than a failure, and to wield power than to be powerless, that news came very late, if at all, to the intellectuals Podhoretz met at Columbia, at Cambridge, and in the New York literary scene. Take, for example, the humiliations that come with the territory of boot camp. In 1953, a scant year after he had bathed in the heady intellectual atmosphere of Cambridge University, Podhoretz found himself serving under a drill instructor's thumb. He did not much like the regimentation or the dehumanization it sought to achieve. In far less than the six weeks designed to turn civilians into disciplined soldiers, Podhoretz readjusted his earlier feelings about power and powerlessness: "*Power was position,* for did not the army teach that one saluted the uniform and not the man?" Significantly enough, that view would change dramatically when, in *My Love Affair with America,* he takes great pleasure in declaring himself "a pretty good solider" and describing the camaraderie that developed between himself and "rednecks" he served with. Apparently, he was popular because, in their words, he "talked so good." Life among the intelligentsia turned out to be considerably more complicated.

Taken together, the cultural figures, so formative in Podhoretz's successive "conversions" from Brooklyn semi-roughneck to sophisticated Manhattanite, represented an ethos that wore its marginality as a badge of honor and that regarded the normal measures of success with haughty contempt. To resist these dictums, as Podhoretz clearly does in *Making It,* is to challenge fundamental tenets, and to bring down the wrath of those who would see the following sentence as betrayal, pure and simple: "On the one hand, we are commanded to become successful—that is, to acquire more of these worldly goods than we began with, and to do so by our own exertions; on the other hand, it is impressed upon us by means both direct and devious that if we obey the commandment, we shall find ourselves falling victim to the radical corruption of spirit which, given the nature of what is nowadays called the 'system,' the pursuit of success requires and which its attainment always bespeaks."

To tell his particular rags-to-riches story (all the more poignant, he argues, because it is grounded in the specifics of the immigrant Jewish experience), Podhoretz spends a good deal of time rehearsing how the success ethic of his immigrant parents eventually clashed with the New York literati he thought of as a second family. How the latter regarded him—indeed, how they took the measure of *anybody* in or out of their tight circle—mattered. With *Making It,* Podhoretz in effect "broke ranks" with those closest to him, long before he would do so a decade later in a memoir of that title. "I will no doubt be accused of self-inflation and therefore of tastelessness," Podhoretz writes in an effort to disarm his critics, but that is precisely what

many New York intellectuals whispered behind his back and what some intimated in their hostile reviews. As Saul Maloff points out in a *Newsweek* review, Podhoretz "persuaded himself that he was writing a kind of *Advertisements for Myself* [Norman Mailer's 1960 account of his own rise to literary prominence] . . . and to undertake that without any of Mailer's gifts for rhetoric and irony is to court disaster." Others commented on sentences that had no ring to them or on paragraphs that were mushy (Mario Puzo in *Book World*), and Daniel Stern, in a review for the pages of *Commonweal* magazine, raced to the bottom line to declare that *Making It* is "at the heart of it a dishonest piece of work." But perhaps the most damning blow of all was delivered by S. L. Goldberg (like Podhoretz, a former Leavisite) who, in his essay "The Education of Norman Podhoretz," declared that Podhoretz's vaunted irony was, in truth, a "mere gesture," and moreover, that:

> . . . all this to-do about Success remains either the untruth or the utter triviality it was from the start since he never applies critical common sense to it. . . . In short, the real objection to Mr. Podhoretz . . . is not that he likes worldly goods or that he finds it hard to draw any line between acquiring them and living in order to acquire them, or even that he merely confuses evident success with proven worth. It is what underlies all this: the crudeness, not to say vulgarity, with which as a professed intellectual, he intellectualizes. It is his thinking that is shoddy.

Joseph Epstein, then editor of the *American Scholar* and one of Podhoretz's staunchest defenders, characterized the "brutal reception" of *Making It* this way: Podhoretz had "committed the crime . . . [of coming] out against the intellectual climate that spawned him." Not doubt the bitter attacks must have been infuriating and helped to push him even further toward the Right, but there were larger, more ominous clouds taking shape in the cultural horizon.

BREAKING RANKS

Breaking Ranks: A Political Memoir (1979) was an occasion to take a measure of what had happened to the left-liberal world he had once tried so hard to penetrate, and what on a more personal level had happened to his own sensibility. As he told *People* magazine, "I came more and more to believe that radicalism—mine and my friends'—was destroying the children." Later, in *Ex-Friends,* he would hold the Beat poet Allen Ginsberg singularly responsible for virtually every countercultural excess of the late 1960s. It is hardly accidental, therefore, that Podhoretz launches *Breaking Ranks* with a letter to his son John, one designed to explain why he once counted himself as a man on the Left, and why he now does not. Unlike *Making It,* this book moves well beyond the petty quarrels that divided a narrow band of New York intellectuals and into the larger world of practical politics. Ideas, Podhoretz came to feel, not only have moral consequences, but also can be genuinely dangerous. The conservative art critic Hilton Kramer, writing in the pages of the *New Republic,* offered this assessment: "In dealing with this fateful link between culture and politics in the period of the Vietnam War and its aftermath, Mr. Podhoretz has few equals among the writers of his time. . . . We are treated to a dazzling account of precisely how the ideas of cultural radicalism, first adumbrated in journals of intellectual debate, succeeded in reshaping the politics of the Democratic Party, and thence the country as a whole."

Nothing shocked and saddened those long committed to the utopian dreams of the Old Left more than the unruly, often anti-intellectual behavior associated with the New Left. America was now commonly written off as "Amerika," the substituted *k* meant to suggest that America had become a fascist state, no different in character or degree from Nazi Germany. Middle-class values seemed everywhere under siege, primarily at American universities, but increasingly in the culture at large as the nation found itself bitterly divided over an unpopular war in Vietnam. The Irish poet William Butler Yeats had, decades earlier, eloquently described the feeling as one in which "things fall apart" and the center no longer holds. Granted, Yeats had the aftermath of World War I in mind, along with intimations of the fascism and communism that he felt would accompany the fast-approaching millennium. Podhoretz, by contrast, did not view the cultural chaos swirling around him as a visionary poet, but rather as a public intellectual growing ever more uncomfortable with an age of giddy abandon.

Breaking Ranks begins with a long letter to his son, a device that allows the author the chance to deliver a history lesson about how and why it was that he once believed "all that [radical] stuff" during the 1950s and early 1960s. For one thing, Podhoretz explains, the ideas *"were new when I first encountered them. They were also daring and a little dangerous; they could get you into trouble. Not so much, I hasten to add, with the FBI or the House of Un-American Activities Committee, as with one's fellow intellectuals."* For another, the complications surrounding who was a hard anti-Communist, who a fellow traveler, and who a liberal (dupe or otherwise) defined the very air that intellectuals of the time breathed. Unpacking these nuances to his young adult son is a way for Podhoretz to set the stage for how he finally had no choice but to bid a bittersweet adieu to his former allies.

Cold war liberalism was among the first of many assumptions that Podhoretz found himself questioning. He was not a "hard" anti-Communist of the sort that had made *Partisan Review* such an important journal during the 1940s and 1950s. Quite to the contrary, when Podhoretz became the editor of *Commentary* he set about creating what would soon be called the "new *Commentary,*" a place where radical thinkers such as the educationists Paul Goodman and Edgar Z. Friedenberg or the historians H. Stuart Hughes and Staughton Lynd would find a congenial home. In retrospect, everything about Podhoretz's early years at *Commentary* seems incredible: he insisted upon—and received—an unheard of amount of editorial freedom, even as he set about turning what had been a narrowly defined "Jewish" periodical into a forum for wide-ranging cultural issues; and even more, he gradually replaced a legacy of left-liberalism with a welcoming embrace of new, radical thinking. The American Jewish Committee, best known for its deep pockets, paid the bills and, at least publicly, allowed the magazine to go where Podhoretz led.

In *Breaking Ranks,* Podhoretz tells us in considerable detail that he was as surprised by this turn of events as anybody:

> The Goodman articles especially [later published to wide acclaim as *Growing Up Absurd*]—but by no means those articles alone—aroused a degree of excitement, and even happiness, that suggested the presence of a hunger that some of us had known was there but which had turned out to be deeper than I or anyone else had suspected: a hunger for something new and something radical that would be free of the disabilities that had crippled radicalism in the past and had left it so discredited.

The fact is that, feigned surprise and qualifications aside, Podhoretz prided himself on being able to articulate what others only felt in inchoate ways. He served, in short, as a bellwether thinker—first as a radical and later as a nascent neoconservative. During his long watch at *Commentary*'s helm, he not only contributed articles under his own name but also commissioned pieces that sharpened the public debate about the proper course that Soviet-American relations should take (even in his radical phase he was never quite comfortable with the prevailing view that "the Russians were merely imitating us in everything we did"), free market economics, the dangers of the New Left, and

the ideologically based assaults against Israel. Podhoretz's detractors were quick to point out that his various sea changes were fueled by ambition, and that his increasingly conservative views made him a power broker during the Reagan administration. Turn the Podhoretz kaleidoscope as one will, however, the result was a serious rupture with the Left:

> But whether it was I who broke with them or they broke with me, the fact remained that becoming an opponent of radicalism effectively cut me off from most of my old friends and acquaintances on the Left—which for all practical purposes meant being cut off from the most fashionable and in some ways the most influential circles in New York. . . . Because everyone who knew anything about the situation recognized that my turn against radicalism was costing me more in the worldly sense than I seemed to be gaining, the theory that I was "selling out" never quite took; and because everyone who knew me or who was paying any attention to the tone of my monthly column in *Commentary* also recognized that I was nevertheless having such a good and happy time, a different theory began to circulate to the effect that I had literally lost my mind.

How else to explain what a nice Jewish Brooklyn boy was doing at cocktail parties with the well-heeled and socially privileged? True, Podhoretz was joined by others who had traveled toward the center and then to the Right from former lives on the Left (indeed, this was the central difference between neoconservatives and those paleoconservatives who had *always* identified themselves with the white shoe crowd and the right wing of the Republican Party), but Podhoretz's subject was always finally conceived in terms of how the intellectual follies affected him. He was, in this sense, a man to the memoir born.

In *Breaking Ranks,* Podhoretz takes a certain glee in "naming names," not as some did during the early 1950s when "Are you now, or were you ever, a member of the Communist Party" was *the* overwhelming culture question for the infamous House Un-American Activities Committee and refusing to provide testimony was to court a jail sentence, but rather as a man eager to set the record straight about where he once was, and where he now is. In the process, Podhoretz's catharsis served a dual purpose: to expiate his own past and to make the current cultural battle lines clear. Not surprisingly, those who had long envied Podhoretz's meteoric rise (it seemed so easy, so effortless) were quick to point out, as Christopher Hitchins did in the pages of the *New Statesman,* that Podhoretz's "review of the reviews of *Making It* gets more space than Vietnam, desegregation, nuclear weaponry, environmentalism and Watergate."

THE PRESENT DANGER AND WHY WE WERE IN VIETNAM

Aspects of Hitchins's charge were repeated when books such as *The Present Danger: Do We Have the Will to Reverse the Decline of American Power?* and *Why We Were in Vietnam* appeared in 1980 and 1982 respectively, but some adjustments in the usual choruses of sniping about Podhoretz's vaulting ambition were now necessary. As Mark Royden Winchell, author of *Neoconservative Criticism: Norman Podhoretz, Kenneth S. Lynn, and Joseph Epstein* (1991), observes: "Norman Podhoretz's ambition to influence American society transcends his literary and cultural writings or even his observations on domestic issues—he aspires to be nothing less than a player in world politics." For good or ill, in the years leading up to these books Podhoretz imagined (often rightly) that *Commentary* magazine had a significant role in shaping America's foreign policy. What was at stake was much larger than even Podhoretz's large ego. The first work, *The Present Danger,* represented a shift of emphasis in the aftermath of the Vietnam War, one that embraced the containment theory outlined in George F. Kennan's "The Sources of Soviet Conduct" (written under the pseudonym "Mr. X" and published in the July 1947 issue of *Foreign Affairs*) and that was promulgated by the United Nations ambassadors Daniel Patrick Moynihan and Jeane Kirkpatrick. The other book directly focused on Podhoretz's second thoughts about Vietnam—that the war was not only moral but also altruistic and heroic because we persisted in fighting even when we could not win—and was an especially vivid case of the lightning rod his arguments could be. Some long-standing Podhoretz critics reminded readers that he once felt quite differently, and that by sweeping his public record of opposition under the rug he was, at the very least, being ingenuous. Others put the matter more baldly: "Nowhere," James Fallows writes, "does the author give a hint that he himself might have fallen short of the high moral standards he now sets. . . . Editors are entitled to change their view . . . [but] they are not entitled to self-righteousness and venom." By contrast, the *Wall Street Journal,* a conservative newspaper, applauded the fact that Podhoretz had once again visited "an epidemic of apoplexy upon Manhattan's literary salons." The first round of opinion, pro as well as con, may be less important than the fact that Podhoretz's Vietnam revisionism opened up a lively debate on the morality of that divisive war. It can be said the jury is still out on this important matter, but Podhoretz's argument is surely part of the record it now has to ponder.

The Bloody Crossroads: Where Literature and Politics Meet (1986) is a collection of nine essays focusing on writers such as George Orwell, Albert Camus, Aleksander Solzhenitsyn, and Milan Kundera. Each stood at an uneasy spot where art and ideology collide, and, as Sidney Blumenthal argues in the *Washington Post Book World,* "the supreme litmus test by which he measures novelists, critics, and poets is where they correctly answer the question: Which side are you on?" As Podhoretz made clear in the collection's introduction: "Writers have been killed by politicians for expressing certain ideas or writing in certain ways; but (what is less often acknowledged) these same politicians have also been inspired by other writers to shed the blood of their fellow writers, and millions of nonwriters as well." What matters then, as one takes the measure of these respective careers at the writing desk, is what the often shivery consequences of their words were. For example, if Orwell were among us, Podhoretz argues, he would be "taking his stand with the neoconservatives and against the Left." On the other hand, Camus is faulted for writing novels [especially *The Rebel*] that are "the record not of growing disillusions with, or transcendence of, convictions expressed, but of an unsuccessful struggle to summon up the full courage of those convictions."

EX-FRIENDS

Ex-Friends: Falling Out with Allen Ginsberg, Lionel and Diana Trilling, Lillian Hellman, Hannah Arendt, and Norman Mailer (1999) reminds us of just how long and protracted Podhoretz's leave-takings have been. After more than thirty years at *Commentary*'s helm one would think that Podhoretz had long ago consigned his former life as a man on the Left to the memory bin, but this is hardly the case. Indeed, he keeps finding new ways to sing the words of the old Jimmy Durante tune, "Did you ever have the feeling that you wanted to go / Still have the feeling that you wanted to stay?" That is why *Ex-Friends* is such a sad and revealing book. In the concluding pages of J. D. Salinger's *The Catcher in the Rye* (1951), the novel's bewildered protagonist makes this bittersweet observation: "About all I know is, I sort of *miss* everybody I told about. . . . It's funny. Don't ever tell anybody anything. If you do, you start missing everyone." Granted, Holden Caulfield, Salinger's hypersensitive

(anti-) hero, suffers from an acute case of adolescent malaise and, as such, hardly seems worth mentioning in the same breath with Norman Podhoretz, an aging New York intellectual who finds himself "missing" old friends even as he is out to settle their hash. With the notable exception of Norman Mailer, all his targets are now safely dead, and thus unable to present their side of the story. The result is an insider account of intellectual life among the New York intellectuals, one that cuts no deals and takes no prisoners.

Nonetheless, one hears more than faint echoes of Holden's plaint in Podhoretz's concluding pages: "I regret the loss of the literary-intellectual world in which I used to live. . . . In spite of what I have said against my ex-friends here, I believe that the absence today of a community like the Family constitutes a great loss for our culture." Thus is *Ex-Friends* wrapped in several contradictory mantles—at once a valentine of self-congratulation and a chronicle of regret. Even readers unfamiliar with the names that drop easily onto his pages (Lionel and Diana Trilling or Hannah Arendt) need not worry because they appear as case studies that, taken together, are meant to show how long-standing Podhoretz's neoconservative instincts in fact were, and how right he was, and is, about American culture.

His complicated relationship with the poet Allen Ginsberg, a fellow Columbia student and ersatz mentor, is a prime example. That Ginsberg had accepted a long Podhoretz poem for the undergraduate literary journal he [Ginsberg] then edited was a coup of the first water—even if many of his original lines ended up on the editorial room floor. No doubt Ginsberg's chaotic, outlaw life once exercised a certain romantic attraction for Podhoretz; but over the years he found himself increasingly uncomfortable with the unhealthy direction that Ginsberg's popular image had taken, especially when its baleful influence on the young became alarmingly clear:

Now, in the mid-1960s, as before, the major difference between us had to do with our wildly contrasting ideas about America. Ginsberg's anti-Americanism of the 1950s had been bad enough, but the form it took in the 1960s as it exfoliated (or perhaps metastasized would be a better word) was even worse. His disciples and friends now extended way beyond the relatively narrow circle of the Beats to encompass the entire world of the counterculture—from rock musicians like Bob Dylan to hippies and yippies like Abbie Hoffman and Jerry Rubin to a variety of "gurus" peddling one form or another of Oriental mysticism. What they all had in common was a fierce hatred of America, which they saw as "Amerika," a country morally and spiritually equivalent to Nazi Germany. America's political system was based on oppression; and its culture was based on repression, to which the only answer was to opt out of middle-class life and liberate the squelched and smothered self through drugs and sexual promiscuity.

Even at his most radical, Podhoretz had always loved America (this would become abundantly clear in *My Love Affair with America*), and that unapologetic patriotism only deepened when he became editor of *Commentary* and turned its direction toward the neoconservative Right. Celebrating America was an important item of the new agenda, as was making an intellectual case for the economics of the free market that, for better of worse, would be the Reagan administration's legacy. About these matters (and many more) Podhoretz not only numbered Allen Ginsberg among the "know nothing bohemians" (as his famous put-down of the Beats would have it), but also came to feel that his ex-friend's 1958 boast/prophecy that "We'll get you through your children!" had, only a decade later, come nightmarishly true. For this, Podhoretz cannot, even now, forgive, despite the fact that an older, mellower Ginsberg was willing to forgive *him*: "But it was because of them [the "children" Ginsberg helped to corrupt, and sometimes to kill, with drugs and sexual promiscuity], as well as all the others

waiting in the wings, that I could not bring myself to forgive him, not even now that he was dead."

By contrast, Podhoretz's realization that even brilliant social commentary might, in the long run, be worse leads him to a chapter-length rumination about why the social philosopher Hannah Arendt took a terribly wrong direction in her controversial book *Eichmann in Jerusalem* (1964), and why their friendship cooled considerably after Arendt's study of Jewish complicity in the Holocaust was published. For Arendt to cast blame on the helpless victims of Nazism, and then go on to argue that Eichmann represents the "banality of evil" rather than evil incarnate, was more than Podhoretz (and many other Jewish intellectuals, for that matter) could bear.

Much the same beat goes on in *Ex-Friends* as one debunking profile blends almost seamlessly with another. Thus we learn how difficult it was for Podhoretz to remain on friendly terms with his Columbia mentor, the magisterial literary critic Lionel Trilling—especially as Lionel's left-leaning wife, Diana, poisoned the atmosphere between them—or how he had no choice when his journal was among the first to air the truth about the systematic lies Hellman had told in such nonfiction books as *Pentimento* (1973) or *Scoundrel Time* (1976). Podhoretz readily admits that, in Hellman's case, he still feels a certain nostalgic tug as he remembers the lavish meals and parties she regularly served up, but politics is, well, politics—and Hellman was always on the wrong side of the aisle: "The plain truth is that I remain proud of the part I went on to take in the fight against the political ideas and attitudes in whose service she corrupted her work and brought, as I now see it, lasting dishonor to her name."

In the final analysis, however, *Ex-Friends* is about people who, in Nathan Glazer's famous definition of the public intellectual, live "for, by, and off ideas." True enough, the usual aspects of friendship can also play a part, but they will, perforce, always be secondary. What matters—and matters passionately—are ideas and their public consequences. The Family, as Podhoretz described his circle in *Making It,* was at once a roll call of the very bright and extremely talented, as well as a recipe for personal disaster. No doubt oversized egos account for part of the friction *Ex-Friends* describes, but acts of ideological betrayal were far more serious, and much more damaging.

Podhoretz's effort to explain why he abandoned the left liberalism of his youth had repercussions that even its author did not fully imagine at the time. True enough, the neoconservative *Commentary* crowd he assembled had more than its fair share of luminaries, such as Irving Kristol, but things, as they say, were never the same—either for those who rallied around Podhoretz's vision of a better, more conservatively inclined American politics or those who continued the good fight for such liberal causes as welfare or affirmative action. Indeed, everything seemed different from the mid-1960s onward: socializing wasn't as exciting or as good as the hard-drinking, freewheeling parties of the 1950s were. A meaner spirit, fueled by heavy doses of political correctness, gradually replaced the intellectual world in which Podhoretz had once scrambled (some would say shamelessly) to make a place for himself.

One could argue that what Podhoretz *really* misses is his youth. Perhaps, but as with most generalizations (and labels) affixed to the New York intellectuals, this commonsensical view is, at best, a partial truth—for what *Ex-Friends* finally comes to is cultural history as it filters itself through Podhoretz's consciousness. That, indeed, is what Podhoretz's string of autobiographies and his most important articles always come to.

MY LOVE AFFAIR WITH AMERICA

My Love Affair with America, the fourth installment of what threatens to become an ongoing series, is ostensibly about "America" and how it deserves the support, yea, the *celebration,* of its citizens. Podhoretz writes as an unembarrassed patriot, partly in the spirit of Jewish gratitude that the once-popular journalist Harry Golden expressed in titles such as *Only in America* (1958), and partly as a recurring theme in his own experience. Describing the various sea changes that took him from a young boy who spoke with a thick Brooklyn-Jewish dialect to one who was able to read and write about the great works of literature, Podhoretz cannot resist taking a swipe at what has replaced the world that formed him as a Jew and an American. In his childhood, cultural pluralism allowed for equal measures of difference and consensus. Public education, for example, was designed to provide all citizens with the academic skills and civic attitudes necessary to become successful Americans, while in the private sphere children could learn as much (or as little) about ethnic or religious traditions as their parents deemed appropriate. In Podhoretz's case, this meant learning correct English in school, learning Hebrew in the late afternoons, and hearing Yiddish around the family dinner table. No longer, at least so far as Mr. Podhoretz is concerned:

> In the age of multiculturalism that dawned on America a half-century later, any teacher doing to a black or Latino or Asian kid what that teacher did to me would (I exaggerate only slightly) have been surrounded in a trice by federal marshals materializing out of the very walls of the school, arrested for attempted cultural genocide, read her Miranda rights, and carted off in handcuffs to the applause of the child's parents and sundry liberal spokesmen.

Something of the same spirit, call it "playful" or simply the "pass" one earns after four decades of nonstop cultural warfare, collects around other sections of this often witty but deeply avuncular book. In discussing, for example, the first time he actually saw—this in the middle 1970s—the "purple mountain majesties" of patriotic song, Podhoretz's deeply rooted love of country gushes out: ". . . they supplied a living connection between this relatively young nation and the most ancient stages of creation itself." One hears echoes of the psalmist in the sentence, but the less beautiful, Midwestern "amber waves of grain" affect him even more:

> Driving through that endless sea of feed, most of it produced by the allegedly villainous "agribusiness"—that is, a very small number of people—I could only marvel at the immense richness of the American soil and the endless ingenuity of those who cultivated it, and I could only laugh derisively at the idea prevalent among my fellow intellectuals that America was a nation in decline.

Podhoretz's credentials as a patriot are clearly not in question, even as one hastens to add that a love of country can express itself in many forms, including criticism; but his glib comment about agribusiness is quite another matter given the steady decline of the family farm (once as much a staple of American life as the little red schoolhouse) and a host of other economic complexities he simply ignores in an effort to paint the rosiest possible picture of the America that has been mighty good to him (and as Podhoretz himself remarks again and again, to countless other Jewish Americans).

To his credit, Podhoretz not only uses *My Love Affair with America* to rehash his quarrels with the Left, ones that we have already heard about in great detail in previous books, but also to make it clear that he can be equally upset when his new allies on the Right bash away at America from their side of the political aisle. As with *Breaking Ranks,* he names names, admonishing Father Richard John Neuhaus, the fiery editor of the neoconservative, religious-culture journal *First Things,* for running a

controversial, deeply upsetting symposium about the "end" of democracy, and worrying that even such a staunch conservative ally as William Bennett can come to doubt American democracy when public opinion polls did not share his moral outrage over the Bill Clinton–Monica Lewinsky scandal. To his credit, Podhoretz is willing to risk alienating friends from the Right just as he was once willing to cut his ties with the Left. Fortunately, Podhoretz hastens to assure us, the flaps died down, ruffled feathers were soothed, and he could look forward to not spending his golden years at the barricades. Even more encouraging, Podhoretz sees evidence, despite his continuing tirades against the folly of affirmative action and the balkanizing tendencies of multiculturalism, that the cultural warfare which provided so much fodder for intellectuals like himself may be coming to an end.

It may even be that patriotism, a sentiment that causes most intellectuals, regardless of their ideology, to roll their eyeballs (corny at its most benign, the refuge of scoundrels at its worst), may yet make a comeback. *My Love Affair with America* might be an important first step—just as Podhoretz's other writing predicted cultural shifts in the country, and in Podhoretz himself, for nearly five decades.

In recent years, Podhoretz has written a number of essays reassessing the legacy of novelists such as Joseph Heller, Ralph Ellison, Saul Bellow, and Philip Roth. In each case, there is the usual amount of repetition as Podhoretz takes us back to the early days when his attention-grabbing reviews made him a Manhattan household name as well as a sense that what is finally important about a novel is its political correctness as neoconservatives define the term.

One feels in all of this a continuation of the young Podhoretz who learned his critical moves at the knee of the very opinionated F. R. Leavis and a reflection of his years as a conservative culture warrior. What has been largely lost, however, is the fascination with imaginative writing that was once the hallmark of Podhoretz's most insightful work. Instead, what we see is the mellow, increasingly "cheerful" conservatism that marks *My Love Affair with America,* a book that ends with a litany of *dayyenus* (roughly translated as "That alone would have been enough for us") that are recited during the Passover service. It would have been enough, the hymn goes, if God had taken us out of bondage in Egypt, and it would have been enough had God given us the Torah. In Podhoretz's Americanized version, it would have been enough if "America had only granted me the inheritance of the English language," or "provided me with three wonderful years at another great university across the sea" or "opened the way for me to meet and mingle and live my life with some of the most interesting people of my time." Or, of course, made it possible for him to edit *Commentary* during its decades of high visibility and importance. *My Love Affair with America* ends in gushes of love and gratitude. In other hands, the sentiments would be suspicious at best and dishonest at worst. But Podhoretz has earned them—not only because of the battles he has found since he wrote his early reviews and commentary, but also because of the fascinating life he unfolds in a culturally important series of memoirs.

Selected Bibliography

WORKS OF NORMAN PODHORETZ

BOOKS

Doings and Undoings: The Fifties and After in American Writing. New York: Farrar, Straus, 1964.

The Commentary Reader: Two Decades of Articles and Stories. New York: Atheneum, 1966. (Edited by Podhoretz.)

Making It. New York: Random House, 1968. New ed., New York: Harper, 1980.

Breaking Ranks: A Political Memoir. New York: Harper, 1979.

The Present Danger: Do We Have the Will to Reverse the Decline of American Power? New York: Simon & Schuster, 1980.

Why We Were in Vietnam. New York: Simon & Schuster, 1982.

The Bloody Crossroads: Where Literature and Politics Meet. New York: Simon & Schuster, 1986.

Ex-Friends: Falling Out with Allen Ginsberg, Lionel and Diana Trilling, Lillian Hellman, Hannah Arendt, and Norman Mailer. New York: The Free Press, 1999.

My Love Affair with America: The Cautionary Tale of a Cheerful Conservative. New York: The Free Press, 2000.

A SAMPLING OF UNCOLLECTED CRITICISM

"The Hate That Dare Not Speak Its Name." *Commentary* 82, no. 5:21–32 (November 1986).

"On Being a Jew." *Commentary* 88, no. 4:28–36 (October 1989).

"What Is Anti-Semitism?" *Commentary* 93, no. 2:15–20 (February 1992).

"Neoconservatism: A Eulogy." *Commentary* 101, no. 3:19–27 (March 1996).

"On the Future of Conservatism." *Commentary* 103, no. 2:35–37 (February 1997).

"Is Affirmative Action on the Way Out? Should It Be?" *Commentary* 105, no. 3:45–47 (March 1998).

"Israel and the United States: A Complex History." *Commentary* 105, no. 5:28–43 (May 1998).

"The Adventures of Philip Roth." *Commentary* 106, no. 4:25–36 (October 1998).

"Clinton, the Country, and the Political Culture." *Commentary* 107, no. 1:39–41 (January 1999).

"What Happened to Ralph Ellison?" *Commentary* 108, no. 1:46–58 (July/August 1999).

"Looking Back at *Catch-22*." *Commentary* 109, no. 2:32–37 (February 2000).

"America Abroad." *Commentary* 109, no. 4:5–10 (April 2000).

"Learning from Isaiah." *Commentary* 109, no. 5:32–39 (May 2000).

"Bellow at 85, Roth at 67." *Commentary* 110, no. 1:35–43 (July/August 2000).

CRITICAL AND BIOGRAPHICAL STUDIES

BOOK

Winchell, Mark Royden. *Neoconservative Criticism: Norman Podhoretz, Kenneth S. Lynn, and Joseph Epstein.* Boston: Twayne, 1991.

ARTICLES

Adler, Renata. "Polemic and the New Reviewers." In *The Young American Writer.* Edited by Richard Kostelanetz. New York: Funk and Wagnalls, 1967. Pp. 3–24.

Bradford, M. E. "The Vocation of Norman Podhoretz." In *The Reactionary Imperative: Essays Literary and Political.* Peru, Ill.: Sherwood Sugden, 1990. Pp. 27–38.

Enright, D. J. "Articles of Use." In *Conspiracies and Poets.* London: Chatto & Windus, 1966. Pp. 19–26.

Garrett, George. "My Silk Purse and Yours: *Making It,* Starring Norman Podhoretz." In *The Sounder Few.* Edited by R. H. W. Dillard, George Garrett, and John Rees Moore. Athens: University of Georgia Press, 1971. Pp. 327–342.

Goldberg, S. L. "The Education of Norman Podhoretz; or, I Was a Teen–Age Intellectual." *Critical Review* 12:83–106 (1969).

Jumonville, Neil. "The New York Intellectuals' Defense of the Intellect." *Queen's Quarterly* 97, no. 2:290–304 (summer 1990).

Mailer, Norman. "Up the Family Tree." In *Existential Errands.* Boston: Little, Brown, 1972. Pp. 171–197.

Pinsker, Sanford. "Revisionism with Rancor: The Threat of the Neoconservative Critics." *The Georgia Review* 38, no. 2:243–261 (summer 1984).

Schuessler, Jennifer. "Norman Podhoretz: Making Enemies." *Publishers Weekly* 246, no. 4:67–68 (January 25, 1999).

ARCHIVAL SOURCES
The Library of Congress

—SANFORD PINSKER

May Sarton

1912–1995

*I*N THE 1980 filmed interview *World of Light* May Sarton describes what she terms the "vision of life" reflected in her writing: that original way of looking at the world that is uniquely May Sarton's. For Sarton, her European roots, her life in America, and her temperament—a combination of passion and a critical mind—coalesce to create this imaginative lens through which she sees and interprets the world. This collection of influences—Europe and America, passion and critical thinking—hold in a balance worlds that could, at first glance, appear to be quite different. Perhaps Sarton's ability to incorporate these disparate elements into her vision of life is the quality the critic Singrid Fowler perceives in Sarton's vision of poetry as well. Fowler writes: "To name distinctive elements of May Sarton's poetry, one would probably mention . . . a characteristic tension of mood, the clash of opposites in imagery . . . the poet's predilection for . . . the oxymoron." But Fowler goes on to suggest that despite the "restlessness of such a mode," it is euphony rather than cacophony that one hears and feels in Sarton's poetry. Sarton achieves this through her "emphasis on the balance rather than the conflict of widely differing elements and her creation of large categories within which apparent irreconcilables can be brought together."

ROOTS IN EUROPE

Sarton's work balances a strong connection to her European heritage with the life she knew in America, demonstrating the poet's ability to bring together and benefit from the richness of two very different worlds. Sarton's European roots are outlined in the autobiographical sketches collected as *I Knew a Phoenix* (1959). The opening two chapters, "'In My Father's House,'" and "A Wild Green Place," describe the early years of her father and mother, George Sarton in Belgium and Mabel Elwes in Wales. The youthful years of both her father and mother were difficult. George Sarton's mother died shortly after he was born, and "loneliness haunted his memories of babyhood." George Sarton—inquisitive, imaginative, independent— grew up in Ghent, a fascinating city that "opened passionate hours of discovery." Mabel Elwes was born in Suffolk, England, but when she was seven, her parents left to work for two years in Canada and Mabel was sent to a farm in Wales, in what her father thought would be a suitable landscape for his daughter's wild and unconventional disposition. Mabel's foster family turned out to be two women—"Grannie" and her high-strung daughter, Aunt Mollie. Mabel, the English girl, was viewed as an outsider, a "foreigner" by these Welsh women. The child was often left alone, deprived of companionship, poorly fed, and, at times, beaten. What Mabel Elwes gained from this experience—and what ultimately her daughter, May, came to inherit—was compassion, intolerance for injustice, and unsentimental truth of perceptions.

A later chapter in *I Knew a Phoenix* describes Wondelgem, Belgium, the place of May Sarton's birth on May 3, 1912. Unlike her father's somber home in Ghent, the country house three miles outside the city was "all light and sunshine." The same year May was born, George Sarton founded *Isis,* a review that was to be devoted to the history of science and civilization. May describes their life in Wondelgem as happy and independent. Her mother, a talented seamstress, designed rugs, curtains, and furniture and was working at the time for a firm in Brussels. George Sarton, a philosopher and scientist, was doing research to fulfill his dream of writing a history of scientific thought. Sarton describes her infancy: "As I grew up from a basket to an outdoor crib, my father's notes for the *History of Science* grew in their boxes, and the garden was growing all the time." But the year was 1914 and German forces were bearing down on the Belgian border. May's father became part of the resistance, but it was clear that completing his own research and writing in the midst of the chaos would be almost impossible, and the Sartons decided to move out of Belgium. What May Sarton recalls in her autobiographical sketches is the hasty leave-taking—without so much as a backward glance "at the garden, at the beloved house," a leave-taking that came full circle to "another deep green garden in Cambridge [Massachusetts]." For the next year, however, May Sarton and her mother stayed in England with fellow refugees and friends, while her father went on to the United States to pursue his dream of writing a major work on the history of science, learn a new language, and explore possible teaching assignments. After a brief period at George Washington University in Washington, D.C., in 1916 George Sarton moved his family one more time to Cambridge, where he took the position of part-time instructor at Harvard and full-time scholar on his research project. For May Sarton, this move was to the garden and home she recalls in her sketches.

Sarton's memories of family often find their focus in an image of gardens and houses. Perhaps the natural world of flowers and plants connected Sarton to her mother's early roots in the wild landscape of Wales; houses, on the other hand, seem more linked to her father, whose city home became the focus of her memories of him. Sarton's subsequent love of gardening and nature, together with the impor-

tance she placed on establishing a home with companion, friends, solitude, and writing, mirror the two worlds, the outside and inside, that fuse in her parents' roots.

In 1968 Sarton inherited money that allowed her to buy a home in Nelson, New Hampshire. The introduction to her 1968 memoir *Plant Dreaming Deep* is entitled "The Ancestor Comes Home." Here Sarton describes two of her ancestors, Duvet de la Tour of Normandy and John Elwes of England. Sarton hangs the former's portrait prominently above the Flemish chest of drawers with an approving, "Well old boy, here we are!" His English contemporary, her ancestor John Elwes, balances for her a critical dichotomy: Elwes, Sarton writes, "was a true English eccentric, at the opposite pole from the French man of reason." Sarton's home becomes the space where these two worlds come together; later in the introduction to *Plant Dreaming Deep* she writes: "I enjoy beginning this chronicle with an evocation of the two ancestors because in this house all the threads I hold in my hands have at last been woven together into a whole—the threads of the English and Belgian families from which I spring (Flanders and Suffolk), the threads of my own wanderings in Europe and the United States, and those shining threads, the values willed to me by my two remarkable parents. Here they all weave their way in to a single unfolding and unifying design."

EDUCATION

Her "wanderings in Europe and the United States" included educational experiences that had a profound influence on May Sarton's vision of life. As a young girl in Cambridge, Massachusetts, Sarton attended Shady Hill School from 1917 to 1926, with a one-year hiatus in 1924–1925, when Sarton accompanied her parents to Belgium during her father's sabbatical leave. At Shady Hill School Sarton was greatly influenced by Agnes Hocking, the founder of the school and Sarton's poetry instructor. Sarton describes Shady Hill—which defined itself as an "open air" school—as having "a spiritual climate as bracing, as rich and unpredictable, as that of New England itself." Agnes Hocking made poetry centrally active; she did not simply teach poetry but inspired her students to "live its life."

During her one-year stay in Belgium, Sarton studied at the Institut Belge de Culture Française. Here she met another major influence, Marie Closset, founder of the school and a well-known poet herself, writing under the pseudonym Jean Dominique. The Belgian school was a polar opposite to Sarton's experience at Shady Hill: here memorization was valued over independent thinking; textbooks were learned quite literally by heart, and fear and trembling replaced the atmosphere of freedom that pervaded Shady Hill. But Sarton saw the value of these opposing viewpoints— and recognized that in combination, the skills she could gain from each would only benefit her, especially as a writer: she suggests that while she suffered at times under this new regime, she learned to respect the memory and the "exact, instead of the almost exact, word." Marie Closset became a powerful presence for Sarton. Her range of knowledge in the arts and literature instilled in Sarton and in all her students an "enlightened homage—homage enriched by intellectual analysis but rooted in passion." The connection of intellect and passion was clearly integral to what was to become Sarton's "vision of life." This teacher, mentor, and friend became the subject of Sarton's first novel, *The Single Hound.*

In 1926 Sarton returned to Cambridge to graduate from Shady Hill School with her twelve classmates and begin her education at the High and Latin, Cambridge's public high school. In ninth grade she began writing poems more seriously and under the tutelage of her former teacher Katharine Taylor, she began to

understand the need to temper her emotions and "discipline the heart," helping her "emerge from a sentimental vision . . . to something harder, clearer, and more honest."

Upon graduation from the High and Latin in 1929, Sarton won a scholarship to Vassar but decided to pursue a career in theater, having been inspired by a trip with her father to Boston when she was fifteen for her first experience of serious theater. In August 1929 Sarton left home to attend Eva La Gallienne's Civic Repertory Theatre in New York City, spending the year studying diction, attending classes in fencing, and learning the basics of theater. Sarton participated in the Civic Repertory for three years. In the winter of 1931–1932, while her parents were at the American University in Beirut, Sarton continued to study theater in Paris. What felt like "a period of illness or even insanity" became for her a rich period of developing friendships and gaining independence. Her learning now took the form of "sudden flashes," including a theater experience of the beauty and strangeness of a controversial artistic movement: surrealism. This winter in Paris also marked the beginning of annual trips to England and Europe where she associated with extraordinary people—Juliette and Julian Huxley, Virginia Woolf, Elizabeth Bowen, and S. S. Koteliansky.

With the close of the Civic Repertory Theatre in 1933, Sarton joined with friends to start an independent theater company. After productions in New York and Boston, the company ultimately disbanded: but for Sarton this "failure" became a source of strength, that despite such losses and disappointments, "human beings have unquenchable resources within them." Throughout her years in theater, Sarton had continued writing poetry; her first poems had already appeared in *Poetry* magazine. Sarton now turned her focus to poetry.

Sarton concludes *I Knew a Phoenix* with a description of time spent in England in 1936 and 1937. Not long after meeting Virginia Woolf, Sarton reads a report of Woolf's suicide; in the same paragraph she recalls the death of a baby giraffe dying of fright in a bombing. She writes of the two: "In an instant of acute grief and recognition, the two images slid together for me." Images sliding together could be characterized as an integral component of May Sarton's "vision of life." Belgium and England; Wondelgem and Cambridge; gardens and houses; outsiders and insiders; solitude and communion: all separate but fused, like the fabric whose threads are diverse but blend to create a work of art (no doubt learned firsthand from her mother's embroidery business). In her work Sarton diffuses the polarities, highlighting the gray area where borders are not so clearly defined.

TEACHING AND LECTURING

Sarton's teaching career was comprised of a series of one-year appointments or contracts to teach specific courses. While she enjoyed teaching, Sarton often sought such positions because of pressing financial need or desire for recognition. But life in the academic world often exacerbated her own feeling of being an outsider. Early in her career, Sarton found a job teaching writing at Stuart School in Rockport, Massachusetts. With no college degree, full-time teaching was almost impossible, but for Sarton, who "loathed the idea of commercial job," college teaching provided status and a sense of self-worth, as well as an opportunity to immerse herself in the literature she loved.

In 1946 Sarton accepted a position as poet-in-residence at Southern Illinois University in Carbondale. According to her biographer Margot Peters, lecturing tours and teaching opportunities changed Sarton: "They satisfied her need to talk, to dominate, to influence." College teaching also gave Sarton the recognition that she longed for—and rarely won—from the critics.

She was known and appreciated for the rigor of her classes and the demands she made of her students. During the 1950s, Sarton taught composition courses at Harvard as a Briggs-Copeland appointee, courses on the short story and the novel at Bread Loaf writer's conference in Vermont, and adult writing classes at Radcliffe; the fact that such prestigious institutions hired Sarton without a college degree is a testament to the quality of her teaching and her skills as a creative writer. Ironically, this same non-degreed status could have contributed to her feeling of marginalization in the academic world.

In January 1960 Sarton took a position at Wellesley, where she taught creative writing classes. During this period, she published *The Small Room,* a novel that chronicles the challenges and frustrations of a new English professor, Lucy Winter, who begins her teaching career at a small, prestigious women's college. The novel explores the politics of academia through candid portrayals of plagiary cover-ups, homoerotic affairs, and power struggles with the college benefactors. Clearly, the novel did not win friends for Sarton at Wellesley. Despite the fact that she was contracted for poetry readings at prestigious institutions like Radcliffe, Bryn Mawr, and New York University, Sarton's teaching career at Wellesley ended disastrously. While Sarton was urging for a three-year appointment, the college terminated her contract altogether. This blow could be attributed to a number of factors—certainly the jealousy of Sarton's colleagues is among them—but Sarton's angry outbursts, her sexual pursuits of the college's president, Margaret Clapp, and the crushes she encouraged from her students all contributed to her departure. The dismissal wounded Sarton deeply.

In 1965 Sarton began teaching at Lindenwood College in St. Charles. That same year, *Mrs. Stevens Hears the Mermaids Singing* (1965), Sarton's "coming out" novel, received a great deal of critical attention—much of it negative. Consequently, she was ostracized by some faculty members at Lindenwood, she was denied fellowships, and lecture tours were cancelled. Her final teaching position at Agnes Scott College in Georgia could have offered some relief since this was a campus where Sarton had previously been hired on several occasions for readings or individual lectures. Here, too, however, Sarton encountered difficulties with her colleagues, leading her to conclude, "I do not really fit into the academic world at all," according to her biographer.

THE NOVELS

In Sarton's imagination, outsiders have a unique vantage point—and in most cases, these outsiders are women. In the film *World of Light*, Sarton addresses three connections among her work and her focus on women and women's art: first, for her, women have acted as muses—that is, women have given focus to her world; second, as a woman writer, she has felt "outside the center" and deprived of critical acclaim; and last, as a lesbian, she has confronted the issue of coming out in her autobiographical fiction, *Mrs. Stevens Hears the Mermaids Singing.*

One of May Sarton's earliest novels, *The Bridge of Years,* published in 1946, introduces this theme of insider and outsider, along with Sarton's proclivity to blur the boundaries that differentiate the two. The story centers on a family living in Belgium between the world wars. Melanie, the matriarch of the family, is also a businesswoman. Much like Sarton's own mother, Melanie designs furniture and fabric to decorate houses. Foreshadowing a theme that will continue to evolve in Sarton's later writing, particularly in the journals, houses are central to the story. If fact, the house in Melanie's case becomes a bridge of sorts between the inside world she nurtures as a mother and the outside world she creates in her business. The story's narrator relates that Melanie's "art" was "composed as much of a genius for personal relations as of a genius for color and texture, for dressing a house as if it were a person in its own character and still in perfect taste." But outside worlds and inside worlds interface on a much broader and foreboding context: World War II has begun. Early in the story, Melanie's husband, Paul, a philosopher and a poet, admits to wanting no more children for fear of the tragic world they will inherit. The outside world of war and prejudice comes crashing into the family's domestic sphere later in the novel, when a German family friend comes to visit and the servants, Marie and Lou-lou, refuse to serve him: "now right here in her own house Melanie was forced to face [the war] in reality." Sarton personalizes the issues that war raises, and in so doing highlights the fact that black and white categories of guilt or blame are difficult to establish. Sarton's story illustrates the devastation of war—to an individual family and to a whole nation—with wounds that penetrate far deeper than the flesh, with stories that narrate the wounds of the heart.

A much later novel, *Kinds of Love* (1970), presents another strong matriarchal figure in the character of Christina Chapman. Unlike her *Bridge of Years,* here Sarton chronicles one year in the lives of the folks who come and go from Willard, New Hampshire, but this "history" is blended from several narrative viewpoints, adding layers and depth to the story of this small rural town. For example, Christina keeps a journal throughout the novel, ending each chapter with her own reflections on the events of her mountain haven, creating a personalized history made up of anecdotes and insights. The novel's narrator tells another version of the story, recounting the interconnections among the town's friendships and family, strangers and outcasts. The novel is about this tapestry of humanity that Sarton weaves together—but it is also about the creative act of writing. At one point in the novel, Christina writes in her journal: "I don't know why I have written all of this down, as if it were a letter to someone interested in all our doings. I suppose gathering it all up for a moment does make me feel a sense of the whole tapestry of life, and not just a thread here or there." Like Christina, Sarton, gathers it all up in her narrative—a story of love growing older and deeper in Christina and her sickly husband, Cornelius, a story of the mental ravages of war in Nick and Old Pete, a story of young love in the next generation represented by the romance between Christina's granddaughter Cathy and a stranger to Willard, Joel.

Sarton dramatizes the "inside" and "outside" worlds of Willard through one more "history" being written: as a backdrop to the story, one of the townsfolk, Eben Fifield, is organizing the writing of a more formal history of Willard, with several townspeople taking responsibility for a portion of the research and writing. Histories ostensibly mean that a private world is to be made public, and this theme extends to the inability of outsiders to really understand the life of Willard based only on appearance. Christina notes that visitors to the town, like Joel and Cathy, cannot really see the "inside"— that is, what makes these townspeople "real": "What Joel and Cathy cannot see is the struggle of course. They see the reality of it all as beauty, wildness, and freedom—'escape,' as Eben would say." Christina's journal provides the texture for another, more personal, study of Sarton's inside and outside worlds and the process of aging that is such a central theme in the novel. Christina reflects as she looks into a mirror, seeing the wrinkles that mark her years: "Inside, the person I really am has no relation to this mask age is slowly attaching to my face. I feel so young, so exposed under it. I simply cannot seem to learn to behave like the very old party I am. The young girl, arrogant, open, full of feelings she cannot analyze, longing to be told she is beautiful—that young girl lives inside this shell." The novel becomes a testament to the struggle to age gracefully, to engage in different "kinds of love," to celebrate, as Christina relates in her journal, "the extraordinary people here . . . whatever they are has had to be created from the inside out, against great odds."

Joanna and Ulysses (1963) takes Sarton's focus on strong women in a different direction: Joanna, the protagonist, has played the matriarchal role in her father's household ever since her mother died helping prisoners escape during the war. Joanna's father has become closed and repressed after his wife's death. Joanna has assumed her mother's responsibilities, but as an artist, she longs to paint and to be valued for her talent. For her more pragmatic father, art as authentic work is difficult to understand. Joanna decides to leave home for a month and sail to the Greek island of Santorini, where she will devote herself to developing her artistic talent. Soon after arriving, however, Joanna comes upon a donkey, sick, wounded, and homeless. She buys the donkey, names him Ulysses, and begins her quest for a space to paint. But Ulysses' wounds need attention and finding a space for herself and a sick donkey is not easy. The challenge, however, forces Joanna to be independent and resourceful; once she finds a place to stay, her art flourishes.

Joanna's growth takes place simultaneously in an outside world that is quite bewildered by this single woman and her donkey and in an inside world, where she slowly builds the internal resources needed to believe in herself as an artist. Joanna's search for freedom and independence in the outside world ultimately brings her to a newfound freedom within herself. Her art improves, and she begins to appreciate herself for the work she has accomplished. She identifies the mission for her art—"to see the essence of a few stones—and communicate it at least to myself"—and Ulysses becomes a metaphor for her, a symbol of true life and joy. At the end of her month in Santorini, Joanna returns a different person: she spontaneously decides minutes before departure home that she cannot leave her companion, Ulysses, behind, and so she takes him to her father's apartment. Her newly discovered confidence in her artwork and the quality of her creations takes her father by surprise. He, too, begins to change, and by the end of the story, his stoicism dissolves. Not only can he speak of his beloved wife once again, but he can see Joanna in a new way, as an artist whose work is valuable.

In *The Small Room,* Lucy Winter, another single woman and aficionado of the arts, finds herself at the center of a plagiarism scandal at a small private college for women. Here Sarton explores the line between the outside appearance of the academic world, with its esoteric discussions and manicured lawns, and the inside world where turbulent emotions and moral debates disrupt the placid facade. Recently separated from her husband, Lucy Winter arrives to teach literature at a selective school for women in New England. Her "small room" of an office becomes the space where students pour out their personal lives to Lucy, a practice with which she feels very uncomfortable. For Lucy, their personal lives are very separate from the academic world; teachers should not become confidantes to help their students sort out personal issues. That is the role for a psychiatrist. Rather, Lucy longs to be free to teach—"without all this personal stuff."

Early in the novel Lucy compares this "inside world" of her office with the academic world of white pillars and stately buildings: "How cool and discreet the world outside looked compared to the confused, upset, muddled world of this small room where so much happened and did not happen." But these two worlds converge when Lucy plays a pivotal role in exposing a plagiarism scandal involving one of the bright-

est and most promising students on campus, Jane Seaman. Formidable Carryl Cope, professor of English, becomes involved in the drama because she is Jane's friend and mentor—and has covered up the discovery of Jane's plagiarism in order to save her from inevitable expulsion. The campus discussion on the issue becomes Sarton's podium for dispelling the notion that clear-cut conclusions can be made about the infraction. Debate among faculty, administration, and students includes issues of fairness in student treatment, as well as Jane's mental instability—caused by the intense pressure to succeed that such "stars" are subject to. Carryl Cope is certainly guilty in this regard. But the water gets muddied further in an underlying erotic fascination Carryl feels toward her protégée as well. Add to the moral quagmire Olive Hunt, a major contributor to the school and involved in a sexual and very closeted affair with Carryl Cope. Olive Hunt insists that the school does not need a resident psychiatrist and threatens to cut off her financial support if the administration does not comply. In Jane Seaman's case, however, professional help could have directed her to a better course of action.

Sarton creates a world where the "outside" and "inside" collide and careen throughout the novel: the facade of "universal truth" in this intellectual world versus the truth of students' lives that Lucy discovers in her "small room"; intellectual brilliance versus emotional breakdown in Jane Seaman; a benefactor's notion of what college should provide in academic programs versus students' need for psychiatric help; relationship of benefactor to teacher and teacher to student versus hidden and forbidden homoerotic fascination. Lucy discovers that it is in the small room of her office where "the real teaching is done." But it also becomes where Lucy faces her students as real people, not simply as students. Pippa, for example, a confused, terrified, and insecure student who looks for Lucy to befriend and console her, blossoms under Lucy's mentoring and advice.

On a broader scale Sarton critiques the notion that education takes place in a sterile world of ideas; in fact, the action of the novel supports Lucy's reflection that crisis is necessary in order for "real" education to flourish—creating a climate "that forces honesty out, breaks down the walls of what ought to be, and reveals what is instead." We get glimpses of Sarton's philosophy of good teaching in a heated debate between Lucy's colleagues Hallie and Maria: that professors are faced everyday with the choice to teach out of vulnerabilities or out of strength, to teach only the mind or the whole person.

In her 1982 novel *Anger,* Sarton explores the relationship between another female artist, Anna Lindstrom—a world renowned singer—and her husband, Ned. The outside world of appearance matters here as well: early in the novel, Anna, so "perfectly in control," admits to another side of pressure under which an artist suffers: "What nobody understands is that an artist, a performer, has to prove herself over and over again. . . . In professional life outside the arts there are no critics in on every move you make. But we are targets. We are judged every time we open our mouths, sometimes by ignoramuses at that, and the public takes any critic's word as gospel truth." Throughout the novel Anna echoes many of Sarton's own frustrations with the critics who, she claimed, failed to recognize the intellect behind her work or dismissed her because she had not followed the conventional academic track of most poets.

This novel, too, is a story of opposites. Ned, Anna's husband, is outwardly composed, unlike Anna, whose temper flies, whose emotions run close to the surface. But as the plot unfolds, Ned's own anger, deep-seated and repressed, becomes as much of a block to the marital communication as Anna's outbursts. The novel explores the ways the couple expresses anger, and the effect that rage, whether articulated or repressed, has on their relationship. Bad reviews become a catalyst for Anna's stormy outbursts; for Ned, "conditioned never to allow [himself] anger," anger is kept well below the surface. The couple is faced with a choice: to stay on the surface of life and keep conversation "pleasant" or dare to talk about the "real" and face the turbulent emotions that may erupt. Ultimately both agree that living with the real is worth the risk. Ned admits to a family tragedy that has always been kept secret. Through tears the two realize that "the closing off, the fear of feeling" does not have to go on from generation to generation. Sarton's journals, particularly *Journal of a Solitude* (1973), suggest that she, too, grappled with establishing the balance between extremes when it came to anger.

Sarton's autobiographical infusion into her fiction is best revealed in *Mrs. Stevens Hears the Mermaids Singing.* The story takes place as the writer F. Hilary Stevens is being interviewed by two young journalists, Peter Selversen and Jenny Hare. Like *Kinds of Love,* where several types of narratives converge, here too layers of the writer's life are revealed: first, in a more public, "outside" way to the interviewers, and second, in a personal and internal way, through Hilary's reflections between the interviewers' questions. Hilary's internal/private narrative is so emotionally explosive that at times during the interview she steps away, ostensibly for a breath of air or a drink, but in fact to manage or process the flood of memories the interview prompts: the emotions, disappointments, inspirations, and relationships behind the events. She chronicles for the interviewers, and for herself, the women who inspired her—her muses, or (to use Sarton's phrase from *A World of Light: Portraits and Celebrations,* 1976) "women who give focus to the world."

As Mrs. Stevens recalls each woman, it is clear each taught her a valuable lesson about tensions being held in the balance. Hilary recalls at fifteen asking her first muse, Phillippa Munn, her governess, "Why wasn't I born a boy, Miss Munn? It's so unfair!" Phillippa awakens a passion within Hilary, a "huge inner reverberation, which stretched all her powers." For the first time, Hilary experiences herself as two people: one caught up in this fascination with Phillippa Munn; the other experiencing the "outer world" with a new excitement. For Hilary, "it was as if the whole outer world also resounded in her . . . landscape, literature, everything had become alive in a wholly new way."

Inner and outer worlds simultaneously come alive for Hilary, but writing cannot be sustained by passion alone. In the story of Willa McPherson, the second muse Hilary reflects upon, Hilary recalls a conversation she had with Willa about a disastrous love affair Willa had had with a young Irish Catholic man who found Willa's passion frightening. He ended the relationship rather cruelly, and Willa still laments the deep hurt she suffered because of the betrayal. Hilary consoles her: "It has made you what you are. It's why you do what you do for everyone who comes into your house. It's the other side of your detachment, of your power to include everyone and everything." Hilary's relationship with Willa inspires her to recognize poetry in a new way. More specifically, Hilary suddenly recognizes the importance of form. The sonnet, for example, "is not a discipline imposed from outside by the intellect, but grappled with from inner necessity as a means of probing and dealing with powerful emotion." But Hilary discovers the muse is detached, separate, offering another kind of intimacy—that of poetic inspiration. Caught between love for this woman and recognition that it cannot be reciprocated with like passion, Hilary struggles to accept the gift that Willa offers: "that the poem itself was the reality . . . that together for some mysterious reason, they made possible the act of creation."

For Hilary Stevens, relating to her next muse, Dorothea, the anti-mystic sociologist, is like "plunging into a huge exhilarating ocean, as if

the very difference in their vision of life gave an exciting enhancement to their meetings." Dorothea helps Hilary develop another side of herself—as Hilary recalls it, "the boy in her gave way to other more feminine activities— arranging flowers, making curtains, etc." But the differences between them defy the healthy balance and instead become a source of antagonism. Dorothea's aggressive questions, her straightforward, no-nonsense attitude is at first a catalyst for Hilary's artistic creation—poems began to pour out as Hilary recalls. The "true love" they imagined, however, turns into devastating, destructive rage. "Their summer ended in mutual relief at going back to separate apartments in New York. It had been a costly indulgence in primary emotion."

The novel becomes a platform for Sarton's own struggle as a woman writer—as Sarton viewed her own situation, she saw herself as being caught between the masculine world of critical acceptance and the world of feminine domesticity. The novel was daring for Sarton's honest exploration of homoerotic desire; it represents the earliest place in her fiction where she speaks openly about love for women and moves toward less privateness in revealing the nature of her own emotional support.

The Education of Harriet Hatfield (1989), Sarton's final novel, takes the openness about her lesbian status one step farther. This portrayal of an older lesbian, Harriet Hatfield, grapples openly with issues of coming out, AIDS, harassment, and lesbian partnership. The first-person narrative written in present tense gives the prose a certain energy and gives Harriet, the speaker, a presence, an agency that is unique to this novel.

Because of a small inheritance left by her longtime companion, Vicky, Harriet Hatfield has enough capital to start a business. "Vicky never felt more at home than in a bookstore," Harriet relates to Mr. Fremont, the executor of Vicky's will. But for Harriet, the bookstore is a space for women to find themselves in books—and the adventure begins! Money means real power, and for the first time Harriet sees the possibility for her "vision" to be realized. As a history major at Smith College, Harriet was fascinated by what was emerging as "herstory," all that had been buried about women's lives in the past and was now being discovered. Harriet chooses to locate the store in a section of town that is relatively off the beaten track, in order to make it more accessible to all walks of life. Openness and accessibility, however, make Harriet vulnerable as well. Because of Harriet's willingness to share personal stories with the women who come into the store, her customers learn that Harriet is a lesbian. Attacks soon begin, and Harriet receives anonymous letters calling the books in her store pornographic. When Harriet is interviewed by the local newspaper, the resulting story focuses on Harriet's own lesbian status and the importance the storeowner places on older women coming out—rather than vilifying the letter as a form of harassment. After the story is published, Harriet receives a visit from the women's auxiliary, whose members fear gays "and their possible influence on our children."

The bigotry and cruelty converge when Harriet's dog, Patapouf, is shot by someone in the neighborhood. Hatred is frightening but also illuminating for Harriet, who has never herself felt like an outcast. Harriet reflects: "People need someone to hate—or is the homosexual ordeal partly that it threatens almost everyone. If you are black then you are black and it's quite clear you are, but if you are a homosexual you can rather easily lead a completely secret life . . . and how many people do?" Hate creates polarities: people take sides with what are seemingly opposite viewpoints. But Sarton diffuses the polarities and raises the gray issues. Rose Donovan, for example, is identified as the woman who shot Harriet's dog. At the same time, Harriet discovers that Rose has recently allowed her married son, wife, and child to move in with her and another daughter. Such a crowd in the cramped space of their small apartment would push anyone to the edge. After the killing of the dog, Rose's son wants her committed, and Harriet is infuriated at his reaction. "Women never get a break," she retorts. Despite her neighbor's prejudice and homophobia, Harriet can relate to Rose and feel compassion. Despite the harassment, Harriet stays in the neighborhood and the store feeling more free and more connected to the "outsiders," the minorities, than she ever had before.

THE POETRY

May Sarton felt that to be a poet one was chosen or called. She believed that to be a poet at all is a mystery. "It's given. . . . There is something divine in it, if you will, or something from the subconscious that you cannot control," she once told an interviewer. But for Sarton, crossing the line from conscious to subconscious did not mean creating abstract or theoretical poetry. Always her poems are rooted in the concrete—and for her, this meant finding an anchor for deep feeling in the real world around her. Thus images become very important in her poetry; in fact, Sarton once asserted that the greatest quality of a poet is to think in images. The critic Lois Rosenthal writes that "to Sarton, a poem is the result of a collision between an object and a state of awareness that registers sensation." Collision is an appropriate descriptor, for often Sarton's images present the oxymoron noted by Singrid Fowler earlier in this essay. Poetry enabled her to be in "dialogue with the self," clarifying how she felt rather than what she thought. Thus the inside and outside worlds become more personal in her poetry as literal expressions of her core, the deep levels of her unconscious. Perhaps this explains Sarton's propensity to rely on traditional rhymes and poetic forms, her own effort to place order on the emotions she grapples with. But form frees Sarton rather than restricts her.

A very early poem from her 1939 collection *Inner Landscape* introduces image in form as integral to Sarton's poetry. The poem "Landscape" opens with the assertion: "it is a different landscape to the one you know." This landscape of poetry and the inner landscape the words describe is clearly the product of deep feeling: "Here is the fire that burns through ice warmly and still, / here the mind frozen up can never intercede." But Sarton reminds her reader that poetry is not only passion, but also form that captures emotion: "Passion that takes a perfect form and stays inviolate, / spirit accompanied in the wilderness: I give you these."

Form and feeling combined permeate Sarton's first volume, *Encounter in April* (1937), which opens with a series of sonnets under the title "Encounter in April." Sarton presents a speaker longing for connection: "We came together softly like two deer." But this is also a poem of leave-taking and the grief and pain associated with it. Sarton's image of human relationship mirrors her commitment to poetry: "I have poured myself without reserve, / telling you all and holding nothing back. . . . I did it for the sake of love, my dear."

In the 1967 volume *As Does New Hampshire, and Other Poems,* the poet celebrates images rooted in New Hampshire; the poems celebrate life in a New Hampshire village: "The House in Winter," "Stone Walls," and "Minting Time," for example. Echoing Robert Frost's poetry of New England, Sarton's images represent lessons of life and death, courage and endurance. In "Stone Walls" Sarton explores issues of invention and persistence. The narrator asserts that many left New Hampshire to find the "easy plain":

Those who stayed learned to grow some rock
  inside
To build hard substance out of loss and pain.

. . . .
Stark need fostered the old inventive genius.

In another poem, "Reflections by a Fire," Sarton describes a house, but the house becomes a symbol of poetry's form that also shapes and orders the experience being described. Windows of this house "frame a world." Like poetry's sonnet or villanelle,

Windows select the form and hold it still.
Almost their shape defines the shape of thought,
That spaciousness in a small region caught.

The poet dares herself

. . . within this native shell
To live close to the marrow, weather well,
Structure the bursts of love and poetry
So that both life and art may come to be
As strict and spacious as this house to me.

A Grain of Mustard Seed (1971) adds a new sense of spaciousness to May Sarton's verse. In this volume the poet turns to the political and explores the viewpoint of the marginalized, epitomized in a clash of opposites and ironies depicted in her "Ballad of the Sixties": "For only the sick are well; / The mad alone have truth to tell."

Another poem in the collection, "The Ballad of Ruby," describes the race issues searing the nation at the time, but rather than staying on the abstract level, Sarton tells the story of prejudice's crippling effects on a young girl. Ruby is a black child psychologically pummeled by a culture that tells her that black is ugly and white is beautiful. "Her mother dressed the child in white" and "white mothers screamed 'Black scum!'" The poem explores the power of words and language, for Ruby herself begins to see black as ugly:

And when the teacher let them draw,
Ruby made all black people lame,
White people tall, strong, without flaw.

While Sarton's rhyme suggests harmony and fusion, the poem's words tell a story of self-hate and exile.

"Invocation to Kali," another poem with strong political themes, invokes the black goddess, a "built-in destroyer, the savage goddess." Kali symbolizes

> . . . this brute power
> That cannot be tamed.
>
> I am the cage where poetry
> Paces and roars.

This muse represents the strength that emerges from the hard lessons of life; as Sarton phrases it, "every creation is born out of the dark. / Every birth is bloody." Section three of the poem, entitled "The Concentration Camps," directly alludes to the ravages of the Holocaust. Sarton opens this section with a question that calls for accountability beyond the prison guards or Nazi soldiers: "Have we managed to fade [the camps] out like God? / Simply eclipse the unpurged images?" The fourth section of the poem, "The Time for Burning," interprets burning on several levels: the burning of the Holocaust victims, but also burning that implies a purging or cleansing: "It is the time of burning, hate exposed." The poem concludes with an invocation to Kali as the source of healing and forgiveness, the one who enables us to transform anger into creative change:

> Kali, be with us.
> . . . .
> To lift out the pain, the anger,
> Where it can be seen for what it is—
> The balance wheel for our vulnerable, aching love.
> Put the wild hunger where it belongs,
> Within the act of creation,
> Crude power that forges a balance
> between hate and love.

In her 1972 volume *A Durable Fire*, Sarton develops this same theme, of new growth emerging from darkness, but here she shifts from the political to the personal. The theme becomes her own story in "Gestalt at Sixty." This poem about time, aging, and solitude, opens with Sarton's disclaimer on the joy of solitude:

> I can tell you that solitude
> Is not all exaltation, inner space
> Where the soul breathes and work can be done.
> . . . .
> Who wakes in the house alone
> Wakes to moments of panic.
> . . . .
> Solitude swells the inner space
> Like a balloon.

Sarton's trepidations, however, are set against the backdrop of nature, her companion and friend for ten years. The poet calls on nature to transform her inside world of turmoil to match what she sees in the outside world that is "strong, renewable, fertile": "Learn to clear myself as I have cleared the pasture." But as a poet Sarton knows she is never really alone as she salutes her inspirations ("Yeats, Valéry stalk through this house. / No day passes without a visitation— / Rilke, Mozart"). Nature remains her constant teacher, her guide. A simple walk can represent lessons in life and death:

> Climb the long hill to the cemetery
> in autumn,
> Take another road in spring
> Toward newborn lambs.

At sixty, one recognizes that time is to be treasured: "How rich and long the hours become, / How brief the years." For Sarton, this milestone represents

> . . . moving
> Toward a new freedom
> Born of detachment,
> And a sweeter grace—
> Learning to let go.

In *Halfway to Silence* (1980), Sarton explores themes of freedom and groundedness in the opening poem, "Airs above the Ground." A sculpture of a Lipizzan horse in Central Park becomes the image through which Sarton wrestles with her own artistic creation and the nature of art's ability to depict life. The art of this horse freezes life: the "muscles look engraved . . . / A furious gallop arrested in mid-air." For Sarton, "Dressage, control create a miracle." Sarton's final stanza returns more directly to issues of writing. Just as the horse is guided through its routine, so too, is the poet guided with language:

> . . . to catch a chancy rhyme,
> And craft that may sometimes harness strange powers,
> Those airs above the ground that banish time.

Like "Airs above the Ground," another poem, "Late Autumn," fuses images of freedom and groundedness, art and nature. The poem opens with an image of autumn's endings: "On random wires the rows of summer swallows / Wait for their lift-off." Sarton's focus on "wires" and "rows," suggests a sense of order and linearity. But the poem is about lines being blurred, most obviously between life and death. In this autumnal season, Sarton recalls the feasts of All Saints and All Hallows. But both feasts commemorate saints and ghosts breaking through the safe border between life and death as they are remembered by those on earth. This is the time "[w]hen we are so transparent to the dead / There is no wall. We hear their voices speak." Nature, too, reflects the foreboding mood, with trees "naked," "dark, precarious days," and "troubled skies over tumultuous seas." What is most frightening are our own vulnerabilities in the face of death: "How to believe that all will not be lost?" Sarton turns to the solace of love to quell the fears and bridge the divided worlds: "Love, leave me your South against the frost. / Say 'hush' to my fears, and warm the night."

In *Letters from Maine* (1984) Sarton's images continue to elucidate her struggles with her own writing. Her opening poem, "Contemplation of Poussin," presents a reflection on this seventeenth-century classical painter whose work is characterized by emphasis on order, clarity, and reason, rather than the sensual. Sarton opens the poem with a description of a world in chaos—from her desk (no order even there) to the romantic impulse "stained like dirty snow." "Nothing is clear," the poet admits. The outside world reflects the disorder inside her, where all is "muddied and unclear." Reason and emotion are also split, for the tears she sheds "spring from below / Where reason cannot touch their source." "Mozart, come back," she calls. "Poussin, come to redeem." Sarton's invocation: to recapture the "Romantic impulse, classic symmetry / Married in the holistic mystery." The poet realizes that both are needed; "Without the wine, without the wild-eyed goat / Where would creation start, or generate?" Her final stanza reasserts the need for passion combined with reason in her work: "Celestial harmony would never move / Us earthlings if it had not sprung from blood."

In the long title poem of the volume, "Letters from Maine," Sarton chronicles coming home to a place, but the mood of the poem signals exile and displacement more than homecoming. The nature Sarton describes reflects a somber, more deflated Sarton: in "sad November woods," "maples are stripped," cherries paled. ". . . All the safe doors have come unlocked." This outside world mirrors the sense of desolation she feels as a writer as she calls on her muse to ". . . meet me in the silence . . . / The long silence of winter when I shall / Make poems out of nothing . . ." The poet moves through emotional upheavals, at times expressing elation at feeling connected with her muse, but often confessing to desolation when no letters arrive. For Sarton, "The muse is there / To let the kite fly as high as it can . . ."

In the preface to *Coming into Eighty* (1994), Sarton describes her love of W. B. Yeats especially because he changed his style dramatically after the age of eighty. She, too, changes her style in this, her final volume of poetry. Unlike earlier volumes, where form is important to the content, here Sarton describes poems as "minimal." This haiku-like poem, "A Thought," is a good example:

The steamroller
That crushes a butterfly
In its path has not won
Anything
Only destroyed something.

Brute power
Is not superior
To a flower.

Images in the poem are stark and focused; very simply, Sarton reimagines the definition of power. The title "A Thought" is intriguing. Is Sarton's notion of power "the thought"? Or are the flower and butterfly the thoughts that are overpowered and lost? Or is "the thought" the crushing instrument itself? Even in this final volume, Sarton's poetry sustains opposing forces, here destruction and life, beauty and power, fragility and aggression. In the title poem of the volume, "Coming into Eighty," Sarton likens herself to a ship which she slows down for a safe landing. The image of the battered, wobbly ship is a testament to eighty years of learning. But Sarton is not to be stopped. In the poem she asserts that she cannot stay anchored, that she must keep sailing, this time on one "last mysterious voyage / Everybody takes . . ."

JOURNALS, LETTERS, AND OTHER WRITINGS

In the film *World of Light,* Sarton describes solitude as her last great love. Once again, Sarton is drawn to that space in which opposites come together and interface; she remarks in the film that for her it is in solitude where the barrier between the conscious and subconscious is released. May Sarton's journals chronicle this blending of the conscious and unconscious in her own life: whether she is grappling with anger and critical rejection during her year in Nelson, New Hampshire (*Journal of a Solitude,* 1973), celebrating her move to Maine and her life by the sea that inspires her writing (*The House by the Sea,* 1977), describing the emotional upheaval that follows her stroke (*After the Stroke,* 1988), or processing the loss of her longtime companion Judith Matlock (*Recovering,* 1980). In addition to providing a space where she can work through a particular issue or emotion, Sarton's journals become a platform for her to articulate her philosophy about women and writing in general; her own insecurities and hopes for her own writing; her relationship to nature, her animals, her neighbors and friends; and the risks that her honesty and openness about her sexuality meant in her personal and professional life.

In *Journal of a Solitude* Sarton describes the year in Nelson, New Hampshire, where she moves apart "from friends, even passionate love," in order to do some serious self-questioning "about my dangerous and destructive angers." At the time she was writing this journal, Sarton was embroiled in two tumultuous relationships: one with a college educator who had begun a correspondence with Sarton about her poetry, and the other with her psychotherapist, Marynia Farnham. The volatile nature of both relationships certainly contributed to Sarton's need to retreat to Nelson, where she could explore with some distance her rage. In her journal, however, Sarton blames her anger on more professional sources: that she has not been recognized by the critics, that the critics accuse her of sentimentality, that they do not appreciate the intellect she brings to her writing. Sarton goes on to describe in a personal way why she writes: "I have written every poem, every novel, for the same purpose—to find out what I think, to know where I stand." She admits that her 1968 memoir *Plant Dreaming Deep,* also about her life in Nelson, describes buying the dilapidated farmhouse in Nelson and her efforts to repair the house itself, but Sarton recognizes that she also wants to write about an "inside" life. What she was experiencing at the time, the "anguish of my life here"—its "rages"—were never really explored. Her desire to be alone to undertake this intimidating task is not without an element of fear and risk: not knowing what will happen "when suddenly I enter the huge empty silence if I cannot find support there." In silence Sarton confronts a range of emotions: she confesses to being "close to both suicide and a mystical experience of unity with the universe"; and true to her propensity to bring such divergent worlds together, Sarton admits that these polar states resemble each other. For Sarton, solitude is "making space for that intense hungry face at the window, starved cat, starved person. . . . 'Can I trust?'" she asks. Through journal writing Sarton hopes to "break through into the rough, rocky depths, to the matrix itself."

What issues emerge that comprise this matrix? First, Sarton's need to believe in her work. She describes coming to this silence to feel the validity of her struggle: "that it is meaningful whether I ever 'succeed' as a writer or not, and that even its failures . . . can be meaningful." The struggle for Sarton can be as individual as finding the personal discipline to put order on a day of her own writing or as general as her ruminations on great writing versus best-seller writing. Great writers have had best-sellers and very great writers have not—Virginia Woolf, for example. Woolf becomes the frame for another of Sarton's reflections, on feminine art versus masculine art. In Sarton's view, one cannot pick up one of Woolf's works and read a page without feeling more alive. Later Sarton touches on this theme again, in her discussion

of women poets versus men. Sarton describes men as needing to find a persona to write through; women, instead, are far more interested in issues of self-actualization.

Sarton's journals are not limited to discussions of such esoteric topics. She confesses to the "dark moods" brought on by bad reviews or by friends who fail to respond to new collections she has published. She admits: "Now it is the old struggle to survive, the feeling that I have created twenty-four 'children' and every one has been strangled by lack of serious critical attention. . . . What a lonely business it is . . . from the long hours of uncertainty, anxiety, and terrible effort while writing such a long book *[Kinds of Love],* to the wild hopes . . . and the inevitable disaster at the end."

Neither are Sarton's journals all about writing; the political world also enters in, with entries about the Kennedy assassination in Dallas, the turbulent atmosphere of the civil rights era, the shift in race relations in the South from old southern loyalty between master and slave to a more militant black power. Sarton reflects on her book of new and more political poems, *A Grain of Mustard Seed*: "an odd book, for an odd time, the devastating sixties of the assassinations and the grinding down of hope about the war, the ghettos, the unemployed, all that plagues and haunts us."

Politics become more personal when Sarton reflects on her desire to be more honest about her sexuality. She cites Willa Cather's refusal to have letters published after her death in comparison to Virginia Woolf's open admission that *Orlando* was based on her friendship with Vita Sackville-West. For Sarton, how one lives as a private person is intimately bound in the work: "At some point, I believe one has to stop holding back for fear of alienating some imaginary reader or real relative or friend, and come out with the personal truth." About her own willingness to take risks and openly write about her homosexuality, she writes: "On the surface my work has not looked radical, but perhaps it will be seen eventually that in a 'nice, quiet, noisy way' [Mrs. Stevens Hears the Mermaids Singing] I have been trying to say radical things gently so that they may penetrate without shock."

In *The House by the Sea,* Sarton describes her first year and a half on the coast of Maine near York as "the happiest year I can remember." Paradoxically, Sarton opens the journal with a story of loss, that of putting her pet cat Scabble to sleep. The cat's death becomes the symbol for Sarton of the losses she experienced on a personal level (saying good-bye to friends in their eighties and nineties) and on a broader, more cosmic plane (witnessing decline in Europe). She mourns the "breakup about which we are helpless, which we have to witness in others, and in ourselves, year by year. How does one deal with it?"

Mourning loss becomes the focus of a later journal, *Recovering,* in which Sarton describes the impact of the death of her longtime companion and friend, Judith Matlock. Relying on her journal writing to help her "sort myself out," Sarton introduces the journal as a way to commemorate "with something better than tears." The journal chronicles her bouts with "undertows of depression," her anxiety about her work under fire by critics, who according to Sarton, have "little understanding" of her work, and her own grappling with her status as a lesbian. Another journal of healing, *After the Stroke,* also focuses on coping with loss, in this case, the loss of her health. Sarton opens her journal: "It may prove impossible because my head feels so queer and the smallest effort, mental or physical, exhausts, but I feel so deprived of my self being unable to write, cut off since early January from all that I mean about life, that I think I must try to write a few lines every day." Sarton's glorious solitude has become painful, debilitating loneliness: "I feel abandoned and desolate," she admits. But gradually through the

journal, Sarton becomes stronger; she begins her readings again, at first with some trepidation, but her confidence builds. Travels take her to a Carmelite monastery near Indianapolis, and later, to Nashville and San Antonio. Sarton celebrates an anniversary at the end of the journal, a year of getting well, and the chronicle of another kind of journey, one that took her inward. Nearing her seventy-fifth birthday, Sarton concludes: "There is much I still hope to do."

In *At Eighty-two* (1996), Sarton explores a myriad of topics, from lamenting the bombings in Bosnia, to being awestruck at the beauty of nature, from admitting to her own depressions, to remembering her mother and her own recollections of being a refugee. This journal reflects Sarton's unfaltering need for independence, her ongoing struggle with depression, and her insistence on staying active and alert despite the times she feels fearful about dependency or death. Her effort to maintain activity at times falters and, as she recognizes the breakdown of her body, she becomes despondent: "I seem to be totally absorbed now in my body and what it is doing, and this is miserable." But a little more than a week later, Sarton reports "going to go on a cheerful errand to get some white sneakers."

Sarton's journals certainly make her interior life accessible in a very overt way. But her children's book is subtler in its depiction of issues toward which the poet is drawn. Here, too, Sarton blends different worlds, specifically that of humans and animals, in *The Fur Person* (1957), a story of a cat transformed through love. But the whimsical story has an underside and, indicative of Sarton's own sense of exile, is a tale of the cat's coping with displacement, his life as an outsider, his fear of showing feelings, and the motto he lives by: don't act too attached. Initially the "Cat about Town" is presented as independent, distrustful and haughty: "glorious in conquests, but rather too thin for comfort." The cat seeks a home but is picky about where he will stay. Proud of status, he decides what is considered "unworthy" for him to eat and lives by the ten commandments of a gentleman cat: for example, he approaches his food slowly, is never hasty when choosing a housekeeper, and when frightened, looks bored. Adopted by two women known only as Gentle Voice and Brusque Voice, the cat experiences a real homecoming with just the right space, a garden, and haddock for dinner. This is a story of growing attachments; for the fur person this translates as people becoming more important than place. The women name him Tom Jones—plain but distinguished, and notable in the history of letters, suggests Brusque Voice. Tom survives a move (he was so angry!), the "great Change" when the old women have him fixed, and his transformation to a cat of peace. By the end of the story, Tom becomes "a fur person," not an ordinary cat, but a cat who is also a person, "whom human persons love in the right way, allowing him to keep his dignity, his reserve and his freedom." Homecoming, human companionship, and acceptance for who one is—all are central themes in Sarton's life that find their way into this tale of a cat and his finding a home.

A prolific letter writer, May Sarton's letters to Juliette Huxley, published in a 1999 collection called *Dear Juliette,* provides another insight into the intimate passions of May Sarton. Sarton met Juliette in the 1930s and began an affair with her husband Julian that was tolerated by Juliette. In 1948 Sarton professed her love for Juliette. Juliette withdrew from the relationship at this point, and the silence between them lasted until 1970s when Julian died and the two women resumed the correspondence. Sarton's editor Susan Sherman asserts that the author's obsession with Juliette was as a muse rather than as a sexual fascination. Sarton believed strongly in the muse's power that would inspire her to write. For Sarton, "No other woman in

her life ever again focused the world or called forth the Muse as consistently as did Juliette Huxley."

The letters give us insight into Sarton's thoughts about her writing and her hopes for achievement. Describing her first novel, *The Single Hound* (1938), Sarton writes to Juliette: "It is all the things I care about and *feel* most about now. For example, the possibility of depth and adventure in an apparently tiny scope of living." But the letters are not all about writing; woven into this love affair in letters are Sarton's ideas on politics and stories of her affairs with Muriel Rukeyser and Elizabeth Bowen, among others. She recounts to Juliette her meeting Judith Matlock during this time, the woman who represented peace and stability in Sarton's life, as opposed to the torment and passion elicited in the relationship with Juliette.

Another collection of letters appeared in 1997, entitled *May Sarton: Selected Letters 1916–1954.* Also edited and introduced by Susan Sherman, this collection illuminates Sarton's life from childhood to middle age. Even as a child, Sarton was a letter writer; she began correspondence with her parents when she was four and continued this epistolary relationship with them connected between continents. This collection includes letters to her parents, along with a voluminous collection of letters to Sarton's friends and acquaintances, including Virginia Woolf, Elizabeth Bowen, and Louise Bogan. Through the letters we get an insight into Sarton's personal world as she chronicles a range of emotions that at times takes her to near ecstasy or deep depression. A letter to her teacher Marie Closset in 1938 reads "I feel bathed in light—Dear God! What a treasure this brief life we are given." Writing to her friend S. S. Koteliansky after Virginia Woolf's death, Sarton writes: "I had so hoped I would someday do something she would like—one of the few people who mattered for work's sake, she was." Sarton also includes in these personal communiqués her own ideas on the political issues of the time, from pressures of communism to American capitalism to fear of war.

May Sarton died from a reoccurrence of breast cancer and congestive heart failure on July 16, 1995, in York, Maine; she had requested cremation and burial in the Nelson cemetery, with a phoenix as her headstone. During her active writing career, Sarton had been asked about her attraction to this image and responded, "I think I have died and been reborn quite a few times." One cannot help but think that Sarton's writing was a critical part of her rebirth, her way to communicate a vision that will remain in the memories and hearts of those who read her works. In Sarton's epigraph to her bibliography edited by Lenora Blouin, she attests to this aspiration: "It is my hope," she writes, "that all the novels, the books of poems, and the autobiographical works may come to be seen as a whole, the communication of a vision that is unsentimental, humorous, passionate, and, in the end, timeless."

Selected Bibliography

WORKS OF MAY SARTON

NOVELS

The Single Hound. Boston: Houghton Mifflin, 1938.

The Bridge of Years. Garden City, N.Y.: Doubleday, 1946.

Shadow of a Man. New York: Rinehart, 1950.

A Shower of Summer Days. New York: Rinehart, 1952.

Faithful Are the Wounds. New York: Rinehart, 1955.

The Fur Person. Illustrated by Barbara Knox. New York: Norton, 1957. Reprint, illustrated by David Canright. New York: Norton, 1978.

The Birth of a Grandfather. New York: Rinehart, 1957. Reprint, Norton, 1989.

The Small Room. New York: Norton, 1961.

Joanna and Ulysses: A Tale. Illustrated by James Spanfeller. New York: Norton, 1963.

Mrs. Stevens Hears the Mermaids Singing. New York: Norton, 1965. Reprint, with introduction by Carolyn G. Heilbrun. New York: Norton, 1974.

Miss Pickthorn and Mr. Hare: A Fable. New York: Norton, 1966.

The Poet and the Donkey. Illustrated by Stefan Martin. New York: Norton, 1969.

Kinds of Love. New York: Norton, 1970.

As We Are Now. New York: Norton, 1973.

Crucial Conversations. New York: Norton, 1975.

A Reckoning. New York: Norton, 1978.

Anger. New York: Norton, 1982.

The Magnificent Spinster. New York: Norton, 1985.

The Education of Harriet Hatfield. New York: Norton, 1989.

POETRY

Encounter in April. Boston: Houghton Mifflin, 1937.

Inner Landscape. Boston: Houghton Mifflin, 1939.

The Lion and the Rose. New York: Rinehart, 1948.

The Leaves of the Tree. Mount Vernon, Iowa: Cornell College Chapbooks, 1950.

The Land of Silence. New York: Rinehart, 1953.

In Time Like Air. New York, Rinehart, 1959.

Cloud, Stone, Sun, Vine: Poems, Selected and New. New York: Norton, 1961.

A Private Mythology. New York: Norton, 1966.

As Does New Hampshire, and Other Poems. Peterborough, N.H.: R. R. Smith, 1967.

A Grain of Mustard Seed. New York: Norton, 1971.

A Durable Fire. New York: Norton, 1972.

Halfway to Silence. New York: Norton, 1980.

Letters from Maine. New York: Norton, 1984.

The Silence Now. New York: Norton, 1988.

Coming into Eighty. New York: Norton, 1994.

NONFICTION

I Knew a Phoenix: Sketches for an Autobiography. New York: Rinehart, 1959.

Plant Dreaming Deep. New York: Norton, 1968.

Journal of a Solitude. New York: Norton, 1973.

A World of Light: Portraits and Celebrations. New York: Norton, 1976.

The House by the Sea: A Journal. New York: Norton, 1977.

Recovering: A Journal. New York: Norton, 1980.

Writings on Writing. Orono, Maine: Puckerbrush Press, 1980.

At Seventy: A Journal. New York: Norton, 1984.

May Sarton: A Self-Portrait. Edited by Martha Wheelock and Marita Simpson. New York: Norton, 1986.

After the Stroke: A Journal. New York: Norton, 1988.

Honey in the Hive: Judith Matlock, 1898–1982. Boston: Warren Publishing, 1988.

Endgame: A Journal of the Seventy-ninth Year. New York: Norton, 1992.

Among the Usual Days: A Portrait: Unpublished Poems, Letters, Journals, and Photographs. Edited by Susan Sherman. New York: Norton, 1993.

Encore: A Journal of the Eightieth Year. New York: Norton, 1993.

At Eighty-two: A Journal. New York: Norton, 1996.

CORRESPONDENCE

May Sarton: Selected Letters. Vol. 1, *1916–1954.* Edited and introduced by Susan Sherman. New York: Norton, 1997.

Dear Juliette: Letters of May Sarton to Juliette Huxley. Selected and edited by Susan Sherman. New York: Norton, 1999.

COLLECTED WORKS

Collected Poems, 1930–1973. New York: Norton, 1974.

Collected Poems, 1930–1993. New York: Norton, 1993.

CRITICAL AND BIOGRAPHICAL STUDIES

Anderson, Dawn Holt. "May Sarton's Women." In *Images of Women in Fiction: Feminist Perspectives.* Edited by Susan Koppelman Cornillon. Bowling Green, Ohio: Bowling Green University Popular Press, 1972.

Ascher, Carol, Louise DeSalvo, and Sara Ruddick,

eds. *Between Women: Biographers, Novelists, Critics, Teachers, and Artists Write about Their Work on Women.* New York: Routledge, 1993.

Blouin, Lenora. *May Sarton: A Bibliography.* Metuchen, N.J.: Scarecrow Press, 1978. 2d ed., 2000.

DeShazar, Mary. *Inspiring Women: Reimagining the Muse.* New York: Pergamon Press. 1986.

Evans, Elizabeth. *May Sarton Revisited.* Boston: Twayne, 1989.

Fowler, Singrid. "A Note on May Sarton's Use of Form." In *May Sarton: Woman and Poet.* Edited by Constance Hunting. Orono, Maine: National Poetry Foundation, 1982. Pp. 173–178.

Hunting, Constance, ed. *May Sarton, Woman and Poet.* Orono, Maine: National Poetry Foundation, 1982.

———, ed. *A Celebration for May Sarton: Essays and Speeches from the National Conference "May Sarton at Eighty: A Celebration of Her Life and Work": Westbrook College, Portland, Maine, June 11–13, 1992.* Orono, Maine: Puckerbrush Press, 1994.

Ingersoll, Earl G., ed. *Conversations with May Sarton.* Jackson: University Press of Mississippi, 1991.

Kallet, Marilyn. *A House of Gathering: Poets on May Sarton's Poetry.* Knoxville: University of Tennessee Press, 1993.

Peters, Margot. *May Sarton: A Biography.* New York: Knopf, 1997.

Rule, Jane. "May Sarton." In *Lesbian Images.* Garden City, N.Y.: Doubleday, 1975.

Schade, Edith Royce, ed. and photographer. *From May Sarton's Well: Writings of May Sarton.* Watsonville, Calif.: Papier-Mache Press, 1994.

Sherman, Susan, ed. *Forward into the Past: For May Sarton on her Eightieth Birthday.* Concord, N.H.: William B. Ewert, 1982.

Sibley, Agnes. *May Sarton.* New York: Twayne, 1972.

Swartzlander, Susan, and Marilyn R. Mumford, eds. *That Great Sanity: Critical Essays on May Sarton.* Ann Arbor: University of Michigan Press, 1992.

Wheelock, Martha, and Marita Simpson, eds. *May Sarton: A Self-Portrait.* New York: Norton, 1982.

FILMS

Saum, Karen. *She Knew a Phoenix.* Women's Media Network, 1980.

Wheelock, Martha, and Marita Simpson. *World of Light: A Portrait of May Sarton.* Ishtar Films, 1980.

—*PATRICIA M. DWYER*

Charles Simic

1938–

Since the publication of his first book in 1967, Charles Simic's poetry has generated an impressive amount of criticism—academic essays, chapters in books, dissertations, and book reviews. This eagerness on the part of critics to explore and explain Simic's poetry stems from its distinctive blend of complexity and simplicity. His ability to locate the "mystery of all that is familiar" has made him a consistently surprising and unsettling poet; and this quality, along with his accessibility of style and devotion to the lyric mode, have helped to build Simic's critical audience. Yet, as Bruce Weigl stated in his introduction to *Charles Simic: Essays on the Poetry,* "Charles Simic remains an enigma, even within the eclectic tradition of postmodern American poetry. He is a poet difficult to categorize, difficult to generalize about. . . ." Part of this difficulty stems from Simic's uniqueness within the field of American poetry. Neither traditional nor avant-garde, his poetry does not confirm the tenets of any prevailing school or camp. Eschewing rhyme and meter, complex syntax, and heightened diction, Simic fashions poems primarily from imagination, imagery, and metaphor. His originality, then, arises less from his use of language than from his poetic vision, which has been influenced by a childhood in Yugoslavia during World War II, a strong interest in surrealism, and a fascination with folklore.

Simic's background and immersion in European poetry, especially that from Eastern and Central Europe, have given him a distinct voice in English. The diction of his poems is most often simple, the syntax straightforward. By omitting verbal pyrotechnics from his poems, he has arrived at the essence of the English language, as "a few words surrounded by much silence," thus commanding a reader's close attention. Simic wants to repay that attention; interested in communicating in his poetry, he has said in an interview with Rod Steier that he writes poems in order to "remind people of their human and mortal predicament . . . to let them reexperience what is right in front of their senses . . . to restore strangeness to the most familiar aspects of existence." Indeed, his poems brim with strangeness, and many spring from his belief that "it is the ordinary, the overlooked, the quotidian, the supposedly familiar and commonplace that is the place of the miraculous, the numinous" ("Streets Strewn With Garbage," *The Uncertain Certainty,* 1985). He believes his task is finding, and illuminating, what hides in the shadows.

But Simic also writes in order to celebrate the individual, to privilege the solitary voice over the din of "the tribe." In this, as in the poetry of Walt Whitman and William Carlos Williams, Simic's work is quintessentially American— iconoclastic, individualistic, brazen. Many of Simic's poems seek to deflate and defame organized religion, governments, and the machines of history and of death, thereby perpetuating the lyric poet's championing of the individual. Throughout his career, he has been chiefly concerned with the individual's position in the midst of impersonal and dehumanizing forces. Simic's oeuvre proves the wisdom of his statement that "only through poetry can human solitude be heard in the history of humanity" ("The Minotaur Loves His Labyrinth," *The Unemployed Fortune-Teller,* 1994).

SIMIC'S LIFE AND CAREER

Born in Belgrade, Yugoslavia, on May 9, 1938, to George and Helen Simic, Charles Simic is truly "a child of History," as he states in "Fried Sausage" (in *The Unemployed Fortune-Teller*). In an interview with Sherod Santos from *The Uncertain Certainty,* he refers to himself as "the product of chance, the baby of ideologies, the orphan of history," claiming that "Hitler and Stalin conspired to make me homeless." While such an upbringing is alarmingly common in Europe, Simic's background makes him unique among American poets, whose historical and political pasts, as a whole, have not included the threat of invasion or physical displacement. As a child during World War II, Simic experienced hunger and flight, fear and arrest; he saw young amputees, "tanks, piles of corpses, and people strung from lampposts" ("Fried Sausage"); he stole food to avoid starving. Because Simic's life affects and informs his poetry in numerous and profound ways, his autobiography is unusually relevant to his poetry.

The combination of the brashness of youth and the horrors of war made for a vivid childhood, as Simic attests in several autobiographical essays, among them "In the Beginning . . ." from *Wonderful Words, Silent Truth: Essays on Poetry and a Memoir* (1990): "The Germans bombed Belgrade in April of 1941, when I was three years old. The building across the street was hit and destroyed. I don't remember anything about that bomb, although I was told later that I was thrown out of my bed and across the room when it hit." The themes of loss and violence recur throughout Simic's poetry, partly in response to the dehumanizing effects of twentieth-century politics and war. Though not a didactic poet, Simic seeks to point out that the individual is inevitably in conflict with institutions. As a child, he had more than ample opportunity to witness the enormous capacity for cruelty that human beings collectively possess. While this type of experience frequently produces disenchantment, despair, and indignation in writers, Simic has not become a solemn or negative-minded poet. In "The Minotaur Loves His Labyrinth," he writes, "It's the desire for irreverence as much as anything else that brought me first to poetry. The need to make fun of authority, break taboos, celebrate the body and its functions, claim that one has seen angels in the same breath as one says that there is no god."

This irreverent temperament has benefited Simic's poetry by enabling him to simultaneously pursue comedy and tragedy. Simic believes that "comedy says as much about the world as does tragedy. In fact, if you seek true seriousness, you must make room for both comic and tragic vision" ("Cut the Comedy," *Orphan Factory: Essays and Memoirs,* 1997). For Simic, comedy also has political ramifications: "The whole notion of hierarchy and its various supporting institutions depends on the absence of humor. The ridiculousness of authority must not be mentioned" ("Cut the Comedy"). This irreverence makes his poems refreshingly subversive and honest.

The comedy in Simic's poetry also serves as an antidote to the pain of his childhood. The poet's father, an electrical engineer for an American telephone company with business in Yugoslavia, escaped Belgrade in 1944, was arrested by the Gestapo in Italy as a spy, and was later freed by the American Army. Instead of returning to Belgrade, he stayed in Italy, eventually immigrating to the United States in 1950. In 1948 Simic left Belgrade with his mother and infant brother and surreptitiously crossed the border from Yugoslavia into Austria in an attempt to join his father in Italy. They were caught and returned to Yugoslavia, where they were arrested and passed from prison to prison for two weeks until Simic and his brother were returned to Belgrade and placed in their grandmother's custody; his mother remained in prison for four months. In 1953 she finally obtained a passport and took her sons to Paris to wait for a visa permitting them to immigrate to the United States. They lived in Paris for a year, where Simic, ignorant of French, performed poorly in school, failing every subject but drawing and music.

In 1954 Simic, his mother, and his brother joined his father in the United States. They arrived in New York, the sharp contrasts and contradictions of which immediately attracted him to American life. Simic attended Newtown High School in Queens until his father was transferred to his company's headquarters in Chicago, which "was the garage sale of all the contradictions America could contain." According to Simic, "Chicago gave me a better sense of what America was than some small town would have. Its mixture of being, at the same time, very modern and progressive and very provincial is our national specialty" ("Fearful Paradise," *Orphan Factory*). In 1956 Simic graduated from high school in Oak Park, a suburb of Chicago.

Simic started writing poems in high school in Oak Park after two of his friends admitted to writing poetry and showed Simic some of their work. He was not impressed, so he decided to write his own poems "in order to demonstrate to them how it's supposed to be done." As Simic explains in "In the Beginning," he was shocked to see that his own poems were as awful as his friends', and this puzzling situation compelled him to read more poetry and, gradually, to view poetry differently. "To be sure," he points out, "it all began with my wanting to impress my friends, but then, in the process of writing, I discovered a part of myself, an imagination and a need to articulate certain things, that I could not afterwards forget."

After graduating from high school, Simic worked as a proofreader for the *Chicago Sun Times* and attended night classes at the University of Chicago. During this period, he notes in "In the Beginning," "poetry was my secret ambition. I was getting obsessed with it. I wanted to know everything about it instantly. I read all the time." Simic's influences were wideranging and powerful: "A friend introduced me to the poems of [Robert] Lowell and [Randall] Jarrell. Another gave me the works of [Wallace] Stevens and [Ezra] Pound. At night, when I was not attending classes, I went to the Newberry Library to read the French Surrealists and literary magazines." Simic moved to New York City in 1958, and his first published poems appeared in the winter 1959 issue of *Chicago Review*. He held various jobs in New York, selling men's apparel in Stern's department store, typing address labels for New York University Press, and working at the Doubleday Bookstore, until 1961, when he was drafted into the U.S. Army. Simic received his military training at Fort Dix and Fort Gordon, and he spent two years in the Army, most of it in France—in Lunéville, Toul, and Nancy—as a military police officer and interpreter.

After his stint in the army, the twenty-five-year-old Simic returned to New York, working in the payroll office at New York University and studying for his Bachelor of Arts degree in Russian, which he received from New York University in 1966. Simic married Helen Dubin in 1964, and they lived in the city until 1970, when Simic was offered a job at California State University in Hayward. He taught for two years and then received a Guggenheim Fellowship in 1972. In 1973 he was offered a teaching position by the University of New Hampshire, where he is currently a professor of English. Simic is the father of two children, Philip and Anna Nicolleta (Nicky), and he and his wife continue to live in southern New Hampshire.

In an active career spanning three decades, Simic has achieved a substantial following among readers, critics, and other writers. His poems appear regularly in the nation's leading magazines, and he has received numerous honors for his poetry, including the 1980 di-Castagnola Award from the Poetry Society of America for *Classic Ballroom Dances* and the

1990 Pulitzer Prize for Poetry for *The World Doesn't End,* as well as fellowships and awards from the American Academy of Arts and Letters, the National Institute of Arts and Letters, the National Endowment for the Arts, and the MacArthur Foundation. All of his books have been well received by critics, the occasional attack greatly outnumbered by enthusiastic reviews.

Simic is exceptional among American poets in his devotion to and success in nonfiction prose. His essay "Reading Philosophy at Night" was selected for inclusion in *The Best American Essays 1988,* edited by Annie Dillard, and "Dinner at Uncle Boris's" appeared in *The Best American Essays 1997,* edited by Ian Frazier. In addition to substantial autobiographical pieces, Simic has written essays on insomnia, history, surrealism, Yugoslav politics, prose poetry, humor, jazz, the blues, food, and the pleasures of reading philosophy. He also has written intelligently on the poetry of Emily Dickinson, William Carlos Williams, Pablo Neruda, Octavio Paz, and Jane Kenyon, as well as on the art of Sigmund Abeles, Bata Mihailovitch, Saul Steinberg, Paul Strand, and Holly Wright. Simic has penned introductions for poetry books by Thomas Campion, Vasko Popa, Benjamin Péret, Ingeborg Bachmann, Aleksandar Ristovic, Ivan V. Lalic, Novica Tadic, and Aleš Debeljak. In addition to four collections of prose, all printed in the Poets on Poetry Series at the University of Michigan Press, he has published a book of creative art criticism, *Dime-Store Alchemy: The Art of Joseph Cornell.*

Simic is also an accomplished and acclaimed translator who has learned from translation "techniques, attention to detail," and the value of "entering somebody else's head and submitting to another's vision" ("Interview with Rod Steier"). He has submitted to the visions of some of Europe's strongest poets, among them Vasko Popa and Tomaz Salamun, and has carried the fruits of those visions into the English language. Simic's anthology *The Horse Has Six Legs* collects the work of eighteen Serbian poets, including Popa, Lalic, Ristovic, and Tadic, thereby adding even more richness to English-language poetry in the United States. Through his numerous books of poetry, prose, and translations, Simic has become one of American poetry's most significant and enduring figures.

DISMANTLING THE SILENCE, RETURN TO A PLACE LIT BY A GLASS OF MILK AND *WHITE*: THE EARLY POEMS

Proceeding from book to book, a reader sees that Simic is a remarkably consistent poet. His concerns, style, and strategies have remained similar since he started publishing; there are no radical departures, no swearings off, no formal breaks of the kind found in the work of many of Simic's peers—John Ashbery, Charles Wright, Adrienne Rich, and Louise Glück, to name just a few. Simic has not written any weak books, partly because he takes fewer large-scale risks than some other poets, but also because he has an exceptionally cohesive vision. His earlier poems differ from his later poems only in minor ways. From the beginning of his career, Simic has favored the short lyric poem; pursued comedy alongside tragedy; avoided the pitfalls of confessionalism, sentimentality, and straightforward realism; focused on the personal element of history; embraced the absurd and illogical; searched for mystery through clarity; and written exclusively in free verse. A book might offer individual surprises, but each book seems a logical companion to, or extension of, the one preceding it.

Simic's poetry is all-embracing and complex; it will not be contained in any set category. Many critics have observed the coexistence of seemingly opposed dualities in his poetry, as Andrew Zawacki pointed out in *Verse*: "Simic's poetry exists within the dark space of tension between the dull real and the wildly imaginary, between the familiar and the alien, between the hopelessly mundane and the thrillingly grotesque." This straddling of borders, along with a fondness for understatement and fragment, are what make Simic's works captivating yet resistant to conventional understanding. Although most of his poems include narratives, the poems' plots are so entwined with image and metaphor that any paraphrase necessarily omits the poems' most central elements. Simic's poetry also thwarts most searches for deeper meaning and symbols since his work, no matter how outlandish, demands to be read literally. Because his tone modulates between melancholy and exuberance, between grimness and insouciance, a reader might have difficulty pinning down the emotional tenor of a Simic poem; but his goal is to capture the intricate, ever-changing emotions of human beings, not to re-create a flat emotional register.

While Simic's focus on the self places him squarely in the tradition of Romantic poetry extending from William Wordsworth and John Keats to the poets writing in the so-called confessional mode, Simic destabilizes the lyric "I" by distorting, hiding, fracturing, and losing it. Although a recognizable personality governs his poems, his works do not present a consistent persona. Rather, they offer monologues, riddles, prophecies, prayers, histories, and cosmologies without transparently autobiographical first-person narratives.

Now that Simic has achieved so much acclaim, it is worth recalling that his early poems represented a distinctive new presence for American poetry. Introducing Simic's first full-length collection, Richard Howard wrote, "*Dismantling the Silence* reinstates an ancient wisdom, as well as an ancient fooling, which, by its presence, we suddenly realize has been absent from recent American verse—a gnomic utterance, convinced in accent, collective in reference, original in impulse." When it appeared in 1971, *Dismantling the Silence* announced a startling and singular voice in American poetry, one that apparently had absorbed an encyclopedic amount of folklore and folk wisdom. No one was writing poems like these, and many critics and fellow poets quickly took notice: Simic was immediately praised, puzzled over, and imitated.

The first poem in *Dismantling the Silence*, "Forest," announces the arrival of both the poet and the forest, which Simic personifies and speaks for. The poem highlights the primitive quality of Simic's early poems—their devotion to trees and stones, to grass and silence—while subtly forcing the reader to acknowledge the relevance of all that the poet cherishes: "There'll be plenty of time / When an acorn grows out of your ear / To accustom yourself to my ways." Like "Forest," most of Simic's early poems are concerned primarily with imagery, metaphor, and myth; they have a distinct mythic element and effectively omit other people from their sparse landscapes. As Howard's introduction also notes, "Simic's poems come to us . . . from an enormous otherness . . . wrought out of remote elements of the imagination of hinterlands, a diction tinged with menace and with grotesquerie."

One of the primary elements of Simic's early poetry is its atmosphere: menacing and grotesque, as Howard commented, but also sinister, voyeuristic, and primordial. Some poems are marked by ritualistic and historical violence, which can be metaphorical, as in "Dismantling the Silence," in which the poet exhorts the readers to physically undo silence and "slit its belly open," or can be literal, as in "Butcher Shop"— "There is a wooden slab where bones are broken, / Scraped clean." The prevalence of violence in these poems has attracted attention from critics, and Simic himself noted in *The Uncertain Certainty* that these poems "try to understand [the] origins [of violence], to see its consequences, to exorcise its demons." Despite the violence and macabre imagery of these poems, Simic frequently manages to infuse them with humor. His refusal to glorify himself results in a self-effacing posture that paradoxically fixes the poet's persona in his readers' memories: "I'm Joseph of the Joseph of the Joseph who rode on a donkey, / A wind-mill on the tongue humming with stars, / . . . I'm anyone looking for a broom closet," he writes in "Psalm" (in *Dismantling the Silence*). Though humorous and irreverent, Simic's poems generally avoid flippancy by acknowledging the weight of suffering behind them.

The world of Simic's poetry, as demonstrated so aptly by his early work, is "a world where magic is possible, where chance reigns, where metaphors have their supreme logic, where imagination is free and truthful" ("Composition," *The Uncertain Certainty*). Weigl has noted "the expansive vistas" of Simic's imagination, its ability to simultaneously establish and traverse great distances, but most critics have labeled this atmosphere Surrealist or "neo-surrealist." Simic clearly has been influenced by surrealism but claimed in an interview in *The Uncertain Certainty*: "I don't think of myself as a surrealist. . . . But I would say my greatest debt is to surrealism." This attraction to surrealism occurred early for Simic, who encountered the work of Eastern European and South American poets in the late 1950s. In Pablo Neruda's poetry, for example, he found "a freedom of the imagination that was completely absent in the American poetry I was seeing in the journals of the day" and "a way to be joyfully subversive, to be funny and serious at the same time" ("Caballero Solo," *Wonderful Words*). The Surrealists, Simic said in another interview from *The Uncertain Certainty,* "satisfied my hunger for adventure, risk. I wanted to leap out of the familiar, invent new worlds."

While Simic's poems are often fantastic, they are not technically Surrealist. Surrealist poetry makes no room for the ordinary; but in Simic's poetry, the situation is frequently ordinary, though altered through the poet's mode of perception. His poems demonstrate more interest in "the small lovely realm / of the possible" ("Ode," *Charon's Cosmology,* 1977) than in the realm of surrealism, in which randomness and chance reign. On the other hand, Simic's poems carry some of the trappings of realism, but make no attempts at mimesis. His technique of recapturing an event is to misremember in an effort to be more faithful to the event. Instead of rendering past events *factually,* he distorts and embellishes the events in order to render them *truthfully.* What many critics have identified as surrealism in Simic's poetry, then, would be more accurately termed imaginative realism.

Some of Simic's most celebrated poems from *Dismantling the Silence* and *Return to a Place Lit by a Glass of Milk* (1974) are those that focus on quotidian objects and transform them through imagination. In "Bestiary for the Fingers of My Right Hand" (from *Dismantling the Silence*), Simic creates metaphors for each of his fingers, such that his thumb becomes "loose tooth of a horse. / Rooster to his hens. / Horn of a devil." The thumb continues to change throughout the poem until it becomes a threat—"It takes four to hold him down"—and an outcast—"Cut him off. He can take care / Of himself." The other fingers have distinct, less mutable purposes: one "points the way," one "has backache," another "is mystery," and the last "takes the mote out of the eye." The metaphoric transformations the fingers undergo also depend on imagery, which is one of Simic's great strengths as a poet. Through imagery, he notes in an essay called "Images and 'Images'" in *The Uncertain Certainty,* he seeks "to reenact the act of attention." Because his images are often startling as well as vivid, he succeeds in forcing the reader to pay attention not only to the image itself—the visual—but also to the action that occurs around, and because of, the image. By packing his poems with images and metaphors, Simic simultaneously highlights and masks the poetic process: he calls attention to the making of metaphors and images and then erases his initial tracks through the multiplication of metaphors and images. This excess creates a productive friction when it rubs against the poems' sparseness of language.

While "Bestiary for the Fingers of My Right Hand" foregrounds Simic's talent for metaphor, his transformative gaze appears even more strongly in his "object" poems—"The Spoon," "Fork," "Knife," "My Shoes," "Needle," "Brooms," and "Breasts." Among these poems, "Fork" from *Dismantling the Silence* is particularly effective in altering the reader's perception of the object: "This strange thing must have crept / Right out of hell. / It resembles a bird's foot / Worn around the cannibal's neck." One of his most well-known poems, "Breasts" stands at the apex of Simic's object poetry. Collected in *Selected Poems, 1963–1983* (1985), the poem spins deliriously yet logically from metaphor to metaphor, each intended to delight the reader and honor the poem's subject. "Breasts" begins simply enough—"I love breasts, hard / Full breasts, guarded / By a button"—but builds complexity as it lays figurative language on its subject. Simic makes breasts seem forbidden, wise, physical, and spiritual. This spiritual element of "Breasts," along with its metaphoric splendor, emerge as Simic's primary achievements in the poem:

> I insist that a girl
> Stripped to the waist
> Is the first and last miracle,
>
> That the old janitor on his deathbed
> Who demands to see the breasts of his wife
> For one last time
> Is the greatest poet who ever lived.

Simic's longest poem, "White" (1972; rev. 1980, 1997), is also his most experimental, abstract and challenging work of poetry to date.

Because it consists of 240 lines in 21 distinct sections, "White" cannot be considered a long poem in the tradition of Whitman's *Leaves of Grass,* Williams' *Paterson,* and John Ashbery's *Flow Chart.* "White" is a sequence, in two parts, of 20 ten-line poems, with an envoi ("What the White Had to Say") of two twenty-line poems. The poem meditates on numerous aspects of white, which serves as a muse for Simic, who devotes his energies in the poem to seducing the muse. The paradox of "White" is that Simic simultaneously seeks and evades white, as if the search for absolute meaning required a flight from meaning. Throughout the poem, he lingers on the thresholds between silence and speech, between the abstract and the concrete; and he relies heavily on juxtaposition rather than on linearity or narrative. Simic's penchant for metaphor emerges forcefully in the poem, which explores numerous aspects of white by transforming it: white becomes "the color of the bride / And that of blindness," "bride of the first / Windless, Spring day," and a "mild nurse." White is also the color of the page onto which the poet casts language.

The poem's opening lines—"Out of poverty / To begin again"—signal a spiritual birth for a poem ultimately about the rebirth of imagination. The poet announces that he is moving from spiritual and imaginative poverty in a seemingly incongruous effort to renew his spiritual and imaginative life. In the second part of "White," Simic complicates the structure of the poem by engaging white in dialogue and using repetition to further estrange the poem from the ordinary. White begins to defeat the poet, who admits, "No use, it preceeds me / Wherever I go" [sic]; and he eventually realizes the poem has begun to obscure white instead of illuminating it: "White—let me step aside / So that the future may see you." The end of the poem offers no resolution, no answers to all the questions posed throughout the poem: "White sleeplessness, / No one knows its weight."

In its response to the poet, "What the White Had to Say," white refutes all the poet has said, every idea he has offered. White speaks in the languages of paradox and riddle: "with my tail I swing at the flies. / But there is no tail and the flies are your thoughts." Itself "the most beautiful riddle," white claims it is "the bullet / That has gone through everyone already" and "the bullet / That has baptized each one of your senses." When white asserts "the sea in which you are sinking / And even this night above it, is myself," the poet realizes he has been defeated. "White" presents Simic at his most spare and enigmatic.

CHARON'S COSMOLOGY, CLASSIC BALLROOM DANCES, AUSTERITIES, UNENDING BLUES: SIMIC'S MIDDLE PERIOD

In the poems in *Charon's Cosmology, Classic Ballroom Dances* (1980), *Austerities* (1982), and *Unending Blues* (1986), Simic becomes more forthrightly autobiographical than in his earlier poems. More populated than the earlier poems, the poems of his middle period revisit the poet's childhood and war experiences, tracing the intersections of the personal and the historical with sensitivity and boldness. What is perhaps most striking about these poems is Simic's move from the prehistory of *Dismantling the Silence* and *Return to a Place Lit By a Glass of Milk* to the twentieth century without any loss of power. His interest in the historical opens to embrace the innumerable and anonymous people who compose the backbone of history, further reinforcing his belief in the importance of the individual.

Simic's fascination with the interaction between the personal and the historical emerges in a variety of ways. In "My Weariness of Epic Proportions" from *Austerities*, he is less interested in mythological heroes—Achilles, Patroclus, "that hothead Hector"—than in an unknown girl who asks her mother for permission to go to the well "by that lovely little path / That winds through / The olive orchard." This preference for the nameless and faceless figures of history—and, in the case of this poem, mythology—reflects Simic's strong connection to the individual and his suspicion of icons of any sort.

In fact, subversion becomes a constant aspiration for Simic, who believes, "Lyric poetry remains the place where the individual asserts himself or herself against the gods and demons of history and the tribe. In that sense the lyric poem remains potentially the most subversive of literary forms" ("Aleš Debeljak," *The Unemployed Fortune-Teller*). In "Rough Outline" from *Austerities*, he illuminates the bureaucracy of political machines, which leads "the famous torturer" to deny a prisoner's fiancée's request for clemency—"I will not give back your bridegroom / He must be tortured tonight"—reminding readers that torturers and executioners, too, have orders to follow. In "Baby Pictures of Famous Dictators" from *Classic Ballroom Dances,* the poet imagines the childhood of those who later will become extremely powerful. The most striking element of these childhoods is their banality; nothing in the lives portrayed in the poem suggests what the infants will become, what they will unleash upon the world.

Simic's subversiveness arises in part from his belief that everything, even the seemingly trivial or mundane, possesses significance. The first poem of *Classic Ballroom Dances,* "The Table of Delectable Contents," is an announcement of the book's concerns, which include *"The invisible's account of the way in which it escaped from the visible"* and *"all manner of matters of little import and lethal consequence."* This focus on "matters of little import" is often what gives Simic's poems their "lethal consequence." Simic is adept at noticing the most minute detail, as when he writes in "Happy End" (from *Charon's Cosmology*): "even a stick used in childbeating / Blossomed by a little crooked road." In the title poem of *Classic Ballroom Dances,* Simic envisions quotidian actions as carefully orchestrated and beautifully executed dance steps. This vision, reminiscent of Williams' in its elevation of the ordinary to the marvelous, imbues the everyday with majesty. Thus, "Grandmothers who wring the necks / Of chickens" are as lissome as the "pickpockets / Working the crowd of the curious / At the scene of an accident." The only figures in the poem literally dancing are "the ancient lovers, cheek to cheek, / On the dancefloor," but in Simic's eyes, everyone has the capacity for gracefulness.

Simic's humor and irreverence also contribute to his subversiveness. The title poem of *Austerities* is as humorous as it is grotesque. An unspecified "they" have made a child's head "from the heel / Of a half loaf / Of black bread," but have nothing from which to make eyes, ears, or a nose. However, they use a knife to make a mouth—at least a replica of a mouth—in the child's face. This, they tell the child, should be a consolation: "You can grin, / You can eat, / Spit the crumbs / Into our faces." The black humor of the poem does not disguise or undermine the seriousness of the poverty that the poem portrays. In "Great Infirmities" from *Classic Ballroom Dances,* Simic extracts humor from a discussion of war wounds: "Everyone has only one leg. / So difficult to get around, / So difficult to climb the stairs / Without a cane or a crutch to our name." While the poem does not ridicule suffering, its refusal to, as Simic says in *Unending Blues'* "Toward Nightfall," succumb to "the weight of tragic events / On everyone's back" and its determination to find humor in the midst of pain make it both touching and disturbing. In a poem from *Austerities,* Simic engages in a discussion of historical atrocities with a friend over dinner: "It wasn't half as bad then as it is today. / In fact, the sufferings were almost lyrical in comparison." This

poem's title, "East European Cooking," emerges as ironic in that the poem is not about food at all, but about the ubiquity of history in the lives—and dinners—of East Europeans. Simic's point is that an East European meal is as much about history as it as about food.

While Simic's considerations of history can be humorous, they also emerge as grim and harrowing. "I have a certain pessimism about history that is very Balkan," he told Molly McQuade in an interview for *Publishers Weekly,* and elsewhere he has written, "I'm surprised that there is no History of Stupidity. I envision a work of many volumes, encyclopedic, cumulative, with an index listing millions of names" ("Elegy in a Spider's Web," *The Unemployed Fortune-Teller*). His interest in revising history, religious history in particular, emerges in "Begotten of the Spleen" in *Classic Ballroom Dances*: "The Virgin Mother walked barefoot / among the land mines. / She carried an old man in her arms. / The dove on her shoulder // barked at the moon." The purposes of such a vision, aside from indulging the imagination, are blasphemy and iconoclasm. Although the startling nature of such poems provides pleasure, the poet's concern with rewriting history is serious-minded. By displacing the Virgin Mary and other New Testament figures (Judas, Joseph, Peter, Mary Magdalene) and situating them in a contemporary war zone with land mines, bedpans, "German bayonets," and guard towers, Simic is making a point about the timelessness of war: the methods might change, but human violence remains a constant. The fact that much large-scale violence arises from religious disputes and hatred lends Simic's approach additional relevance.

Violence frequently lurks at the edges of Simic's poems, and the threat and actuality of war are omnipresent. In *Austerities'* "The Work of Shading," for example, the view outside a school window consists of a "stretch of weed-choked marshland / On a far side of which is a city / With a plume of black smoke." In "Prodigy," from *Classic Ballroom Dances,* the poet describes how as a boy he learned chess from a retired professor. Simic connects the pleasant memories of learning chess to the traumatic memories of the war: "I'm told but do not believe / that that summer I witnessed / men hung from telephone poles." His mother, however, tries to stop him from seeing such atrocities: "She had a way of tucking my head / suddenly under her overcoat." By linking his memories of chess to those of war, however, Simic succeeds in conquering terror through the memory of pleasure.

"Whispers in the Next Room," also included in *Classic Ballroom Dances,* presents a different kind of terror. It displays a personal situation simple in appearance but harrowing in its implications. The poem's only figure, a hospital barber, leads a lonely existence; he is "a widower, has a dog waiting / At home, a canary from a dimestore . . . / Eats beans cold from a can." The poem, divided into three quatrains, presents three sketches of the barber's life in each stanza—his profession, his home life, and his mental life. The poem's achievement is its ability to render a psychologically and emotionally complex situation in such a small space. The ending of the poem—"No one has seen me today, / Oh Lord, as I too have seen / No one, not even myself, / Bent as I was, intently, over the razor"—introduces an ontological crisis in the barber.

Other poems in Simic's middle period place him on city streets at night, navigating by "the street-light / of [his] insomnia" ("Euclid Avenue," *Charon's Cosmology*). The poet is immensely attracted to "the streets with their pawnshops, groceries, poolhalls" in "Auction" (in *Charon's Cosmology*); he wanders, later recalling strange sights: a cat and a mouse "lapping milk / From the same saucer" in "Avenue of the Americas" (in *Unending Blues*); the tarot card readers "Madame Olga and Madame Es-

meralda in spiked heels / Outside a storefront church on a windy night" in "Rosalia" (in *Austerities*); dogs serving "as ushers and usherettes" at the "Angelic Breeders Association's Millennial Company Picnic" in "Strictly Bucolic" (also in *Austerities*). Simic personifies animals in many poems, most strikingly in "Animal Acts" from *Charon's Cosmology,* which includes "rats who do calculus" and "a bedbug who suffers, who has doubts / About his existence." Similarly, in "Progress Report," rats in a maze "study the stars" and "make valentines." This focus on street life and animals becomes a constant element of Simic's poetry from this point onward.

While *Unending Blues* resembles the other books of Simic's middle period in its amplification of the poet's historical concerns, the book is his most personal to date and his first book to include tender love poems ("To Helen," "Dear Helen") and poems overtly set in New Hampshire, his home since 1973. Simic often combines the personal and the historical with quiet sincerity, as when the historian in "The Fly" (from *Unending Blues*), writing the History of Optimism in Time of Madness, "found a bit of blue sky on the day of the Massacre of the Innocents. / . . . a couple of lovers, / A meadow strewn with flowers. . . ." This historian clearly represents the poet, who shuffles through old texts and memories to locate the individual moment in history.

Unending Blues' "For the Lovers of the Absolute" conveys this dynamic between the historical and the personal. In Simic's exquisite sketch of a man and a woman in bed, the woman is "naked and stretching herself / As if still convulsed / By passionate embraces," while the man sleeps at her side. The poem is evocative and touching because of the woman's solitary sensuality and the man's obliviousness to that sensuality; but the poem's final stanza discloses the intrusion of history into this intensely personal scene: "instead of snores she hears / The distant artillery fire / That makes the blinds rattle / Ever so slightly . . . / And then she's fast asleep herself."

As personal as "For the Lovers of the Absolute" but more tonally complex, "History" (also from *Unending Blues*) shows how the lives of an ordinary couple are destroyed by history: "Then came History. He was arrested and shot." Simic parodies the attempts of literature to confront such a scene even as he makes his own attempt at confrontation: "Do they speak in heroic couplets as he's dragged away looking over his shoulder? / . . . More likely she wipes her eyes and nose with a sleeve, / Asks for a stiff drink, takes her place in the breadline." Even when confronted by tragedy, Simic implies, one must fulfill basic necessities in order to survive.

THE WORLD DOESN'T END: SIMIC AND THE PROSE POEM

The World Doesn't End (1989), Simic's only book to win the Pulitzer Prize for poetry, is also his first and only book of prose poems. The book's receipt of the Pulitzer Prize generated controversy because of its form, which inspired an open letter to the prize's board (printed in *The New Criterion,* 1989) from the poet Louis Simpson objecting to the prize going to a book of prose instead of a book of verse. Despite Simpson's objection and some critics' and poets' agreement with him, *The World Doesn't End* received mostly favorable reviews and has been reprinted eight times, further bolstering Simic's reputation as a significant and original poet.

The originality of *The World Doesn't End* stems mainly from the formal innovations Simic brings to prose poetry. His prose poems are more impressionistic and less narrative-oriented than those most familiar to American readers—those pioneered by the French symbolists and Surrealists and later modified by Americans such as Robert Bly, Russell Edson, and James

Tate. Because the book has no cumulative narrative effect, no continuity or consistent theme, it resembles a gathering of miscellanies; it is filled with the material of legend, folk tales, and dreams. This resistance to genre and generic expectations indicates Simic's creativity within the prose poem form. Describing the prose poem's relationship to established genres, he writes, "Fable, legend, creation myth, bedtime story, travel journal, epistle, diary, dream are just some of its ingredients" ("Aleš Debeljak," *The Unemployed Fortune-Teller*). In Simic's hands, the prose poem becomes either a nongenre or a new genre, depending on how one views the work within the literary tradition.

Simic has written extensively about the prose poem as a form, explaining in "The Minotaur Loves His Labyrinth": "The prose poem is the result of two contradictory impulses, prose and poetry, and therefore cannot exist, but it does." In Simic's hands, this paradox produces a highly charged, compressed prose that thwarts conventional approaches to reading both poetry and fiction, thereby establishing a new genre even as it destroys genre. For him, as he notes in "Aleš Debeljak," "the prose poem reads like a narrative but works like a lyric, since it relies on juxtaposition of images and unexpected turns of phrase." The prose poems in *The World Doesn't End* constantly court the unexpected, and Simic does not make room for the conventionally rational and logical in the book. In one piece, he writes, "The hundred-year-old china doll's head the sea washes up on its gray beach. One would like to know the story. One would like to make it up, make up many stories." *The World Doesn't End* satisfies that imaginative impulse even as it resists the rational mind's push toward comprehension, confirming Simic's belief, as recorded in "Aleš Debeljak," that "a prose poem . . . is an invitation to the imagination."

Indeed, Simic's imagination—with its knack for invention, absurdity, and impossibility—

governs *The World Doesn't End*, which ultimately emerges as a fresh approach to realism. The book presents a world where question marks appear as "greasy ropes with baby nooses," the poet and his wife spend a "week-long holiday in a glass paperweight bought at Coney Island," and "thousands of old men with pants lowered sleeping in public rest rooms" become Christ figures, martyrs with "thousands of Marias, of Magdalenas at their feet weeping." Throughout the book, the poet's perception is skewed, such that "the high heavens were full of little shrunken deaf ears instead of stars" and lizards are found wearing "ecclesiastical robes and speak[ing] French."

The diversity of approaches in *The World Doesn't End* demonstrates a number of Simic's strengths as a poet. The dramatic monologue emerges as a significant mode in the book; Simic loses, confuses, and shuffles his identity throughout: "I am the last Napoleonic soldier"; "My mother was a braid of black smoke"; "I meet other dogs with souls when I'm not lighting firecrackers in heads that are about to doze off." In some of the prose poems, he offers political commentary: "Another century gone to hell—and for what? Just because some people don't know how to bring their children up!" Elsewhere, he makes room for the satirical, as when he writes, "The time of minor poets is coming. Good-by Whitman, Dickinson, Frost. Welcome you whose fame will never reach beyond your closest family, and perhaps one or two good friends gathered after dinner over a jug of fierce red wine. . . ."

As in Simic's other books, images of war—burning cities, soldiers, poverty, starvation—are scattered throughout *The World Doesn't End* but are usually treated lightheartedly, as when Simic explains, "We were so poor I had to take the place of the bait in the mousetrap." The structure of the piece's opening line resembles that of a joke, and the scene is both horrible and hilarious. The child, inedible and therefore inessential, is used as bait for something as negligible as a mouse. The shocking image of a child in a mousetrap becomes absurd when the mouse, nibbling the child's ear, tells him, "'These are dark and evil days.'" Another piece captures the emotional impulse of a child who wants to be loved: "I was stolen by the gypsies. My parents stole me right back. Then the gypsies stole me again. This went on for some time." Simic refracts this emotional need through the absurdity of the situation, spinning it into a farcical drama.

One prose poem in particular approaches normative prose even as it retreats from rationality. A gothic narrative that revels in its own impossibility, the piece begins, "The dead man steps down from the scaffold. He holds his bloody head under his arm." The dead man then walks to the village tavern, where he "takes a seat at one of the tables and orders two beers, one for him and one for his head." The narrator of this piece, whose mother serves drinks at the tavern, then claims, "It's so quiet in the world. One can hear the old river, which in its confusion sometimes forgets and flows backwards." As the dead man reverses the course of life by continuing to walk (and drink) after death, the river forgets its own course and flows the wrong way. Both occurrences are impossible in the real world, but Simic makes such events not only possible but feasible in his writing. *The World Doesn't End* is replete with such plausible impossibilities.

THE BOOK OF GODS AND DEVILS, HOTEL INSOMNIA, A WEDDING IN HELL, WALKING THE BLACK CAT, JACKSTRAWS: SIMIC IN THE 1990s

Simic's rate of poetic production accelerated during the 1990s. He published five substantial books of poems—*The Book of Gods and Devils* (1990), *Hotel Insomnia* (1992), *A Wedding in Hell* (1994), *Walking the Black Cat* (1996), and *Jackstraws* (1999)—at regular intervals, such that the longest gap between books was three years. The books themselves are longer than most of Simic's earlier books, varying between 66 and 85 pages (his books of the previous decade varied between 47 and 64 pages). Whether or not Simic wrote more in the 1990s than in other decades is unclear, but he preserved more poems from that decade than from any other. The result is an incomparably rich and cohesive group of books.

The predominant tones of Simic's later poems are informed by melancholy, angst, nostalgia, fear, and desire. Because of his wish to write less oblique, more straightforwardly autobiographical poems, the later poems employ more narrative techniques than his earlier poems, thus resembling vignettes and anecdotes. History becomes less a presence than a subject, and mortality preoccupies the poet toward the end of the 1990s.

In *The Book of Gods and Devils* Simic returns to the New York City of the early 1960s in an effort to re-create the sense of amazement he felt while living there. Because "New York City is much too complex a place for just one god and one devil," as Simic wrote in "The Minotaur Loves His Labyrinth," he turns from the Christian notion of one God toward a more pagan attitude. Simic has commented on this pagan aspect of the book in his interview with McQuade: "Pagans would invent gods or demons for any place where people had intense experiences. A big city is a home of multiple gods, not just the obvious religions." Throughout *The Book of Gods and Devils,* then, Simic sees gods everywhere, and they are likely to be devils in disguise or cheap, mass-produced statues. Nevertheless, the book is less sinister, more affirmative than its title suggests, mainly because the poet is "thinking constantly of the Divine Love and the Absolute" ("The Initiate"). Simic himself told McQuade: "I don't think the demons are very strong in the book; there is a lot of humor, and there are a lot of gods."

The primary drama of *The Book of Gods and Devils* is that of a narrator on a destinationless odyssey, constantly wandering, solitary and on foot, through New York City at night. Writing of cities in Simic's poems, including New York, Suzanne Matson described them in an article for *Harvard Review* as "places of dislocation, a landscape where the self wanders lost in quest of companionship (real or imagined), the satiation of hungers both philosophical and carnal, and a hoped-for glimpse of the sacred or at least the novel." Therefore, the reader finds the poet squatting in an abandoned factory, sleeping in the public library's reading room and on a park bench, reading "in a dingy coffee shop / With last summer's dead flies on the table" ("Shelley"), and listening to Thelonious Monk at the Five Spot. An habitué of store windows and shopfronts, Simic passes St. John of the Cross on the street and meets a bag lady who claims to be Venus. "Everyone I met / Wore a part of my destiny like a carnival mask," he writes in "St. Thomas Aquinas." Simic's encounters transform ordinary, sometimes grimy urban scenes into sites of magic and bliss. He seeks to honor everything in his poems—rats and insects as well as beggars and drunks—and he joins the beautiful and the grotesque so powerfully that a boundary between the two categories is no longer distinct in the reader's mind. *The Book of Gods and Devils* also continues Simic's long-standing preoccupation with history, which "practic[es] its scissor-clips / In the dark, / So everything comes out in the end / Missing an arm or a leg" ("Frightening Toys"). In the poem "Marching Music" from the same collection, Simic asserts, "Our history is both tragic and comic," echoing earlier writings.

Simic has immortalized his insomnia in earlier poems ("The Traveling Theater of My Insomnia" in *Unending Blues,* for example) and essays, but he gives it full coverage in *Hotel Insomnia,* in which he convenes "The Congress of the Insomniacs" and exclaims (in "Caged Fortuneteller"), "Sleeplessness, you're like a pawnshop / Open late / On a street of failing businesses." Insomnia skews the poet's perceptions, so in "Place at the Outskirts" a waitress becomes "Aphrodite with arms missing dressed as a nun" and Poseidon is the night clerk at the Hotel Starry Sky. Other characters in the book include a six-legged dog and an artist who wears candles in his hat in order to paint the sea in the dark. Given the book's title and Simic's fondness for invention, it is open for conjecture whether these figures are real or are projections of the poet's insomnia.

In *Hotel Insomnia* Simic continues to elevate dross to divinity, writing from "here where flames rise from trash barrels, / And the homeless sleep standing up" ("Lost Glove"). The poems can be ominous, especially when Simic confronts spiritual issues, as he does in "The Old Word": "I believe in the soul; so far / It hasn't made much difference." His works can be harrowing, as well. In "Missing Child," the poet addresses the child from a poster he saw twenty years ago and admits to thinking of the child and "the growing horror of the truth" of the child's death. In "War" he finds that "all our names are included" on the list of casualties of an unnamed war. But Simic also focuses on ephemeral pleasures—food, wine, sex—the fugitive moments that comprise a life.

Although *Hotel Insomnia* contains many unsettling poems, *A Wedding in Hell* emerges as Simic's darkest book, the poet more openly political and despairing than ever before. In "Dream Avenue," for example, he addresses himself as "nothing / But a vague sense of loss, / A piercing, heart-wrenching dread / On an avenue with no name." And in "The World," he writes, "You who torture me / Every day / With your many cruel instruments, / I'm about to confess to / A despair / Darker than all your darkest / Nights" A cloud of disillusionment hangs over the

poems, leading Simic to lament, "we put all / Our trust into the world / Only to be deceived."

The angst in *A Wedding in Hell* arises from the violence surrounding Simic, in life and on television. The poet casts himself against a desolate, sinister backdrop in which "one is always speaking from / Underneath a pile of fresh corpses" ("Grim Contingencies"). In "Raskolnikov," a poem addressed to the homicidal hero of Fyodor Dostoyevsky's *Crime and Punishment,* Simic explains, "Philosophical murderer, times are propitious / For your edifying experiments. / Even in the sunlight the world looks evil." The world does look evil in *A Wedding in Hell,* which is full of menacing images. In "Psalm," Simic consults God on the century's atrocities: "You've been a long time making up your mind, / O Lord, about these madmen / Running the world. Their reach is long / And their claws must have frightened you." Other explicitly political poems in this collection include "Men Deified Because of Their Cruelty," "Paper Dolls Cut Out of a Newspaper," "At Sunset," "Dark TV Screen," "Documentary," and "Empires."

But Simic also makes room for pleasure in *A Wedding in Hell,* whether celebrating sexuality in "Crazy about Her Shrimp," "Transport," and "Divine Collaborator," or revising the crucifixion scene in "Haunted Mind" so it occurs "in a neighborhood dive" with "the Beast of War / Lick[ing] its sex on TV" and "Mary sitting in old Joe's lap, / Her crazy son in the corner / With arms spread wide over the pinball machine." In "The Massacre of the Innocents" Simic describes how he "felt joy / Even at the sight of a crow circling / As [he] stretched out on the grass / Alone now with the silence of the sky." Such moments, though infrequent, become increasingly important to the poet.

With his two most recent books, *Walking the Black Cat* and *Jackstraws,* critics have expressed ambivalence about Simic's prolificness and consistency, acknowledging his accomplishments while wishing for more risk-taking. Paul Breslin, reviewing *Walking the Black Cat* for *Poetry,* commented, "On the whole I have the sense of a style running on automatic pilot, the urgencies that once called it into existence largely forgotten." But most critics have been more forgiving, as when Jason Whitmarsh asserted, "Even when his quirks become characteristic (in a Simic poem, it's always night, the palette is gray, and the bugs are worth talking to), their deft arrangement continues to illumine." Some poems not only give the impression of revisiting old terrain, but do so literally. The first line of *"El libro de la sexualidad"* in *Jackstraws*—"The pages of all the books are blank"—is lifted from the beginning of "Green Lampshade" in *Classic Ballroom Dances*—"All the pages of all the books / are blank." Elsewhere in *Jackstraws,* "My Little Utopia" revises a poem of the same title from *Classic Ballroom Dances,* "Mother Tongue" is a shorter version of the "Mother Tongue" in *Return to a Place Lit by a Glass of Milk,* and the title poem revises a poem called "Jackstraws" in *Austerities.*

Walking the Black Cat and *Jackstraws* differ from Simic's previous books primarily in the poet's increased focus on himself. He frequently casts himself as a pariah, speaking mainly to birds, cats, dogs, and ghosts. Even mirrors avoid his gaze. Throughout *Jackstraws,* he spends much time in rooms "unused to the sound of a voice" ("Vacant Rooms") and claims, "The world beyond / My window has grown illegible, / And so has the clock on the wall" ("Private Eye"). Owner of "a garden with nothing / But barbed wire and cinder blocks" ("The Father of Lies"), Simic's persona becomes paranoid—"These hunches I get, cold shivers / At the way the light / Makes bloodstains on the house wall, / I'm scared to trust a sparrow, / I won't come near the cat" ("Winter Evening," *Walking the Black Cat*)—as well as pessimistic—"Even the rats when they die / Are going to a better world" ("The Preacher Says," *Walk-*

ing the Black Cat). By writing himself as a pathetic figure, Simic has found a refreshing approach to tragicomedy, and his willingness to ridicule himself results in some of his funniest poems to date.

Despite all this attention to the self, Simic persists in confronting history, accusing it of gluttony in *Walking the Black Cat*'s "An Address with Exclamation Points": "O History, cruel and mystical, / You ate Russia as if it were / A pot of white beans cooked with / Sausage, smoked ribs and ham hocks!" The opening line of "What the Gypsies Told My Grandmother While She Was Still a Young Girl"—"War, illness and famine will make you their favorite grandchild"—is just the first item in a catalog of hardship and miseries. In "Modern Sorcery" (from *Jackstraws*) he realizes he "could have been just another maggot / Squirming over history's roadkill"; and in "Cameo Appearance" (from *Walking the Black Cat*) he explains, "I had a small, nonspeaking part / In a bloody epic. I was one of the / Bombed and fleeing humanity." Such imaginative approaches to his obsession with history keep the subject from becoming tiresome over the course of many books.

A more recent obsession—the poet's own mortality—emerges in *Jackstraws,* in which Simic speaks to God more than in any other book. Simic is, predictably, not very reverent, as when he addresses God as "Boss of all bosses of the universe, / Mr. know-it-all, wheeler-dealer, wire-puller" in "To the One Upstairs." As "The Gang of Mirrors" demonstrates, Simic will not remain placid in the face of his own mortality:

And the one that's got it in for you,
That keeps taunting you
In an old man's morning wheeze
Every time you so much as glance at it,
Or blurt something in your defense,
Screaming, raising your chin high,
While it spits and chokes in reply.

One of Simic's most emotive poems, "The Friends of Heraclitus" from the collection *Walking the Black Cat,* reacts to a friend's recent death. The poet, after expressing sadness over his friend's absence, notes, "The world we see in our heads / And the world we see daily, / So difficult to tell apart / When grief and sorrow bow us over." More accustomed to being bowed over by laughter, Simic, and his readers with him, are increasingly moved by the "grief and sorrow" of everyday existence.

Selected Bibliography

WORKS OF CHARLES SIMIC

POETRY

What the Grass Says. Prints by Joan Abelson. San Francisco: Kayak Press, 1967.

Somewhere among Us a Stone Is Taking Notes. San Francisco: Kayak Press, 1969.

Dismantling the Silence. Introduction by Richard Howard. New York: George Braziller, 1971.

White. New York: New Rivers Press, 1972. Rev. ed., Durango, Colo.: Logbridge-Rhodes, 1980.

Return to a Place Lit by a Glass of Milk. New York: George Braziller, 1974.

Charon's Cosmology. New York: George Braziller, 1977.

Classic Ballroom Dances. New York: George Braziller, 1980.

Austerities. New York: George Braziller, 1982.

Shaving at Night: Poems. Woodcuts by Helen Siegl. San Francisco: Meadow Press, 1982. (Limited edition.)

The Chicken without a Head: A New Version. Portland, Ore.: Trace Editions, 1983. (Limited edition of a single poem.)

Weather Forecast for Utopia and Vicinity: Poems 1967–1982. Barrytown, N.Y.: Station Hill Press, 1983.

Selected Poems, 1963–1983. New York: George Braziller, 1985. Rev. and exp. ed., 1990.

Unending Blues. New York: Harcourt Brace Jovanovich, 1986.

The World Doesn't End. New York: Harcourt Brace Jovanovich, 1989.

The Book of Gods and Devils. New York: Harcourt Brace Jovanovich, 1990.

Hotel Insomnia. New York: Harcourt Brace Jovanovich, 1992.

A Wedding in Hell. New York: Harcourt Brace & Company, 1994.

Frightening Toys. London: Faber, 1995. (Selected poems from *Unending Blues, The World Doesn't End, The Book of Gods and Devils,* and *Hotel Insomnia.*)

Walking the Black Cat. New York: Harcourt Brace & Company, 1996.

Looking for Trouble. London: Faber, 1997.

Jackstraws. New York: Harcourt Brace & Company, 1999.

Charles Simic: Selected Early Poems. New York: George Braziller, 1999.

BOOKS OF PROSE

The Uncertain Certainty: Interviews, Essays, and Notes on Poetry. Ann Arbor: University of Michigan Press, 1985.

Wonderful Words, Silent Truth: Essays on Poetry and a Memoir. Ann Arbor: University of Michigan Press, 1990.

Dime-Store Alchemy: The Art of Joseph Cornell. Hopewell, N.J.: Ecco Press, 1992.

The Unemployed Fortune-Teller: Essays and Memoirs. Ann Arbor: University of Michigan Press, 1994.

Orphan Factory: Essays and Memoirs. Ann Arbor: University of Michigan Press, 1997.

A Fly in the Soup: Memoirs. Ann Arbor: University of Michigan Press, 2000.

UNCOLLECTED PROSE

"And What Would Groucho Marx Do with His Cigar?" *Harvard Review* 13:183 (fall 1997).

"From *Notebooks 1996–1997.*" *Harvard Review* 13:166–169 (fall 1997).

"Who Cares?" *New York Review of Books,* October 21, 1999, p. 16.

"Anatomy of a Murderer." *New York Review of Books,* January 20, 2000, pp. 26–29. (Review of *Milosevic: Portrait of a Tyrant,* by Dusko Doder and Louise Branson.)

"Forgotten Games." *New York Review of Books,* April 27, 2000, pp. 4–7. (Review of *Joseph Cornell: Stargazing in the Cinema,* by Jodi Hauptman.)

TRANSLATIONS BY SIMIC

Fire Garden, by Ivan V. Lalic. New York: New Rivers Press, 1970.

The Little Box, by Vasko Popa. Washington, D.C.: Charioteer Press, 1970.

Homage to the Lame Wolf: Selected Poems, 1956–1975, by Vasko Popa. Oberlin, Ohio: Oberlin College Press, 1979. Rev. and exp. ed., 1987.

Roll Call of Mirrors: Selected Poems of Ivan V. Lalic, by Ivan V. Lalic. Middletown, Conn.: Wesleyan University Press, 1988.

Some Other Wine and Light, by Aleksandar Ristovic. Washington, D.C.: Charioteer Press, 1989.

The Bandit Wind, by Slavko Janevski. Takoma Park, Maryland: Dryad, 1991.

The Horse Has Six Legs: An Anthology of Serbian Poetry. Edited by Charles Simic. St. Paul, Minn.: Graywolf Press, 1992.

Night Mail: Selected Poems, by Novica Tadic. Oberlin, Ohio: Oberlin College Press, 1992.

Devil's Lunch: Selected Poems, by Aleksandar Ristovic. London: Faber, 1999.

Feast, by Tomaz Salamun. New York: Harcourt, 2000.

WORKS EDITED

Four Yugoslav Poets. Northwood Narrows, N.H.: Lillabulero Press, 1970.

Another Republic: 17 European and South American Writers. With Mark Strand. New York: Ecco Press, 1976.

The Essential Campion. New York: Ecco Press, 1988.

The Selected Poems of Tomaž Šalamun. New York: Ecco Press, 1988.

The Best American Poetry 1992. New York: Scribners, 1992.

The Horse Has Six Legs: An Anthology of Serbian Poetry. Trans. by Charles Simic. St. Paul, Minn.: Graywolf Press, 1992.

Mermaids Explained: Poems, 1976–1996, by Christopher Reid. New York: Harcourt, 2001.

CRITICAL AND BIOGRAPHICAL STUDIES

Atwan, Robert. *Los Angeles Times Book Review,* December 7, 1986, p. 8. (Review of *Unending Blues.*)

Avery, Brian C. "Unconcealed Truth: Charles Simic's *Unending Blues.*" In *Charles Simic: Essays on the Poetry.* Edited by Bruce Weigl. Ann Arbor: University of Michigan Press, 1996. Pp. 73–95.

Baker, David. "On Restraint." *Poetry* 168, no. 1:36–38 (April 1996). (Review of *A Wedding in Hell.*)

Banks, Russell. "Schooldays." *Harvard Review* 13:21–22 (fall 1997).

Barr, Tina. "The Poet as Trickster Figure: Charles Simic's Pack of Cards." *Harvard Review* 13:84–93 (fall 1997).

Barwell, Jay. "Charles Simic: Visions of Solitude." *Manassas Review* 1, no. 2:33–44 (winter 1978). Reprinted in Bruce Weigl's *Charles Simic: Essays on the Poetry.* Ann Arbor: University of Michigan Press, 1996. Pp. 172–182.

Bond, Bruce. "Immanent Distance: Silence and the Poetry of Charles Simic." *Mid-American Review* 8, no. 1:89–96 (1988). Reprinted in Weigl's *Charles Simic: Essays on the Poetry.* Pp. 156–163.

Breslin, Paul. *Poetry* 170, no. 4:226–228 (July 1997). (Review of *Walking the Black Cat.*)

Buckley, Christopher. "Sounds That Could Have Been Singing: Charles Simic's *The World Doesn't End.*" In *Charles Simic: Essays on the Poetry.* Edited by Bruce Weigl. Pp. 96–113.

Corbett, William. *Poets and Writers Magazine* 24, no. 3:30–35 (May–June 1996). (Interview with Simic.)

———. "We'll Talk." *Harvard Review* 13:23–25 (fall 1997).

Delville, Michel. "Unreal Miniatures: The Art of Charles Simic." In his *The American Prose Poem: Poetic Form and the Boundaries of Genre.* Gainesville: University Press of Florida, 1998. Pp. 169–181.

deNiord, Chard. "He Who Remembers His Shoes, Charles Simic." *Harvard Review* 13:77–83 (fall 1997).

Dobyns, Stephen. "Some Happy Moments, Some Very Tall Language." *New York Times Book Review,* October 18, 1987, p. 46. (Review of *Unending Blues.*)

Dooley, David. Review of *Selected Poems, 1963–1983* and *The World Doesn't End. Hudson Review* 44, no. 1:157–159 (spring 1991).

Doreski, William. "Dusty Storefronts, Rooms Far Back in Time." *Harvard Review* 13:35–46 (fall 1997).

Duffin, K. E. "The Voyeur and the Prisoner: Simic's Windows." *Harvard Review* 13:64–76 (fall 1997).

Flamm, Matthew. "Impersonal Best: Charles Simic Loses Himself." *Village Voice Literary Supplement,* December 1986, pp. 18–19. Reprinted in Weigl's *Charles Simic: Essays on the Poetry.* Pp. 164–171.

Ford, Mark. "The Muse as Cook." *Times Literary Supplement,* July 7, 1995, p. 15. (Review of *Frightening Toys* and *The Unemployed Fortune-Teller.*)

Guimond, James. "Moving Heaven and Earth." *Parnassus: Poetry in Review* 1, no. 1:114–115 (fall/winter 1972). (Review of *White.*)

Hart, Henry. "Story-tellers, Myth-makers, Truth-sayers." *New England Review* 15, no. 4:201–203 (fall 1993). (Review of *The Book of Gods and Devils.*)

Hart, Kevin. "Writing Things: Literary Property in Heidegger and Simic." *New Literary History* 21, no. 1:199–214 (autumn 1989).

Haviaras, Stratis. "Charlie Simic at Large." *Harvard Review* 13:4–7 (fall 1997).

Henry, Brian. Review of *Jackstraws. Boston Review* 24, no. 3–4:49–50 (summer 1999).

Hirsch, Edward. "Joseph Cornell: Naked in Arcadia." *New Yorker,* December 21, 1992, pp. 130–135. (Review of *Dime-Store Alchemy.*)

Ignatow, David. Review of *Charon's Cosmology. New York Times Book Review,* March 5, 1978, pp. 14, 34.

Kirby, David. "Life's Goofy Splendors." *New York Times Book Review,* December 23, 1990, p. 16. (Review of *The Book of Gods and Devils.*)

Libby, Anthony. "Gloomy Runes and Loony Spoons." *New York Times Book Review,* January 12, 1986, p. 17. (Review of *Selected Poems, 1963–1983.*)

Limehouse, Capers, and Megan Sexton. "Visionary Skeptic: An Interview with Charles Simic." *Atlanta Review* 2, no. 1:23–36 (fall 1995).

Longinovic, Tomislav. "Between Serbian and English: The Poetics of Translation in the Works of Charles Simic." *Modern Poetry in Translation,* n.s., 3:167–174 (1993). Reprinted in Weigl's *Charles Simic: Essays on the Poetry.* Pp. 148–155.

Matson, Suzanne. "Strange Cities." *Harvard Review* 13:47–50 (fall 1997).

McClatchy, J. D. "Figures in the Landscape." *Poetry* 138, no. 4:235–236 (July 1981). (Review of *Classic Ballroom Dances.*)

McQuade, Molly. "Charles Simic." *Publishers Weekly,* November 2, 1990, pp. 56–57.

———. "Real America: An Interview with Charles Simic." *Chicago Review* 41, nos. 2–3:13–18 (1995).

Milburn, Michael. "An Interview with Charles Simic." *Harvard Review* 13:156–165 (fall 1997).

Morris, Daniel. "'My Shoes': Charles Simic's Self-Portraits." *Auto/Biography Studies* 11, no. 1:109–127 (1996).

———. "Responsible Viewing: Charles Simic's *Dime-Store Alchemy: The Art of Joseph Cornell.*" *Papers on Language and Literature* 34, no. 4:337–357 (fall 1998).

Plumly, Stanley. "Of Lyricism, Verbal Energy, the Sonnet, and Gallows Humor." *Washington Post Book World,* November 2, 1980, pp. 10–11. (Review of *Classic Ballroom Dances.*)

Schmidt, Peter. "*White:* Charles Simic's Thumbnail Epic." *Contemporary Literature* 23:528–549 (fall 1982).

———. "Notes on Charles Simic's New *White* (1997)." *Harvard Review* 13:138–148 (fall 1997).

Shaw, Robert B. "The Long and the Short of It." *Poetry* 119:351–352 (March 1972). (Review of *Dismantling the Silence.*)

———. "Life among the Cockroaches." *New Boston Review* 6, no. 2:27–29 (March–April 1981). Reprinted in Weigl's *Charles Simic: Essays on the*

Poetry. Pp. 55–61. (Review of *Classic Ballroom Dances.*)

Spalding, J. M. "Interview." *Cortland Review,* www.cortlandreview.com/issuefour/interview4.htm.ne, August 1998.

Stitt, Peter. "Imagination in the Ascendant." *Poetry* 142, no. 1:46–48 (October 1983). Reprinted in Weigl's *Charles Simic: Essays on the Poetry.* Pp. 68–69. (Review of *Austerities.*)

———. "Staying at Home and Going Away." *Georgia Review* 60, no. 2:564–567 (summer 1986). (Review of *Selected Poems, 1963–1983.*)

———. "Poetry in a Time of Madness." In his *Uncertainty and Plenitude: Five Contemporary Poets.* Iowa City: University of Iowa Press, 1997. Pp. 86–118.

Vendler, Helen. "Totemic Sifting." *Parnassus: Poetry in Review* 18, no. 2:86–99 (fall 1993). Reprinted in Weigl's *Charles Simic: Essays on the Poetry.* Pp. 119–132. (Review of *The Book of Gods and Devils, Dime-Store Alchemy,* and *Hotel Insomnia.*)

———. "The Voice at 3 A.M." *New York Review of Books,* June 10, 1999, pp. 24–27. (Review of *Jackstraws.*)

Weigl, Bruce. *Charles Simic: Essays on the Poetry.* Ann Arbor: University of Michigan Press, 1996.

———. "Simic and Whitman at Northwood." *Harvard Review* 13:26–31 (fall 1997).

Whitmarsh, Jason. Review of *Jackstraws. Verse* 16, no. 3, and 17, no. 1:199–202 (2000).

Williamson, Alan. Review of *Charon's Cosmology. Poetry* 133, no. 2:103–105 (November 1978).

———. "Pasts That Stay Present." *New York Times Book Review,* May 1, 1983, pp. 15, 34. (Review of *Austerities.*)

Wood, Susan. *Review of Classic Ballroom Dances. Washington Post Book World,* December 11, 1977, p. E6.

Zawacki, Andrew. Review of *Frightening Toys.Verse* 12, no. 3:114–116 (1995).

Zeidner, Lisa. *Review of Hotel Insomnia.* New York Times Book Review, March 21, 1993, p. 14.

Zweig, Paul. *Review of Return to a Place Lit by a Glass of Milk. Village Voice,* April 4, 1974, pp. 33–34.

BIBLIOGRAPHY
Avery, Brian C. F. "A Simic Bibliography." *Harvard Review* 13:170–180 (fall 1997).

—BRIAN HENRY

Gary Snyder

1930–

GARY SNYDER WAS born on May 8, 1930, in San Francisco, California, to Harold Snyder and Lois Wilkie Snyder. Growing up during the Great Depression in the Pacific Northwest, Snyder moved often during his early life, as his father struggled to earn a living. In 1932 his family moved to the country near Lake City, Washington, to start a small dairy. Ten years later, they moved to Portland, Oregon. During his childhood Snyder often camped in the woods around his home, and from the age of thirteen he began to explore the high country of the Cascade Mountains; his love of the wilderness would remain with him throughout his life.

In 1947 Snyder began undergraduate study at Reed College in Portland; he majored in literature and anthropology and became involved with a literary group whose members worked on the student magazine *Janus,* in which his first poems appeared in 1950. During summers while in college he worked on trail crews and in logging and forest service jobs. In 1951 Snyder graduated from Reed after writing his senior thesis on a North American Indian myth (published in 1979 as *He Who Hunted Birds in His Father's Village: The Dimensions of a Haida Myth*), and in the fall he began a graduate program in linguistics at Indiana University. He stayed at Indiana only a semester, moving to San Francisco in the spring of 1952. In 1953 he enrolled as a graduate student in East Asian languages at the University of California at Berkeley, and in the summers he worked as a lookout in Mount Baker National Forest and on a trail crew in Yosemite National Park—jobs that provided him with material for his poems and deepened his respect for the environment.

THE SAN FRANCISCO RENAISSANCE

In the mid-1950s Snyder was a vigorous participant in the countercultural poetry scene in San Francisco, which came to be popularized (and homogenized) as the beat movement. He subsequently attempted to distance himself from the label "beat," noting in his essay "North Beach" (collected in *The Old Ways: Six Essays,* 1977) that "this emphasis often neglected the deeply dug-in and committed thinkers and artists of the era who never got or needed much media-fame." His persona as a beat is based largely on his appearance as the protagonist Japhy Ryder in Jack Kerouac's 1958 novel *The Dharma Bums.* Despite its mythic dimensions, Kerouac's portrait of Snyder is accurate in some respects: Snyder *was,* as the novel pronounces him to be, a "woods boy, an axman, farmer, interested in animals and Indian lore so that when he finally got to college . . . he was already well equipped for his early studies in anthropology and later in Indian myth." Although at times reticent about his beat past, Snyder freely acknowledges his role in the San Francisco renaissance—a period in which artists expressed their disaffection with the materialism of the dominant culture by rejecting traditional poetic forms and themes.

In 1955 Snyder met Allen Ginsberg and Jack Kerouac in San Francisco and lived for a time with Kerouac in a cabin in Mill Valley. On October 13, 1955, a landmark poetry reading was organized at the Six Gallery in San Francisco. At that auspicious event, Snyder performed his poem "A Berry Feast." In addition to Snyder, the evening featured local poets Kenneth Rexroth (as emcee), Michael McClure, Philip Whalen, Philip Lamantia, and Ginsberg, who read "Howl" for the first time in public. As Snyder remembers in "Poetry, Community and Climax," a text based on talks he gave at Oberlin College and Brown University in 1978 (collected in 1980 in *The Real Work: Interviews and Talks, 1964–1979*), that reading "was a curious kind of turning point in American poetry. . . . Poetry suddenly seemed useful in 1955 San Francisco." As a result of that poetry reading and those it spawned across the country, Snyder was encouraged that the deleterious effects of modern industrial life could be counteracted, since to him the public performance of poetry represents a return to the roots of poetry in primitive culture. As he stated in a 1964 interview with Gene Fowler ("The Landscape of Consciousness," collected in *The Real Work*), "A reading is a kind of communion. I think the poet articulates the semi-known for the tribe. This is close to the ancient function of the shaman." Indeed, Snyder believes that the cultural work of oral poetry constitutes one of the richest legacies of the beats. In 1992 he told Eliot Weinberger (in an interview collected in *The Gary Snyder Reader*, 1999), that such work involves "the building of something closer to a mass audience."

Snyder's desire to fashion such a popular poetry marks a turn away from the elitist poetics of high modernism as exemplified by such figures as T. S. Eliot and Ezra Pound. Chafing at the modernist cult of difficulty, Snyder affirmed in the 1992 interview with Weinberger that "there's a percentage of my poetry—maybe twenty-five percent, maybe forty—that is accessible. I think partly that has been a function of my regard for the audience, my desire to have some poems that I knew that I could share with people I lived and worked with." This democratic sensibility is consistent with the beat poet Lawrence Ferlinghetti's call in his "Populist Manifesto" for a poetry with a "public surface"—that is, a poetry that may include depths of expression but that also can be easily grasped and enjoyed by a general audience in performance. Snyder's enthusiasm about the oral mode of poetry has led the critic Michael Davidson to fault him for his "logocentrism": "Snyder's view of orality (one that he shares with many other contemporary poets) fails to account for the degree to which 'voice' is also a product—as well as a vehicle—of specific Western traditions based on the need for a self-sufficient, unitary ego." However, if Snyder does suffer from a belief in the primacy of the spoken word, he departs from many Western traditions and values in his reach across the Pacific to Far Eastern cultures and practices in his poetry and theory of poetry.

BORDER CROSSING: OPEN-FORM POETICS

Like his beat colleagues, Snyder experimented with new formal arrangements and mythologized poetic voice in part under the influence of the poet Charles Olson's 1950 essay "Projective Verse." In that statement of his poetics, Olson recalls attention to the audible units of syllable and line ("the line comes from the breath, from the breathing of the man who writes, at the moment that he writes"), arguing that projective or open verse provides a "script to its vocalization," with the entire page seen as a field on which to compose. Olson's poetic theory takes aim not only at traditional modes of formatting but also at traditional modes of grammar, as he observes that "the conventions which logic has forced on syntax must be broken open as quietly as must the too set feet of the old line." Snyder explains in a 1973 interview for the *New York Quarterly* (collected in *The Real Work*) that his prosody—what he calls his "open form structuring of the line on the page"—is "with full intention as a scoring—as Charles Olson pointed out some years ago in his essay on projective verse." Although he insists that he is not opposed to closed poetic forms, which, he says, may sometimes be useful, he clearly is most interested in the rhythms of poetry outside of meter and traditional stanzaic patterns. In 1966 Snyder wrote in the essay "Some Yips and Barks in the Dark" (collected in *Naked Poetry: Recent American Poetry in Open Forms,* edited by Stephen Berg and Robert Mezey) that he opts not for "the intensity of straining and sweating against self-imposed bonds" in traditional formal poetry, but rather for "the perfect easy discipline of the swallow's dip and swoop, 'without east or west,'" in the conviction that "Each poem grows from an energy-mind-field-dance, and has its own inner grain." In further explanation of his sense of form, Snyder invokes Pound's concept of *logopoeia,* what Pound defined in his 1929 book *How To Read* as "the dance of the intellect among words," a forerunner of Olson's projective verse, as well as Pound's ideogramic method; that is, the examination and juxtaposition of particular works and passages of literature to elucidate general concepts. However, Snyder is quick to insist that he achieves a clarity that Pound, by virtue of his obscure poetic references, does not.

But it is not only modernist American poetics that shaped Snyder's formal commitments. At the age of twenty-six Snyder left America for Japan, and from 1956 to 1968 he studied Zen Buddhism in Kyoto, returning only occasionally to the United States during these years. Snyder's Buddhist instruction led him to the view, as he articulated it in "Poetry and the Primitive: Notes on Poetry as an Ecological Survival Technique" (collected in *Earth House Hold: Technical Notes and Queries to Follow Dharma Revolutionaries,* 1970), that the universe is "a vast breathing body," that poetry is "the vehicle of the mystery of voice"; thus, his prosody is as influenced by Far Eastern breath-rhythm theory as it is by Olson's theory of projective verse. Indeed, in this same work Snyder analogized his poetic form to the rhythmic mode of Indian music *(thala),* which includes improvisational opportunities within it, even as he confirmed his debt to Olson: "In intrinsic poetic theory: projective verse—I quote that right like everybody else as a starting point for thinking about the line's breath and the poem as a musical phrase or a *thala.*" In a 1975 interview with Lee Bartlett (quoted in *Towards a New American Poetics: Essays and Interviews,* edited by Ekbert Fass, 1979), Snyder pointed up the cultural border crossing that shapes the patterns of his verse:

Then, in terms of poetic craft, one must not only have an ear for daily speech, but the particularly poetic sense of refining, purifying, and compressing daily speech into the kind of compact utterance that a poem becomes. So first of all, in my poetry my craft has a sense of compression, a sense of ellipsis, of leaving out the unnecessary, of sharpening the utterance down to a point where a very precise, very swift message is generated, an energy is transmitted. In doing that, I have paid particular attention to the Anglo-Saxon or Germanic derived aspects of the English language, and have made much use of mono-syllabic words, of compactness and directness of the Anglo-Saxon heritage in the English language, which I have cross-bred with my understanding and ear for Chinese poetry.

Snyder's Buddhist philosophy and practice—in particular the idea of contemplating the void, of emptying one's mind of extraneous thought—inform his principle of compression and ellipsis: Form, he says in "Lookout's Journal" (in *Earth House Hold*), is "leaving things out at the right spot / ellipse, is emptiness." He has remarked, in "Statements on Poetics" in *The New American Poetry,* edited by Donald Allen (1960), on the influence of Chinese poetry on his diction and line length as well: "I tried writing poems of tough, simple, short words, with the complexity far beneath the surface texture. In part the line was influenced by the five- and seven-character line Chinese poems I'd been reading, which work like sharp blows on the mind."

ETHNOPOETICS AND ENVIRONMENTAL POETRY

Along with such poets as David Antin and Jerome Rothenberg, Snyder has been at the forefront of ethnopoetics, the study of the verbal arts in a worldwide range of languages and cultures. Like Rothenberg, Snyder believes that a return to the values of primitive culture is necessary if we are to rekindle a basic communalism as the fundamental form of human society and sustain life on the planet. The title of his essay "Poetry and the Primitive: Notes on Poetry as an Ecological Survival Technique" testifies to his understanding of the primitive worldview and the poetic imagination as "related forces which may help if not to save the world or humanity, at least to save the Redwoods." Snyder further tied his idea of poetic form to his ethnopoetic sense when he remarked to Ekbert Faas in 1975 that he has been affected by "the shamanistic terminology of the magic of words and what that is, the mantric efficacy of sound, and the genres of poetry as derived from Tribal concept: essentially work songs, power vision songs, love songs, courting songs, death songs, war songs, healing songs." Snyder's poetry embodies in its very forms, then, his critique of Western cultural values.

Snyder's spiritual ecology is nourished by several distinct literary traditions in both the East and the West. First, he draws inspiration from classical Chinese nature poetry, including the work of Han-shan, a Buddhist hermit-poet of the Tang dynasty (A.D. 618–906). His translations of that poet appeared in *Evergreen Review* in 1958. Later, Snyder published a group of translations of the Japanese Buddhist poet Miyazawa Kenji (1896–1933), whose work is reminiscent of Han-shan's and contains such potent natural images as "Rolling snow turned peach-color / the moon / left alone in the fading night." In addition to these influences, Snyder takes his place in a vital American line that extends from the transcendentalist writers Ralph Waldo Emerson and Henry David Thoreau to modern nature poets Robinson Jeffers, who also depicted the landscapes of the American West, and Robert Frost.

RIPRAP

In his 1992 interview with Weinberger, Snyder said that he wrote the poems in his first book, *Riprap*, after he had "given up poetry," having burned the poems of his youth—"romantic teenage poetry about girls and mountains" and poetry imitating the modernist masters, W. B. Yeats, Eliot, Pound, William Carlos Williams, and Wallace Stevens. Cid Corman's Origin Press published *Riprap*, which includes poems composed between 1953 and 1956, in Kyoto, Japan, in 1959, and the book was sold through Ferlinghetti's City Lights Books in San Francisco. The book traces a physical and spiritual journey (one that Snyder himself made) from the West Coast of the United States to Japan and back. As the critic Charles Molesworth has observed, *Riprap* is part of the poetic traditions of imagism and objectivism, its concern for concrete details in accord with Pound's belief that "the natural object is always the adequate symbol" and Williams's credo "no ideas but in things." The title of the book is the word for "a cobble of stone laid on steep slick rock to make a trail for horses in the mountains," a definition provided on the title page, and Snyder knew the art of laying riprap well from his trail work in Yosemite National Forest and elsewhere. The forms of Snyder's poetry in *Riprap* bear out his claim, made in "Statements on Poetics" in *The New American Poetry,* that "the rhythms of my poems follow the rhythm of the physical work I'm doing and life I'm leading at any given time."

The imagist technique that serves as Snyder's prosodic bedrock is apparent in the first poem of the book, "Mid-August at Sourdough Mountain Lookout" (he was stationed as a lookout on

Sourdough Mountain in the Northern Cascades of Washington State just south of the Canadian border in 1953):

Down valley a smoke haze
Three days heat, after five days rain
Pitch glows on the fir-cones
Across rocks and meadows
Swarms of new flies.

I cannot remember things I once read
A few friends, but they are in cities.
Drinking cold snow-water from a tin cup
Looking down for miles
Through high still air.

Here Snyder uses no unnecessary words, as he focuses intensively on the scene at hand. Far above the hum of city life, he enters a state where book learning drops away; removed from civilization, Snyder is able to clear his mind and concentrate on reestablishing bonds with wild nature, to achieve an existential purity ("Drinking cold snow-water from a tin cup"). As opposed to the confessional poets, who were his contemporaries, Snyder does not indulge in egotism. Rather, as the critic Michael Davidson has noted: "When the first-person pronoun enters the poem, it is not the expressive 'I' of romantic subjectivity but rather the 'I' as interpreter who establishes relationships between local and universal." In the first stanza of "Mid-August at Sourdough Mountain Lookout," no subject appears, and when it does in the second stanza, it is subsumed, with the present participles of the last lines left without a noun ("I") to modify.

In other poems in *Riprap,* Snyder dwells on the insights into nature available during and in the aftermath of intense manual labor. In "Above Pate Valley," the speaker has just finished clearing a section of trail (a metaphor for his own mental cleansing) and in an alpine meadow he sees the sweep of geological time in a littering of arrowhead remains; at the end of the poem, he narrates:

. . . I followed my own
Trail here. Picked up the cold-drill,
Pick, single-jack, and sack
Of dynamite.
Ten thousand years.

In touch with nature like the American Indians before him, the speaker minds his tools, and the first-person pronoun vanishes as self and world interpenetrate. In "Piute Creek" the poet specifically celebrates the virtue of a "clear, attentive mind," that state attainable through meditation when

All the junk that goes with being human
Drops away, hard rock wavers
Even the heavy present seems to fail
This bubble of a heart.

As Snyder makes clear in the poem, "All the junk" includes "words and books"—the contents of the mind accumulated in Western culture. This poem, like the others in *Riprap,* is guided by principles of linguistic precision and perceptual intensity, principles that hark back to Pound's imagist tenets (direct treatment of the thing, economy of language) as well as to Chinese and Japanese Buddhist poetry. These values of attention and strict observation also structure the title poem, "Riprap," in which Snyder analogizes the art of setting cobbles in a trail with the art of poetic composition:

Lay down these words
Before your mind like rocks.
          placed solid, by hands
In choice of place, set
Before the body of the mind
          in space and time:
Solidity of bark, leaf, or wall
     riprap of things:
Cobble of milky way,
          straying planets,
These poems, people,
          lost ponies with

Dragging saddles—
        and rocky sure-foot trails.
The worlds like an endless
        four-dimensional
Game of *Go.*
        ants and pebbles
In the thin loam, each rock a word
        a creek-washed stone
Granite: ingrained
        with torment of fire and weight
Crystal and sediment linked hot
        all change, in thoughts,
As well as things.

In these lines the poet represents his Zen awareness and detachment, emphasizing the value of concrete words and things while insisting that these universal objects allow the human mind to pass into nature, thus operating as stepping-stones to other "worlds." The precise poetic language symbolizes the mind that has been sharpened to a point in order to connect to and make connections in those worlds, from small ("ants and pebbles") to large ("milky way").

Snyder's orientation toward Eastern religious practices also shapes his lyric "Milton by Firelight," in which he rejects Christian doctrine as embodied by Milton's myth of the fall of man ("No paradise, no fall, / Only the weathering land / The wheeling sky . . ."). Sitting in a camp in the High Sierra, Snyder believes that Milton's theology does not account for our ecstatic response to the world in our everyday experience of it, and so is irrelevant:

Working with an old
Singlejack miner, who can sense
The vein and cleavage
In the very guts of rock, can
Blast granite, build
Switchbacks that last for years
Under the beat of snow, thaw, mule-hooves,
What use, Milton, a silly story
Of our lost general parents,
        eaters of fruit?

The layering of Eastern and Western myth— what Davidson sees as "a version of Pound's ideogramatic method, juxtaposing one cultural tradition on top of another with a minimum of critical commentary"—permits the poet to display the consistency of his values and beliefs with those of preliterate cultures; alert to distant sounds in nature, he declares without alarm, "Fire down / Too dark to read." One troubling aspect of Snyder's tribalism, though, is that it sometimes leads him to a patriarchal point of view, as in "Praise for Sick Women," where he says that "The female is fertile, and discipline / (contra naturam) only / confuses her," that women have "a difficult dance to do, but not in mind."

If he is less attuned to gender politics than he might be, Snyder does include several poems in *Riprap* that exhibit concern for the working class and mount an effective critique of industrial capitalism in America. In "The Late Snow & Lumber Strike of the Summer of Fifty- Four," Snyder observes that "The whole Northwest [is] on strike" and laments,

I must turn and go back:
        caught on a snowpeak
        between heaven and earth
And stand in lines in Seattle.
Looking for work.

Forced to interrupt his meditation on Mount Baker, he knows he must return to work as a logger, relinquishing the transcendence he has experienced in his liminal existence ("between heaven and earth"). In "T-2 Tanker Blues," Snyder again contemplates the economic system that forces him to abandon his communion with nature, but this time it is not logging but work on an oil tanker that distracts him from his spiritual quest. Aboard the tanker, Snyder expresses his "hatred of machinery and money & whoring my hands and back to move this military oil," seeking any chance to be "alone" to "see the Moon, white wake, black water & a few bright stars."

MYTHS AND TEXTS

In 1960 *Myths and Texts* was published by Le-Roi Jones's (Amiri Baraka's) Totem Press. The book is a three-part poem sequence that is interested in, as Snyder stated in his 1996 book *Mountains and Rivers without End,* "interweaving physical life and inward realms." The poems, which were written between 1952 and 1956 at the same time as those in *Riprap,* are informed by Snyder's logging, trail-making, and forest lookout work during the 1950s and by Northwest Indian stories that Snyder discovered in Bureau of Ethnology reports and various collections of American Indian folktales by Edward Sapir, Franz Boas, John Reed Swanton, and others. In the preface to *Myths and Texts,* Snyder asserts his commitment to ancient poetic forms and concepts, appearing in the role of modern shaman: "As a poet I hold the most archaic values on earth. They go back to the upper Palaeolithic: the fertility of the soil, the magic of animals, the power-vision in solitude, the terrifying initiation and rebirth, the love and ecstasy of the dance, the common work of the tribe." By promoting these values, the book radically revises Western attitudes toward the natural world and suggests new ways of living in it.

Myths and Texts is divided into three sections: "Logging," "Hunting," and "Burning." The first of these is based on Snyder's experience in the lumber camps of the Pacific Northwest and reflects his interest in Eastern culture and philosophy. The initial poem of that section hails Io, the maiden loved by Zeus in Greek mythology, as symbol of a season of rebirth ("Green comes out of the ground / Birds squabble / Young girls run mad with the pine bough"). In the second poem we are shown the despoliation of the natural environment by loggers—"tin pisspot hat[s]" driving "crummy truck[s]" and "Cat[s]." The forests of China and Seattle have been logged to pave the way for cities, with the only remnant the lodgepole pine,

which, as Snyder tells us in the third poem of the section, can "endure a fire / which kills the tree without injuring its seed." In poem 2 we see that this tree holds within it the promise of regeneration, but the pillaging has taken its toll:

Someone killed and someone built, a house,
a forest, wrecked or raised
All America hung on a hook
& burned by men, in their own praise.

Against the backdrop of such destruction, a shaman in a later poem pronounces the fate of the white man: "You shall live in square / gray houses in a barren land / and beside those square gray houses you shall starve."

Snyder's incisive critique of commodity culture in the West, especially in the United States, continues in poem 14, where he condemns clear-cutting practices as the desecration of nature:

The groves are down
                        cut down
Groves of Ahab, of Cybele
. . . .
Cut down to make room for the suburbs
Bulldozed by Luther and Weyerhaeuser
Crosscut and chainsaw
        squareheads and finns
        high-lead and cat-skidding
Trees down
Creeks choked, trout killed, roads.

In poem 15 Snyder further exposes the lack of respect for nature that Americans possess, with the Hindu deity (Shiva) coming at the end of time to lay waste to the labor of those who have gutted nature:

Shiva at the end of the kalpa:
Rock-fat, hill-flesh, gone in a whiff.
Men who hire men to cut groves
Kill snakes, build cities, pave fields,
Believe in god, but can't
Believe their own senses
Let alone Gautama. Let them lie.

In the second section ("Hunting") Snyder explores the magic of animals through the cultivation of a primitive consciousness, as he searches for a regenerative vision, a renewal of the values of primitive culture in the face of the mindless mechanization of the State. In the first poem Snyder is surrounded by the destruction represented in the initial section of the book; he sits alone in an old lumber camp—a "village of the dead." Distancing himself from the white world, he attempts to integrate himself with his own primitive spirit and the spirits of the animal world. He goes without food for two days in order to reach a point "without thoughts," to create "a new myth" through meditation and acceptance of Amerindian and Buddhist beliefs about the inhuman realm. In poem 6 a girl encounters a bear, the archetypal wanderer, marries him, and has children with him. The girl's brothers find out and hunt down and kill the bear. This response to the interpenetration of the human and the animal worlds represents, for Snyder, the depravity of Western values. In yet another animal poem, the eighth in the sequence, Snyder confronts his guilt over his association with those values, placing himself in the company of drunken hunters who do not respect the wilderness and its life-forms. Hitting a buck with their car, these men are pictured as aggressive and selfish hunters, perpetrators of thoughtless murder.

In the third section of *Myths and Texts* ("Burning"), Snyder shows man's reintegration with nature and completes his own spiritual odyssey. In poem 13 his senses are filled with nature, and he imagines his creative writing as a concrete symbol of the abstract unconscious, declaring "Poetry a riprap on the slick rock of metaphysics." In poem 8 Snyder represents an experience of John Muir, the founder of the American environmental movement, who in his mountain climbing suddenly comes to a point of attention, a moment when "life blazed / Forth again with preternatural clearness"; "possessed / Of a new sense," Muir is in perfect harmony with his surroundings. The book ends with two poems that record an identical event, but in very different ways. In "the text"—by which Snyder means the phenomenal world—he tells of his experience helping to put out a forest fire in the most straightforward of terms; the lyric begins: "Sourdough mountain called a fire in: / Up Thunder Creek, high on a ridge." In "the myth," on the other hand, Snyder's version of the event is charged with symbolism:

> Fire up Thunder Creek and the mountains—
>   troy's burning!
> The cloud mutters
> The mountains are your mind.

The figures of speech that mark this passage represent the uses to which we put the objective world (our mythmaking) in our search for correspondence. The final line of the poem, "The sun is but a morning star," echoes the last sentence of Thoreau's *Walden* and sounds as a herald of rebirth. It is appropriate that Thoreau should appear here, too, since, like Snyder, he holds a deep interest in both Native American and Eastern practices and traditions.

THE BACK COUNTRY

In 1968 Snyder published *The Back Country,* a book of poems in four sections—"Far West," "Far East," "Kali," and "Back"—that takes the reader on a circular journey from the U.S. West Coast to East Asia to India and back to the West Coast, the same ground Snyder covered between 1956 and 1964. The title of the book is meant to resonate on various levels—as natural wilderness, the "backward" countries, and the back countries of the mind, or the unconscious. In its poems Snyder continues to record the negative effects of political systems and hymn the importance of place as it stands outside of such regimes.

The first poem of the first section is "A Berry Feast," the poem Snyder performed at the Six Gallery reading in San Francisco in 1955. In it he celebrates the spirit of the wild in Coyote, the trickster figure of Amerindian myth; as Snyder observes in his essay "The Incredible Survival of Coyote" (collected in *The Old Ways*), Coyote "belonged to the place and became almost like a guardian, a protector spirit." In the poem Coyote stands between the city and the wilderness, seeing on the one hand a vital landscape ("People gone, death no disaster") and on the other a sterile urban setting ("Dead city in dry summer"). Coyote is seen "Mating with / humankind," and that image of interrelatedness stands in stark ideological contrast to the destruction recorded in the poem ("The Chainsaw falls for boards of pine, / Suburban bedrooms"; "Coyote: shot from the car, two ears, / A tail, bring bounty"). Snyder's desire to escape civilization sets the tone for the entire book (and successive books), and has led to the charge of his "inhumanism," what the critic David Carpenter called his refusal to deal with "the problems of modern existence, as his poetry does not deal with the tensions of urban life." Similarly, in 1976 Charles Altieri argued that "Snyder's images of an ideal society remain mere fictions that do not address themselves to the immediate and varied problems of our society," although others claim that Snyder's utopian vision, while it may not change the world, can change our thinking about it.

Snyder's quest for self-transcendence and his belief in the interpenetration of all beings and things shapes another poem in the first section of the book, "Sixth-Month Song in the Foothills," where he liberates himself from the constraints of ego in line with Buddhist teachings. In the poem Snyder sets down several participial phrases without the noun ("I") they modify ("In the cold shed sharpening saws"; "Grinding the falling axe"; "sharpening tools") in recognition of the speaker's mental freedom. The critic Jody Norton (in *Critical Essays on*

Gary Snyder, edited by Patrick Murphy) has suggested the resemblance of Snyder's poetry based on such ellipses to the *shih,* the standard lyric form of the Chinese Tang Dynasty, and the haiku, a Japanese poetic form with a minimum of descriptive language and fragmented syntax. Indeed, Snyder includes in the first section of *The Back Country* a series entitled "Hitch Haiku"; the productive compression of that form comes through in the following lines:

> Scrap brass
> dumpt off the fantail
> falling six miles

Through presentation rather than statement we are made to witness the careless pollution of nature, our junk cast off into a vast watery wild.

Snyder's concern for nature and his spiritual connection to it are further revealed in the poem "A Walk," where the speaker undertakes a long, hard journey through a landscape of concrete particulars:

> . . . I've eaten breakfast and I'll
> take a walk
> To Benson Lake. Packed a lunch,
> Goodbye. Hopping on creekbed boulders
> Up the rock throat three miles
> Piute Creek—
> In steep gorge glacier-slick rattlesnake country
> Jump, land by a pool, trout skitter,
> The clear sky. Deer tracks.

In this passage, jumps from one image to another metaphorically represent the speaker's quick movement from one rock to another as well as his laser-like focus. When the speaker finally reaches his destination, he records his simple pleasure in the following lines:

> . . . At last.
> By the rusty three-year-
> Ago left-behind cookstove
> Of the old trail crew,
> Stoppt and swam and ate my lunch.

No ordinary lunch, this meal is transformed into a sacramental event. However, the tone of quiet casualness and plain speech distinguish this poem and others like it in the book from the rhetoric of traditional devotional lyric and point to Snyder's comfortable placement in the natural world.

In "Burning the Small Dead" Snyder continues to explore the unconscious realm, tracing the expansion of the mind in meditation through cosmic time and space:

Burning the small dead
          branches
broke from beneath
          thick spreading
                    whitebark pine.

          A hundred summers
Snowmelt   rock   and air

hiss in a twisted bough.

          sierra granite;
                    mt. Ritter—
                    black rock twice as old.

Deneb, Altair

windy fire

The ascendance through the trees up the mountain and beyond (Deneb and Altair are stars of the first magnitude) finds a fit form in the spacing of words on lines and leaps from one stanza to the next, with the final phrase "windy fire" standing for the process of linking these elements of the universe together in thought.

In "Far East," a section of poems written in Japan, Snyder expresses personal doubt about his ability to shed his Western identity, to lay full claim to an ecological conscience. He recognizes his partial understanding of nature ("thought nature meant mountains") and his complicity in American aggression in the world. In "The Public Bath" he senses his physical and moral difference from the Japanese around him, and is haunted by scenes of destruction from World War II:

squatting soapy and limber
smooth dense skin, long muscles—

I see dead men naked
tumbled on beaches,
                    newsreels, the
                              war

Snyder extends his political critique in "Vapor Trails," an invective against U.S. militarism, where we find "Young expert U.S. pilots waiting / The day of criss-cross rockets / And white blossoming smoke of bomb." In the final poem of the section, Snyder, collapsing his time in Japan into a single calendar year, comes to an appreciation of all he has learned in Japan as he makes his way back to America.

The title of the third section, "Kali," refers to the Hindu goddess of destruction and points to Snyder's idea of India, which he visited while living in Japan, as a backward country, particularly in its economic and social modes. Many of the poems of this section are pessimistic, and some are about failed love. In "This Tokyo" he expresses his momentary doubt that an embodiment of Buddhist principles in the world will change reality: "Peace, war, religion, / Revolution, will not help." The city of Tokyo is spiritually and morally desolate, a place of "Hopelessness where love of man / Or hate of man could matter / None." However, in the final poem of the section Snyder finds some measure of hope in rebirth, addressing "Mother"—the principle of regeneration at work in the world—and laying himself open before her:

Snyder says: you bear me, nurse me
I meet you, always love you,
          you dance
          on my chest and thigh

Forever born again.

The poetic mask having fallen away, Snyder announces his desire to be transformed, to reimagine existence in a spirit of "dance."

The final section ("Back"), which includes poems written upon Snyder's return to the United States in 1964, invokes figures of harmony that stand in opposition to the values of Europe and America, with the latter in "For the West" described as a "flowery glistening oil blossom / spreading on water." This figure calls attention to the industrial economy upon which his homeland is built—an economy that has led to the pollution of the environment and a spiritual bankruptcy. In the penultimate poem, "Through the Smoke Hole," Snyder dwells on the figure of the kiva, the early American Indian lodge where religious rituals were enacted, and imagines paths to enlightenment running through the smoke hole and under the kiva ("the way to it is thru the smoke of this one, & the hole that smoke goes through"); as he concludes, our goal should be "to cultivate the fields of our own world without much thought for the others"; that is, to develop deep spiritual practices even if one must go it alone.

REGARDING WAVE

Regarding Wave, published by New Directions in 1970, continues where *The Back Country* leaves off, with the principle of "communionism" a predominant force. Many of the poems in the book reflect changes in Snyder's life prior to its publication. Just before his permanent return to the United States in 1968, Snyder married Masa Uehara in Kyoto, Japan, and lived with her in a collective on an island in the East China Sea. In 1968 his first son, Kai, was born, and the next year he and Masa had another son, Gen. In *Regarding Wave,* which is dedicated to Masa, Snyder reflects on the roles and rewards of husband and father and, in the process, extends his ecological vision.

The first poem, "Wave," begins in a series of moving images, presenting a picture of a dynamic natural world that stands as a symbol for the flux of human consciousness (what he calls at the close of the poem "the dancing grain of things / of my mind!"):

Grooving clam shell,
    streakt through marble,
      sweeping down ponderosa pine bark-scale
        rip-cut tree grain
          sand-dunes, lava
            flow

Wave   wife.

As Snyder points out in his essay "Poetry and the Primitive" (in *Earth House Hold*), in Indo-European etymology "'wife' means 'wave' means 'vibrator,'" and that understanding allows him to make the correspondence between woman and energetic nature that he does in the poem. As he insists, to perceive the dynamism of the environment one must recognize interrelatedness and one's personal involvement in the universe.

The title poem—"Regarding Wave"—stands at the other end of the first three-part section, and imagines the world flooded with the sounds of the dharma (the natural and moral principles that apply to all beings and things), with "the voice of the Dharma" "a shimmering bell / through all." By accepting Buddhist teachings, one is able to see

Every hill,   still.
Every tree alive. Every leaf.
All the slopes flow.

The purified mind makes possible such insights into the fixity and flux of the world. The poem ends in a figure of poetic voice that descends from Indian tradition, where voice is a Goddess named Vak, who is wife to Brahma and the source of his creativity: "The Voice / is a wife / to / him still." Snyder thus points up his own poetic powers as a product of his sense of wholeness with nature. In the poem "Shark Meat" Snyder further remarks on the interdependence of self and universe, this time through contemplation of the food chain. That network binding humans to animals is metaphorically rich, with the shark that the speaker has eaten imagined as

> re-crossing his own paths
> to tangle our net
>   to be part of
>   this loom.

The net that traps the shark represents "the empirically observable interconnectedness of nature," which, Snyder observes in "Poetry and the Primitive," "is but a corner of the vast 'jewelled net' which moves from without to within."

Many of the poems in *Regarding Wave* are erotically charged and express the joys of family life. In such poems as "It Was When" and "The Bed in the Sky," Snyder celebrates the sexual union of husband and wife and the miracle of birth. His appreciation of the smallest details of the domestic scene is registered in the following lines from the latter poem:

> . . . the bed is full and spread and dark
> I hug you and sink in the warm
>   my stomach against your big belly
>
> feels our baby turn

In "Kai, Today" and "Not Leaving the House," Snyder records the birth of his son and the change in him that this event brings. Clearly, the poet's ecological vision bears on his sense of family, and in "Meeting the Mountains" the entwinement of the two is seen through Snyder's eyes when his small son crawls to the edge of a pool by a creek and responds ecstatically to it.

The two final sections of *Regarding Wave* are more overtly political. In the section entitled "Long Hair," a figure that denotes for Snyder the acceptance of appetite and change, the poem "Revolution in the Revolution in the Revolution" takes us to the "back country," that place where "the most ruthlessly exploited class" resides: "Animals, trees, water, air, grasses." As he says, we must pass through the stage of the "'Dictatorship of the Unconscious' before we can / Hope for the withering-away of the states / And finally arrive at true Communionism." Insisting that the power we derive from Buddhist meditational practice is consonant with the power we derive from revolutionary struggle ("POWER / comes out of the seed-syllables [OM and AYNG and AH] of mantras"), Snyder imagines an end of politics and a coincident spiritual and ecological regeneration. The final section ("Target Practice") is made up of short haiku-like poems, with emphasis on the oneness of being and the corrosive effects of civilization.

TURTLE ISLAND

Snyder won the Pulitzer Prize for his 1974 volume *Turtle Island,* the title of which revives the name for the North American continent in Native American creation stories. One recurrent theme among its poems and essays is the need for modern Americans to return to an understanding of the earth as a living organism to whom we are related, to break through geopolitical abstractions (like "the United States") and, as Snyder puts it in his introductory note, to "see ourselves more accurately on this continent of watersheds and life-communities—plant zones, physiographic provinces, culture areas; following natural boundaries." The book issues a rather dire assessment of capitalist culture in North America and its future if a return to "the old ways" does not occur, and is divided into four sections, the last of which, "Plain Talk," is comprised of several short prose essays whose values are embodied in the poems.

Turtle Island begins by invoking the memory of the Anasazi, the aboriginal cliffdwellers who were in North America long before the arrival of the white man. In sympathy with their environmental sense, Snyder exposes the destruction of the wilderness by civilized man in other poems in the section. In "Front Lines" he denounces the rapine tactics of the industrial world and insists that we take a stand against them:

> A bulldozer grinding and slobbering.
> Sideslipping and belching on top of
> The skinned-up bodies of still-live bushes
> In the pay of a man
> From town.
>
> Behind is a forest that goes to the Arctic
> And a desert that still belongs to the Piute
> And here we must draw
> Our line.

Calling attention to the ruthless practices of "Amerika," Snyder insists on the superior ecological values of native peoples, and in "Control Burn" (also in this first section) he expresses his desire for a return to those values, proposing "a hot clean burn" that will purge the land, restoring it to the way it was "Before." Consistent with this critique of dominant (Western) cultural values, Snyder's poem "Steak" castigates those who support the commercialization of slaughtered beef. Another poem—"The Dead by the Side of the Road"—takes aim at the senseless slaughter of animals on highways, as we forsake "our ancient sisters' trails" for roads where "Log trucks run on fossil fuel." In "The Call of the Wild" Snyder again highlights our disrespect of the nonhuman world, as he sneers at a man who has coyotes trapped because they make too much noise. Angry at such behavior, the poet makes the link between U.S. aggression in Vietnam and the extinction of nature:

> All these Americans up in special cities in the sky
> Dumping poisons and explosives

> Across Asia first,
> And next North America,
>
> A war against earth.
> When it's done there'll be
>   no place
>
> A Coyote could hide.

In most of these poems Snyder is not very optimistic about the possibility of forging a new relationship between people and the environment. In "I Went into the Maverick Bar" he expresses despair about the ability of local people to grasp the gravity of the ecological crisis, lamenting "That short-haired joy and roughness— / America—your stupidity." Such an encounter, though, wakes Snyder up to his own responsibilities: "I came back to myself, / To the real work, to / 'What is to be done.'" That final quoted phrase, the title of the Russian Communist leader Vladimir Lenin's 1902 revolutionary tract, highlights the anticapitalist orientation of the entire book.

The second section of *Turtle Island* opens with "Facts," a poem that dispenses with figurative language and whose voice is far from that of traditional romantic lyric. It begins in the following enumerations:

> 1. 92% of Japan's three million ton import of soybeans comes from the U.S.
>
> 2. The U.S. has 6% of the world's population; consumes 1/3 the energy annually consumed in the world.
>
> 3. The U.S. consumes 1/3 of the world's annual meat.

This string of statistics is intended to open eyes and minds to the need to reverse course, to begin acting in ways that will make our "reinhabitation" of the continent a success. In the poem, Snyder also attacks the growing disparity in the United States between those with wealth and those without and the usurpation of the arts by multinational oil corporations. In "Mother Earth: Her Whales," a poem written as an op-ed piece for the *New York Times,* Snyder again calls for a radical break with current practices, denouncing those who "argue how to parcel out our Mother Earth / To last a little longer":

> North America, Turtle Island, taken by
> invaders who wage war around the world.
> May ants, may abalone, otters, wolves, and
> elk
> Rise! and pull away their giving from the
> robot nations.

Here the imperialistic pursuits of the United States are seen in stark contrast to the unselfishness of nature. "L M F B R" likewise sounds an apocalyptic note:

> Death himself,
> (Liquid Metal Fast Breeder Reactor)
> stands grinning, beckoning.
> Plutonium tooth-glow.
> Eyebrows buzzing.
> Strip-mining scythe.

The nuclear reactor on which the future of capitalism is staked and which leads to a police state (as Snyder writes in "Poetry, Community and Climax") brings destructive Kali onto the scene once again, and leads to Snyder's grim forecast of the "end of days" in the last line of the poem.

The pessimistic outlook of *Turtle Island* is partially mitigated by Snyder's attention to family relationships and their curative properties. In "The Egg," Snyder takes a walk with Kai; in "The Bath" he and his wife, Masa, wash Kai in the sauna. In "Gen" the son by that name nurses at Masa's breast. All of these activities give Snyder pleasure, releasing him from the pains inflicted by the larger social order. Snyder also expresses his hope for oneness in "The Hudsonian Curlew," a poem that insists on our identity with the natural world as symbolized by a

hunter's ritualistic (and therefore respectful) killing, cleaning, cooking, and eating of a bird (the curlew of the title). The final poem of the section, "Magpie's Song," also points to the promise of transcendence, with the magpie telling the poet that through meditation nature has the power to make us whole: *"Here in the Mind, Brother, / Turquoise Blue."*

In the third section, "For the Children," Snyder includes more poems about his own family, including one, "Dusty Braces," in which he berates his male ancestors ("you bastards") for harming the environment (they "killd off the cougar and grizzly"). In another poem he suggests that the lack of conscience that allows the continued clear-cutting of forests also leads to the U.S. bombing of Vietnamese children in war. In "What Happened Here Before" Snyder records the destruction brought on by the white man's coming to the continent, going back in time first 300 million years, then 80 million then 3 million then 40,000, and finally 125 years, before arriving in the present, where the voices of the children are drowned out by "military jets head[ing] northeast, roaring, every dawn." The poem ends with a bluejay screeching: "WE SHALL SEE / WHO KNOWS / HOW TO BE." The implication is that the white man, unless he radically transforms his attitudes and practices, is doomed to extinction.

Michael Davidson criticizes many of the poems of *Turtle Island* for adopting a "shrill, hectoring tone that seems intolerant of the reader," as in these lines from "Tomorrow's Song":

> The USA slowly lost its mandate
> in the middle and later twentieth century
> it never gave the mountains and rivers,
> trees and animals,
> a vote.
> all the people turned away from it
> myths die; even continents are impermanent
>
> Turtle Island returned.

My friend broke open a dried coyote-scat
removed a ground squirrel tooth
pierced it, hung it
from the gold ring
in his ear.

We look to the future with pleasure
we need no fossil fuel
get power within
grow strong on less.

Davidson laments what he sees as a lack of artistry in these lines: "It is not that we disagree with any of the ecological or political issues raised here but that they are treated exactly as that: issues." Likewise, Charles Altieri finds that Snyder, while successful in his role as seer (that is, as a poet concerned with discovering values and presenting a moral and social vision to an elite audience of believers) fails when he tries to supplement it with the role of prophet—a role that compels him to win a wide audience through use of a more ordinary discourse so as to effect political and social change. Of course, Snyder would assent to the charge that he is focused on programmatic change and insist that that is a proper poetic goal. In this sense, Snyder actively contests traditional lyric modes, revising Western cultural attitudes about the social function of the poet.

AXE HANDLES

Axe Handles (1983), a book of poems dedicated not to a person but to a place (the San Juan Ridge in the Sierra foothills where Snyder has lived since 1970) is less apocalyptic and more personal than *Turtle Island*. Snyder has said that "If *Turtle Island* was a statement about what life in North America could be . . . *Axe Handles* is a much more low-key presentation of what the moves are when you really make a place your home" (quoted in Patrick Murphy, *Understanding Gary Snyder*). The first section of the book is entitled "Loops," referring to Snyder's

desire to return (loop back) to primitive modes of existence ("the old ways"). The title poem, which opens the first section of the book, is autobiographical, referring in the first lines to Snyder's son Kai, to whom he is going to teach the art of making axe handles. Stressing the continuity of community and culture through that activity, Snyder imagines himself as participating in both Eastern and Western poetic traditions, with two phrases "ring[ing] in his ears": Ezra Pound's "When making an axe handle / the pattern is not far off" and the fourth century A.D. Chinese essayist Lu Ji's "In making the handle / of an axe / By cutting wood with an axe / The model is indeed near at hand," the latter translated for Snyder by his college professor, Shih-hsiang Chen. The poem ends with the title figure turned into a metaphor for interdependence and inheritance:

. . . Pound was an axe,
Chen was an axe, I am an axe
And my son a handle, soon
To be shaping again, model
And tool, craft of culture,
How we go on.

As these lines indicate, instruction and the transmission of culture down through generations are the book's central concerns.

In his lyric "For/From Lew," these concerns are particularly apparent, as Snyder imagines his friend Lew Welch, a roommate at Reed College and a poet who also was involved in the San Francisco renaissance, returning to life (he is thought to have committed suicide, but his body was never found) and telling him: "teach the children about the cycles. The life cycles. All the other cycles." In several poems Snyder explains the practices he is engaged in in a manner that recalls Thoreau, who provides minute detail in his discussion of the economies of life on Walden Pond. In "Bows to Drouth," for instance, Snyder describes with precision the labor required to work a pump ("the handle extended with pipe / sweeps down / six strokes to a gallon"), and in "Fence Posts" he tells us that "With sapwood fenceposts / You ought to soak to make sure they won't rot / In a fifty-five gallon drum with penta 10 to 1 / Which is ten gallons of oil and a gallon of / Termite and fungus poison." These poems of instruction attest to Snyder's deep knowledge of the land and the practices that one must cultivate in order to live productively on it.

In *Axe Handles,* Snyder also analogizes Buddhist mental habits and his environmentalist ethos, and in his poem "On Top" he commands:

> All this new stuff goes on top
> turn it over   turn it over
> wait   and water down.
> From the dark bottom
> turn it inside out
> let it spread through, sift down,
> even.
> Watch it sprout.
>
> A mind like compost.

This poem is reminiscent of a poem by another preeminent American nature poet, Robert Frost, who in his dramatic dialogue "Build Soil" has a character instruct, "Turn the farm in upon itself / Until it can contain itself no more, / But sweating-full, drips wine and oil a little." In a 1977 interview for *East West Journal* (collected in *The Real Work*), Snyder referred to this composting method in relation to his own poetic procedures, distinguishing between those poets "who have fed on a certain kind of destructiveness for their creative glow," and those closer to his own energies, like Wendell Berry and Robert Duncan, "who have 'composted' themselves and turned part of themselves back in on themselves to become richer and stronger." In "Berry Territory," a poem inspired by a walk Snyder took with Tanya and Wendell Berry (the latter another prominent nature poet) on their farm on the Kentucky River, Snyder partakes in the close inspection of the land and celebrates his rootedness in it.

The title of the final section of *Axe Handles*—"Nets"—reaches back to Snyder's metaphor of the "jewelled net" of existence, by which he means the mythic notion of communionism. It also refers to the actual nets in which animals are caught. As opposed to the debased images of hunters we see in earlier books, here Snyder celebrates the reverent hunter who engages in ritual behavior in step with ancient practice. In "Geese Gone Beyond" the speaker kneels in the bow of a cedar canoe "in *seiza,* like tea-ceremony" and when his gun goes off he appears in sympathetic identification with his target: "A touch across, / the trigger, / The one who is the first to feel to go." In the final poem of the book, entitled "For All," Snyder recites his own bioregional oath in parody of the national pledge of allegiance:

> I pledge allegiance to the soil
>   of Turtle Island,
>   one ecosystem
>   in diversity
>   under the sun
> With joyful interpenetration for all.

In another notable poem from this section Snyder invokes Gaia, the Greek earth goddess, setting down in his title the precise time and place that he achieves oneness with nature:

> 24:IV:40075, 3:30 PM,
>   of Coaldale, Nevada,
>   A Glimpse through a Break
>   in the Storm of the Summit
>   of the White Mountains
>
>   O Mother Gaia
>
> sky   cloud   gate   milk   snow
>
>   wind-void-word
>
>   I bow in roadside gravel

His respect for the earth makes this revelation possible, and his insight into the mystery of the universe breathes life not only into himself but into his art ("wind-void-word").

NO NATURE

Snyder's 1986 collection, *Left Out in the Rain: New Poems 1947–1985,* contains previously unpublished poems that echo less expertly earlier published poems. However, in *No Nature: New and Selected Poems* (1992) several of Snyder's new poems figure in creative ways his practices and convictions. In "How Poetry Comes to Me" he suggests the condition that the poet must be in to receive what the world has to offer:

It comes blundering over the
Boulders at night, it stays
Frightened outside the
Range of my campfire
I go to meet it at the
Edge of the light.

The radical enjambments in these lines (articles separated from the nouns that they modify, as in "the / Boulders") imitate the gaps in the poet's consciousness waiting to be filled. In another poem, "Building," Snyder reflects on his construction of his house and on historical and cultural changes in the United States between the time of its construction (the early 1970s) and a time twenty years later, when, in the midst of the Persian Gulf War, "Lies and Crimes in the Government [are] held up as Virtues." The house he has built puts up a resistance to those dominant ideologies:

our buildings are solid, to live, to teach, to sit,
To sit, to know for sure the sound of a bell—
This is history. This is outside of history.

The image of the bell stands for the saturation of his environment with dharma, and the poem speaks to Snyder's concern for informing others in their spiritual quest through those ancient wisdom teachings.

MOUNTAINS AND RIVERS WITHOUT END

Mountains and Rivers without End, a sequence of long poems begun in 1956, was published in its entirety in 1996, with *Six Sections from Mountains and Rivers without End* published by Grey Fox Press as early as 1965. A forty-year-long project, the book is epic in scope, belonging to a modernist tradition that includes such long poems as Pound's *Cantos,* Williams's *Paterson,* and Olson's *Maximus,* but like other of Snyder's work, the sequence also is indebted to Eastern forms, with its overall structure conceived after a Chinese sidewise scroll painting. Kerouac memorialized the inception of the work in *The Dharma Bums,* where Snyder as Japhy Ryder says:

Know what I'm gonna do? I'll do a new long poem called "Rivers and Mountains without End" and just write it on and on on a scroll and unfold on and on with new surprises and always what went before forgotten, see, like a river, or like one of them real long Chinese silk paintings that show two little men hiking in an endless landscape of gnarled old trees and mountains so high they merge with the fog in the upper silk void. I'll spend three thousand years writing it, it'll be packed full of information on soil conservation, the Tennessee Valley Authority, astronomy, geology, Hsuan Tsung's travels, Chinese painting theory, reforestation, Oceanic ecology and food chains.

The wide-ranging source texts should remind us of Pound's imperative to include in poetry "whole slabs of the [historical] record," and Snyder himself has said, in a 1989 interview with David Robertson (in *Critical Essays on Gary Snyder,* edited by Patrick Murphy), that the book includes "more mythological and symbolical material," representing "a different order of poetic" from his previous projects.

Despite these differences, most of Snyder's concerns in *Mountains and Rivers without End* are consistent with those expressed in his earlier books. In "Bubbs Creek Haircut," which commemorates a haircut Snyder got in San Francisco before a hiking trip he took to Bubbs Creek, the speaker meditates on the nature of junk, as he goes to a Goodwill store next to the barbershop to buy secondhand clothes for his trip. Framed by the speaker's image in a double mirror in the barbershop, the poem reflects on the power of memory and the larger patterns of life, what he calls "the crazy web of wavelets," which, "seen from high above," "makes sense." In another poem in the sequence, "The Blue Sky," Snyder explores the lore of healing in Buddhism and Native North America, imagining the realm of "Medicine Old Man Buddha" and the protective and healing powers of the color blue. The concluding poem ("Finding the Space in the Heart") further expresses his sense of the dynamic transformations of the world, and he relates that sense directly to the unwinding field of scroll on which his book is metaphorically inscribed:

> *Walking on walking,*
>   *under foot   earth turns*
>
> *Streams and mountains never stay the same.*
>
> The space goes on.
> But the wet black brush
> tips drawn to a point,
>   lifts away.

As Snyder reflects here, although he must come to an end of writing, the natural world in which he lives does not end, continuing on in its revolutions.

SUMMARY

Snyder is considered one of the most accomplished nature poets of the twentieth century, receiving such prestigious awards as the Pulitzer Prize for Poetry (1975) and the Bol-

lingen Prize (1997). Although, as Molesworth asserts, "many readers find his work either tendentious politically or insufficiently complex in terms of irony, paradox, or other formalist values," many others have found in his poetry a refreshing engagement with contemporary political issues, particularly involving the environment, and a formal clarity that follows from his ethics. Indeed, the interrelatedness of Snyder's lyric forms and the values he celebrates stands as a figure for his conception of the interrelatedness of all beings and things.

Selected Bibliography

WORKS OF GARY SNYDER

POETRY

Riprap. Ashland, Mass.: Origin Press, 1959.

Myths and Texts. New York: Totem/Corinth, 1960; New York: New Directions, 1978.

Six Sections from Mountains and Rivers without End. San Francisco: Four Seasons, 1965; London: Fulcrum, 1967; enlarged edition: *Six Sections from Mountains and Rivers without End Plus One.* San Francisco: Four Seasons, 1970.

A Range of Poems. London: Fulcrum, 1966.

The Back Country. London: Fulcrum, 1967; revised and enlarged edition, New York: New Directions, 1968.

Regarding Wave. Iowa City: Windhover, 1969 [limited edition]; revised and enlarged edition, New York: New Directions, 1970. London: Fulcrum, 1970.

Riprap and Cold Mountain Poems. San Francisco: Four Seasons, 1969; San Francisco: North Point, 1980.

Cold Mountain Poems: Twenty Four Poems by Han Shan Translated by Gary Snyder. Portland, Ore.: Press 22, 1970.

Manzanita. Bolinas, Calif.: Four Seasons, 1972.

The Fudo Trilogy. Berkeley, Calif.: Shaman Drum, 1973.

Turtle Island. New York: New Directions, 1974.

Axe Handles. San Francisco: North Point, 1983.

Left Out in the Rain: New Poems, 1947–1985. San Francisco: North Point, 1986.

No Nature: New and Selected Poems. New York: Pantheon, 1992.

Mountains and Rivers without End. Washington, D.C.: Counterpoint, 1996.

CRITICAL PROSE

"Statements on Poetics." In *The New American Poetry.* Edited by Donald M. Allen. New York: Grove, 1960. Pp. 420–421.

"Some Yips and Barks in the Dark." In *Naked Poetry: Recent American Poetry in Open Forms.* Edited by Stephen Berg and Robert Mezey. Indianapolis: Bobbs-Merrill, 1969.

Earth House Hold: Technical Notes and Queries to Follow Dharma Revolutionaries. New York: New Directions, 1969; London: Jonathan Cape, 1970.

The Old Ways: Six Essays. San Francisco: City Lights, 1977.

He Who Hunted Birds in His Father's Village. Bolinas, Calif.: Grey Fox, 1979.

Passage through India. San Francisco: Grey Fox, 1983.

The Practice of the Wild: Essays by Gary Snyder. San Francisco: North Point, 1990.

A Place in Space: Ethics, Aesthetics, and Watersheds. Washington, D.C.: Counterpoint, 1995.

COLLECTIONS

The Real Work: Interviews and Talks, 1964–1979. New York: New Directions, 1980.

The Gary Snyder Reader: Prose, Poetry, and Translations, 1952–1998. Washington, D.C.: Counterpoint, 1999.

CRITICAL AND BIOGRAPHICAL STUDIES

Altieri, Charles. "Gary Snyder's Turtle Island: The Problem of Reconciling the Roles of Seer and Prophet." *Boundary 2* 4:761–777 (spring 1976).

———. *Enlarging the Temple: New Directions in American Poetry during the 1960's.* Lewisburg, Pa.: Bucknell University Press, 1979.

Bartlett, Lee. "Gary Snyder's Myths and Texts and the Monomyth." *Western American Literature* 17:137–148 (1982).

Carpenter, David A. "Gary Snyder's Inhumanism, from *Riprap* to *Axe Handles.*" *South Dakota Review* 26:110–138 (1988).

Davidson, Michael. *The San Francisco Renaissance: Poetics and Community at Mid-century.* Cambridge: Cambridge University Press, 1989.

Dean, Tim. *Gary Snyder and the American Unconscious: Inhabiting the Ground.* New York: St. Martin's, 1991.

Faas, Ekbert. "Gary Snyder." In his *Towards a New American Poetics: Essays and Interviews.* Santa Barbara: Black Sparrow, 1979.

Folsom, L. Edwin. "Gary Snyder's Descent to Turtle Island: Searching for Fossil Love." *Western American Literature* 15:103–121 (1980).

Kern, Robert. "Clearing the Ground: Gary Snyder and the Modernist Imperative." *Criticism: A Quarterly for Literature and the Arts* 19:158–177 (1977).

———. "Recipes, Catalogues, Open Form Poetics: Gary Snyder's Archetypal Voice." *Contemporary Literature* 18:173–197 (spring 1977).

Molesworth, Charles. *Gary Snyder's Vision: Poetry and the Real Work.* Columbia: University of Missouri Press, 1983.

Murphy, Patrick D., ed. *Critical Essays on Gary Snyder.* Boston: G. K. Hall, 1991.

———. *Understanding Gary Snyder.* Columbia: University of South Carolina Press, 1992.

Paul, Sherman. *In Search of the Primitive: Rereading David Antin, Jerome Rothenberg, and Gary Snyder.* Baton Rouge: Louisiana State University Press, 1986.

Steuding, Bob. *Gary Snyder.* Boston: Twayne, 1976.

—*TYLER HOFFMAN*

Paul Theroux

1941–

*P*AUL THEROUX'S PERSONALLY revealing *Sir Vidia's Shadow: A Friendship across Five Continents* (1998) opens with a vividly described chapter in the day-to-day life of a young expatriate American living and teaching in Uganda. In his twenties, Theroux lived for several years in southeast Africa, in Malawi and Uganda, as a teacher in the Peace Corps and on his own, and the facts and nuances within this introductory narrative mirror those of the author's early life with unmistakable precision, save for a few subtle yet crucial details. While this passage is part of what is billed as a nonfiction autobiographical work, the names—including that of Julian Lavelle, the young male protagonist who is unmistakably a stand-in for the writer himself—are pure invention.

It is not until the start of the second chapter that Theroux abruptly cuts in upon his tale and sets the record straight: "Wait, wait, wait. You know I'm lying, don't you? This is not a novel, it is a memory." He then proceeds to explain this interruption and the casting off of the fictional guise: "I cannot change any of this. I am writing with a ballpoint on a pad at my desk. How can this be a novel? This narrative is not something that would be improved by the masks of fiction. It needs only to be put in order. I am free of the constraint of alteration and fictionalizing."

This declaration is noteworthy for a number of reasons that are key in the examination of the life and writings of Paul Theroux. By the year 2000 Theroux had authored thirty-eight books—twenty-two works of fiction (including seventeen novels and five volumes of short stories), one book of criticism, two essay collections, eleven travel books, two children's

books, and one autobiographical study (*Sir Vidia's Shadow*)—and countless articles and book reviews. Still, he remains an enigmatic, compelling, and often deeply mysterious literary figure.

Theroux might be called a deliberate stranger. Again and again in both his fiction and nonfiction work—much of it highly autobiographical—he takes as his central starting point the voice and life of the outsider, a man not at home in the world. In his fictional works, Theroux's protagonists and narrators include an array of strangers in ever stranger lands: Americans transported to the steamy jungles of Africa and South America; quasi criminals, spies, and government officials lurking in the shadows of southeast Asia; disfranchised Englishmen marooned on their own decaying British isle; husbands and fathers who will not reveal their true personalities and secrets even to their own families; and adventurers whose journeys more often than not end in scenes of solitary repose. They are searchers, off on frequently self-punishing explorations of the interior and exterior worlds. They are faced, finally, with moral dilemmas—choices cloaked in long, dark nights of the soul.

In his nonfiction, most notably in his globe-spanning travel books, Theroux casts himself as the perpetual visitor, the careful observer of people and places, from which he habitually holds himself apart. His role is that of the exiled watcher, creator of the readers' guide to unseen worlds, who examines and records, then moves on without a trace. Because of this, Theroux has been criticized for his detached, ironic, and sometimes bitingly satiric look at the world and its people. Cited are his cool and brutally honest views of the places he visits. He is quick to both admit to and defend himself against these charges: "My life is a paragon of noninvolvement," he told Arthur Lubow in a *People* magazine interview in 1983. Yet several years later, in 1989, he took the opposite tack in an article written for the *New York Times Book Review* titled "Travel Writing: Why I Bother," in which he stated, "I believe I have a sunny disposition, and am not naturally a grouch. It takes a lot of optimism, after all, to be a traveler."

It is in this movement from light to dark, from being very much in a place but never of a place, that Theroux's fictional characters and Theroux himself might best be defined. On one hand, Theroux is an indefatigable traveler who has explored the most remote corners of exotic locales. Yet he admits, freely—and often on the very journeys he faithfully records—to never feeling fully at home and to at times loathing travel in general. In his novels and short stories, his narrators and protagonists suffer from this same sense of dislocation, yet they continue to search and to seek, wandering in difficult, often dangerous landscapes of their own devising. Theroux's answer to this duplicity of feeling— the core emotional contradiction present in nearly all of his work—is the doppelgänger, or double. Borrowing from one of his favorite writers, Joseph Conrad, Theroux has constructed a line of secret sharers, shadow figures who represent a darker side to the conscious and unconscious life. Such figures allow, in a metaphoric sense, for the self meeting the self; they embody the conflict of good versus evil. If Theroux commits a questionable act, thinks a disturbing thought, or goes on a wild adventure, is it Paul Theroux the writer or Paul Theroux the fictional character? It is both and it is neither—the line between what is real and what is imaginary having been extended for the purpose of discovering the what-ifs and what-

might-have-beens, the possibilities present in the previously unexplored, unlived life.

It is the process that all artists and writers must experience on some level in the transformation of life into art, yet Theroux breaks down the barriers between his real and created worlds by deliberately failing to distinguish or spell out easy categories for the reader. There is a direct line between being somewhere else—Theroux the inveterate excursionist and travel writer— and being someone else—Theroux the fictional man. Both incarnations are essentially an act of pilgrimage and reinvention, the remaking of a person given his current surroundings. Travel is an act of discovery, as is writing. Theroux meets the loneliness and isolation present in both with his own creation and rediscovery, his voyages of the body and the spirit.

The shadow characters act out dramas the writer himself may never have literally experienced, yet they allow Theroux to explore a series of possible outcomes in his written work. As he observed in a 1996 interview for the online magazine *Salon,* "The question is not, 'Did it happen?' It is: 'Did it convince you? Did it hold you until the end? Did you like it?' Rather than, 'Is it true?' If all the other things happen—if you read it, like it, remember it, dream about it—in a way it doesn't matter if it's true or not."

In two of Theroux's best-known novels, *My Secret History* (1989) and *My Other Life* (1996), the respective narrators live lives that on the surface are seemingly identical to that of the author himself. Andre Parent, the speaker of *My Secret History,* is a writer and traveler, a man with a life doubling that of Paul Theroux. In *My Other Life* the doubling is even more closely linked: the narrator is named Paul Theroux. Yet it is not Paul Theroux, not exactly, for this is a fiction, an artfully constructed parallel universe in which real people inhabit invented lives. It is through this deliberate obfuscation that Theroux seeks clarity. As he explained in the *Salon* interview: "I'll write a book and call it an autobiography. But it will be all lies. And in fact *My Other Life* is a pack of lies that looks like it amounts to a sort of truth. And I suppose it does."

Explorer of the farthest reaches of the globe, spelunker in the shadowy caverns of the human psyche, chronicler of existing continents and invented nations, teller of truthful lies and fabricated verifications, Theroux is a uniquely American writer. He has captured the dogged optimism of the lone adventurer and the promise of America: to be anyone one wishes to be. Best known for his travel writing, he has moved with ease through varied forms, mastered several disparate and difficult genres, and written more than a book a year since his first published novel in 1967. By turns detached and charming, unknowable yet familiar, he continually revises his own history, and in the process changes our perceptions about the lines between fact and fiction.

CHILDHOOD AND YOUTH

Paul Edward Theroux was born on April 10, 1941, in Medford, Massachusetts, the third son in a family of seven children born to Albert Theroux and Anne Dittami Theroux. Theroux's parents were both one of eight children, and growing up in their respective large families perhaps influenced the value they placed upon the extended familial group and the secure foundation that such a clan can provide. Theroux has observed that coming from a big family forced him, early on, to be both independent—alone in his own private world—and comfortable in the fray of clamoring, boisterous tribes. It is clear that his talent for both isolation and assimilation is rooted in his complex family matrix. As he writes about observing his nieces and nephews at play in "My Extended Family," reprinted in the essay collection *Sunrise with Seamonsters: Travels and Discoveries, 1964–1984* (1985): "Watching these children I am

reminded of my own upbringing, how much freedom I had, how little privacy, how well I was defended and protected. These came as ideas to me quite early in life, for with so much variety around me—such an ideal version of the world—I was able to see the difference between freedom and privacy." Theroux's proclivity for being alone but not lonely, apart from yet very much within the fray, eventually extended to his writing life as well.

Isolation coupled with intense togetherness is a quality long present in the Theroux family history. Theroux's father, Albert, was the descendent of French Canadians who emigrated from Canada in the 1800s into Maine, New Hampshire, Massachusetts, and southward. For many of these early immigrants, their language, strong sense of Catholicism, and close family bonds kept them apart from fellow townspeople. This failure to fully assimilate reached into their educations as well. French Canadian students often attended separate parochial schools in an effort to preserve their French language and distinct heritage. Many of these immigrants found work in New England textile mills. This is the background Albert Theroux had, in Massachusetts, and like those before him, when Albert found work it was in the textile industry, as a salesman for the American Oak Leather Company, which supplied the materials used in the shoe factories of the northeastern United States.

Theroux's mother, Anne Dittami Theroux, was the descendent of Italian immigrants. Her father came to the United States in the early 1900s at the age of twenty-six and soon found work, first in New York, then in Boston, where he opened a tailor shop, married, and raised his children. A graduate of Lowell State College in Massachusetts, Anne Dittami Theroux was a strong believer in both education and creativity; for a time before she married, she was a schoolteacher. Although Albert Theroux did not attend college and never achieved financial prosperity, at times struggling to provide for his family, he loved books and American history, sharing his enthusiasm for both with his children. Meanwhile, Anne Theroux held fast to the American dream. In raising her family, she attempted to impart the importance of success and the promise of limitless possibility, encouraging her children's budding creativity along the way. Anne's wish for greater rewards and a more affluent lifestyle for her children was met with the reality of the Theroux family's modest means, and yet without exception all seven of the Theroux offspring achieved worldly success as adults; three of Paul Theroux's siblings also became writers, most notably his older brother Alexander, the author of several novels and two popular nonfiction books, *The Primary Colors* and *The Secondary Colors,* an exploration of the associative power of color. Alexander, who in the year 2000 continued to teach English at the University of Virginia, had a falling-out with his younger, more successful brother—openly attacking Paul Theroux in the *New York Times*—but there appears to be nothing in the brothers' childhood that anticipated this later animosity.

Medford, Massachusetts, was a stodgily working- and middle-class town, far enough from Boston that it cultivated what might now be seen as traditional, newly suburban, and somewhat oppressive roles and values. Growing up in Medford in the 1950s, Theroux realized early on that he would, without question, have to leave it. Writing in 1980 about his twentieth high school class reunion in a *New York Times Magazine* essay, "The Great Class-Reunion Bazaar," he recalled a youthful sentiment: "I knew only one thing for sure. It was this: Nothing will happen to me in Medford—worse, I will fail here." This is not to suggest that Theroux was a literary prodigy or outwardly ambitious from the start. Far from it; he has acknowledged that he was at best a mediocre student, not particularly interested in literature, influenced much more, he has often joked, by the

countless hours he spent poring over comic books and the L.L. Bean catalog. He has described school as tedious and punishing, and he did not participate in either sports teams or school clubs. In searching for the reasons behind his chosen profession and later literary success, he has said that he is hard-pressed to find evidence of his talent in his early years, yet he has often named his riotous imagination as the source of his writerly invention. But even this he kept a secret from others, later claiming that he feared that any form of creative expression would be perceived as unmanly in a time when masculinity was rather narrowly defined. To this day, Theroux does not believe writing to be a particularly or acceptably masculine profession. He would say that his childhood was full of secrets—truths he hid from others and from himself. Looking back, he would later acknowledge that he had turned his childhood and high school years into a fiction, creating false memories distinctly removed from the reality of the somewhat average youth he appeared on the surface: not bookish, not intellectually curious, and not necessarily bound for success.

Theroux attended public elementary school, played with his brothers and neighborhood children, made play bombs, pulled pranks, and eased into his high school years in the late 1950s. He would later look back and claim that the only event to touch him in all twelve years of his schooling was the launch by the Soviet Union in October 1957 of *Sputnik,* the first artificial satellite sent into Earth orbit, and that he spent most of his adolescence in a state of innocent confusion and mild fear. He has stated that his real education began after he graduated from high school, in 1959, just before the dawn of the great social and political shifts of the 1960s. It was at this time that Theroux, like so many other college students of that era, began to discover his voice, an outspokenness surfacing in the form of protest. Indeed, upon arriving at the University of Maine for the 1959–1960 school year, enrolled as a premed student (the "acceptable" male occupation of physician covering for his still well-hidden dreams), Theroux began writing vehement anti–Vietnam War editorials and refused to register with the Reserve Officers Training Corps (ROTC) as was then required.

Theroux transferred to the University of Massachusetts the following year and settled into a student life of antiwar demonstrations (he was arrested in 1962 for leading a campus demonstration), continuing refusal to join the ROTC, and a developing quest to discover his own core values and beliefs. Theroux did not consider himself part of the pacifist movement, yet he abhorred the military. In 1967 he wrote a short essay titled "Cowardice," collected in *Sunrise with Seamonsters,* in which he admitted his own struggles with fear and anger: "This is really what a coward is, I believe: a person who is afraid of nearly everything and most of all afraid of anger. . . . He accepts his solitary hardship and pays the price of withdrawing."

Uncommitted to a movement he was very much involved in and admittedly fearful of the groups and public faiths he protested, Theroux made two decisions that changed the course of his life. The first was to enroll in a creative writing course at the University of Massachusetts. His instructor, upon reading Theroux's work, put the young student in touch with an editor at Houghton Mifflin, Craig Wiley, who would go on to publish Theroux's first novel, *Waldo* (1967), some four years after their first meeting. The second life-shaping decision Theroux made was to sign up for the Peace Corps, which he did in 1963, after graduating with a bachelor of arts degree during the spring of that year. It is in this move that Theroux embraced, in a decisively dramatic gesture, the desire for travel, for a life far removed from anything he had known, and for, it might be said, a place for his interior or emotional sense of alienation

to find its exterior corollary. If he felt like an outsider, he would truly *be* an outsider.

EARLY TRAVELS AND WRITINGS

Theroux was not immediately accepted into the Peace Corps; he was seen as a potential troublemaker and security risk due to his anti–Vietnam War activities. But after a lengthy interview process, he was signed on as a volunteer and sent to the University of Urbino, in Italy, where he served briefly as a lecturer before being transferred to Malawi (then governed by the British as the protectorate Nyasaland) in eastern Africa.

Theroux has said that before going to Africa he did not know where Malawi was, yet he quickly fell into his new life, teaching English at Soche Hill College and penning what were to be the precursors of his most popular travel writings: short, observational pieces about the people and places he encountered in his exotic new home. These personal essays—about the Great Rift Valley, government activities, a leper colony, his teaching experiences—were published in the *Christian Science Monitor* in a letters-from-Africa series. They were Theroux's first serious, published work, and displayed the same minutely detailed landscapes, wry observations, and deep sense of separateness present in his subsequent travel writings. In these early essays, Theroux seems to be testing his own voice, tentatively at times, and exploring his newfound sense of freedom, his role as an outsider, perhaps as a rebel, and reveling in the act of discovery both in writing and in life. If he comes off as impressionably jejune in some of his pronouncements—he contemptuously dismisses people who take photographs as a way of preserving memories in "The Cerebral Snapshot" and titles one piece "Tarzan Is an Expatriate"—it is because Theroux was quite young—in his early twenties—when they were written.

As he continued to teach and travel within Malawi and southeastern Africa, fulfilling his two-year commitment to the Peace Corps, Theroux also continued to write, branching out into a number of genres—poems, articles, and short stories that appeared in a number of African, British, and American magazines, including *Esquire* and the *Atlantic Monthly*. He was consciously and unconsciously gathering material— the sights, smells, characters, places, and events—that would fill three novels: *Fong and the Indians* (1968), *Girls at Play* (1969), and *Jungle Lovers* (1971), but that would not be written until he had left Africa for good, several years later. Theroux has remarked that he can write about a place only after he has moved on to someplace else, and he has maintained this practice of setting each of his novels in the locale in which he last lived. This is reflected in his travel writings as well; his modus operandi as an explorer is to pass through countries, not settling in any one destination but being ever on the move—usually by train—formulating his impressions and conclusions once he has arrived safely back at his current home. But "home" is a relative term in considering Theroux, for it may be everywhere and nowhere at once.

Near the end of his stay in Malawi, in 1964, Theroux was involved, if unintentionally, in the overthrowing of that country's government. Although the exact details and charges are sketchy—Theroux allegedly aided the guerrilla fighters by helping a rebel leader flee to Uganda—there was enough evidence to persuade Peace Corps officials to expel him from that organization, fine him for several months of unsatisfactory work, and deport him, in 1965, back to Washington D.C. Theroux looked back on his service in the Peace Corps with a mixture of anger and affection in the 1986 article "When the Peace Corps Was Young": "At an uncertain time in my life I joined. And up to a point— they gave me a lot of rope—the Peace Corps al-lowed me to be myself. I realized that it was much better to be neglected than manipulated, and I had learned that you make your own life."

Spending little time back in the United States, Theroux returned to Africa that same year, signing a four- year contract to teach at Makerere University in Kampala, Uganda. There, Theroux lived in a house replete with servants and gardeners (typical for visiting Westerners at that time and place), taught his classes, and worked on what would become his first novel, *Waldo*. It was in Kampala that Theroux met two important figures in his life—Anne Castle, a young British teacher from a neighboring Kenyan girls' school who became his wife—and the writer V. S. Naipaul, with whom Theroux formed a long friendship, until a dramatic and public break in the 1990s. The impact Naipaul and his writing had upon Theroux cannot be underestimated. Theroux's thoughts on the subject would later fill two books: the critical study *V. S. Naipaul* and *Sir Vidia's Shadow*, which traced the friendship to its embittered end. At the time of their first meeting Theroux was twenty-four, and in the thirty-four-year-old Naipaul, he had found his literary mentor, the first person who would call him a writer, and believe, so Theroux felt, in his future success. At nine years Theroux's senior, Naipaul read Theroux's earliest writings—essays and poems—and offered editorial suggestions. During this time, Theroux was also at work on a novel about life under the politically shaky conditions of Uganda during the late 1960s. This work was never published, but *Waldo* appeared in 1967 in the United States and in 1968 in London.

Waldo is very much a first novel—revealing a young writer's familial concerns and demonstrating somewhat wooden plotting and characterization—but it also introduced the hallmarks of both style and subject matter that Theroux would come to be known by: careful attention to the minute, telling detail, use of the ironic aside, and the presence of an isolated male protagonist set against an alien landscape. *Waldo* takes place in a surreally realized Massachusetts and concerns the eponymous antihero Waldo, who is being held in a juvenile reform school as the novel opens. After his release, Waldo—a violently raging adolescent who harbors great hatred for his ineffectual father and weak-willed mother—is off on a series of adventures, sometimes grotesque, at times deadly. It is on this personal odyssey that Waldo falls in with a wealthier older woman, Clovis Techy, who becomes his mistress and patron and sends Waldo to college, where he continues to fight to locate the truth in life.

Through this struggle for meaning and insight, Waldo rejects and attacks all figures of familial and institutional authority—his parents, psychiatrists, school officials—and ends up, fittingly, a writer. Finally, through a series of shadowy twists and turns, Waldo, now a famous and celebrated author, finds himself dangling aloft in a cage as part of a nightclub's feature entertainment:

> He got into his glass writer's-cage and set immediately to work. As he typed . . . he was raised in the air, higher than the night before. But he did not notice it just as he did not notice the locked doors of the cage or the small size of the glass box which was now his home. He had already begun the story, dazzling, uproarious, hilarious, original, vivid.

In this passage, the themes present in nearly all of Theroux's works—the belief in the transformative power of art and its ability to literally and figuratively lift us from our lives; the reinvention of the isolated self; the protagonist's personal remove and detachment—are vividly rendered in clear detail. Theroux would later demonstrate, again and again in both fiction and nonfiction, the writer's ability to be in the world but not part of the ensuing action—never *of* the world. The writer's avocation and devotion separates him from others by an invisible yet ever present shield. In this case, it is a cage

made of glass. For Theroux the narrator and for Theroux's protagonists, the truth is only to be found in pure isolation.

SINGAPORE AND THE NOVELS OF AFRICA

Waldo sold about four thousand copies in the United States and England and received solidly positive reviews, if little literary fanfare. In 1967, while teaching at Makerere University, Theroux married Anne Castle; the couple remained in Africa until 1968, and their first son, Marcel, was born in Kampala that year. But due to increasingly dangerous conditions within Uganda—violent demonstrations, frequent gun battles, a disintegrating governmental structure, and attempted coups—and owing to the fact that his four-year contract at the university was drawing to an end, Theroux accepted a job teaching at the University of Singapore. Late in 1968 he and his family left Africa and resettled in the Far East, living in a small house on the outskirts of Singapore.

Subsequently, in three thematically linked novels—*Fong and the Indians, Jungle Lovers,* and *Girls at Play*—Theroux drew upon his experiences in Africa to continue his exploration of the isolated soul, populating his writing with drifters, American and British expatriates, foreigners, and lost dreamers, all of whom search for, and by turns identify themselves against, their adopted African home. The books were interrupted by what is technically Theroux's third novel, in scope more of a novella, *Murder in Mount Holly.* Published in England in 1969 and never reprinted, the book differs stylistically as well as thematically from the three Africa novels. *Murder in Mount Holly* is a dark, quasi-surrealistic tale, not unlike *Waldo,* and it can be read as a striking back against American conservatism and militarism. Its young hero or antihero, Herbie, is caught up in situations he neither agrees with nor fully understands, including a sudden conscription into the army, which ultimately proves deadly. The novel is what reviewers delicately referred to as "slight" or lacking in fully realized intent. Within the body of Theroux's writings, it registers as a minor misstep.

Theroux had begun gathering material for what would later become his first two Africa novels, *Fong and the Indians* and *Jungle Lovers,* while still in Africa, using a method of writing and revision he has since practiced in all of his work: completing a first draft in notebooks, copying it longhand onto lined paper, typing a third draft, making corrections, and finally turning the manuscript over to someone else to type up the fourth and final draft. This was the method he used for his Africa novels, writing them amid the distractions of the Singaporean heat and noise, while shouldering the demands of his new roles as a husband and father and his duties as a college professor. If Theroux felt the resident outsider while in Africa, this feeling only deepened in Singapore, a conservative and restrictive environment for the young writer; while there, Theroux was warned by the chair of his department not to write about what he had experienced.

Fittingly, all three of Theroux's Africa novels concern outsiders and their innocent and at times misguided, and therefore dangerous, actions, against the backdrop of an exotic landscape. Through a willful misreading of their own limitations, given the set of societal rules implicit within African culture—self-congratulatory neocolonialists out to show the poor villagers the correct way to do things—these Americans and Brits blunder along, often causing, in turn, their own untimely deaths. These three novels form a trilogy of dark secrets and quiet, sure annihilation in the tropics, and they owe not a passing nod to Conrad's *Heart of Darkness.* The novels were published together in 1996 as *On the Edge of the Great Rift: Three Novels of Africa.*

The central characters of *Fong and the Indians, Girls at Play,* and *Jungle Lovers* are men and women who are cut adrift from lives they led within the safe confines of their native countries, yet all expect to find second chances—success, excitement, even redemption—in exotic lands. Instead, these men and women become increasingly disenchanted as Africa refuses to bend to their expectations; often they end up dead. Anything can happen to these unprepared yet high-minded visitors, and a sense of gothic doom, issuing from the dark underpinnings of imminent violence, deceptive appearances, and twisted logic, permeates the novels.

For these unsettled exiles—a Chinese grocer and the only Chinese citizen living in Uganda in *Fong and the Indians*; the naive, alternately destructive and destroyed Western school teachers of *Girls at Play*; and an American insurance salesman in Malawi, in *Jungle Lovers*—order, understanding, and meaning are replaced by the unknowable and deadly dictates of the law of the jungle: the strong survive and the weak and foolhardy are dispatched in the time it takes a lion to bring down a frightened gazelle. Expatriate professors, nuns and priests, runaways, shadowy government officials, and nefarious capitalist adventurers round out the supporting characters. Their dreams involve, in some small fashion, taming a corner of the African continent; their mistakes are ones of entitlement and hubris. When these once hopeful men and women are broken, they often arrive at moments of futile clarity. Sam Fong, the title character of *Fong and the Indians,* comes to this moment when he realizes that his grocery store is a failure:

Fong took a mystified look around the dark, boarded-up shop; what seemed most strange to him was that so much time, so many years could have passed and now, old, with children scuttling around his ankles, in his closed grocery store he had a dumb lonely vision of all those years in Africa.

The vision was foreign, plainly odd rather than shocking: he lacked what the Chinese call "the necessary grains"—he had nothing; he was among neither friends nor strangers, but enemies. . . . Another look at the empty shop, now buzzing with one underfed fly, and it came to him again: *I have nothing, I am owned, I am a slave in a strange country.*

In *Girls at Play,* chapters alternate among characters, following, in turn, a promiscuous young British teacher, Heather Monkhouse; Bettyjean (B. J.) Lebow, a naive, enthusiastic Peace Corps volunteer; and Miss Poole, the rigid colonialist headmistress of the East African girls' school at which the ensuing action takes place. The setting itself—a British boarding school deep in the Kenyan bush country—suggests both mannered civility and order and their Therouxian flip side of natural destruction and violence. It is a setup for danger and an unraveling of a more serious sort than that found in *Fong and the Indians,* involving rape and murder, but the plot of *Girls at Play* charts a similar equation: strangers in a strange land find at first promise, then are broken—not by the uncaring landscape but by their own actions. And when they realize that they are in a place far different from their homeland, as Bettyjean does, it is with a mixture of self-serving and self-congratulatory glee—a rejection of Africa as inferior: "Her good humor returned and she made jokes about Africa, not nasty ones, but ones that showed she did not belong. And one day she said to Miss Mael, 'Really Pam, you should visit the States. It's the greatest place on earth. We've invented so many things. You know, *we* invented Africa.'" It is not entirely a shock when Bettyjean ends up savagely murdered.

Jungle Lovers, the last novel in Theroux's Africa trilogy, combines elements of the two previous works—the outsider in an alien land, the opposition of hope and powerlessness, the constantly shifting definitions of good and evil—in even sharper contrast and with more attention to subplot and complex characterization, and it introduces the figure of the double or doppelgänger. Calvin Mullet is an American insurance agent intent on getting rich by selling life insurance in Malawi. Marais, his double, is a white revolutionary who plots to overthrow the Malawian dictatorship and return the government to the Africans. Both men are outsiders, seeking success, and both feel that they are doing something to help the African people— one offering security, the other political freedom. As the novel progresses, Mullet and Marais battle for their lost causes, and each in his own separate path to despair ends up imperiled and finally broken. The revolutionary and the traveling salesman—the yin and yang of the displaced adventurer—are both idealists and both crushed by their ideals as day gives way to night. There are no happy endings here, only hard lessons and an exacting price: a human life.

The opposition of sunny hopes and dark realism, of dreams and desires matched up against a harsh reality, was a constant in Theroux's own life. By 1971 he was thirty years old. He had taught, unhappily so, for three years at the University of Singapore and in that time had managed to publish four works of fiction. Each of his Africa novels met with increasingly positive reviews, yet Theroux still did not feel he had attained lasting success in either a literary or financial sense. His novels received only small advances—usually a few thousand dollars—and could not be depended upon for steady income. In 1969 Theroux and his wife had added a second son, Louis, to their family; their first child, Marcel, was almost two. Theroux continued his struggle to make ends meet, writing book reviews and articles for a variety of American and British magazines, and short stories, all while teaching his courses in Jacobean drama at the university. But the pressure of raising a family, teaching full time, and writing, all while living in an inhospitable environment—Theroux was one of only a very few expatriate lecturers at the university, all the others having been replaced by native Chinese and Singaporean teachers—proved too much. Theroux journeyed alone on a trip through Borneo, but upon returning to Singapore, he vowed to leave the country and to never again accept another teaching position, or any job other than that of full-time writer. It was a vow he would break only once by the end of the century. In 1971 Theroux and his wife and children left Asia and moved to a small cottage in Dorset, England.

ENGLAND AND *THE GREAT RAILWAY BAZAAR*

Theroux would later say that he moved to England because it was his wife's native country and because it offered a pleasant contrast to Singapore, but it bears noting that after eight years away from the United States, Theroux, ever the peripatetic observer, was in no rush to return to his native land. England was also the home of Naipaul, who continued to advise and encourage Theroux and who introduced him to a number of British authors. It was in England that Theroux's fate as a writer would forever change, for it was there, in 1973, that he conceived of and set out upon a journey by train from London to Asia and back again, recording his thoughts and observations of this extended sojourn in what would become the best-selling *The Great Railway Bazaar: By Train through Asia* (1975). True to form, Theroux's imagination had taken him someplace far from his current home, on a literal excursion. Theroux the inveterate wanderer had hit upon what was for him a fitting and hugely successful form: travel writing. But this was not before he had written and published several other works.

After arriving in England in November 1971, Theroux settled into work on three distinctly different writing projects. Living in the English countryside, at a far remove from the climates of Singapore and Africa, Theroux looked back upon his eight years in these exotic locales and began gathering the various short stories he had written during that period. The resulting work was his first collection of short fiction, *Sinning with Annie, and Other Stories,* published in 1972. The characters present in these stories are familiar from those in his novels: disaffected men and women living isolated lives in foreign countries—Peace Corps volunteers, consulate workers, teachers, willful men whose marriages and friendships have gone wrong and whose personal and political maneuverings often end in futile despair. Written in a deliberate, dryly realistic style that had come to characterize Theroux's narrative tendencies, the stories follow the ins and outs of the expatriate life; the humor found here is biting and ironic. The characters who populate *Sinning with Annie* are outsiders—all careful watchers and observers. In their experiences and personalities, they may be examined as extensions, shadowy doubles, of Theroux himself. Indeed, when these and later stories were gathered in *The Collected Stories,* published in 1997, Theroux raised the issue of the overlapping of life and art in his introduction to the work: "People who have no idea who they are talking to have told me they love Paul Theroux's stories; yet I can see they aren't impressed with me. Of course! Other people have told me to my face that they dislike my stories, but that I am a good sort. Why is this? As a person I am hurt and incomplete. My stories are the rest of me." Stories told the story of his life, with a few careful twists of fact.

During 1971 Theroux also completed *V. S. Naipaul: An Introduction to His Work,* published in 1972. This book, an exhaustive critical study of Naipaul's fiction and nonfiction, was written, Theroux would later say, as a form of thanks and admiration, a tribute to his mentor. It was released in a small press run and is now considered a rare edition, of interest primarily to scholars.

The third project Theroux completed during his first year in England was the manuscript for the novel *Saint Jack*. Published in 1973, this work displays two of Theroux's characteristic hallmarks: it is set in his previous home—in this case, Singapore—and it utilizes the figure of the double in mining the territory between the overlapping worlds of fiction and life. The title character is Jack Fiori, a middle-aged Boston native who runs a brothel in Singapore. The novel charts Jack's attempts to pen a novel featuring a main character named Jack Flowers (in a move similar to Theroux's own author/character flipping), but Jack soon gives up this pursuit and focuses instead upon the Singaporean underworld of which he is a part. Befriended by William Leigh, an older American accountant, to whom Jack confesses his secrets and desires and in whom Jack sees his own inevitable decline, Jack begins to explore dreams of what his life might have been. Leigh acts as Jack Fiori's double—a possible life—and when Leigh dies suddenly, Jack must come to terms with his own life of misdeeds. Yet as the title ironically suggests, Jack does not see himself as a bad or evil man, just a doggedly optimistic one. When Jack contemplates his own poverty, it is not without the great hope of a dreamer, that characteristically American orientation: "Being poor was the promise of success; the anticipation of fortune, a fine conscious postponement, made the romance, for to happen best it would have to come all at once, as a surprise, with the great thud a bag of gold makes when it's plopped on a table."

Theroux doubtless saw the conditions of his own life within these lines. At thirty, he had published eight books; *Saint Jack* was his ninth and the one he hoped would bestow on him financial solvency. Despite his successes, however, he was no closer to becoming the moneyed, independent writer he had dreamed of becoming when he quit his teaching post in Singapore. *Saint Jack* would go on to sell about

seventy-five hundred copies in its initial release, and in 1979 it was made into a motion picture starring Ben Gazzara. But the Theroux family was still financially strapped. Theroux's wife, Anne, decided to accept a job as a broadcaster with the British Broadcasting Corporation, and the couple and their two children moved into a small apartment in London. Theroux broke his vow of never teaching again, and took a one-semester appointment in the English Department of the University of Virginia, teaching creative writing as a writer-in-residence during the fall term of 1972.

While in Virginia, Theroux completed his seventh novel, *The Black House,* published in 1974. Set in his last home base, Dorset, England, the story concerns Alfred Munday, a retired anthropologist who has moved to the English countryside with his wife after ten years in the African bush. Part gothic ghost story, part psychological thriller, *The Black House* is first and foremost a novel about obsession, fear, and the condition of the untrusting outsider—all familiar themes. Like so many of Theroux's protagonists before him, Munday is haunted by his past and unwilling and unable to reconcile himself with his present surroundings. Thus isolated, he must face responsibility for his own demise or redemption, and in this dark novel, death is everywhere. Written during a bleak and perhaps despairing period of Theroux's life, it would be his last work before he achieved unquestionable critical and financial success with *The Great Railway Bazaar.*

The Black House received respectful reviews, though it sold only modestly, and after his brief reentry into teaching, Theroux hit upon the idea for a new writing project. He would leave from Victoria Station in London and journey to Paris, on to Istanbul, through Afghanistan, India, the Far East, and Japan, then return via the Soviet Union, all by train. He would weave together his thoughts and observations in one narrative, describing what he saw on this railway expedition; it would be his first travel book. It was not a calculated or even well-planned journey—Theroux undertook the trip and the book that resulted simply as a way to make money. But *The Great Railway Bazaar* marks a definitive turning point for Theroux. It was the book that forever changed his life and career, and in travel writing Theroux was able to bring together the disparate elements he had explored within his fiction and his life: the figure of the outsider in strange, often threatening locales; stark and unflinching observation and attention to detail; ironic, self-deprecating humor; the mysterious inner self; the kaleidoscope of possible lives that the world provides.

Theroux has said repeatedly that he abhors travel writing that attempts to paint a too-pretty picture, writing that is replete with syrupy or laudatory postcard sentiments. In his travel writings, Theroux often takes the opposite tack, exposing every blemish and incongruity associated with the places he sees. In his description of a settlement in Burma in *The Great Railway Bazaar,* he neither romanticizes nor overlooks even the homeliest details:

> The "canteen" . . . was one of these grass-roofed huts: inside was a long table with tureens of green and yellow stew, and Burmese, thinly clad for such a cold place, were warming themselves beside caldrons of rice bubbling over braziers. It looked like the field kitchen of some Mongolian tribe retreating after a terrible battle: the cooks were old Chinese women with black teeth [who] . . . ladled the stews onto large palm leaves and plopped down a fistful of rice; this the travelers ate with cups of hot weak tea. The rain beat on the roof and crackled on the mud outside, and Burmese hurried to the train with chickens bound so tightly in feather bundles, they looked like a peculiar kind of native handicraft. I bought a two-cent cigar, found a stool near a brazier, and sat and smoked until the next train came.

In the many travel books he would subsequently write—charting his journeys through South America and Patagonia, China, the Mediter-

ranean, the South Pacific—the trip itself, going from point A to point B, becomes the mode by which Theroux can explore the minutiae of each moment, each exposed and exposing detail. As he relates his experiences, he adopts the voice of a knowledgeable if prickly visitor. Many critics came to criticize this narrative approach, calling Theroux everything from dyspeptic to grumpy to misanthropic, yet Theroux would also become perhaps the best-known contemporary travel writer in the world. His refusal to sugarcoat his descriptions of the world's sights and peoples is the very reason so many readers find him a compelling raconteur, a trustworthy provider of outpost dispatches and field notes. But it is more than simply honest recounting: for Theroux, travel is a means to an end. There is no arrival or clear destination, only more places to see. In this sense, the journey is the backdrop: the true exploration concerns Theroux's own perceptions, his revelations, his hopes and fears.

There is never any question in his works that these are Theroux's journeys. His is a singular vision: one man alone, making his way through utterly foreign landscapes, and while exploring the far corners of the globe he is recognizable only to himself and the unfamiliar—everything and everyone else remains at a slight remove. This distance is not unlike the glass writer's cage that Waldo finds himself held within at the end of Theroux's first novel, and it is present on journeys in which he is both watcher and watched, a lone figure always passing through on his way to someplace else, but never pausing long enough to become part of the lives and places he observes. The search is for the ever elusive, mythical homeland; he is a pilgrim on a never-ending quest. As he writes near the end of his journey in *The Great Railway Bazaar* of traveling through the then-Soviet Union:

> All morning the tree trunks, black with dampness, were silhouettes in the fog, and the pine groves at the very limit of visibility in the mist took on the

appearance of cathedrals with dark spires. In places the trees were so dim, they were like an afterimage on the eye. I had never felt close to the country, but the fog distanced me even more, and I felt, after 6,000 miles and all those days in the train, only a great remoteness . . . I wanted to be home.

The Great Railway Bazaar opened up a whole new world for Theroux, both literally and figuratively. Published in 1975, it immediately went into a third printing and quickly sold thirty-five thousand copies. It has since sold many multiples of that figure. It received the highest critical praise of Theroux's career—including a laudatory front-page review in the *New York Times Book Review*—and was chosen as a Book-of-the-Month Club main selection. It also earned Theroux considerable financial reward; from that time on he was able to earn a living solely as a writer. As he wrote in 1998 in *Sir Vidia's Shadow* of this turning point: "I was out from under. I never again worried about money—that freedom from worry was wealth to me. No more drudging. I was free. I was thirty-two."

The Great Railway Bazaar was significant for another reason as well. In the coming years Theroux, though he continued to publish novels, was identified primarily as a travel writer. In fact, as he has frequently pointed out in interviews, many readers have never read his fiction nor do they realize that he has written fiction. After penning *The Great Railway Bazaar*, Theroux continued to publish weighty travel tomes, several of which also became best-sellers. Still, none of Theroux's subsequent travel books would have quite the impact of *The Great Railway Bazaar*. It stands as a unique and defining endeavor in Theroux's life, both in terms of outward public and critical success and his own interior creative life. In his writing as in his life, Theroux is a searcher, continually on the move—defining, redefining, and reinventing. And in this searching he has created the perfect means of expression: the travel book written as a mapped exploration of one man's soul. Eccentric, eclectic, and entirely his own person, it is through Theroux that the reader experiences the world, and it is through the world that Theroux searches for himself.

THE BENEFITS OF ACCLAIM

After the freeing financial success and critical acclaim of *The Great Railway Bazaar*, Theroux turned his attention back to fiction. This was to be a pattern he followed in his later writing life, moving from travel books to novels with even progression, much like his practice of setting his novels in the place of his previous residence. Predictably, Theroux set his fiction of this period primarily in England, while he himself set off on literal journeys.

Although he continued to make his primary home in London, albeit in a much larger house, he purchased a secondary residence on Cape Cod in Massachusetts. There, he began spending summers and vacations near his boyhood home, reacquainting himself with his family and old friends. This would be his first significant return to American life since leaving it some fifteen years before. Theroux's wife, Anne, continued her work at the BBC, while his sons attended London schools.

Far from enticing him to rest on his laurels, Theroux's success and recognition only made him more prolific. He maintained his book-a-year rate and often published two or more works in the same year, and he continued to write fiction even after it became clear that his nonfiction travel writing would be the source of greater prosperity and advancement. Herein lies another of Theroux's contradictions: while most readers have come to think of Theroux as a travel writer, he regards himself primarily as a novelist. While none of his fictions can match the public reception of his nonfiction work—save perhaps for *The Mosquito Coast* (1982)—he has never slackened in his pursuit of what others deem his secondary genre. The novels and short stories written during this period contain the types of characters readers had come to expect of Theroux's fictions—isolated expatriates and outsiders coming to terms with their own beliefs and personal illusions: Valentine Hood, the dangerously embittered ex-consulate worker involved with a group of London terrorists in *The Family Arsenal* (1976); Maude Coffin Pratt, the unforgiving New England photographer of *Picture Palace* (1978), who at the end of her years realizes that her only true life has been that captured in her pictures, that her art has eclipsed her own personal failures; Dr. Lauren Slaughter and Dr. Gerald DeMarr, the main characters of *Half Moon Street: Two Short Novels* (1984), physicians who lead double lives, their respectable daytime occupations hiding shady nighttime pursuits. By turns dark and light, Theroux's characters engage in continuing, often unsuccessful, personal struggles to reconcile the conflicting halves of their personalities.

In 1977 Theroux was presented with an award in literature from the American Academy and Institute of Arts and Letters, and in 1978, *Picture Palace* won that year's prestigious Whitbread Award in England. These were the first significant literary prizes Theroux had received. For most of his career as a writer, he had been denied artistic support in the form of grants or awards, several times applying for, but never receiving, either a National Endowment for the Arts or a Guggenheim Foundation grant. The awards were a significant boost to his morale, for just as he refused to rest on the commercial success of his travel writing, he sought critical and scholarly approbation for his less recognized novels and short stories.

Setting forth on his next extended journey, the trip that saw book form in *The Old Patagonia Express: By Train through the Americas* (1979), Theroux left from Boston during the winter of 1978 and traveled by rail for weeks through Central and South America to the tip of Argentina—the desolate ends of Patagonia. In *The Old Patagonia Express,* Theroux again focuses, even more acutely than he does in *The Great Railway Bazaar,* upon the journey itself—his fellow passengers, each momentary gesture and frozen scene through a blurred window—rather than upon any particular place or final destination. Small wonder: the Patagonia of the book's title is an empty, unpeopled, and unforgiving moonscape. It is in such environs that the traveler must confront himself, or else keep moving. Theroux chooses a bit of both, as he acknowledges near the end of his journey: "I knew I was nowhere, but the most surprising thing of all was that I was still in the world after all this time, on a dot at the lower part of the map. The landscape had a gaunt expression, but I could not deny that it had readable features and that I existed in it. This was a discovery—the look of it. I thought: *Nowhere is a place.*" This last line provided the title for a collaborative work Theroux authored with fellow travel writer Bruce Chatwin some years later, a photographic and text compilation, *Nowhere Is a Place: Travels in Patagonia,* published in 1986.

The Old Patagonia Express secured Theroux's reputation as one of—if not the—preeminent travel writers in the world. Critics praised the work's depth, perceptive commentary, and startlingly honest vision. True to form, Theroux, pleased but exhausted from his journey, subsequently turned to fiction, publishing two children's books that he had written for his sons, *A Christmas Card* (1978) and *London Snow: A Christmas Story* (1979), and a collection of short fiction, *World's End and Other Stories* (1980). During this period, Theroux also began work on what would become his most acclaimed novel to date, *The Mosquito Coast.* The idea for the novel had come to the author on his travels through Central America; in writing it he was also heavily influenced by the 1978 Jonestown,

Guyana, massacre presided over by the messianic cult leader Jim Jones. The intersecting themes of travel and death are basic and recurring motifs in Theroux's works, and in *The Mosquito Coast,* he brings together much of what he had explored in his writing up to that point: naive, foolhardy outsiders (Americans) plopped down in a dangerous jungle locale; the clash between belief and myth; the interior journey paralleling the exterior quest; and personal will and false triumph versus nature's inevitable destruction. In Allie Fox, *The Mosquito Coast*'s egomaniacal inventor/father protagonist, Theroux had created his ultimate portrait of a man at once at war with and wedded to his world. Narrated by Allie's fourteen-year-old son, Charlie, the novel follows the Fox family as Allie moves them from Massachusetts—to escape the modern world's dangers of strip malls and corrupt politicians—to the Honduran jungle. Allie's absurdity and hubris is heightened by his dream of bringing ice to the jungle natives, and when the Fox family—after a series of twisting revelations and natural tragedies of biblical proportions—are left struggling for life, there is no one and nothing left either to fear or believe in except themselves. The novel ends on a note of simultaneous hope and obliteration.

The Mosquito Coast, published in 1982, earned Theroux the strongest reviews he had received thus far for a novel. At last, Theroux's fiction was heralded with a reception equal to that of his nonfiction travel works. The novel would go on to sell well and to win the James Tait Black Award and the *Yorkshire Post* Best Novel of the Year award in Britain. In 1986 it was made into a motion picture starring Harrison Ford as Allie Fox. The movie received mixed reviews, but Ford's performance as the crazed father-figure Fox was almost unanimously praised. Theroux was formally inducted into the American Academy and Institute of Arts and Letters and became a member of the Royal Society of Literature and the Royal Geographical Society in England. At forty-one, he had arrived at what might be considered the pinnacle of his career.

THE CONTINUING SEARCH FOR THE SELF

Following publication of *The Mosquito Coast,* Theroux began the start of what would become an even more introspective period in his life and work. He set off on another journey, this time around the coast of his adopted homeland. The resulting work, *The Kingdom by the Sea: A Journey around Great Britain* (1983), was an unflinchingly harsh look at England and the British coast. The book was met with an equally cool critical reception. Some British critics took Theroux to task for what they saw as his lampooning of a country that had been kind to him over the years. It marked the beginning of the end of Theroux's time in the United Kingdom, and by the late 1980s, he had left England altogether and begun to divide his time between his home on Cape Cod and a residence on Oahu, Hawaii.

The years 1983 and 1984 saw the publication of the short story collection *The London Embassy* (1983) and of *Half Moon Street.* Theroux's journeys down the Yangtze River in China and through India by train provided the material for two slim travel books, *Sailing through China* (1984) and *The Imperial Way: By Rail from Peshawar to Chittagong* (1985). In 1985 Theroux published a collection of essays and articles written over the previous twenty years as *Sunrise with Seamonsters.* Then, in a somewhat mysterious move, Theroux, picking up on ideas of false utopia and destruction he had worked on in *The Mosquito Coast,* produced his first—and so far only—science fiction work, *O-Zone,* published in 1986. The novel paints a bleak picture of a decimated and contaminated twenty-first-century America and the various groups who fight for survival within it. *O-Zone* was met with mixed reviews and left many critics curious as to what Theroux was up to with his experimentation in the science fiction genre. Was it simply a journey of another sort, or was this the work of a writer reaching too far afield and missing his intended mark? Theroux, ever more elusive, did not provide many answers.

By then, he was off on another extended journey, this time a nearly yearlong excursion in Asia. *Riding the Iron Rooster: By Train through China* (1988) was the resulting book, and while this would be one of Theroux's most popular works among all his travel books—spending sixteen weeks on the *New York Times* best-seller list—it was also his most cutting, sardonic, and dark travelogue to date. Critics pointed out Theroux's increasingly ironic and detached outlook, and reviews for the book bore titles such as "He Hated Sightseeing" and rejected its author's complaining tone and grumpiness. In interviews and in his own essays Theroux defended his work as an honest appraisal of what he had witnessed on his travels.

Theroux followed his adventures in China with what would be the first of a pair of somewhat controversial if highly successful novels—*My Secret History* and *My Other Life*—both of which fall into the intentionally cloudy area of autobiographical fiction. He was now exploring the landscape of his own lived life with the fervor and intensity with which he had explored so many remote and uncharted territories. In *My Secret History,* Theroux's alter ego, Andre Parent, lives a life that is a familiar version of Theroux's own existence, but there are two double lives at work here—that of author and his protagonist-creation and that of the protagonist's own secret, private life. In *My Other Life,* Theroux journeys down the same path, but simultaneously clarifies and distorts the facts by calling his narrator Paul Theroux, and by giving him a life that is identical to the life Paul Theroux himself had lived up to that point. Theroux called the work an "imaginary memoir" in the author's note that opens the novel, stating: "The man is fiction, but the mask is real." Even though Theroux uses actual names and incidents throughout, the outcomes are all slightly shifted from those in reality. Even before publication, *My Other Life* met with protest. Readers and critics—indeed, Theroux's own family members—were concerned with his intentional blurring of the boundaries between fact and fiction, life and imagination. Theroux, once more, made no apologies for his invention of a hypothetical life, his truthful lie, even if it was at the expense of others' reputations.

During this period, Theroux produced the novel *Chicago Loop* (1990), which added yet another double-sided figure to Theroux's gallery of duplicitous rogues: Parker Jagoda, Chicago businessman and father by day, psychopath by night. Simultaneously, a collection of Theroux's previous travel writings appeared in *To the Ends of the Earth: The Selected Travels of Paul Theroux* (1990), and Theroux set off on his most prolonged and dangerous journey to date, voyaging alone by kayak through the islands of the South Pacific. The trip began with the end of Theroux's marriage to Anne—they divorced in 1993—and continued on, with few breaks, for two years. The product of this journey, *The Happy Isles of Oceania: Paddling the Pacific,* published in 1992, weighed in at 528 pages and, as its ironically coded title suggests, painted a largely gloomy portrait of a characteristically sunny area of the globe. Theroux, whether due to internal concerns—"My soul hurt, my heart was damaged, I was lonely," he remarks—or the more external incidents he encounters along the way, comes off as weary, but he had lost none of his sharp eye's searching sense of detail. *The Happy Isles of Oceania* received praise for its literary quality and subject matter, but it was frequently criticized for its overridingly negative tone.

Inspired by something he witnessed on this journey—Trobri and Islanders who followed the

Seventh-Day Adventist religion—Theroux wrote *Millroy the Magician* (1994). The novel follows the exploits of an evangelical road-show performer—the Millroy of the title—and his personal quest to introduce a biblically inspired health-food diet to Americans. The novel received mixed reviews. Following fiction with travel in his typical form, Theroux left for an extended tour of the Mediterranean coastline, travels that he would weave together in the work *The Pillars of Hercules: A Grand Tour of the Mediterranean* (1995). His subsequent novel, *Kowloon Tong* (1997), takes place in Hong Kong and charts the lives of one English family and the effect of the Chinese takeover of that longtime British colony.

By this point in Theroux's career, readers seemed to fall into two distinct camps with respect to his travel writing: devoted readers, those who appreciated Theroux's discursive, irony-laden narratives, and critics, who derided his at times peevish or cantankerous assessments of the places he visited. Theroux addressed this division in print, writing on the opening page of *The Pillars of Hercules*: "I had traveled past clumps of runty stunted trees and ugly houses (the person who just muttered, 'Oh, there he goes again!' must read no further)." and Theroux's readership was secure enough by the 1990s that he was perhaps unmoved by critical complaint.

This ongoing critical debate extended to other genres in which Theroux wrote as well, developing into a full-blown literary contretemps with the publication in 1998 of *Sir Vidia's Shadow*. The highly personal and scrutinizing memoir of Theroux's friendship and later falling out with Naipaul drew almost unanimous criticism for its tone and subject matter, while winning praise for its crystalline prose. Theroux had turned his unflinching eye upon a former friend, and the resulting portrait disturbed and confused many. At the same time, Theroux had provided an equally severe portrait of himself. The question

remains unanswered as to whether or not Theroux, with his love of and obsession for the hidden, unknowable self, is aware of how much he had revealed, if anything at all.

CONCLUSION

In the year 2000, at the age of fifty-nine, Theroux published a collection of his travel articles and essays, *Fresh Air Fiend: Travel Writings, 1985–2000*. There were few areas of the globe he had not set foot upon, and with the release of this work he showed no sign of slowing in his journeys, both literal and imaginative, in fact and in fiction. In 1995 he was married again, to Sheila Donnely. His oldest son, Marcel, had become a writer too, following in what had become a Theroux family tradition. Theroux continued to write, explore, and probe the solitary reaches of his own soul and that of the earth's most alien landscapes, both distanced from and a part of what he views, within and without the world. He continued to pursue the questions he had asked himself at the beginning of his travels, those he had posed, at the age of twenty-three, in the essay "The Edge of the Great Rift," reprinted in *Sunrise with Seamonsters*:

> I stand on the grassy edge of the Great Rift. I feel it under me and I expect soon a mighty heave to send us all sprawling. The Great Rift. And whom does this rift concern? Is it perhaps a rift with the stars? Is it between earth and man, or man and man? Is there something under this African ground seething still?
>
> We like to believe that we are riding it and that it is nothing more than an imperfection in the crust of the earth. We do not want to be captive to this rift, as if we barely belong, as if we were scrawled on the landscape by a piece of chalk.

In elucidating the Great Rift, Theroux offers a definition of identity in the absence of place and belonging. He illuminates the constant exiled state: self in the presence of nothingness, the writer as watcher, wanderer, messenger, and fugitive, everywhere and nowhere at once.

Selected Bibliography

WORKS OF PAUL THEROUX

NOVELS AND SHORT STORY COLLECTIONS

Waldo. Boston: Houghton Mifflin, 1967.

Fong and the Indians. Boston: Houghton Mifflin, 1968.

Girls at Play. Boston: Houghton Mifflin, 1969.

Murder in Mount Holly. London: Alan Ross, 1969.

Jungle Lovers. Boston: Houghton Mifflin, 1971.

Sinning with Annie and Other Stories. Boston: Houghton Mifflin, 1972.

Saint Jack. Boston: Houghton Mifflin, 1973.

The Black House. Boston: Houghton Mifflin, 1974.

The Family Arsenal. Boston: Houghton Mifflin, 1976.

The Consul's File. Boston: Houghton Mifflin, 1977. (Short story collection.)

Picture Palace. Boston: Houghton Mifflin, 1978.

World's End and Other Stories. Boston: Houghton Mifflin, 1980.

The Mosquito Coast. Boston: Houghton Mifflin, 1982.

The London Embassy. Boston: Houghton Mifflin, 1983. (Short story collection.)

Half Moon Street: Two Short Novels. Boston: Houghton Mifflin, 1984. (Contains *Doctor Slaughter* and *Doctor DeMarr.*)

O-Zone. New York: G. P. Putnam's Sons, 1986.

My Secret History. New York: G. P. Putnam's Sons, 1989.

Chicago Loop. New York: Random House, 1990.

Millroy the Magician. New York: Random House, 1994.

My Other Life. Boston: Houghton Mifflin, 1996.

On the Edge of the Great Rift: Three Novels of Africa. New York: Penguin, 1996. (Contains *Fong and the Indians, Girls at Play,* and *Jungle Lovers.*)

The Collected Stories. New York: Viking, 1997.

Kowloon Tong. Boston: Houghton Mifflin, 1997.

TRAVEL BOOKS

The Great Railway Bazaar: By Train through Asia. Boston: Houghton Mifflin, 1975.

The Old Patagonia Express: By Train through the Americas. Boston: Houghton Mifflin, 1979.

The Kingdom by the Sea: A Journey around Great Britain. Boston: Houghton Mifflin, 1983.

Sailing through China. Boston: Houghton Mifflin, 1984.

The Imperial Way: By Rail from Peshawar to Chittagong. Photographs by Steve McCurry. Boston: Houghton Mifflin, 1985.

Nowhere Is a Place: Travels in Patagonia. San Francisco: Yolla Bolly Press, 1986. (A text and photo work, coauthored with Bruce Chatwin, with photographs by Jeff Gnass.)

Riding the Iron Rooster: By Train through China. New York: G. P. Putnam's Sons, 1988.

To the Ends of the Earth: The Selected Travels of Paul Theroux. New York: Random House, 1990.

The Happy Isles of Oceania: Paddling the Pacific. New York: G. P. Putnam's Sons, 1992.

The Pillars of Hercules: A Grand Tour of the Mediterranean. New York: G. P. Putnam's Sons, 1995.

Fresh Air Fiend: Travel Writings, 1985–2000. Boston: Houghton Mifflin, 2000.

OTHER WORKS

V. S. Naipaul: An Introduction to His Work. London: Andre Deutsch, 1972.

A Christmas Card. Boston: Houghton Mifflin, 1978. (A children's book.)

London Snow: A Christmas Story. Wilton, England: Michael Russel, 1979. (A children's book.)

Sunrise with Seamonsters: Travels and Discoveries, 1964–1984. Boston: Houghton Mifflin, 1985.

Sir Vidia's Shadow: A Friendship across Five Continents. Boston: Houghton Mifflin, 1998.

UNCOLLECTED ESSAYS AND ARTICLES

"The Great Class-Reunion Bazaar." *New York Times Magazine,* September 14, 1980, pp. 88+.

"When the Peace Corps Was Young." *New York Times,* February 25, 1986, p. 31A.

"Travel Writing: Why I Bother." *New York Times Book Review,* July 30, 1989, pp. 7–8.

"Memory and Creation: Reflections at Fifty." *Massachusetts Review* 32:381–400 (fall 1991).

"The Other Wife—One Man Asks the Eternal, Nagging Question: Where Would I Be Now if I Had Married Her? Paul Theroux Imagines the Answer." *Vogue,* May 1996, p. 308.

"Bookend: Memory and Invention." *New York Times Book Review,* November 1, 1998, p. 39.

CRITICAL AND BIOGRAPHICAL STUDIES

Coale, Samuel. "A Quality of Light: The Fiction of Paul Theroux." *Critique: Studies in Contemporary Fiction* 22, no. 3:5–30 (1981).

———. *Paul Theroux.* Boston: Twayne, 1987.

Epstein, Joseph. "Poison Pen-Pals." *Commentary* 107, no. 3:36–41 (March 1999).

Glaser, E. "The Self-Reflexive Traveler: Paul Theroux on the Art of Travel and Travel Writing." *Centennial Review* 33:193–206 (1989).

Krist, Gary. "Me, Myself, and I." *New Republic* 201:40–42 (July 17, 1989). (Review of *My Secret History.*)

Naipaul, V. S. "Letters to a Young Writer." *The New Yorker,* June 26 and July 3, 1995, pp. 144–154. (Naipaul's letters to Paul Theroux.)

Santelmann, Neal. "Touring Pro." *Forbes* 153, no. 6:34–37 (March 14, 1994).

Weller, Anthony. "Paul Theroux: The Writer of Fine Fiction and Travel Literature Tells What Separates the Tourists from the Explorers." *Geo* 5:12–18 (November 1983).

Wheeler, Edward T. "What the Imagination Knows: Paul Theroux's Search for the Second Self." *Commonweal* 121:18–22 (May 20, 1994).

INTERVIEWS

Baumgold, Julie. "Fellow Traveler: Blending Fact with Fiction with Paul Theroux." *Esquire* 126, no. 3:184–186 (September 1996).

Garner, Dwight. "Paul Theroux: His Secret Life." *Salon,* September 2, 1996.

Lubow, Arthur. "Paul Theroux: Casting a Cold Eye on the Land Where He Lives, an American Writer Makes Waves in Great Britain." *People Weekly,* December 12, 1983, pp. 124–125.

Noble, Holcombe B. "A Novel Gives You a Second Chance." *New York Times Book Review,* June 4, 1989, p. 28.

FILMS BASED ON THE WORKS OF PAUL THEROUX

Saint Jack. Screenplay by Peter Bogdanovich. Directed by Peter Bogdanovich. Paramont, 1979.

The Mosquito Coast. Screenplay by Paul Schrader. Directed by Peter Weir. Warner, 1986.

Half Moon Street. Screenplay by Bob Swaim. Directed by Bob Swaim. RKO, 1986.

—LIESEL LITZENBURGER

August Wilson

1945–

*F*EW PLAYWRIGHTS HAVE garnered the popular and critical accolades that have been bestowed upon African American dramatist August Wilson. Though some might misguidedly attribute his ascension to the pantheon of great American playwrights as evidence of our culture's proclivity for praising fulsomely, Wilson's meteoric rise stems from the originality and vibrancy of his voice and the scope of his artistic imagination. That Wilson has been positioned alongside our most lionized dramatists—Eugene O'Neill, Arthur Miller, Tennessee Williams—bears out that his penetrating forays into the psyches of African Americans and their history is currently unrivaled. Moreover, while Lorraine Hansberry (*A Raisin in the Sun*) and Amiri Baraka (*Dutchman*) have heretofore been regarded as America's most accomplished black dramatists, Wilson's multiple Pulitzer Prizes, New York Drama Critics' Circle Awards, Tony Awards, and artistic fellowships make him the most critically, popularly, and financially successful black dramatist of this or preceding generations. The playwright's stated goal of composing a ten-play cycle representing each decade of the African American experience, as outlined in an interview with Kim Powers, encapsulates the ambitiousness of this unique and eloquent voice:

> Somewhere along the way it dawned on me that I was writing one play for each decade. Once I became conscious of that, I realized I was trying to focus on what I felt were the most important issues confronting Black Americans for that decade, so ultimately they could stand as a record of Black experience over the past hundred years presented in the form of dramatic literature.

LIFE AND EARLY CAREER

August Wilson was born Frederick August Kittel on April 27, 1945, in Pittsburgh, Pennsylvania, to Daisy Wilson Kittel, a black cleaning woman, and Frederick Kittel, a white German baker. He was the fourth of their six children. Wilson's relationship with his father was at best strained, for the elder Frederick never lived with the family and was little more than an occasional presence in his children's lives. Daisy Wilson later wed David Bedford, who then moved the family from the racially diverse "Hill" community to a white suburb; the racial animosity that greeted them is eerily reminiscent of that faced by the Hansberrys when Lorraine's father, Carl, challenged racially discriminatory housing covenants by moving his family to an all-white Chicago suburb. Wilson's relationship with his stepfather was also prickly. Significantly, David Bedford's life served as a model for Troy Maxson, the embittered protagonist of *Fences* (1986). Like his fictionalized counterpart, Bedford had athletic ambitions that were thwarted by racism; he then turned to crime and served twenty-three years for robbery and murder. An important moment in Wilson's youth occurred during his sophomore year at Gladstone High School: a teacher accused him of plagiarizing a paper on Napoleon, and a distraught Wilson immediately dropped out. But his subsequent informal "education" in the Hill district's gritty restaurants, bar, and barbershops would give him a command of the language and overall cultural ethos which would become the trademark of each of his works. A year after his departure from high school, Wilson spent a year in the army and was discharged in 1963.

The year 1965 represented a turning point in young August's life: he moved into a rooming house and purchased his first typewriter. However, the most artistically transformative event was his purchase of a Bessie Smith record. "Nobody in Town Can Bake a Sweet Jelly Roll Like Mine" introduced Wilson to the music and language that would become the bedrock of every play he would author. He recalled in the preface to *Fences*:

> I put that record on, and I'll tell you, I felt as though she was talking directly to me. The universe stuttered when I heard her voice. I played it again, and again, over and over. The world began to change in front of my eyes. The other records disappeared. The people around me suddenly began to look different. . . . The sound of Bessie Smith's voice represented something else in the world that I needed to find out about. She was a link, in the same way that discovering the Negro section in the library was a link—to the richness of black culture. I went from Bessie Smith to Malcolm X.

The blues would provide Wilson his artistic template: characters such as Ma Rainey, Troy Maxson, Boy Willie, and Floyd Barton metamorphose into larger-than-life figures whose lives are replete with the grim experiences that define the blues. The latter part of the 1960s marked the burgeoning of Wilson's nascent artistic identity. He began to write poetry and cofounded with Rob Penny the Black Horizons on the Hill theater company in the Hill community; they staged all of Baraka's *Four Black Revolutionary Plays*. Buoyed by the overt politicizing of black theater that Baraka inaugurated in Newark, New Jersey, Wilson conceived of drama as a vehicle for the heartfelt black nationalism that held sway during that period. Another significant event was his decision to officially change his name to August Wilson, signaling his embracing of his mother's culture and a repudiation of his father's. The decade concluded with his marriage to Brenda Burton,

a Muslim, in 1969; they divorced three years later when Wilson found her religious principles incompatible with his own. This union produced his first daughter, Sakina Ansari, in 1970.

The late 1960s and early 1970s witnessed the further flowering of Wilson's artistic voice. He continued to write poetry, a medium that would be instrumental in his life and one he would call the "bedrock of my playwriting." He wrote poems on Muhammad Ali and Malcolm X, mammoth black icons whose bold stands against malignant racial attitudes moved and motivated the young Wilson. In 1976 Wilson attended a performance of South African playwright Athol Fugard's *Sizwe Bansi Is Dead* and gained further creative inspiration. The year 1976 marked the first time that one of his works was staged: a local amateur group performed *The Homecoming,* a play based on the life of blues singer Blind Lemon Jefferson. The following year Wilson wrote *Black Bart and the Sacred Hills,* a musical satire about Black Bart, a legendary black stagecoach robber whose outlaw behavior recalls Stagolee and other archetypal "bad Negroes." Wilson embarked on a radical relocation in 1978 to St. Paul, Minnesota, at the behest of his mentor and fellow Pittsburgh native, the producer Charles Purdy. Wilson held a variety of jobs while residing in the American heartland, the most significant being that of cook (an experience he drew upon for the 1993 play *Two Trains Running*) and scriptwriter for the Science Museum of Minnesota. In 1979 Wilson authored *Jitney,* a play about black cabdrivers in Pittsburgh that he would continually revise over the next twenty years.

The early 1980s brought the germination of Wilson's artistic gifts, evidenced by a flurry of personal and professional activities. In 1980 he became affiliated with the Playwrights' Center of Minneapolis, which accepted *Jitney* for a staged reading. His friend and Horizons theater cofounder Rob Penny encouraged Wilson to submit plays to the Eugene O'Neill Theater

Center National Playwrights Conference. Though *Black Bart, Jitney,* and *Fullerton Street* (a play about the collapse of a marriage due to alcoholism, economic exigency, and relocation from South to North) would all be rejected, the O'Neill center accepted *Ma Rainey's Black Bottom* for workshop production in 1982, another cardinal year in Wilson's life. Not only would *Ma Rainey* go on to become his first Broadway play, but Wilson also met Lloyd Richards, then dean of the Yale School of Drama and artistic director at the O'Neill Theater Center. This meeting would profoundly impact Wilson's artistic evolution, for he found in Richards a mentor and friend who would subsequently direct the plays that established Wilson's reputation as America's foremost dramatist since O'Neill. During this same year, Pittsburgh's Allegheny Repertory Theatre produced *Jitney,* marking his spiritual homecoming. In fact, Wilson would continue to mine his native landscape, setting all but one of his plays there. He also married for a second time in 1981, wedding the social worker Judy Oliver. A crushing personal event was the death of Wilson's beloved mother Daisy in 1983; one sees his reverence for her in plays such as *Fences* and *Seven Guitars,* where mothers—living and dead—figure prominently in their sons' lives.

The acceptance of *Ma Rainey* would amount to the playwright's "big break" and establish a pattern for his plays' development: most would first be staged at Yale and then proceed to Broadway. Appropriately enough, Wilson's first Broadway play, which dramatizes the blues not only as a way of living but as a life philosophy, illuminates a core element of the playwright's artistic schema. In a 1991 *New York Times* article, Wilson articulated what would become the nucleus of all of his works: "In terms of influence on my work, I have what I call my four B's: Romare Bearden; Imamu Amiri Baraka, the writer; Jorge Luis Borges, the Argentine short-story writer; and the biggest B

of all: the blues." The preponderance of his plays foregrounds the blues literally through performance or emotionally through the characters' lived experiences. His plays often depict blues artists who are shamelessly exploited by perfidious white recording executives. Nevertheless, these bluespeople possess the psychic and cultural resources blacks have traditionally drawn from when faced with seemingly insurmountable obstacles. He articulated this point in an interview with Bill Moyers: "The blues are important primarily because they contain the cultural responses of blacks in America to the situation that they find themselves in. Contained in the blues is a philosophical system at work."

Though acclaimed as the most popular American playwright since Edward Albee, Wilson has never shied away from controversy. His racial and artistic positions throughout the 1980s and 1990s have placed him in more than one imbroglio, the most widely known being his running squabble with Robert Brustein, the former dean of the Yale School of Drama and a venerable theater critic. Brustein has been summarily unimpressed with Wilson's "cycle": "This single-minded documentation of American racism is a worthy if familiar social agenda, and no enlightened person would deny its premise, but as an ongoing artistic program it is monotonous, limited, locked in a perception of victimization." Their caustic feud reached its nadir in a 1997 "debate" at New York's Town Hall, which was spawned by Wilson's keynote address at the Theatre Communications Group National Conference at Princeton University in June 1996. Titled "The Ground on Which I Stand," Wilson's speech decried the lack of financial resources available for black theater companies and forthrightly assailed as "sophomoric" Brustein's belief that cultural "diversity" in grant-awarding criteria has resulted in the compromising of artistic standards. The resulting Town Hall din was roundly denigrated by supporters of both men; spectators felt that what might have been a potentially enriching exchange on the state of contemporary American theater devolved into an acrimonious, ad hominem harangue which was heated but far from enlightening. Despite a few detractors and the playwright's occasionally austere stances, however, Wilson has secured a place on the hallowed stage of great world, American, and African American drama: the myriad comparisons to Sophocles, Anton Chekhov, O'Neill, and Baraka are a testament to his wrenchingly eloquent plays of black Americans' internal and external land- and lifescapes. Wilson resides in Seattle with his third wife, the costume designer Constanza Romero, and their daughter, Azula Carmen.

MA RAINEY'S BLACK BOTTOM

Wilson's first Broadway hit, *Ma Rainey's Black Bottom,* was initially performed at the Yale Repertory Theatre in April 1984 before it premiered at the Cort Theatre on October 11 of the same year. The ensemble cast was led by the veteran television actress Theresa Merritt and Charles S. Dutton, a budding stage actor and a graduate of the Yale School of Drama whom Wilson met at the O'Neill center in 1982. *Ma Rainey* ran for 275 performances and garnered the New York Drama Critics' Circle Award.

As do all of Wilson's dramas, *Ma Rainey* defies the parameters of the well-made play. Instead, Wilson's first Broadway success unfurls as a series of stories. The drama is set in Chicago in 1927 at a recording studio and concentrates not on the eponymous blues diva of the 1920s, but instead on the four musicians who will accompany her on the recording date: Cutler, the leader of the backup band "because he is the most sensible"; Slow Drag, "perhaps the one most bored by life" but who is nevertheless "deceptively intelligent"; Toledo, the only

literate member of the group who is "self-taught but misunderstands and misapplies his knowledge"; and Levee, the youngest of the band, who is alternatively "flamboyant," "rakish," and "buffoonish." In fact, Ma Rainey does not appear until midway through the first act, with full entourage in tow: her current love interest, Dussie Mae, and her speech-impaired nephew, Sylvester. The play's only white characters are Mel Sturdyvant and Irvin, two rapacious producers conducting the recording date. The primary "action" of the play involves Irvin and Sturdyvant's attempts to record Ma's songs amidst myriad conflicts. When Ma finally arrives, she is escorted by a policeman who accuses her of "creating a disturbance" after a minor traffic infraction; she then berates the record producers on several counts (the studio is too cold, they haven't supplied her with Coca-Cola, they've tampered with her song selection). After endless false starts and technical glitches, the recording session is completed. The play ends when Levee, despondent when Sturdyvant pays him a mere five dollars for some songs Levee has written and performed for him, misdirects his anger and stabs Toledo, ostensibly for stepping on his new Florsheims. Despite the concluding violence, the play is anchored in the men's verbal jousts and personal confessions—their attempts to assert their voices in an abjectly oppressive milieu. *Ma Rainey* is ultimately a meditation on the ways that black artists attempt to find meaning in their meager if not meaningless existences in a culture that exploits them with impunity.

One pervasive issue concerns the black artist's dependence on an often unscrupulous and predatory white recording apparatus. Levee, a songwriter and self-proclaimed artist who often draws the other band members' ire, envisions himself on the cutting edge of a musical shift. Unlike their southern counterparts, northerners prefer a more up-tempo, dance hall–style blues, which differs markedly from what Levee derides as the "old jug band shit"—the southern-honed blues that Ma has parlayed into popular success. Though Cutler testily reminds Levee that "this ain't none of them hot bands. This is an accompaniment band," Levee dreams of starting his own group. Upon Sturdyvant's request that Levee present him more of his original compositions, Levee responds "Yessir!," a reply that draws a strong rebuke from Cutler and especially Toledo; in fact, the latter observes that Levee's fawning behavior is symptomatic of blacks' general self-devaluation that results from being "spooked up with the white men."

Toledo's response is particularly germane, for it conveys his role as the play's racial consciousness: as an uncompromising "race man," he articulates the plight of black artists specifically and African Americans historically. His aria on "leftovers" bespeaks his keen awareness of blacks' marginal status:

> Everybody come from different places in Africa, right? Come from different tribes and things. Soonawhile they began to make one big stew. You had the carrots, the peas, and potatoes and whatnot over here. And over there you had the meat, the nuts, the okra, corn . . . and then you mix it up and let it cook right through to get the flavors flowing together . . . then you got one thing. You got a stew. Now you take and eat the stew. You take and make your history with that stew. Alright. Now it's over. Your history's over and you done ate the stew. But you look around and you see some carrots over here, some potatoes over there. That stew's still there. You can't eat it all. You done made your history and it's still there. So what you got? You got some leftovers. That's what it is. You got leftovers and you can't do nothing with it. . . . See, we's the leftovers. The colored man is the leftovers. . . . But first we gotta know we the leftovers. . . . The problem ain't with the white man. The white man knows you just a leftover. Cause he the one who done the eating and he know what he done ate. But we don't know that we been took and made history out of. Done went and filled the white man's belly and now he's full and tired and wants you to get out the

way and let him be by himself. . . . And if you wanna find out, you just ask Mr. Irvin what he had for supper yesterday.

On its face, Toledo's analogy incisively illustrates blacks' peripheral status in a country that consistently and willfully denigrates them. However, his somewhat opaque logic evinces a problem that consistently dilutes Toledo's blues voice: his inability to make his storytelling accessible to his audience. Slow Drag incredulously asks, "What's eating got to do with how the white man treat you?" while Levee comically rejoins, "I got lost right there trying to figure out who puts nuts in their stew."

If Toledo is the drama's voice of racial reason, then Levee by comparison is its most emotionally menaced figure. As an eight-year-old living on his father's farm in Natchez, Mississippi, Levee witnessed his mother's brutal gang rape at the hands of marauding white men; as a result of his futile attempts to defend her, he bears a "long ugly scar" on his chest. Though his father feigns acceptance of the crime by "smil[ing] in the face of one of them crackers who had been with my mama," his father subsequently ambushes the men in retaliation, killing four of them before being lynched. Physical scarring will become a dominant trope in Wilson's works, a point he subsequently noted in an interview with the scholar Sandra Shannon: "I think in almost every play most of my male characters have scars." Indeed, this physical wounding emblematizes Levee's crippling psychospiritual wounds that cause his ultimate demise. His obsessive competitiveness reflects a gnawing desire to reclaim the manhood that was seized when he helplessly witnessed his mother's violation.

Though some critics chided Wilson for what they viewed as "false advertising"—their belief that he gave Ma Rainey's music short shrift in not featuring it more prominently—the 1920s blues matriarch nevertheless maintains a pivotal role once she arrives. A walking volcano, she alternatively excoriates her white "handlers" ("I'm gonna tell you something, Irvin . . . and you go on up there and tell Sturdyvant. What you all say don't count with me. You understand?") and cautions the sidemen: her upstart trumpet player's sexual interest in Dussie Mae provokes Ma's wrath ("Levee's got his eyes in the wrong place. You better school him, Cutler"). Quite clearly, Ma Rainey's popularity as blues icon and her attendant economic success endow her with a modicum of power in a virulently racist and hegemonic recording industry. Moreover, Ma Rainey echoes Toledo's stinging cultural observations, bemoaning her exploitation by men like Sturdyvant and Irvin: "As soon as they get my voice down on them recording machines, then it's just like if I'd be some whore and they roll over and put their pants on." As well, it is she who functions as the author's surrogate, voicing his sentiments about the indispensability of the blues vis-à-vis black cultural and personal epistemology:

> White folks don't understand about the blues. They hear it come out, but they don't know how it got there. They don't understand that's life's way of talking. You don't sing to feel better. You sing cause that's a way of understanding life.

Anticipating characters such as Bertha Holly in *Joe Turner's Come and Gone* (1988), Ma Rainey is a resonant voice, a culturally vital one that reverberates whether she is physically on stage or not.

Though the play replicates many male-authored dramas in that it concludes with paroxysmal, male-on-male violence, *Ma Rainey*'s denouement in which Levee kills Toledo expresses how black men have historically internalized and displaced anger. This internecine racial violence demonstrates one of Wilson's dramatic aims: to depict vividly how blacks must force themselves to revisit and reconcile personal and collective racial animus in healthier, more constructive ways. His own

comments about Levee's catastrophic act are enlightening: "His [Levee's] question is, 'How can I live this life in a society that refuses to recognize my worth, that refuses to allow me to contribute to its welfare—how can I live this life and remain a whole and complete person?'" This compelling question provides the dramatic scaffolding for Wilson's next play.

FENCES

While many critics heralded Wilson as a refreshing, vibrant new voice in American theater, others felt that his first play suffered from "talkiness" and "plotlessness." Unlike *Ma Rainey's Black Bottom,* which foregrounds a panoply of voices and stories, *Fences* is more "traditional" in that it examines more closely the life of a single character. The play chronicles the life of fifty-three-year-old Troy Maxson, an embittered former Negro league baseball star who currently toils as a garbage collector struggling to support his wife and their adolescent son. The drama was a star vehicle for veteran stage and film star James Earl Jones, whose poignant portrayal elevated Troy's ostensibly mundane life to tragipoetic heights reminiscent of Miller's deluded dreamer Willy Loman and O'Neill's self-destructive, alcoholic Tyrone men. *Fences* opened on March 26, 1987, at the 46th Street Theatre and ran for 526 performances, earning more money in its first year ($11 million) than any nonmusical in Broadway history. The drama earned a plethora of prizes: another New York Drama Critics' Circle Award, a Tony for best play, and Wilson's first Pulitzer Prize. Plans to adapt the play into a motion picture engendered much rumor and speculation, fueled by the playwright's declaration that only a black director could vivify the sensibilities and sensitivities of his black family's experience. The black-director "controversy" stalled the adaptation, though Wilson reportedly sold the film rights to Paramount Pictures in the late 1980s.

The play opens with Troy and his best friend and coworker, Jim Bono, engaging in what the stage directions identify as "a ritual of talk and drink," the male-to-male interactions that provide the foundation for most of Wilson's dramas. Troy is recapitulating his encounter with his white boss, Mr. Rand, against whom he has filed a complaint: he asks, "Why you got the white mens driving and the colored lifting?" during garbage pickups. While characters allude to interracial conflicts throughout the drama, the play focuses primarily on intraracial relationships. Wilson examines Troy's gravitational pull and those in his orbit: his wife of eighteen years, Rose; their son Cory, who harbors athletic dreams comparable to Troy's unfulfilled ones; Bono, whom Troy met when both were incarcerated; Gabriel, his brother who incurred irreparable physical and psychic damage fighting in World War II; and Lyons, his thirty-four-year-old son from a previous relationship whom Troy failed to help rear.

Fences's epigraphic poem, penned by Wilson, illumines one of the play's dominant themes: "When the sins of our fathers visit us / We do not have to play host. / We can banish them with forgiveness / As God, in His Largeness and Laws." Generational conflicts among fathers and sons abound, cyclical and seemingly irreparable. Troy casts such an immense shadow over Cory that the younger Maxson cannot help but emulate his father, hence Cory's enthusiastic desire to play a professional sport. However, Troy's scabrous experiences of racial discrimination—in addition to his present workplace complaints, he was too old to play professional baseball when the major leagues finally integrated—have left lacerations so deep that he equates sports with white perfidy. Despite Cory's attempts to persuade Troy to sign the forms that would permit him to play college football, Troy not only squelches his son's budding hopes of obtaining a scholarship but has him removed from his high school team so that he can concentrate solely on his job at the A&P supermarket. An exchange in the first act exposes the crux of this disharmonious father-son relationship and adumbrates its inevitable collapse.

During an argument in which Cory implores Troy to let him remain on his high school football team, Troy imparts a maxim (a possible source for his surname) that in effect has become a lifelong mantra: "You've got to take the crooked with the straights." Cory then poses a question that in its simplicity gets to the root of the historical chasm separating fathers and sons generally and African American fathers and sons specifically: "How come you ain't never liked me?" Troy replies stringently:

> Like you? I go out of here every morning . . . bust my butt . . . putting up with them crackers every day . . . cause I like you? You about the biggest fool I ever saw. It's my job. It's my responsibility! You understand that? A man got to take care of his family. You live in my house . . . sleep you [sic] behind on my bedclothes . . . fill you belly up with my food . . . cause you my son. You my flesh and blood. Not cause I like you! Cause it's my duty to take care of you. I owe a responsibility to you!

This speech attests to Troy's alternatively anachronistic and admirable construction of American fatherhood, which mandates that men's contributions to family should be financial, not emotional. His conceptualization of masculine identity on the one hand disrupts portraitures of black men as shiftless and perpetually absent; conversely, however, it signals the limitations of such a philosophy given the emotional exigencies of young black men, whose need for nourishment far exceeds bread alone. Hence, Troy's understanding of his role permits him to parcel out meager loans to his struggling jazz musician son Lyons, but he adamantly refuses to attend Lyons' performances.

The final encounter between Troy and his youngest son, which begins with Cory taunting and taking swings at Troy with Troy's baseball bat but ends with Troy having wrested control of the bat away from his son and standing poised to hit him, eventuates the dissolution of the relationship. The prodigal Cory, whom Troy in effect banishes—he bellows to his son that his clothes will "be on the other side of that fence"—will disappear from Troy's life. This acrimonious parting is part of a vicious cycle, for it reenacts Troy's own physical confrontation with his father, which resulted in his leaving home at age fourteen. Only when Rose convinces Cory to reverse his decision not to attend Troy's funeral do we see a disruption of the spiritually splintered father-son relationships and evidence of the "forgiveness" of the father's sins which the play's epigraphic poem foretold.

Not coincidentally, the exchange that ends their relationship ensues during Cory and Troy's constructing of the fence that Rose has insisted be built around the yard. As the play's dominant symbol, the fence functions contrapuntally: on the one hand, the ritual of constructing the fence fosters a bond between Troy and Bono. Conversely, the same ritual occasions Troy's speech on responsibility and Cory's growing disillusionment with his father's rigid, martinet-like mien. As well, Rose's intermittent humming and singing of "Jesus, be a fence all around me every day" illustrates Wilson's representations of black women as wedded to traditional conceptions of Christianity. Bono helps Troy to grasp not so much the religious dimensions of Rose's connection to the fence as much as the emotional ones: "Some people build fences to keep people out . . . and other people build fences to keep people in. Rose wants to hold on to you all. She loves you." Ironically, however, the completion of the fence has the opposite effect. Troy's infidelity and fathering of a child out of wedlock hastens the emotional though not legal end of his and Rose's marriage; she proceeds to immerse herself in church activities, though she also agrees to raise the baby,

whose mother (Alberta) died during childbirth. As mentioned earlier, Troy vows to put Cory's belongings outside the fence, signaling the demise of their relationship. Also, Jim Bono, Troy's boon companion to whom Troy even felt compelled to proclaim "I love you, nigger," has drastically curtailed their relationship in light of Troy's willingness to commit adultery despite Bono's remonstrations; Troy completes the fence without Bono's assistance or companionship. And as cultural symbol, the fence concretizes Troy's home run–hitting acumen but also the impenetrable boundary between him and all-white major-league baseball, as well as the broader social boundaries restricting blacks in the 1940s and 1950s.

Fences develops through a series of violations—racial, economic, filial, and sexual. Two such transgressions which merit brief commentary are Troy's adultery and his economic and personal betrayal of his mentally impaired brother, Gabriel. Though some critics accused Wilson of depicting in Rose the stereotypical long-suffering, God-fearing black woman whose self-effacing gestures border on the masochistic, she is quite multifaceted. One of the play's most impassioned moments occurs when Rose agrees to raise Raynell, the child Troy sires with Alberta: "From right now . . . this child got a mother. But you a womanless man." Having fulfilled her promise, Rose also experiences an epiphany upon Troy's death as she acknowledges her own flaws:

> I took on his life as mine and mixed up the pieces so that you couldn't hardly tell which was which anymore. It was my choice. It was my life, and I didn't have to live it like that.

Like Ma Rainey, Rose evolves into an empowered black feminist voice, one who takes responsibility for her actions and resists patriarchal constrictions which render black women perpetual victims.

During Troy's confession of infidelity to Rose, Gabriel offers her a rose in a comforting display. Indeed, like Rose, Gabriel has borne the brunt of Troy's myopic, self-absorbed actions. For example, Troy used part of Gabriel's war compensation to build a roof. Even more dastardly, and in a paradoxical contrast to his refusal to sign papers to permit Cory to play college football, Troy signs a release form that results not only in Gabriel's institutionalization, but in Troy's ability to feather his nest: Gabriel's war benefits will now be divided between the hospital to which he is confined and Troy. However, the conclusion of the play brings a sort of cosmological correcting of this travesty. Gabriel outlives Troy and, reminiscent of his archangel namesake, tries to herald Troy's arrival at the pearly gates with his mouthpiece-less trumpet, a gesture that gives way to a dance that the stage directions describe as "a slow, strange dance, eerie and life-giving. A dance of atavistic signature and ritual." This conclusion is apropos, given Troy's own contradictory and paradoxical modus vivendi; the combination of Gabriel's soundless trumpet and the ritualistic dance that ensues commemorates Troy's misguided attempts to locate his voice and the ill-fated actions he undertakes to assert his manhood.

Fences demonstrated Wilson's ability to depict a profoundly tragic figure while further illuminating his belief in the dramaturgical value of the blues, as well as rituals such as storytelling and dance. Indeed, Troy is the consummate blues hero, one who perpetually invents and reinvents his identity to combat the obdurate conditions facing black men in the 1940s and 1950s. Whether it be the stories he weaves in which he battles the specter of "Mr. Death" and the devil (Bono declares, "I know you [Troy] got some Uncle Remus in your blood") or the song he sings about his dog "Blue" that he learned from his own father and bequeaths both Cory and Raynell (they sing it at the end of the drama), Troy's rootedness in African American vernacular and performative traditions renders

him the archetypal Wilson protagonist, one who despite tragic flaws leaves an indelible imprint on everyone he touches.

JOE TURNER'S COME AND GONE

Wilson's third Broadway drama may in fact be his most sophisticated and ambitious in scope; he himself deems it his "favorite play." In *Joe Turner's Come and Gone* he fuses his core dramatic elements. He dexterously weaves a lyrical blues collage, replete with music, African dance, Christian and African myths, tall tales, folklore, African American history, and the *supernatural*—this reflecting the artist's willingness to experiment with different extra-realistic vehicles for presenting the black experience he so assiduously works to excavate and depict. The result is a profound epic of blacks' individual and collective fortitude in the face of seemingly intractable circumstances. *Joe Turner* opened March 26, 1988, at the Ethel Barrymore Theatre, running for 105 performances and earning Wilson his third New York Drama Critics' Circle Award.

Joe Turner's Come and Gone was inspired by disparate texts: *Mill Hand's Lunch Bucket,* a Romare Bearden painting depicting a boardinghouse in Pittsburgh in the 1920s; "Restoring the House," a series of poems Wilson had been composing which traced the life of a male slave in search of his wife who had been sold; a W. C. Handy recording; and Wilson's interest in the historical figure Joe Turner, whom he identifies as "the brother of Pete Turner, governor of Tennessee, who pressed Blacks into peonage." Wilson's dramatic methodology is expressly syncretic, for he assembles multiple cultural, literary, and historical sources to shape the play's characterization, themes, and structure.

The Pittsburgh of 1911, the play's setting, is a brash, lean steel town that, potentially at least, fosters in its inhabitants a sense of progress and optimism. However, this bustling milieu of change and growth, where three rivers converge, does not bring the coalescence of blackness and the fulfillment of the American dream. Wilson unequivocally makes this point in the stage directions: these neo-northern denizens who have trekked from the South are now "[i]solated, cut off from memory," and have arrived "carrying Bibles and guitars, their pockets lined with dust and fresh hope, marked men and women seeking to scrape from the narrow, crooked cobbles and the fiery blasts of the coke furnace a way of bludgeoning and shaping the malleable parts of themselves into a new identity as free men of definite and sincere worth." Indeed, this optimism is tentative and chimerical, for again the urban North fails to salve the economic and racial wounds that the South inflicted upon scores of southern blacks. The geographic setting, coupled with the fact that a mere forty-six years separate these "freed" blacks from the end of slavery, gives rise to the play's central question: How do physically unshackled Africans in America reconcile countless binaries—the slave past and the free present, their abiding double consciousness as Africans and Americans, their southern, rural ethos and the steely, inflexible urban northern environ which does not accommodate their bucolic roots?

Given the peripatetic lives of these neo-northern blacks, the boardinghouse becomes the quintessential setting, allowing Wilson to present a panoramic view of black life in the early twentieth century. More critically, it functions as a concrete metaphor for black displacement—spiritual, communal, familial. The wayfarers who pass through Seth and Bertha Holly's home become cultural pilgrims whose sense of self and family has been so battered that they seek an oasis, no matter how transitory. That most of the boarders are in some way connected to the South buttresses the theme of migration and its crushing impact on blacks' perpetual search for personal and collective identity.

The first act presents an amalgam of attitudes toward history, race, and self-fulfillment. Seth fashions himself as the archetypal self-made man; he proudly identifies himself a "free northern man" and has harnessed his energy and optimism into a comfortable, middle-class existence. As the proprietor of what he repeatedly labels a "respectable house," he exults not only in the fact that it was bequeathed him by his father, but that he "ain't never picked no cotton. I was born here in the North. My daddy was a freedman. I ain't never even seen no cotton!" Moreover, Seth is a skilled craftsman whose father also taught him how to "take these hands and make something out of nothing. Take that metal and bend and twist whatever way I want." Clearly, Seth is an entrepreneur, though racist attitudes about blacks in business prevent him from obtaining a loan; hence he sells his products to the white peddler Rutherford Selig, a middleman who in turn sells Seth's pots and pans. Through Seth, Wilson depicts blacks' racial and economic hardships amidst an inexorable desire to enjoy the accoutrements of the American dream.

Countering Seth's adherence to American materialist values is Bynum Walker, a conjure man in his early sixties and one of the boardinghouse residents. An omnipowerful figure sought by many blacks, Bynum embodies the playwright's insistence that traditions from both the rural South and the African homeland are indispensable in the North, despite pressures to discount those beliefs. Counseling women seeking to rekindle relationships with erstwhile lovers and others desiring to reconnect with lost family members, Bynum radiates a wisdom and power that attracts blacks from many distant locations, including the South.

Bynum's story about the derivation of his name becomes a guidepost for grasping what Wilson has called the play's "mythic base," one that he argued supersedes its realistic one. The conjurer fantastically re-creates a pivotal moment in his life: a journey in which he encounters a figure he calls "John" who metamorphoses into the "Shiny Man," who then leads Bynum to his father. His self-creation story is an arabesque of mythic and cosmic proportions, beginning with the "road" John guides Bynum down in showing him "The Secret of Life":

> We got near this bend in the road and he told me to hold out my hands. Then he rubbed them together with his and I looked down and see they got blood on them. Told me to take and rub it all over me . . . say that was a way of cleaning myself. . . . I turned around to look at this fellow and he had this light coming out of him. I had to cover up my eyes to keep from being blinded. He shining like new money with that light. He shined until all the light seemed like it seeped out of him and then he was gone and I was by myself in this strange place where everything was bigger than life.

Upon the Shiny Man's disappearance, Bynum encounters his father, who conducts the remainder of his journey toward spiritual enlightenment:

> My daddy called me to him. Said he had been thinking about me and it grieved him to see me in the world carrying other people's songs and not having one of my own. Told me he was gonna show me how to find my song. Then he carried me further into this big place until we come to this ocean. . . . I stayed in that place awhile and my daddy taught me the meaning of this thing I had seen and showed me how to find my song. I asked him about the shiny man and he told me he was the One Who Goes Before and Shows the Way. Said there was lots of shiny men and if I ever saw one again before I died then I would know that my song had been accepted and worked its full power in the world and I could lay down and die a happy man. A man who done left his mark on life. On the way people cling to each other out of the truth they find in themselves. Then he showed me how to get back to the road. I came out where everything was its own size and I had my song. I had the Binding Song. I chose that song because that's what I seen most when I was

traveling . . . people walking away and leaving one another. So I takes the power of my song and binds them together.

This preternatural story approximates African and African American folktales, which bear as their trademarks exaggerations, strange encounters between the "folk" and supernatural, otherworldly figures, and journeys in which one engages persons who both help and hinder. Wilson thus imbues Bynum with cosmic dimensions, inserting him as the play's spiritual life force and the character who stimulates others' "finding of their songs"—the drama's central metaphor which involves blacks' self-manumission from an ensnaring history that cripples them physically and spiritually. Finally, Bynum's references to "blood" and "cleaning," clear allusions to Christian rituals of sacrifice and cleansing, will figure prominently when he stimulates the personal journey of another psychically enslaved boardinghouse dweller, Herald Loomis.

Paradoxically, Bynum tells his story to Selig, whose own background is equally revelatory. Selig, referred to throughout the play as the "People Finder," is a descendent of slave traffickers and catchers: his great grandfather "used to bring Nigras across the ocean on ships" and his father "used to find runaway slaves for the plantation bosses." After Abraham Lincoln signed the Emancipation Proclamation, Selig went into the business of reuniting former slaves, though "it don't pay as much." Though Wilson has adduced that Selig is "not evil at all," it is difficult not to view him as one who, like his ancestors, profits from black misery. While he might ostensibly be a benign figure who "records" blacks' names in his "book" with the promise of locating them (Loomis pays him a dollar to reunite him with his wife, Martha), Bertha Holly articulates the more nefarious side of Selig's enterprise: "You [Bynum] can call him a People Finder if you want to. I know Rutherford Selig carries people away too. He done carried a whole bunch of them away from here." Bertha's condemnation distills Selig's past and present, exposing not only a history of white perfidy but something much more ominous: blacks' proclivity for ceding their power to whites, who reap financial rewards over generations.

The title *Joe Turner's Come and Gone* refers specifically to a blues song about the notorious bounty hunter who captured and exploited black men for their labor. Herald Loomis, a thirty-two-year-old man who is described as being "at times possessed," unable to "harmonize the forces that swirl around him," is the character most tormented by a history of exploitation and abuse. When he arrives at the Holly's with his eleven-year-old daughter Zonia, he is alternatively deranged and paranoid. However, he reveals the sources of his distemper: Joe Turner captured and enslaved him for seven years (1901–1908). In his interview with Powers, Wilson sheds light on the inspiration for one of his most emotionally disfigured characters:

> There is a figure in the painting *[Mill Hand's Lunch Bucket]* that my attention was drawn to. The figure of a man sitting at a kitchen table in a posture of defeat or abandonment. And I wondered, "Who is this man and why is he sitting there and what are the circumstances of his life?" That became Herald Loomis. It occurred to me that at the time and particularly after slavery there was a lot of dispersement among Blacks. Families were separated.

Correspondingly, Loomis' capture results in the physical, financial, and emotional rupturing of his family. Martha and Zonia were evicted from the land on which the family eked out a meager living as sharecroppers; mother and daughter were then forced to live with Martha's mother; and, upon being freed, Loomis retrieved Zonia, who had remained with her grandmother while Martha ventured north to assist in the relocating of her church. Loomis' fervent desire to reunite his family epitomizes the plight of countless black men and women trying to reform families in the aftermath of slavery. That Loomis procures Selig's help in finding Martha attests to his ongoing mental bondage despite his physical freedom.

The conclusion of act 1 represents the play's epicenter, explosively bringing together its core thematic concerns. First, the scene reflects Wilson's multitextual dramaturgical strategies, where he assembles an array of cultural forms. Here, the dancing of the Juba flowers into a communal ritual, one that supplies the boarding-house residents the sense of cohesion that many have found elusive. Though Africa as a nurturing psychocultural space may be accessible only through memory, the Juba becomes a tangible cultural rite that helps to preserve and perpetuate a rich, generative history. As the stage directions iterate, "The Juba is reminiscent of the Ring Shouts of the African slaves. It is a call and response dance. . . . It should be as African as possible." Even Seth, so opposed to vernacular expressions such as the blues, plays his harmonica as Bynum "calls the dance." The ornate Juba set piece reifies Wilson's insistence that blacks preserve their spiritual ties to Africa and locate within such traditions the power to withstand the onslaught of Eurocentric values and beliefs.

However, this revivifying communal act is violently disrupted when Loomis appears: he denounces the participants for mentioning the "Holy Ghost" during the dance and then begins speaking in tongues and dancing around the kitchen. This scene reaches its frenetic apex when Bynum, the spiritual healer, coaxes Loomis into revealing the visions and experiences Loomis has proclaimed he "ain't got words to tell you." Loomis' harrowing revelations of seeing "bones rise up out the water," bones that "begin to walk on top of it," ostensibly alludes to the biblical "Valley of Dry Bones" in which the Jewish nation is physically and spiritually renewed. But with Bynum's urging, Loomis exclaims that in his visions the bones "got flesh on them!" and "[t]hey black." This scene is paradigmatic, for it illustrates Wilson's appropriation and subversion of Christian and biblical narratives and his recoloring of them in a sepia hue. Unequivocally, Loomis' story becomes a plaintive commemoration of those Africans whose "bones" did not survive the physically and psychically eviscerating journey to the Americas. In an interview with Richard Pettengill, the author himself identified this scene as a tour de force in his prodigious body of work:

> The bones rising out of the ocean—when I wrote that I thought, okay that's it, if I die tomorrow I'll be satisfied and fulfilled as an artist that I wrote that scene. I think you can go a lifetime and not arrive at that scene which for me crystallized everything, because it was a symbolic resurrection of those Africans who were lost, tossed overboard during the Middle Passage, and whose bones right now still rest at the bottom of the Atlantic Ocean.

Wilson effectively transforms this testimony to Christ's restorative powers into a culturally specific and resonant theatrical moment that forces his audience to recognize how the sins of the past are inevitably visited upon those in the present.

Hence, Loomis' misinterpretation of and disaffection with African cultural practices is symptomatic of a devitalized spirit; his emotional deformity becomes representative of African Americans who have amputated parts of themselves both historically and culturally. His act-concluding cry, "My legs won't stand up! My legs won't stand up!," is the byproduct of his physical enslavement to Joe Turner and his continuing insistence on measuring himself by whites' devaluative yardsticks. As he dispiritedly expresses in the second act, "He [Joe Turner] told me I was worthless." The dramatic action in act two shifts primarily to Loomis' past travails, and the play reaches its climax

with the arrival of his lost wife, Martha, who has now assumed the surname "Pentecost" as a testimony to her unswerving commitment to Christian principles. Indeed, Wilson's characterization of Martha's Christian rhetoric and Loomis' repudiation of it reflects the playwright's distaste for blacks' inculcation with what he considers oppressive Western Christianity. During Martha's attempted "conversion" of her wayward husband, Loomis, a former deacon in the "Abundant Life Church," fumes against Martha's "Great big old white man . . . your Mr. Jesus Christ," as well as men such as Joe Turner who have kept him psychically captive. This volatile denunciation of what he deems secular and sacred enslavers catalyzes Loomis' self-resuscitative act: he "slashes himself across the chest" and "rubs the blood over his face" and proclaims, "I don't need nobody to bleed for me! I can bleed for myself." This reversal of traditional Christian rites of cleansing, purification, and rebirth marks Loomis' transcendence of his own debased history and a reclamation of his body, psyche, and spirit. As Wilson has said about the character, "Loomis accepts responsibility for his presence in the world, and the responsibility for his own salvation. . . . Because your god should resemble you. When you look in the mirror you should see your god. If you don't, then you have the wrong god."

Joe Turner's Come and Gone reverberates as Wilson's strongest artistic-cultural statement, bearing out what he sees as blacks' abilities to achieve self-worth in a relentlessly hostile Eurocentric environment. Bynum, the binder-cum-shaman-cum-exorcist, transports Loomis to his spiritual center and bestows upon him the play's blessing that elucidates his new luminous, spiritually enlightened self: "Herald Loomis, you shining! You shining like new money!" The "singing of one's own song," both symbolically and literally, dominates Wilson's next exploration of blacks' psychospiritual deprivation and regeneration.

THE PIANO LESSON

For Wilson's fourth play in his ten-play cycle documenting African Americans' history in America, he returns to the black family as his dramatic terrain. *The Piano Lesson* depicts the weight of the horrific racial past and its potential to fracture family relations in the present. Taking place in Pittsburgh in the 1930s, the play's central conflict pits Boy Willie Charles against Berniece Charles, siblings who debate the fate of a piano. Though the piano has remained with Berniece at the house she shares with her uncle, Doaker Charles, Boy Willie travels from Mississippi to claim this valuable heirloom that has been a part of the family since their ownership by the Sutter family. Like Wilson's other works, this one was staged at both the O'Neill Theater and Yale Repertory Theatre before it opened at the Walter Kerr Theatre on April 16, 1990, with Charles Dutton starring as Boy Willie. His second Pulitzer Prize–winning drama, *The Piano Lesson* is also Wilson's first work to be made into a film: CBS produced it as part of its Hallmark Hall of Fame series.

Again, the work of artist Romare Bearden provided Wilson with the dramatic kernel from which the play spawned—this time Bearden's collage entitled *The Piano Lesson*. Wilson explained that he "got the idea from the painting that there would be a woman and a little girl in the play. And I thought that the woman would be a character who was trying to acquire a sense of self-worth by denying her past." At the heart of this play lies a basic concern with how blacks should negotiate the afflictive cultural legacy of slavery, which again reflects Wilson's overarching concern with African Americans' need to reconcile and even embrace an almost genocidal racial experience.

The series of entanglements that underlie the play illuminate how the harrowing slave past produces conflicts that transcend geographic and psychic space and time. The play opens with Boy Willie and his partner, Lymon, boisterously awakening Doaker, Berniece, and her daughter, Maretha, in the predawn hours. That Boy Willie and Lymon arrive via a ramshackle truck with a cargo of watermelons they hope to sell to whites is apropos, for it particularizes the themes of travel, relocation, and displacement, all of which transpire on geographic as well as personal fronts. When it is revealed that Boy Willie's goal is to seize and sell the piano in order to purchase property from the grandson of the Sutters, Wilson establishes the instrument as the device through which he will present the depths of each character's geographic and emotional dislocations.

Storytelling is again Wilson's primary epistemological device, as the siblings' Uncle Doaker furnishes the piano's contentious history. His brother Wining Boy, a downtrodden alcoholic blues singer, corroborates Doaker's tale and also supplies a few details. The piano had been owned by Robert Sutter, the patriarch of the family that owned the Charles family. Lacking enough money to purchase an anniversary present for his wife, Ophelia, Sutter trades Doaker's grandmother (also Boy Willie and Berniece's great-grandmother for whom Berniece is named) and her nine-year-old son (Doaker's father) to Joel Nolander in exchange for a piano. However, the loss of Miss Ophelia's trusted mammy and confidante brings about a deep depression and sparks Sutter's attempted reacquisition of both mother and son. When Nolander refuses, Sutter forces Ophelia's husband Willie Boy—a "worker of wood" so accomplished that Sutter parlays his labor and talent into profits by having him make furniture for whites—to carve their pictures into the piano. But Willie Boy takes it upon himself to transform the piano into a visual family history: he carves etchings of his mother and father as well as pictures commemorating his marriage to Mama Berniece and his mother's funeral. Willie Boy performs a type of artistic resistance and affirmation, keeping alive the memories of a wife who has been so inhumanely bartered alongside the monumental events in their lives.

Subsequently, Boy Charles—Doaker's brother and father of Boy Willie and Berniece—decides to claim the heirloom because "it was the story of our whole family and as long as Sutter had it . . . he had us." With the assistance of brothers Doaker and Wining Boy, Boy Charles takes the piano from the Sutters' home during a Fourth of July picnic; Wining Boy and Doaker then carry the piano to the next county and leave it with relatives of Mama Ola, Boy Charles's wife. What Sutter considers a theft touches off a spate of violent episodes: the burning of Boy Charles's house and then the torching of a "Yellow Dog" railroad boxcar on which he was escaping—a blaze that kills him along with four hobos. Though the murderer is never identified, the townspeople suspect any number of white men, including Sutter himself and the sheriff. Doaker's story comes full circle when he reveals that Boy Charles's death precipitates the mysterious deaths of several white men; significantly, Boy Willie arrived bearing the news that Sutter's 340-pound grandson had just fallen down his own well. The piano becomes the play's unifying symbol, its labyrinthine history and the characters' visceral reactions to it signifying the link between past and present, the extent to which blacks' and whites' personal histories are intertwined, and the best ways to preserve artifacts steeped in personal and familial misery.

Sutter's ghost, like the eponymous infant-apparition in Toni Morrison's *Beloved,* becomes an indefatigable, ominous presence: all of the inhabitants of the Charles household claim to have seen the ghost upstairs. Though Sutter's ghost instills fear in Berniece and Maretha, another ghost story, which involves Boy Charles and the men killed in the boxcar, is the basis of the "Ghosts of the Yellow Dog." According to this piece of local lore, the ghosts of Boy Charles and his fellow victims have metamor-

phosed into a presence that is now avenging his death—thus the white men inexplicably falling into wells. Wining Boy further illuminates this inscrutable story, revealing that he ventured to the place where the Yellow Dog and Southern railroads intersect to commune with the "ghosts of the yellow dog." Conjuring up images of Bynum's magic-tinged story of finding his "Shiny Man," Wining Boy declares that he called out the dead men's names, an act of ancestor worship which proves regenerative: "I walked away from there feeling like a king." Though the three years of good luck he experiences give way to an emotional inertia that even leads him to give up playing piano professionally, Wining Boy's tale becomes an integral part of Wilson's folkloric and supernatural design, which illustrates how blacks' access to different forms of cultural knowledge can effect change. The Yellow Dog ghosts become the symbolic counterpart of the piano, for the characters invest them with the ability to empower and, alternatively, the potential to disrupt.

Recalling Hansberry's *A Raisin in the Sun,* Wilson vividly foregrounds sibling conflict in *The Piano Lesson.* The piano functions as the objective correlative, concretizing Boy Willie and Berniece's diametrically opposite attitudes about everything—family history, religion, economics, the South, even child rearing. For Boy Willie, the proceeds from its sale will enable him to live out the American patriarchal dream of ownership:

> I ain't talking about selling my soul. I'm talking about trading that piece of wood for some land. Get something under your feet. . . . The only thing that make that piano worth something is them carvings Papa Willie Boy put on there. That's what make it worth something. That was my great-granddaddy, Papa Boy Charles brought that piano into the house. Now I'm supposed to build on what they left me.

Boy Willie imagines the piano as the linchpin in a grand patriarchal lineage that connects him with ancestors who, emotionally or physically or both, were denied existences as strong, liberated black men. He eschews what he calls Berniece's "sentimental value," which he feels reduces the piano to a static historical object whose monetary value is wasted.

Contesting Boy Willie's strictly utilitarian approach to the past, Berniece offers a sustained countervoice. Not only does she vow to prevent its sale, but she decides that the most fruitful way to preserve its legacy is not to play it herself, though she insists that her daughter play it. Berniece also offers a different interpretation of her father's claiming of the piano: while Boy Willie views it solely in terms of male lineage and ownership, Berniece extrapolates from its wrenching history the irremediable heartache it brought to their mother, Mama Ola:

> You always talking about your daddy but you ain't never stopped to look at what his foolishness cost your mama. Seventeen years' worth of cold nights and an empty bed. For what? For a piano? For a piece of wood? To get even with somebody?

Berniece further reveals her own tortured childhood relationship with the piano, one that sheds light on her self-imposed exile in which she "just stay home most of the time. Take care of Maretha":

> When my mama died I shut the top on that piano and I ain't never opened it since. I was only playing it for her. When my daddy died seem like all her life went into that piano. She used to have me playing on it . . . say when I played it she could hear my daddy talking to her. I used to think them pictures came alive and walked through the house. Sometime late at night I could hear my mama talking to them. I said that wasn't gonna happen to me. I don't play that piano cause I don't want to wake them spirits. They never be walking around in this house.

That Berniece forces Maretha to play the piano marks Wilson's variation on the standard literary plot which foregrounds sons wrestling with their fathers' ghosts: Mama Ola has bequeathed her emotional stasis to Berniece, who similarly inflicts her pain upon her own daughter. Through his characterizations of Boy Willie and Berniece, Wilson not only *races* family history, but he *genders* it in some especially compelling ways.

The play's conclusion brings about a final confrontation regarding the siblings' flawed interpretations of the piano's meaning. Though one might assume that Boy Willie is Wilson's surrogate (recall the author's observation that the mother in Bearden's collage "is trying to acquire a sense of self-worth by denying her past"), certain scholars do not ultimately see the author as necessarily endorsing either character's mindset. That the piano proves to be literally immovable (it withstands Lymon and Boy Willie's assiduous attempts to remove it) would suggest that Wilson does not wholly side with Boy Willie's unabashed commodification of the heirloom. Brother and sister must confront the enshackling legacy of Sutter's ghost head-on, a seemingly intractable presence that not only frightens Berniece and Maretha, but one that becomes more formidable as the play reaches its climax. When Boy Willie determines that he will expel the ghost from his uncle's home (significantly, the attempted exorcism performed by Berniece's lover, Reverend Avery, proves totally ineffectual), the stage directions capture the immense power of the white man whose apparitional presence continues to plague the Charles family: "The sound of SUTTER's GHOST is heard. As BOY WILLIE approaches the steps he is suddenly thrown back by the unseen force, which is choking him. As he struggles he frees himself, then dashes up the stairs." Like the ghosts of the Yellow Dog, Sutter's proves to be omnipowerful and omnipresent. Though the ghost appears victorious—it continually throws Boy Willie down the stairs—Boy Willie wages a valiant battle with it. However, it is Berniece who delivers both the fatal blow and the healing balm.

The distaff version of Loomis' finding his song at the conclusion of *Joe Turner's Come and Gone,* Berniece "crosses to the piano. She begins to play. The song is found piece by piece. . . . It is intended as an exorcism and a dressing for battle." Her feverish playing of the piano accompanies an African ritual of ancestor calling: she invokes the names of several deceased relatives while fervidly singing "I want you to help me." Her praise song not only rids the house of Sutter's demonic presence, but it purges from her and Boy Willie the racial and familial demons that had made them inflexible and oppositional. Singing one's song, not solely the purview of Wilson's male protagonists, inaugurates both siblings' healing on several fronts. Wilson masterfully enmeshes the racial, personal, familial in *The Piano Lesson,* showing that painful racial memories can neither be sold off nor spirited away if they are ignored long enough.

TWO TRAINS RUNNING

In response to Pettengill's query on why Wilson's play representing the 1960s does not foreground cataclysmic events and cultural icons such as the March on Washington and Martin Luther King Jr., he replied, "The play itself does not speak to the so-called red lettered events of the sixties, because at the time all of that was going on—the assassination of Martin Luther King and Bobby Kennedy and all the anti-war administrations [sic], etc.— people were still living their lives." *Two Trains Running* renders the 1960s by an almost indirect method: it dramatizes not black luminaries or cultural conflagrations but the seemingly pedestrian lives of black Americans embroiled in myriad crises, persons for whom the turbulent 1960s provided only the backdrop for their own emotional upheavals. *Two Trains Running*

opened at Broadway's Kerr Theatre on April 13, 1992, and starred Laurence Fishburne and Roscoe Lee Browne; the play won Wilson his fourth New York Drama Critics' Circle Award.

The title, taken from bluesman Muddy Waters' "Still a Fool," again expresses Wilson's concentration on trains, a recurring conceit throughout his works. The notion of "two trains running" is rife with meanings: the author himself explained to Pettengill, "There were two ideas in the play, or at least two ideas that have confronted black America since the Emancipation, the ideas of cultural assimilation and cultural separatism. These were, in my mind, the two trains." Though the play certainly buttresses this point, Wilson's observation belies the rather somber if not moribund tone of most of the play, for it is a mourning play. In fact, the "running" the title delineates might more aptly be categorized as a *passing*: the literal death of the black cultural icon Malcolm X, whose memory figures prominently, the degeneration and outright implosion of the black community, the characters' psychospiritual demise. The play examines the detritus of a motley crew of African Americans. Its restaurant setting, like the boardinghouse in *Joe Turner,* enables Wilson to bring together a disparate group of wayfarers—an ex-con, a mortician, a floundering businessman, a waitress with self-inflicted wounds, a mentally incapacitated man whose unutterable pain has all but left him speechless, a sagacious but ineffectual observer who grasps at some sort of meaning if not order. Like the spiritually bereft barflies in O'Neill's *The Iceman Cometh,* the play depicts men and women who have been battered black and blue: as restaurant owner Memphis laments, "Every nigger I know got bad luck."

Memphis' restaurant, once a thriving business, is now a shadow of its former self. As part of its urban renewal plan, the city is purchasing and razing businesses on his block; hence, Memphis spends more time haggling with the city over his asking price, $25,000, than he does running the diner. Two of the few remaining businesses are adjacent to his: a meat market owned by Lutz, one of the play's off-stage white characters who nevertheless figures prominently in the characters' lives; and West, a black undertaker and Memphis' nemesis whose business is flourishing. The imminent demolition of this block reflects the reality of many large cities in the late 1960s. Memphis' eulogy early in the play establishes its elegiac tone:

> Ain't nothing to do. Unless I do like West and go into the undertaking business. I can't go out there in Squirrel Hill and open up a restaurant. Ain't nothing gonna be left around here. Supermarket gone. Two drugstores. The five and ten. Doctor done moved out. Dentist done moved out. Shoe store gone. Ain't nothing gonna be left but these niggers killing one another. That don't never go out of style. West gonna get richer and everybody else gonna get poorer. At one time you couldn't get a seat in here. . . . It ain't nothing like that now. I'm lucky if I go through a case a chicken a week.

Enervated by racial and economic struggles, the tattered inner city is now a wasteland town whose remaining denizens self-destructively turn their frustrations inward. Though Wilson may be recalling the squalid Hill neighborhood of his youth, the crumbling Pittsburgh ghetto that Memphis mourns could in fact be any number of American cities from Newark to Detroit to Washington, racial war zones whose damaged physical infrastructures emblematized the decayed emotional infrastructures of many residents. Despite West's offers to purchase the restaurant, Memphis vehemently insists on being justly compensated.

Two Trains Running hearkens back to *Ma Rainey's Black Bottom* in that the characters' inner struggles constitute the main action. Each character brings with him or her a blues-inflected history. Risa, the play's only woman character and the sole waitress in Memphis'

diner, literally bears the lacerations that mirror the community's looming demolition: in an effort to make herself unattractive to men, she has taken a razor blade to her legs. Memphis weighs in on her act of self-mutilation, characterizing her as "a mixed-up personality" who was briefly institutionalized after her scarring. He attributes her emotional paralysis to her six years of manlessness. In fact, most of the characters' lives are marred by an absence of companionship: all of the women in the male characters' lives have either died or abandoned them. A potential lover for Risa surfaces in Sterling, a thirty-year-old with whom she grew up who has just been released from the penitentiary. Other regulars in Memphis' diner include Wolf, the numbers runner who uses the restaurant as his base of operations, and Hambone, whose failure to be remunerated by the white storeowner Lutz has left him verbally and emotionally debilitated.

Rounding out the restaurant patrons is Holloway, a former house painter who is more an observer and commentator than a participant in the action. Reminiscent of Toledo in *Ma Rainey*, Holloway is the resident sage and race man; Wilson designated him "the character who knows everything." As the community's oral historian, he supplies information about characters on- and offstage, demonstrating Wilson's belief that blacks' personal and collective stories must be kept alive and transmitted from generation to generation. A wellspring of information, he provides key details about Prophet Samuel, whose funeral takes place offstage during the course of the play. He reveals that Samuel began as "Reverend" Samuel, the prototypical "jack-leg" preacher who "[h]ad him a truck . . . had him a loudspeaker, and he'd go out and preach the word of the gospel and sell barbecue on the side." Samuel's accurate prediction of the stock market's decline and eventual revival garners favor with wealthy white businessmen such as Mellon, who "sent Prophet Samuel a five-hundred-dollar donation and a brochure advertising his banking services." From this point Samuel is catapulted into a cult figure, a robe-wearing, barefoot messiah—"That's when Prophet Samuel went big." The charlatan-like Samuel dispenses dubious promises of economic prosperity to destitute blacks. Like West, who formerly ran numbers and gambled before deciding that burying African Americans was more lucrative, Prophet Samuel represents a pseudospiritual figure who nevertheless cultivates a substantial following in the spiritually and economically ravaged black community. Risa's membership card reveals the guiding principle of Samuel's "ministry": "This certifies that Risa Tomas is a member in good standing of the First African Congregational Kingdom, having duly paid all tithing. . . . Signed, Prophet Samuel."

The other major offstage source of spiritual uplift is Aunt Ester, whom Holloway describes as 322 years old. An oracle and spiritual advisor who, unlike Prophet Samuel, "won't take no money for herself," she usually counsels her clients to throw money into the river to bring about good fortune. Holloway credits her with preventing him from killing his obsequious, white-worshiping grandfather; conversely, West and Memphis place little stock in her, though Memphis ultimately visits her and is subsequently offered $35,000 for his restaurant, $10,000 more than his asking price. The self-fashioned proverb she recites to Memphis contains one of the play's central themes, for it relates to personal and collective recuperation and reconciliation of the past: "If you drop the ball, you got to go back and pick it up." She emerges as an ethereal but forceful presence in the drama, one who counterpoises Prophet Samuel's meretricious if not fraudulent brand of evangelism. Wilson explained in his interview with Pettengill that he fashioned her as representing "the entire 349 [the corrected age Sterling later reveals] years that blacks have

been in America. She represents our tradition, our philosophy, our folk wisdom, our hobbies, our culture, whatever you want to call it."

Another character that Wilson feels embodies the spirit of the drama is Hambone, a human hieroglyph who elicits multiple interpretations and responses; when the undertaker West retrieves Hambone's corpse, he divulges that it contains "so many scars. . . . All on his back, his chest . . . his legs." Hambone maniacally repeats two phrases throughout the play: "He gonna give me my ham. I want my ham." Holloway and Memphis give conflicting accounts, but it can be extrapolated that Hambone had agreed to paint Lutz's fence in exchange for a ham (note Wilson's return to his metaphorical fence). Unsatisfied with the job, Lutz offered Hambone a chicken; the latter then began a nine-year crusade for personal justice. Despite Memphis's fervent objections, Risa feeds Hambone, and Sterling attempts to commune with him; Sterling even has limited success in teaching him quixotic, 1960s catchphrases such as "Black is beautiful" and "United we stand, divided we fall." Though Memphis derides Hambone's campaign against Lutz as "that old backward southern mentality," Holloway applauds his refusal to accept "whatever the white man throw at him." He becomes the play's symbol of black resistance in the face of protracted white venality.

That Hambone's sudden death stimulates Sterling's regeneration bears out Wilson's emphasis not on the turbulent struggles that have come to define the 1960s, but on personal and intimate acts that foster connectedness in a world that Sterling—orphaned and institutionalized as a child—desolately concludes "done gone crazy. I'm sorry I was ever born into it." Despite having been incarcerated and being slightly "unbalanced" (according to the stage directions), Sterling emerges as one of the play's most prescient and reflective voices. At times, he articulates the community's existential alienation: "People don't pay you half as much mind as you think they do. That just be in your head. Most people so busy trying to live their own lives they ain't got time to pay attention to nobody else." Alternatively, however, he represents the ineradicable hope and commitment to change that also marked the black zeitgeist. He eagerly prepares to attend a rally commemorating Malcolm X's death, and he dares to challenge the invisible white power structure represented by "the Alberts," the local racketeering family who "cut the number," thereby sharply decreasing the amount of money Sterling's winning number would have brought. The event that ends the play—Sterling, soaked with blood after breaking into Lutz's market, presents West with a ham to place in Hambone's casket—animates Sterling's personal redemption and epitomizes the empowerment and activism championed by Malcolm X. The author's reflections on both Sterling and Hambone in an interview with Sandra Shannon attest to the quasi-spiritual heights to which both men ascend:

> So Hambone's presence . . . and his death affect the whole play, and then Sterling can resurrect and redeem Hambone's life by taking the ham. This produces the man of action. Without Hambone, you don't have a Sterling. And also it's the demonstration of his willingness to shed blood in order to get the ham.

Two Trains Running is Wilson's most meditative play—perhaps this accounts for the plotlessness or amorphousness some critics disparaged. Unencumbered by the parameters of the well-made play, Wilson embroiders a collage of black voices that at once express wrenching pain and guarded optimism. The dramatist ingeniously crafts a play about the 1960s that explores cultural and psychic fragmentation while concomitantly celebrating the lives of ordinary African Americans who are on the brink of personal and collective annihilation.

SEVEN GUITARS

For his 1940s play, Wilson mines familiar thematic terrain, though he experiments formally with a flashback and flashfoward technique. *Seven Guitars* recounts the interwoven stories of seven black men and women in Pittsburgh in 1948. In his interview with Pettengill, Wilson adduces that the play was originally based on a short story he had written "about a guy who was killed. By going through all the boxes of papers in his room, you discover who he was simply by looking at the contents of his life." In fact, he singles out the fiction of the Argentine writer Jorge Luis Borges as a structural model for *Seven Guitars,* specifically his technique of "tell[ing] you exactly what is going to happen." Chronicling the short and tragic life of a blues singer named Floyd "Schoolboy" Barton, *Seven Guitars* is less about who kills Floyd than it is about the profound impact his life has upon those closest to him: Vera, a lover he had formerly abandoned and has returned to woo; her confidante Louise, a world-weary woman whose husband deserted her several years earlier; Red Carter and Canewell, members of Floyd's fledgling band; Hedley, a combination peddler and mystic whose visions and dreams ominously portend doom; and Ruby, Louise's niece whose "little fast behind" arrives from Alabama fleeing a tawdry murder in which one of her suitors shot another. The drama premiered in Chicago, though Wilson revised it prior to its opening at the Walter Kerr Theatre on March 28, 1996; the play received yet another New York Drama Critics' Circle Award.

Seven Guitars might be considered a primer for students and critics of Wilson's oeuvre. He interlards the drama with his signature narrative concerns: the tumultuous lives of blacks negotiating an urban North that is racially hostile and economically discommoding, ailing relationships between men and women, the brazen exploitation of black artists, the irrepressible and irreplaceable folk and vernacular culture that sustains those who would otherwise drown amidst a current of insurmountable circumstances, and the simmering violence that defines so many black men's lives and devastates when it is finally unleashed. Though the play approximates the aforementioned Borges technique of openly revealing key plot information very early, *Seven Guitars* more closely resembles James Baldwin's sprawling 1962 novel *Another Country,* which similarly explores the life of a musician whose premature death spawns the novel's action.

The play opens with Floyd's friends remembering their deceased compatriot with anecdotes and songs in "the Yard," a rear portion of the duplex and the primary setting. Several claim to have glimpsed angels in black spiriting Floyd's body away to heaven, a claim that continues Wilson's interest with otherworldliness and black folk and religious beliefs. The combination of celebration and commemoration establishes the play's overall elegiac feel, for the characters' remembrances quickly flash backward to Floyd's complex relationships with several of them. His only hit single, "That's All Right," which Wilson took from a line in a song by the legendary blues artist Blind Lemon Jefferson, is the musical bridge that transports us to the past. As with most Wilson plays, this one progresses as a series of interconnected stories and songs. But unlike *Ma Rainey's Black Bottom,* with which it shares several similarities, *Seven Guitars* concentrates more extensively on Floyd, a black artist who failed to receive commensurate payment for his musical labor and the calamitous end he meets when attempting to recoup those rewards in order to acquire material possessions.

Floyd Barton is the quintessential portrait of the Wilson artist. The litany of woes that bedevil

him are endemic of a blues life—false imprisonment, financial exigency, woman trouble. We are introduced to him as he attempts to rekindle his relationship with Vera, whom he spurned when he went to Chicago to record his hit record in the company of Pearl Brown. His lengthy entreaties subsequently pay off when she decides to marry him and return to Chicago, though she purchases a return ticket to Pittsburgh and hopes "I never have to use it." In fact, women, present and past, are pressing concerns in Floyd's life. He is haunted by memories of Maude Avery Barton, a mother whom he loved unfailingly; he poignantly recalls her favorite spiritual, "Old Ship of Zion," which leads him to sing the Lord's Prayer in her memory at the end of act 1, scene 4. However, her unabating poverty has left him resentfully materialistic. Still reconciling this unresolved relationship, Floyd devotes his energies to earning enough money to purchase a headstone; she had been buried in a pauper's cemetery in an unmarked grave that took Floyd three hours to find. At this moment he asserts, "I get her that marker and I won't owe nobody nothing." A strange nexus surfaces between Floyd's increasingly insatiable materialism and this filial relationship that continually vexes and anguishes him. In one soliloquy, he forebodingly declares:

> I am going to Chicago. If I have to buy me a graveyard and kill everybody I see. I am going to Chicago. I don't want to live my life without. . . . My mama ain't had two dimes to rub together. . . . Floyd Barton gonna make his record. Floyd Barton is going to Chicago.

On some level, Floyd links his mother's unalterable poverty with his own feelings of emasculation. Thus, recording another hit and purchasing a gravestone simultaneously mark the material fulfillment of his titular role as "man" and the paying off of a debt—his mother's poverty and the heretofore eternal memory of it—which has weighed on his consciousness like an unmovable boulder.

Reminiscent of the male rituals that undergird *Ma Rainey's Black Bottom* and *Fences,* Wilson layers *Seven Guitars* with the culturally evocative traditions of performance—blues and gospel singing, sermon-like personal testimonies, folk rhymes, and dance. The play's kinetic energy derives from the men's philosophizing, confessing, signifying. Buffeted by racial, economic, and artistic breaches, most of the men tell a blues tale of sound and fury. Floyd laments his three-month imprisonment in a workhouse for what was termed "vagrancy" and "worthlessness." He is then exploited by his white manager T. L. Hall, who fails to help Floyd and fellow band members Red Carter and Canewell retrieve their instruments from the pawnshop. An offstage menace, "Mr. T. L. Hall," like Sturdyvant and Irvin in *Ma Rainey,* ruthlessly commodifies black musicians: the play suggests that he has been swindling Floyd out of royalties and performance fees, and he is subsequently convicted of peddling false insurance policies to unsuspecting black clients. Canewell, whose name bears out a southern heritage in which his father cut sugarcane in Louisiana, has suffered many of the same indignities that have befallen Floyd—mainly his arrest in Chicago for performing on the street. But unlike Floyd, Canewell voices a healthy contempt for bloodsucking hegemonic operatives such as Savoy (the label that recorded "That's All Right") and T. L. Hall. He unsuccessfully tries to educate "Schoolboy" on the music business: "I told Floyd to get a cut of the money. They paid him a flat rate." His vehement refusal to return to Chicago unless he is paid "up front" reflects a keen awareness of the unethical practices of a recording industry that routinely parlays black talent into white profits.

The other most complexly drawn character in *Seven Guitars* is Hedley, a fifty-nine-year-old Haitian who sells sundry items—cigarettes, chicken sandwiches, eggs—and, more importantly, fantasizes that he is "gonna be a big man." Throughout the play, he and Floyd engage in a sort of call-and-response riddle about Buddy Bolden, a renowned New Orleans jazz trumpeter in the early twentieth century:

> FLOYD [singing]: "I thought I heard Buddy Bolden say . . ."
> HEDLEY: What he say?
> FLOYD: He said, "Wake up and give me the money."
> HEDLEY: Naw. Naw. He say, "Come here. Here go the money."

This exchange reveals both men's tragic flaw: a compulsive quest for economic fulfillment which is constantly thwarted. Bolden's personal history is also germane here: known for his immodest appetites for women and alcohol, he suffered severe mental breakdowns and was institutionalized for much of his life. Hedley also has a penchant for alcohol, though part of his own malaise stems from his inability to marry and produce male offspring. His body racked with a tuberculosis that he refuses to treat, Hedley weaves elaborate stories about personal indignities (he is tormented by his father's violent rejection of him), economic longing (he persistently dreams that his father has bequeathed him money that Bolden will deliver), and a desire to ascend to Christ-like power and majesty. Most vexing are Hedley's copious references to a melange of messiah-like figures of biblical and historical proportions—Christ, Moses, Marcus Garvey, Toussaint-Louverture—whom he deifies and emulates.

Wilson clearly configures Hedley as a disturbing presence who might ostensibly be mentally unbalanced but who is also stridently oppositional in matters of race: "The black man is not a dog." Though the play will end tragically with a deranged Hedley killing Floyd over money that Floyd and another man have stolen from a bank, it is clear that both men are more alike than different. To their detriment, they use white patriarchal masculinity as their benchmark, and when they fail to attain the material accoutrements of success, they resort to violence. Hedley's killing of his neighbor Mrs. Tillery's rooster at the end of act 1 portends not only the police's murder of Poochie, her son and Floyd's accomplice in the bank robbery, but it marks the death of the southern communal folk culture that is eclipsed by a corrosive, distinctly northern form of materialism. One can interpret Hedley as a conundrum: he embodies the immigrant dream of America as the gateway to opportunity; he abjures Western medicine and instead embraces folk remedies and natural healing; and he imagines himself as a faux white patriarch who will use his power to elevate himself from the bottom of the racial totem pole. One can see in his killing of Floyd materialism run amok, but, almost paradoxically, one also sees Hedley's severing of Floyd's windpipe with a machete as an act of cosmic retribution, as Floyd repudiates a religious-spiritual base (at one point he tells Hedley, "I don't want to hear nothing about no Bible"). As a potential messiah whose art could save himself and his community, Floyd degenerates into a money-driven miscreant, and it is Hedley who becomes a cosmologically corrective force. Perhaps this might account for the play's conclusion, which returns to the opening scene in the Yard following Floyd's funeral: Hedley's act is not revealed to Floyd's friends and goes unpunished.

Wilson's refusal to offer moral judgments of the characters' actions, along with his violation of murder mystery conventions which mandate that the culprit be exposed and punished, makes *Seven Guitars* one of his most unsettling works. Far more than a rags–to–modest success–to–death story of a foundering crooner, the play is a blues poem whose seven voices express in lyrical prose their own personal trials and tribulations, which are balanced by an unflag-ging spirit and perseverance. Floyd's sole hit record, "That's All Right," becomes a paean to all of Wilson's characters—men and women whose southern roots, geographic displacement, and commitment to struggle reflect the souls of all the black folk whom Wilson has committed to inscribing, dramatizing, and commemorating. August Wilson continued to solidify his position at the pinnacle of American dramatic letters with the New York production of *Jitney* in April 2000, a work on which he expended exhaustive creative energy but one which he credits as shaping his artistic voice.

Selected Bibliography

WORKS OF AUGUST WILSON

PLAYS
Ma Rainey's Black Bottom. New York: New American Library, 1985.
Fences. New York: New American Library, 1986.
Joe Turner's Come and Gone. New York: New American Library, 1988.
The Piano Lesson. New York: Plume, 1990.
Three Plays. Pittsburgh: University of Pittsburgh Press, 1991. (Includes *Ma Rainey's Black Bottom, Fences,* and *Joe Turner's Come and Gone.*)
Two Trains Running. New York: Plume, 1993.
Seven Guitars. New York: Plume, 1997.

POETRY
"For Malcolm X and Others." *Negro Digest* 18:58 (September 1969).
"Bessie." *Black Lines* 1:68 (summer 1971)
"Morning Song." *Black Lines* 1:68 (summer 1971)
"Muhammad Ali." *Black World* 1:60–61 (September 1972).
"Theme One: The Variations." In *The Poetry of Black America: Anthology of the Twentieth Century.* Edited by Arnold Adoff. New York: Harper and Row, 1973.

ARTICLES
"How to Write a Play like August Wilson." *New York Times,* March 10, 1991, pp. 5, 17.

"The Legacy of Malcolm X." *Life,* December 1992, pp. 84–94.

"I Want a Black Director." In *May All Your Fences Have Gates: Essays on the Drama of August Wilson.* Edited by Alan Nadel. Iowa City: University of Iowa Press, 1994. Pp. 200–204.

Preface to *Fences.* In *Swing Low: Black Men Writing.* Edited by Rebecca Carroll. New York: Crown Trade Paperbacks, 1995. Pp. 246–254.

"The Ground on Which I Stand." *American Theatre* 13:50–52, 71–74 (September 1996).

CRITICAL AND BIOGRAPHICAL STUDIES

Awkward, Michael. "'The Crookeds with the Straights': *Fences,* Race, and the Politics of Adaptation." In Nadel. Pp. 205–229.

Bogumil, Mary L. *Understanding August Wilson.* Columbia: University of South Carolina Press, 1999.

Brustein, Robert. *Reimagining American Theater.* New York: Wang, 1991.

Elkins, Marilyn, ed. *August Wilson: A Casebook.* New York: Garland, 1994.

Fishman, Joan. "Romare Bearden, August Wilson, and the Traditions of African Performance." In Nadel. Pp. 133–149.

Glover, Margaret E. "Two Notes on August Wilson: The Songs of a Marked Man." *Theater* 19, no. 3:69–70 (1988).

Harrison, Paul Carter. "August Wilson's Blues Poetics." In *Three Plays,* by August Wilson. Pp. 291–318.

Kubitschek, Missy Dehn. "August Wilson's Gender Lesson." In Nadel. Pp. 183–199.

Marra, Kim. "Ma Rainey and the Boyz: Gender Ideology in August Wilson's Broadway Canon." In Elkins. Pp. 123–160.

McDonough, Carla J. *Staging Masculinity: Male Identity in Contemporary American Drama.* Jefferson, N.C.: McFarland, 1997.

Nadel, Alan, ed. *May All Your Fences Have Gates: Essays on the Drama of August Wilson.* Iowa City: University of Iowa Press, 1994.

O'Neill, Michael. "August Wilson." In *American Playwrights since 1945: A Guide to Scholarship, Criticism, and Performance.* Edited by Philip C.

Kolin. Westport, Conn.: Greenwood, 1989. Pp. 175–177.

Pereira, Kim. *August Wilson and the African-American Odyssey.* Urbana: University of Illinois Press, 1995.

Plum, Jay. "Blues, History, and the Dramaturgy of August Wilson." *African American Review* 27, no. 4:561–567 (winter 1993).

Reed, Ishmael. "In Search of August Wilson: A Shy Genius Transforms the American Theater." *Connoisseur* 217:92–97 (March 1987).

Rocha, Mark William. "August Wilson and the Four B's: Influences." In Elkins. Pp. 3–16.

Rothstein, Mervyn. "Round Five for a Theatrical Heavyweight." *New York Times,* April 15, 1990, pp. 1, 8.

Shafer, Yvonne. *August Wilson: A Research and Production Sourcebook.* Westport, Conn.: Greenwood, 1998.

Shannon, Sandra G. *The Dramatic Vision of August Wilson.* Washington, D.C.: Howard University Press, 1995.

Werner, Craig. "August Wilson's Burden: The Function of Neoclassical Jazz." In Nadel. Pp. 21–50.

Wolfe, Peter. *August Wilson.* New York: Twayne, 1999.

INTERVIEWS

Lyons, Bonnie. "An Interview with August Wilson." *Contemporary Literature* 40:1–21 (spring 1999).

Moyers, Bill. "August Wilson: Playwright." In his *A World of Ideas: Conversations with Thoughtful Men and Women about American Life Today and the Ideas Shaping Our Future.* New York: Doubleday, 1989. Pp. 167–180.

Pettengill, Richard. "The Historical Perspective: An Interview with August Wilson." In *August Wilson: A Casebook.* Edited by Marilyn Elkins. New York: Garland, 1994. Pp. 207–226.

Powers, Kim. "An Interview with August Wilson." *Theatre* 16:50–55. (fall/winter 1984).

Rocha, Mark William. "A Conversation with August Wilson." *Diversity* 1:24–42 (fall 1992).

Shafer, Yvonne. "An Interview with August Wilson." *Journal of Dramatic Theory and Criticism* 4:161–173 (fall 1989).

Shannon, Sandra G. "August Wilson Explains His Dramatic Vision: An Interview." In her *The Dramatic Vision of August Wilson.* Washington, D.C.: Howard University Press, 1995. Pp. 201–235.

—KEITH CLARK

Index

Index

Arabic numbers printed in bold-face type refer to extended treatment of a subject.

"Apology, An" (Malamud), **Supp. I, Part 2,** 435, 437

"Apology for Bad Dreams" (Jeffers), **Supp. II, Part 2,** 427, 438

"Apology for Crudity, An" (Anderson), **I,** 109

Apology for Poetry (Sidney), **Supp. II, Part 1,** 105

"Apostle of the Tules, An" (Harte), **Supp. II, Part 1,** 356

"Apostrophe to a Dead Friend" (Kumin), **Supp. IV, Part 2,** 442, 451, 452

"Apostrophe to a Pram Rider" (White), **Supp. I, Part 2,** 678

"Apostrophe to Man (on reflecting that the world is ready to go to war again)" (Millay), **III,** 127

"Apostrophe to Vincentine, The" (Stevens), **IV,** 90

"Apotheosis" (Kingsolver), **Supp. VII,** 208

"Apotheosis of Martin Luther King, The" (Hardwick), **Supp. III, Part 1,** 203–204

Appalachia (Wright), **Supp. V,** 333, 345

"Appalachian Book of the Dead III" (Wright), **Supp. V,** 345

"Appeal to Progressives, An" (Wilson), **IV,** 429

Appeal to Reason (journal), **Supp. V,** 281

Appeal to Reason (Paine), **I,** 490

Appeal to the World, An (Du Bois), **Supp. II, Part 1,** 184

Appearance and Reality (Bradley), **I,** 572

Appel, Alfred, Jr., **III,** 266; **IV,** 284

"Appendix to 'The Anniad'" (Brooks), **Supp. III, Part 1,** 77

Apple, Max, **Supp. VIII,** 14

"Apple, The" (Kinnell), **Supp. III, Part 1,** 250

Applegarth, Mabel, **II,** 465, 478

Appleseed, Johnny (pseudonym), *see* Chapman, John (Johnny Appleseed)

Appleton, **Retro. Supp. I,** 381

Appleton, Frances, *see* Longfellow, Mrs. Henry Wadsworth (Frances Appleton)

Appleton, Nathan, **II,** 488

Appleton, Thomas Gold, **Supp. I, Part 1,** 306, **Part 2,** 415

"Applicant, The" (Plath), **Supp. I, Part 2,** 535, 544, 545

"Applications of the Doctrine" (Hass), **Supp. VI, 100–101**

Appointment in Samarra (O'Hara), **III,** 361, 363–364, 365–367, 371, 374, 375, 383

"Approach to Thebes, The" (Kunitz), **Supp. III, Part 1,** 265–267

"Approaches, The" (Merwin), **Supp. III, Part 1,** 350

"Approaching Artaud" (Sontag), **Supp. III, Part 2,** 470–471

"Approaching Prayer" (Dickey), **Supp. IV, Part 1,** 175

"Après-midi d'un faune, L'" (Mallarmé), **III,** 8

"April" (Williams), **Retro. Supp. I,** 422

"April" (Winters), **Supp. II, Part 2,** 788

"April Galleons" (Ashbery), **Supp. III, Part 1,** 26

April Galleons (Ashbery), **Supp. III, Part 1,** 26

April Hopes (Howells), **II,** 285, 289

"April Lovers" (Ransom), **III,** 489–490

"April Showers" (Wharton), **Retro. Supp. I,** 361

"April Today Main Street" (Olson), **Supp. II, Part 2,** 581

April Twilights (Cather), **I,** 313; **Retro. Supp. I,** 5

"Apt Pupil" (King), **Supp. V,** 152

Aptheker, Herbert, **IV,** 118

Aquinas, Saint Thomas, **I,** 13, 14, 265, 267; **III,** 270; **Supp. IV, Part 2,** 526

Arab Observer (publication), **Supp. IV, Part 1,** 8

Arabian Nights, **I,** 204; **II,** 8; **Supp. I, Part 2,** 584, 599; **Supp. IV, Part 1,** 1

"Araby" (Joyce), **I,** 174; **Supp. VIII,** 15

Aragon, Louis, **I,** 429; **III,** 471

Aramco World Magazine, **Supp. IV, Part 2,** 599

Arana-Ward, Marie, **Supp. VIII,** 84

Ararat (Glück), **Supp. V,** 79, 86–87

Arbuthnott, John (pseudonym), *see* Henry, O.

Arch, The (magazine), **Supp. IV, Part 1,** 168

Archaeologist of Morning (Olson), **Supp. II, Part 2,** 557

"Archaic Maker, The" (Merwin), **Supp. III, Part 1,** 357

"Archaically New" (Moore), **Supp. I, Part 1,** 97

Archer, William, **IV,** 131; **Retro. Supp. I,** 228

Archer (television show), **Supp. IV, Part 2,** 474

Archer at Large (Macdonald), **Supp. IV, Part 2,** 473

Archer in Hollywood (Macdonald), **Supp. IV, Part 2,** 474

"Archibald Higbie" (Masters), **Supp. I, Part 2,** 461

"Architect, The" (Bourne), **I,** 223

"Architecture of Walter Mitty's Secret Life, The" (Sundell), **Supp. I, Part 2,** 627

Archives of Maryland, **I,** 131

Arctic Dreams (Lopez), **Supp. V,** 211

"Are You a Doctor?" (Carver), **Supp. III, Part 1,** 139–141

Arena (publication), **I,** 407

Arendt, Hannah, **II,** 390, 544; **Retro. Supp. I,** 87; **Supp. I, Part 2,** 570; **Supp. IV, Part 1,** 386; **Supp. VIII,** 98, 99, 100, 243

Arensberg, Walter, **IV,** 408; **Retro. Supp. I,** 416

Aren't You Happy for Me? (Bausch), **Supp. VII,** 42, 51, 54

Areopagitica (Milton), **Supp. I, Part 2,** 422

Argonaut (publication), **I,** 196

"Argonauts of 49, California's Golden Age" (Harte), **Supp. II, Part 1,** 353, 355

Aria da Capo (Millay), **III,** 137–138

Ariel (Plath), **Supp. I, Part 2,** 526, 539, 541; **Supp. V,** 79

"Ariel" (Plath), **Supp. I, Part 2,** 542, 546

227, 229–231, 231, 232, 233, 238

Billy Bathgate (film), **Supp. IV, Part 1,** 236

Billy Budd, Sailor (Melville), **III,** 40, 93–95; **IV,** 105; **Retro. Supp. I,** 249, **258–260**

Billy Phelan's Greatest Game (Kennedy), **Supp. VII,** 131, 132, 134, 135, 142–147, 149, 151, 153, 155

Billy the Kid, **Supp. IV, Part 2,** 489, 490, 492

Biloxi Blues (Simon), **Supp. IV, Part 2,** 576, 577, 584, 586–587, 590

"Bimini" (Hemingway), **II,** 258

Bingham, June, **III,** 312

Bingham, Millicent Todd, **I,** 470, 472, 473; **Retro. Supp. I,** 36

Bingo Palace, The (Erdrich), **Supp. IV, Part 1,** 259, 260, 261, 263–264, 265, 266–267, 268–269, 270, 271–273, 274, 275

"Binsey Poplars" (Hopkins), **Supp. I, Part 1,** 94; **Supp. IV, Part 2,** 639

Bio-Bibliography of Langston Hughes, 1902–1967, A (Dickinson), **Supp. I, Part 1,** 348

Biographia Literaria (Coleridge), **II,** 10; **Retro. Supp. I,** 308

"Biography" (Pinsky), **Supp. VI,** 235, 236, 239, 241, **243,** 249, 250

Biography and Poetical Remains of the Late Margaret Miller Davidson (Irving), **II,** 314

Biography of William Cullen Bryant, with Extracts from His Private Correspondence, A (Godwin), **Supp. I, Part 1,** 173

"Birchbrook Mill" (Whittier), **Supp. I, Part 2,** 699

"Birches" (Frost), **II,** 154; **Retro. Supp. I,** 132

Bird, Alan, **Supp. I, Part 1,** 260

Bird, Robert M., **III,** 423

"Bird came down the Walk, A" (Dickinson), **Retro. Supp. I,** 37

"Bird Frau, The" (Dove), **Supp. IV, Part 1,** 245

"Bird, the Bird, the Bird, The" (Creeley), **Supp. IV, Part 1,** 149

Birdoff, Harry, **Supp. I, Part 2,** 601

Birds of America (McCarthy), **II,** 579–583

"Bird-Witted" (Moore), **III,** 214

Birkerts, Sven, **Supp. IV, Part 2,** 650; **Supp. V,** 212; **Supp. VIII,** 85

Birkhead, L. M., **III,** 116

"Birmingham Sunday" (Hughes), **Supp. I, Part 1,** 343

Birney, James G., **Supp. I, Part 2,** 587, 588

Birstein, Ann, **Supp. VIII,** 100

Birth of a Nation, The (film), **Supp. I, Part 1,** 66

"Birth of the Water Baby, The" (Jong), Supp. V, 131

Birth of Tragedy, The (Nietzsche), **Supp. IV, Part 1,** 105, 110, **Part 2,** 519; **Supp. VIII,** 182

"Birth of Venus, The" (Botticelli), **IV,** 410

"Birth of Venus, The" (Rukeyser), **Supp. VI,** 281

"Birthday Cake for Lionel, A" (Wylie), **Supp. I, Part 2,** 721

"Birthday of Mrs. Pineda, The" (Ríos), **Supp. IV, Part 2,** 542, 546

"Birthday Present, A" (Plath), **Supp. I, Part 2,** 531

"Birthmark, The" (Ellison), **Supp. II, Part 1,** 237–238

"Birth-mark, The" (Hawthorne), **Retro. Supp. I,** 152

Birth-mark, The: Unsettling the Wilderness in American Literary History (Howe), **Supp. IV, Part 2,** 422, 431, 434

Bisch, Louis E., **Supp. I, Part 2,** 608

Bishop, Elizabeth, **II,** 390; **III,** 217; **Retro. Supp. I,** 140, 296, 303; **Supp. I, Part 1, 79–97;** **Supp. III, Part 1,** 6, 7, 10, 1–8, 64, 239, 320, 326, **Part 2,** 541, 561; **Supp. IV, Part 1,** 249, 257, **Part 2,** 439, 626, 639, 641, 644, 647, 651, 653; **Supp. V,** 337

Bishop, Ferman, **II,** 413

Bishop, John Peale, **I,** 119, 432, 440; **II,** 81, 85, 86–87, 91, 209; **III,** 384; **IV,** 35, 140, 427; **Retro.**

Supp. I, 109; **Supp. I, Part 2,** 709

Bishop, John W., **Supp. I, Part 1,** 83

Bishop, Morris, **Supp. I, Part 2,** 676, 681

Bishop, William Thomas, **Supp. I, Part 1,** 83

Bismark, Otto von, **Supp. I, Part 2,** 643

"Bistro Styx, The" (Dove), **Supp. IV, Part 1,** 250–251

Bitov, Andrei, **Retro. Supp. I,** 278

"Bitter Drink, The" (Dos Passos), **Supp. I, Part 2,** 647

"Bitter Farce, A" (Schwartz), **Supp. II, Part 2,** 640, 657–658

"Bitter Pills for the Dark Ladies" (Jong), **Supp. V,** 118

Bitter Victory (Hardy, trans. Kinnell), **Supp. III, Part 1,** 235

Bittner, William, **III,** 432

Bixby, Horace, **IV,** 194

Bjorkman, Frances Maule, **Supp. V,** 285

Björnson, Björnstjerne, **II,** 275

Black, Jeanette, *see* Norris, Mrs. Frank (Jeanette Black)

Black, John, **IV,** 353

Black, Stephen A., **Supp. I, Part 2,** 626

"Black Aesthetic in White America, The" (Daniels), **Supp. I, Part 1,** 70

Black Armour (Wylie), **Supp. I, Part 2,** 708, 709, 712–714, 729

"Black Art" (Baraka), **Supp. II, Part 1,** 49, 50–51, 59, 60

"Black Art, The" (Sexton), **Supp. II, Part 2,** 682

Black Arts Movement, **Supp. II, Part 1,** 34, 53

Black Bart and the Sacred Hills (Wilson), **Supp. VIII,** 330, 331

Black Beetles in Amber (Bierce), **I,** 204, 209

"Black Birch in Winter, A" (Wilbur), **Supp. III, Part 2,** 561

Black Boy (Wright), **IV,** 477, 478, 479, 480–482, 488, 489, 494; **Supp. II, Part 1,** 235–236; **Supp. IV, Part 1,** 11

"Black Boys and Native Sons" (Howe), **Supp. I, Part 1,** 70

(Millay), **III,** 127–128
"Epithalamium" (Auden), **Supp. II, Part 1,** 15
Epoch (magazine), **Supp. VIII,** 12
Epstein, Jason, **Supp. VIII,** 233
Epstein, Joseph, **Supp. IV, Part 2,** 692; **Supp. VIII,** 236, 238
"Epstein" (Roth), **Supp. III, Part 2,** 404, 406–407, 412, 422
"Equal in Paris" (Baldwin), **Supp. I, Part 1,** 52
"Equilibrists, The" (Ransom), **III,** 490, 494
"Erat Hora" (Pound), **III,** 463; **Retro. Supp. I,** 413
Erdrich, Louise, **Supp. IV, Part 1,** **259–278,** 333, 404
"Ere Sleep Comes Down to Soothe the Weary Eyes" (Dunbar), **Supp. II, Part 1,** 199, 207–208
Erikson, Erik, **I,** 58, 214, 218
Erisman, Fred, **Supp. VIII,** 126
Erkkila, Betsy, **Retro. Supp. I,** 42
"Ernest: or Parent for a Day" (Bourne), **I,** 232
"Eros at Temple Stream" (Levertov), **Supp. III, Part 1,** 278–279
"Eros Turannos" (Robinson), **III,** 510, 512, 513–516, 517, 518
"Errand" (Carver), **Supp. III, Part 1,** 149
Erskine, Albert, **IV,** 261
Erskine, John, **I,** 223
Erstein, Hap, **Supp. IV, Part 2,** 589, 590
"Escape" (MacLeish), **III,** 4
Espey, John, **III,** 463, 468, 478
Esprit (publication), **III,** 352, 355, 356, 358
Esquire (magazine), **I,** 139; **II,** 78, 97, 98, 591; **III,** 38, 351; **IV,** 97, 461; **Retro. Supp. I,** 98, 113, 114, 115; **Supp. I, Part 1,** 50, 295, 329, **Part 2,** 664; **Supp. IV, Part 1,** 102, 198, 201, 205, 383, **Part 2,** 678; **Supp. V,** 237, 238; **Supp. VIII,** 12, 39, 231, 314
Essais (Renouvier), **II,** 344–345
Essay Concerning Human Understanding, An (Locke), **I,** 554; **II,** 8, 348–349
Essay on American Poetry (Brown), **Supp. I, Part 1,** 156

"Essay on Aristocracy" (Paine), **Supp. I, Part 2,** 515
Essay on Man (Pope), **II,** 111; **Supp. I, Part 2,** 516
Essay on Our Changing Order (Veblen), **Supp. I, Part 2,** 629, 642
"Essay on Poetics" (Ammons), **Supp. VII,** 29–31
Essay on Projects (Defoe), **II,** 104
"Essay on Psychiatrists" (Pinsky), **Supp. VI,** 237, 238, 241, 242, 249, 250
Essay on Rime (Shapiro), **I,** 430; **Supp. II, Part 2,** 702, 703, 708–711
"Essay on the Character of Robespierre" (Paine), **Supp. I, Part 2,** 515
Essay on the Chinese Written Character (Fenollosa), **III,** 474
"Essay Toward a Point of View, An" (Brooks), **I,** 244
Essays (Emerson), **II,** 1, 7, 8, 12–13, 15, 21
Essays in Anglo-Saxon Law (Adams), **I,** 5
Essays in London (James), **II,** 336
Essays in Radical Empiricism (James), **II,** 356–357, 355
Essays on the Nature and Principles of Taste (Alison), **Supp. I, Part 1,** 151
Essays, Speeches, and Public Letters by William Faulkner (Meriweather, ed.), **Retro. Supp. I,** 77
Essays to Do Good (Mather), **II,** 104; **Supp. II, Part 2,** 461, 467
Essence (magazine), **Supp. VIII,** 214
Essential Haiku, The (Hass), **Supp. VI,** 102
Essential Keats (Levine, ed.), **Supp. V,** 179
"Essential Oils—are wrung" (Dickinson), **I,** 471; **Retro. Supp. I,** 43, 46
"Essentials" (Toomer), **Supp. III, Part 2,** 486
Essentials: A Philosophy of Life in Three Hundred Definitions and Aphorisms (Toomer), **Supp. III, Part 2,** 486

"Essentials of Spontaneous Prose" (Kerouac), **Supp. III, Part 1,** 227–228
Essex Gazette (newspaper), **Supp. I, Part 2,** 683, 684
Esslin, Martin, **I,** 95
Estess, Sybil, **Supp. IV, Part 2,** 449, 452
Esther (Adams), **I,** 9–10, 20
"Esthétique du Mal" (Stevens), **IV,** 79; **Retro. Supp. I,** 300, 311, 312
"Estoy-eh-muut and the Kunideeyahs (Arrowboy and the Destroyers)" (film), **Supp. IV, Part 2,** 560
"Estrangement, Betrayal & Atonement: The Political Theory of James Baldwin" (Daniels), **Supp. I, Part 1,** 70
Esty, William, **III,** 358; **Supp. I, Part 1,** 198
"Etching, An" (Masters), **Supp. I, Part 2,** 458
Eternal Adam and the New World Garden, The (Noble), **Supp. I, Part 1,** 70
"Eternal Goodness, The" (Whittier), **Supp. I, Part 2,** 704
"Eternity, An" (Williams), **Retro. Supp. I,** 423
"Eternity Is Now" (Roethke), **III,** 544–545
"Ethan Brand" (Hawthorne), **II,** 227
Ethan Frome (Wharton), **IV,** 316–317, 327; **Retro. Supp. I,** 372–373
Ethics (Spinoza), **IV,** 12
Etulain, Richard, **Supp. IV, Part 2,** 597, 601, 604, 606, 607, 608, 610, 611
Euclid, **III,** 6; **III,** 620
"Euclid Alone Has Looked on Beauty Bare" (Millay), **III,** 133
Eudora Welty Society, **Retro. Supp. I,** 354
Eudora Welty Writers' Center, **Retro. Supp. I,** 354
Eugene Onegin (Pushkin), **III,** 246, 263
Eugene Onegin (Pushkin; trans. Nabokov), **Retro. Supp. I,** 266, 267, 272

"Father" (Levine), **Supp. V,** 188
"Father" (Walker), **Supp. III, Part 2,** 522
"Father, The" (Carver), **Supp. III, Part 1,** 137, 140
"Father Abraham" (Faulkner), **Retro. Supp. I,** 81, 82
"Father and Daughter" (Eberhart), **I,** 539
Father and Son (Gosse), **Supp. VIII,** 157
"Father and Son" (Eberhart), **I,** 539
Father and Son (Farrell), **II,** 34, 35, 290, 291
"Father and Son" (Hughes), **Retro. Supp. I,** 204; **Supp. I, Part 1,** 329, 339
"Father and Son" (Kunitz), **Supp. III, Part 1,** 262
"Father and Son" (Schwartz), **Supp. II, Part 2,** 650
Father Bombo's Pilgrimage to Mecca (Freneau), **Supp. II, Part 1,** 254
"Father out Walking on the Lawn, A" (Dove), **Supp. IV, Part 1,** 246
"Fathers" (Creeley), **Supp. IV, Part 1,** 157–158
Fathers, The (Tate), **IV,** 120, 127, 130, 131–133, 134, 141
"Fathers and Sons" (Hemingway), **II,** 249, 265–266; **Retro. Supp. I,** 175
"Father's Body, The" (Dickey), **Supp. IV, Part 1,** 176
"Father's Story, A" (Dubus), **Supp. VII,** 88
Fatout, Paul, **I,** 213
Faulkner, Mrs. William (Estelle Oldham), **II,** 57
Faulkner, William, **I,** 54, 97, 99, 105, 106, 115, 117, 118, 119, 120, 123, 190, 204–205, 211, 288, 289, 291, 292, 297, 305, 324, 374, 378, 423, 480, 517; **II,** 28, 51, **54–76,** 131, 174, 194, 217, 223, 228, 230, 259, 301, 306, 431, 458–459, 542, 594, 606; **III,** 45, 70, 108, 164, 218, 220, 222, 236–237, 244, 292, 334, 350, 382, 418, 453, 454, 482, 483; **IV,** 2, 4, 33, 49, 97, 98, 100, 101, 120, 131, 203, 207,

211, 217, 237, 257, 260, 261, 279, 280, 352, 461, 463; **Retro. Supp. I, 73–95,** 215, 339, 347, 356, 379, 382; **Supp. I, Part 1,** 68, 196, 197, 242, 372, **Part 2,** 450, 621; **Supp. III, Part 1,** 384–385, 396; **Supp. IV, Part 1,** 47, 130, 257, 342, **Part 2,** 434, 463, 468, 502, 677, 682; **Supp. V,** 58, 59, 138, 210, 226, 237, 261, 262, 334–336; **Supp. VIII,** 37, 39, 40, 104, 105, 108, 175, 176, 180, 181, 183, 184, 188, 189, 215
Faulkner: A Collection of Critical Essays (Warren), **Retro. Supp. I,** 73
Faulkner at Nagano (ed. Jelliffe), **I,** 289; **II,** 63, 65
Faulkner-Cowley File, The: Letters and Memories 1944–1962 (Cowley, ed.), **Retro. Supp. I,** 73, 92; **Supp. II, Part 1,** 140, 141
"Faun" (Plath), **Supp. I, Part 2,** 537
"Fauna" (Jeffers), **Supp. II, Part 2,** 415
Fauset, Jessie, **Supp. I, Part 1,** 321, 325; **Supp. IV, Part 1,** 164
Fausset, Hugh I'Anson, **IV,** 354
Faust, Clarence H., **I,** 564, 565; **II,** 20, 23
Faust (Goethe), **I,** 396; **II,** 489; **III,** 395; **Supp. II, Part 1,** 16
Faute de l'Abbé Mouret, La (Zola), **III,** 322
Favor Island (Merwin), **Supp. III, Part 1,** 346, 347
Fay, Bernard, **IV,** 41
"Fear & Fame" (Levine), **Supp. V,** 192
Fear of Fifty: A Midlife Memoir (Jong), **Supp. V,** 114, 115, 116, 131
Fear of Flying (Jong), **Supp. V,** 113, 115, 116, 119–123, 124, 129
"Fear, The" (Frost), **Retro. Supp. I,** 128
"Feast, The" (Kinnell), **Supp. III, Part 1,** 239, 250
Feast of All Saints, The (Rice), **Supp. VII,** 299–301

Feather Crowns (Mason), **Supp. VIII, 146–147**
"Featherbed for Critics, A" (Blackmur), **Supp. II, Part 1,** 93, 151
"Feathers" (Carver), **Supp. III, Part 1,** 145
Feathers (Van Vechten), **Supp. II, Part 2,** 736, 749
"Feathers, The" (Hogan), **Supp. IV, Part 1,** 416
"February" (Ellison), **Supp. II, Part 1,** 229
"February 14th" (Levine), **Supp. V,** 194
"February: Thinking of Flowers" (Kenyon), **Supp. VII,** 171
Fechner, Gustav, **II,** 344, 355, 358, 359, 363, 364
Feder, Lillian, **IV,** 136, 142
Federal Arts Project, **Supp. III, Part 2,** 618
Federalist, The, **II,** 8
Federigo, or, The Power of Love (Nemerov), **III,** 268, 276, 282, 283–284, 285
"Fedora" (Chopin), **Supp. I, Part 1,** 220
Fedorko, Kathy A., **Retro. Supp. I,** 361, 374
"Feel Like a Bird" (Swenson), **Supp. IV, Part 2,** 639
"Feel Me" (Swenson), **Supp. IV, Part 2,** 647
Feeley, Sister Kathleen, **II,** 221
"Feeling and Precision" (Moore), **III,** 206
"Feeling of Effort, The" (James), **II,** 349
Feibleman, James K., **I,** 119–120
Feidelson, Charles, Jr., **II,** 23, 245
Feied, Frederick, **II,** 484
Fein, Richard, **II,** 390
Feldman, Irving, **IV,** 23
Felheim, Marvin, **Supp. I, Part 1,** 297
Felheim, Melvin, **II,** 608
"Fellow Citizens" (Sandburg), **III,** 553
Fellows, John, **Supp. I, Part 2,** 520
"Felo de Se" (Wylie), **Supp. I, Part 2,** 727, 729

Supp. IV, Part 2, 678; **Supp. VIII,** 98, 101, 102

Howells, Winifred, **II,** 271

"Howells as Anti-Novelist" (Updike), **Retro. Supp. I,** 334

Howells: His Life and World (Brooks), **I,** 254

Howgate, George W., **III,** 622

Howl (Ginsberg), **Retro. Supp. I,** 426; **Supp. III, Part 1,** 92; **Supp. IV, Part 1,** 90; **Supp. V,** 336; **Supp. VIII,** 290

Howl and Other Poems (Ginsberg), **Supp. II, Part 1,** 308, 317–318, 319

Howlett, William, **Retro. Supp. I,** 17

Hoyer, Linda Grace (pseudonym), *see* Updike, Mrs. Wesley

Hoyle, James F., **Supp. I, Part 2,** 548

Hoyt, Charles A., **Supp. I, Part 1,** 148

Hoyt, Constance, **Supp. I, Part 2,** 707

Hoyt, Elinor Morton, *see* Wylie, Elinor Hoyt, Henry (father), **Supp. I, Part 2,** 707

Hoyt, Henry (son), **Supp. I, Part 2,** 708

Hoyt, Henry Martyn, **Supp. I, Part 2,** 707

Hoyt, Nancy, **Supp. I, Part 2,** 730

Hubbard, Elbert, **I,** 98, 383

Hubbell, G. S., **II,** 23

Hubbell, Jay B., **III,** 431; **Supp. I, Part 1,** 372

"Hubbub, The" (Ammons), **Supp. VII,** 35

Huber, François, **II,** 6

Huckleberry Finn (Twain), **Retro. Supp. I,** 188; **Supp. I, Part 1,** 247; **Supp. V,** 131

Hud (film), **Supp. V,** 223, 226

Hudson, Henry, **I,** 230

Hudson Review (periodical), **Supp. IV, Part 1,** 285; **Supp. V,** 344

Hudson River Bracketed (Wharton), **IV,** 326–327; **Retro. Supp. I,** 382

"Hudsonian Curlew,The" (Snyder), **Supp. VIII,** 302

Huebsch, B. W., **III,** 110

Hueffer, Ford Madox, **Supp. I,**

Part 1, 257, 262; *see also,* Ford, Ford Madox, *see* Ford, Ford Madox

Huftel, Sheila, **III,** 169

Hug Dancing (Hearon), **Supp. VIII, 67–68**

Huge Season, The (Morris), **III,** 225–226, 227, 230, 232, 233, 238

"Hugh Harper" (Bowles), **Supp. IV, Part 1,** 94

Hugh Selwyn Mauberley (Pound), **I,** 66, 476; **III,** 9, 462–463, 465, 468; **Retro. Supp. I, 289–290,** 291, 299

Hughes, Catharine R., **IV,** 23

Hughes, Frieda, **Supp. I, Part 2,** 540, 541

Hughes, Glenn, **II,** 533; **Supp. I, Part 1,** 255, 275

Hughes, H. Stuart, **Supp. VIII,** 240

Hughes, James Nathaniel, **Supp. I, Part 1,** 321, 332

Hughes, Langston, **Retro. Supp. I, 193–214; Supp. I, Part 1, 320–348; Supp. II, Part 1,** 31, 33, 61, 170, 173, 181, 227, 228, 233, 361; **Supp. III, Part 1,** 72–77; **Supp. IV, Part 1,** 15, 16, 164, 168, 169, 173, 243, 368; **Supp. VIII,** 213

Hughes, Mrs. Ted, *see* Plath, Sylvia

Hughes, Nicholas, **Supp. I, Part 2,** 541

Hughes, Ted, **IV,** 3, 23; **Supp. I, Part 2,** 536, 537, 538, 539, 540, 541, 548

Hughes, Thomas, **Supp. I, Part 2,** 406

Hughie (O'Neill), **III,** 385, 401, 405

Hugo, Richard, **Supp. VI, 131–134,** 135–148

Hugo, Victor, **II,** 290, 490, 543; **Supp. IV, Part 2,** 518

Hui-neng, **III,** 567

Huis Clos (Sartre), **Supp. IV, Part 1,** 84

Huizinga, Johan, **I,** 225; **II,** 416–417, 418, 425

Hul-House Maps and Papers, **Supp. I, Part 1,** 7

Hull-House Settlement, **Supp. I, Part 1,** 1, 2, 3, 4, 7, 11, 12, 16,

17, 19, 21, 22

Hulme, Thomas E., **I,** 68, 69, 475; **III,** 196, 209, 463–464, 465; **IV,** 122; **Supp. I, Part 1,** 261, 262

"Human Culture" (Emerson), **II,** 11–12

Human Factor, The (Greene), **Supp. V,** 298

"Human Immortality" (James), **II,** 353–354

"Human Life" (Emerson), **II,** 11–12

"Human Things" (Nemerov), **III,** 279

"Human Universe" (Olson), **Supp. II, Part 2,** 565, 567

Human Universe (Olson), **Supp. II, Part 2,** 571

Human Wishes (Hass), **Supp. VI,** 105–106, 107

Humanism, **I,** 577; **II,** 542; **III,** 231, 600, 613; **IV,** 117, 165, 435, 437, 438, 439, 474, 491

Humble Inquiry into the Rules of the Word of God, An, Concerning the Qualifications Requisite to a Complete Standing and Full Communion in the Visible Christian Church (Edwards), **I,** 548

Humboldt, Alexander von, **III,** 428

Hume, David, **I,** 125; **II,** 349, 357, 480; **III,** 618

Humes, Harold, **Supp. V,** 201

"Hummingbirds, The" (Welty), **IV,** 273

Humphreys, Christmas, **Supp. V,** 267

Humphreys, David, **Supp. II, Part 1,** 65, 69, 70, 268

Humphries, Rolfe, **III,** 124, 144; **Retro. Supp. I,** 137

Hunchback of Notre Dame, The (film), **Supp. IV, Part 1,** 101

Hundred Camels in the Courtyard, A (Bowles), **Supp. IV, Part 1,** 90

"Hundred Collars, A" (Frost), **Retro. Supp. I,** 128

Hundred White Daffodils, A: Essays, Interviews, Newspaper Columns, and One Poem (Kenyon), **Supp. VII,** 160–162, 165, 166, 167, 174

Huneker, James, **III,** 102

Keating, AnnLouise, **Supp. IV, Part 1,** 330

Keaton, Buster, **I,** 31; **Supp. I, Part 2,** 607; **Supp. IV, Part 2,** 574

Keats, John, **I,** 34, 103, 284, 314, 317–318, 385, 401, 448; **II,** 82, 88, 97, 214, 368, 512, 516, 530–531, 540, 593; **III,** 4, 10, 45, 122, 133–134, 179, 214, 237, 272, 275, 469, 485, 523; **IV,** 360, 405, 416; **Retro. Supp. I,** 91, 301, 313, 360, 395, 412; **Supp. I, Part 1,** 82, 183, 266, 267, 312, 349, 362, 363, 365, **Part 2,** 410, 422, 424, 539, 552, 675, 719, 720; **Supp. III, Part 1,** 73; **Supp. IV, Part 1,** 123, 168, 325, **Part 2,** 455; **Supp. VIII,** 41, 273

"Keela, the Outcast Indian Maiden" (Welty), **IV,** 263

"Keen Scalpel on Racial Ills" (Bruell), **Supp. VIII,** 126

"Keep A-Inchin' Along" (Van Vechten), **Supp. III, Part 2,** 744

"Keeping Informed in D.C." (Nemerov), **III,** 287

Keeping Slug Woman Alive: A Holistic Approach to American Indian Texts (Sarris), **Supp. IV, Part 1,** 329

"'Keeping Their World Large'" (Moore), **III,** 201–202

"Keeping Things Whole" (Strand), **Supp. IV, Part 2,** 624

Kees, Weldon, **Supp. I, Part 1,** 199

Kegley, Charles W., **III,** 313

Keith, Brian, **Supp. IV, Part 2,** 474

Keith, Minor C., **I,** 483

Keller, A. G., **III,** 108

Keller, Dean H., **Supp. I, Part 1,** 147

Keller, Helen, **I,** 254, 258

Keller, Karl, **Supp. I, Part 2,** 705

Keller, Lynn, **Supp. IV, Part 2,** 423; **Supp. V,** 78, 80

Kelley, David, **Supp. IV, Part 2,** 528, 529

Kelley, Florence, **Supp. I, Part 1,** 5, 7

Kellogg, Paul U., **Supp. I, Part 1,** 5, 7, 12

Kellogg, Reverend Edwin H., **III,** 200

Kelly, **II,** 464

Kemble, Fanny, **Retro. Supp. I,** 228

Kemble, Gouverneur, **II,** 298

Kemble, Peter, **II,** 298

Kemler, Edgar, **III,** 121

Kempton, Murray, **Supp. VIII,** 104

Kempton-Wace Letters, The (London and Strunsky), **II,** 465

Kendle, Burton, **Supp. I, Part 1,** 199

Kennan, George F., **Supp. VIII,** 241

Kennard, Jean E., **I,** 143

Kennedy, Albert J., **Supp. I, Part 1,** 19, 27

Kennedy, Arthur, **III,** 153

Kennedy, Burt, **Supp. IV, Part 1,** 236

Kennedy, John F., **I,** 136, 170; **II,** 49, 152–153; **III,** 38, 41, 42, 234, 411, 415, 581; **IV,** 229; **Supp. I, Part 1,** 291, **Part 2,** 496; **Supp. VIII,** 98, 104, 203

Kennedy, John Pendleton, **II,** 313

Kennedy, Mrs. John F., **I,** 136

Kennedy, Raymond A., **IV,** 425

Kennedy, Richard S., **IV,** 472, 473

Kennedy, Robert, **Supp. V,** 291

Kennedy, Robert F., **I,** 294; **Supp. I, Part 1,** 52

Kennedy, William, **Supp. VII,** 131–133

Kennedy, William Sloane, **Supp. I, Part 2,** 705

Kennedy, X. J., **Supp. V,** 178, 182

Kenner, Hugh, **I,** 590; **III,** 217, 475, 478; **IV,** 412, 424, 425; **Supp. I, Part 1,** 255, 275; **Supp. IV, Part 2,** 474

Kenneth Millar/Ross Macdonald: A Checklist (Bruccoli), **Supp. IV, Part 2,** 464, 469, 471

Kenny, Maurice, **Supp. IV, Part 2,** 502

Kent, Charles W., **Supp. I, Part 1,** 373

Kent, George, **Supp. IV, Part 1,** 11

Kent, Rockwell, **III,** 96

Kenton, Edna, **I,** 263; **II,** 340

Kenyon, Jane, **Supp. VII,** 159–162; **Supp. VIII,** 272

Kenyon Review (publication), **I,** 170, 174; **II,** 536–537; **III,** 497, 498; **IV,** 141; **Supp. IV, Part 2,** 550; **Supp. V,** 187, 324

Keokuk Evening Post (newspaper), **IV,** 194

Kepler, Johannes, **III,** 484; **IV,** 18

Keppel, Frederick P., **I,** 214

"Kéramos" (Longfellow), **II,** 494

Kéramos and Other Poems (Longfellow), **II,** 490

Kermode, Frank, **IV,** 95, 133, 143, 449; **Retro. Supp. I,** 301

Kern, Jerome, **II,** 427

Kerner, David, **I,** 143

Kerouac, Jack, **III,** 174; **Retro. Supp. I,** 102; **Supp. II, Part 1,** 31, 307, 309, 318, 328; **Supp. III, Part 1,** 91–94, 96, 100, 217–234; **Supp. IV, Part 1,** 90, 146; **Supp. V,** 336; **Supp. VIII,** 42, 138, 289, 305

Kerr, Orpheus C. (pseudonym), *see* Newell, Henry

Kerr, Walter, **III,** 407; **Supp. IV, Part 2,** 575, 579

Kesey, Ken, **III,** 558; **Supp. III, Part 1,** 217; **Supp. V,** 220, 295

Kessler, Jascha, **I,** 189

"Key, The" (Welty), **IV,** 262

Key to Uncle Tom's Cabin, A (Stowe), **Supp. I, Part 2,** 580

"Key West" (Crane), **I,** 400

Key West: An Island Sheaf (Crane), **I,** 385, 399–402

Khrushchev, Nikita, **I,** 136

Kid, The (Aiken), **I,** 61

Kid, The (Chaplin), **I,** 386

Kidder, Tracy, **Supp. III, Part 1,** 302

Kidwell, Clara Sue, **Supp. IV, Part 1,** 333

Kielsky, Vera Emuma, **Supp. V,** 273

Kiely, Benedict, **I,** 143

Kieran, John, **II,** 417

Kierkegaard, Søren Aabye, **II,** 229; **III,** 292, 305, 309, 572; **IV,** 438, 491; **Retro. Supp. I,** 326; **Supp. V,** 9; **Supp. VIII,** 7–8

Kiernan, Robert F., **Supp. IV, Part 2,** 684

Kieseritsky, L., **III,** 252

"Killed at Resaca" (Bierce), **I,** 202

Killens, John Oliver, **Supp. IV, Part 1,** 8, 369

"Killer in the Rain" (Chandler), **Supp. IV, Part 1,** 122

"Killers, The" (Hemingway), **II,** 249; **Retro. Supp. I,** 188, 189

Killing Mister Watson (Matthiessen), **Supp. V,** 212, 214

"Killing of a State Cop, The" (Ortiz), **Supp. IV, Part 2,** 499

Killing of Sister George, The (Marcus), **Supp. I, Part 1,** 277

"Killing the Plants" (Kenyon), **Supp. VII,** 167, 168

"Killings" (Dubus), **Supp. VII,** 85–86

Kilmer, Joyce, **Supp. I, Part 2,** 387

Kilvert, Francis, **Supp. VIII,** 172

Kim, Kichung, **Supp. I, Part 1,** 70

Kimball, Arthur, **Supp. I, Part 1,** 148

Kimball, J. Golden, **Supp. IV, Part 2,** 602

Kimbrough, Mary Craig, *see* Sinclair, Mary Craig (Mary Craig Kimbrough)

"Kin" (Welty), **IV,** 277; **Retro. Supp. I,** 353

Kincaid, Jamaica, **Supp. VII, 179–182**

Kind of Order, A Kind of Folly, A: Essays and Conversations (Kunitz), **Supp. III, Part 1,** 262, 268

"Kind Sir: These Woods" (Sexton), **Supp. II, Part 2,** 673

Kindred Spirits: Knickerbocker Writers and American Artists, 1807–1855 (Callow), **Supp. I, Part 1,** 173

Kinds of Love (Sarton), **Supp. VIII, 253–254,** 256

Kindt, Kathleen A., **Supp. I, Part 1,** 70

Kinfolk (Buck), **Supp. II, Part 1,** 126

King, Alexander, **IV,** 287

King, Clarence, **I,** 1

King, Ernest, **Supp. I, Part 2,** 491

King, Fisher, **II,** 425

King, Lawrence T., **II,** 222

King, Martin Luther, Jr. **Supp. I, Part 1,** 52, 60, 65; **Supp. IV, Part 1,** 5; **Supp. V,** 291; **Supp. VIII,** 204

King, Starr, **Supp. II, Part 1,** 341, 342

King, Stephen, **Supp. IV, Part 1,** 102, 104, **Part 2,** 467; **Supp. V, 137–155**

King, Tabitha (Mrs. Stephen King), **Supp. V,** 137

King Coal (Sinclair), 286–288; **Supp. V,** 276, 282

King Coffin (Aiken), **I,** 53–54, 57

King Jasper (Robinson), **III,** 523

King Kong (film), **Supp. IV, Part 1,** 104

King Lear (Shakespeare), **I,** 538; **II,** 540, 551; **Retro. Supp. I,** 248; **Supp. IV, Part 1,** 31, 36

King Leopold's Soliloquy (Twain), **IV,** 208

King of Babylon Shall Not Come Against You, The (Garrett), **Supp. VII,** 110–111

"King of Folly Island" (Jewett), **II,** 394

King of Kings (film), **Supp. IV, Part 2,** 520

"King of the Bingo Game" (Ellison), **Supp. II, Part 1,** 235, 238, 240–241

"King of the Clock Tower" (Yeats), **III,** 473

"King of the Desert, The" (O'Hara), **III,** 369

King of the Mountain (Garrett), **Supp. VII,** 96, 97

"King of the River" (Kunitz), **Supp. III, Part 1,** 263, 267–268

"King of the Sea" (Marquand), **III,** 60

"King over the Water" (Blackmur), **Supp. II, Part 1,** 107

"King Pandar" (Blackmur), **Supp. II, Part 1,** 92, 102

King, Queen, Knave (Nabokov), **III,** 251; **Retro. Supp. I,** 270

King, The (Barthelme), **Supp. IV, Part 1,** 47, 52

"King Volmer and Elsie" (Whittier), **Supp. I, Part 2,** 696

Kingdom by the Sea, The: A Journey around Great Britain (Theroux), **Supp. VIII,** 323

Kingdom of Earth (Williams), **IV,** 382, 386, 387, 388, 391, 393, 398

"Kingdom of Earth, The" (Williams), **IV,** 384

"Kingfishers, The" (Olson), **Supp. II, Part 2,** 557, 558–563, 582

King's Henchman, The (Millay), **III,** 138–139

"King's Missive, The" (Whittier), **Supp. I, Part 2,** 694

Kingsblood Royal (Lewis), **II,** 456

Kingsbury, John, **Supp. I, Part 1,** 8

Kingsley, Sidney, **Supp. I, Part 1,** 277, 281

Kingsolver, Barbara, **Supp. VII, 197–199**

Kingsport Times-News, **Supp. V,** 335, 342

Kingston, Earll, **Supp. V,** 160

Kingston, Maxine Hong, **Supp. IV, Part 1,** 1, 12; **Supp. V, 157–175,** 250

Kinmont, Alexander, **Supp. I, Part 2,** 588–589

Kinnaird, John, **Retro. Supp. I,** 399

Kinnamon, Kenneth, **Supp. I, Part 1,** 69

Kinnell, Galway, **Supp. III, Part 1, 235–256, Part 2,** 541; **Supp. IV, Part 2,** 623; **Supp. V,** 332; **Supp. VIII,** 39

Kinsey, Alfred, **IV,** 230

Kipling, Rudyard, **I,** 421, 587–588; **II,** 271, 338, 404, 439; **III,** 55, 328, 508, 511, 521, 524, 579; **IV,** 429; **Supp. IV, Part 2,** 603

"Kipling" (Trilling), **Supp. III, Part 2,** 495

Kirk, Clara M., **II,** 292, 293, 294

Kirk, Rudolf, **II,** 292, 293, 294

Kirk, Russell, **I,** 590

Kirkham, Edwin Bruce, **Supp. I, Part 2,** 601

Kirkland, Jack, **I,** 297

Kirkpatrick, Jeane, **Supp. VIII,** 241

Kirkus Review, **Supp. V,** 62; **Supp. VIII,** 124

Kirstein, Lincoln, **Supp. II, Part 1,** 90, 97; **Supp. IV, Part 1,** 82, 83

Marshall, Paule, **Supp. IV, Part 1,** 8, 14, 369

"Marshes of Glynn, The" (Lanier), **Supp. I, Part 1,** 364, 365–368, 370, 373

"'Marshes of Glynn, The': A Study in Symbolic Obscurity" (Ross), **Supp. I, Part 1,** 373

Marsman, Henrik, **Supp. IV, Part 1,** 183

Marston, Ed, **Supp. IV, Part 2,** 492

Marta y Maria (Valdes), **II,** 290

Marthe, Saint, **II,** 213

Martial, **II,** 1, 169

Martian Chronicles, The (Bradbury), **Supp. IV, Part 1,** 102, 103, 106–107

Martien, Norman, **III,** 48

Martin, Benjamin, **Supp. I, Part 2,** 503

Martin, Carter W., **III,** 360

Martin du Gard, Roger, **Supp. I, Part 1,** 51

Martin Eden (London), **II,** 466, 477–481

Martin, Ernest, **II,** 509

Martin, Jay, **I,** 55, 58, 60, 61, 67, 70, 426, 590; **III,** 307

Martin, John Stephen, **Supp. I, Part 1,** 319

Martin, Judith, **Supp. V,** 128

Martin, Nell, **Supp. IV, Part 1,** 351, 353

Martin, R. A., **III,** 169

Martin, Stephen-Paul, **Supp. IV, Part 2,** 430

Martin, Terrence, **II,** 318; **Supp. I, Part 1,** 148

Martineau, Harriet, **Supp. II, Part 1,** 282, 288, 294

Martinelli, Sheri, **Supp. IV, Part 1,** 280

Mart'nez, Rafael, **Retro. Supp. I,** 423

Martone, John, **Supp. V,** 179

Martson, Frederic C., **II,** 293

"Martyr, The" (Porter), **III,** 454

Martz, Louis L., **IV,** 151, 156, 165, 166; **Supp. I, Part 1,** 107

Martz, William J., **I,** 189; **II,** 557; **III,** 550

Marvell, Andrew, **IV,** 135, 151, 156, 161, 253; **Retro. Supp. I,** 62, 127; **Supp. I, Part 1,** 80

Marvell family, **IV,** 318

"Marvella, for Borrowing" (Ríos), **Supp. IV, Part 2,** 551

Marx, Arthur "Harpo", **Supp. IV, Part 1,** 384

Marx, Herbert "Zeppo", **Supp. IV, Part 1,** 384

Marx, Julius Henry "Groucho", **Supp. IV, Part 1,** 384

Marx, Karl, **I,** 60, 267, 279, 283, 588; **II,** 376, 462, 463, 483, 577; **IV,** 429, 436, 443–444, 469; **Retro. Supp. I,** 254; **Supp. I, Part 2,** 518, 628, 632, 633, 634, 635, 639, 643, 645, 646; **Supp. III, Part 2,** 619; **Supp. IV, Part 1,** 355; **Supp. VIII,** 196

Marx, Leo, **Supp. I, Part 1,** 233, 252

Marx, Leonard "Chico", **Supp. IV, Part 1,** 384

Marxism, **I,** 371, 488, 518; **II,** 26, 34, 39, 567; **III,** 3, 17, 27, 30, 262, 297–298, 304, 580, 602; **IV,** 5, 7, 288, 302, 349, 363, 428, 429, 441; **Supp. I, Part 2,** 493, 518, 600, 628, 633, 635, 643, 645

"Marxism and Monastic Perpectives" (Merton), **Supp. VIII,** 196

Marxist Quarterly (publication), **Supp. I, Part 2,** 645

Mary (Jesus' mother), **IV,** 152; **Supp. I, Part 2,** 581

Mary (Nabokov), **Retro. Supp. I,** 267–268, 270, 277

Mary, Queen, **IV,** 145, 163

Mary Magdalene, **I,** 303

"Mary O'Reilly" (Anderson), **II,** 44

"Mary's Song" (Plath), **Supp. I, Part 2,** 541

Masefield, John, **II,** 552; **III,** 523

Mask for Janus, A (Merwin), **Supp. III, Part 1,** 339, 341, 342

Maslow, Abraham, **Supp. I, Part 2,** 540

Mason, Bobbie Ann, **Supp. VIII, 133–149**

Mason, David, **Supp. V,** 344

Mason, Lowell, **I,** 458

Mason, Marsha, **Supp. IV, Part 2,** 575, 586

Mason, Otis Tufton, **Supp. I, Part 1,** 18

Mason, Ronald, **III,** 97

"Mason Jars by the Window" (Ríos), **Supp. IV, Part 2,** 548

Masque of Mercy, A (Frost), **II,** 155, 165, 167–168; **Retro. Supp. I,** 131, 140

"Masque of Mummers, The" (MacLeish), **III,** 18

Masque of Pandora, The (Longfellow), **II,** 490, 494, 506

Masque of Poets, A (ed. Lathrop), **Retro. Supp. I,** 31; **Supp. I, Part 1,** 365, 368

Masque of Reason, A (Frost), **II,** 155, 162, 165–167; **Retro. Supp. I,** 131, 140

"Masque of the Red Death, The" (Poe), **III,** 412, 419, 424

"Masquerade" (Banks), **Supp. V,** 7

"Mass for the Day of St. Thomas Didymus" (Levertov), **Supp. III, Part 1,** 283

Massa, Ann, **Supp. I, Part 2,** 402

"Massachusetts 1932" (Bowles), **Supp. IV, Part 1,** 94

Massachusetts, Its Historians and Its History (Adams), **Supp. I, Part 2,** 484

Massachusetts Quarterly Review (publication), **Supp. I, Part 2,** 420

Massachusetts Review (publication), **Supp. IV, Part 1,** 208

"Massachusetts to Virginia" (Whittier), **Supp. I, Part 2,** 688–689

"Massacre and the Mastermind, The" (Bausch), **Supp. VII,** 49

"Massacre at Scio, The" (Bryant), **Supp. I, Part 1,** 168

"Massacre of the Innocents, The" (Simic), **Supp. VIII,** 282

Masses (publication), **I,** 105

Masses and Man (Toller), **I,** 479

Massey, Raymond, **Supp. IV, Part 2,** 524

Massie, Chris, **Supp. IV, Part 2,** 524

Massing, Michael, **Supp. IV, Part 1,** 208

"May Day Dancing, The" (Nemerov), **III,** 275

"May Day Sermon to the Women of Gilmer County, Georgia, by a Woman Preacher Leaving the Baptist Church" (Dickey), **Supp. IV, Part 1,** 182

"May Sun Sheds an Amber Light, The" (Bryant), **Supp. I, Part 1,** 170

"May Swenson: The Art of Perceiving" (Stanford), **Supp. IV, Part 2,** 637

"May 24, 1980" (Brodsky), **Supp. VIII,** 28

May Sarton: Selected Letters 1916–1954, **Supp. VIII,** 265

Maybe (Hellman), **Supp. IV, Part 1,** 12

"Maybe" (Oliver), **Supp. VII,** 239

"Mayday" (Faulkner), **Retro. Supp. I,** 80

Mayer, Elizabeth, **Supp. II, Part 1,** 16; **Supp. III, Part 1,** 63

Mayer, John, **Retro. Supp. I,** 58

Mayfield, Julian, **Supp. I, Part 1,** 70

Mayflower, The (Stowe), **Supp. I, Part 2,** 585, 586

Maynard, Joyce, **Supp. V,** 23

Maynard, Theodore, **I,** 263

Maynard, Tony, **Supp. I, Part 1,** 65

Mayo, Robert, **III,** 478

Mayorga, Margaret, **III,** 167; **IV,** 381

"Maypole of Merrymount, The" (Hawthorne), **II,** 229

"Maze" (Eberhart), **I,** 523, 525–526, 527

Mazzaro, Jerome, **II,** 390, 557

Mazzini, Giuseppe, **Supp. I, Part 1,** 2, 8; **Supp. II, Part 1,** 299

"Me and the Mule" (Hughes), **Supp. I, Part 1,** 334

"Me, Boy Scout" (Lardner), **II,** 433

"Me Decade and the Third Great Awakening, The" (Wolfe), **Supp. III, Part 2,** 581

Me, Vashya! (Williams), **IV,** 381

Mead, Elinor, *see* Howells, Mrs. William Dean (Elinor Mead)

Mead, George Herbert, **II,** 27, 34; **Supp. I, Part 1,** 5, **Part 2,** 641

Mead, Margaret, **Supp. I, Part 1,** 49, 52, 66

Meaders, Margaret Inman, **III,** 360

Meadowlands (Glück), **Supp. V,** 88–90

"Mean, Mrs." (Gass), **Supp. VI,** 83

Mean Spirit (Hogan), **Supp. IV, Part 1,** 397, 404, 407–410, 415, 416–417

"Meaning of a Literary Idea, The" (Trilling), **Supp. III, Part 2,** 498

"Meaning of Death, The, An After Dinner Speech" (Tate), **IV,** 128, 129

"Meaning of Life, The" (Tate), **IV,** 137

"Meaningless Institution, A" (Ginsberg), **Supp. II, Part 1,** 313

Mearns, Hughes, **III,** 220

"Measure" (Hass), **Supp. VI,** 99–**100,** 101

"Measuring My Blood" (Vizenor), **Supp. IV, Part 1,** 262

"Mechanism" (Ammons), **Supp. VII,** 28

"Mechanism in Thought and Morals" (Holmes), **Supp. I, Part 1,** 314

Mecom, Mrs. Jane, **II,** 122

"Meddlesome Jack" (Caldwell), **I,** 309

Medea (Jeffers), **Supp. II, Part 2,** 435

Medea and Some Poems, The (Cullen), **Supp. IV, Part 1,** 169, 173

"Médecin Malgré Lui, Le" (Williams), **IV,** 407–408

"Medfield" (Bryant), **Supp. I, Part 1,** 157

Medical History of Contraception, A (Himes), **Supp. V,** 128

"Medicine Song" (Gunn Allen), **Supp. IV, Part 1,** 326

Médicis, Marie de, **II,** 548

Medina (McCarthy), **II,** 579

"Meditation 1.6" (Taylor), **IV,** 165

"Meditation 1.20" (Taylor), **IV,** 165

"Meditation 2.102" (Taylor), **IV,** 150

"Meditation 2.112" (Taylor), **IV,** 165

"Meditation 20" (Taylor), **IV,** 154–155

"Meditation 40" (Second Series) (Taylor), **IV,** 147

"Meditation 2.68A" (Taylor), **IV,** 165

"Meditation, A" (Eberhart), **I,** 533–535

"Meditation at Lagunitas" (Hass), **Supp. VI,** 104–105

"Meditation at Oyster River" (Roethke), **III,** 537, 549

Meditations (Descartes), **III,** 618

"Meditations for a Savage Child" (Rich), **Supp. I, Part 2,** 564–565

Meditations from a Movable Chair (Dubus), **Supp. VII,** 91

"Meditations of an Old Woman" (Roethke), **III,** 529, 540, 542, 543, 545–547, 548

Meditations on the Insatiable Soul (Bly), **Supp. IV, Part 1,** 72–73

Meditative Poems, The (Martz), **IV,** 151

"Mediterranean, The" (Tate), **IV,** 129

"Medium of Fiction, The" (Gass), **Supp. VI,** 85–86

"Medusa" (Bogan), **Supp. III, Part 1,** 50, 51

Meehan, Thomas, **Supp. IV, Part 2,** 577–578, 586, 590

Meek, Martha, **Supp. IV, Part 2,** 439, 440, 441, 442, 445, 447, 448

Meeker, Richard K., **II,** 190, 195

Meet Me at the Morgue (Macdonald), **Supp. IV, Part 2,** 472

"Meeting South, A" (Anderson), **I,** 115

"Meeting the Mountains" (Snyder), **Supp. VIII,** 300

"Meeting-House Hill" (Lowell), **II,** 522, 527

Meiners, R. K., **IV,** 136, 137, 138, 140, 143

Meister, Charles W., **II,** 112, 125

"Melancholia" (Dunbar), **Supp. II, Part 1,** 194

"Melanctha" (Stein), **IV,** 30, 34, 35, 37, 38–40, 45

"Melancthon" (Moore), **III,** 212, 215

135–136

Millay, Edna St. Vincent, **I,** 482; **II,** 530; **III, 122–144; IV,** 433, 436; **Supp. I, Part 2,** 707, 714, 726; **Supp. IV, Part 1,** 168, **Part 2,** 607; **Supp. V,** 113

Miller, Arthur, **I,** 81, 94; **III, 145–169; Supp. IV, Part 1,** 359, **Part 2,** 574; **Supp. VIII,** 334

Miller, Brown, **Supp. IV, Part 1,** 67

Miller, C. William, **II,** 125

Miller, Carol, **Supp. IV, Part 1,** 400, 405, 409, 410, 411

Miller, Edwin H., **IV,** 354

Miller, Henry, **I,** 97, 119, 157; **III,** 40, **170–192; IV,** 138; **Supp. I, Part 2,** 546; **Supp. V,** 119, 131

Miller, Herman, **Supp. I, Part 2,** 614, 617

Miller, J. Hillis, **IV,** 424; **Supp. IV, Part 1,** 387

Miller, James E., Jr., **I,** 404; **II,** 100; **III,** 241; **IV,** 352, 354

Miller, Jeffrey, **Supp. IV, Part 1,** 95

Miller, Joaquin, **I,** 193, 195, 459; **Supp. II, Part 1,** 351

Miller, John Duncan, **Supp. I, Part 2,** 604

Miller, Jordan Y., **I,** 96; **III,** 406, 407

Miller, Mrs. Arthur (Ingeborg Morath), **III,** 162–163

Miller, Mrs. Arthur (Marilyn Monroe), **III,** 161, 162–163

Miller, Mrs. Arthur (Mary Grace Slattery), **III,** 146, 161

Miller, Orilla, **Supp. I, Part 1,** 48

Miller, Perry, **I,** 546, 547, 549, 550, 560, 564, 566; **II,** 23, 460; **III,** 407; **IV,** 166, 186, 188; **Supp. I, Part 1,** 31, 46, 104, **Part 2,** 484; **Supp. IV, Part 2,** 422; **Supp. VIII,** 101

Miller, R. B., **Supp. I, Part 1,** 348

Miller, R. Baxter, **Retro. Supp. I,** 195, 207

Miller, Robert Ellis, **II,** 588

Miller, Rosamond, **IV,** 47

Miller, Russell H., **I,** 143

Miller of Old Church, The (Glasgow), **II,** 175, 181

"Miller's Tale" (Chaucer), **III,** 283

Millet, Kate, **III,** 48, 192

Millgate, Michael, **Retro. Supp. I,** 91

"Million Young Workmen, 1915, A" (Sandburg), **III,** 585

Millroy the Magician (Theroux), **Supp. VIII,** 325

Mills, Benjamin Fay, **III,** 176

Mills, C. Wright, **Supp. I, Part 2,** 648, 650

Mills, Florence, **Supp. I, Part 1,** 322

Mills, Ralph J., Jr., **I,** 542; **II,** 557; **III,** 549, 530; **Supp. IV, Part 1,** 64

Mills family, **IV,** 311

"Mills of the Kavanaughs, The" (Lowell), **II,** 542–543

Mills of the Kavanaughs, The (Lowell), **II,** 542–543, 546, 550; **III,** 508

Milne, A. J. M., **I,** 278

Milosz, Czeslaw, **Supp. III, Part 2,** 630; **Supp. VIII,** 20, 22

Milton, Edith, **Supp. VIII,** 79

Milton, John, **I,** 6, 138, 273, 587–588; **II,** 11, 15, 113, 130, 411, 540, 542; **III,** 40, 124, 201, 225, 274, 468, 471, 486, 487, 503, 511, 525; **IV,** 50, 82, 126, 137, 155, 157, 241, 279, 347, 422, 461, 494; **Retro. Supp. I,** 60, 67, 127, 360; **Supp. I, Part 1,** 124, 150, 370, **Part 2,** 412, 422, 491, 501, 522, 622, 722, 724; **Supp. IV, Part 2,** 430, 634; **Supp. VIII,** 294

Milton, John R., **Supp. IV, Part 2,** 503

"Milton by Firelight" (Snyder), **Supp. II, Part 1,** 314; **Supp. VIII,** 294

"Miltonic Sonnet, A" (Wilbur), **Supp. III, Part 2,** 558

Milwaukee Journal (newspaper), **III,** 580

Milwaukee Leader (newspaper), **III,** 580

Milwaukee News (newspaper), **III,** 580

Milwaukee Sentinel (newspaper), **III,** 580

Mimesis (Auerbach), **III,** 453

Mims, Edwin, **Supp. I, Part 1,**

362, 364, 365, 371, 373

"Mind" (Wilbur), **Supp. III, Part 2,** 554

Mind Breaths: Poems 1972–1977 (Ginsberg), **Supp. II, Part 1,** 326

"Mind in the Modern World" (Trilling), **Supp. III, Part 2,** 512

"Mind Is Shapely, Art Is Shapely" (Ginsberg), **Supp. II, Part 1,** 327

"Mind, The" (Kinnell), **Supp. III, Part 1,** 245

Mindlin, Henrique, **Supp. I, Part 1,** 92

"Mind-Reader, The" (Wilbur), **Supp. III, Part 2,** 561–562

Mind-Reader, The (Wilbur), **Supp. III, Part 2,** 560–562

Mindwheel (Pinsky), **Supp. VI,** 235

"Mine Own John Berryman" (Levine), **Supp. V,** 179–180

"Mined Country" (Wilbur), **Supp. III, Part 2,** 546–548

Miner, Bob, **Supp. V,** 23

Miner, Earl, **III,** 466, 479

Miner, Ward L., **II,** 76

"Minerva Writes Poems" (Cisneros), **Supp. VII,** 63–64, 66

Ming Yellow (Marquand), **III,** 56

"Minimal, The" (Roethke), **III,** 531–532

Minimalism, **Supp. V, Supp. V,** 23

"Minions of Midas, The" (London), **II,** 474–475

Minister's Charge, The, or The Apprenticeship of Lemuel Barber (Howells), **II,** 285–286, 287

"Minister's Wooing, The" (Stowe), **Supp. I, Part 2,** 592–595

Minister's Wooing, The (Stowe), **II,** 541

"Ministration of Our Departed Friends, The" (Stowe), **Supp. I, Part 2,** 586–587

"Minneapolis Poem, The" (Wright), **Supp. III, Part 2,** 601–602

Minneapolis Star and Tribune, **Supp. V,** 250

"Minnesota Transcendentalist" (Peseroff), **Supp. IV, Part 1,** 71

III, Part 2, 595

"Old Man on the Hospital Porch" (Ríos), **Supp. IV, Part 2,** 546–547

Old Man Rubbing His Eyes (Bly), **Supp. IV, Part 1,** 65

"Old Man's Winter Night, An" (Frost), **Retro. Supp. I,** 126, 131

"Old Manse, The" (Hawthorne), **II,** 224

"Old Meeting House, The" (Stowe), **Supp. I, Part 2,** 586

"Old Memory, An" (Dunbar), **Supp. II, Part 1,** 198

"Old Men, The" (McCarthy), **II,** 566

"Old Mortality" (Porter), **III,** 436, 438–441, 442, 445, 446

"Old Mrs. Harris" (Cather), **I,** 332; **Retro. Supp. I,** 19

Old New York (Wharton), **IV,** 322; **Retro. Supp. I,** 381

"Old, Old, Old, Old Andrew Jackson" (Lindsay), **Supp. I, Part 2,** 398

Old One-Two, The (Gurney), **Supp. V,** 98

"Old Order, The" (Porter), **III,** 443, 444–445, 451

"Old Osawatomie" (Sandburg), **III,** 584

Old Patagonia Express, The: By Train through the Americas (Theroux), **Supp. VIII,** 322

"Old People, The" (Faulkner), **II,** 7172

"Old Poet Moves to a New Apartment 14 Times, The" (Zukofsky), **Supp. III, Part 2,** 628

"Old Red" (Gordon), **II,** 199, 200, 203

Old Red and Other Stories (Gordon), **II,** 157

Old Régime in Canada, The (Parkman), **Supp. II, Part 2,** 600, 607, 608–609, 612

"Old Saws" (Garrett), **Supp. VII,** 96–97

Old Testament, **I,** 109, 181, 300, 328, 401, 410, 419, 431, 457, 458; **II,** 166, 167, 219; **III,** 270, 272, 348, 390, 396; **IV,** 41, 114, 152, 309; **Retro. Supp. I,** 122,

140, 249, 311, 360; **Supp. I, Part 1,** 60, 104, 106, 151, **Part 2,** 427, 515, 516; *see also names of Old Testament books*

"Old Things, The" (James), **Retro. Supp. I,** 229

"Old Times on the Mississippi" (Twain), **IV,** 199

"Old Trails" (Robinson), **III,** 513, 517

"Old Tyrannies" (Bourne), **I,** 233

Old Vic, **Retro. Supp. I,** 65

"Old West" (Bausch), **Supp. VII,** 48

"Old Whorehouse, An" (Oliver), 235

"Old Woman" (Pinsky), **Supp. VI,** 238, **239**

"Old Word, The" (Simic), **Supp. VIII,** 282

Olderman, Raymond M., **I,** 143

Old-Fashioned Girl, An (Alcott), **Supp. I, Part 1,** 29, 41, 42

Oldham, Estelle, *see* Faulkner, Mrs. William (Estelle Oldham)

Oldtown Folks (Stowe), **Supp. I, Part 2,** 587, 596–598

Oldys, Francis, *see* Chalmers, George

Olendorf, Donna, **Supp. IV, Part 1,** 196

"Olga Poems, The" (Levertov), **Supp. III, Part 1,** 279–281

Oliver, Bill, **Supp. VIII,** 138

Oliver, E. S., **III,** 95

Oliver, Mary, **Supp. VII, 229–231**

Oliver, Sydney, **I,** 409

Oliver Goldsmith: A Biography (Irving), **II,** 315

Oliver Twist (Dickens), **I,** 354; **Supp. IV, Part 2,** 464

"Oliver Wendell Holmes" (Leary), **Supp. I, Part 1,** 319

"Oliver Wendell Holmes" (Menikoff), **Supp. I, Part 1,** 319

Oliver Wendell Holmes (Small), **Supp. I, Part 1,** 319

Olivieri, David (pseu. of Wharton, Edith), **Retro. Supp. I,** 361

Ollive, Elizabeth, *see* Paine, Mrs. Thomas (Elizabeth Ollive)

Ollive, Samuel, **Supp. I, Part 2,** 503

Olmsted, Frederick Law, **Supp. I,**

Part 1, 355

Olsen, Lance, **Supp. IV, Part 1,** 54, **Part 2,** 623

Olsen, Tillie, **Supp. V,** 114, 220

Olson, Charles, **III,** 97; **Retro. Supp. I,** 209; **Supp. II, Part 1,** 30, 328, **Part 2, 555–587; Supp. III, Part 1,** 9, 271, **Part 2,** 542, 624; **Supp. IV, Part 1,** 139, 144, 146, 153, 154, 322, **Part 2,** 420, 421, 423, 426; **Supp. VIII,** 290, 291

O'Malley, Frank, **II,** 53

Omar Khayyam, **Supp. I, Part 1,** 363

Omensetter's Luck (Gass), **Supp. VI, 80–82,** 87

"Ominous Baby, An" (Crane), **I,** 411

Ommateum, with Doxology (Ammons), **Supp. VII,** 24–26, 27, 28, 36

"Omnibus Jaunts and Drivers" (Whitman), **IV,** 350

Omoo: A Narrative of Adventures in the South Seas (Melville), **III,** 76–77, 79, 84; **Retro. Supp. I,** 247

"On a Certain Condescension in Foreigners" (Lowell), **Supp. I, Part 2,** 419

On a Darkling Plain (Stegner), **Supp. IV, Part 2,** 598, 607

"On a Hill Far Away" (Dillard), **Supp. VI,** 28

"On a Honey Bee, Drinking from a Glass and Drowned Therein" (Freneau), **Supp. II, Part 1,** 273

"On a Proposed Trip South" (Williams), **Retro. Supp. I,** 413

"On a Tree Fallen across the Road" (Frost), **Retro. Supp. I,** 134

"On a View of Pasadena from the Hills" (Winters), **Supp. II, Part 2,** 795, 796–799, 814

"On Acquiring Riches" (Banks), **Supp. V,** 5

"On an Old Photograph of My Son" (Carver), **Supp. III, Part 1,** 140

On Becoming a Novelist (Gardner), **Supp. VI,** 64

"On Being an American" (Toomer), **Supp. III, Part 2,** 479

"Spain" (Auden), **Supp. II, Part 1,** 1213, 14

"Spain in Fifty-Ninth Street" (White), **Supp. I, Part 2,** 677

Spangler, George, **Supp. I, Part 1,** 226

Spanish Background of American Literature, The (Williams), **Supp. I, Part 1,** 173

Spanish Ballads (trans. Merwin), **Supp. III, Part 1,** 347

Spanish Earth, The (film), **Retro. Supp. I,** 184

Spanish Papers and Other Miscellanies (Irving), **II,** 314

"Spanish Revolution, The" (Bryant), **Supp. I, Part 1,** 153, 168

Spanish Student, The (Longfellow), **II,** 489, 506

"Spanish-American War Play" (Crane), **I,** 422

Spanking the Maid (Coover), **Supp. V,** 47, 48, 49, 52

Spargo, John, **Supp. I, Part 1,** 13

"Spark, The" (Wharton), **Retro. Supp. I,** 381

"Sparkles from the Wheel" (Whitman), **IV,** 348

Sparks, Jared, **Supp. I, Part 1,** 156

Sparrow, Henry, **III,** 587

Sparrow, Mrs. Henry, **III,** 587

Speak, Memory (Nabokov), **III,** 247–250, 252; **Retro. Supp. I,** 264, 265, 266, 267, 268, 277

Speaking and Language (Shapiro), **Supp. II, Part 2,** 721

"Speaking of Counterweights" (White), **Supp. I, Part 2,** 669

Speaking of Literature and Society (Trilling), **Supp. III, Part 2,** 494, 496, 499

Spear, Roberta, **Supp. V,** 180

Spears, Monroe K., **I,** 404

"Special Kind of Fantasy, A: James Dickey on the Razor's Edge" (Niflis), **Supp. IV, Part 1,** 175

"Special Pleading" (Lanier), **Supp. I, Part 1,** 364

"Special Problems in Teaching Leslie Marmon Silko's *Ceremony*" (Gunn Allen), **Supp. IV, Part 1,** 333

Special View of History, The

(Olson), **Supp. II, Part 2,** 566, 569, 572

Specimen Days (Whitman), **IV,** 338, 347, 348, 350; **Retro. Supp. I,** 408

Specimens of the American Poets, **Supp. I, Part 1,** 155

"Spectacles, The" (Poe), **III,** 425

Spectator, The (college newspaper), **Retro. Supp. I,** 344

Spectator, The (journal), **II,** 104–105, 106

Spectator (London) (publication), **II,** 314

Spectator (publication), **Supp. IV, Part 2,** 685

Spectator Bird, The (Stegner), **Supp. IV, Part 2,** 599, 604, 606, 611–612

Spectorsky, A. C., **IV,** 235

"Spectre Bridegroom, The" (Irving), **II,** 304

"Spectre Pig, The" (Holmes), **Supp. I, Part 1,** 302

"Speech to a Crowd" (MacLeish), **III,** 16

"Speech to the Detractors" (MacLeish), **III,** 16

"Speech to the Young" (Brooks), **Supp. III, Part 1,** 79, 86

"Speech to Those Who Say Comrade" (MacLeish), **III,** 16

Speed of Darkness, The (Rukeyser), **Supp. VI,** 274, 281

Spence, Thomas, **Supp. I, Part 2,** 518

Spence + Lila (Mason), **Supp. VIII,** 133, **143–145**

Spencer, Edward, **Supp. I, Part 1,** 357, 360, 373

Spencer, Herbert, **I,** 515; **II,** 345, 462–463, 480, 483, 536; **III,** 102, 315; **IV,** 135; **Supp. I, Part 1,** 368, **Part 2,** 635

Spencer, T. J., **Supp. I, Part 1,** 348

Spencer, Theodore, **I,** 433, 450; **Supp. III, Part 1,** 2

Spender, Natasha, **Supp. IV, Part 1,** 119, 127, 134

Spender, Stephen, **II,** 371; **III,** 504, 527, 550; **Retro. Supp. I,** 216; **Supp. I, Part 1,** 71, **Part 2,** 536; **Supp. II, Part 1,** 11; **Supp. IV, Part 1,** 82, 134, **Part 2,** 440

Spengler, Oswald, **I,** 255, 270; **II,** 7, 577; **III,** 172, 176; **Supp. I, Part 2,** 647

Spens, Sir Patrick, **Supp. I, Part 2,** 404

Spenser, Edmund, **I,** 62; **III,** 77, 78, 89; **IV,** 155, 453; **Retro. Supp. I,** 62; **Supp. I, Part 1,** 98, 152, 369, **Part 2,** 422, 719

"Spenser's Ireland" (Moore), **III,** 211, 212

Sperry, Margaret, **Supp. IV, Part 1,** 169

Sphere: The Form of a Motion (Ammons), **Supp. VII,** 24, 32, 33, 35, 36

"Sphinx" (Hayden), **Supp. II, Part 1,** 373

"Spiced Plums" (Ríos), **Supp. IV, Part 2,** 553

"Spider and the Ghost of the Fly, The" (Lindsay), **Supp. I, Part 2,** 375

Spider Bay (Van Vechten), **Supp. II, Part 2,** 746

Spider Woman's Granddaughters: Traditional Tales and Contemporary Writing by Native American Women (ed. Gunn Allen), **Supp. IV, Part 1,** 320, 326, 332–333, **Part 2,** 567

"Spiders" (Schwartz), **Supp. II, Part 2,** 665

Spider's House, The (Bowles), **Supp. IV, Part 1,** 87–89, 90, 91

Spiegelberg, Herbert, **II,** 366

Spiegelman, Willard, **Supp. I, Part 1,** 97

Spillane, Mickey, **Supp. IV, Part 2,** 469, 472

Spiller, Robert E., **I,** 241, 357, 520; **II,** 125, 413, 533; **III,** 408; **IV,** 188, 448; **Supp. I, Part 1,** 104, 148, **Part 2,** 601

Spillway (Barnes), **Supp. III, Part 1,** 44

Spingarn, Amy, **Supp. I, Part 1,** 325, 326

Spingarn, Joel, **I,** 266; **Supp. I, Part 1,** 325

Spinoza, Baruch, **I,** 493; **II,** 590, 593; **III,** 600; **IV,** 5, 7, 11, 12, 17; **Supp. I, Part 1,** 274, **Part 2,** 643

"Tracing Life with a Finger" (Caldwell), **I,** 291

"Track Meet, The" (Schwartz), **Supp. II, Part 2,** 665

Tracks (Erdrich), **Supp. IV, Part 1,** 259, 262–263, 269, 272, 273–274, 274, 275

"Tract" (Williams), **Retro. Supp. I,** 414

"Tract against Communism, A" (Twelve Southerners), **IV,** 125, 237

Tracy, Lee, **IV,** 287, 288

Tracy, Steven, **Retro. Supp. I,** 195

"Trade, The" (Levine), **Supp. V,** 193

"Tradition and Industrialization" (Wright), **IV,** 489–490

"Tradition and the Individual Talent" (Eliot), **I,** 441, 574, 585; **Retro. Supp. I,** 59, 286

Tragedies, Life and Letters of James Gates Percival (Swinburne), **Supp. I, Part 2,** 422

Tragedy of Don Ippolito, The (Howells), **II,** 279

"Tragedy of Error, A" (James), **II,** 322; **Retro. Supp. I,** 218

Tragedy of Pudd'nhead Wilson, The (Twain), **IV,** 206–207

"Tragic Dialogue" (Wylie), **Supp. I, Part 2,** 724

Tragic Ground (Caldwell), **I,** 297, 306

"Tragic Mulatto Theme in Six Works of Langston Hughes, The" (Davis), **Supp. I, Part 1,** 348

Tragic Muse, The (James), **Retro. Supp. I,** 227

Traherne, Thomas, **IV,** 151; **Supp. III, Part 1,** 14; **Supp. V,** 208

Trailerpark (Banks), **Supp. V,** 12

"Trailing Arbutus, The" (Whittier), **Supp. I, Part 2,** 691

"Train Rising Out of the Sea" (Ashbery), **Supp. III, Part 1,** 22

"Train Tune" (Bogan), **Supp. III, Part 1,** 64

"Trains" (Banks), **Supp. V,** 8

"Traits of Indian Character" (Irving), **II,** 303

Tramp Abroad, A (Twain), **IV,** 200

Tramping With a Poet in the Rock-ies (Graham), **Supp. I, Part 2,** 397, 402

Tramp's Excuse, The (Lindsay), **Supp. I, Part 2,** 379, 380, 382

Transactions of the Royal Society (publication), **IV,** 163

"Transatlantic" (Toomer), **Supp. III, Part 2,** 486

Transatlantic Review (publication), **II,** 68, 435; **III,** 471; **IV,** 27; **Retro. Supp. I,** 178

Transatlantic Sketches (James), **II,** 324; **Retro. Supp. I,** 219

"Transcendental Etude" (Rich), **Supp. I, Part 2,** 576

Transcendentalists, **Supp. II, Part 1,** 279, 289, 291

Transcendentalists, The: An Anthology (ed. Miller), **Supp. I, Part 1,** 46

"Transcontinental Highway" (Cowley), **Supp. II, Part 1,** 141

"Transducer" (Ammons), **Supp. VII,** 28

"Transfigured Bird" (Merrill), **Supp. III, Part 1,** 320–321

Transformations (Sexton), **Supp. II, Part 2,** 689–691; **Supp. IV, Part 2,** 447

transition (publication), **III,** 434; **IV,** 31; **Supp. III, Part 2,** 611; **Supp. IV, Part 1,** 80

"Translation and Transposition" (Carne-Ross), **Supp. I, Part 1,** 268–269, 275

"Translation of a Fragment of Simonides" (Bryant), **Supp. I, Part 1,** 153, 155

"Translations" (Rich), **Supp. I, Part 2,** 563

Translations of Ezra Pound, The (ed. Kenner), **III,** 463

"Trans-National America" (Bourne), **I,** 299, 230

Transparent Things (Nabokov), **Retro. Supp. I,** 266, 270, 277

"Transport" (Simic), **Supp. VIII,** 282

Transport to Summer (Stevens), **IV,** 76, 93; **Retro. Supp. I,** 309–312

Tranströmer, Thomas, **Supp. IV, Part 2,** 648

"Traps for the Unwary" (Bourne), **I,** 235

Trash Trilogy (McMurtry), **Supp. V,** 225–226, 231

Traubel, Horace, **IV,** 350, 353

"Travel: After a Death" (Kenyon), **Supp. VII,** 169

"Travel Writing: Why I Bother" (Theroux), **Supp. VIII,** 310

"Traveler, The" (Stegner), **Supp. IV, Part 2,** 605

Traveler at Forty, A (Dreiser), **I,** 515

Traveler from Altruria, a Romance A, (Howells), **II,** 285, 287

"Traveling" (Paley), **Supp. VI,** 230

"Travels in Georgia" (McPhee), **Supp. III, Part 1,** 293–294

Travels in the Congo (Gide), **III,** 210

"Travels in the South" (Ortiz), **Supp. IV, Part 2,** 506

Travels with Charley (Steinbeck), **IV,** 52

Travis, Merle, **Supp. V,** 335

Trawick, Leonard M., **Supp. I, Part 2,** 706

Tre Croce (Tozzi), **Supp. III, Part 2,** 616

"Treasure of the Redwoods, A" (Harte), **Supp. II, Part 1,** 337

Treasury of the Theatre, A (Gassner), **Supp. I, Part 1,** 292

Treasury of Yiddish Stories, A (eds. Howe and Greenberg), **Supp. I, Part 2,** 432

Treat 'Em Rough (Lardner), **II,** 422–423

Treatise Concerning Religious Affections (Edwards), **I,** 547, 552, 554, 555, 557, 558, 560, 562

Treatise Concerning the Lord's Supper (Doolittle), **IV,** 150

"Treatise on Poetry" (Milosz), **Supp. VIII,** 20

Treatise on Right and Wrong, A (Mencken), **III,** 110, 119

"Treatise on Tales of Horror, A" (Wilson), **IV,** 438

Treatise on the Gods, A (Mencken), **III,** 108–109, 119

"Tree, The" (Pound), **Retro. Supp. I,** 286; **Supp. I, Part 1,** 255

"Tree, a Rock, a Cloud, A" (McCullers), **II,** 587

Valley of the Moon, The (London), **II,** 467, 481

"Valley of Unrest, The" (Poe), **III,** 411

Valli, Alida, **Supp. IV, Part 2,** 520

"Valor" (Bausch), **Supp. VII,** 54

Valparaiso (DeLillo), **Supp. VI,** 4, 12

"Values and Fictions" (Toomer), **Supp. III, Part 2,** 485–486

Values of Veblen, The: A Critical Appraisal (Rosenberg), **Supp. I, Part 2,** 650

Vampire Armand, The (Rice), **Supp. VII,** 290, 294–295

Vampire Chronicles, The (Rice), **Supp. VII,** 290

Vampire Lestat, The (Rice), **Supp. VII,** 290–292, 298, 299

Van Buren, Martin, **II,** 134, 312; **III,** 473

Van Dine, S. S., **Supp. IV, Part 1,** 341

Van Doren, Carl, **I,** 252–253, 423; **II,** 103, 111, 112, 125, 461; **III,** 144; **IV,** 143; **Supp. I, Part 2,** 474, 478, 486, 707, 709, 717, 718, 727, 730; **Supp. II, Part 1,** 395; **Supp. VIII,** 96–97

Van Doren, Mark, **I,** 70, 168; **II,** 245; **III,** 4, 23, 589, 598; **IV,** 143; **Supp. I, Part 2,** 604, 626; **Supp. III, Part 2,** 626; **Supp. VIII,** 231

Van Dyke, Annette, **Supp. IV, Part 1,** 327

Van Dyke, Henry, **I,** 223; **II,** 456

Van Gelder, Robert, **III,** 73

Van Ghent, Dorothy, **I,** 334

Van Gogh, Vincent, **I,** 27; **IV,** 290; **Supp. I, Part 2,** 451; **Supp. IV, Part 1,** 284

Van Gogh's Room at Arles (Elkin), **Supp. VI,** 56

Van Matre, Lynn, **Supp. V,** 126

Van Nostrand, Albert, **III,** 384

Van Rensselaer, Stephen, **I,** 351

Van Rensselaer family, **IV,** 311

Van Schaick, John, Jr., **II,** 509–510

Van Vechten, Carl, **I,** 295; **IV,** 76; **Supp. I, Part 1,** 324, 327, 332, **Part 2,** 715; **Supp. II, Part 2,** 725–751

Vande Kieft, Ruth M., **IV,** 260, 284

Vanderbilt, Cornelius, **III,** 14

Vanderbilt family, **IV,** 311

Vandover and the Brute (Norris), **III,** 314, 315, 316, 320–322, 328, 333, 334

"Vanisher, The" (Whittier), **Supp. I, Part 2,** 691

"Vanity" (B. Diop), **Supp. IV, Part 1,** 16

Vanity Fair (magazine), **I,** 429; **III,** 123; **IV,** 427; **Supp. I, Part 2,** 709

Vanity Fair (Thackeray), **I,** 354; **II,** 91; **III,** 70

"Vanity of All Wordly Things, The" (Bradstreet), **Supp. I, Part 1,** 102, 119

Vanity of Duluoz (Kerouac), **Supp. III, Part 1,** 221, 222

"Vanity of Existence, The" (Freneau), **Supp. II, Part 1,** 262

Vanquished, The (Faulkner), **I,** 205

Vanzetti, Bartolomeo, **I,** 482, 486, 490, 494; **II,** 38–39, 426; **III,** 139–140; **Supp. I, Part 2,** 446, 610, 611; **Supp. V,** 288–289

"Vapor Trail Reflected in the Frog Pond" (Kinnell), **Supp. III, Part 1,** 242–243

"Vapor Trails" (Snyder), **Supp. VIII,** 298

"Variation: Ode to Fear" (Warren), **IV,** 241

"Variation on a Sentence" (Bogan), **Supp. III, Part 1,** 60

"Variation on Gaining a Son" (Dove), **Supp. IV, Part 1,** 248

"Variation on Pain" (Dove), **Supp. IV, Part 1,** 248

"Variations: The air is sweetest that a thistle guards" (Merrill), **Supp. III, Part 1,** 321

"Variations: White Stag, Black Bear" (Merrill), **Supp. III, Part 1,** 321

"Varick Street" (Bishop), **Supp. I, Part 1,** 90, 92

Varieties of Metaphysical Poetry, The (Eliot), **Retro. Supp. I,** 65

Varieties of Religious Experience, The: A Study in Human Nature (James), **II,** 344, 353, 354, 359–360, 362; **IV,** 28, 291

Variety (publication), **Supp. VIII,** 129

Variorum (Whitman), **Retro. Supp. I,** 406

"Various Miracles" (Shields), **Supp. VII,** 318–319, 324

Various Miracles (Shields), **Supp. VII,** 318–320, 323, 324

Vasari, Giorgio, **Supp. I, Part 2,** 450; **Supp. III, Part 1,** 5

Vasilievskaya, O. B., **I,** 427

Vasquez, Robert, **Supp. V,** 180

Vassall Morton (Parkman), **Supp. II, Part 2,** 595, 597–598

Vasse, W. W., **III,** 478

Vaudeville for a Princess (Schwartz), **Supp. II, Part 2,** 661–662

Vaughan, Henry, **IV,** 151

"Vaunting Oak" (Ransom), **III,** 490

Veblen, Andrew, **Supp. I, Part 2,** 640

Veblen, Mrs. Thorstein (Ellen Rolfe), **Supp. I, Part 2,** 641

Veblen, Oswald, **Supp. I, Part 2,** 640

Veblen, Thorstein, **I,** 104, 283, 475–476, 483, 498, 511; **II,** 27, 272, 276, 287; **Supp. I, Part 2,** 628–650; **Supp. IV, Part 1,** 22

Veblen (Hobson), **Supp. I, Part 2,** 650

Veblenism: A New Critique (Dobriansky), **Supp. I, Part 2,** 648, 650

"Veblen's Attack on Culture" (Adorno), **Supp. I, Part 2,** 650

Vechten, Carl Van, **Retro. Supp. I,** 199

Vedas, **IV,** 183

Vega, Lope de, **Retro. Supp. I,** 285; **Supp. III, Part 1,** 341, 347

Vegetable, The (Fitzgerald), **Retro. Supp. I,** 105

Vegetable, The, or From President to Postman (Fitzgerald), **II,** 91

Vein of Iron (Glasgow), **II,** 175, 186, 188–189, 191, 192, 194

Veinberg, Jon, **Supp. V,** 180

Velie, Alan R., **Supp. IV, Part 2,** 486

"Velorio" (Cisneros), **Supp. VII,** 66

"Velvet Shoes" (Wylie), **Supp. I,**

A Complete Listing of Authors in *American Writers*